MAN'S RELIGIOUS QUEST

A READER

The following is a list of authors of units of the Open University Course AD208, *Man's Religious Quest*, who co-operated in the selecting of material for the Course Reader:

Dr Stuart Brown	The Open University
Dr Francis Clark	The Open University
Bishop Kenneth Cragg	University of Sussex
Professor John Ferguson	The Open University
Dr Ruth Finnegan	The Open University
Dr David Goldstein	The British Library
Miss Margaret Hall	The Open University
Mr John R. Hinnells	University of Manchester
Professor Joseph Masson	The Pontifical Gregorian University, Rome, and the University of Louvain.
Dr Robert McDermott	City University of New York
Professor Eric J. Sharpe	University of Sydney
Professor Ninian Smart	University of Lancaster
Dr Kenneth Thompson	The Open University
Mr D.A.T. Thomas	The Open University
Mr Simon Weightman	School of Oriental and African Studies, University of London

MAN'S RELIGIOUS QUEST

A READER

Edited by WHITFIELD FOY
at the Open University

CROOM HELM
London & Sydney
in association with
The Open University Press

200.8
MAN

Selection and editorial material copyright
©The Open university 1978
Reprinted 1982 and 1985
Croom Helm Ltd, Provident House, Burrell Row,
Beckenham, Kent BR3 1AT

Croom Helm Australia Pty Ltd, First Floor, 139 King Street,
Sydney, NSW 2001, Australia

British Library Cataloguing in Publication Data

Man's religious quest. — (Open University.
  Set Books).
  1. Religions — Addresses, essays, lectures
  I. Foy, Whitfield II. Series
  200'.8   BL87

  ISBN 0-85664-548-6
  ISBN 0-85664-599-0 Pbk

Printed and bound in Great Britain
by Billing & Sons Limited, Worcester.

7.8.87

CONTENTS

3. THE NOBLE PATH OF BUDDHISM

8. ISLAM AND THE MUSLIM

INTRODUCTION

This book is not a general anthology of material from world religions. It is a resource volume for use in the Open University's Course AD208, *Man's Religious Quest*. The course of study for which the book has been produced lasts for one academic year. During that time Open University students will be receiving, and working at, a steady supply of original writing, produced by the Course Unit authors who are listed on another page. They will also be listening to and watching specially made radio and television broadcasts and they will have the regular assistance of Course Tutors. This book is therefore only one of the students' several tools for the job.

Although designed for students following a particular Course the Reader will nevertheless, we believe, be of interest to a wider readership. Such readers can have the benefit of radio and television programmes in Britain as well as being able to buy (or borrow from libraries) the Course Units themsevles.

The structure of the Course, and therefore of the Course Reader, is clear enough. There is a general introductory section dealing with the overall question of religious study. This is followed by the very large central block in which most of the major world religions (plus what are sometimes referred to as 'substitute' religions) will be looked at closely. Then a final section deals with the encounter of religions. The course itself provides reflective concluding matter, but the Reader material stops at the subject of encounter.

Two other points are worth a brief mention. One is that the study of World religions compels a student to come to terms with a specialised vocabulary. Open University students will have special assistance in this matter, particularly through the provision of a new Glossary. Secondly, the material in the Reader comes from many very different sources and is inevitably of varying quality and interest. It is therefore necessary to ask readers not to be daunted by any one piece; the next piece will probably be much more readable.

We make explicit here our gratitude to the Course Unit authors who are largely responsible for the choice of material for the Reader. And the Editor expresses warm thanks to the small group of people without whose generously offered help the book could not have been produced.

ACKNOWLEDGEMENTS

We are grateful to the following for permission to reproduce copy-right material:

The Oriel Press for 'The Comparative Study of Religion in Historical Perspective' by Dr E.J. Sharpe from *Comparative Religion in Education*, ed. J.R. Hinnells, 1970. The Royal Anthropological Institute of Great Britain and Ireland for 'Theodicy and the Doctrine of Karma' by Dr Ursula M. Sharma from *Man*, Vol.8, No.3, 1973 and for 'Status and Evaluation in the Hindu Caste System' by H.N.C. Stevenson from *Proceedings of the Royal Anthropological Institute of Great Britain and Ireland*, No. 84, 1954, pp.63-4. Professor W. Cantwell Smith for *The Meaning and End of Religion* by W. Cantwell Smith, 1964, pp.61, 63, 130. The Free Press of Glencoe for 'Sociological Dilemmas: Five Paradoxes of Institutionalization' by Thomas F. O'Dea, from *Sociological Theory, Values and Socio-cultural Change*, ed. E.A. Tiryakian, pp.71-89. Vikas Publishing House for 'The Problem of Village Hinduism' by Dr. Ursula M. Sharma from *Contributions to Indian Sociology*, 1973, pp.1-21. Weidenfeld and Nicolson the University of Chicago Press (USA) for *Homo Hierarchicus* by L. Dumont, 1972, pp.123-9. Harper & Row for the *Bhagavad Gita*, trans. F. Edgerton, 1944, pp.2-8, 9-16, 38-41, 55-61, 83-91. The Navajivan Publishing House for *Hindu Dharma* by M.K. Gandhi, 1950, pp.3, 6-9, 13, 158-60 and 220-28. The Sri Aurobindo Ashram for selections from the *Birth Centenary Library* of Sri Aurobindo, 1972. The Pali Text Society for extracts from *Gradual Sayings, Middle Length Sayings* and *Kindred Sayings* by F.L. Woodward, I.B. Horner and Mrs. Rhys Davids, 1917, 1927, 1930, 1932, 1954 and 1957 and for *Dialogues of the Buddha* by F.L. Woodward, Vol.II, 1972, pp.81-5. W. Heffer & Sons, for *Lamaism* by L.A. Wadell, 1934, pp.435-7. Hutchinson Publishing Group for *A Critical Survey of Indian Philosophy* by C. Sharma, 1960, pp.101-2, for 'The Ox Herd' from *Essays in Zen Buddhism* (1st Series), Plates I to X and for extracts from the *Manual of Zen Buddhism*, 1955, both by D.T. Suzuki. Weatherhill for 'Bassui's Sermon' from *The Three Pillars of Zen*, ed. P. Kapleau, 1967. Bruno Cassirer for *Buddhist Texts through the Ages* by E. Conzè *et al.*, 1954, pp.180, 253-54. Harvard University Press for *Buddhism in Translations* by H.C. Warren, 1963, pp.289, 298-9. The

2

Chicago University Press for *Religious Observances in Tibet*, by R.B. Ekvall, 1964, p.31. Chion-in, Kyoto for *Honen, the Buddhist Saint*, trans. H.H. Coates and R. Ishizuka, 1925, pp.402-6 and 542-5. Allen & Unwin for *A Moslem Saints of the Twentieth Century*, by M. Lings, 1961, pp.107, 112-14, 117, and for *The Koran Interpreted*, trans. A.J. Arberry, 1964, Surahs, 2, 17, 23, 24, 57, 59, 90-114. Oxford University Press for 'Sikhism' by H. McLeod from *Cultural History of India*, ed. A.L. Basham, 1975, pp.294-302, for *Rome* by W. Warde Fowler, 1972, pp.7-15, for *The Mishnah* by H. Danby, 1933, pp.387-8, *Nuer Religion* by E.E. Evans-Pritchard, 1956, pp.1-27, 44-7, 98-9, for *Divinity and Experience* by R.G. Lienhardt, 1961, pp.28-32, 147-50, 156-70, for *The Dinka and Their Songs* by F.M. Deng, 1973, pp.238-42 The American Philosophical Society for 'Religious Attitudes of the Ancient Greeks' by A.D. Nock from *Proceedings of the American Philosophical Society* 85 (1942) pp.472-82, and the Oxford University Press for the same essay in *Essays on Religion in the Ancient World* by A.D. Nock, 1972, Vol.II, pp.534-550. The Oxford and Cambridge University Presses for Passages from the Old Testament in the New English Bible. Singer's Prayer Book Publication Committee for *The Authorised Daily Prayer Book*, ed. S. Singer, 1963, pp.6, 8, 9 and 251-54. The Hebrew Publishing Company for *Hamadrikh, the Rabbi's Guide* by J. Goldin, 1956, pp.142ff. Prentice-Hall for *Judaism* by A. Hertzberg, 1961, pp.82-6, 221-2 and 231-3. The Union of Liberal and Progressive Synagogues for *Service of the Heart*, 1967, pp.364-6. David Higham Associates for *The Jewish Poets of Spain*, trans. D. Goldstein, 1971, pp.39-40, 97 and 158. Schocken Books for *The Hasidic Anthology*, ed. C. Newman, 1963, pp.175-6, and for *Days of Awe*, ed. S.Y. Agnon, 1948, p.116. Holt, Rinehart & Winston for *This People Israel* by L. Baeck, 1964, pp.199-200 and 215-16. The Leo Baeck Institute, Mr. Z. Kolitz and Rabbi A.H. Friedlander for *Out of the Whirlwind*, ed. A.H. Friedlander, 1968, pp.231-2, 396,-7 and 484-6. The East and West Library for *Letters of Jews through the Ages*, ed. F. Kobler, 1952, Vol.I, pp.194-6. Darton, Longman & Todd and Dr. Louis Jacobs (USA) for *A Jewish Theology*, 1973, pp.269-75. Nelson & Sons for biblical passages from the Old and New Testaments. The Scripture quotations from p.419 to p.455 publication are from the Revised Standard Version of the Bible copyrighted 1946 and 1952 by the Division of Christian Education of the National Council of the Churches of Christ in the U.S.A. The Daystar Press for *the Names of God*, trans. R.C. Stade,

4   Acknowledgements

1970, pp.36-8, 44-5, 49-50, 68, 69, 75-6. Orientalis for *Pearls of Faith* by E. Arnold, 1954, pp.41-6 and 80-81. Beshara Publications for *The Wisdom of the Prophets* by Muhyi al-Din Ibn 'Arabi', 1975, pp.27-9. Cassell for *The Living Thoughts of the Prophet Mohammad*, ed. Muhammad Ali, 1947, pp.62, 68, 71, 75, 83-85, 89, 92, 110, 114-115, 117, 123, 125-6, 135-7. Gateway Publications for *Ijma and the Gate of Ijtihad* by K.A. Faruki, 1954, pp.8-20. The Muslim World Quarterly for *'Uyub Al-Nafs*, trans. A.J. Arberry, Vol.30, 1940, pp.140-43. Emery Walker for *Poem of the Way* by Ibn al-Farid, trans. A.J. Arberry, 1952, lines 2137-2199. Islamic Council of Europe for *Islam*, 1976. Collier-Macmillan for *Secular Alternatives to Religion* by J.M. Yinger, 1970, pp.191-202. Prof. M. Boyce for *The Continuity of the Zoroastrian Quest* (unpublished). Cambridge University Press for selected passages from *The Avestan Hymn to Mithra*, trans. I. Gershevitch. Philo Press for *Early Zoroastrianism* by J.H. Moulton, 1972, pp.347-87. Sheldon Press for *The Teachings of the Magi, by R.C. Zaehner*, 1975, pp. 59-61 and 146-50. Mrs. B.T. Anklesaria for *Zand-i Vohuman Yasn* and *Two Pahlavi Fragments,* 1957, pp.106-13 and 116-20. S.K. Hodivala for selections from the Kissah-i-Sanjan, from *Parsis of Ancient India,* 1920, pp.99-106. M.M. Murzban for *The Parsis in India,* 1917, pp-67-70. H.T. Anklesaria for *Homage unto Ahura Mazda* by M.N. Dhalla, 1970, pp.4, 5, 52, 67, 83, 84, 85-186, 101, 131, 138, 144, 176, 197, 206 and 212. The P.N. Mehta Educational Trust for selections from *A Handbook of Information on Zoroastrianism,* by K.S. Dabu, 1969, pp.2, 3, 4, and 28. The Parsi Punchayet Press for selections from *A Catechism of the Zoroastrian Religion* by J.J. Modi, 1961. Brill Publishing Company for *A History of Zoroastrianism* by M. Boyce, 1975, pp.252-7. The World Council of Churches for 'Liberation for Social Justice' by J. de Santa Ana from *Living Faiths and Ultimate Goals,* ed. S.J. Samartha, 1974, pp.90-107, and for 'The Meaning of *Moksha* in Contemporary Hindu Thought and Life' by K. Sivaraman from *Living Faiths and Ultimate Goals,* ed. S.K. Samartha, 1974, pp.2-11. The Christian Institute for the study of Religion and Society, Bangalore, for 'Major Issues in the Hindu-Christian Dialogue in India today' by S.J. Samartha from *Inter-Religious Dialogue, ed.,* H.J. Singh, 1967, pp.141-65. Temple University, Philadelphia, for, 'A Hindu-Christian Dialogue on Truth' by Klaus K. Klostermaier from L. Swidler, ed., *The Journal of Ecumenical Studies,* 1975, Vol.12 Part 2, pp.157-71. Harper for extracts from *Original Teachings of Ch'an Buddhism* by C.Y. Chang, 1971. The Islamic Council of Europe for *Islam: a Contemporary Statement,* 1976.

1 SEEKERS AND SCHOLARS

[*Editor's Note:* No area of life or thought has been charged with emotion more than that of religious enquiry. Reaction to religious material — written, liturgical, or in any other form — is often very vigorous.

It is expected, however, that serious students of the subject will seek to be as objective as possible in their approach to the matter: such objectivity is required if the full value of the Open University Course for which this Reader is a textbook is to be grasped.

The first part of the Course deals, not with any single religion, but with the whole question of the how and why of the study of *any* religion. And in the Reader there are two essays to provide supportive material, essays which are quite different. Dr Sharpe writes on what has for long been known as the Comparative Study of Religion; while Dr Sharma's essay might perhaps have been expected to appear to the Hinduism section of the Course. Careful reading of the latter will show, however, that the essay is pointing to a problem common to all religious study.

Students should note that the original spelling and use of diacritical marks have been retained in all the extracts used in the Reader. This practice is extended even to the wording of such foot-notes as are retained.

Readers will therefore note inconsistencies both in the spelling and accenting of words. This inconsistency, however, does not interfere with a ready understanding on the part of the Reader.

This note, though produced in the first section of the Reader, applies to the Book's entire material.]

1.1 THE COMPARATIVE STUDY OF RELIGION IN HISTORICAL PERSPECTIVE

Eric J. Sharpe

It is scarcely necessary at the present time to draw attention to the 1.1.1 remarkable popularity of 'world religions' as a subject for academic and semi-academic study in Western educational institutions. Universities, colleges of education, seminaries and theological colleges, secondary schools and part-time classes are all, in their various ways, attempting to meet what is in process of becoming a widespread popular desire for insights into the beliefs and practices of religions other than Christianity. The cause of this upsurge of enthusiasm for a subject which until only a few years ago remained the province of a very few specialists would provide a fascinating study in itself. Briefly (for this is not a subject we can undertake to examine in detail here) it seems that improved travel and communications, insistent questioning of the role of the West *vis-à-vis* non-Western nations and peoples, increased availability of information on the popular level, and the presence in the midst of Western societies of ever larger numbers of adherents of non-Western religious traditions, have combined with a growing feeling of disillusionment with organised Christianity and with the intellectual foundations of Western society to turn increasing numbers of people – and not least young people – towards a new quest for 'light from the East'. This phenomenon, particularly in its more extreme aspects may be ephemeral. But for the present it is a fact of experience, which the educationalist would be unwise to attempt to ignore. And in view of the current crisis in religious education, it is imperative that we should know what may be involved in this new and apparently exotic orientation. Equally we must know what is not involved, since newness and the quality of the exotic are poor recommendations for an academic subject.

It is, however, undeniable (however unfortunate it may be) that the words 'comparative religion' have long suggested something unorthodox and off-beat, and therefore, perhaps a possible alternative to orthodoxy in a period when all orthodoxies are suspect. There are good historical reasons for this. But there are much better reasons for looking upon a comparative study of religion (CSR) as both a highly individual and a highly necessary field of study, related only incidentally to current emphasis in popular religious culture.

1.1.2   CSR is neither a very new nor a very old subject. If two of its constituent elements are a degree of detachment from one's own religious tradition (i.e. the tradition of the society in which one happens to be placed) and a degree of interest in religious traditions other than one's own, then a good case might be made out for the subject having its origins in classical antiquity. But an academic subject, if it is to be studied at all consistently, must have an adequate method, and until the third quarter of the nineteenth century, this was precisely what it lacked. There had of course been earlier studies of certain world religions; but the motives from which these studies were undertaken varied greatly. For instance, eighteenth-century France was passionately interested in the religious traditions of China. This interest stemmed more or less directly from the work and observations of Jesuit missionaries in China during the previous century, but owed its existence less to any genuine concern for Chinese culture than to the belief that in China was to be found a prototype of 'natural religion', i.e. that religion, without miracle and without 'priestcraft', which the Deists had believed to be religion in its pristine purity. In the early nineteenth century, various representatives of the Romantic movement — Emerson and Thoreau in America and Schopenhauer in Germany being typical examples — studied oriental religions to the best of their ability, but again less with a view to understanding oriental cultures than to bolstering a particular type of individualist, 'transcendental' philosophy. In neither case can one accord these studies the name 'academic'.

1.1.3   The turning point, as far as CSR as a scholarly discipline is concerned, came in the years immediately following the publication (in 1859) of Darwin's *Origin of Species,* as the evolutionary hypothesis came to be applied to all areas of human existence, religion not excepted. This hypothesis provided a principle on which previously amorphous bodies of miscellaneous material could be organised and classified. The motive for the study was already there; bodies of *material* were at hand, and growing rapidly, with the development of anthropology, archæology, philology and kindred disciplines; now to these was added a *method,* the evolutionary method, which appeared to be the key which would unlock every door. The idea of evolution struck the late nineteenth century with the force of revelation: in the words of J.H. Moulton, 'A revelation of the Reign of Law invaded every field of thought'.[1] A new class of scholar emerged: men such as Max Müller, E.B. Tylor, J.G. Frazer, R.R. Marett and many more — analysing, with the help of the evolutionary 'key', philosophy, ritual, myth, folklore and all the other ingredients of 'religion'. A new interest grew up in what might be called 'religious prehistory', or the origins of religion, religion viewed by this time not as a body of revealed doctrine but as a human function, and a rash of theories concerning religious origins broke out. Obviously this could not have happened had it not been believed that religion, in common with all other expressions of human existence, exhibits a largely unbroken evolution from lower forms to higher. J. Estlin Carpenter expressed the original dependence of CSR on the evolutionary hypothesis in these words, written just before the First World War:

> It is on this great idea [evolution] that the whole study of the history of religion is now firmly established. At the foundation of all endeavours to classify the multitudinous facts which it embraces lies the conviction that whatever may be the occasional instances of degeneration or decline, the general movement of human things advances from the cruder and less complex to the more refined and developed.[2]

So it came to be virtually axiomatic that clear stages of development could be discerned, from (using the new language of the new discipline) animatism to animism to polydaemonism to polytheism to henotheism to monotheism. In some cases it was held that the crown and culmination of the whole process was that largely undogmatic, moralistic Christianity since called, among other things, 'Liberal Protestantism'.

1.1.4 These details are worth bearing in mind, since it is sometimes forgotten that CSR was born and raised under the optimistic auspices of evolutionary theory, and that for years it was concerned mainly with the discerning and elaboration of evolutionary patterns in the area of religion. This, for instance, goes a long way towards accounting for the traditional suspicion in which 'comparative religion' has been held by certain types of Christian, to whom the very mention of 'evolution' has been tantamount to a confession of heresy. Not that CSR was only concerned with this, of course: it was first of all necessary to gather, edit and sift masses of material from a wide variety of cultures, and this task was done with great conscientiousness, as Max Müller's series of *Sacred Books of the East* bears witness; but the passing of value judgements was never far from the minds of the first practitioners of the new science. They might attempt to persuade themselves that the labelling of one religion as 'primitive' (or a 'survival') and another as 'higher' was a scientific procedure; in fact it was the fruit of the application of an *a priori* theory, and was therefore nowhere near as scientific as the convinced evolutionist tends to suppose.

1.1.5   But if we are thus disposed, with all the wisdom of hindsight, to criticise the scientific basis of 'comparative religion' as originally practised, what guarantee have we that in a few years (if not at present) someone will not turn round and accuse us of being equally unscientific? To put it as sharply as possible, is CSR a scientific discipline at all?

Certainly, CSR has always found it somewhat difficult to achieve academic respectability, not least because over the past fifty years or so its exponents have been less than unanimous when it came to trying to express the precise aims they had in view. There has been uncertainty as to whether it ought to be treated as a theological discipline or whether its place ought to be among the humanities; and there have been those who have dismissed it impatiently as merely a 'fringe activity' having no academic relevance. The root of the trouble is the question of method. Methodological uncertainty has been paraded for all to see in the variety of names the subject (allowing for the moment that it is a subject) has carried during its brief academic life: comparative religion, comparative religions, the science of religion (*Religionswissenschaft*), the history of religion (*Religionsgeschichte*), the history of religions, the phenomenology of religion, religious studies, and so on. 'The comparative study of religion' is perhaps a compromise and may not be ideal; but for the present it will serve our purpose.

It is only in very recent years that CSR has left the university and begun to enjoy independent existence on other, less exalted, academic levels. But it is illuminating to look back to see how the universities originally stood in relation to the development of CSR as a non-theological discipline. The theological faculties were, with very few exceptions, at first suspicious of what seemed to them to be illegitimate trespassing on their preserves. Some in fact still are. Most tended to look upon comparative religionists much as the landed gentry once looked upon poachers — as resourceful villains who knew the terrain extraordinarily well, but were totally lacking in respect for property. They were not able to prevent the development of the new discipline, although they did succeed in considerably retarding it in some areas.

The honour of establishing the first chair in the subject belongs 1.1.6 to Switzerland, and the University of Geneva (1873); in Holland, the theological faculties of the four Dutch universities were separated in 1877 from the Dutch Reformed Church and turned into institutes of religious studies, each with a chair in the history of religion. In 1879 a chair was established at the Collège de France, and in 1886 the subject was introduced, in ten separate sections, in the Ecole des Hautes Etudes of the Sorbonne. The Free University of Brussels appointed its first professor of the subject in 1884. In the United States, by 1895, chairs had been created at Harvard, Cornell and the University of Chicago. In Scotland, the Gifford Lectures were started in 1888, but these were concerned mainly with the philosophy of religion, and with comparative religion only secondarily, and as a matter of apologetics.

The English universities were in a very peculiar position. On the 1.1.7 one hand, they could boast of having some of the world's outstanding representatives of the new discipline. Max Müller, Robertson Smith, Jevons, Tylor, Lubbock, Lang, Frazer and others. But on the other hand, not one of these occupied a chair of comparative religion: they were either philologists, anthropologists, or (as in the case of Lang and Frazer) essentially freelancers. It is true that in 1904 a chair of comparative religion was set up in the University of Manchester; but despite the subsequent establishment of two chairs of religious studies at Lancaster, and personal chairs of comparative religion at Leeds and London, it has remained, strictly speaking, the only one of its kind in the country. Departments were set up in time at other universities, and some of the concerns of comparative religion were cared for in some cases by other chairs (for example the Spalding Professorship at Oxford), but the range and effectiveness of such centres was strictly limited. It is also worth mentioning that there were some theological colleges that did offer some teaching in the subject – Manchester and Mansfield, Oxford, spring immediately to mind, though these were not the only ones – but again, there was considerable dependence on the presence of gifted and enlightened individuals, such as, in the early days, A.M. Fairbairn and J. Estlin Carpenter.

Turning for a moment to continental Europe, the Scandinavian 1.1.8

countries and Germany have traditionally entrusted the training of their ministers of religion to Lutheran confessional faculties of theology. In Sweden, a chair with the elaborate name of Theological Propaedeutics and Theological Encyclopaedia had been in existence in the University of Uppsala since the 1870s and its occupants had taught some comparative religion under the aspect of Christian apologetics. In 1901 Nathan Söderblom was appointed to the chair, having received his training in the heady atmosphere of the Sorbonne, and although an expert on Iranian religion, covered more ground in the thirteen years of his professorship than most teachers would expect to cover in a lifetime, his subjects ranging from primitive religion to Catholic Modernism. However, in the same year, 1901, Adolph von Harnack opposed the setting up of just such a chair in the theological faculty of the University of Berlin on the grounds that it would surely lead to the production of religious dilettantes. What Harnack said in effect was that unless you have a thorough grounding in the language and culture of a people, you cannot begin even to approach their religion with any hope of understanding. The Christian cobbler ought, he maintained, to stick to his Biblical last, and leave other religious traditions to those who are able to deal with them in depth.

The differences between these two attitudes is fundamental. Söderblom was interested in everything having to do with that universal phenomenon called (rightly or wrongly) 'religion'; Harnack mainly in the Christian tradition. For Harnack, historical scientific method was everything; for Söderblom, it was a tool, to be sharpened and polished, but ultimately to be used in the interests of a better understanding of something fundamentally and inalienably human. In his inaugural lecture he had asked:

> How can any education deserving of the name avoid knowing about religion? How are we to describe and understand the history of mankind without insight into that mighty, incommensurable factor in human aspiration and the destiny of peoples which we call religion? How are we to attain to any real understanding of the deepest secrets of human life in all ages and of the great present-day conflicts and questions in the world without coming up against religion?[3]

How indeed?

1.1.9   It would be tempting simply to set these two alternative approaches as the two with which CSR is faced today; but this would be something of an oversimplification. The discipline today is not what it was at the turn of the century, and the alternatives are perhaps not quite so clear-cut as they might seem.

We have already drawn attention to the close connection which originally existed between 'comparative religion' and the evolutionary hypothesis. Now while it is no part of our intention to question the biological theory of evolution, increasingly of late scholars have come to question whether it can be successfully applied to the area of human thought, and, in this case, to the area of religion. The idea of unbroken (or, at any rate, steady) progress from lower forms to higher seems less self-evident, in the light of *inter alia* two world wars, than it once did. And as a result the method on which CSR once rested has fallen upon evil days. The early comparative religionists have been severely criticised for their cavalier treatment of the sparse and enigmatic material which they once advanced as proof of one or another theory of the origins of religion. The anthropologists in particular have been taken to task for assuming that the religions of pre-literate peoples can without more ado be equated with (to quote a popular, though inaccurate phrase) 'Stone age religion'.

Furthermore, the past sixty years have seen the breakdown of a number of academic disciplines into their constituent elements as a result of the well-known process of increasing specialisation. The subject which was once called 'natural philosophy' is now studied under such varied headings as botany, chemistry, physics and zoology. Anthropology was once categorised unhesitatingly as 'the science of man', but has since divided into its constituent elements of prehistoric archaeology, linguistics, physical anthropology, social anthropology, folklore, and the rest. Similarly, the sheer weight of material which has accumulated under the general heading of comparative religion is now often broken down into the history of religion, the phenomenology of religion, the psychology of religion, the sociology of religion and the philosophy of religion (not to mention a host of auxiliary disciplines), any one of which might occupy the normal scholar for rather more than his allotted three score years and ten. 1.1.10

This means in practice that the optimism which once characterised the comparative religionist has now given place to extreme caution. It has been stressed repeatedly of late, in tones reminiscent of Harnack, that no student can ever hope to cover the entire field of 1.1.11

religion. It is simply too large and too diffuse. However, to treat, say, Hinduism as representing the universal category of 'religion' is to do far less than justice to its distinctive features as an aspect of Indian culture. Each religion must, in other words, be dealt with separately, historically and scientifically, on the basis of its own primary sources and against its own specific background. And in the cultivation of such a field of study, linguistic proficiency plays a very important part indeed.

1.1.12   What this means in practice is that in most European universities, any name involving the word 'comparative' is firmly rejected, partly in order to make clear the extent of the break with the past that has in fact taken place. Usually the subject is there called 'the history of religion', and extreme pains are taken to emphasise that its legitimacy as a scientific discipline rests entirely on its historical method. Occasionally, an additional factor contributing to this attitude has been the position which certain faculties of theology have been forced to adopt in face of the attacks of what might be called militant secularists. Sweden is a case in point, where the very existence of university faculties of theology has been challenged repeatedly this century, and where members of those faculties have asserted their own right to full academic citizenship primarily as historians. And since the average historian finds the greatest satisfaction in the intensive cultivation of a small and circumscribed area, the tendency has been to study religion microscopically, to the virtual (though by no means complete) exclusion of theorising concerning 'religion-as-such'. It goes without saying that this kind of university discipline presupposes that the university is first and foremost a centre of scholarship, geared primarily to the needs of its professors, lecturers and research students. In this kind of climate, undergraduates may be regarded either as a necessary evil, or as potential research students, to be taught the relevant languages and the rudiments of scientific method as quickly and painlessly as possible, against the day when they are able to put away childish things.

1.1.13   This is of course not the only way to teach religion in a university; and it would be possible to bring forward examples of a much wider and more comprehensive approach from many parts of the world. However, the sharpest contrast at present is perhaps to be seen in the United States. In 1901, Morris Jastrow of the University of Pennsylvania, while lamenting that so little was being done to teach religion in American schools and colleges, wrote that:

The main purposes. . .for which the study of religions should be introduced into the curriculum of American colleges, and of the higher schools on the Continent leading to the university proper, are two – as part of the equipment of a liberal education, and as a necessary adjunct for appreciating and understanding the religious needs of the present time.[4]

These words are remarkably reminiscent of Söderblom's statement of the same year; and while not all scholars would probably now want to claim that we study religion in order to understand 'the religious needs of the present time', the other motif – that of the place of religion in liberal education – is being stressed in America more strongly than ever. Take, for instance, these words of Robert Michaelsen:

Religion is a fact. It is a fact which the community of learning cannot responsibly ignore. To be sure, one can debate whether religion is phenomenon or epiphenomenon; whether religious behaviour is normal or aberrant; whether religion is *sui generis* or merely the function of something else more fundamental. These are important debates which are of significance to the study of religion and will inevitably be raised in connection with such a study. But to deny the fact of religion by ignoring it is to engage in a kind of irresponsibility which does not befit the proud heritage of the community of learning. The question, then, is not *whether* to study religion, but *how* to study it.[5]

Once more we are faced with the question of methodology. This question is at present being hotly debated in the United States, as it is in Europe, but it would probably not be too much of an exaggeration to claim that most American scholars would tend to agree with the Chicago professor Joseph M. Kitagawa, who follows Joachim Wach in demanding some 'integral understanding' of the area of religion as a whole. Kitagawa has written in a recent article: 1.1.14

We must. . .be crystal clear concerning the basic distinction between the study of specific religions and the history of religions. We are all aware, of course, that in the popular mind the history of religions is often thought of as a convenient semantic umbrella that covers all the independent studies of specific religions. But the objective of the history of religions (*Religionswissenschaft*), in the technical sense in which we use this term, must be nothing short of scholarly inquiry into the nature and structure of the religious experience of the human race and its diverse manifestations in history.[6]

1.1.15   Although this is admittedly a tall order, it need not for that reason be ruled out as inacceptable in principle. However, it is questionable whether it is at all practical, as things are at present, to consider this to be part of the *teaching* function of the university, college or school. We all know that we are living in a society in which ignorance of even the basic concepts and terminology of religion is so widespread as to be almost universal, even among nominal Christians. If it were the case that university students were to come to the subject with even a modicum of accurate knowledge (which many of them, by and large, do not), then we might attempt to extend and integrate that knowledge, with the help of such disciplines as sociology, social anthropology and psychology, into something approaching a 'scholarly inquiry into the nature and structure of the religious experience of the human race'. As it is however, it seems unlikely that we shall be in a position to adopt the grand synoptic view for some time to come.

1.1.16   But the situation at present is anything but static. We began by mentioning the remarkable upsurge of interest in CSR which is currently taking place on both sides of the Atlantic. Between about 1960 and 1975, the size of most undergraduate classes has increased spectacularly; and although there appear to be signs, at least in America and Canada, that the peak may have been passed, the level of popular demand for courses in comparative religion is still high. But what is to be done to satisfy this demand? It seems that we are faced with the broad alternatives of following the path of sober descriptive instruction, taking one religious area at a time under conditions of great scientific stringency, or of seeking, with some at least of the Americans, for an insight into 'the nature and structure of the religious experience of the human race'.

1.1.17   Both alternatives, if elevated into absolute principles, are, however, beset with serious pitfalls. The 'pure' historian of religion runs the risk of losing sight of the living reality of religion in the experience of a great many human beings, and may unwittingly transmute his subject into a species of antiquarianism. The cosmic visionary may know everything about religion in general and embarrassingly little about any religion in particular; lacking the patience for detailed historical and linguistic study, he may lead his students into a 'cloud-cuckoo land' in which nothing is explicable save as inspiration or aberration. The classroom is not the place for an intense dialogue of religions, while both Christian and anti-Christian apologetics are equally illegitimate in the educational setting.

Among the various practical teaching alternatives at present open 1.1.18 to departments of CSR or religious studies, the tendency appears to be either to emphasise the present situation of religion (with which must be reckoned the recent past), endeavouring to provide a cross-section of religious and anti-religious opinion in various parts of the world, or to work in the broad sense historically, limiting courses to certain specific religious areas which can be dealt with in a couple of hours a week. Again, neither is fully satisfactory if isolated arbitrarily from the other – in the first case because of the danger of the proliferation of shallow and undifferentiated judgements, and because those who claim to be 'contemporary' are frequently in bondage to the fairly recent past; in the second, because we are not antiquarians, and must at all costs avoid becoming departments of old wives' tales and miscellaneous exotic superstitions.

Ideally, of course, when CSR is taught, at whatever level, some 1.1.19 attempt should be made to combine description with interpretation. But since there are diversities of gifts and inclinations, some teachers of the subject will inevitably feel more drawn to the one side than to the other, and this may place a considerable strain on a one-man department. However, we do not live in an ideal world, and we have to face up to the seriously limited time that is normally available for the teaching of CSR. And this being so, our first priority must be to inform students concerning the history and phenomenology of specific religious traditions. It may be that in another decade, when CSR is more widely accepted on the secondary level, that the universities and colleges will need to spend less time teaching students the ABC of Christianity, Hinduism, Buddhism and Islam. But for the present, this must have first call upon our teaching energies.

The question inevitably arises at this point whether and to what 1.1.20 extent the attempt should be made to compare religions. It must be recognised, in the first place, that comparison with a view to assigning religions relative places on the evolutionary ladder is no longer an acceptable option; and that comparison with a view to demonstrating the superiority of one or other religion over all its 'competitors' is illegitimate in the framework of secular education.

More seriously, there are good grounds for objecting that the comparison of religious systems *as systems* is a thoroughly unprofitable exercise, partly because excessive systematisation is never in the interests of accurate understanding and may (e.g. in the case of Hinduism) promote complete misunderstanding and partly because such comparisons are always ultimately between abstractions. We may compare our *understanding* of, say, Judaism and Christianity, Vedānta and Zen Buddhism; what we are not doing is to compare these phenomena as they are in themselves. This is not, however, to say that there is no place for comparison in CSR (which would be an extreme paradox); but comparison should be between comparables, for instance phenomena such as sacrifice, iconography, prayer, music and the like. This is one of the concerns of the phenomenology of religion, and ought to be given its rightful place within the discipline.

It is doubtful, however, whether we ought to waste too much time looking for 'the origins of religion', or that we should spin too many high-flown theories concerning the nature and function of 'religion-as-such': someone will always be found to pick up this particular fallen mantle.

Nor should we let our new-found popularity go to our heads; Kitagawa, in the article to which reference has already been made, is perfectly right when he says that

> It takes a considerable amount of determination for a historian of religions in-the-making to work towards creative scholarship without succumbing to the temptation to produce instant relevance either as a pseudo-Orientalist or as a quasi-theologian.[7]

The warning is timely: there is no surer formula for instant irrelevance tomorrow than instant relevance today.

1.1.21   At present, CSR is mainly taught in the university setting and a university is a centre of scholarship as well as a teaching institution. This means that university teachers of CSR, as well as producing *oeuvres de vulgarisation* (for which there has never been a better market) should constantly be hard at work both perfecting and using the tools of their trade, within their chosen field of specialist study. But we all have to recognise our limitations. We have already had occasion to speak of the increasing degree of academic specialisation that has led to the breakdown of the monolithic field of comparative religion, and we have referred to the fact that no single scholar can ever hope to master the entire field of religion. So, for instance, the scholar whose training has been in Oriental languages is unlikely to want (or be able) to concern himself at any depth with problems of philosophy; and it must be accepted that the same scholar may not be in a position both to edit and interpret, say, the *Brahma Sūtras* or *Tao Te Ching*. There is, then, ample scope for teamwork, not only within departments, but between departments and between universities.

Another area in which cooperation might well be extended is that 1.1.22 of library resources. In a field as vast as that of CSR, no single provincial library can hope to accumulate a complete range of primary sources, texts, theses, monographs and journals. This is perhaps not so much of a burden for undergraduates, but it may constitute a serious hindrance to research projects, and it is embarrassing to have to turn potential research students away on the grounds that the relevant literature is unavailable. There is of course the Inter-Library Loan System, but this is both expensive and slow, and a comprehensive system of mutual availability might be of very great benefit indeed.

So far we have been concerned almost entirely with CSR within 1.1.23 the framework of secular education; something must now be said about CSR in the explicitly Christian setting.

Many Christians have traditionally felt that CSR has no business to be taught in Christian institutions, perhaps because they feel, like the nineteenth-century divine, that 'there may be comparative religions, but Christianity is not one of them', or like Ronald Knox, that there is nothing like comparative religion for making a person comparatively religious. At all events, CSR has long had a bad image among Christians, particularly, though not exclusively, among Christians of the Evangelical type. An Anglican Bishop (not an Evangelical) wrote, for instance, in 1919, that 'The comparative study of religion is ... a new obsession of the liberal mind. We are supposed to set out in parallel columns the beliefs and customs of all known religions contemporary with, or antecedent to, Christianity, to note their similarities, and to account for them all by labelling them products of the human mind.'[8] The distortion is scarcely worth refuting; yet the image has persisted, of CSR as a curious, rationalist, eclectic discipline (if this is the right word), dedicated to the devaluation and relativisation of all absolutes, the slaughter of all sacred cows, and the humanisation of all religions.

But the time has long since passed when the Christian could live in the world as though other religions than Christianity did not exist;

this was always a dangerous delusion, and it is doubly dangerous in today's so-called 'global village'.

So to my mind it goes without saying that every Christian student (and particularly those in training for the ministry or priesthood) should receive some instruction in at least the rudiments of non-Christian religious belief and practice, ideally on the same conditions of sympathy and (as far as possible) objectivity as those obtaining in the university. A second requirement should be a course in the history of Christian attitudes to non-Christian religions — a course, incidentally, from which many historians, Christian and non-Christian alike, might profit. This would certainly give the lie to the common misapprehension that the Christian Church has in the past refused to concern itself with other religious traditions, and it might give a more balanced picture of the history of Christian missions — a subject on which ignorance in this country is so widespread as to be almost barbaric.

1.1.24   Let me make it quite clear that I have no quarrel whatsoever with the attempt from the side of the Christian Church to work out a theology of confrontation with other religions; in view of the actual situation of the Church in many parts of the world, this is an imperative necessity, and methodologically, it is perfectly legitimate, provided always that it is made quite explicit on what criteria the Christian is passing judgement. But in this, theological college and secular university part company; it is a confessional concern, and I hold no brief for Christian apologetics masquerading as CSR.

1.1.25   There is one point, however, at which university and theological college should be motivated by a similar concern. Granted that they are not identical types of institution, and that the theological college may legitimately enter upon matters which must remain for the most part closed to the university, they share one educational ideal. No study, and certainly no religious study, can entirely overlook the question of religious presuppositions; faith is itself a basic religious presupposition (though not the only one) to which no student is altogether immune. Although there are, of course, many possible answers to the question 'What is it all *for?*' I am tempted to say that the study of exotic and foreign religious traditions, past and present, is of value precisely in that it enables the individual, as well as discovering something about the religious presuppositions of others, to find out something of importance about his own presuppositions. It may bring them out into the light of day — perhaps for the first time — where they can be more easily weighed in the balances. That is why it is essential that in all our enthusiasm for Hinduism and Buddhism and the rest, we should not forget that Christianity is a world religion, with its own history and its own claims. It would be the height of irresponsibility for a department of religious studies or CSR deliberately to suppress such an important tradition (or, for that matter, the humanist tradition which serves as its antithesis) merely in the mistaken belief that it was giving the customer what the customer wanted.

I want to end with one severely practical matter. Time and time 1.1.26 again in these days one hears the lament that there is such a shortage of teachers of CSR that many ideal programmes simply cannot be put into practice. The theological courses which were mentioned are for the most part entirely impracticable, since there is no one to teach them; colleges of education are aware, almost without exception, of the need for instruction in the major non-Christian traditions, not least because of the growing immigrant population: few are able to provide such instruction, because of the shortage of qualified staff. Departments of CSR in the universities are the only ones who can do anything about this problem. It is necessary that we take our responsibilities in this regard with the utmost seriousness, both by laying firm and accurately-constructed foundations, and by discouraging students from following the attractive byways of dilettantism. It would be little short of tragic if, when the tide is running so strongly in our favour, we were to miss the opportunity of influencing the course of religious education in this country for years to come.

Notes

1. J.H. Moulton, *Religions and Religion,* London 1911, p.7.
2. J. Estlin Carpenter, *Comparative Religion,* London 1913, p.33.
3. N. Söderblom, *Om studiet av religionen,* reprinted Lund 1951, p.15.
4. M. Jastrow, *The Study of Religion,* London 1901, p.364.
5. R. Michaelsen, *The Scholarly Study of Religion in College and University,* New Haven 1964, p.7.
6. J.M. Kitagawa, 'The Making of a Historian of Religion', in *Journal of the American Academy of Religion,* XXXVI/3 Sept. 1968, p.199.
7. Kitagawa, op. cit., p.201.
8. F. Weston, *The Christ and His Critics,* London 1920, p.57.

Source: From J.R. Hinnells, ed., *Comparative Religion in Education,* Oriel Press, 1970, pp.1-9.

1.2 THEODICY AND THE DOCTRINE OF KARMA

Ursula Sharma

1.2.1 In this article I shall take as my starting point the general problem of the need for a cultural resolution for the problem of suffering, which Max Weber terms the need for 'theodicy'; in particular I shall examine the ways in which this need is fulfilled in popular Hinduism, using data from a field study carried out in a Himachal Pradesh village.

1.2.2 The idea that religion can primarily be seen as a means of comfort (spurious or genuine, according to one's view) in a world of suffering is not a new one. One of the earlier sociological versions of this idea was suggested by Marx; religion reconciles the oppressed to their uncomfortable roles in this life by dignifying their suffering and promising spiritual rewards in a world to come. But apart from the psychological problem, the existence of suffering also poses a cognitive problem, albeit in practice the two are often closely related or even confused with each other. Religion does not only have to provide the promise of some kind of escape or salvation from suffering but also some kind of moral vindication of its distribution in this world.

> Thou art indeed just, Lord, if I contend
> With thee; but, sir, what I plead is just.
> Why do sinners' ways prosper? and why must
> Disappointment all I endeavour end?
>
> (Gerard Manley Hopkins)

Geertz suggests that 'the strange opacity of events, the dumb sense-lessness of intense or inexorable pain, and the enigmatic unaccountability of gross iniquity all raise the uncomfortable suspicion that perhaps the world, and hence man's life in the world, has no genuine order at all — no empirical regularity, no emotional form, no moral coherence.'[1] Religion provides a solution for this problem, since it offers 'a formulation by means of symbols, of an image of such a genuine order of the world which will account for, and even celebrate the perceived ambiguities, puzzles and paradoxes in human experience'. Geertz's presentation of the problem implies that it is a universal function of religion to provide such an answer to the problematic nature of the world around us, since suffering is a universal fact, and in no place is it distributed entirely according to merit (allowing for the different interpretations which we may place upon the word 'merit'). On the whole, Geertz says, the religious answers to this problem do not try to deny that the just suffer sometimes, in spite of their righteousness, but only deny that their suffering is inexplicable, or without either value or meaning — even if that meaning is not fully accessible to human comprehension.

If this kind of approach to religion is less popular amongst 1.2.3 anthropologists (perhaps still embarrassed by early attempts to explain the origins of religion as a kind of primitive and speculative substitute for science), it has established a respectable position in the sociological camp, where Weber and (latterly) Parsons[2] have been its main exponents. Weber takes as given the need for an explanation of the distribution of fortune — what he calls the 'ineradicable need for a theodicy' and shows how different religious systems have offered contributions to a solution of this problem. They have supplied different sorts of answer according to the kinds of evil which men have seen as being in most need of explanation, and where they have failed to satisfy these needs, often new religious movements have risen. Often, for instance, the theory which has satisfied the privileged strata of society has failed to meet the needs of the depressed and poor, and hence redemption religions have appealed to the latter, giving a positive evaluation to their sufferings (e.g. Weber[3]). The provision of a theodicy according to such views, then, would by implication appear to be a functional necessity, if not from the point of view of the survival of the entire society in question, then at least so far as the persistence of the religious system itself is concerned. Thus it has sometimes been argued that failure to satisfy the need for a theodicy could well be one of the factors accounting for the failure of Christianity to maintain its hold in countries like Britain, where participation in institutionalised forms of religion is low. Weber himself cites the evidence gathered from German workers which showed that the 'rejection of the God idea was motivated not by scientific arguments but by the difficulty in reconciling the idea of providence with the injustice and imperfections of the social order'.[4] If this has really been an important factor in the general movement away from religion in its institutionalised form, at least in modern Europe, it is difficult to see why it did not take effect earlier since injustice and suffering have not been limited to any particular period.

1.2.4   Interesting as this question is, however, it is somewhat of a red
herring so far as my main argument here is concerned, my
contention being that the problem of suffering, which Weber,
Geertz, Parsons and others have presented as central to the relationship between doctrine and religious needs, is itself a complex one;
rather it involves two, or maybe three, connected problems.

1.2.5   Obeyesekere recognises this fact when he points out that Weber
has in fact used the term theodicy in more than one sense. He uses
it to refer to the 'existential need to explain suffering and evil; and
. . . to mean the resolution of these needs in statements of moral
meaning'.[5] But the 'classical' sense of the term is a vindication of the
goodness and mercy of God in the face of suffering and misery in
the world he is said to have created. The need for a theodicy in this
sense only exists in those dogmatically monotheistic religions for
which the ethical righteousness of God is an indispensable dogma –
for only in such systems is the tension pronounced between
observed reality (an imperfect world) and *a priori* assumptions (a
perfect God). It follows from this that there are really three aspects
to the problem of evil and suffering which must be resolved in every
religious interpretation of the world. There is (1) the cognitive
problem (why does the sinner prosper and the good man suffer?);
there is (2) the psychological problem (assurance of comfort, or
perhaps ultimate termination of suffering); and (3) the theological
problem just referred to in the case of certain monotheistic religions.
(Let us refer to these as problems 1, 2 and 3 to avoid repetition.) But
if problem 3 is confined only to those religions in which the
goodness and omnipotence of God are both essential dogmas, then
even problem 1, the cognitive problem, is not a universal one. For
as Obeyesekere points out, if a man once accepts a theory like that
of *karma* then the need for a theodicy in this sense will never arise; if
all suffering is the result of past sins then no suffering can be unjust.
The rationally closed belief systems which Weber describes as the
only three truly rational theodicies (*karma,* dualism and
predestination) suppress problem 2 altogether. But if they preclude
the rise of any intellectual problem because of their extreme
theoretical consistency, does it follow that they are satisfactory
from the psychological point of view, that is, do they provide
workable answers to problem 2? Obeyesekere refers to this problem
when he states that 'even more important is the fact that *karma,* as a

theory of causation, is *psychologically* indeterminate. The past determines the present which (combined with the past) determines the future.'[6] Not knowing what his actions have been in past lives, the individual is therefore in the dark so far as his future is concerned. 'Anything could happen to me; sudden changles or alternations of fortune are to be expected for my present existence is determined by past *karma* regarding which I know nothing. Today I may be in perfect health, but tomorrow I may be suddenly struck down by fatal disease. It is my fault that it is so, but my conscious experience cannot tell me what this fault is.'[7] At least, this is the case if he really does accept the doctrine of *karma* in its scriptural form as, say, expounded in the *Bhagavad Gita*. I add this word of precaution since, as M.S.A. Rao has pointed out, there is nothing more dangerous for the sociologist than what he calls the 'hypothetico-deductive approach'.[8] We should not, he says, assume that once a particular belief is held it will have a determining effect on behaviour. (Indeed we should not assume that it is held at all merely on the strength of its existence in ancient texts.) We cannot understand the meaning of a particular belief if we depend only upon scriptural statements, or any other cultural expression of creed, until we have discovered its position in the total belief system of its adherents and seen how it operates in its social context. If we expect the sacred literature of Hinduism to supply us with the context of beliefs we are expecting something which it cannot provide and are liable to further confusion, for as Dumont has pointed out, the scriptures record the ideas and the experiences of the renouncer rather than those of the 'man-in-the-world'.[9]

According to Rao, we cannot judge the consequences of the adherence to the doctrine of *karma* for the individual believer until we know, for instance, whether the notion of *karma* enters the thought process as a cause of action or as a rationalising afterthought. 'More often when a person fails to succeed in business he rationalises his failure in terms of *karma* rather than think of it in advance. Conversely, when he achieves success, he hardly attributes it to *karma*. Hence it is difficult to trace the causal relationship between beliefs and human motivations for what is presented as a cause might well be treated as a justification'.[10] We would be rash then to assert that the problem of *karma must* cause the Hindu to feel anxious or uncomforted about his future without conducting empirical investigation to ascertain whether this is really so. However, we could go so far as to say that such a hypothesis would be worth testing.

1.2.6   So far, my discussion of the problem may seem to be somewhat abstract, theological rather than sociological. But I think such a discussion must form a necessary preliminary to the study of the problem of theodicy in Hinduism. For one thing, as should be abundantly clear by now, the particular form which the problem of suffering takes will vary in different societies. Whilst problem 2 (psychological) in some form could be assumed to be universal, the nature and magnitude of problem 1 (cognitive) and the very existence or non-existence of problem 3 (theological) depend on the kind of solution given to problem 2. Thus the precise nature of the questions to be resolved has to be reformulated in each cultural case. In Hinduism, as we have seen, problem 3 would hardly seem to arise, for as Weber has pointed out, the doctrine of *karma* is one of the most rational of all possible theodicies at the theological level. But problem 2 might be assumed to be fairly acute. Secondly, the fact that in reality Hindus very often do not behave quite as we should expect them to behave if they were to hold strictly to such scriptural beliefs as *karma, dharma* etc., suggests that we should not make assumptions in the first place as to what they really do believe as adherents of the Hindu religion. Indeed, some empirical studies show that some Hindus quite definitely claim that they do not accept certain beliefs like *karma* or the existence of a supreme deity. Individuals may reject certain 'orthodox' beliefs, or at any rate adhere to modified forms or idiosyncratic interpretations of these beliefs. (I record here my reservations about the terms 'modified' and 'interpretations', as they imply that the scripturally 'orthodox' beliefs existed *first* and that villagers and other laymen having once received, then subsequently adapted them to suit their own tastes. I shall return to this point later.) Indeed, it would seem that sociologists were naïve to assume that there would be any less diversity of belief and cosmology among Hindu peasants than among educated Christian Europeans.

1.2.7   Both the points I have raised here indicate that further progress will not be made unless we conduct empirical (and preferably numerous) studies of what Hindus of various types actually do believe about such problems as the causes of misfortune and the relationship of misfortune to behaviour. I will therefore forbear from further theoretical dalliance and present the information which I was able to gather in Ghanyari, a Himachal Pradesh village, during the course of fieldwork carried out in 1966 and 1967. I do not think it will be necessary for me to give a preliminary account of this village except to mention a couple of salient points. First, the dominant caste there is a group of Brahmins; they do not practise priestcraft, being chiefly engaged in agriculture as a full-time source of livelihood. Secondly, the district in which the village lies, whilst not 100 per cent Hindu, has a very strong Hindu majority and has been relatively little exposed to the belief systems of Islam, Sikhism, Christianity or Buddhism. There is only one Muslim family in Ghanyari, which has a population of roughly 350, and is thus large by local standards. The Muslims in this area share many customs with their Hindu heighbours and even celebrate some Hindu festivals. Indeed, being a somewhat isolated area with a very low level of literacy, there has been little possibility for the exposure to any external intellectual influences until recently.

How, then, do villagers account for misfortune and the 1.2.8 distribution of suffering in the world? When speaking in general terms, that is, without reference to any particular instance of good or bad fortune, informants invariably explained the distribution of good and bad fortune in terms of the *karma* theory in its familiar form. The universe is peopled with beings in different stages of spiritual advancement; those who do meritorious deeds in this life will be reborn in favourable circumstances, and similarly those who are sinful will be punished by being reborn in wretched circumstances or as some low form of life. Every deed, good or bad, will eventually bear its fruits, and the individual cannot escape from them. He is thus totally responsible for his fate. The concepts of merit (*pun*) and sin (*pap*), it should be noted, are very broad categories and include ritual conformity and ritual offences respectively, although, as we shall see, this does not mean that ethical and ritual offences are confused, since the distinction between them is clearly made in other contexts. Sometimes the *karma* theory is elaborated in such a way as to personalise the process of judgement and retribution; thus the dead person's soul is judged by Dharmraj, the Lord of the Dead, who assigns to it whatever future status it deserves. Before his soul is reborn in mundane form, one who has done excessive evil may be condemned by Dharmraj to spend some time in whichever of the various hells is appropriate to his offence. Similarly, one whose virtue has been outstanding may dwell for a time in *svarg*, or heaven, before resuming the round of mundane birth and rebirth. These elaborations of the basic theory, however, do not in any way negate the idea that merit is automatically rewarded and sin automatically punished.

1.2.9   Considered thus *in abstracto,* the process of karmic retribution is generally seen as a long-term affair. As one Brahmin priest explained, 'If a man has led a very wicked life he may be happy enough at first, but he will certainly be reborn as a snake or a *bhut* (malevolent ghost) or a dog after his death. He may have to undergo rebirth in such a dreadful form several times before he can expiate his sin and be born in some more auspicious form'. Could he not escape this by being a very good dog, snake, etc., I asked? No, the priest replied, because these creatures have no *dharma* (religious duty attached to their status or condition). Only human beings have *dharma* and if they do not fulfil it, they may take several rebirths in lower non-human forms before they are sufficiently punished for their omissions. Though this informant's view that only men have *dharma* may have been idiosyncratic, his recognition that the operation of *karma* may not be immediate was typical of the views of other villagers whom I questioned on the subject.

1.2.10   Next, let us examine some actual instances in which the theory of *karma* was explicitly invoked to account for misfortune. Here again we find some variations, as it were, on the scriptural themes. For instance, *karma* is sometimes described as not merely the total result of a person's actions — good and bad — for himself (the actor), but as a kind of influence which attaches to his person by virtue of these actions, and which can affect others also. When a boat crowded with pilgrims bound for the shrine of a local saint sank in a lake near to Ghanyari, and all the passengers were drowned, one informant remarked that there must have been some very sinful person aboard for such a terrible disaster to have occurred. When a youth who had been born with a slight deformity of the leg, so that he walked with a limp, found difficulty in getting a bride because of this disability, his father said that this trouble must have been due to the bad *karma* of *both father and son* in past lives. In another family the eldest son of Atma Ram had died in his early twenties, leaving a widow still in her teens, but no children; Atma Ram's cousin commented that this trouble must have been due to the bad *karma* of someone in the household (not necessarily the boy himself). In yet another case a Brahmin, Basala, who had been very much feared and disliked during his lifetime, died, leaving two sons and a married daughter. A series of misfortunes beset the family during the years following his death. First of all the younger son died quite suddenly when he was only sixteen. The elder son married, but his first child died within a few days of birth. Various quarrels took place within the household, both between the Brahmin's two widows (he had married twice, as his first wife had borne no children), and between the elder widow and the son. As a result of these troubles the son and his young wife attempted to commit suicide by drowning themselves in the lake, but were rescued by passers-by. Several neighbours attributed these misfortunes and domestic strife to the bad *karma* of the dead Brahmin which was causing suffering in his family even after his decease.

When I asked a Brahmin priest to explain the concept of *karma* 1.2.11 he stated quite explicitly that the *karma* of one person could affect another, and used a well-known story to illustrate this idea. In this story, a professional burglar is teaching his son the best way to break into a rich man's house. The father points out a house where every window is bright with light from within and where all the inhabitants seem to be enjoying themselves, dressed in fine garments and eating good food, and he remarks to his son that he has burgled this house many a time. But the son observes that the inmates of the house which has provided them with their livelihood appear prosperous and happy in spite of the father's depredations, while their own house remains a gloomy and miserable place. This makes the father think again and he comes to the conclusion that his past life has indeed been futile and sinful, and that the joylessness of his life is due to his wickedness. He takes heed of his son's words and reforms his ways, albeit late in life. This, explained the priest, illustrates how the good *karma* of the son affected that of the father for the virtue and wisdom of the son (expressions of his arrival at a superior stage of karmic evolution) counteracted the sin of the father, enabling the latter to reform before he was inextricably ensnared in the effects of his own bad *karma*.

It will be noted that many of the instances I have cited refer to 1.2.12 members of the same household or kin group being affected by each other's *karma*. In this connection it may be worth noting that many villagers expressed the idea that when a couple marry the wife will henceforth tend to reap the results of her husband's *karma* as well as her own. That is, if he is generous in almsgiving or diligent in keeping fasts, some of the good *karma* he acquires will accrue to the wife, and similarly she would automatically be affected by his bad deeds. The converse, however, did not hold, for her own deeds affect her own fate alone, and would not become part of the *karma* of her husband.

1.2.13   If bad *karma* can exert an influence on those associated with or related to the doer, so also can good *karma* affect others. For example, one villager described how he had been riding in one of a convoy of trucks during the monsoon season. One of the trucks had been swept into the churning waters of a river when the bridge it had been crossing collapsed. But the truck in which he himself had been riding arrived safely at the far side of the bridge just at the very moment before this disaster occurred, and he observed that someone among the company must have had very good *karma* to counteract the danger of the situation.

1.2.14   In the above instances, *karma* has usually been referred to as a general influence, having its origin in unspecified and indeed unknown offences (or good deeds) in the past lives of individuals. Very often, however, misfortunes are seen as the karmic consequences of some known, and usually fairly recent offence in this life.

An interesting example was that of an elderly Brahmin who had been living for some time with the widow of a washerman. His caste fellows had disowned him for associating with such a low-caste woman, and had ceased to eat, drink or smoke with him when he refused to give her up. More than once I heard Brahmins in the village explain the blindness which afflicted his latter years as a punishment for his breach of caste rules. His metaphorical blindness (failure to perceive or take account of caste differences) had become, as it were, a real physical disease. This idea can be compared with the widespread belief that lameness may be the result of having kicked either a cow or a Brahmin in some past life. There are also various legends and stories in which wrongdoers are punished in ways explicitly appropriate to their crimes in some future rebirth.

1.2.15   A similar example of ritual offence being punished with physical disease was the case of another villager, Ramanand, who suffered from such severe rheumatism that he was virtually bed-ridden. His neighbours attributed this to the fact that the year before he had felled a *pipal* tree growing on his land in order to extend one of his meadows (the *pipal* tree being regarded as sacred). Misfortunes suffered by entire groups of people can similarly be attributed to offences or omissions for which they were collectively responsible, as in the case of a *jag*, or feast, organised for the whole village in honour of the deity Thakur, the lord of the rains, during a period of severe drought. The rite failed. The rain which the rite was expected to procure did not fall, or at least not as soon as expected, and this was explained by some as being due to the fact that some of the Chamars (low-caste leather workers) had been turned away rather brusquely by the men in charge of the distribution of the food. The drought itself, incidentally, was regarded by some as a punishment dealt to the village as a whole for its general wickedness, and in particular the quarrelling and disunity of its Brahmin members.

Specific offences, ritual or otherwise, are not related to misfortunes solely retrospectively. Sometimes the commission of a particular offence would give rise to the expectation that some misfortune or disaster would overtake the wrongdoer. For example two brothers cut down a *pipal* tree in order to clear a site for their new house. They satisfied themselves by performing a ritual of worship before the tree before actually taking the axe to it, but their neighbours did not consider this to be a sufficient precaution (as one man remarked, 'what difference does it make to the *pipal* whether you have worshipped it or not when you begin to lop its branches?') and expressed the opinion that some kind of trouble was surely in store for the brothers by way of retribution for this offence. 1.2.16

So far we have been dealing with explanations of misfortune in terms of the moral consequences of offences of an ethical or ritual nature, either specific and known (committed in this life) or putative and unknown (committed in some past life). But perhaps the commonest mode of accounting for misfortunes, especially illness or injury, is not in terms of *karma,* but of the malice of some other person, deity or personalised agent. Thus physical ailments which are chronic or do not respond to treatment are readily attributed to the sorcery (*tuna*) of a near kinsman or affine, and resort may be made to a *chela,* a ritual specialist who will attempt to detect the origin of the trouble and suggest protective measures (such as wearing special charms or amulets). Much more could be said about the techniques used in the practice and cure of sorcery and about the role of the *chela* as diviner, but I will not go into further detail as we are concerned here with the intellectual status of the theory of *tuna* as used to explain misfortune. Alternatively, the afflicted person may view his suffering as due to the anger (*khota*) of some deity or spirit, but here the misfortune is not so readily seen as the result of undeserved or unprovoked spite. Deities as a general rule only send illness or misfortune to those who offend them in some way. A 1.2.17

deity may be offended by an individual's failure to worship him, his failure to fulfil vows he has made to the deity or otherwise neglecting the cult. These offences may be specific and known or only presumed.

1.2.18   These kinds of explanation of suffering are rather different from that which appeals to the principle of *karma* pure and simple, without the involvement of any other agent, as they interpret the individual's suffering in such a way as to indicate some positive and immediate steps which he can take to attempt to remove his troubles – to consult the diviner if he suspects *tuna,* to restore good relations with any deity he feels he has offended or neglected, in whatever may be the appropriate way.

1.2.19   A villager who is suffering from some chronic ailment or trouble which is particularly persistent may invoke both *tuna* and *khota* to explain his problems, either simultaneously or consecutively. For instance one Brahmin woman suffered from some kind of skin disease which would not respond to medication. This convinced her that her sufferings were traceable to more than mere physical causes, but sometimes she favoured the idea that her sister-in-law was causing her sufferings through *tuna* (the two women were not on very good terms at the time) and at others considered the displeasure of the goddess Durga a more likely cause. She was aware of having made a vow to donate charitable gifts to unmarried girls in honour of Durga (a common means of fêting the goddess) which she had not yet been in a position to fulfil, and recalled several dreams she had had in which the goddess had appeared to her, angry and accusing. To cover the possibility of *tuna* she ceased to take food in her sister-in-law's house (*tuna* can often, according to villagers' accounts, be performed by putting magical objects in a person's food which are then consumed without his being aware of the fact.) But she also arranged to conduct rites in honour of Durga as soon as was practicable, so as to take care of the possibility of this goddess's anger being the prime cause of her troubles. Whilst taking these ritual precautions, she did not give up her attempts to find an effective medical treatment, as she continued to try out numerous different kinds of medication and folk remedy.

1.2.20   Usually explanations of suffering in terms of *tuna* and *khota* are used only by the sufferer himself to explain his own misfortune, and not as a means to account for the misfortune of others. After all, family tensions and jealousies or violations of good relations with particular deities are matters known best to the individual concerned.

But in some cases this kind of explanation is used to rationalise the sufferings of another, as in the case of Sibbi, an elderly woman who had become sick and senile. Her mind had begun to wander and she behaved in a very eccentric way, causing her family much embarrassment. Her neighbours attributed her sufferings to the fact that she was apparently known to have made a vow to Gugga, a local saint, to make an offering of Rs.10 at his shrine if her daughter-in-law was safely delivered of a son. In fact two sons were born during the next five years, but Sibbi still had not fulfilled her promise and therefore Gugga was causing her suffering to remind her of this vow.

This would seem a suitable point to summarise some points which   1.2.21
emerge from the material presented so far.

1. The theory of *karma* in its classical form, at least, is not the only concept used to rationalise the occurrence of suffering. Variants of this theory as well as other theories, apparently unconnected, may be used.
2. These theories imply differing degrees of responsibility on the part of the subject, and where responsibility is implied, the offence which is thought to have provoked the affliction in questions may be more or less remote in time, more or less specific, known or unknown to the subject.
3. The explanation for particular events or misfortunes given by the afflicted person and by those amongst whom he lives may not be identical in every case.

What does all this tell us about the ways in which Hinduism as   1.2.22
practised provides solutions to the cognitive and psychological problems of suffering?

I suggested earlier than whilst Hinduism certainly provides an answer to the cognitive problem of suffering (indeed a multiplicity of possible answers at the popular level, as my material shows) it might be supposed that the kind of answer it provides would intensify rather than resolve the psychological problem, i.e. that of providing comfort and justification for the suffering. In theory, Hinduism teaches that suffering is deserved, therefore the sufferer is afflicted by both misfortune *and* guilt. In practice, our material shows that the kinds of explanation given for various kinds of misfortune can be placed on a hypothetical continuum, according to the degree of responsibility allowed to the sufferer, and the immediacy of the responsibility:

karma;   known offence in this life
khota;   known offence against deity
khota;   unintentional or unknown offence against deity
karma;   of others and generalised *karma*
tuna;   sorcery.

Where a misfortune is attributed to the retributive karmic effect of some offence committed in this life, in theory the maximum responsibility is borne by the actor. Where his troubles are attributed to *tuna* his responsibility would be minimal since it is in no way necessarily his fault if he has jealous or malicious kinsmen or neighbours. It is only in the first three instances listed above that we should expect the question of moral guilt to complicate the problem of actual suffering seriously. In practice, as we have seen, there are ways in which individuals can protect themselves from the psychological consequences which might be presumed to follow from such moral propositions.

1.2.23   First, as my material should make clear, there are cases in which the explanation given by the actual sufferer differs from that given by others who witness his suffering in such a way as to remove the responsibility from himself to a degree, or altogether. Thus Ramanand's neighbours attributed his problems to the fact that he had felled a *pipal* tree; but Ramanand himself merely attributed them to generalised bad *karma,* earned in some previous incarnation. One cannot give more than subjective impressions in matters like this, but I should say that villagers do not show signs of deep anxiety or acute remorse over unknown offences committed in past lives. Such offences were theoretically committed by the same self incarnated in a different body, but in practice village sseem to feel immediate responsibility only for offences committed in the present incarnation. Past incarnations are in theory the same self, but it is a rather remote kind of self, differently constituted. Thus Ramanand did not appear to be unduly anxious about the presumed offences which had earned him bad *karma,* on the principle that one can hardly feel guilt about offences that one is unaware of. This kind of multiple explanation is also found in other kinds of case. For instance in the case of Sibbi, whilst her neighbours explained her illness in terms of her responsibility for an offence against a deity, Sibbi herself was more inclined to either a straightforward explanation in mundane physical terms, or in terms of *tuna* practised by her daughter-in-law, thus removing direct moral responsibility from herself. We may add that where villagers use ideas of ritual offence or omission to explain particular troubles, this does not necessarily imply a burden of guilt being placed upon the offender. Whilst it would be untrue to say that ritual errors or omissions are morally entirely neutral, a clear distinction is made between the kind of ethical or ritual offence which is knowingly committed (telling lies, felling a *pipal* tree) and the kind of ritual error which can be made unwittingly, such as omitting some ritual act expected by the deity in question. (This distinction is maintained in practice in spite of the fact that both kinds of offence are subsumed under the concept of *pap*). This kind of omission is a familiar theme in legend and folk stories. For instance there is a story current in Ghanyari concerning a blacksmith who was afflicted with nightmares and sickness because he had used a large boulder, in which (unknown to him) the deity Thakur had chosen to reside, as a weight to secure the jute stems which he was soaking in a local stream. Fortunately Thakur revealed his offence to him in a dream, and he was able to make good his error by building a shrine to the deity in which the stone in question was given a place of honour. In a case like this, unintentional ritual offence implies no moral opprobrium and therefore an individual might own to having (presumably) committed some such error without implying any moral culpability on his own part. Again, where the bad deeds of some member of the family – known (as in the case of Basala) or unknown (as in the case of Atma Ram) – are involved the acceptance of the working of *karma* does not oblige the sufferer to accept disturbing guilt feelings, since he himself has not committed the acts which provoked the karmic retribution. The effects of karmic retribution have, as it were, become diffused to include him through no direct fault of his own. Occasionally we even hear villagers employ the Islamic term *kismet,* to account for events and fortunes, thus approaching a purely fatalistic interpretation. Also, it is not uncommon to hear villagers account for events by saying 'It is God's will', although I believe that this is more often proffered as a kind of conventional consolation to, for example, someone suffering from a bereavement, rather than a thought-out explanation of the misfortune in question.

From observation, therefore, we may say that whilst the concept of *karma* is accepted in theory by the villagers, in actual operation it is either supplemented by other notions of causation, or it is implemented in such a way that the afflicted person is protected from a heavy sense of responsibility or feelings of anxiety about past deeds. I do not mean that the Hindu villager has side-stepped the problem of moral guilt altogether, or that due to some sort of intellectual cheating he never feels this emotion; I mean that for him it does not constitute a *special* problem, such as a naïve view of the existence of the *karma* theory as an explanation of suffering might lead us to expect.

1.2.24   But what about the future? Does not the Hindu feel insecure in whatever good fortune he may enjoy, by virtue of the fact that he may yet have to receive punishment for unknown offences in past lives? In practice, I would say that this does not seem to be a subject which causes the villager to lose much sleep. The very 'supplementary' theories of causation which he used to explain suffering imply, as I have already observed, techniques for attempting to improve one's lot in future or averting trouble and suffering, and on the whole it is the fairly immediate future with which the villager concerns himself. Thus the idea of *khota* is balanced by the idea that deities can also be placated and won over by offerings and worship to provide positive good fortune to their devotees. If ritual offences bring misfortune, the punctilious observance of fasts and other religious rituals ensure happiness and welfare. If neighbours and relatives can cause trouble through the practice of *tuna* then the diviner and his various skills are there to be used to counteract this. So the villager does not by any means see himself as helpless in the face of fortune, even though according to a strict interpretation of the *karma* theory he is in fact highly vulnerable to the effects of deeds committed in this and other lives.

1.2.25   It will be noticed that the words 'in theory' and 'in practice' are continually juxtaposed and contrasted. I have mentioned the existence of 'supplementary' theories — supplementary, that is, to the scriptural notion of *karma*. What is the status of that theory if it is frequently negated in practice, and apparently competes with other theories?

On the face of it, it would seem that to claim in the first place that *karma* accounts for the differential distribution of good and bad fortune, and then to explain a particular misfortune in terms of, say, *tuna*, would amount to a logical inconsistency. If the individual is ultimately responsible for his own fate, how can the will of others influence this fate for good or ill? The operative word here, however, is 'ultimately'. When I put this question to villagers directly they answered that explanations of bad fortune in terms of one's relationships with the deities or one's kinsmen do not negate the theory of *karma*. One might suffer from some illness on account of the machinations of some jealous kinsman who practised sorcery, to be sure, but this was only an explanation in terms of immediate causes. If the sufferer's *karma* had been good, he would not have succumbed to his kinsman's *tuna*. To put it another way, it must be the *karma* of the individual which explains why he in particular is fated to be the victim of such malice. Again, a person might suffer from financial troubles or ill health because of his neglect of a particular deity, but in the final analysis it is the *karma* which he has accumulated in this and previous lives which determines the degree to which he is successful in his dealings with the gods. In short, we encounter here the familiar distinction between the 'cause' and the 'meaning' of misfortune.

The practice of astrology would also appear to imply a rejection 1.2.26 of the principle of karmic determination, for if the events in one's life are determined by the conjunction of stars at one's birth, how can they also be shaped by one's moral activity in previous lives? But, I was told, this is only a contradiction at the superficial level; the very moment of one's birth is determined by one's past *karma,* so that if a person is born at an astrologically inauspicious time this must be because of his sinfulness in a past life. The stars therefore *predict* a man's future rather than *determine* it. I have not dwelt on the phenomenon of astrology because whilst the horoscope is of great importance at weddings (when the horoscopes of the bride and groom must be matched and found compatible), I did not find that particular instances of misfortune were often attributed to inauspicious planetary influences. For one thing, horoscopes and astrological predictions seldom foretell good or bad events in a very specific way; the fact that some kind of trouble is predicted in a person's horoscope may diminish the surprise element when trouble eventually occurs, but some other more precise explanation is generally sought in addition, if the trouble is felt to be problematic.

The admission of immediate causes of suffering for which the 1.2.27 victim is not directly responsible should not therefore be taken as a denial of his long-term responsibility for his fate according to the principle of *karma*. The various types of explanation given for suffering and misfortune have not been integrated by the villagers into a tidy and logically coherent system of metaphysics, but they should not therefore be regarded as entirely discrete and unrelated. The principle of *karma* is prior to the others in several senses. First, it is logically prior to all other possible explanations in the sense that the latter can be reduced to or made compatible with the *karma* doctrine in the final analysis. Secondly, whilst the *karma* principle need not be the theory which the villager turns to first of all in his search for a meaning for the misfortune he suffers, it is generally the last which he will abandon. By this I mean that he is more likely to express scepticism towards the cult of the gods or towards the idea of *tuna* than he is explicitly to reject the doctrine of *karma*. This at least was the impression I received when talking to some of the more educated and sophisticated members of the village.

1.2.28   As we have seen, in times of stress or trouble, a villager is more likely to act on the assumption that his suffering is not inevitable and that it can be dealt with by applying whichever of the other possible kinds of explanations seems appropriate, or even more than one theory simultaneously. Since the logical paramountcy of the *karma* theory does not in any way preclude the existence of other beliefs, it is tempting to treat these beliefs as distinct and incongruent bodies of theory, especially in view of the fact that the philosophy of *karma* is elaborated in some of the Hindu Texts, whereas the other theories receive less authoritative treatment or none at all. The temptation to treat the theories as disparate or conflicting is the greater in view of the fact that each kind of theory is associated with its own system of ritual practice or 'technology' and its separate set of specialists. To the level of ultimate karmic explanation belongs all that body of ritual (*kathas,* fasts, charitable donations, feeding of Brahmins) which is directed to improving one's store of personal merit and thereby warding off the misfortunes which may arise from bad *karma.* To the more immediate level of explanation (in terms of malevolent deities) correspond the cults of the gods with all their priests and ritual paraphernalia, all the ritual designed to improve a person's fortune by ensuring that the gods are well-disposed towards him. At a more mundane level there are explanations of misfortune in terms of the sufferer's relationship with other human beings; associated with this kind of belief we find the institution of the *chela* and the remedies for the effects of *tuna* which he can prescribe. Alongside all these 'supernatural' kinds of belief and procedure there are all the various kinds of material technology available to the villager through which he can try to better his lot and ward off misfortune, including at least three different systems of medicine known and practised locally. (This may seem an obvious point, but it would be misleading if our interest in religious and philosophical interpretations of misfortune were to lead us to assume that the Hindu himself is only interested in this kind of explanation and ignores the various material techniques of cure and prevention which are at his disposal.)

Having made these distinctions, the anthropologist may be further tempted to regard the well-known 'classical' version of the *karma* theory as 'orthodox', from which it will follow that the various other kinds of explanation which I have described must be regarded as heterodox variations of, or even departures from the basic theory. The temptation is especially acute for the educated western observer whose prior knowledge of Hinduism before he arrives in the field may largely be derived from scriptural texts which he has read in translation. Yet in Ghanyari it is very difficult to talk about orthodoxy. For one thing whilst the Brahmin priest certainly has a monopoly in the performance of some key rituals and may be regarded as having a special competence to pronounce on matters of doctrine, he cannot be said to have final authority in the case of the latter. Respect for his judgement is based on his superior learning (although most priests in the area are not particularly erudite) rather than on his authority *qua* priest. 1.2.29

Secondly, whilst the theory of *karma* may be expounded by the priests when they recite the Sanskrit texts as scripture recitals and other religious occasions, it is my impression that the doctrine does not depend on this channel of information for its survival and propagation. In practice the individual receives the concept of *karma* as part of a living folk tradition which includes equally the other ideas which I have described, such as those concerning the pantheon, or the effects of *tuna*. In other words, the villager is not much concerned with the different sources of authority for these various strands in local Hindu thought. Indeed, far from regarding the *karma* concept in any passive way, the villager, as we have seen, is liable to elaborate or reinterpret the theory actively, resulting in variations and idiosyncrasies of interpretation. (This applies equally to the Brahmin priest.) The existence of scriptural expositions of the kind of idea which we have been discussing cannot simply be left out of account, since the villager is aware of their existence and prestige even though he is not very likely to have read them; the scriptures are constantly referred to in a vague manner as the epitome of Hindu metaphysics and law, even though few have a very precise idea of their contents. On the other hand, the villager does not let this 1.2.30

interfere with his right to reinterpret received doctrines in the light of his own personal ideas and experiences. This, at least, is true of Ghanyari, although I am aware that a different situation might obtain, in, say, an area where there were influential groups of learned Brahmins or sectarian scholars, or centres of traditional Hindu learning and culture.

1.2.31 The problem of the relationship of the *karma* theory to other theories used to interpret suffering and misfortune is not peculiar to the Hindu world. In fact it has been studied more extensively with reference to Buddhism. The Buddhists of south and south-east Asia have in common with the Hindus of Ghanyari both a belief in *karma* (albeit in a slightly different form), and a religious tradition which is conducive to heterogeneity, being decentralised and multi-stranded. In Thailand, Tambiah notes that the merit-making ceremonies which are associated with scriptural beliefs in *karma* coexist with the cults addressed to deities which are also believed to be capable of influencing the affairs of men. At first sight an inconsistency would seem to exist in the religious thinking of these Buddhists, for Tambiah comments that 'if the doctrine of *karma* gives an explanation for present suffering and squarely puts the burden of release on individual effort then the doctrine that super-natural agents can cause or relieve suffering and that relief can come through propitiating them contradicts the *karma* postulate'.[11] But Tambiah goes on to say that it is not helpful to regard these two theories as being, as it were, in competition with each other, for 'while this categorical opposition is present in Thailand I see it as one which operates within a total field that expresses other relations as well of complementarity and hierarchical ordering between Buddhism and the spirit cults. To emphasise one aspect at the expense of others seems to me to be a partial analysis; to go further and assert that there are in fact two contradictory religions in uneasy coexistence appears to me to be a misunderstanding'.[12] Tambiah is referring here to Spiro's study of Buddhism in Burma where Buddhism and the cult of the *nats* (powerful and often malevolent spirits capable of causing illness and misfortune to humans) provide answers to different kinds of moral or personal crises. To the extent that they seem to embody different moral values, Spiro regards them as being in conflict and points out that his Burmese informants themselves were aware of the tension between the values of the two cults. But we may concur with Tambiah that this does not justify the assertion that there are two distinct religions. Presumably it might be possible for Burmese Buddhists to square their performance of *nat* rituals with the belief in the operation of the moral law of *karma*, much as the Hindus of Ghanyari are capable of ironing out the inconsistencies between their worship of the Hindu deities and their belief in the Hindu version of *karma*. But unlike Tambiah's Thai Buddhists, Spiro's informants seemed to be acutely aware of their dilemma and entertained a highly ambivalent attitude to the *nat* cults. The more educated especially deprecated them as being not really 'religion' at all, yet in spite of professed scepticism few omitted to propitiate them, including the educated sceptics. Thus, for these Burmese Buddhists the problem of the discontinuities in their belief system is a real one, and not simply an academic one manufactured by the anthropologist. But in this respect Spiro's material would seem to differ from the other studies discussed here; as Tambiah points out, it is more common for the anthropologist to take as his starting point the scriptural expressions of the *karma* theory and then note how these differ from the 'popular' religion. This orientation dictates its methodology and shapes the final conclusions, for the analyst accordingly seeks to see how 'non-doctrinal' facts are adapted, modified, and rationalised in relation to 'doctrinal' ideas.

Gombrich has tackled the same problem in Ceylon. There, as in Ghanyari, the effects of a rigorous interpretation of the *karma* doctrine are mitigated by a number of practices which would seem to imply modification of the strict *karma* theory. For instance, to make a *prarthanu* religious wish – for instance to wish that all the hearers of a particular sermon may attain nirvana, would seem to contradict the *karma* theory; at least this would be the case if the maker of the wish had any faith in the efficacy of his prayer really to affect the spiritual fortunes of others. How can the hearers of a sermon attain nirvana except by their own efforts? 'This is not strictly in contradiction to *karma* theory because it can be said that the wish will only be fulfilled if the *karma* is good enough, and the merit gained just before a *prarthana* is made should ensure this. However, there is little doubt that affectively the donor feels that he is achieving a certain result by a certain action in an automatic, magical way.'[13] So for Gombrich's Buddhists, the real tensions lie not between the various intellectual expressions of their religious ideas, since notions which on the face of it appear undoctrinal can generally be assimilated to canonical doctrines, albeit sometimes

1.2.32

with difficulty. The important tensions lie between what Gombrich calls 'cognitive' religion (what people say about their beliefs and practices) and 'affective' religion (the religion of the heart, the ideas that are implied by actual behaviour).

1.2.33   Whilst a comparison with Buddhist cases is obviously interesting here, we must not lose sight of certain important differences between the religious organisations of Buddhism and Hinduism. Here I return to the points I made earlier about orthodoxy. As Gombrich shows, it does make sense to talk about 'canonical' Buddhism provided that we understand that this does not mean that there is any enforcement of intellectual conformity, merely a body of scriptures which are agreed to be authoritative above all others. But of Hinduism one could only say that of the great body of religious literature, some texts are better known and regarded as more authoritative than others, or are regarded as authoritative for certain sects only. Yet as Gombrich shows, some of the tensions between affective and cognitive religion are present within canonical Buddhism itself. Certainly it would not be legitimate to characterise some of the popular ideas and practices which he describes as being in any way heterodox departures from canonical doctrine since, as he points out, some of the very ideas and practices which he refers to would seem to date back to the very beginning of Buddhist history and are even mentioned in early Buddhist writings. They reflect the inevitable tension between the cognitive propositions of Buddhism and the affective needs of the Buddhist rather than the heterodoxy of the latter. This is an important point since it has always been a besetting sin of western scholars (and indeed of some oriental ones) to impute to Buddhism and Hinduism a stronger and more rigid sense of orthodoxy than actually exists, and therefore to regard very readily the latitude with which the uneducated Buddhist or Hindu interprets received religious ideas as departures from 'orthodoxy'. The very term 'orthodoxy' can, I feel, be applied to Indian Hinduism only in certain very specific contexts, as for instance, when we are speaking of the doctrines of particular monastic orders or sects. I hope I have demonstrated this satisfactorily already so far as Ghanyari itself is concerned.

What the Buddhist material which I have mentioned does illustrate very clearly, I think, is that when we set out to discover the relationship between doctrinal tenets and affective needs, we are not by any means creating a pseudo-problem. The danger of creating 'pseudo-problems' is an ever-present one, especially where a 'hypothetico-deductive' approach is used. The study of belief systems is particularly difficult because it is all too easy for the anthropologist to assume that beliefs *are* arranged in systems, instead of feeling obliged to demonstrate that this is in fact the case. Discontinuities or inconsistencies among the ideas expressed by the subject then become a problem to the researcher even though they may not be at all problematic to the subject. Most human beings after all, seem able to tolerate some areas of uncertainty or confusion in their belief systems, though obviously the problems which appear to need precise resolution and those which can safely be left unresolved or even imperfectly formulated will vary in different societies. Yet, if the questions posed at the beginning of this article were perhaps formulated in an ethnocentric manner, I do not think that they were foolish ones. Approaching the question of theodicy solely in terms of the possible doctrinal conflict between the various theories put forward to explain suffering would not seem to be the most appropriate method of approach in the case of Hinduism, as the material shows, since intellectual conformity is not a matter of great concern to the Hindu villager. It was found more appropriate to define the question in terms of 'tensions' rather than 'conflict' or 'contradiction'. But the very diversity and complexity of the various resolutions to the problem of suffering which can be found within Buddhist and Hindu villages, even such a small and isolated village as Ghanyari, are surely of great interest, not to mention the more general questions about the structure of belief systems which are raised by these studies of Hinduism and Buddhism.

Appendix

Karma and caste   1.2.34

Mention may be made here of the role of the *karma* theory in interpreting the social order. Low-caste status may be conceived as a special form of misfortune or suffering, entailing as it does a position of ritual and frequently economic disprivilege. In Hindu writings the idea is often expressed that low-caste status is to be accounted for by sins in a past life, and sociologists have often assumed that this theory is in fact current as a rationale for the caste system (e.g. Weber). Studies of particular low castes such as those conducted by Cohn, Mahar and others show (not surprisingly) that members of low castes do not in fact use this theory to explain their own low-caste status. Rather they explain it in secular or historical terms (e.g.

that they are really descended from a high-caste person who contracted a misalliance, they were outcasted unjustly, etc.). Of the sweepers whom she studied, Kolenda says that their 'conception of why they have a low-caste status protects them from anxiety which would result if they accepted the full *karma* theory with its require- ments that members of the lowest caste must have been those who were most sinful in past incarnations.'[14] So far, my experiences in Ghanyari would confirm this observation, for the untouchable castes there used similar mythical explanations for the status of their caste. What is interesting is the fact that when asked to account for the existence of the caste system, Brahmins also tended to explain it primarily in secular terms, usually in terms of the need for a division of labour in society. For instance, one Brahmin farmer said, 'caste arose because one man alone cannot do all the work himself. One person cannot do the work of a teacher, farmer, priest, smith, soldier – he would never have time. Therefore different castes were created to perform these different tasks. Another Brahmin explained the system in terms of the differential prestige of various occupations. 'Low castes came into existence because some tasks, like sweeping out latrines or skinning dead animals, are dirty and repulsive; ordinary people do not wish to associate with those who do such work, and therefore separate castes were formed.' Responses of a secular kind were given by both high and low caste persons to the question as to why the caste system exists. But when asked to account for a particular individual's birth in a low-caste family, villagers answered in terms of past *karma* and here again, I noticed no great differences between the responses given by members of high or low castes. A member of a low caste said to me, 'You are dressed in fine clothes and are seated upon a chair wherever you go. I am dressed in rags and people only bid me sit on the floor because I am of low caste; surely it must all be due to *karma* in our past life.' This informant did not seem to feel the suggestion that she had been sinful in her past life unacceptable, presumably because – as I have shown – unknown offences committed in a past life are regarded as too remote from the individual who is presumed to have committed them to activate very acute feelings of guilt or responsibility. The theory of *karma* need not therefore pose any greater problem to low castes than it does to anyone else who feels that his situation is unenviable or unfortunate.

Notes

Ursula Sharma, *Man*, Vol.8, No.3, Royal Anthropological Institute, September 1973, pp.347-64.

1. C. Geertz, 'Religion as a cultural system', in *Anthropological Approaches to the Study of Religion*, ed. M. Banton (Assoc. Social Anthrop. Monogr.) London: Tavistock 1966.

2. T. Parsons, 'The theoretical development of the sociology of religion', in *Essays in Sociological Theory, pure and applied*, Glencoe: Free Press 1949, pp.52-66.

3. M. Weber, *The Sociology of Religion*, london: Associated Book Publishers 1966, p.107.

4. M. Weber, 'The social psychology of the world religions', in *From Max Weber*, eds. H.H. Gerth and C. Wright Mills, London: Routledge and Kegan Paul 1948, p.276.

5. G. Obeyesekere, 'Theodicy, sin and salvation in a sociology of Buddhism', in *Practical Religion*, ed. E.R. Leach, Cambridge University Press 1968, p.11.

6. G. Obeyesekere, *op.cit.* p.21.

7. *Ibid.*

8. M.S.A. Rao, 'Religion and economic development' in *Tradition, Rationality and Change*, Bombay: Popular Prakashan 1972, p.630.

9. L. Dumont, *Religion, Politics and History in India*, The Hague: Mouton 1970, p.41.

10. M.S.A. Rao, *op.cit.* p.66.

11. S.J. Tambiah, *Buddhism and the Spirit Cults in North East Thailand*, CUP 1970, p.41.

12. *Ibid.*

13. R.F. Gombrich, *Precept and Practice*, Oxford: Clarendon Press 1971, p.220.

14. P.M. Kolenda, Religious Anxiety and Hindu fate, in *Journal of Asian Studies*, No.23, pp.71-9.

2 ASPECTS OF HINDUISM

[*Editor's Note:* Hinduism is marked off from religions such as Christianity, Buddhism and Islam by its having no founder. In addition it has to a large extent remained the religion of one specific part of the world — though for centuries there have been some adherents outside India. But like Christianity and Judaism, and indeed most of the major religions of mankind, Hinduism has a very considerable body of sacred writings and we are concerned in the Reader with two forms of those writings. The Upanishads, one form of sacred writing represented in the Reader, come from the great creative period of world religion — about the middle of the first millennium B.C. They are a reaction against the Vedic hymns which had been in use for a thousand years and which were polytheistic in their theology. In the Bhagavad Gita, chapters of which are also found within the Reader, a more devotional theology comes to birth. Gods from the long past become objects of popular devotion; and this almost human relationship with a personal god remains an important strain in modern Hinduism. Passages in the Reader, additional to the Upanishads and the Bhagavad Gita, relate to Hindu belief in its historical and social context in India and also to aspects of Hindu spirituality up to the twentieth century.

Students will encounter a number of new and somewhat strange sounding words in the material of this section. Any difficulty over these terms can be dispelled by the use of the special Glossary which all Open University students will receive and which will make clear the meaning of all unusual words of major importance.]

2.1   THE CONCEPT 'HINDUISM'

W. Cantwell Smith

The term 'Hinduism' is, in my judgement, a particularly false 2.1.1
conceptualisation, one that is conspicuously incompatible with any
adequate understanding of the religious outlook of Hindus. Even the
term 'Hindu' was unknown to classical Hindus. 'Hinduism' as a
concept certainly they did not have. And indeed one only has to
reflect on the situation carefully to realise that it would necessarily
have been quite meaningless to them.

As we have previously observed, the classical Hindus were 2.1.2
inhibited by no lack of sophistication or self-consciousness. They
thought about what we call religious questions profusely and with
critical analysis. But they could not think of Hinduism because that
is the name that we give to a totality whatever it might be that they
thought, or did, or thought worth doing. . .

My objection to the term 'Hinduism', of course, is not on the 2.1.3
grounds that nothing exists. Obviously an enormous quantity of
phenomena is to be found that this term covers. My point, and I
think that this is the first step that one must take towards understanding something of the vision of Hindus, is that the mass of
religious phenomena that we shelter under the umbrella of that
term, is not a unity and does not aspire to be. It is not an entity
in any theoretical sense, let alone any practical one.

'Islam' and 'Christianity', as we shall subsequently consider, are 2.1.4
also in fact, in actual practice, internally diverse, and have been
historically fluid. They, however, have included a tendency to wish
not to be so; this is not how they conceptualise themselves. Many
Christians and many Muslims have come to believe that there is one
true Christianity and one true Islam. Hindus, on the other hand,
have gloried in diversity. One of their basic and persistent
affirmations has been that there are as many aspects of the truth as
there are persons to perceive it.

Or, if some proclaimed a dogmatic exclusivism, insisting on their 2.1.5
own version of the truth over against alternatives, it was always on a
sectarian basis, one fraction of the total Hindu complex affirmed
against other fractions — not of one transcending Hindu scheme as a
whole. Some Hindus have been tolerant of diversity, and indeed have

made a principle of it; those who have not, have adhered to a particularist position that thereby segmented the Hindu tradition as a possible theoretic unity. In either case, 'Hinduism' has not been a feasible concept for them in any essentialist sense. . .

2.1.6   What obstructs a definition of Hinduism, for instance, is precisely the richness of what exists, in all its extravagant variety from century to century and from village to village. The empirical religious tradition of the Hindus developing historically in the minds and hearts and institutions and literature and societies of untold millions of actual people is not a form, but a growing congeries of living realities. It is not to be compressed within or eviscerated into or confused with any systematic intellectual pattern.

2.1.7   'Hinduism' refers not to an entity; it is a name that the West has given to a prodigiously variegated series of facts. It is a notion in men's minds — and a notion that cannot but be inadequate. To use this term at all is inescapably a gross oversimplification.

Source: From W. Cantwell Smith, *The Meaning and End of Religion*, Mentor Religious Classics, 1964, pp.61, 63 and 130.

2.2 THE PROBLEM OF VILLAGE HINDUISM: 'FRAGMENTATION' AND INTEGRATION

Ursula Sharma

The Theoretical Problem and the 'Fragmentary' Approach

Anyone who studies Hinduism in its village context is liable to be 2.2.1
more immediately impressed by the diversity of its local forms than
by their unity. In the first place, the pantheon of any particular
village is likely to be complex enough; the deities of the place may
include gods and goddesses whose cults are sanctioned in the Vedas
themselves alongside local godlings whose names are barely heard of
outside a restricted area. The rituals used in worshipping these
deities may be just as diverse; they will include relatively informal
and private acts of worship on the part of individual devotees, whilst
on other occasions highly formalised ritual procedure defined in
Sanskrit texts must be used. Again, some rites are performed at the
initiative of the individual and are directed to ends personal to
himself, whilst others are associated with fixed dates in the calendar.

This diversity poses the following problem for the sociologist: to 2.2.2
what extent do these various forms of religious activity form any
kind of system? How are they related to each other in terms of
either common underlying values or consistency of purpose? If
Hinduism can indeed be envisaged as a system of social behaviour (as
opposed to a mere collection of heterogeneous, and uncoordinated
ritual activities, which we associate with each other merely through
the force of tradition) then what gives coherence to this system?
Hinduism is not sustained as a whole by any ecclesiastical or
sectarian organisation; in the absence of such an institutional framework, at what level ought we to seek continuities between the
diverse elements of which it is made?

Hitherto, the majority of sociologists who have made field 2.2.3
studies of Hinduism have attempted to deal with this bewildering
variety of its local forms by trying to arrange them in some scheme
of classification, usually according to more or less culturological
criteria. The origins of this kind of method can be seen in the
preoccupation of nineteenth-century ethnographers with the
distinction between 'Aryan' and 'pre-Aryan' deities but the most
prominent example of this type of approach in modern sociology is

51

Srinivas's formulation of the 'Sanskritic'/'non-Sanskritic' dichotomy, and also his distinction between 'all-India' and 'local' Hinduism. Another leading example is Marriott's division of Hindu cultural features into the 'great traditional' and the 'little traditional'. This kind of approach is unsatisfactory in that it tends to deal with the individual elements of Hindu religious behaviour (cults, deities, rites) as discrete cultural traits, capable of being considered in isolation from each other. This is no doubt justifiable if our interest does not go beyond the cultural origins of these features; but for the sociologist it is hardly legitimate to treat them as independent entities, since in doing so he is obliged to lift them from their social context of meaning and purpose. Encumbered by frames of reference more suited to culturological investigation than to sociology, these writers have been able to pay little attention to such questions as whether for the individual Hindu his religious activities have any kind of underlying purpose or rationale integrating their diversity. Because the kind of approach which I have described emphasises, on the contrary, the ways in which the Hindu's religious experience and activity can be broken down and pigeon-holed into different categories I shall term this the 'fragmentary' method.

2.2.4   The most influential exponent of this kind of method has been M.N. Srinivas. In his study of the Coorgs he analyses their religion in terms of the distinction between, on the one hand, those forms which they share with Hindus everywhere in India (all-India Hinduism) and, on the other hand, those which they share only with members of a restricted locality (regional and local Hinduism). There are also forms which are entirely peculiar to themselves as a caste. Besides this formal distinction, Srinivas also distinguishes between those elements in Coorg religion which are Sanskritic (a term which he never adequately or explicitly defines, but by which he seems to mean 'sanctioned in scriptural texts written in Sanskrit') and those which are non-Sanskritic. In practice, for Srinivas, these two dichotomies often amount to one and the same distinction, since on the whole Sanskritic Hinduism and all-India Hinduism are the same thing. The process of Sanskritisation consists of the adoption of Sanskritic cults and practices and the giving up of purely local non-Sanskritic forms. In so far as Sanskritic forms (being associated with the Brahmans and the high castes) bear prestige, they may be copied by castes who wish to improve their status in the local caste hierarchy. The Coorgs, claims Srinivas, have Sanskritised many of their practices in recent times. Their participation in reformist

movements such as the Ramakrishna Mission and the Lingayat sect
are cited as evidence of this process, also the fact that they have
begun to honour their ancestors by observing the annual *shraddha*
ritual under the direction of a Brahman priest where before they
made offerings of meat and wine to their ancestors through a low
caste oracle. Because of his tendency to fragment Coorg religious
experience, Srinivas is unable to tell us whether this Sanskritisation
represents any kind of qualitative change in the mode of Coorg
religiosity, or whether it is a purely formal change; that is, when
Coorg offer *shraddha* through Brahman priests instead of meat and
wine through low-caste oracles, does this mean that they have in any
way altered their ideas about the after-life or their attitudes towards
their ancestors, or are these simply new manifestations of the same
religious attitudes? If their acquaintance with the Lingayat sect has
influenced the Coorgs to observe Shivratri and erect images of
Shiva's Nandi bull, does this adoption of Sanskritised practice
indicate the development of new religious ideas or sentiments, or
simply the adoption of different cultural forms of expression? Does
it mean that the Coorgs have changed the way in which they view
their pantheon, or the relative importance which they give to its
various members? Such questions cannot be answered so long as the
practices in question are considered separately from Coorg religion
in general. Whilst the sociologist ought not to concentrate
exclusively on the subjective aspects of religion, Srinivas's over-
concentration on ritual (as a self-acknowledged follower of
Radcliffe-Brown) leads him to neglect the role of attitudes and
values. Hence it is impossible to tell whether or in what way the
Sanskritic elements in their religion and the non-Sanskritic elements
are related to each other so far as the Coorgs themselves are
concerned.

Even supposing that this kind of classification is useful, it still
poses many problems of definition. In the absence of any clear
statement of what exactly constitutes Sanskritic Hinduism, are we
to use the term only to refer to rites sanctioned in the Hindu
scriptures? Srinivas seems to imply this. Yet, if by Sanskritic deities
we mean scriptural deities, how can we term Bheru (generally
identified as a form of Shiva) and Chamunda (a form of Devi) as
non-Sanskritic? At other times Srinivas seems to identify Sanskritic
Hinduism with the forms of ritual and belief characteristic of the
Brahmans as a caste.[1] But if this identification is valid it is hardly
consistent to refer to sects which explicitly challenge the authority

of the traditional Brahman priesthood as agents of Sanskritisation. Mahar describes the Arya Samaj as a Sanskritising influence on the group of sweepers which she studied, yet it is questionable whether such a term ought to be used of a movement which has aroused much bitter opposition from orthodox Brahmans. If we are to apply the term Sanskritic to sects which have rejected the religious value of the Sanskrit language and which have encouraged the development of vernacular religious literature — as Cohn does when he states that the Shiv Narayan sect has assisted the Sanskritisation of a group of Chamars — then we are quite evidently not using the term in a literal sense to mean 'connected with the Sanskrit language' (a point which Cohn does recognise himself).

Srinivas himself cannot, of course, be blamed if others have used the concepts which he originated somewhat lavishly and loosely. But the fact that he never gives a strict definition of what the term Sanskritic is supposed to comprise leaves it open to this kind of use, and especially when he himself seems to use it to embrace what is actually quite a hetereogeneous group of concepts. Staal makes the same point in his critique of Srinivas's use of the term Sanskritic when he complains that 'Sanskritisation is a complex concept or class of concepts' which covers a wide variety of phenomena. To be useful to the sociologist, therefore, any typology of Hindu religious forms needs a much narrower and better defined set of categories.

2.2.5   An approach to the problem of the diversity of local Hinduism which is very similar to Srinivas's in certain respects is that of McKim Marriott. He distinguishes between those cultural features of a North Indian village which belong to what he calls the great traditional culture (the culture of the wider community of which the village is a part) and those belonging to the little tradition (the parochial culture of a particular locality). Just as Srinivas recognises that there is communication between the Sanskritic and the non-Sanskritic levels of Hinduism (for instance non-Sanskritic deities such as village gods and goddesses may be assimilated to the Sanskritic tradition by being identified with forms of Sanskritic deities), so Marriott recognises that there is continual communication between the great and little traditions. Features of the great tradition develop local peculiarities and accretions and likewise what were once no doubt purely local forms and customs come to have more universal reference and eventually become assimilated to the great tradition. But no more than Srinivas does Marriott make it clear whether these changes have more than formal significance. For instance, if the festival of Charm Tying can be regarded as a great traditional version of the little traditional festival of Saluno (which also celebrates the brother-sister relationship), is the transformation one of cultural form alone or is it accompanied by a reinterpretation of the values and beliefs which Saluno expresses? If, on the other hand, Saluno and Charm Tying are simply different ways of expressing the same set of beliefs and values, why does the more universalised form have an attraction for the villagers when, after all, their own local culture already provided them with an occasion for celebrating the brother-sister bond? What function, if any, does this cultural duplication fulfil? It could be that the adoption of the priestly great traditional form of the festival signifies something about changing attitudes to caste and status rather than to the sibling relationship. But it is impossible to come to any conclusions about what such changes represent in terms of the meaning of the rites for their participants so long as we consider the rites in isolation from the rest of the religious activity of the village. Were Marriott to give us further information about, for instance, local attitudes to the Brahman priesthood, any recent extensions in the villagers' religious knowledge or experience, which may have come about through (for instance) education or greater opportunities for travel, the nature of the brother-sister relationship and any changes which it may have undergone in recent times, we might then be in a position to assess the sociological significance of this transformation. But as long as this festival is treated only as an isolable fragment we are permitted to view it in cultural terms alone.

Some progress towards a more integrated view of Hinduism has 2.2.6 been made by E.B. Harper. Describing the 'supernaturals' worshipped by the members of a South Indian village he divides these beings into three groups. First, there are the vegetarian, Sanskritic *devaru;* secondly, there are the meat-eating *devate* or local gods; thirdly, there are the blood-thirsty and demonic *devva.* On the whole the divinities of the first group are worshipped predominantly by the Brahmans and the high castes; on the other hand the Brahmans never participate directly in the non-vegetarian cults of the *devva.* The deities thus form a kind of hierarchy according to the status of their devotees. But Harper recognises that this kind of classification on its own does not explain very much. He therefore further distinguishes the three classes of deity on the basis of the different functions they fulfil in village religion. The *devaru* are primarily viewed as benevolent beings and are worshipped chiefly for the purpose of acquiring spiritual merit. The *devate* are generally worshipped with more this-wordly ends in view; they are believed to be able to use their powers both to help and to harass human beings, and correct worship can persuade them to act benevolently. The *devva*, on the other hand, are purely hostile beings and never anything but malevolent in disposition. They are worshipped only by way of appeasement in order to avert the terrible results of their displeasure. Harper leaves unanswered the question of whether the villager himself visualises his pantheon as a structured hierarchy in this manner, or how he relates these cults to each other. To this extent he still treats the supernaturals as detachable elements in the religious tradition of the village. But at least he presents these culturally transmitted elements − i.e., beliefs in different kinds of deity − in the context of the purposes and activities associated with them by the members of this tradition.

Harper avoids the fragmentary approach more successfully in a later article in which he describes the same supernaturals as members of a hierarchy of beings which includes both human beings as well as deities and spirits. The 'pure' (vegetarian) deities stand in a similar relationship to the 'impure' (carnivorous) deities as that of the high castes among human beings to the low castes. The services of the members of any level in the cosmic hierarchy are necessary to the members of the next ascending level if the latter are to maintain their superior ritual status. Thus, just as the members of the middle castes are only able to retain their purity if members of the lowest castes perform tasks for them which would be polluting were they to carry them out themselves, so the deities in turn require the services of the priestly (high) caste among men to act as their ritual servants or 'purifiers'. Since on the whole the same kind of things are held to be polluting for the gods as are thought to be polluting to men, the purity-pollution principle provides a theme which does not only relate the different elements in the Hindu's religious life to each other, but also integrates his religious activities as a total system to the rest of his social life.

2.2.7   Some years earlier, Louis Dumont had reached a very similar conclusion on the basis of fieldwork carried out in another part of South India. Writing on the religion of the Pramalai Kallar he observes that the deities worshipped by the Kallar are seldom considered in isolation from each other; where they are represented in temples, it is always as members of a pantheon. Temples contain not one deity but groups of deities − traditionally twenty-one, though sometimes fewer than twenty-one can actually be identified by name. What is important about these temple pantheons, Dumont says, is the fact that they are invariably divided into two sections, the pure deities and the impure deities. The impure (carnivorous) deities are seen as standing in a relationship to the pure (vegetarian) deities which is subordinate and yet complementary. The pure deities are above the impure deities but yet dependent on them both practically (for the services which the impure deities are held to perform as doorkeepers and guardians of the temples) and conceptually (in that purity can only be said to exist in relationship to impurity, and hence the existence of pure beings has no meaning unless impure beings are also held to exist). The division between the pure and the impure deities is reflected both in their separate accommodation in the same temples and in the different kinds of offering made to them, often also in the existence of dual sets of cultic instruments and a dual priesthood. This dichotomy or polar opposition between the pure and the impure at the divine level is for Dumont not just a projection of caste values or an intrusion of secular values into the religious sphere; the principle which activates the caste system is actually identical with that which gives the pantheon its structure. 'La caste mêle les hommes et les dieux. . . le dieu véritable c'est le Brahmane' (Dumont). Herein, according to Dumont, lies the unity of Hindu religious life, since it amounts to a consistent expression of faith in the polarity of the pure and the impure. For the worship of impure deities does not constitute a lower or separate level or tradition of Hinduism which has yet to be assimilated to some more universal or Sanskritic mainstream, but rather an indispensable adjunct to the worship of the pure deities – an inseparable part of the same system of activity.

The objection may be raised, however, that Dumont and Harper no doubt come to these conclusions as a result of the fact that they have both done their fieldwork in South India; it is well-known that in peninsular India the ritual distance between different castes is maintained in a more literal and rigid manner than in other parts of the subcontinent. Thus it is hardly a matter of surprise if we find that South Indian Hindus carry this purity-pollution principle into the religious sphere also. But will we find the same principle operating as an integrating factor in the religion of, say, Punjabi or Pahari Hindus, who observe a much looser system of caste restrictions? Can we argue that the opposition of the pure and the impure is a universally valid principle of Hindu religious experience?

I hope to show from some field material of my own that the religious activities of the Hindus of a North Indian hill village can indeed be equally successfully interpreted according to these terms.

2.2.8 Purity and Pollution in Practice: The Case of Ghanyari

Ghanyari lies in District Kangra in the lower ranges of the Himalyan foothills, a few miles from the border dividing Himachal Pradesh from the Punjab. The numerically preponderant and economically dominant caste in the village is a group of Saraswat Brahmans. These Brahmans, however, perform no priestly functions but are mainly engaged in agriculture, working their own landholdings. The other inhabitants of the village are the members of five intermediate service castes and the untouchable Chamars, whose hamlet lies at a little distance from the main settlement area. The difference in ritual status between the Brahmans and the artisan castes is not very conspicuous in everyday activities. There are no strongly marked dietary differences between castes since, unlike Brahmans in most other parts of India, the Brahmans of Ghanyari may eat meat. (Few in fact do, but this is for economic rather than ritual reasons; there is no caste prohibition on their taking meat if they wish to do so.) Brahmans take *pakka* food from members of all the artisan castes and will take *kaccha* food and water from most of them. Only in the case of Chamars is there a very conspicuous emphasis on ritual distance in daily dealings, since none of the other castes in the village will take food of any kind or water from a Chamar. Even physical contact with a Chamar is polluting and strictly avoided, except in cases where it is quite inevitable, such as when men of different castes travel together in a crowded bus or when men of different castes are engaged in work alongside each other (e.g., house construction or harvesting grain). Nevertheless, the purity-pollution principle is certainly not absent. If pollution puts less distance between man and man than in other parts of India, the sources which are held to give rise to ritual pollution are essentially those which other Hindus believe in. Lack of space prevents me from giving a detailed account of how the purity-pollution principle operates in daily life, but in general the ritual idiom is that of what Stevenson calls the 'Hindu Pollution Concept', even if this concept operates somewhat less rigorously compared with the nicety with which it is applied elsewhere. To take but one example, spittle is generally treated as a source of pollution. Srinivas mentions the fact that among the Coorgs it is considered necessary for a person to wash his hands if he has so much as touched his tongue or teeth. Otherwise he is regarded as having fallen from his normal state of ritual purity. In Ghanyari no one, not even the Brahmans, would consider it necessary to wash one's hands after casually putting a finger in one's mouth. But in the context of a mealtime the transmission of food to the mouth is considered to pollute the hands and a person who is in the process of eating food ought not to touch any food or vessels other than his own until he has washed his hands. If he does so, these vessels must be purified before they can be used again by others by being scoured with ashes, and any food or drink they contain should be thrown away. These Hindus therefore observe the same principle as the Coorgs of South India but they apply it in a more narrowly defined set of situations.

Similarly we find that, as among the Coorgs, the Hindus of Ghanyari regard death as a strong source of pollution, especially for members of the family of the dead person. In Coorgs this principle is applied to the extent that relatives of the deceased must avoid even touching other people during the period of mourning. In Ghanyari the restriction on bodily contact is observed only on the day of death itself. During the rest of the mourning period it is only the cooking of food and eating together which is thought to transmit pollution to non-relatives. 2.2.9

In brief, the Hindus of Ghanyari, as in other parts of India, regard themselves as each having a normal ritual status which can be threatened or preserved by certain kinds of contact. They differ from other Hindus only in the degree of detail and rigidity with which they apply these principles of purity and pollution in daily life, and not in the nature of the principles themselves. 2.2.10

The Range of Religious Activity

How then do these rules apply to the religious sphere, and to what extent can they be said to order the diversity of religious activities in Ghanyari? Certainly this diversity is not less apparent here than in other Indian villages for which we have information. We find the same variety of cults, deities, festivals, etc. that other field investigators have reported. However, for descriptive purposes we can divide the religious activities of Ghanyari into two broad categories. Firstly, there are private acts of devotion performed by individuals to deities of their own choice. These acts are carried out without the aid of priests, either in the home or at a shrine or temple. They are usually performed at the initiative of the worshipper on a 2.2.11

particular occasion, generally either because he has reason to suppose that the deity in question is troubling him in some way and demands to be appeased with an offering, or because he hopes to seek some positive favour which he believes the deity has in his power to grant. This kind of ritual act of devotion can however also be performed on festival days to the deities to which the feasts are dedicated.

2.2.12   The second main category of religious activity consists of rituals addressed to deities through the offices of a Brahman priest according to forms laid down in Sanskrit texts and accompanied by the chanting of these sacred verses by the priest. The rituals which fall into this class are mainly rites of passage but the preliminary worship which always precedes the reading of a *katha* (scripture recital) is also of this kind.

2.2.13   I should emphasise that this scheme is not exhaustive; there are religious activities (such as for instance the full moon fast which women keep for their husbands' welfare) which cannot conveniently be placed in either of these categories. I must also point out most emphatically that this division is not intended to have any theoretical significance whatsoever; it is a purely ad hoc scheme which I have introduced simply in order to reduce the complexity of the data to proportions manageable in a paper. If I were to ascribe to it more than this empirical significance I might justly be accused of adopting the very 'fragmentary' approach which I have just deplored. However, this division has the virtue of corresponding in fact roughly with some of the typologies made by other sociologists and hence is useful for comparative purposes. The 'individual' rites are mainly addressed to what Srinivas would call non-Sanskritic deities and belong to what Marriott would call the little tradition. 'Priestly' rites are Sanskritic and great traditional, and are further-more confined to the upper castes since Chamars are unable to hire Brahman priests to serve them and depend on ritual specialists of their own caste to perform their life-cycle rites for them. If therefore, we can show that there is a common theme or set of values which integrate these two types of religious activity we shall also have demonstrated the continuity between the levels of Hinduism which other writers have distinguished.

I therefore propose now to describe first an example of an individual ritual of worship and then an example of priestly ritual. We shall then be in a position to see whether they truly express different kinds of religious value or tradition.

Individual Ritual and the Structure of the Pantheon

Villagers assert that their deities number thirty-three crore but this is   2.2.14
more an expression of the general belief that *devatas* (deities) are
legion than the outcome of any kind of divine census-taking. The
number of *devatas* which are actually worshipped or of whom the
villagers have a detailed knowledge is much smaller. The *devatas* with
whom any one villager will have regular dealings of any kind will
rarely exceed about a dozen in number and he may know about a
dozen more by repute. These *devatas*, it is often asserted, are but
forms of the Supreme Spirit, Paramatma or Bhagvan. God, the
villagers say, is really above these manifestations of his, but in fact
practically no institutionalised religious activities are directed purely
to God conceived as Bhagvan. The various *devatas* are held to have
various characteristics ranging from the generally benevolent (such as
the local saint Baba Ludru) via the mildly annoying (exemplified by
the mountain spirit Baba Sindhu) to the downright dangerous (such
as the Chamar *devata* Siddh Channo). But all the *devatas* are
considered to be both potentially troublesome if their wishes are
ignored and potentially helpful if their goodwill is solicited in the
right manner. The correct way to avert their anger as well as to seek
their active aid in a particular project or dilemma is to make
offerings to them accompanied by the performance of certain simple
ritual acts. (The orientation of these cults is therefore decidedly
pragmatic rather than directed to any species of other-worldly
salvation.) The making of such offerings is the most commonly
observed form of religious activity in the village and such acts are
undertaken by individuals according to their own needs and circumstances. A *devata* may be worshipped in order to secure a good
harvest for the next year, to seek a cure for some troublesome
disease, to obtain offspring, or in thanksgiving for some fortunate
event such as the birth of a child or the passing of an examination.
Not being directed by a priest, nor carried out with reference to any
written text, the details of the worship can be varied by the
individual worshipper; he is at liberty to omit certain acts and to
include others at least to a limited extent; but the general pattern
which these rites follow is fairly constant and is exemplified
adequately in the case I shall describe.

I shall give an account of the ritual acts carried out by Ratno, a   2.2.15
Tarkhan woman, on the occasion of the maize harvest of 1966. She
worshipped the *devata* Baba Balak Nath in thanksgiving for the help
which she believed him to have given in ensuring that the harvest was

a good one, and in the hope that a pleasing offering would induce him to render the same aid in future years. I shall outline the ritual acts which she performed in the sequence in which they took place.

1. Ratno rises early and takes a bath. She puts on clean clothes and begins a fast which she keeps until the ritual of worship has been completed.

2. She replasters her kitchen floor and hearth with cowdung. On the newly plastered hearth she prepares a quantity of *karah* – a kind of sweet pudding which is to be used as the offering.

3. She takes out an image of Baba Balak Nath from the inner room where it is generally kept. She smears a small area of the verandah floor with the same plaster of cowdung which she used in the kitchen. She sets up the image on a small wooden stool placed on this area. No one in the household now approaches this area unless they have first removed their shoes.

4. Ratno removes her shoes before she bathes the image with fresh water.

5. She bows before the image and offers flowers and incense before it. She takes a quantity of red powder and applies it to the 'forehead' of the *devata* in the form of a *tika*. She ties a length of the sacred red thread known as *moli* round the 'waist' of the image.

6. Finally she offers a small quantity of the pudding before the image, pressing a little of it to the 'mouth' of the *devata*.

7. She distributes the remaining portion of the food prepared for the offering – which is now known as *prasad*, i.e. the transmitter of the grace of the devata – amongst the members of her household and to a few close neighbours who happen to be around. She then sets the rest aside. It is later offered to other friends and relatives who happen to call at the house during the course of the day. Great care is taken that no crumb of this *prasad* should fall to the ground or be left where it might accidentally come into contact with any impure substance, such as leather shoes.

8. Later in the day Ratno removes the image and puts it away. She clears the area where the worship has been carried out of its ritual debris. The remains of the items offered are taken and thrown into a nearby stream.

The *devata* to whom this worship was addressed may be described as belonging to the regional Hinduism of Punjab and Himachal Pradesh. Baba Balak Nath is said to have been born on earth in a Brahman family some hundreds of years ago and to have lived the life of an ascetic at Shah Talai, a village some twenty miles from

Ghanyari. After completing the span of his mortal life on earth he achieved a state of liberation from the body through his asceticism and saintliness. The god Shiva then conferred upon him the gift of immortality, whereupon he attained the status of a *devata* himself. He is well known to the villagers of this region, many of whom have visited his cult centre at Shah Talai. Those who are literate will have read, and may perhaps own, copies of the popular booklets relating the story of his life, his exploits, the miracles he is supposed to have performed and the words of hymns sung in his praise. These booklets are obtainable at stalls selling religious literature, almanacs, etc. in many towns of the Punjab and District Kangra. His cult is not recorded in Sanskrit literature as far as I know, however, and the rituals which are carried out in his honour (whether at home or at the village shrines dedicated to him) do not need the services of a Brahman, or indeed of any kind of ritual specialist. Members of any caste may and do worship him in the way described, and according to my observation he is not worshipped by members of any particular caste more than others.

Unlike the Pramalai Kallar, the villagers of Ghanyari do not rank   2.2.16 the members of their pantheon explicitly in any kind of hierarchy. The vegetarian/non-vegetarian distinction in any case hardly exists there. I was told that goats used to be sacrificed to certain *devatas* but that this practice has been discontinued for the past forty years or more. Interestingly enough, goats are still presented to Baba Balak Nath at his shrine at Shah Talai, but they are never killed nowadays. They are simply offered live before the image of the *devata*, and once the latter has shown his approval of the gift by causing the animal to shiver and tremble it is then released. Therefore the pure-impure dichotomy cannot be applied to the pantheon of this village at the present time, whatever the case might once have been. What, however, one does find is that villagers tend to rank their *devatas* after a fashion, according to the strength of the powers they believe them to have. Thus some of the *devatas*, mainly the great traditional deities like Vishnu, Shiva and Durga, are attributed more universal powers than the lesser local, or little traditional deities such as Baba Balak Nath himself. Certain more educated villagers sometimes dismiss the latter class of deity, not as having no existence, but as having little power to influence the lives of men (with the implication that their worship is therefore a waste of time if not a positive distraction from the true path to salvation, which consists of doing good *karma* and revering Bhagvan through inner prayer). The point which I am trying to emphasise here is that the pantheon of Ghanyari can only with difficulty be divided into Sanskritic and non-Sanskritic, pure and impure, great and little traditional levels; but to the extent that any such distinction can be made, or is in fact made by the villagers themselves, we are obliged to classify the cult of Baba Balak Nath as belonging to the inferior (non-Sanskritic, little traditional) level.

Priestly Ritual: Public Worship

2.2.17   In contrast to the ritual which I have just described, let us now look at a rite which can only be classified as Sanskritic and great traditional (no matter how we choose to define these terms). A popular form of religious activity in the village is the *katha,* or scripture recital. This consists of a reading by a Brahman priest of some story of moral import taken from the scriptures. The text is recited in Sanskrit and then expounded line by line in the vernacular by the priest. The reading itself is preceded by a formal rite of worship in which the householder who is sponsoring the reading worships Ganesh and the nine planets and seeks their blessing for the meritorious act which he is about to have performed. This ritual is carried out under the direction of the priest who has been hired to read the *katha.* I shall describe here the form of this ritual as carried out by a Brahman farmer, Ramanand, when he held a *katha* to celebrate the completion of the new house he had been building. However, there is, as far as I could observe at least, almost no variation in the way this ritual is performed on different occasions (as there can be in the case of individual rites of worship) for the very reason that it depends on a written text. This text is regarded as sacred and hence any intentional variation is not even envisaged, let alone approved.

2.2.18   The acts constituting the ritual of worship on this occasion were as follows:

1. On returning from the fields on the evening of the day when the *katha* is to be held (the auspicious day and time has been ascertained beforehand from the Brahman priest who has consulted his almanac for the purpose) Ramanand takes a bath and changes into clean clothes.

2. Ramanand's wife replasters her kitchen hearth and the place in the main room of the house where the worship is to be offered by resmearing them with cowdung. She then prepares the *prasad* which is to be distributed after the *katha* (in this case a kind of sweet made

from flour fried in *ghi* and sweetened with crude sugar).

3. The priest arrives. He has also bathed and changed his clothes before leaving his house and on arrival once more washes his hands. He then begins to prepare a *mandala,* that is a sacred diagram, on the area of the floor which Ramanand's wife has previously replastered. This diagram consists of symbolic representation of the nine planets and other deities or sacred beings. These include Ganesh, Tridev (Vishnu, Shiva and Brahman), Suraj Devata (the sun), Shesh Nag (the serpent who upholds the world) the sixty-four Yoginis (the wives of the deity Bhairon) and Onkar (the sacred syllable Om conceived as a divine being). The symbols of these deities are traced on the floor in white flour.

4. The invited guests begin to arrive. The priest blows a blast on his conch shell to signify that the worship is about to begin. He bids Ramanand sit down beside him before the *mandala* which he has prepared. He ties a length of red *moli* to Ramanand's wrist and tufts of the sacred kusha grass to the third finger of each of his hands.

5. The priest recites the appropriate lines from the Sanskrit text which he has opened in front of him as he directs Ramanand in the worship of the symbols represented in the *mandala.* To each in turn various substances are offered: water, rice, flowers, incense. Ritual gestures, such as bowing with folded hands, are made to the various symbols.

6. After this the reading itself begins. The priest chants the Sanskrit verses and then explains what they mean to his listeners. The text includes various anecdotes concerning the sage Narada which illustrate the effectiveness of righteous conduct and the diligent observance of fasting and other ritual practices as means of obtaining salvation. After the reading is completed the *prasad,* which has been placed beside the *mandala,* is distributed to all present. Great care is taken that no portion of the *prasad* should be trodden under foot.

7. After the guests have departed, Ramanand's wife scrapes up what is left of the sacred diagram and the items offered to it and puts them by on a tray. They are removed later by Ramanand and thrown into a stream.

In certain striking respects this ritual quite obviously belongs to a 2.2.19 different strand of the Hindu tradition from the private ritual carried out by Ratno to Baba Balak Nath, and fulfils a different kind of religious function. The ritual has a fixed form, as has been pointed out, and depends on a written text. Moreover this text is not written in the vernacular but in a language which is incomprehensible to the ordinary villager. The services of a Brahman priest are essential to the villager for this kind of ritual, not merely because only the priest has the requisite training to understand the directions for worship contained in the text, but also because only a Brahman is considered fit, by virtue of his special ritual status, to utter and expound the holy verses in question. The ritual therefore cannot take place without his aid, or at least without the presence of a Brahman who can read enough Sanskrit to stumble through the text. (One *katha* which I attended was read by a Brahman villager, who had a little education, when the priest who had been invited failed to turn up.)

2.2.20   Furthermore, the ritual preceding a *katha*, unlike the rite conducted by Ratno in her home, is public. It is carried out in the presence of guests formally invited, whose attendance is considered essential as witnesses that the ritual has been carried out in the proper manner. The rite is performed by the head of the household on behalf of his whole family. Individual rites of worship may be carried out in order to further aims which are of interest or benefit to the whole household, as indeed was Ratno's worship of Baba Balak Nath; but in such cases the worshipper is still acting on his own individual initiative and not because of his structural position in the kinship group. In such cases any member of the family may equally legitimately perform the worship. Priestly rituals seldom involve women (except in cases such as weddings and naming rites, when the bride and the mother of the new baby have a certain part to play). A *katha* could, I was told, be sponsored by a woman in the last resort in the absence of any male member of the household, but no one could recall such an occasion. Normally a woman's inferior ritual status debars her from taking part in this kind of ritual. One priest said, 'A woman can never be as pure as a man and therefore if there is a man in her household, he should perform the necessary rites'. Individual acts of worship to *devatas* can be performed by members of either sex with equal legitimacy and effectiveness.

2.2.21   The deities worshipped through priestly ritual also tend to belong to a different category. Whilst Shiva, Vishnu and Ganesh are sometimes worshipped through individual rites of the type described already, the other divinities depicted on the *mandala* which Ramanand worshipped are not worshipped by individual villagers privately. Indeed many of them are only known to the villagers at all because they feature in the worship effected at weddings, namely rites, *kathas* and other priestly rituals. If they are known outside these contexts at all it is as scriptural figures, but as most of the villagers are illiterate this means that these beings belong to a literary tradition to which they have little direct access. Deities like Baba Balak Nath, on the other hand, belong to the oral traditions of the place and knowledge of them does not depend on written sources (although written sources in the forms of books and pamphlets may amplify the villager's information concerning them if he is literate).

There is also, as I have mentioned, a functional difference 2.2.22 between the two kinds of rite. Individual rites are oriented towards the attainment of highly specific and this-worldly ends rather than towards the attainment of salvation (in the sense of liberation from this world). Priestly rites to be sure, certainly have a this-worldly reference also; *kathas* can be held (as Ramanand's was) to celebrate the achievement of some material or this-worldly end, and life cycle rites such as weddings obviously have a this-worldly reference. But the completion of these rituals is also conceived as a worthy end in itself, and an aid on the path to salvation. Life cycle rites should be performed duly and correctly, since this is fulfilment of one's *dharma* and hence a religious necessity. As for *kathas,* one informant told me, 'In former times, in the Sat Yug, a man who sponsored a *katha* accumulated so much merit through the deed that he was not reborn in mortal form for thousands of years; even now there is great merit in performing a *katha*'. Individual rites of worship are obviously directed to much more immediate ends.

Continuities and Common Principles

Having outlined the differences between the two classes of religious 2.2.23 activity which I have described I ought now, if I am to fulfil the intention which I expressed in the beginning of this paper, to point out where the continuities between them lie. If we choose to analyse Hinduism in terms of types or levels then the two rituals which I have described certainly belong to different levels of the religious culture of Ghanyari. But it is not difficult to find a definite consistency in the idiom they employ if we examine the ritual procedure followed in either case. Obvious similarities, for instance, can be seen in the fact that in both kinds of ritual the main participant(s) had first to bath themselves and change their clothes; in both rituals the site where worship was to take place was first smeared with cowdung; in both rituals this area was not approached without shoes being first removed; in either case the ritual equipment used was disposed of after the worship was over by being immersed in running water; in both cases certain precautions were observed in the disposal of the *prasad*. When we take into account both these regularities in practice and the statements which villagers make in explanation of these practices, it becomes clear that there is a basic likeness in the rules observed in both contexts which underlies the more conspicuous differences in their content and purpose.

2.2.24   The rules which govern both kinds of ritual alike can be summarised according to the following scheme:

(a) Rules which maintain or maximise the purity of the worshipper(s)

These comprise the taking of a preliminary ritual bath, changing clothes, washing hands, fasting. (Fasting can be seen as a means of purification in that the consumption of food always conveys a certain degree of pollution, and by avoiding eating one is also avoiding an occasion for pollution.)

(b) Rules directed towards maintaining or preserving the purity of the deity or deities to be worshipped

These include smearing the site of worship with cowdung, removing shoes before coming near this area, bathing the image with water. All these acts can be interpreted in terms of the preservation of the purity of the gods (or more specifically the images and symbols which are used to represent their presence). Indeed they are so interpreted by the villagers themselves.

(c) Rules governing the purity of the offering

These include the obligation on the woman who is to cook the *prasad* to take a bath (whether or not she will participate in the ritual worship herself), the purification of the hearth before the cooking takes place, and the precautions taken about the disposal of the *prasad* after it has been presented to the gods. Under this heading we may also include the practice of immersing the remains of the other offerings in running water; this is also explicitly described by villagers as being carried out in order to ensure that the substances offered to and accepted by the gods should not become defiled accidentally by being left lying about where they might come into contact with sources of pollution.

2.2.25   It is clear that the substances which are considered to be sources of pollution in this context (whether it is the purity of the deity which they threaten or that of his worshipper) are no different from those which are thought to transmit pollution in other contexts. For instance, leather (especially in the form of footwear) is polluting and should not be brought near the area where worship is to take place. Exactly the same principle is at work when villagers remove their shoes before entering a kitchen or cooking area, except that in the latter case it is the purity of the household's cooking utensils and foodstuffs which is at stake rather than purity of a deity or his devotee. And the same rule is in operation when villagers place ritual distance between themselves and the low caste Chamars, whose traditional work is the preparation of leather from the hides of dead cattle.

Similarly the substances which are conceived as purifiers in the religious context are also those which are used for purificatory purposes in non-religious contexts. Cowdung, as the product of that extraordinarily pure animal, the cow, is used to purify the area where the image or symbols of the deities are to be placed for worship and to purify the hearth where *prasad* is to be prepared. When a housewife smears her kitchen floor and hearth with cowdung as a regular practice, even when no ritual is to take place, or when a new mother is made to drink cow's urine after the birth of her child in order to remove the pollution which the very act of parturition brings upon her, the very same principle is being observed. Likewise there is consistency between the religious and non-religious use of water as an agent of purification. Villagers bathe themselves and the images of their gods with water and immerse the remains of their offerings in water in order that everything associated with the divine should remain pure. In accordance with the same principle, a villager will purify himself by bathing in clean water if he ever becomes polluted through accidental contact with a person of unclean caste. Bathing is also used as a means of purification when a birth or death in the household involves its members in pollution of another kind.

Now that I have made them, these remarks may seem rather 2.2.26 obvious – especially to anyone who has spent any time in an Indian village. But it has been necessary to make them in order to counter the effects of the 'fragmentary' approach which has hitherto dominated the study of Hindu religion in its village context. I hope I have shown that in spite of the distinctions which can be made between the different types of Hindu religious activity on the basis of their different cultural origins or their different functions, there is also an underlying consistency of idiom. The purity-pollution principle is applied in the conduct of religious rituals of all types in exactly the same manner.

The Cosmic Hierarchy

2.2.28 It should also be obvious from material I have presented that there is in addition a consistency between application of the purity-pollution principle in the religious sphere and its application in the non-religious context. The evidence from Ghanyari tends to confirm the ideas expressed by Harper and Dumont, namely that the Hindu pantheon can be viewed as an upwards extension of the caste system. In Ghanyari, as in the South Indian villages which these writers studied, the man-*devata* relationship emerges as being of a similar character to the low caste-high caste relationship in certain important respects. The rules of ritual procedure followed in the examples I have described are in both cases oriented to the maintenance of the superior ritual purity of the *devata*(s). The purity of the worshipper is instrumental in this context, not an object in itself, for the villagers state that only if the worshipper makes himself pure will his worship be acceptable to the deities he addresses. More than this, in both kinds of ritual the intrusion of any source of pollution may even excite the anger of the offended *devata*. The purity of the *prasad* is interpreted by the villagers as being necessary also in order to make it an acceptable offering to the gods, a principle which is consistent with the fact that in the human sphere only food which is pure can be passed from ritual inferior to ritual superior (in so far as men can accept food from their ritual inferiors at all). Thus only a ritual inferior will accept polluted food; only Chamars will accept the scraps left over from the plates of members of the higher castes. The exclusion of leather articles from the area of worship can be compared with the custom according to which (at least until about forty years ago) Chamars were not allowed to enter the main settlement area of the village where the other castes lived unless they first removed their shoes as a mark of respect. Even nowadays a Chamar will not enter the courtyard of a member of the higher castes without first leaving his shoes at the gate or entrance. There are obvious parallels here between the way a low-caste man treats a high-caste man and the way a worshipper treats the deity he worships.

2.2.29 Theoretically attractive, the analogy between caste relationships and man-*devata* relationships does have certain common-sense limitations in actual practice. For instance, a Brahman (unlike a *devata*) can take certain measures himself to maintain his normal ritual status, by avoiding contacts with members of low castes. (He can move away if a Chamar approaches him; if he has to give food to an untouchable he can insist that the latter provide his own vessels.) Of course, it is doubtful whether a Brahman could protect himself effectively from a deliberate attempt to pollute him on the part of a low-caste man who was quite bent on seeing him ritually degraded. However, I imagine such a flagrant and calculated effort to violate a ritual superior's ritual purity would be a rather rare occurrence, at least on the part of persons very low in the hierarchy, because any such step could be met with punishment; the ritual superior is usually also superior in political and economic status and thus has effective sanctions at his disposal.[2]

Even so, unlike the *devata's* worshipper, the low-caste man might   2.2.30
even be said to have a certain interest in reducing his superior's ritual status to the extent that if the ritual distance between them is diminished he may be able to obtain recognition of a higher rank for himself in the hierarchy. (The worshipper has no possible interest in changing his *devata's* status.) Thus where members of a caste which is ritually low, but on the ascendant in socio-economic terms, succeed in inducing members of a higher caste to take food from them where there had been no inter-dining before, this might pave the way for confirmation of a shift in their relative ritual positions. But the literature on village Hinduism suggests that it is far more common for a mobile caste to try to pull themselves up the ritual ladder by purifying their own customs — giving up meat, liquor, etc. — than by making deliberate assaults on the purity of their superiors such that the latter would find hard to avoid.

A *devata* — in spite of the greater power with which he is credited   2.2.31
to shape the progress of events and fortunes at a more general level — can only react passively by punishing the person who violates his purity after the offence has been committed; punishment is within his power but not active avoidance (although of course this power to punish should not be underestimated as a form of sanction).

To summarise this discussion, which is admittedly somewhat of a   2.2.32
digression from our main argument, we could perhaps say that the main limitation to our analogy is that in caste relationships both sides are active agents and both can help to effect readjustments in the ritual distance which separates them, especially over periods of time. In particular, the ritual superior may lose out to his inferior, the more so if he loses the economic and political power which enabled him to punish the low-caste man for breaches of caste etiquette and get away with it. The man-*devata* relationship is asymmetrical in that the superior partner is partly passive; he can

punish but not forestall or avoid outrages to his purity. The relationship is a simpler one in a sense, for it is not complicated by the economic and political considerations which are the secular concomitants of the ritual side of caste relationships.

2.2.33   It must also be stressed that villagers recognise the superior purity of their *devatas* only indirectly and implicitly. That is, when asked to describe their pantheon, they will make statements such as 'the *devatas* are powerful' rather than 'the *devatas* are pure'. But when asked to account for the details of the worship they offer to these *devatas* act by act, they will state, for example, 'we bathe to make ourselves pure' or 'we remove our shoes because they are made of leather and are not pure'.

Conclusions

2.2.34   It is only with certain qualifications, therefore, that we can agree with Harper and Dumont as regards the similarity between the application of the purity-pollution principle in the religious sphere and in the caste context. However, this does not prejudice our agreement with these authors concerning the importance of this principle as an integrator of the Hindu's experience and activity within the religious sphere. The villager is, as we have seen, acting on similar principles whether he worships some local little traditional *devata* privately or whether he sits besides his *purohit* to perform some *puja* before a *mandala* prepared by the priest. Whether the little tradition is a parochialised version of the great tradition, or whether the great tradition is a more generalised version of a prior folk culture — this is a matter for the cultural historian to decide and need not concern us here. What the sociologist has to determine is the relationship of these strands of cultural activity to each other in the context of modern social organisation. For the practical purposes of description I have found it necessary to divide religious activity in the village into two broad categories, and indeed the villager himself sometimes makes such a distinction between priestly and non-priestly ritual. But, as I have shown, the differences between these two kinds of activities, or 'traditions' (if one wishes to use the term) is greater in terms of their mode of transmission and superficial style than in terms of thematic content and underlying values. The hierarchical aspect of the purity-pollution principle is emphasised again and again — from the explicit exhortation to fast and be pure contained in the priestly *kathas* to the practical regard for the *devatas'* purity implicit in the villager's very action as he worships his domestic *devatas*. Indeed the need to mark off the pure from the impure not only pervades the Hindu's social and religious life but also his attitudes to all the members of his cosmos. Within almost any category which he distinguishes, the Hindu will rank some items as more pure than others. Thus among animals the cow is most pure; among trees the *pipal* and the *bor* are pure and the *lasura* is impure — a 'Musulman' tree, too polluted to be used for timber. Among vegetables, carrot and turnips are less pure than pumpkins and potatoes, which is why it is permissible to eat the latter on fast days but not the former. Of beverages, milk and clean water (especially Ganges water) are pure, and alcoholic drinks are impure. These distinctions are not of equal practical significance, although of course, the distinctions among foodstuffs are of considerable importance in the ritual sphere. But they are all of potential religious importance in that during worship the devotee wishes to exclude what is not pure and to include what is pure as far as he is able. On the conceptual level these distinctions illustrate the broad dominion of the purity-pollution principle which we have been discussing. A detailed study of the cosmology of popular Hinduism and the way in which the Hindu villager frames his world view might reveal further elaboration of the purity-pollution theme and would be a rewarding subject for further research. However our conclusions in this paper must be limited to the religious sphere, and we can summarise them by stating that we find in Ghanyari, just as others have found in South India, that the link between the different cultural levels of religious tradition and activity lies in the consistent application of the rules of purity and pollution to the relationship between man and the forces which he reveres as divine.

Source: Ursula Sharma, *Contributions to Indian Sociology*, Vikas Publishing House 1973, pp.1-21.

2.3 CASTE, FOOD AND COMMENSALITY WITHIN HINDUISM

Louis Dumont

A Local Example (Central India)

2.3.1 In order to take an accurate view of the way in which the hierarchical principle is expressed in the caste system, one must obviously study what happens at a given place among the actual castes which co-exist there. On the other hand, it will have been noticed that the rules which lay down for the members of each caste from whom they may or may not accept such and such a kind of food, or simply drinking-water, without degradation, are one of the most convenient manifestations of the hierarchical principle from the point of view of recording and observing. I say 'recording and observing', for it is not enough to list the rules which the witnesses recite. One must also know if and under what circumstances these presumptive rules are applied in practice. In the first period of inquiries into these questions, people were too often content to ask informants and reproduce the rules which they mentioned. But what can a rule like the following signify: 'I may, or may not, take water from X', if the witness cannot cite a single moment in his life when the question has really arisen for him? From this point of view, there are different kinds of food which, as McKim Marriott has rightly said, are suitable for different situations: ordinary everyday food based, according to region, on wheat cakes or boiled rice, is essentially for the family, and is accepted only by servants of a distinctly inferior rank, and so on this level is food for service. By contrast, food fried in butter (or certain equivalent foods) is the food of feasts: its greater purity, or rather, its greater resistance to impurity, enables a greater number of castes than in the preceding case to accept it, and it is thus suitable for banquets to which one invites neighbours; if these include superiors, it is advisable that the cook should himself be of high caste. Akin to this type are certain special preparations which can be called food for travelling; these too are relatively resistant to impurity in virtue of their composition and preparation, and they make it possible to eat in circumstances where it is preferable not to have to do any cooking. Finally, if one remunerates a superior – a Brahman, say – in food, this will be raw food which is immune from pollution and which he will cook himself (*sīdhā*); Marriott rightly calls this the food of gifts. Our aim here was not to study food in itself, but to throw just as much light on the question as is required in order to use the corresponding rules for the study of caste ranking.

A good study of this topic is available: Mayer's book[1] about a   2.3.2 village in Southern Malwa (Central India). Perhaps it is not perfect, but one must take into account the complexity of the phenomena and the difficulty of recording them correctly, which is what this writer has done. He cannot be reproached for not having pursued his analysis far enough, for it is open to the reader to do so. The village includes twenty-three castes, and their relationships will be studied under three headings: use of the same pipe, and the provision of ordinary food, called *kachā*, and of perfect food, called *pakkā*. In the north-west of India, men of castes of similar status are wont to meet round a hookah (*hukkā*), which is smoked in turn. This would be inconceivable in the south in view of the contact between the lips, and hence saliva, and the mouthpiece of the pipe, even if a cloth or a hand is placed between. Here the pipe smoked is of clay without a tube (*cilam*), and a cloth is interposed between lips and mouthpiece. The pipe is shared among roughly the same castes as those from whom one accepts water, and there is considerable tolerance. The data are to be found in figure 1b. Higher castes share the pipe with almost all castes excluding, apart from the Untouchables (F), only four other castes (Mayer's category 4, category E here) and, in a varying way, certain of the lower castes included (D). In some cases, a different cloth must be placed between the pipe and the lips of the smoker. Briefly, between twelve and sixteen castes smoke together; in the first place, this is very remarkable by comparison with other regions, and in the second it indicates a cleavage which is higher than that marked by Untouchability, and is obviously important. Let us also note that lower castes either do not share the pipe (these are Untouchables, and their exclusiveness is not exceptional), or else do so only with one or two castes immediately below (the two castes of my category E).

For the rest, and to see it more clearly, we must arrange Mayer's   2.3.3 material in a hierarchical way. The facts about the food for feasts, pakkā, are not essential, for it is not really used in its true function in this locality. Indeed, one reads that at a banquet the food was partly kachā and party pakkā: in such a case the pakkā has no more than a gastronomic significance since all those who could eat pakkā alone but not kachā could obviously not partake of it. There remains the ordinary food, kachā. There are two ways in which it may be considered here: from whom do I accept kachā, and who accepts it from me. The two are not necessarily connected, for I may be punctilious in my acceptance, and yet at the same time possess other characteristics which make others refuse kachā from me. The essential thing here is the common opinion which others have of me, and not my own opinion of them. Hence we shall take as the essential criterion for the order in which we shall rank the castes: *what castes accept kachā from the caste in question?* Thus we ohtain the table (Figure 1a) in which the caste under consideration is placed on the diagonal; the castes which take kachā from it are read vertically, forming a kind of ladder from left to right at the bottom of the diagram; the castes from which it accepts kachā are read horizontally.

2.3.4   The choice of our main criterion leads to a slight modification of the grouping proposed by Mayer, namely, to the division of category 2 into B and D. For the rest, his 3 corresponds to our C, his 4 becomes our E and his 5 our F (untouchables). Still considering only kachā, it will be seen from the table that the castes of category B have a peculiarity which distinguishes them from all the others; the other castes, except the very last, F, will accept (horizontally) kachā only from very superior castes. By contrast, the castes of category B form a compact rectangle in this respect: B1, B2, B3, B4, B5 eat the ordinary food together! Now B1 represents the Rajputs, the dominant caste, which in this instance may be called the royal caste, and group B as a whole represents what Mayer calls as a result the 'allied castes'. The commensality of the group is even more remarkable because it includes 'serving' castes like the potters B4, who accept kachā from a caste outside the group, the carpenters, and especially the barbers, B5, who, as a necessary result of their domestic functions, accept it from four of the castes in category C, which are themselves very exclusive. This is in general an admission of inferiority, and one might expect to see the B castes dissociate themselves from B5 in order to preserve their status. This is far from the case, and one may even observe that an inferior caste, D3, makes no distinction between them and accepts kachā from the barbers, B5, just as from the other members of B. Further, castes of category C, who accept kachā only from the Brahmans, are classed by three castes (D3, E1, E2) below the barber (except for the carpenter, C1,

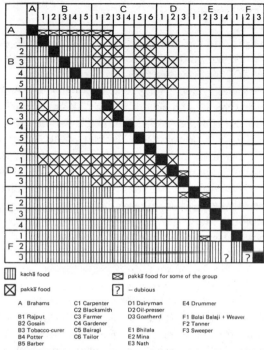

Fig. 1a. Status ranking on the basis of exchange of food in a Malwa village (from the data in A.C. Mayer, *Caste and Kinship,* pp. 33-40).

For each caste (■), the castes from whom it accepts such-and-such a food are read horizontally, those who accept the food from it are read vertically.

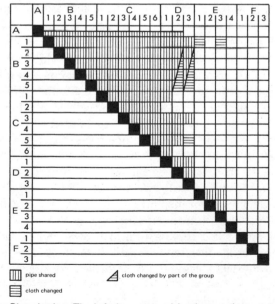

Figure 1b. Pipe sharing. The inferior castes with whom a given caste will share a pipe are read horizontally, starting from the caste in question (■). Same locality. [Castes and categories as detailed under Figure 1a]

who is thought inferior only by D3). Now the ˙C castes are vegetarian, while the B castes eat meat. Hence in this case the promiscuity of meat eaters prevails over the separatism of vegetarians in public esteem (the esteem not only of inferiors, but even of the Brahmans, who accept pakkā only up to and including C2). Here, to all appearances, the principle of the pure and the impure is in abeyance. In this form the fact is, I believe, unique up to this date. To understand it, it must be remembered that the B castes are united around the power caste, B1. (Moreover, some of them are dominant in neighbouring villages.) This is the point at which, in the manner we have already hinted at, power participates in purity, although the latter negates it in theory; in other words, this is the point at which the solidarity between the first two varnas reveals itself.

2.3.5   Consideration of the purer food, pakkā, brings out two points: (1) as has been mentioned, it is not used here in its full capacity as food for festivals, which should normally allow for the commensality between the B castes and the C castes which are close in status; (2) the distinctive feature of the exclusiveness of C castes is that they refuse almost all pakkā as well as kachā (which is absurd), while by contrast the B castes generally accept pakkā from the C castes (C4 seems to be inferior to the other C castes, but I do not intend to make any modifications in detail to the order given by the author); the D castes, on the contrary, behave normally in accepting pakkā from all the superior categories; pakkā is scarcely used among the E and F castes.

2.3.6   In short, the main lesson of this investigation concerns the opposition of the B and C castes, whose behaviour must be seen together. Faced with the 'allied castes', allied around power, who here display exceptional carefreeness and solidarity, the C castes seem to exaggerate the reserve and self-containment of vegetarians, to such a degree that even the Brahmans scarcely take them seriously. We are told that the B castes are lavish and freely invite other castes to their family ceremonies, followed in this by the carpenters (C1). By contrast, the farmers (C3) are niggardly and scarcely invite any except members of their own caste; at the same time, they pose as puritans, if they are invited they insist on receiving raw food and cooking it in their own homes. That it is a question of asserting themselves in face of the B castes is the more clear in that in other villages this same caste is part of the group of 'allies'.

We have seen how, in an actual situation, power may victoriously offset purity. In a less spectacular form this is a very widespread phenomenon. This is why we have been at pains to indicate above how the theory of varnas opens the road to this possibility.

Note

1. *Caste and Kinship*, pp.33-40.

Source: Louis Dumont, *Homo Hierarchicus,* Weidenfeld and Nicolson, 1972, pp.123-9.

2.4 STATUS EVALUATION IN THE HINDU CASTE SYSTEM

H.N.C. Stevenson

Conclusions

2.4.1 The following tentative hypotheses emerge from this survey of Hindu status evaluation:

(1) There are two categories of status — secular status and ritual status — each derived from different sources and socially manifested in different ways.

(2) Whereas secular status is derived from such criteria as skill, education, wealth, land ownership and economic 'lines of demarcation' in occupation, ritual status is derived from behaviour patterns linked with mystical beliefs, of which the most important are those subsumed under the title 'The Hindu Pollution Concept'.

(3) The principal constituent beliefs of the Pollution Concept are: (i) that group behaviour patterns establish group-derived natal ritual status; (ii) that this group ritual status cannot be altered so long as the person concerned conforms to the group pattern of behaviour; (iii) that there is another category of ritual status — personal ritual status — which is derived from personal rather than group conduct, and which provides the individual with the means of achieving higher natal ritual status in subsequent rebirths; (iv) that a rise or fall in personal ritual status above or below the level of group ritual status involves deviation from the group pattern of behaviour.

(4) The main principles governing evaluation of natal status through group behaviour are: (i) that the life principle is sacred, and that destruction of life for a living (as in oil-seed-crushing) is polluting; (ii) that death and decay are polluting and therefore occupational association with them is polluting; (iii) that all human emissions are polluting, and therefore occupational association with these, too, is polluting; (iv) that the cow is sacred above all creatures, and that killing it, or flaying it, or dealing in skins or eating its flesh is sinful, and therefore polluting; (v) that certain other creatures — some monkeys, cobras, squirrels, etc. — are also sacred in varying degrees or in some localities, and that killing or eating them is polluting; and (vi) that the drinking of alcohol is polluting.

(5) Pollution may be permanent or temporary, being subdivisible into voluntary pollution, the result of wrong behaviour, and involuntary pollution, the result of such natural crises as birth, death and menstruation. Pollution may also be subdivided into external and internal pollution, the latter being much the less easily expunged.

(6) Permanent pollution is a function of the relations between commensal and endogamous groups; between man and the phenomena of the natural world, and among these phenomena themselves.

(7) Temporary pollution is situational, and in general is a function of the relations between an individual and the commensal, endogamous and local groups of which he or she is a member.

(8) Group ritual status is socially manifested mainly through ritual avoidances which may arise from: (i) social activation of a single group (or category, e.g. *sannyasis*) by one or more beliefs; or, (ii) social activation of a number of groups – from the family through its associated endogamous and commensal groups to the caste system as a whole – by one or more beliefs.

(9) There is no fixed hierarchy of 'castes' and 'sub-castes'. Group status – both secular and ritual – is *variable* and *relative* in time, space and interaction. Relativity and fission are the characteristics which make possible the status mobility of endogamous groups. Observance of different combinations of status principles makes possible fine differentiations of status at all levels.

(10) Change of group ritual status by endogamous groups may be both upward and downward, upward change being secured only by generations of conformation to behaviour patterns which avoid pollution, and by severing marital and commensal relations with any non-conforming section.

(11) Ritual status is of different orders at different structural levels. (i) *At the level of endogamous and commensal groups,* group ritual status vis-à-vis like groups can be changed, and is evaluated on the basis of (a) the observance of certain standards of behaviour, mainly concerning occupation, diet and marriage, by reference to the Pollution Concept; (b) the right to perform certain rites, of which the most important is the orthodox initiation rite of *upanayana,* which divides the *duija,* or 'twice-born' groups, from the lower orders. (ii) *At the level of exogamous groups,* group ritual status vis-à-vis like groups cannot be changed, and is evaluated according to (a) the ritual status of the endogamous group to which

the exogamous group belongs; (b) mythical origin; (c) difference in protecting deities. (iii) *At the level of the individual,* group-derived ritual status vis-à-vis the whole Hindu system is inherited and cannot be changed except by deviation from the group behaviour pattern of the endogamous group to which the individual belongs. It is evaluated (a) within the caste system, according to the status of the endogamous and commensal groups to which the individual belongs; (b) within the endogamous group, according to the exogamous group to which the individual belongs; (c) within the local community, according to ritual roles undertaken by his status group in local group ritual. On the other hand, personal ritual status, achieved through such deviations from the group pattern of behaviour as asceticism or breach of pollution rules, is variable upwards and downwards. A permanent rise or fall in personal ritual status involves severance of social ties with the natal group.

Source: H.N.C. Stevenson, *Proceedings of the Royal Anthropoligical Institute of Great Britain and Ireland,* No.84. Royal Anthropological Institute 1954, pp.63-4.

2.5 FROM THE UPANISHADS

Iśā Upanishad

Translated by R.E. Hume

2.5.1
Recognition of the unity underlying the diversity of the world
1. By the Lord (*īśā*) enveloped must this all be —
   Whatever moving thing there is in the moving world.
   With this renounced, thou mayest enjoy.
   Covet not the wealth of anyone at all.

2.5.2
Non-attachment of deeds on the person of a renouncer
2. Even while doing deeds here,
   One may desire to live a hundred years.
   Thus on thee — not otherwise than this is it —
   The deed (*karman*) adheres not on the man.

2.5.3
The forbidding future for slayers of the Self
3. Devilish (*asurya*) are those worlds called,
   With blind darkness covered o'er!
   Unto them, on deceasing, go
   Whatever folk are slayers of the Self.

2.5.4
The all-surpassing, paradoxical world-being
4. Unmoving, the One is swifter than the mind.
   The sense-powers reached not It, speeding on before.
   Past others running, This goes standing.
   In It Mātariśvan places action.
5. It moves. It moves not.
   It is far, and It is near.
   It is within all this,
   And It is outside of all this.
6. Now, he who on all beings
   Looks as just in the Self (Ātman),
   And on the Self as in all beings —
   He does not shrink away from Him.
7. In whom all beings
   Have become just the Self of the discerner —
   Then what delusion, what sorrow (*śoka*) is there.
   Of him who perceives the unity!

2.5.5 *Characteristics of the world-ruler*
   8. He has environed. The bright, the bodiless, the scatheless,
      The sinewless, the pure, unpierced by evil!
      Wise, intelligent, encompassing, self-existent.
      Appropriately he distributed objects through the eternal years.

2.5.6 *Transcending, while involving, the antithesis of knowing*
   9. Into blind darkness enter they
      That worship ignorance;
      Into darkness greater than that, as it were, they
      That delight in knowledge.
   10. Other, indeed, they say, than knowledge!
      Other, they say, than non-knowledge!
      — Thus we have heard from the wise
      Who to us have explained It.
   11. Knowledge and non-knowledge —
      He who this pair conjointly knows,
      With non-knowledge passing over death,
      With knowledge wins the immortal.

2.5.7 *The inadequacy of any antithesis of being*
   12. Into blind darkness enter they
      Who worship non-becoming;
      Into darkness greater than that, as it were, they
      Who delight in becoming.
   13. Other, indeed — they say — than origin.
      Other — they say — than non-origin!
      — Thus to us we heard from the wise
      Who to us have explained It.

2.5.8 *Becoming and destruction a fundamental duality*
   14. Becoming and destruction —
      He who this pair conjointly knows,
      With destruction passing over death,
      With becoming wins the immortal.

2.5.9 *A dying person's prayer*
   15. With a golden vessel
      The Real's face is covered o'er.
      That do thou, O Pūshan, uncover.
      For one whose law is the Real to see.
   16. O Nourisher, the sole Seer, O Controller, O Sun, offspring of
      Prajāpati, spread forth thy rays! Gather thy brilliance! What is
      thy fairest form — that of thee I see. He who is yonder, yonder

Person (*purusa*) — I myself am he!

17. [My breath (*vāyu*) to the immortal wind *(anila)*! This body then
ends in ashes! *Om*!
O Purpose, remember! The deed remember!
O Purpose, remember! The deed remember!

General prayer of petition and adoration   2.5.10

18. O Agni, by a goodly path to prosperity (*rai*) lead us,
Thou god who knowest all the ways!
Keep far from us crooked-going sin!
Most ample expression of adoration to thee would we render!

Source; Robert Ernest Hume, trans., *The Thirteen Principal Upanishads,* OUP
1931, pp.362-5.

Chandogya Upanishad

Translated by M. Müller

Sixth Prapathaka

2.5.11 **First Khanda**

1. Harih, Om. There lived once Svetaketu Âruneya (the grandson of Aruna). To him his father (Uddâlaka, the son of Aruna) said: 'Svetaketu, go to school; for there is none belonging to our race, darling, who, not having studied (the Veda), is, as it were, a Brâhmana by birth only.'

2. Having begun his apprenticeship (with a teacher) when he was twelve years of age, Svetaketu returned to his father, when he was twenty-four, having then studied all the Vedas — conceited, considering himself well-read, and stern.

3. His father said to him: 'Svetaketu, as you are so conceited, considering yourself so well-read, and so stern, my dear, have you ever asked for that instruction by which we hear what cannot be heard, by which we perceive what cannot be perceived, by which we know what cannot be known?'

4. 'What is that instruction, Sir?' he asked.

The father replied: 'My dear, as by one clod of clay all that is made of clay is known, the difference being only a name, arising from speech, but the truth being that all is clay;

5. 'And as, my dear, by one nugget of gold all that is made of gold is known, the difference being only a name, arising from speech, but the truth being that all is gold;

6. 'And as, my dear, by one pair of nail-scissors all that is made of iron is known, the difference being only a name, arising from speech, but the truth being that all is iron — thus, my dear, is that instruction.'

7. The son said: 'Surely those venerable men (my teachers) did not know that. For if they had known it, why should they not have told it me? Do you, Sir, therefore tell me that.' 'Be it so', said the father.

2.5.12 **Second Khanda**

1. 'In the beginning, my dear, there was that only which is, one only, without a second. Others say, in the beginning there was that only which is not, one only, without a second; and from that which

is not, that which is was born.

2. 'But how could it be thus, my dear?' the father continued. 'How could that which is, be born of that which is not? No, my dear, only that which is, was in the beginning, one only, without a second.

3. 'It thought, may I be many, may I grow forth. It sent forth fire.

'That fire thought, may I be many, may I grow forth. It sent forth water.

'And therefore whenever anybody anywhere is hot and perspires, water is produced on him from fire alone.

4. 'Water thought, may I be many, may I grow forth. It sent forth earth (food).

'Therefore whenever it rains anywhere, most food is then produced. From water alone is eatable food produced.

Third Khanda   2.5.13

1. 'Of all living things there are indeed three origins only, that which springs from an egg (oviparous), that which springs from a living being (viviparous), and that which springs from a germ.

2. 'That Being (i.e. that which had produced fire, water, and earth) thought, let me now enter those three beings (fire, water, earth) with this living Self, and let me then reveal (develop) names and forms.

3. 'Then that Being having said, Let me make each of these three tripartite (so that fire, water, and earth should each have itself for its principal ingredient, besides an admixture of the other two) entered into those three beings with this living self only, and revealed names and forms.

4. 'He made each of these tripartite; and how these three beings become each of them tripartite, that learn from me now, my friend!

Fourth Khanda   2.5.14

1. 'The red colour of burning fire is the colour of fire, the white colour of fire is the colour of water, the black colour of fire the colour of earth. Thus vanishes what we call fire, as a mere variety, being a name, arising from speech. What is true are the three colours (or forms).

2. 'The red colour of the sun is the colour of fire, the white of water, the black of earth. Thus vanishes what we call the sun, as a mere variety, being a name, arising from speech. What is true are the

three colours.

3. 'The red colour of the moon is the colour of fire, the white of water, the black of earth. Thus vanishes what we call the moon, as a mere variety, being a name, arising from speech. What is true are the three colours.

4. 'The red colour of the lightning is the colour of fire, the white of water, the black of earth. Thus vanishes what we call the lightning, as a mere variety, being a name, arising from speech. What is true are the three colours.

5. 'Great householders and great theologians of olden times who knew this, have declared the same, saying "No one can henceforth mention to us anything which we have not heard, perceived, or known". Out of these (three colours or forms) they knew all.

6. 'Whatever they thought looked red, they knew was the colour of fire. Whatever they thought looked white, they knew was the colour of water. Whatever they thought look black, they knew was the colour of earth.

7. 'Whatever they thought was altogether unknown, they knew was some combination of those three beings.

'Now learn from me, my friend, how those three beings, when they reach man, become each of them tripartite.

2.5.15 Fifth Khanda

1. 'The earth (food) when eaten becomes threefold; its grossest portion becomes feces, its middle portion flesh, its subtilest portion mind.

2. 'Water when drunk becomes threefold; its grossest portion becomes water, its middle portion blood, its subtilest portion breath.

3. 'Fire (i.e. in oil, butter, etc.) when eaten becomes threefold; its grossest portion becomes bone, its middle portion marrow, its subtilest portion speech.

4. 'For truly, my child, mind comes of earth, breath of water, speech of fire.'

'Please, Sir, inform me still more', said the son.

'Be it so, my child', the father replied.

2.5.16 Sixth Khanda

1. 'That which is the subtile portion of curds, when churned, rises upwards, and becomes butter.

2. 'In the same manner, my child, the subtile portion of earth (food), when eaten, rises upwards, and becomes mind.

3. 'That which is the subtile portion of water, when drunk, rises upwards, and becomes breath.

4. 'That which is the subtile portion of fire, when consumed, rises upwards, and becomes speech.

5. 'For mind, my child, comes of earth, breath of water, speech of fire.'

'Please, Sir, inform me still more', said the son.

'Be it so, my child', the father replied.

Seventh Khanda
2.5.17

1. 'Man, my son, consists of sixteen parts. Abstain from food for fifteen days, but drink as much water as you like, for breath comes from water, and will not be cut off, if you drink water.'

2. Svetaketu abstained from food for fifteen days. Then he came to his father and said: 'What shall I say?' The father said: 'Repeat the *Rig*, *Yajus*, and *Sâman* verses.' He replied: 'They do not occur to me, Sir.'

3. The father said to him: 'As of a great lighted fire one coal only of the size of a firefly may be left, which would not burn much more than this (i.e. very little), thus, my dear son, one part only of the sixteen parts (of you) is left, and therefore with that one part you do not remember the Vedas. Go and eat!

4. 'Then wilt thou understand me.' Then Svetaketu ate, and afterwards approached his father. And whatever his father asked him, he knew it all by heart. Then his father said to him:

5. 'As of a great lighted fire one coal of the size of a firefly, if left, may be made to blaze up again by putting grass upon it, and will thus burn more than this,

6. 'Thus, my dear son, there was one part of the sixteen parts left to you, and that, lighted up with food, burnt up, and by it you remember now the Vedas.' After that, he understood what his father meant when he said: 'Mind, my son, comes from food, breath from water, speech from fire.' He understood what he said, yea, he understood it.

Eighth Khanda
2.5.18

1. Uddâlaka Âruni said to his son Svetaketu: 'Learn from me the true nature of sleep. When a man sleeps here, then, my dear son, he becomes united with the True, he is gone to his own (Self). Therefore they say, *svapiti*, he sleeps, because he is gone (*apita*) to his own (*sva*).

2. 'As a bird when tied by a string flies first in every direction, and finding no rest anywhere, settles down at last on the very place where it is fastened, exactly in the same manner, my son, that mind, after flying in every direction, and finding no rest anywhere, settles down on breath; for indeed, my son, mind is fastened to breath.

3. 'Learn from me, my son, what are hunger and thirst. When a man is thus said to be hungry, water is carrying away (digests) what has been eaten by him. Therefore as they speak of a cow-leader, a horse-leader, a man-leader, so they call water (which digests food and causes hunger) food-leader. Thus (by food digested etc.),my son, know this offshoot (the body) to be brought forth, for this (body) could not be without a root (cause).

4. 'And where could its root be except in food (earth)? And in the same manner, my son, as food (earth) too is an offshoot, seek after its root, viz. water. And as water too is an offshoot, seek after its root, viz. fire. And as fire too is an offshoot, seek after its root, viz. the True. Yes, all these creatures, my son, have their root in the True, they dwell in the True, they rest in the True.

5. 'When a man is thus said to be thirsty, fire carries away what has been drunk by him. Therefore as they speak of a cow-leader, of a horse-leader, of a man-leader, so they call fire *udanyâ*, thirst, i.e. water-leader. Thus (by water digested etc.), my son, know this offshoot (the body) to be brought forth: this (body) could not be without a root (cause).

6. 'And where could its root be except in water? As water is an offshoot, seek after its root, viz. fire. As fire is an offshoot, seek after its root, viz. the True. Yes, all these creatures, O son, have their root in the True, they dwell in the True, they rest in the True.

'And how these three beings, fire, water, earth, O son, when they reach man, become each of them tripartite, has been said before. When a man departs from hence, his speech is merged in his mind, his mind in his breath, his breath in heat (fire), heat in the Highest Being.

7. 'Now that which is that subtile essence (the root of all), in it all that exists has its self. It is the True. It is the Self, and thou, O Svetaketu, art it.'

'Please, Sir, inform me still more', said the son.

'Be it so, my child', the father replied.

2.5.19 **Ninth Khanda**

1. 'As the bees, my son, make honey by collecting the juices of

distant trees, and reduce the juice into one form.

2. 'And as these juices have no discrimination, so that they might say, I am the juice of this tree or that, in the same manner, my son, all these creatures, when they have become merged in the True (either in deep sleep or in death), know not that they are merged in the True.

3. 'Whatever these creatures are here, whether a lion, or a wolf, or a boar, or a worm, or a midge, or a gnat, or a mosquito, that they become again and again.

4. 'Now that which is that subtile essence, in it all that exists has its self. It is the True. It is the Self, and thou, O Svetaketu, art it.'

'Please, Sir, inform me still more', said the son.

'Be it so, my child', the father replied.

Tenth Khanda

2.5.20

1. 'These rivers, my son, run, the eastern (like the Gangâ) toward the east, the western (like the Sindhu) toward the west. They go from sea to sea (i.e. the clouds lift up the water from the sea to the sky, and send it back as rain to the sea). They become indeed sea. And as those rivers, when they are in the sea, do not know, I am this or that river,

2. 'In the same manner, my son, all these creatures, when they have come back from the True, know not that they have come back from the True. Whatever these creatures are here, whether a lion, or a wolf, or a bear, or a worm, or a midge, or a gnat, or a mosquito, that they become again and again.

3. 'That which is that subtile essence, in it all that exists has its self. It is the True. It is the Self, and thou, O Svetaketu, art it.'

'Please, Sir, inform me still more', said the son.

'Be it so, my child', the father replied.

Eleventh Khanda

2.5.21

1. 'If some one were to strike at the root of this large tree here, it would bleed, but live. If he were to strike at its stem, it would bleed, but live. If he were to strike at its top, it would bleed, but live. Pervaded by the living Self that tree stands firm, drinking in its nourishment and rejoicing;

2. 'But if the life (the living Self) leaves one of its branches, that branch withers; if it leaves a second, that branch withers; if it leaves a third, that branch withers. If it leaves the whole tree, the whole tree withers. In exactly the same manner, my son, know this.' Thus

he spoke:

3. 'This (body) indeed withers and dies when the living Self has left it; the living Self dies not.

'That which is that subtle essence, in it all that exists has its self. It is the True. It is the Self, and thou, Svetaketu, art it.'

'Please, Sir, inform me still more', said the son.

'Be it so, my child', the father replied.

2.5.22 Twelfth Khanda

1. 'Fetch me from thence a fruit of the Nyagrodha tree.'

'Here is one, Sir.'

'Break it.'

'It is broken, Sir.'

'What do you see there?'

'These seeds, almost infinitesimal.'

'Break one of them.'

'It is broken, Sir.'

'What do you see there?'

'Not anything, Sir.'

2. The father said: 'My son, that subtle essence which you do not perceive there, of that very essence this great Nyagrodha tree exists.

3. 'Believe it, my son. That which is the subtle essence, in it all that exists has its self. It is the True. It is the Self, and thou, O Svetaketu, art it.'

'Please, Sir, inform me still more', said the son.

'Be it so, my child', the father replied.

2.5.23 Thirteenth Khanda

1. Place this salt in water, and then wait on me in the morning.'

The son did as he was commanded.

The father said to him: 'Bring me the salt, which you placed in the water last night.'

The son having looked for it, found it not, for, of course, it was melted.

2. The father said: 'Taste it from the surface of the water. How is it?'

The son replied: 'It is salt.'

'Taste it from the middle. How is it?'

The son replied: 'It is salt.'

'Taste it from the bottom. How is it?

The son replied: 'It is salt'.

The father said: 'Throw it away and then wait on me.'

He did so; but salt exists for ever.

Then the father said: 'Here also, in this body, forsooth, you do not perceive the True, my son; but there indeed it is.

3. 'That which is the subtile essence, in it all that exists has its self. It is the True. It is the Self, and thou, O Svetaketu, art it.'

'Please, Sir, inform me still more', said the son.

'Be it so, my child'. the father replied.

Fourteenth Khanda 2.5.24

1. 'As one might lead a person with his eyes covered away from the Gandhâras, and leave him then in a place where there are no human beings; and as that person would turn towards the east, or the north, or the west, and shout: "I have been brought here with my eyes covered, I have been left here with my eyes covered,"

2. 'And as thereupon some one might loose his bandage and say to him, "Go in that direction, it is Gandhâra, go in that direction"; and as thereupon, having been informed and being able to judge for himself, he would by asking his way from village to village arrive at last at Gandhâra – in exactly the same manner does a man, who meets with a teacher to inform him, obtain the true knowledge. For him there is only delay so long as he is not delivered (from the body); then he will be perfect.

3. 'That which is the subtile essence, in it all that exists has its self. It is the True. It is the Self, and thou, O Svetaketu, art it.'

'Please, Sir, inform me still more', said the son.

'Be it so, my child', the father replied.

Fifteenth Khanda 2.5.25

1. If a man is ill, his relatives assemble round him and ask: "Dost thou know me? Dost thou know me?" Now as long as his speech is not merged in his mind, his mind in breath, breath in heat (fire), heat in the Highest Being, he knows them.

2. 'But when his speech is merged in his mind, his mind in breath, breath in heat (fire), heat in the Highest Being, then he knows them not.

'That which is the subtile essence, in it all that exists has its self. It is the True. It is the Self, and thou, O Svetaketu, art it.'

'Please, Sir, inform me still more', said the son.

'Be it so, my child', the father replied.

2.5.26 Sixteenth Khanda

1. 'My child, they bring a man hither whom they have taken by the hand, and they say: "He has taken something, he has committed a theft." (When he denies, they say) "Heat the hatchet for him." If he committed the theft, then he makes himself to be what he is not. Then the false-minded, having covered his true Self by a falsehood, grasps the heated hatchet — he is burnt, and he is killed.

2. 'But if he did not commit the theft, then he makes himself to be what he is. Then the true-minded, having covered his true Self by truth, grasps the heated hatchet — he is not burnt, and he is delivered.

'As that (truthful) man is not burnt, thus has all that exists its self in That. It is the True. It is the Self, and thou, O Svetaketu, art it.' He understood what he said, yea, he understood it.

Source: M. Müller, trans. SBE, OUP 1879, Vol.X, pp.92-109.

2.6 FROM THE BHAGAVAD GITA

Translated by Franklin Edgerton

Chapter I

Dhrtarāstra said:

1. In the Field of Right, the Kuru-field,
      Assembled ready to fight,
   My men and the sons of Pāndu as well,
      What did they do, Samjaya?

   Samjaya said:

2. Seeing however the host of the sons of Pāndu
      Arrayed, Duryodhana then
   Approached the Teacher (Drona),
      And spoke a word, the prince:

3. Behold of Pāndu's sons this
      Great host, O Teacher!
   Arrayed by Drupada's son,
      Thy skilful pupil.

4. Here are heroes, great archers,
      Like unto |Bhima and Arjuna in battle,
   Yuyudhāna, and Virāta,
      And Drupada of the great car;

5. Dhrstaketu, Cekitāna,
      And the heroic king of Benares,
   Purujit, and Kuntibhoja,
      And the Śibi-king, bull of men;

6. Yudhāmanyu the valorous,
      And Uttamaujas the heroic,
   The son of Subhadrā, and the sons of Draupadi,
      All, aye all, men of great cars.

7. But of our men, who are the most distinguished
    Learn from me, best of brahmans —
    Who are the leaders of my host;
    To name them, I declare them to thee.

8. Thy good self, and Bhīṣma, and Karṇa,
    And battle-winning Kṛpa,
    Aśvatthāman, and Vikarṇa,
    And the son of Somadatta too;

9. And many other heroes,
    Giving up life for my sake;
    With various weapons and arms,
    All skilled in conflict.

10. (Altho) insufficient (in number) this our
    Host is protected by (the wise) Bhīṣma;
    On the other hand, (while) sufficient, this their
    Host is protected by (the unskilled) Bhīma.

11. And (so) in all movements,
    Stationed in your several places,
    Guard Bhīṣma above all,
    Each and every one of you.

12. Producing joy in his heart,
    The aged grandsire of the Kurus
    Roared a lion's roar on high,
    And blew his conch-shell, full of valor.

13. Then conch-shells and drums,
    Kettle-drums, cymbals and trumpets,
    All at once were sounded;
    The sound was tremendous.

14. Then on the white-horse-yoked
    Mighty car standing,
    Mādhava (Kṛṣṇa) and the son of Pāṇḍu (Arjuna)
    Blew their wondrous conch-shells:

15. Hṛṣīkeśa (Kṛṣṇa) blew Pāñcajanya,
    Dhanaṃjaya (Arjuna) blew Devadatta,
    The great shell Pauṇḍra blew
    Wolf-belly (Bhīma) of terrible deeds.

16. (The shell) Anantavijaya (blew) the king
    Yudhiṣṭhira, Kuntī's son;
    Nakula and Sahadeva
    (Blew) Sughoṣa and Maṇipuṣpaka.

17. And the king of Benares, supreme archer,
    And Śikhaṇḍin, of the great car,
    And Dhṛṣṭadyumna and Virāṭa,
    And the unconquered Sātyaki,

18. Drupada and the sons of Draupadī,
    All together, O king,
    And the great-armed son of Subhadrā,
    Blew their conch-shells severally.

19. That sound Dhṛtarāṣṭra's men's
    Hearts did rend;
    And both sky and earth
    It made to resound, swelling aloft.

20. Then seeing arrayed
    Dhṛtarāṣṭra's sons, the ape-bannered (Arjuna),
    When the clash of arms had already begun,
    Lifted up his bow, the son of Pāṇḍu,

21. And to Hṛṣīkeśa then words
    Like these spoke, O king.
    Between the two armies
    Halt my chariot, O unshaken one,

22. Until I espy these
    That are drawn up eager to fight,
    (And see) with whom I must fight
    In this warlike enterprise

23. I will see those who are going to fight,
    Who are here assembled,
    For Dhṛtarāṣtra's ill-minded son
    Eager to do service in battle.

24. Hṛṣīkeśa, thus addressed
    By Gudākeśa, O son of Bhārata,
    Between the two armies
    Halted the excellent car,

25. In front of Bhīṣma and Droṇa
    And all the kings,
    And said: Son of Pṛthā, behold these
    Assembled Kurus!

26. There the son of Pṛthā saw stationed
    Fathers and grandsires,
    Teachers, uncles, brothers,
    Sons, grandsons, and comrades too,

27. Fathers-in-law and friends as well,
    In both the two armies.
    The son of Kuntī, seeing them,
    All his kinsmen arrayed,

28. Filled with utmost compassion,
    Despondent, spoke these words:
    Seeing my own kinsfolk here, Kṛṣṇa,
    That have drawn near eager to fight,

29. My limbs sink down,
    And my mouth becomes parched,
    And there is trembling in my body,
    And my hair stands on end.

30. (The bow) Gāndīva falls from my hand,
    And my skin, too, is burning,
    And I cannot stand still,
    And my mind seems to wander.

31. And I see portents
    That are adverse, Keśava;
    And I foresee no welfare,
    Having slain my kinsfolk in battle.

32. I wish no victory, Kṛṣṇa,
    Nor kingdom nor joys;
    Of what use to us were kingdom, Govinda.
    Of what use enjoyments or life?

33. For whose sake we desire
    Kingdom, enjoyments, and happiness,
    They are drawn up here in battle,
    Giving up life and wealth;

34. Teachers, fathers, sons,
    Grandsires as well,
    Uncles, fathers-in-law, grandsons,
    Brothers-in-law, and (other) kinsfolk.

35. Them I do not wish to slay,
    Even tho they slay (me), O slayer of Madhu,
    Even for three-world-rulership's
    Sake; how much less for the sake of the earth!

36. Having slain Dhṛtarāṣṭra's men, to us
    What joy would ensue, Janārdana?
    Evil alone would light upon us,
    Did we slay these (our would-be) murderers.

37. Therefore we should not slay
    Dhṛtarāṣṭra's men, our own kinsfolk.
    For how, having slain our kinsfolk,
    Could we be happy, Mādhava?

38. Even if they do not see,
    Because their intelligence is destroyed by greed,
    The sin caused by destruction of family,
    And the crime involved in injury to a friend,

39. How should we not know enough
    To turn back from this wickedness,
    The sin caused by destruction of family
    Perceiving, O Janārdana?

40. Upon the destruction of the family, perish
    The immemorial holy laws of the family;
    When the laws have perished, the whole family
    Lawlessness overwhelms also.

41. Because of the prevalence of lawlessness, Krsna,
    The women of the family are corrupted;
    When the women are corrupted, O Vrsni-clansman,
    Mixture of caste ensues.

42. Mixture (of caste) leads to naught but hell
    For the destroyers of the family and for the family;
    For their ancestors fall (to hell),
    Because the rites of (giving) food and water are interrupted.

43. By these sins of family-destroyers,
    (Sins) which produce caste-mixture,
    The caste laws are destroyed,
    And the eternal family laws.

44. When the family laws are destroyed,
    Janārdana, then for men
    Dwelling in hell certainly
    Ensues: so we have heard (from the Holy Word).

45. Ah woe! 'Twas a great wickedness
    That we had resolved to commit,
    In that, thru greed for the joys of kingship,
    We undertook to slay our kinsfolk.

46. If me unresisting,
    Weaponless, with weapons in their hands
    Dhrtarāstra's men should slay in battle,
    That would be a safer course for me.

47. Thus speaking Arjuna in the battle
    Sat down in the box of the car,
    Letting fall his bow and arrows,
    His heart smitten with grief.

Chapter II   2.6.2

    Saṃjaya said:
1. To him thus by compassion possessed,
    His eyes tear-filled, blurred,
    Despondent, this word
    Spoke the Slayer of Madhu.

    The Blessed One said:
2. Whence to thee this faintheartedness
    In peril has come,
    Offensive to the noble, not leading to heaven,
    Inglorious, O Arjuna?

3. Yield not to unmanliness, son of Pṛthā;
    It is not meet for thee.
    Petty weakness of heart
    Rejecting, arise, scorcher of the foe!

    Arjuna said:
4. How shall I in battle against Bhīṣma,
    And Droṇa, O Slayer of Madhu,
    Fight with arrows,
    Who are both worthy of reverence, Slayer of Enemies?

5. For not slaying my revered elders of great dignity
    'Twere better to eat alms-food, even, in this world;
    But having slain my elders who seek their ends, right in this world
    I should eat food smeared with blood.

6. And we know not which of the two were better for us,
    Whether we should conquer, or they should conquer us;
    What very ones having slain we wish not to live,
    They are arrayed in front of us, Dhṛtarāṣṭra's men.

7. My very being afflicted with the taint of weak compassion,
      I ask Thee, my mind bewildered as to the right:
   Which were better, that tell me definitely;
      I am Thy pupil, teach me that have come to Thee (for
      instruction).

8. For I see not what would dispel my
      Grief, the witherer of the senses,
   If I attained on earth rivalless, prosperous
      Kingship, and even overlordship of the gods.

   Samjaya said:
9. Thus speaking to Hrsīkeśa,
      Gudākeśa the Slayer of the Foe
   'I'll not fight!' to Govinda
      Said, and was silent.

10. To him spoke Hrsīkeśa,
       With a semblance of a smile, son of Bhārata,
    Betwixt the two armies
       As he was despondent, these words:

    The Blessed One said:
11. Thou hast mourned those who should not be mourned,
       And (yet) thou speakest words about wisdom!
    Dead and living men
       The (truly) learned do not mourn.

12. But not in any respect was I (ever) not,
       Nor thou, nor these kings;
    And not at all shall we ever come not to be,
       All of us, henceforward.

13. As to the embodied (soul) in this body
       Come childhood, youth, old age,
    So the coming to another body;
       The wise man is not confused herein.

14. But contacts with matter, son of Kuntī,
    Cause cold and heat, pleasure and pain;
    They come and go, and are impermanent;
    Put up with them, son of Bhārata!

15. For whom these (contacts) do not cause to waver,
    The man, O bull of men,
    To whom pain and pleasure are alike, the wise,
    He is fit for immortality.

16. Of what is not, no coming to be occurs;
    No coming not to be occurs of what is;
    But the dividing-line of both is seen,
    Of these two, by those who see the truth.

17. But know that that is indestructible,
    By which this all is pervaded;
    Destruction of this imperishable one
    No one can cause.

18. These bodies, come to an end,
    It is declared, of the eternal embodied (soul),
    Which is indestructible and unfathomable.
    Therefore fight, son of Bhārata!

19. Who believes him a slayer,
    And who thinks him slain,
    Both these understand not:
    He slays not, is not slain.

20. He is not born, nor does he ever die;
    Nor, having come to be, will he ever more come not to be.
    Unborn, eternal, everlasting, this ancient one
    Is not slain when the body is slain.

21. Who knows as indestructible and eternal
    This unborn, imperishable one,
    That man, son of Pṛthā, how
    Can he slay or cause to slay — whom?

22. As leaving aside worn-out garments
    A man takes other, new ones,
    So leaving aside worn-out bodies
    To other, new ones goes the embodied (soul).

23. Swords cut him not,
    Fire burns him not,
    Water wets him not,
    Wind dries him not.

24. Not to be cut is he, not to be burnt is he,
    Not to be wet nor yet dried;
    Eternal, omnipresent, fixed,
    Immovable, everlasting is he.

25. Unmanifest he, unthinkable he,
    Unchangeable he is declared to be;
    Therefore knowing him thus
    Thou shouldst not mourn him.

26. Moreover, even if constantly born
    Or constantly dying thou considerest him,
    Even so, great-armed one, thou
    Shouldst not mourn him.

27. For to one that is born death is certain,
    And birth is certain for one that has died;
    Therefore, the thing being unavoidable,
    Thou shouldst not mourn.

28. The beginnings of things are unmanifest,
    Manifest their middles, son of Bhārata,
    Unmanifest again their ends:
    Why mourn about this?

29. By a rare chance one may see him,
    And by a rare chance likewise may another declare him,
    And by a rare chance may another hear (of) him;
    (But) even having heard (of) him, no one whatsoever knows
    him.

30. This embodied (soul) is eternally unslayable
    In the body of every one, son of Bhārata;
    Therefore all beings
    Thou shouldst not mourn.

31. Likewise having regard for thine own (caste) duty
    Thou shouldst not tremble;
    For another, better thing than a fight required of duty
    Exists not for a warrior.

32. Presented by mere luck,
    An open door of heaven —
    Happy the warriors, son of Pṛthā,
    That get such a fight!

33. Now, if thou this duty-required
    Conflict wilt not perform,
    Then thine own duty and glory
    Abandoning, thou shalt get thee evil.

34. Disgrace, too, will creatures
    Speak of thee, without end;
    And for one that has been esteemed, disgrace
    Is worse than death.

35. That thou hast abstained from battle thru fear
    The (warriors) of great chariots will think of thee;
    And of whom thou wast highly regarded,
    . Thou shalt come to be held lightly.

36. And many sayings that should not be said
    Thy ill-wishers will say of thee,
    Speaking ill of thy capacity:
    What, pray, is more grievous than that?

37. Either slain thou shalt gain heaven,
    Or conquering thou shalt enjoy the earth.
    Therefore arise, son of Kuntī,
    Unto battle, making a firm resolve.

38. Holding pleasure and pain alike,
    Gain and loss, victory and defeat,
    Then gird thyself for battle:
    Thus thou shalt not get evil.

39. This has been declared to thee (that is found) in Reason-method,
    This mental attitude: but hear this in Discipline-method,
    Disciplined with which mental attitude, son of Pṛthā,
    Thou shalt get rid of the bondage of action.

40. In it there is no loss of a start once made,
    Nor does any reverse occur;
    Even a little of this duty
    Saves from great danger.

41. The mental attitude whose nature is resolution
    Is but one in this world, son of Kuru;
    For many-branched and endless
    Are the mental attitudes of the irresolute.

42. This flowery speech which
    Undiscerning men utter,
    Who take delight in the words of the Veda, son of Pṛthā,
    Saying that there is nothing else,

43. Whose nature is desire, who are intent on heaven,
    (The speech) which yields rebirth as the fruit of actions,
    Which is replete with various (ritual) acts
    Aiming at the goal of enjoyment and power —

44. Of men devoted to enjoyment and power,
    Who are robbed of insight by that (speech),
    A mental attitude resolute in nature
    Is not established in concentration.

45. The Vedas have the three Strands (of matter) as their scope;
    Be thou free from the three Strands, Arjuna,
    Free from the pairs (of opposites), eternally fixed in goodness,
    Free from acquisition and possession, self-possessed.

46. As much profit as there is in a water-tank
      When on all sides there is a flood of water,
    No more is there in all the Vedas
      For a brahman who (truly) understands.

47. On action alone be thy interest,
      Never on its fruits;
    Let not the fruits of action be thy motive,
      Nor be thy attachment to inaction.

48. Abiding in discipline perform actions,
      Abandoning attachment, Dhanamjaya,
    Being indifferent to success or failure;
      Discipline is defined as indifference.

49. For action is far inferior
      To discipline of mental attitude, Dhanamjaya.
    In the mental attitude seek thy (religious) refuge;
      Wretched are those whose motive is the fruit (of action).

50. The disciplined in mental attitude leaves behind in this world
      Both good and evil deeds.
    Therefore discipline thyself unto discipline;
      Discipline in actions is weal.

51. For the disciplined in mental attitude, action-produced
      Fruit abandoning, the intelligent ones,
    Freed from the bondage of rebirth,
      Go to the place that is free from illness.

52. When the jungle of delusion
      Thy mentality shall get across,
    Then thou shalt come to aversion
      Towards what is to be heard and has been heard (in the Veda).

53. Averse to traditional lore ('heard' in the Veda)
      When shall stand motionless
    Thy mentality, immovable in concentration,
      Then thou shalt attain discipline.

Arjuna said:
54. What is the description of the man of stabilized mentality,
    That is fixed in concentration, Keśava?
    How might the man of stabilized mentality speak,
    How might he sit, how walk?

    The Blessed One said:
55. When he abandons desires,
    All that are in the mind, son of Pṛthā,
    Finding contentment by himself in the self alone,
    Then he is called of stabilized mentality.

56. When his mind is not perturbed in sorrows,
    And he has lost desire for joys,
    His longing, fear, and wrath departed,
    He is called a stable-minded holy man.

57. Who has no desire towards any thing,
    And getting this or that good or evil
    Neither delights in it nor loathes it,
    His mentality is stabilized.

58. And when he withdraws,
    As a tortoise his limbs from all sides,
    His senses from the objects of sense,
    His mentality is stabilized.

59. The objects of sense turn away
    From the embodied one that abstains from food,
    Except flavor; flavor also from him
    Turns away when he has seen the highest.

60. For even of one who strives, son of Kuntī,
    Of the man of discernment,
    The impetuous senses
    Carry away the mind by violence.

61. Them all restraining,
    Let him sit disciplined, intent on Me;
    For whose senses are under control,
    His mentality is stabilized.

62. When a man meditates on the objects of sense,
    Attachment to them is produced.
    From attachment springs desire,
    From desire wrath arises;

63. From wrath comes infatuation,
    From infatuation loss of memory;
    From loss of memory, loss of mind;
    From loss of mind he perishes.

64. But with desire-and-loathing-severed
    Senses acting on the objects of sense,
    With (senses) self-controlled, he, governing his self,
    Goes unto tranquillity.

65. In tranquillity, of all griefs
    Riddance is engendered for him;
    For of the tranquil-minded quickly
    The mentality becomes stable.

66. The undisciplined has no (right) mentality,
    And the undisciplined has no efficient-force;
    Who has no efficient-force has no peace;
    For him that has no peace how can there be bliss?

67. For the senses are roving,
    And when the thought-organ is directed after them,
    It carries away his mentality,
    As wind a ship on the water.

68. Therefore whosoever, great-armed one,
    Has withdrawn on all sides
    The senses from the objects of sense,
    His mentality is stabilized.

69. What is night for all beings,
    Therein the man of restraint is awake;
    Wherein (other) beings are awake,
    That is night for the sage of vision.

70. It is ever being filled, and (yet) its foundation remains unmoved —
    The sea: just as waters enter it,
    Whom all desires enter in that same way
    He attains peace; not the man who lusts after desires.

71. Abandoning all desires, what
    Man moves free from longing,
    Without self-interest and egotism,
    He goes to peace.

72. This is the fixation that is Brahmanic, son of Pṛthā;
    Having attained it he is not (again) confused.
    Abiding in it even at the time of death,
    He goes to Brahman-nirvāṇa.

2.6.3 Chapter VII

The Blessed One said:
1. With mind attached to Me, son of Pṛthā,
    Practising discipline with reliance on Me,
    Without doubt Me entirely
    How thou shalt know, that hear!

2. Theoretical knowledge to thee along with practical
    I shall now expound completely;
    Having known which, in this world no other further
    Thing to be known is left.

3. Among thousands of men
    Perchance one strives for perfection;
    Even of those that strive and are perfected,
    Perchance one knows Me in very truth.

4. Earth, water, fire, wind,
    Ether, thought-organ, and consciousness,
    And I-faculty: thus My
    Nature is divided eight-fold.

5. This is My lower (nature). But other than this,
    My higher nature know:
   It is the Life (soul), great-armed one,
   By which this world is maintained.

6. Beings spring from it,
    All of them, be assured.
   Of the whole world I am
   The origin and the dissolution too.

7. Than Me no other higher thing
    Whatsoever exists, Dhanaṃjaya;
   On Me all this (universe) is strung,
   Like heaps of pearls on a string.

8. I am taste in water, son of Kuntī,
    I am light in the moon and sun,
   The sacred syllable (ōm) in all the Vedas,
   Sound in ether, manliness in men.

9. Both the goodly odor in earth,
    And brilliance in fire am I,
   Life in all beings,
    And austerity in ascetics am I.

10. The seed of all beings am I,
     The eternal, be assured, son of Pṛthā;
    I am intelligence of the intelligent,
    Majesty of the majestic am I.

11. Might of the mighty am I, too,
     (Such as is) free from desire and passion;
    (So far as it is) not inconsistent with right, in creatures
     I am desire, O best of Bhāratas.

12. Both whatsoever states are of (the Strand) goodness,
     And those of (the Strands) passion and darkness too,
    Know that they are from Me alone;
     But I am not in them; they are in Me.

13. By the three states (of being), composed of the Strands,
    These (just named), all this world,
    Deluded, does not recognize
    Me that am higher than they and eternal.

14. For this is My divine strand-composed
    Trick-of-illusion, hard to get past;
    Those who resort to Me alone
    Penetrate beyond this trick-of-illusion.

15. Not to Me do deluded evil-doers
    Resort, base men,
    Whom this illusion robs of knowledge,
    Who cleave to demoniac estate.

16. Fourfold are those that worship Me,
    (All) virtuous folk, Arjuna:
    The afflicted, the knowledge-seeker, he who seeks personal ends,
    And the possessor of knowledge, bull of Bhāratas.

17. Of these the possessor of knowledge, constantly disciplined,
    Of single devotion, is the best;
    For extremely dear to the possessor of knowledge
    Am I, and he is dear to Me.

18. All these are noble;
    But the man of knowledge is My very self, so I hold.
    For he with disciplined soul has resorted
    To Me alone as the highest goal.

19. At the end of many births
    The man of knowledge resorts to Me;
    Who thinks 'Vāsudeva (Kṛṣṇa) is all,'
    That noble soul is hard to find.

20. Deprived of knowledge by this or that desire,
    Men resort to other deities,
    Taking to this or that (religious) rule,
    Constrained by their own nature.

21. Whatsoever (divine) form any devotee
     With faith seeks to worship,
   For every such (devotee), faith unswerving
     I ordain that same to be.

22. He, disciplined with that faith,
     Seeks to propitiate that (divine being),
   And obtains therefrom his desires,
     Because I myself ordain them.

23. But finite fruition for them
     That becomes, (since) they are of scant intelligence;
   The worshipers of the gods go to the gods,
     My devotees go to Me also.

24. Unmanifest, as having come into manifestation
     Fools conceive Me,
   Not knowing the higher essence
     Of Me, which is imperishable, supreme.

25. I am not revealed to every one,
     Being veiled by My magic trick-of-illusion;
   'Tis deluded and does not recognize
     Me the unborn, imperishable — this world.

26. I know those that are past,
     And that are present, Arjuna,
   And beings that are yet to be,
     But no one knows Me.

27. It arises from desire and loathing,
     The delusion of the pairs (of opposites), son of Bhārata;
   Because of it all beings to confusion
     Are subject at their birth, scorcher of the foe.

28. But those whose sin is ended,
     Men of virtuous deeds,
   Freed from the delusion of the pairs,
     Revere Me with firm resolve.

29. Unto freedom from old age and death
Those who strive, relying on Me,
They know that Brahman entire,
And the over-soul, and action altogether.

30. Me together with the over-being and the over-divinity,
And with the over-worship, whoso know,
And (who know) Me even at the hour of death,
They (truly) know (Me), with disciplined hearts.

2.6.4 Chapter XI

Arjuna said:
1. As a favor to me the supreme
Mystery, called the over-soul,
The words which Thou hast spoken, thereby
This delusion of mine is dispelled.

2. For the origin and dissolution of beings
Have been heard by me in full detail
From Thee, Lotus-petal-eyed One,
And also (Thine) exalted nature unending.

3. Thus it is, as Thou declarest
Thyself, O Supreme Lord.
I desire to see Thy form
As God, O Supreme Spirit!

4. If Thou thinkest that it can
Be seen by me, O Lord,
Prince of mystic power then do Thou to me
Reveal Thine immortal Self.

The Blessed One said:
5. Behold My forms, son of Prthā,
By hundreds and by thousands,
Of various sorts, marvelous,
Of various colors and shapes.

6. Behold the Ādityas, Vasus, Rudras,
   The Aśvin-pair and the Maruts too;
   Many before-unseen
   Marvels behold, son of Bharata.

7. Here the whole world united
   Behold today, with moving and unmoving things,
   In My body, Gudākeśa,
   And whatsoever else thou wishest to see.

8. But thou canst not see Me
   With this same eye of thine own;
   I give thee a supernatural eye:
   Behold My mystic power as God!

   Samjaya said:
9. Thus speaking then, O king,
   Hari (Visṇu), the great Lord of Mystic Power,
   Showed unto the son of Pṛthā
   His supernal form as God:

10. Of many mouths and eyes,
    Of many wondrous aspects,
    Of many marvelous ornaments,
    Of marvelous and many uplifted weapons;

11. Wearing marvelous garlands and garments,
    With marvelous perfumes and ointments,
    Made up of all wonders, the god,
    Infinite, with faces in all directions.

12. Of a thousand suns in the sky
    If suddenly should burst forth
    The light, it would be like
    Unto the light of that exalted one.

13. The whole word there united,
    And divided many-fold,
    Beheld in the God of Gods'
    Body the son of Pāṇḍu then.

14. Then filled with amazement,
       His hair standing upright, Dhanamjaya
    Bowed with his head to the God,
       And said with a gesture of reverence:

    Arjuna said:
15. I see the gods in Thy body, O God,
       All of them, and the hosts of various kinds of beings too,
    Lord Brahmā sitting on the lotus-seat,
       And the seers all, and the divine serpents.

16. With many arms, bellies, mouths, and eyes,
       I see Thee, infinite in form on all sides;
    No end nor middle nor yet beginning of Thee
       Do I see, O All-God, All-formed!

17. With diadem, club, and disc,
       A mass of radiance, glowing on all sides,
    I see Thee, hard to look at, on every side
       With the glory of flaming fire and sun, immeasurable.

18. Thou art the Imperishable, the supreme Object of Knowledge;
       Thou art the ultimate resting-place of this universe;
    Thou art the immortal guardian of the eternal right,
       Thou art the everlasting Spirit, I hold.

19. Without beginning, middle, or end, of infinite power,
       Of infinite arms, whose eyes are the moon and sun,
    I see Thee, whose face is flaming fire,
       Burning this whole universe with Thy radiance.

20. For this region between heaven and earth
       Is pervaded by Thee alone, and all the directions;
    Seeing this Thy wondrous, terrible form,
       The triple world trembles, O exalted one!

21. For into Thee are entering yonder throngs of gods;
       Some, affrighted, praise Thee with reverent gestures;
    Crying 'Hail!' the throngs of the great seers and perfected ones
       Praise Thee with abundant laudations.

22. The Rudras, the Ādityas, the Vasus, and the Sādhyas,
    All-gods, Aśvins, Maruts, and the Steam-drinkers ('fathers'),
    The hosts of heavenly musicians, sprites, demons, and perfected
    ones,
    Gaze upon Thee, and all are quite amazed.

23. Thy great form, of many mouths and eyes,
    O great-armed one, of many arms, thighs and feet,
    Of many bellies, terrible with many tusks —
    Seeing it the worlds tremble, and I too.

24. Touching the sky, aflame, of many colors,
    With yawning mouths and flaming enormous eyes,
    Verily seeing Thee (so), my inmost soul is shaken,
    And I find no steadiness nor peace, O Viṣṇu!

25. And Thy mouths, terrible with great tusks,
    No sooner do I see them, like the fire of dissolution (of the
    world),
    Than I know not the directions of the sky, and I find no refuge;
    Have mercy, Lord of Gods, Thou in whom the world dwells!

26. And Thee yonder sons of Dhṛtarāṣtra,
    All of them, together with the hosts of kings,
    Bhīṣma, Droṇa, and yonder son of the charioteer (Karṇa) too,
    Together with our chief warriors likewise,

27. Hastening enter Thy mouths,
    Frightful with tusks, and terrifying;
    Some, stuck between the teeth,
    Are seen with their heads crushed.

28. As the many water-torrents of the rivers
    Rush headlong towards the single sea,
    So yonder heroes of the world of men into Thy
    Flaming mouths do enter.

29. As moths into a burning flame
    Do enter unto their destruction with utmost impetuosity,
    Just so unto their destruction enter the worlds
    Into Thy mouths also, with utmost impetuosity.

30. Devouring them Thou lickest up voraciously on all sides
    All the worlds with Thy flaming jaws;
    Filling with radiance the whole universe,
    Thy terrible splendors burn, O Visnu!

31. Tell me, who art Thou, of awful form?
    Homage be to Thee: Best of Gods, be merciful!
    I desire to understand Thee, the primal one;
    For I do not comprehend what Thou hast set out to do.

    The Blessed One said:
32. I am Time (Death), cause of destruction of the worlds, matured
    And set out to gather in the worlds here.
    Even without thee (thy action), all shall cease to exist,
    The warriors that are drawn up in the opposing ranks.

33. Therefore arise thou, win glory,
    Conquer thine enemies and enjoy prospered kingship,
    By Me Myself they have already been slain long ago;
    Be thou the mere instrument, left-handed archer!

34. Drona and Bhisma and Jayadratha,
    Karna too, and the other warrior-heroes as well,
    Do thou slay, (since) they are already slain by Me; do not
    hesitate!
    Fight! Thou shalt conquer thy rivals in battle.

    Samjaya said:
35. Hearing these words of Kesava,
    Making a reverent gesture, trembling, the Diademed (Arjuna)
    Made obeisance and spoke yet again to Krsna,
    Stammering, greatly affrighted, bowing down:

    Arjuna said:
36. It is in place, Hrsikesa, that at Thy praise
    The world rejoices and is exceeding glad;
    Ogres fly in terror in all directions,
    And all the hosts of perfected ones pay homage.

37. And why should they not pay homage to Thee, Exalted One?
      Thou art greater even than Brahman; Thou art the First
        Creator;
    Of infinite Lord of Gods, in whom the world dwells,
      Thou the imperishable, existent, non-existent, and beyond
        both!

38. Thou art the Primal God, the Ancient Spirit,
      Thou art the supreme resting-place of this universe;
    Thou art the knower, the object of knowledge, and the highest
      station,
      By Thee the universe is pervaded, Thou of infinite form!

39. Vāyu, Yama, Agni, Varuṇa, the moon,
      Prajāpati art Thou, and the Greatgrandsire;
    Homage, homage be to Thee a thousand fold,
      And again be yet further homage, homage to Theei

40. Homage be to Thee from in front and from behind,
      Homage be to Thee from all sides, Thou All!
    O Thou of infinite might, Thy prowess is unmeasured;
      Thou attainest all; therefore Thou art All!

41. Whatever I said rashly, thinking Thee my boon-companion,
      Calling Thee 'Krsna, Yādava, Companion!',
    Not knowing this (truth, namely) Thy greatness,
      Thru careless negligence, or even thru affection,

42. And if I treated Thee disrespectfully, to make sport of Thee,
      In the course of amusement, resting, sitting, or eating,
    Either alone, O unshaken one, or in the presence of those
      (others),
      For that I beg forgiveness of Thee, the immeasurable one.

43. Thou art the father of the world of things that move and move
      not,
      And Thou art its revered, most venerable Guru;
    There is no other like Thee — how then a greater?
      Even in the three worlds, O Thou of matchless greatness!

44. Therefore, bowing and prostrating my body,
      I beg grace of Thee, the Lord to be revered:
    As a father to his son, as a friend to his friend,
      As a lover to his beloved, be pleased to show mercy, O God!

45. Having seen what was never seen before, I am thrilled,
      And (at the same time) my heart is shaken with fear;
    Show me, O God, that same form of Thine (as before)!
      Be merciful, Lord of Gods, Abode of the World!

46. Wearing the diadem, carrying the club, with disc in hand,
      Just (as before) I desire to see Thee;
    In that same four-armed shape
      Present Thyself, O Thousand-armed One, of universal form!

      The Blessed One said:
47. By Me showing grace towards thee, Arjuna, this
      Supreme form has been manifested by My own mysterious
        power;
    (This form) made up of splendor, universal, infinite, primal,
      Of Mine, which has never been seen before by any other than
        thee.

48. Not by the Vedas, by acts of worship, or study, or gifts,
      Nor yet by rites, nor by grim austerities,
    In the world of men can I in such a form
      Be seen by any other than thee, hero of the Kurus.

49. Have no perturbation, nor any state of bewilderment,
      Seeing this so awful form of Mine;
    Dispel thy fear; let thy heart be of good cheer; again do thou
      Behold that same (former) form of Mine: here!

      Samjaya said:
50. Having thus spoken to Arjuna, Vāsudeva
      Again revealed his own (natural) form,
    And comforted him in his fright
      By once more assuming his gracious aspect, the Exalted One.

Arjuna said:

51. Seeing this human form
Of Thine, gracious, O Janārdana,
Now I have become
Possessed of my senses, and restored to normal state.

The Blessed One said:

52. This form that is right hard to see,
Which thou hast seen of Mine,
Of this form even the gods
Constantly long for the sight.

53. Not by the Vedas nor by austerity,
Nor by gifts or acts of worship,
Can I be seen in such a guise,
As thou hast seen Me.

54. But by unswerving devotion can
I in such a guise, Arjuna,
Be known and seen in very truth,
And entered into, scorcher of the foe.

55. Doing My Work, intent on Me,
Devoted to Me, free from attachment,
Free from enmity to all beings,
Who is so, goes to Mc, son of Pāṇḍu.

Chapter XVIII   2.6.5

Arjuna said:

1. Of renunciation, great-armed one,
I desire to know the truth,
And of abandonment, Hṛṣīkeśa,
Severally, Slayer of Keśin.

The Blessed One said:

2. The renouncing of acts of desire
   Sages call renunciation.
   The abandonment of all action-fruits
   The wise call abandonment.

3. That it must be abandoned as sinful, some
   Wise men say of action;
   That actions of worship, gift, and austerity
   Must not be abandoned, say others.

4. Hear my decision in this matter
   Of abandonment, best of Bhāratas;
   For abandonment, O man-tiger,
   Is reputed to be threefold.

5. Actions of worship, gift, and austerity
   Must not be abandoned, but rather performed;
   Worship, gift, and austerity
   Are purifiers of the wise.

6. However, these actions
   With abandonment of attachment and fruits
   Must be performed: this, son of Pṛthā, is My
   Definite and highest judgment.

7. But abandonment of a (religiously) required
   Action is not seemly;
   Abandonment thereof owing to delusion
   Is reputed to be of the nature of darkness.

8. Just because it is troublesome, what action
   One abandons thru fear of bodily affliction,
   Such a man performs an abandonment that is of the nature of
   passion;
   By no means shall he get any fruit of (this) abandonment.

9. Simply because it ought to be done, when action
   That is (religiously) required is performed, Arjuna,
   Abandoning attachment and fruit,
   That abandonment is held to be of goodness.

10. He loathes not disagreeable action,
    > Nor does he cling to agreeable (action),
    The man of abandonment who is filled with goodness,
    > Wise, whose doubts are destroyed.

11. For a body-bearing (soul) can not
    > Abandon actions without remainder;
    But he who abandons the fruit of action
    > Is called the man of (true) abandonment.

12. Undesired, desired, and mixed —
    > Threefold is the fruit of action
    That ensues after death for those who are not men of
    abandonment,
    > But never for men of renunciation.

13. O great-armed one, these five
    > Factors learn from Me,
    Which are declared in the reason-method doctrine
    > For the effective performance of all actions.

14. The (material) basis, the agent too,
    > And the instruments of various sorts,
    And the various motions of several kinds,
    > And just Fate as the fifth of them.

15. With body, speech, or mind, whatever
    > Action a man undertakes,
    Whether it be lawful or the reverse,
    > These are its five factors.

16. This being so, as agent herein
    > Whoso however the self alone
    Regards, because his intelligence is imperfect,
    > He does not see (truly), the fool.

17. Whose state (of mind) is not egoized,
    > Whose intelligence is not stained,
    He, even tho he slays these folk,
    > Does not slay, and is not bound (by his actions).

18. Knowledge, the object of knowledge, the knower,
   Form the threefold impellent cause of action;
   Instrument, action, and the agent,
   Form the threefold summary of action.

19. Knowledge, and action, and the agent
   Are of just three kinds, according to difference of Strands;
   So it is declared in the theory of the Strands;
   Hear of them also, how they are.

20. Whereby in all beings one
   Unchanging condition men perceive,
   Unmanifold in the manifold,
   Know that that knowledge is of goodness.

21. But what knowledge in various fashion
   Different conditions of various sorts
   Sees in all beings,
   Know that that knowledge is of passion.

22. But what knowledge to one — as it were all —
   Thing to be done is attached, unconcerned with causes,
   Not dealing with the true nature of things, and insignificant,
   That is declared to be of darkness.

23. Obligatory, free from attachment,
   Done without desire or loathing,
   By one who seeks no fruit from it, action
   Such as this is called of goodness.

24. But action which by one seeking desires,
   Or again by one who is selfish,
   Is done, with much weary labor,
   That is declared to be of passion.

25. Consequences, loss, injury (to others),
   And (one's own) human power disregarding,
   Owing to delusion, when action is undertaken,
   It is declared to be of darkness.

26. Free from attachment, not talking of himself,
    Full of steadfastness and energy,
    Unchanged in success or failure,
    Such an agent is called one of goodness.

27. Passionate, seeking the fruits of action,
    Greedy, injurious, impure,
    Full of joy and grief, such an agent
    Is celebrated as one of passion.

28. Undisciplined, vulgar, arrogant,
    Tricky, dishonest, lazy,
    Despondent, and procrastinating,
    Such an agent is said to be of darkness.

29. The distinction of intelligence and of firmness also,
    Threefold according to the Strands, hear
    Fully expounded
    In their several forms, Dhanaṃjaya.

30. Activity and cessation from it,
    Things to be done and not to be done, danger and security,
    Bondage and release, that which knows these
    Is the intelligence that is of goodness, son of Pṛthā.

31. Whereby right and unright,
    And things to be done and not to be done,
    Are understood incorrectly,
    That intelligence, son of Pṛthā, is of passion.

32. Right as unright what
    Conceives, obscured by darkness,
    And all things contrary (to the truth),
    That intelligence, son of Pṛthā, is of darkness.

33. The firmness with which one holds fast,
    The activities of the mind, life-breaths, and senses,
    And which is unswerving in discipline,
    That firmness is of goodness, son of Pṛthā.

34. But when to religion, love, and wealth
    With firmness he holds fast, Arjuna,
    With attachment, desirous of the fruits,
    That firmness is of passion, son of Pṛthā.

35. Whereby sleep, fear, sorrow,
    Despondency, and pride,
    The foolish man does not let go,
    That firmness is of darkness, son of Pṛthā.

36. But now the threefold happiness
    Hear from Me, bull of Bhāratas.
    That in which he comes to delight thru long practice (only),
    And comes to the end of suffering,

37. Which in the beginning is like poison,
    But in maturity like nectar,
    That is called the happiness of goodness,
    Sprung from serenity of soul and of intellect.

38. (Springing) from union of the senses and their objects,
    That which in the beginning is like nectar,
    In maturity like poison,
    That happiness is recorded as of passion.

39. Which both in the beginning and in its consequence
    Is a happiness that deludes the self,
    Arising from sleep, sloth, and heedlessness,
    That is declared to be of darkness.

40. There is no thing, whether on earth,
    Or yet in heaven, among the gods,
    No being which free from the material-nature-born
    Strands, these three, might be.

41. Of brahmans, warriors, and artisans,
    And of serfs, scorcher of the foe,
    The actions are distinguished
    According to the Strands that spring from their innate nature.

42. Calm, (self-) control, austerities, purity,
    Patience, and uprightness,
 Theoretical and practical knowledge, and religious faith,
    Are the natural-born actions of brahmans.

43. Heroism, majesty, firmness, skill,
    And not fleeing in battle also,
 Generosity, and lordly nature,
    Are the natural-born actions of warriors.

44. Agriculture, cattle-tending, and commerce
    Are the natural-born actions of artisans;
 Action that consists of service
    Is likewise natural-born to a serf.

45. Taking delight in his own special kind of action,
    A man attains perfection;
 Delighting in one's own special action, success
    How one reaches, that hear!

46. Whence comes the activity of beings,
    By whom this all is pervaded —
 Him worshipping by (doing) one's own appropriate action,
    A man attains perfection.

47. Better one's own duty, (even) imperfect,
    Than another's duty well performed.
 Action pertaining to his own estate
    Performing, he incurs no guilt.

48. Natural-born action, son of Kuntī,
    Even tho it be faulty, one should not abandon.
 For all undertakings by faults
    Are dimmed, as fire by smoke.

49. His mentality unattached to any object,
    Self-conquered, free from longings,
 To the supreme perfection of actionlessness
    He comes thru renunciation.

50. Having attained perfection, how to Brahman
       He also attains, hear from Me,
    In only brief compass, son of Kuntī;
       Which is the highest culmination of knowledge.

51. With purified mentality disciplined,
       And restraining himself with firmness,
    Abandoning the objects of sense, sounds and the rest,
       And putting away desire and loathing.

52. Cultivating solitude, eating lightly,
       Restraining speech, body, and mind,
    Devoted to the discipline of meditation constantly,
       Taking refuge in dispassion,

53. From egotism, force, pride,
       Desire, wrath, and possession
    Freed, unselfish, calmed,
       He is fit for becoming Brahman.

54. Having become Brahman, serene-souled,
       He neither grieves nor longs;
    Alike to all beings,
       He attains supreme devotion to Me.

55. Thru devotion he comes to know me,
       What My measure is, and who I am, in very truth;
    Then, knowing Me in very truth,
       He enters into (Me) straightway.

56. Even tho all actions ever
       He performs, relying on Me,
    By My grace he reaches
       The eternal, undying station.

57. With thy thoughts all actions
       Casting upon Me, devoted to Me,
    Turning to discipline of mentality,
       Keep thy mind ever fixed on Me.

58. If thy mind is on Me, all difficulties
    Shalt thou cross over by My grace;
    But if thru egotism thou
    Wilt not heed, thou shalt perish.

59. If clinging to egotism
    Thou thinkest 'I will not fight',
    Vain is this thy resolve;
    (Thine own) material nature will coerce thee.

60. Son of Kuntī, by thine own natural
    Action held fast,
    What thru delusion thou seekest not to do,
    That thou shalt do even against thy will.

61. Of all beings, the Lord
    In the heart abides, Arjuna,
    Causing all beings to turn around
    (As if) fixed in a machine, by his magic power.

62. To Him alone go for refuge
    With thy whole being, son of Bhārata;
    By his grace, supreme peace
    And the eternal station shall thou attain.

63. Thus to thee has been expounded the knowledge
    That is more secret than the secret, by Me;
    After pondering on it fully,
    Act as thou thinkest best.

64. Further, the highest secret of all,
    My supreme message, hear.
    Because thou art greatly loved of Me,
    Therefore I shall tell thee what is good for thee.

65. Be Me-minded, devoted to Me;
    Worshipping Me, revere Me;
    And to Me alone shalt thou go; truly to thee
    I promise it – (because) thou art dear to Me.

66. Abandoning all (other) duties,
    Go to Me as thy sole refuge;
    From all evils I thee
    Shall rescue: be not grieved!

67. This on thy part to no one not endowed with austerity,
    Nor ever to one not devoted,
    Nor to one not obedient, must be told,
    Nor to one who murmurs against Me.

68. Whoso this supreme secret
    Shall make known to My devotees,
    Showing utmost devotion to Me,
    Shall go just to Me, without a doubt.

69. And not than he among men
    Is there any who does things more pleasing to Me;
    Nor shall there be than he to Me
    Any other dearer on earth.

70. And whoso shall study this
    Colloquy on duty between us two,
    By him with knowledge — worship I
    Would be worshiped: so I hold.

71. With faith, and not murmuring against it,
    What man even hears it,
    He too shall be released, and the fair worlds
    Of men of virtuous deeds shall he attain.

72. Has this been heard, son of Pṛthā,
    By thee with concentrated thought?
    Has the confusion of ignorance
    In thee been destroyed, Dhanaṃjaya?

         Arjuna said:
73. Destroyed the confusion; attention (to the truth) is won,
    By Thy grace, on my part, O Changeless One;
    I stand firm, with doubts dispersed;
         I shall do Thy word.

Samjaya said:

74. Thus I of Vāsudeva
    And the exalted son of Pṛthā
    This colloquy have heard,
    Marvelous and thrilling.

75. By the grace of Vyāsa have I heard
    This supreme secret,
    This discipline, from Kṛṣṇa the Lord of Discipline,
    Speaking it Himself in very person.

76. O king, as I recall again and again
    This marvelous colloquy,
    And holy, of Keśava and Arjuna,
    I thrill with joy at every moment.

77. And as I recall again and again that
    Most wondrous form of Hari,
    Great is my amazement, O king,
    And I thrill with joy again and again.

78. Where is Kṛṣṇa the Lord of Discipline,
    And where is the Bowman, the son of Pṛthā,
    There fortune, victory, prosperity,
    And statecraft are firmly fixed, I ween.

Source: Franklin Edgerton, trans., *The Bhagavad Gītā*, New York, Harper and Row 1944, pp.2-8, 9-16, 38-41, 55-61, 83-91.

2.7 THE MEANING OF *MOKSHA* IN CONTEMPORARY HINDU THOUGHT AND LIFE

K. Sivaraman

2.7.1 I have been asked to discuss *moksha,* the Hindu counterpart of salvation, and its meaning for the 'contemporary' Hindu. In view of my specialised interest and supposed competence, my approach will be from the perspective of 'theistic' Hinduism. Accordingly, I wish first to comment briefly on 'contemporaneity' and, at more length, on 'theism' in relation to Hinduism. My comments will of course bear on the theme of *moksha.* I shall then analyse the implication of *moksha* by a bold appropriation of terms and ideas to which I have been exposed.

2.7.2 **I**

Does *moksha* have any meaning for the thought and life of the present-day Hindu? The normal attitude is to treat it as part of traditional Hindu culture and therefore as accepted today, if at all, out of sheer cultural habit. It is true that many Hindus in their scholarly discussions exhibit this attitude. As in the rest of the world many Hindus too have no kind of contact with any form of religion or its modes of thought. They grow up as strangers to the terms and meaning of religion. If Hinduism as a living religion interests them little, its transcendent claims focused in a concept like *moksha* interest them even less.

But we do not have to search for a greatest or lowest common measure of acceptance in order to justify the claim of meaningfulness. To those to whom it is meaningful it is profoundly meaningful. To them, *moksha* is a living reality of their experience. The contemporary Hindu may not be exercised to the extent of prophesying about religious problems being the principal problem of the end of the century. But he certainly values *moksha,* whether actively or implicitly, and seeks to find a place for it in his view of human life and purposes. To many it presents itself as an 'esoteric' possibility open through submission to the rigour of spiritual discipline and discipleship. To some it is a kind of transient mystical ecstasy that is induced as the culmination of devotion, group-singing meditation, etc. To the philosophically lettered, *moksha* is an abstract, formal, intellectual possibility and despite its abstractness, that is as something that one has not yet 'had', its real value is still assumed as a possible experience for oneself.

All this is interesting as information but I do not think that these are the points which really concern us. What matters for contemporary Hindu thought is the Hindu self-understanding of his tradition in terms of growth and regeneration in response to the requirements of modern living and thinking. The contemporary Hindu is heir to systems of ideas of the Hindu East and of the non-Hindu West, both of which serve as sources of his way of looking at things. He achieves assimilation of the foreign not by a rejection of his own standpoint or ideal but by a deepening of it with increasing reverence through infinite patience and humility until what was foreign reveals its kinship with his own. The outcome is a reassessment of his heritage and a continual recreation or renewal of his faith. What remains 'traditional' about the tradition is its continuity, not its conservatism. Hindu tradition is a continuous process of evolution by a free use of reason and experience. This is how a Hindu, today, 'liberated' from his native medievalism, looks at his own faith. It is in this spirit that my personal reflections and reassessments of the meaning of *moksha,* quickened by closeness to a particular phase of Hinduism, are offered in this paper and made to pass for 'contemporary' views.

I now pass on to 'theistic' Hinduism. The theistic-absolutistic polarisation of standpoints is one of the significant features of Hindu thought and life, and to accord recognition to this is to take a major step towards truly encountering Hinduism. Present from the very dawn of its history, this polarisation emerged with greater self-consciousness and philosophic sophistication under the stimulus of the challenge of Buddhism.

The great divide between Hinduism and Buddhism seems to be, to put it in relation to our present concern, between the point of view according to which the love of a personal God is the very crown of the experience of liberation from bondage to which man has been subject, and a point of view where the love of God is acclaimed only as a preparation, even if a necessary one, for realising the goal of such liberation. In both, it may be noted, liberation or deliverance stands for the ultimate goal of life's endeavour. The difference is in respect of what is entailed by the two standpoints, theoretically and also in practice. For the theist, spiritual liberation is identified with the love which becomes central and persuasive in the sphere of experience. God, none other than love itself (cf. the oft-quoted Tamil verse 'Love is God'), is the exact expression of perfect deliverance. God's self-revelation and man's liberation from self-estrangement coincide in the moment of the experience of love. The love of God means avowedly a corresponding love towards the concrete, individual, unique here and now. It is in the meeting of these two that *moksha* liberates and enlarges human existence. In contrast, the absolutist sees 'liberation' as, unequivocally, liberation from time, from the world and all that is conditioned by time. Spiritual liberation, itself no doubt a positive experience as the perfect expression of self or self-hood, is negative in respect of all those values associated with human life: history, personality, freedom, community, progress, etc. Self is, precisely, 'not this, not this'.

2.7.3 **II**

What gives a real edge to the 'absolutist' Hindu attitude is his severely theoretical veto of everything that is 'not-self'. Falsity — this is his key-concept — includes within its sweep the worlds of nature and of culture alike. The latter is denied not merely as a value. For the theistic world-view also devalues the world on account of its evanescence. The absolutist denies it as a real given. Lapse of value means lapse of reality. As one of the Hindu classics puts it, 'the snake is false at the very place and in the very moment that it appeared, substituting as it did, demonically, for the rope'.

One of the outcomes of this attitude, of great consequence for Hindu thought and life as a whole, is to view reality not horizontally but as a pyramid of levels succeeding each other in a vertical direction, according to their degree of value and of their consequent power of being. The world's encountered diversities and pluralities, its change, all that goes with freedom and action are all alike 'levelled' as belonging together under a common verdict. Unity, however, stands on a 'higher' level not contradicted by but contradicting diversity, so that movement is possible from below to above but not vice versa. 'From death to immortality' is the pattern. Not the other way round. Again, in the asymmetrical movement from one level to another, there is no organic transition implied in so far as the higher does not literally 'fulfil' the lower. *Telos* or fulfilment does not have a horizontal sense of lying at the end of the road. It is vertical, involving an 'ascent' or leap. 'Liberation', comparable to waking up from a dream, is an essential possibility present for man always, and at no time in particular. It is not, strictly, accomplishing something. Indeed, it is waking up from the illusion of accomplishment.

The model of 'waking from dream' likewise contains implicit answers to the problems of individuality, community or social obligation. When I 'wake up' from a dream I realise that all the individuals I saw in the dream were 'false', but I also realise that the person I call myself, with the body and behaviour I had in the dream, was equally 'false'. There is illusion, there is freedom from illusion, but individuals are not freed from illusion. Individuals are the products of illusion. Individuality is itself precisely the illusion from which we seek to be freed. You and I differ in our bodies, in the minds and egos associated with bodies, but we do not differ in self. It is by falsely identifying the self with the body that we suffer the illusion of individuality. The self is in the world as the sleeper is in his dream-world; he is not really in it, he only seems to be. Similarly, the ethical problem simply does not arise for the 'liberated'. While dreaming, the dreamer has moral obligations to the persons in the dream. But after he wakes up from his dream he feels no obligation to go back to sleep in order to recover his dream and help those persons further, because he knows that they no longer exist — in fact they never did exist.

I have dwelt at some length on the absolutist's uncompromising views only to set off negatively the Hindu theist's frame of reference. Theistic Hinduism of all shades stands defined by its repudiation of the theory of falsity, and of the distinction of levels implied by it. In effect it may be said to affirm freedom, love, personality, community, history and moral obligation, and to rediscover their deeper spiritual significance for man. Their positive role in the service of man's freedom from the thraldom of unfreedom can be duly appreciated once man is 'liberated' from the penumbra of falsity. There is a spiritual purpose in history: to reclaim man estranged from himself and from others in consequence of his estrangement from the ground of his very being. God's cosmic functions are, to generalise the theology of Hindu theism, to help us to grow into full spiritual manhood. History as the sphere of man's conscious, deliberate and collective striving is what makes possible the realisation of his values, though this is not itself viewed as 'accomplishment' but as an aspect of cosmic history.

Two kinds of eschatologies — under the categories of 'bondage' and 'liberation' — are used. In contrast to the generality of absolutistic thought, theism is sensitive of the continuity between the two. Bondage, or *samsara,* includes the conception of an 'after-life' which remains on the same level as the present life, and though comprising all forms of life, sub-human and super-human alike, is typified in regard to moral responsibility uniquely by human life. The corollary to this 'after-life' concept is *karma.* The individual continues from life to life in an embodied existence, the contents and forms of his life dependent on what the individual has performed in former lives, yet affording some scope for growth and gradual perfection by the performance of meritorious actions. This is the sphere of *dharma.*

The second eschatology consists of the assumption of a 'liberation' (*moksha*), from bondage into unending embodied existence. Negatively, it is the de-conditioning of the individual, subject to multiple conditionings or bonds; positively, it is unhindered conformity to the gracious will of God, not in spite of but in due compliance with the individual's freedom, and a consequent experience of blessedness in the wake of fulfilment and freedom.

Cosmic action on the part of the divine will is conceived imaginatively to consist of two phases. The initial phase involves the self-veiling of God, even while He is witness to the obstructing function of human ignorance. God is thus not only the ground but the hidden meaning and motive of history. The endless sequence of life and death, of wakefulness and sleep, of memory and oblivion, of creation and destruction, is really the grand work of God's construction, in free complicity with man obstructed in his vision and constricted in his action. History is not a series of meaningless recurrences of the 'natural' world but a process pointing and moving toward a fuller disclosure and realisation of life's essential meaning. That this is so becomes apparent retrospectively in the experience of *moksha.* This marks the second phase of God's cosmic function. This is the self-revelation of God coinciding with the termination of bondage, which is of the nature of revelation. The entire sweep of man's existence thus stands in relation to God and as a preparation for *moksha.* No special religious sphere need be set apart from the secular world. Ordinary life as such takes on religious meaning. *Dharma* and *moksha* are continuous, the continuity of course being perceptible only from the perspective of the second.

It is also to be noted here that though bondage and liberation from bondage are alike 'caused' for man from without man, the decision however rests with man and depends on his preparation. Full scope is thus provided for man's being motivated to exert himself individually and collectively toward the common goal of liberation.

The essence of Hindu religiosity is often thought to be the immanent conception of Truth. Truth is something which cannot be introduced from without in time but is within the individual. The individual's task is accordingly to strive to appropriate the God within. This is the 'infinite resignation' of the ascetic who renounces the temporal for the sake of the eternal. Even the teacher cannot directly teach but only serve as a stimulus or occasion for the individual to help himself. He can, to use Socrates' words, stimulate but not 'beget'.

This view can, however, bear reassessment and reconstruction in the light of the reoriented understanding of the problem in Hindu theism, which conceives the individual to be transcendentally conditioned, as the being primordially divided from the truth by an infinite qualitative gulf. He neither has the truth nor is he able to acquire it. The teacher must supply the condition as well as the truth. This particular teacher can only be God. He acts in history, confronting man as the 'thou', exemplifying personal relationship and investing time with decisive significance. His action gives the temporal eternal significance. Man, tied to the temporal, is redeemed in time, 'at the appropriate moment' which is filled with the significance of the eternal.

Lastly, *moksha*, contrary to the belief that it cries halt to all dynamism, may be interpreted with the support of the authentic theistic tradition as implying the eternal conquest of the negative. *Eternal* blessedness involves the presence of three factors: the 'giver' and the 'enjoyer' and the 'occasioner'. By 'occasioner' is meant the negative factor which also paradoxically contributes to and even constitutes the experience of blessedness. An example may be useful. Light dispels darkness. But does the latter become nonexistent? When the light is withdrawn the darkness returns. This shows that darkness continues to exist even in the presence of the light. The latter continuously prevails against the continuously existent darkness by continuously dispelling it. Bondage is 'privation' of one's will, a thwarting of compliance with one's own unrestrained will which fulfils itself by conforming to Divine will. Liberation is a privation of this privation, a thwarting of the thwarting of will or, positively, a free unhampered exercise of will as in 'Thy will be done', which is joy itself. Even after attaining to the highest, life receives its content by 'repetition' or forward recollection. As Augustine says, commenting on the Psalm 'Seek His Face ever more', 'Finding should not end that seeking by which love is testified but with the increase of love, the seeking of the found one should also increase.'

2.7.4 **III**

The basic polarity which colours the meaning of *moksha* is the polarity of its negative and positive aspects. Liberation is liberation from pain, suffering and loss. From estrangement of every kind. From the dubious and vulnerable character of human existence. Yet for the precise theistic sense, one must also look into its positive aspect. It is liberation or freedom *to do*. The free man, religiously speaking, is one who is unhindered in his freedom of volitional conformity or coincidence with the Divine. It is the freedom of enjoying union with God. Freedom to enjoy is another way of saying freedom from any sort of engagement or impediment that stands in the way of fulfilling one's will to enjoy. It is freedom from impediments of both commission and omission. Again, the expression 'free from' suggests that one is happy and *relieved* to be without those things one is freed from. A set of circumstances become constraining only when one wants to do something that these circumstances prevent. The world is a bondage to the extent that the circumstances of worldly existence hinder the accomplishment of the desire for freedom to enjoy. Without the implication of will to enjoy we should hardly know the meaning of freedom. Bondage is a thwarting of one's will and liberation is a thwarting of bondage. The liberating agent merely arrests the arresting of the constraint or opposes its opposing.

The second polarity of meaning that gives substance to the theistic understanding of *moksha* is the polarity of the divine and the human. The factors involved are Divine grace and human freedom. Acknowledging either without the other leads to the partial emphasis of *moksha* as a prize to be won by one's efforts or as a gift freely given but not earned. This conflict runs through the entire Indian culture and is present in the West too, in the form of opposition between grace and self-reliance.

Grace supplies the essential transcendent element but it does not present itself as a total stranger; rather as a welcome guest whose appearance was not only awaited but intensively aspired or craved with the whole of our centred self.

Theistic Hinduism affirms the paradox that in affirming God man affirms his selfhood. It is genuine self-affirmation rather than self-negation that is entailed by God-affirmation. Saving knowledge is of the form of overcoming of alienation. One becomes aware of the sense of alienation, of being lost to oneself and consequently to the world, paradoxically, in the God-consciousness which at the same time involves the overcoming of this alienation.

To acknowledge a polar relation between self-effort and grace as a feature characteristic of *moksha* enables the avoidance of the extremes of moral legalism and graceless moralism on the one side and amoral lawlessness and a supra-ethical mysticism on the other. It is the affirmation of moral conscience but as having a more than moral foundation. Being precedes action in everything that is, including man, although in man as the bearer of freedom previous action determines present being. *Moksha,* therefore, phenomenologically at least, understood strictly from the self-restricted perspective of the striving seeker, is not exclusively God's work utterly apart from man's latent resources and endowment. The latter must be utilised, transformed and transmuted. God must accept us if we are to accept God. This is not so much an external necessity placed upon God as the inner logic of the situation in which man stands before God, the situation presupposed by the distinction of bondage and freedom from bondage.

Hindu spirituality is thus able to appreciate the theme of how God's 'forgiveness' concretely comes to the fore, because it itself acknowledges Divine initiative in the sphere of knowledge and being, an initiative which does not contradict human freedom but rather assumes it and builds upon it. Hindus will simply add that man's real freedom to be himself comes by the surrender of all claims to isolated independence and self-willedness. Precisely this is what man contributes to his own deliverance which he must 'work out by fear and trembling', for the very reason that 'deliverance' belongs to God. We become aware that this is so in so far as we make ourselves open to the power of God which God makes available to us. Accepting God's acceptance of us, love answering love — this is also the profound theme of Hindu theism. *This* is liberation. Overcoming of suffering, escaping the round of rebirth, all these are circumstantial to it.

The words of Irenaeus about Christ 'as God becoming what we

are that he might make us what he himself is' is also exactly the note of praise and prayer addressed by the pupil to his spiritual Master:

I have seen His mercy's feet
See His roseate Feet this earth hath trod
Seen Him, even I have known the Blessed one
Seen in grace He made me His.

(*Thiruvacakam,* a Tamil classic)

I shall close by briefly referring to two other sets of polarities of meaning in respect of *moksha,* the polarity of means and end and the polarity of the individual and the universal. These are what makes *moksha* a *spiritual* experience; in the secular world there can only be conflict between them. The concept of the spiritual involves the identity of means and end. This is the paradox of spiritual realisation. Realisation is eternal realisation. The goal of spiritual life is also a kind of life — life eternal, life divine or life universal, call it by any name. It involves no change in the modes of existence or even in the behaviour of the 'liberated' man. What he has been doing with a sense of 'ought' he now does spontaneously. The example that is given is significant. Milk is taken by the convalescent as a means of nourishment, and also by the healthy for conserving health. *Moksha* is also an eternal conservation of spiritual value, and is continuous with its means. Conversely, knowledge, work, devotion are all involved in the accomplished character of *moksha.* The dawn of saving faith is itself in principle coincident with the advent of *moksha.*

The polarity is also exemplified by the equation of Revelation with liberation. The history of Divine self-disclosure and the 'history' of man's liberation from bondage are one and the same history. The bestowal of revelatory grace is *moksha,* just as the veiling of it is bondage. Lastly, 'liberation' does not imply fulfilment of the individual in isolation. A limited fulfilment of separate individuals would not be fulfilment at all, not even for the individuals, for no person is separated from other persons and from the whole of reality in such a way that he could be 'liberated' apart from the liberation of everyone and everything. This is the polarity of individual and universal.

This demand is implicitly present in classical Hinduism and becomes explicitly articulated in medieval and modern Hinduism, thus giving a religious urgency to community and institutional life. *Moksha* is conceived as an 'empire' where one's autonomy is truly regained. It is an empire of emperors in complete possession of their empire which is only to say: of themselves in conscious conformity with God. There is complete transparency of everything for the divine to shine through, so that there is no tension of claim and counterclaim. Just as *moksha* may he conceived as life that finally triumphs over what restricts it (death), it can also be viewed as a Divine universe or kingdom, triumphing over the demonic power structure that is the world.

In this paper, I have purposefully highlighted those areas of interest in connection with a discussion on the meaning of *moksha* that will be of significance for dialogue between Hindu and Christian religions. Even at the risk of a certain measure of oversimplification and blurring of distinctions, to which charge I shall plead guilty, I have striven to indicate certain structural affinities between the ideas of 'Salvation in history' and 'Liberation from bondage'. The convergences and divergences which follow should provide the grist for fruitful dialogue.

Source: From S.J. Samartha, ed., *Living Faiths and Ultimate Goals,* World Council of Churches, Geneva 1974, pp.2-11.

2.8   HINDU DHARMA

M.K. Gandhi

2.8.1   Gandhi on his Mission

I do not consider myself worthy to be mentioned in the same breath
with the race of prophets. I am a humble seeker after truth. I am
impatient to realise myself, to attain moksha in this very existence.
My national service is part of my training for freeing my soul from
the bondage of flesh. Thus considered, my service may be regarded
as purely selfish. I have no desire for the perishable kingdom of
earth. I am striving for the Kindom of Heaven which is moksha. To
attain my end it is not necessary for me to seek the shelter of a cave.
I carry one about me, if I would but know it. A cave-dweller can
build castles in the air whereas a dweller in a palace like Janak has no
castles to build. The cave-dweller who hovers round the world on the
wings of thought has no peace. A Janak though living in the midst of
'pomp and circumstance' may have peace that passeth understanding.
For me the road to salvation lies through incessant toil in the service
of my country and therethrough of humanity. I want to identify
myself with everything that lives. In the language of the Gītā I want
to live at peace with both friend and foe. Though therefore a
Mussulman or a Christian or a Hindu may despise me and hate me, I
want to love him and serve him even as I would love my wife or son
though they hate me. So my patriotism is for me a stage in my
journey to the land of eternal freedom and peace. Thus it will be
seen that for me there are no politics devoid of religion. They
subserve religion. Politics bereft of religion are a deathtrap because
they kill the soul.

2.8.2   Gandhi on Gandhism

There is no such thing as 'Gandhism', and I do not want to leave any
sect after me. I do not claim to have originated any new principle or
doctrine. I have simply tried in my own way to apply the eternal
truths to our daily life and problems. There is, therefore, no
question of my leaving any code like the *Code of Manu*. There can

be no comparison between that great lawgiver and me. The opinions I have formed and the conclusions I have arrived at are not final. I may change them tomorrow. I have nothing new to teach the world. Truth and non-violence are as old as the hills. All I have done is to try experiments in both on as vast a scale as I could do. In doing so I have sometimes erred and learnt by my errors. Life and its problems have thus become to me so many experiments in the practice of truth and non-violence. By instinct I have been truthful, but not non-violent. As a Jain *muni* once rightly said I was not so much a votary of *ahimsa* as I was of truth, and I put the latter in the first place and the former in the second. For, as he put it, I was capable of sacrificing non-violence for the sake of truth. In fact it was in the course of my pursuit of truth that I discovered non-violence. Our scriptures have declared that there is no *dharma* (law) higher than Truth. But non-violence they say is the highest duty. The word *dharma* in my opinion has different connotations as used in the two aphorisms.

Well, all my philosophy, if it may be called by that pretentious name, is contained in what I have said. You will not call it 'Gandhism'; there is no *ism* about it. And no elaborate literature or propaganda is needed about it.

Gandhi on the Gītā   2.8.3

Questioner: I am told you recite the Bhagavadgita daily?
Gandhi: Yes, we finish the entire Gītā reading once every week.
Questioner: But at the end of the Gītā Krishna recommends violence.
Gandhi: I do not think so. I am also fighting. I should not be fighting effectively if I were fighting violently. The message of the Gītā is to be found in the second chapter of the Gītā where Krishna speaks of the balanced state of mind, of mental equipoise. In nineteen verses at the close of the second chapter of the Gītā, Krishna explains how this state can be achieved. It can be achieved, he tells us, after killing all your passions. It is not possible to kill your brother after having killed all your passions. I should like to see that man dealing death — who has no passions, who is indifferent to pleasure and pain, who is undisturbed by the storms that trouble

mortal man. The whole thing is described in language of beauty that is unsurpassed. These verses show that the fight Krishna speaks of is a spiritual fight.

Questioner: To the common mind it sounds as though it was actual fighting.

Gandhi: You must read the whole thing dispassionately in its true context. After the first mention of fighting, there is no mention of fighting at all. The rest is a spiritual discourse.

Questioner: Has anybody interpreted it like you?

Gandhi: Yes. The fight is there, but the fight as it is going on within. The Pandavas and Kauravas are the forces of good and evil within. The war is the war between Jekyll and Hyde, God and Satan, going on in the human breast. The internal evidence in support of this interpretation is there in the work itself and in the Mahabharata of which the Gītā is a minute part. It is not a history of war between two families, but the history of man — the history of the spiritual struggle of man.

Questioner: Is the central teaching of the Gītā selfless action or non-violence?

Gandhi: I have no doubt that it is *anasakti* — selfless action. Indeed I have called my little translation of the Gītā Anasaktiyoga. And anasakti transcends ahimsa. He who would be *anasakta* (selfless) has necessarily to practise non-violence in order to attain the state of selflessness. Ahimsa is, therefore, a necessary preliminary, it is included in anasakti, it does not go beyond it.

Questioner: Then does the Gītā teach himsa and ahimsa both?

Gandhi: I do not read that meaning in the Gītā. It is quite likely that the author did not write it to inculcate ahimsa, but as a commentator draws innumerable interpretations from a poetic text, even so I interpret the Gītā to mean that if its central theme is anasakti, it also teaches ahimsa. Whilst we are in the flesh and tread the solid earth, we have to practise ahimsa. In the life beyond there is no himsa or ahimsa.

Questioner: But Lord Krishna actually counters the doctrine of ahimsa. For Arjuna utters this pacifist resolve:

Better I deem it, if my kinsmen strike,
To face them weaponless, and bear my breast
To shaft and spear, than answer blow with blow.

And Lord Krishna teaches him to 'answer blow with blow'.

Gandhi: There I join issue with you. Those words of Arjuna were words of pretentious wisdom. 'Until yesterday', says Krishna to him, 'you fought your kinsmen with deadly weapons without the slightest compunction. Even today you would strike if the enemy was a stranger and not your own kith and kin!' The question before him was not of non-violence, but whether he should slay his nearest and dearest.

Ashram Vows
2.8.4

[Gandhi sent during 1930 a series of weekly discourses from Yeravda Jail (which he called *mandir* or temple) to members of his Ashram at Sabarmati. Four of these, dealing with the Ashram vows of Truth, Non-violence, Chastity and Non-possession are given here. The remaining seven vows of the Ashram are: Control of the Palate, Non-stealing, Fearlessness, Removal of Untouchability, Bread Labour, Equality of Religions and Swadeshi. Gandhi's discourses on these also will be found in the booklet *From Yeravda Mandir* (published by the Navajivan Press, Ahmedabad).]

Importance of Vows

Taking vows is not a sign of weakness, but of strength. To do at any cost something that one ought to do constitutes a vow. It becomes a bulwark of strength. One, who says that he will do something 'as far as possible', betrays either his pride or his weakness. I have noticed in my own case, as well as in the case of others, that the limitation 'as far as possible' provides a fatal loophole. To do something 'as far as possible' is to succumb to the very first temptation. There is no sense in saying that one would observe truth 'as far as possible'. Even as no businessman will look at a note in which a man promises to pay a certain amount on a certain date 'as far as possible', so will God refuse to accept a promissory note drawn by one, who would observe truth 'as far as possible'.

God is the very image of the vow. God would cease to be God if He swerved from His own laws even by a hair's breadth. The sun is a great keeper of observances; hence the possibility of measuring time and publishing almanacs. All business depends upon men fulfilling their promises. Are such promises less necessary in character-building or self-realisation? We should therefore never doubt the necessity of vows for the purpose of self-purification and self-realisation.

Truth

I deal with Truth first of all, as the Satyagraha Ashram owes its very existence to the pursuit and the attempted practice of Truth.

The word *Satya* (Truth) is derived from *Sat*, which means 'being'. Nothing is or exists in reality except Truth. That is why *Sat* or Truth is perhaps the most important name of God. In fact it is more correct to say that Truth is God, than to say that God is Truth. But as we cannot do without a ruler or a general, names of God such as 'King of Kings' or 'the Almighty' are and will remain generally current. On deeper thinking, however, it will be realised, that *Sat* or *Satya* is the only correct and fully significant name for God.

And where there is truth, there also is knowledge which is true. Where there is no Truth, there can be no true knowledge. That is why the word *Chit* or knowledge is associated with the name of God. And where there is true knowledge, there is always bliss (*Ananda*). There sorrow has no place. And even as Truth is eternal, so is the bliss derived from it. Hence we know God as *Sat-chit-ananda,* One who combines in Himself Truth, Knowledge and Bliss.

Devotion to this Truth is the sole justification for our existence. All our activities should be centred in Truth. Truth should be the very breath of our life. When once this stage in the pilgrim's progress is reached, all other rules of correct living will come without effort, and obedience to them will be instinctive. But without Truth it would be impossible to observe any principles cr rules in life.

Generally speaking, observation of the law of Truth is understood merely to mean that we must speak the truth. But we in the Ashram should understand the word *Satya* or Truth in a much wider sense. There should be Truth in thought, Truth in speech, and Truth in action. To the man who has realised this Truth in its fulness, nothing else remains to be known, because all knowledge is necessarily included in it. What is not included in it is not Truth, and so not true knowledge; and there can be no inward peace without true knowledge. If we once learn how to apply this never-failing test of Truth, we will at once be able to find out what is worth doing, what is worth seeing, what is worth reading.

But how is one to realise this Truth, which may be likened to the philosopher's stone or the cow of plenty? By single-minded devotion (*abhyasa*) and indifference to all other interests in life (*vairagya*) — replies the *Bhagavadgita*. In spite, however, of such devotion, what may appear as truth to one person will often appear as untruth to another person. But that need not worry the seeker. Where there is honest effort, it will be realised that what appear to be different truths are like the countless and apparently different leaves of the same tree. Does not God Himself appear to different individuals in different aspects? Yet we know that He is one. But Truth is the right designation of God. Hence there is nothing wrong in every man following Truth according to his lights. Indeed it is his duty to do so. Then if there is a mistake on the part of any one so following Truth, it will be automatically set right. For the quest of Truth involves *tapas* — self-suffering, sometimes even unto death. There can be no place in it for even a trace of self-interest. In such selfless search for Truth nobody can lose his bearings for long. Directly he takes to the wrong path he stumbles, and is thus redirected to the right path. Therefore the pursuit of Truth is true *bhakti* (devotion). It is the path that leads to God. There is no place in it for cowardice, no place for defeat. It is the talisman by which death itself becomes the portal to life eternal.

Ahimsa or *Love*

We saw last week how the path of Truth is as narrow as it is straight. Even so is that of *ahimsa*. It is like balancing oneself on the edge of a sword. By concentration an acrobat can walk on a rope. But the concentration required to tread the path of Truth and *ahimsa* is far greater. The slightest inattention brings one tumbling to the ground. One can realise Truth and *ahimsa* only by ceaseless striving.

But it is impossible for us to realise perfect Truth so long as we are imprisoned in this mortal frame. We can only visualise it in our imagination. We cannot, through the instrumentality of this ephemeral body, see face to face Truth which is eternal. That is why in the last resort we must depend on faith.

It appears that the impossibility of full realisation of Truth in this mortal body led some ancient seeker after Truth to the appreciation of *ahimsa*. The question which confronted him was: 'Shall I bear with those who create difficulties for me, or shall I destroy them?' The seeker realised that he who went on destroying others did not make headway but simply stayed where he was, while the man who suffered those who created difficulties marched ahead, and at times even took the others with him. The first act of destruction taught him that the Truth which was the object of his quest was not outside himself but within. Hence the more he took to violence, the more he receded from Truth. For in fighting the imagined enemy without, he neglected the enemy within.

We punish thieves, because we think they harass us. They may leave us alone; but they will only transfer their attentions to another victim. This other victim however is also a human being, ourselves in a different form, and so we are caught in a vicious circle. The trouble from thieves continues to increase, as they think it is their business to steal. In the end we see that it is better to endure the thieves than to punish them. The forbearance may even bring them to their senses. By enduring them we realise that thieves are not different from ourselves, they are our brethren, our friends, and may not be punished. But whilst we may bear with the thieves, we may not endure the infliction. That would only induce cowardice. So we realise a further duty. Since we regard the thieves as our kith and kin, they must be made to realise the kinship. And so we must take pains to devise ways and means of winning them over. This is the path of *ahimsa*. It may entail continuous suffering and the cultivating of endless patience. Given these two conditions, the thief is bound in the end to turn away from his evil ways. Thus step by step we learn how to make friends with all the world; we realise the greatness of God — of Truth. Our peace of mind increases in spite of suffering; we become braver and more enterprising; we understand more clearly the difference between what is everlasting and what is not; we learn how to distinguish between what is our duty and what is not. Our pride melts away, and we become humble. Our wordly attachments diminish, and the evil within us diminishes from day to day.

Ahimsa is not the crude thing it has been made to appear. Not to hurt any living thing is no doubt a part of *ahimsa*. But it is its least expression. The principle of *ahimsa* is hurt by every evil thought, by undue haste, by lying, by hatred, by wishing ill to anybody. It is also violated by our holding on to what the world needs. But the world needs even what we eat day by day. In the place where we stand there are millions of micro-organisms to whom the place belongs, and who are hurt by our presence there. What should we do then? Should we commit suicide? Even that is no solution if we believe, as we do, that so long as the spirit is attached to the flesh, on every destruction of the body it weaves for itself another. The body will cease to be only when we give up all attachment to it. This freedom from all attachment is the realisation of God as Truth. Such realisation cannot be attained in a hurry. The body does not belong to us. While it lasts, we must use it as a trust handed over to our charge. Treating in this way the things of the flesh, we may one day expect to become free from the burden of the body. Realising the limitations of the flesh, we must strive day by day towards the ideal with what strength we have in us.

It is perhaps clear from the foregoing, that without *ahimsa* it is not possible to seek and find Truth. *Ahimsa* and Truth are so intertwined that it is practically impossible to disentangle and separate them. They are like the two sides of a coin, or rather of a smooth unstamped metallic disc. Who can say, which is the obverse, and which is the reverse? Nevertheless *ahimsa* is the means; Truth is the end. Means to be means must always be within our reach, and so *ahimsa* is our supreme duty. If we take care of the means, we are bound to reach the end sooner or later. When once we have grasped this point, final victory is beyond question. Whatever difficulties we encounter, whatever apparent reverses we sustain, we may not give up the quest for Truth which alone is, being God Himself.

Brahmacharya or *Chastity*

The third among our observances is *brahmacharya*. As a matter of fact all observances are deducible from Truth, and are meant to subserve it. The man, who is wedded to Truth and worships Truth alone, proves unfaithful to her, if he applies his talents to anything else. How then can he minister to the senses? A man, whose activities are wholly consecrated to the realisation of Truth, which requires utter selflessness, can have no time for the selfish purpose of begetting children and running a household. Realisation of Truth through self-gratification should, after what has been said before, appear a contradiction in terms.

If we look at it from the standpoint of *ahimsa* (non-violence), we find that the fulfilment of *ahimsa* is impossible without utter selflessness. *Ahimsa* means Universal Love. If a man gives his love to one woman, or a woman to one man, what is there left for all the world besides? It simply means, 'We two first, and the devil take all the rest of them.' As a faithful wife must be prepared to sacrifice her all for the sake of her husband, and a faithful husband for the sake of his wife, it is clear that such persons cannot rise to the height of Universal Love, or look upon all mankind as kith and kin. For they have created a boundary wall round their love. The larger their family, the farther are they from Universal Love. Hence one who would obey the law of *ahimsa* cannot marry, not to speak of gratification outside the marital bond.

Then what about people who are already married? Will they never be able to realise Truth? Can they never offer up their all at the altar of humanity? There is a way out for them. They can behave as if they were not married. Those who have enjoyed this happy condition will be able to bear me out. Many have to my knowledge successfully tried the experiment. If the married couple can think of each other as brother and sister, they are freed for universal service. The very thought that all the women in the world are his sisters, mothers or daughters will at once ennoble a man and snap his chains. The husband and wife do not lose anything here, but only add to their resources and even to their family. Their love becomes free from the impurity of lust and so grows stronger. With the disappearance of this impurity, they can serve each other better, and the occasions for quarrel become fewer. There are more occasions for quarrelling where the love is selfish and bounded.

If the foregoing argument is appreciated, a consideration of the physical benefits of chastity becomes a matter of secondary importance. How foolish it is intentionally to dissipate vital energy in sensual enjoyment! It is a grave misuse to fritter away for physical gratification that which is given to man and woman for the full development of their bodily and mental powers. Such misuse is the root cause of many a disease.

Brahmacharya, like all other observances, must be observed in thought, word and deed. We are told in the *Gītā,* and experience will corroborate the statement, that the foolish man, who appears to control his body, but is nursing evil thoughts in his mind, makes a vain effort. It may be harmful to suppress the body, if the mind is at the same time allowed to go astray. Where the mind wanders, the body must follow sooner or later.

It is necessary here to appreciate a distinction. It is one thing to allow the mind to harbour impure thoughts; it is a different thing altogether if it strays among them in spite of ourselves. Victory will be ours in the end, if we non-cooperate with the mind in its evil wanderings.

Non-possession or Poverty

Possession implies provision for the future. A seeker after Truth, a follower of the law of Love, cannot hold anything against tomorrow. God never stores for the morrow; He never creates more than what is strictly needed for the moment. If therefore we repose faith in His providence, we should rest assured, that He will give us every day our daily bread, meaning everything that we require. Saints and devotees, who have lived in such faith, have always derived a justification for it from their experience. Our ignorance or negligence of the Divine Law, which gives to man from day to day his daily bread and no more, has given rise to inequalities with all the miseries attendant upon them. The rich have a superfluous store of things which they do not need, and which are therefore neglected and wasted; while millions are starved to death for want of sustenance. If each retained possession only of what he needed, no one would be in want, and all would live in contentment. As it is, the rich are discontented no less than the poor. The poor man would fain become a millionaire, and the millionaire a multi-millionaire. The rich should take the initiative in dispossession with a view to a universal diffusion of the spirit of contentment. If only they keep their own property within moderate limits, the starving will be easily fed, and will learn the lesson of contentment along with the rich. Perfect fulfilment of the idea of Non-possession requires, that man should, like the birds, have no roof over his head, no clothing and no stock of food for the morrow. He will indeed need his daily bread, but it will be God's business, and not his, to provide it. Only the fewest possible, if any at all, can reach this ideal. We ordinary seekers may be repelled by the seeming impossibility. But we must keep the ideal constantly in view, and in the light thereof, critically examine our possessions, and try to reduce them. Civilisation, in the real sense of the term, consists not in the multiplication, but in the deliberate and voluntary reduction of wants. This alone promotes real happiness and contentment, and increases the capacity for service. Judging by this criterion, we find that in the Ashram we possess many things, the necessity for which cannot be proved, and we thus tempt our neighbours to thieve.

From the standpoint of pure Truth, the body too is a possession. It has been truly said, that desire for enjoyment creates bodies for the soul. When this desire vanishes, there remains no further need for the body, and man is free from the vicious cycle of births and deaths. The soul is omnipresent; why should she care to be confined within the cagelike body, or do evil and even kill for the sake of that cage? We thus arrive at the ideal of total renunciation, and learn to use the body for the purpose of service so long as it exists, so much so that service, and not bread, becomes with us the staff of life.

2.8.5 Sanatana Dharma

I have asserted my claim to being a *Sanatani* Hindu, and yet there are things which are commonly done in the name of Hinduism, which I disregard. I have no desire to be called a *Sanatani* Hindu or any other if I am not such. It is therefore necessary for me once for all distinctly to give my meaning of *Sanatana* Hinduism. The word *Sanatana* I use in its natural sense.

I call myself a *Sanatani* Hindu, because,

(1) I believe in the *Vedas,* the *Upanishads,* the *Puranas* and all that goes by the name of Hindu scriptures, and therefore in *avataras* and rebirth;

(2) I believe in the *varnashrama dharma* in a sense, in my opinion, strictly *Vedic* but not in its present popular and crude sense;

(3) I believe in the protection of the cow in its much larger sense than the popular;

(4) I do not disbelieve in idol-worship.

The reader will note that I have purposely refrained from using the word divine origin in reference to the *Vedas* or any other scriptures. For I do not believe in the exclusive divinity of the *Vedas.* I believe the Bible, the Quran, and the Zend Avesta to be as much divinely inspired as the *Vedas.* My belief in the Hindu scriptures does not require me to accept every word and every verse as divinely inspired. Nor do I claim to have any first-hand knowledge of these wonderful books. But I do claim to know and feel the truths of the essential teaching of the scriptures. I decline to be bound by any interpretation, however learned it may be, if it is repugnant to reason or moral sense. I do most emphatically repudiate the claim (if they advance any such) of the present *Shankaracharyas* and *shastris* to give a correct interpretation of the

Hindu scriptures. On the contrary I believe that our present knowledge of these books is in a most chaotic state. I believe implicitly in the Hindu aphorism, that no one truly knows the *shastras* who has not attained perfection in Innocence (*ahimsa*), Truth (*satya*) and Self-control (*brahmacharya*) and who has not renounced all acquisition or possession of wealth. I believe in the institution of *gurus*, but in this age millions must go without a *guru*, because it is a rare thing to find a combination of perfect purity and perfect learning. But one need not despair of ever knowing the truth of one's religion, because the fundamentals of Hinduism, as of every great religion, are unchangeable, and easily understood. Every Hindu believes in God and His oneness, in rebirth and salvation.

I can no more describe my feeling for Hinduism than for my own wife. She moves me as no other woman in the world can. Not that she has no faults. I dare say she has many more than I see myself. But the feeling of an indissoluble bond is there. Even so I feel for and about Hinduism with all its faults and limitations. Nothing elates me so much as the music of the *Gītā* or the *Ramayana* by Tulsidas, the only two books in Hinduism I may be said to know. When I fancied I was taking my last breath the *Gītā* was my solace. I know the vice that is going on today in all the great Hindu shrines, but I love them in spite of their unspeakable failings. There is an interest which I take in them and which I take in no other. I am a reformer through and through. But my zeal never takes me to the rejection of any of the essential things of Hinduism. I have said I do not disbelieve in idol-worship. An idol does not excite any feeling of veneration in me. But I think that idol-worship is part of human nature. We hanker after symbolism. Why should one be more composed in a church than elsewhere? Images are an aid to worship. No Hindu considers an image to be God. I do not consider idol-worship a sin.

It is clear from the foregoing, that Hinduism is not an exclusive religion. In it there is room for the worship of all the prophets of the world. It is not a missionary religion in the ordinary sense of the term. It has no doubt absorbed many tribes in its fold, but this absorption has been of an evolutionary imperceptible character. Hinduism tells every one to worship God according to his own faith or *dharma*, and so it lives at peace with all the religions.

That being my conception of Hinduism, I have never been able to reconcile myself to untouchability. I have always regarded it as an excrescence. It is true that it has been handed down to us from generations, but so are many evil practices even to this day. I should be ashamed to think that dedication of girls to virtual prostitution was a part of Hinduism. Yet it is practised by Hindus in many parts of India. I consider it positive irreligion to sacrifice goats to Kali and do not consider it a part of Hinduism. Hinduism is a growth of ages. The very name, Hinduism, was given to the religion of the people of Hindustan by foreigners. There was no doubt at one time sacrifice of animals offered in the name of religion. But it is not religion, much less is it Hindu religion. And so also it seems to me, that when cow-protection became an article of faith with our ancestors, those who persisted in eating beef were excommunicated. The civil strife must have been fierce. Social boycott was applied not only to the recalcitrants, but their sins were visited upon their children also. The practice which had probably its origin in good intentions hardened into usage, and even verses crept into our sacred books giving the practice a permanence wholly undeserved and still less justified.

Whether my theory is correct or not, untouchability is repugnant to reason and to the instinct of mercy, pity or love. A religion that establishes the worship of the cow cannot possibly countenance or warrant a cruel and inhuman boycott of human beings. And I should be content to be torn to pieces rather than disown the suppressed classes. Hindus will certainly never deserve freedom, nor get it, if they allow their noble religion to be disgraced by the retention of the taint of untouchability. And as I love Hinduism dearer than life itself, the taint has become for me an intolerable burden. Let us not deny God by denying to a fifth of our race the right of association on an equal footing.

Source: From M.K. Gandhi, *Hindu Dharma,* Navajivan Publishing House, Ahmedabad 1950. The extracts make use of pages in the following order: p.13; p.3; pp.158-60; pp.220-8; pp.6-9.

2.9   FROM THE WRITINGS OF SRI AUROBINDO

His Teaching   2.9.1

The teaching of Sri Aurobindo starts from that of the ancient sages of India: that behind the appearances of the universe there is the reality of a being and consciousness, a self of all things, one and eternal. All beings are united in that one self and spirit but divided by a certain separativity of consciousness, an ignorance of their true self and reality in the mind, life, and body. It is possible by a certain psychological discipline to remove this veil of separative consciousness and become aware of the true Self, the divinity within us all.

Sri Aurobindo's teaching states that this one being and consciousness is involved here in matter. Evolution is the process by which it liberates itself; consciousness appears in what seems to be inconscient, and once having appeared is self-impelled to grow higher and higher and at the same time to enlarge and develop toward a greater and greater perfection. Life is the first step of this release of consciousness; mind is the second. But the evolution does not finish with mind; it awaits a release into something greater, a consciousness which is spiritual and supramental. The next step of the evolution must be toward the development of Supermind and spirit as the dominant power in the conscious being. For only then will the involved divinity in things release itself entirely and it become possible for life to manifest perfection.

But while the former steps in evolution were taken by nature without a conscious will in the plant and animal life, in man nature becomes able to evolve by a conscious will in the instrument. It is not, however, by the mental will in man that this can be wholly done, for the mind goes only to a certain point and after that can only move in a circle. A conversion has to be made, a turning of the consciousness by which mind has to change into the higher principle. This method is to be found through the ancient psychological discipline and practice of yoga. In the past, it has been attempted by a drawing away from the world and a disappearance into the height of the self or spirit. Sri Aurobindo teaches that a descent of the higher principle is possible which will not merely release the spiritual

Self out of the world, but release it in the world, replace the mind's ignorance or its very limited knowledge by a supramental Truth-Consciousness which will be a sufficient instrument of the inner self, and make it possible for the human being to find himself dynamically as well as inwardly and grow out of his still animal humanity into a diviner race. The psychological discipline of yoga can be used to that end by opening all the parts of the being to a conversion or transformation through the descent and working of the higher, still-concealed supramental principle.

This, however, cannot be done at once or in a short time or by any rapid or miraculous transformation. Many steps have to be taken by the seeker before the supramental descent is possible. Man lives mostly in his surface mind, life and body, but there is an inner being within him with greater possibilities to which he has to awake – for it is only a very restricted influence from it that he receives now and that pushes him to a constant pursuit of a greater beauty, harmony, power and knowledge. The first process of yoga is therefore to open the ranges of this inner being and to live from there outward, governing his outward life by an inner light and force. In doing so he discovers in himself his true soul, which is not this outer mixture of mental, vital, and physical elements, but something of the reality behind them, a spark from the one divine fire. He has to learn to live in his soul and purify and orientate by its drive toward the truth the rest of the nature. There can follow afterwards an opening upward and descent of a higher principle of the being. But even then it is not at once the full supramental light and force. For there are several ranges of consciousness between the ordinary human mind and the supramental Truth-Consciousness. These intervening ranges have to be opened up and their power brought down into the mind, life and body. Only afterwards can the full power of the Truth-Consciousness work in the nature. The process of this self-discipline or *sādhanā* is therefore long and difficult, but even a little of it is so much gained because it makes the ultimate release and perfection more possible.

There are many things belonging to older systems that are necessary on the way – an opening of the mind to a greater wideness and to the sense of the self and the infinite, an emergence into what has been called the cosmic consciousness, mastery over the desires and passions: an outward asceticism is not essential, but the conquest of desire and attachment and a control over the body and its needs, greeds and instincts are indispensable. There is a combination of the principles of the old systems, the way of knowledge through the mind's discernment between reality and the appearance: the heart's way of devotion, love and surrender; and the way of works, turning the will away from motives of self-interest to the truth and the service of a greater reality than the ego. For the whole being has to be trained so that it can respond and be transformed when it is possible for that greater light and force to work in the nature.

In this discipline the inspiration of the master and, in the difficult stages, his control and his presence are indispensable — for it would be impossible otherwise to go through it without much stumbling and error which would prevent all chance of success. The master is one who has risen to a higher consciousness and being and he is often regarded as its manifestation or representative. He not only helps by his teaching and still more by his influence and example, but by a power to communicate his own experience to others.

This is Sri Aurobindo's teaching and method of practice. It is not his object to develop any one religion or to amalgamate the older religions or to found any new religion — for any of these things would lead away from his central purpose. The one aim of his yoga is an inner self-development by which each one who follows it can in time discover the One Self in all and evolve a higher consciousness than the mental, a spiritual and supramental consciousness which will transform and divinise human nature.

The Hour of God

2.9.2

There are moments when the Spirit moves among men and the breath of the Lord is abroad upon the waters of our being; there are others when it retires and men are left to act in the strength or the weakness of their own egoism. The first are periods when even a little effort produces great results and changes destiny; the second are spaces of time when much labour goes to the making of a little result. It is true that the latter may prepare the former, may be the little smoke of sacrifice going up to heaven which calls down the rain of God's bounty.

Unhappy is the man or the nation which, when the divine moment arrives, is found sleeping or unprepared to use it, because the lamp has not been kept trimmed for the welcome and the ears are sealed to the call. But thrice woe to them who are strong and ready, yet waste the force or misuse the moment; for them is irreparable loss or a great destruction.

In the hour of God cleanse thy soul of all self-deceit and hypocrisy and vain self-flattering that thou mayst look straight into thy spirit and hear that which summons it. All insincerity of nature, once thy defence against the eye of the Master and the light of the ideal, becomes now a gap in thy armour and invites the blow. Even if thou conquer for the moment, it is the worse for thee, for the blow shall come afterwards and cast thee down in the midst of thy triumph. But being pure cast aside all fear; for the hour is often terrible, a fire and a whirlwind and a tempest, a treading of the winepress of the wrath of God; but he who can stand up in it on the truth of his purpose is he who shall stand; even though he fall, he shall rise again; even though he seem to pass on the wings of the wind, he shall return. Nor let worldly prudence whisper too closely in thy ear; for it is the hour of the unexpected.

2.9.3 Integral Perfection

A Yoga of integral perfection regards man as a divine spiritual being involved in mind, life and body; it aims therefore at a liberation and a perfection of his divine nature. It seeks to make an inner living in the perfectly developed spiritual being his constant intrinsic living and the spiritualised action of mind, life and body only its outward human expression. In order that this spiritual being may not be something vague and indefinable or else but imperfectly realised and dependent on the mental support and the mental limitations, it seeks to go beyond mind to the supramental knowledge, will, sense, feeling, intuition, dynamic initiation of vital and physical action, all that makes the native working of the spiritual being. It accepts human life, but takes account of the large supraterrestrial action behind the earthly material living, and it joins itself to the divine Being from whom the supreme origination of all these partial and lower states proceeds so that the whole of life may become aware of its divine source and feel in each action of knowledge, of will, of feeling, sense and body the divine originating impulse. It rejects nothing that is essential in the mundane aim, but enlarges it, finds and lives in its greater and its truer meaning now hidden from it, transfigures it from a limited, earthly and mortal thing to a figure of intimate, divine and immortal values.

The integral Yoga meets the religious ideal at several points, but goes beyond it in the sense of a greater wideness. The religious ideal looks, not only beyond this earth, but away from it to a heaven or even beyond all heavens to some kind of Nirvana. Its ideal of perfection is limited to whatever kind of inner or outer mutation will eventually serve the turning away of the soul from the human life to the beyond. Its ordinary idea of perfection is a religio-ethical change, a drastic purification of the active and the emotional being, often with an ascetic abrogation and rejection of the vital impulses as its completest reaching of excellence, and in any case a supraterrestrial motive and reward or result of a life of piety and right conduct. In so far as it admits a change of knowledge, will, aesthesis, it is in the sense of the turning of them to another object than the aims of human life and eventually brings a rejection of all earthly objects of aesthesis, will and knowledge. The method, whether it lays stress on personal effort or upon divine influence, on works and knowledge or upon grace, is not like the mundane a development, but rather a conversion; but in the end the aim is not a conversion of our mental and physical nature, but the putting on of a pure spiritual nature and being, and since that is not possible here on earth, it looks for its consummation by a transference to another world or a shuffling off of all cosmic existence.

But the integral Yoga founds itself on a conception of the spiritual being as an omnipresent existence, the fullness of which comes not essentially by a transference to other worlds or a cosmic self-extinction, but by a growth out of what we now are phenomenally into the consciousness of the omnipresent reality which we always are in the essence of our being. It substitutes for the form of religious piety its completer spiritual seeking of a divine union. It proceeds by a personal effort to a conversion through a divine influence and possession; but this divine grace, if we may so call it, is not simply a mysterious flow or touch coming from above, but the all-pervading act of a divine presence which we come to know within as the power of the highest Self and Master of our being entering into the soul and so possessing it that we not only feel it close to us and pressing upon our mortal nature, but live in its law, know that law, possess it as the whole power of our spiritualised nature. The conversion its action will effect is an integral conversion of our ethical being into the Truth and Right of the divine nature, of our intellectual into the illumination of divine knowledge, our emotional into the divine love and unity, our dynamic and volitional into a working of the divine power, our aesthetic into a plenary reception and a creative enjoyment of divine beauty, not excluding even in the end a divine conversion of the vital and physical being. It regards all the previous life as an involuntary and unconscious or half-conscious preparatory growing towards this change and Yoga as the voluntary and conscious effort and realisation of the change, by which all the aim of human existence in all its parts is fulfilled, even while it is transfigured. Admitting the supracosmic truth and life in worlds beyond, it admits too the terrestrial as a continued term of the one existence and a change of individual and communal life on earth as a strain of its divine meaning.

To open oneself to the supracosmic Divine is an essential condition of this integral perfection; to unite oneself with the universal Divine is another essential condition. Here the Yoga of self-perfection coincides with the Yogas of knowledge, works and devotion; for it is impossible to change the human nature into the divine or to make it an instrument of the divine knowledge, will and joy of existence, unless there is a union with the supreme Being, Consciousness and Bliss and a unity with its universal Self in all things and beings. A wholly separative possession of the divine nature by the human individual, as distinct from a self-withdrawn absorption in it, is not possible. But this unity will not be an inmost spiritual oneness qualified, so long as the human life lasts, by a separative existence in mind, life and body; the full perfection is a possession, through this spiritual unity, of unity too with the universal Mind, the universal Life, the universal Form which are the other constant terms of cosmic being. Moreover, since human life is still accepted as a self-expression of the realised Divine in man, there must be an action of the entire divine nature in our life; and this brings in the need of the supramental conversion which substitutes the native action of spiritual being for the imperfect action of the superficial nature and spiritualises and transfigures its mental, vital and physical parts by the spiritual ideality. These three elements, a union with the supreme Divine, unity with the universal Self, and a supramental life action from this transcendent origin and through this universality, but still with the individual as the soul-channel and natural instrument, constitute the essence of the integral divine perfection of the human being.

Man a Transitional Being 2.9.4

Man's greatness is not in what he is, but in what he makes possible. His glory is that he is the closed place and secret workshop of a living labour in which supermanhood is being made ready by a divine Craftsman. But he is admitted too to a yet greater greatness and it is that, allowed to be unlike the lower creation, he is partly an artisan of this divine change; his conscious assent, his consecrated will and participation are needed that into his body may descend the glory that will replace him. His aspiration is earth's call to the supramental creator.

If earth calls and the Supreme answers, the hour can be even now for that immense and glorious transformation.

But what shall be the gain to be won for the Earth-consciousness we embody by this unprecedented ascent from mind to supermind and what the ransom of the supramental change? To what end should man leave his safe human limits for this hazardous adventure?

First consider what was gained when Nature passed from the brute inconscience and inertia of what seems inanimate Matter to the vibrant awakening of sensibility of plant range. Life was gained; the gain was the first beginnings of a mite groping and involved, reaching a consciousness that stretches out dumbly for growth, towards sense vibration, to a preparation for vital yearnings, a living joy and beauty. The plant achieved a first form of life but could not possess it, because this first organised life-consciousness had feeling and seeking but was blind, dumb, deaf, chained to the soul and involved in its own nerve and tissue; it could not get out of them, could not get behind its nerve self as does the vital mind of the animal; still less could it turn down from above upon it to know and realise and control its own motions as does the observing and thinking mind in man. This was an imprisoned gain, for there was still a gross oppression of the first Inconscience which had covered up with the brute phenomenon of Matter and of Energy of Matter all signs of the Spirit. Nature could in no wise stop here, because she held much in her that was still occult, potential, unexpressed, unorganised, latent; the evolution had perforce to go farther. The animal had to replace the plant at the head and top of Nature. And what then was gained when Nature passed from the obscurity of the plant kingdom to the awakened sense, desire and emotion and the free mobility of animal life? The gain was liberated sense and feeling and desire and courage and cunning and the contrivance of the objects of desire, passion and action and hunger and battle and conquest and the sex-call and play and pleasure, and all the joy and pain of the conscious living creature. Not only the life of the body which the animal has in common with the plant but a life-mind that appeared for the first time in the earth-story and grew from form to more organised form till it reached in the best the limit of its own formula.

The animal achieved a first form of mind, but could not possess it, because this first organised mind-consciousness was enslaved to a narrow scope, tied to the full functioning of the physical body and brain and nerve, tied to serve the physical life and its desires and needs and passions, limited to the insistent uses of the vital urge, to material longing and feeling and action, bound in its own inferior instrumentation, its spontaneous combinings of association and memory and instinct. It could not get away from them, could not get behind them as man's intelligence gets behind them to observe them; still less could it turn down on them from above as do human reason and will to control, enlarge, re-order, exceed, sublimate.

At each capital step of Nature's ascent there is a reversal of consciousness in the evolving spirit. As when a climber turns on a summit to which he has laboured and looks down with an exalted and wider power of vision on all that was once above or on a level with him but is now below his feet, the evolutionary being not only transcends his past self, his former now exceeded status, but commands from a higher grade of self-experience and vision, with a new apprehending feeling or a new comprehending sight and effectuating power in a greater system of values, all that was once his own consciousness but is now below him and belongs to an inferior creation. This reversal is the sign of a decisive victory and the seal of a radical progress in Nature.

The new consciousness attained in the spiritual evolution is always higher in grade and power, always larger, more comprehensive, wider in sight and feeling, richer and finer in faculties, more complex, organic, dominating than the consciousness that was once our own but is now left behind us. There are greater breadth and space, heights before impassable, unexpected depths and intimacies. There is a luminous expansion that is the very sign-manual of the Supreme upon his work.

Mark that each of the great radical steps forward already taken by Nature has been infinitely greater in its change, incalculably vaster in its consequences than its puny predecessor. There is a miraculous opening to an always richer and wider expression, there is a new illuminating of the creation and a dynamic heightening of its significances. There is in this world we live in no equality of all on a flat level, but a hierarchy of ever-increasing precipitous superiorities pushing their mountain shoulders upwards towards the Supreme.

Because man is a mental being, he naturally imagines that mind is the one great leader and actor and creator or the indispensable agent in the universe. But this is an error; even for knowledge mind is not the only or the greatest possible instrument, the one aspirant and discoverer. Mind is a clumsy interlude between Nature's vast and precise subconscient action and the vaster infallible superconscient action of the Godhead.

There is nothing mind can do that cannot be better done in the mind's immobility and thought-free stillness.

When mind is still, then Truth gets her chance to be heard in the purity of the silence.

Truth cannot be attained by the Mind's thought but only by identity and silent vision. Truth lives in the calm wordless Light of the eternal spaces; she does not intervene in the noise and cackle of logical debate.

Conditions for the Coming of a Spiritual Age   2.9.5

A change of this kind, the change from the mental and vital to the spiritual order of life, must necessarily be accomplished in the individual and in a great number of individuals before it can lay any effective hold upon the community. The Spirit in humanity discovers, develops, builds into form in the individual man: it is through the progressive and formative individual that it offers the discovery and the chance of a new self-creation to the mind of the race. For the communal mind holds things subconsciently at first or, if consciously, then in a confused chaotic manner: it is only through the individual mind that the mass can arrive at a clear knowledge and creation of the thing it held in its subconscient self. Thinkers, historians, sociologists who belittle the individual and would like to lose him in the mass or think of him chiefly as a cell, an atom, have got hold only of the obscurer side of the truth of Nature's workings in humanity. It is because man is not like the material formations of Nature or like the animal, because she intends in him a more and more conscious evolution, that individuality is so much developed in him and so absolutely important and indispensable. No doubt what comes out in the individual and afterwards moves the mass, must have been there already in the universal Mind and the individual is only an instrument for its manifestation, discovery, development; but he is an indispensable instrument and an instrument not merely of subconscient Nature, not merely of an instinctive urge that moves the mass, but more directly of the Spirit of whom that Nature is itself the instrument and the matrix of his creations. All great changes therefore find their first clear and effective power and their direct shaping force in the mind and spirit of an individual or of a limited number of individuals. The mass follows, but unfortunately in a very imperfect and confused fashion which often or even usually ends in the failure or distortion of the thing created. If it were not so, mankind could have advanced on its way with a victorious rapidity instead of with the lumbering hesitations and soon exhausted rushes that seem to be all of which it has yet been capable.

Therefore if the spiritual change of which we have been speaking is to be effected, it must unite two conditions which have to be simultaneously satisfied but are most difficult to bring together. There must be the individual and the individuals who are able to see, to develop, to re-create themselves in the image of the Spirit and to communicate both their idea and its power to the mass. And there must be at the same time a mass, a society, a communal mind or at the least the constituents of a group-body, the possibility of a group-soul which is capable of receiving and effectively assimilating, ready to follow and effectively arrive, not compelled by its own inherent deficiencies, its defect of preparation to stop on the way or fall back before the decisive change is made. Such a simultaneity has never yet happened, although the appearance of it has sometimes been created by the ardour of a moment. That the combination must happen some day is a certainty, but none can tell how many attempts will have to be made and how many sediments of spiritual experience will have to be accumulated in the subconscient mentality of the communal human being before the soil is ready. For the chances of success are always less powerful in a difficult upward effort affecting the very roots of our nature than the numerous possibilities of failure. The initiator himself may be imperfect, may not have waited to become entirely the thing that he has seen. Even the few who have the apostolate in their charge may not have perfectly assimilated and shaped it in themselves and may hand on the power of the Spirit still farther diminished to the many who will come after them. The society may be intellectually, vitally, ethically, temperamentally unready, with the result that the final acceptance of the spiritual idea by the society may be also the beginning of its debasement and distortion and of the consequent departure or diminution of the Spirit. Any or all of these things may happen, and the result will be, as has so often happened in the past, that even though some progress is made and an important change effected, it will not be the decisive change which can alone re-create humanity in a diviner image.

What then will be that state of society, what that readiness of the common mind of man which will be most favourable to this change, so that even if it cannot at once effectuate itself, it may at least make for its ways a more decisive preparation than has been hitherto possible? For that seems the most important element, since it is that, it is the unpreparedness, the unfitness of the society or of the common mind of man which is always the chief stumbling-block. It is the readiness of this common mind which is of the first importance; for even if the condition of society and the principle and rule that govern society are opposed to the spiritual change, even if these belong almost wholly to the vital, to the external, the economic, the mechanical order, as is certainly the way at present with human masses, yet if the common human mind has begun to admit the ideas proper to the higher order that is in the end to be, and the heart of man has begun to be stirred by aspirations born of these ideas, then there is a hope of some advance in the not distant future. And here the first essential sign must be the growth of the subjective idea of life – the idea of the soul, the inner being, its powers, its possibilities, its growth, its expression and the creation of a true, beautiful and helpful environment for it as the one thing of first and last importance. The signals must be there that are precursors of a subjective age in humanity's thought and social endeavour.

Source: From Sri Aurobindo, *Birth Centenary Library,* Pondicherry. Sri Avrobindo Ashram 1972-5. Extracts make use of volumes and pages in the following order: Vol.1, pp.59-62; Vol.17, p.1; Vol.24, pp.594-6; Vol.17, pp.9-11; Vol.15, pp.231-3.

2.10   AUROVILLE

The Mother of Sri Aurobindo Ashram

2.10.1 A Dream

There should be somewhere upon earth a place that no nation could claim as its sole property, a place where all human beings of good will, sincere in their aspiration, could live freely as citizens of the world, obeying one single authority, that of the supreme Truth, a place of peace, concord, harmony, where all the fighting instincts of man would be used exclusively to conquer the causes of his sufferings and miseries, to surmount his weakness and ignorance, to triumph over his limitations and incapacities; a place where the needs of the spirit and the care for progress would get precedence over the satisfaction of desires and passions, the seeking for material pleasures and enjoyment. In this place, children would be able to grow and develop integrally without losing contact with their soul. Education would be given not with a view to passing examinations and getting certificates and posts but for enriching the existing faculties and bringing forth new ones. In this place titles and positions would be supplanted by opportunities to serve and organise. The needs of the body will be provided for equally in the case of each and everyone. In the general organisation intellectual, moral and spiritual superiority will find expression not in the enhancement of the pleasures and powers of life but in the increase of duties and responsibilities. Artistic beauty in all forms, painting, sculpture, music, literature, will be available equally to all, the opportunity to share in the joys they give being limited solely by each one's capacities and not by social or financial position. For in this ideal place money would be no more the sovereign lord. Individual value would have a greater importance than the value due to material wealth and social position. Work would not be there as the means for gaining one's livelihood, it would be the means whereby to express oneself, develop one's capacities and possibilities, while doing at the same time service to the whole group, which on its side would provide for each one's subsistence and for the field of his work. In brief, it would be a place where the relations among human beings, usually based almost exclusively upon competition and strife, would be replaced by relations of emulation for doing better, for collaboration, relations of real brotherhood.

The earth is certainly not ready to realise such an idea, for mankind does not yet possess the necessary knowledge to understand and accept it nor the indispensable conscious force to execute it. That is why I call it a dream.

Yet, this dream is on the way to becoming a reality. That is exactly what we are seeking to do at the Ashram of Sri Aurobindo on a small scale, in proportion to our modest means. The achievement is indeed far from being perfect but it is progressive; little by little we advance towards our goal, which, we hope, one day we shall be able to hold before the world as a practical and effective means of coming out of the present chaos in order to be born into a more true, more harmonious new life.

Auroville, the Cradle of a New World   2.10.2

In April 1956 the Mother declared:

> The manifestation of the Supramental upon earth is no longer a promise but a living fact, a reality. It is at work here. And one day will come when the most blind, the most unconscious, even the most unwilling shall be obliged to recognise it.

Replacing the future tense of her 1914 vision by the present, the Mother announced:

> A new light breaks upon the earth.
> A new world is born.
> All that were promised are fulfilled.

The following year, the Mother delivered a talk in the Ashram, about this event:

> You must leave behind whatever has been designed, whatever has been built up, and then proceed on the march into the unknown. Come what may.

2.10.3 Auroville Charter

1. Auroville belongs to nobody in particular. Auroville belongs to humanity as a whole. But to live in Auroville one must be a willing servitor of the Divine Consciousness.
2. Auroville will be the place of an unending education, of constant progress and a youth that never ages.
3. Auroville wants to be the bridge between the past and the future. Taking advantage of all discoveries from without and from within Auroville will boldly spring towards future realisations.
4. Auroville will be a site of material and spiritual researches for a living embodiment of an actual Human Unity.

2.10.4 To Be a True Aurovillian

1. The first necessity is the inner discovery by which one learns who one really is behind the social, moral, cultural, racial and hereditary appearances.

At our inmost centre there is a free being, wide and knowing, who awaits our discovery and who ought to become the acting centre of our being and our life in Auroville.

2. One lives in Auroville in order to be free of moral and social conventions; but this liberty must not be a new slavery to the ego, its desires and its ambitions.

The fulfilment of desires bars the route to the inner discovery which can only be attained in peace and the transparency of a perfect disinterestedness.

3. The Aurovillian must lose the proprietary sense of possession.

For our passage in the material world, that which is indispensable to our life and to our action is put at our disposal according to the place we should occupy there. The more conscious our contact is with our inner being, the more exact are the means given.

4. Work, even manual work, is an indispensable thing for the inner discovery. If one does not work, if one does not inject his consciousness into matter, the latter will never develop. To let one's consciousness organise a bit of matter by way of one's body is very good. To establish order, around oneself, helps to bring order within oneself.

One should organise life not according to outer, artificial rules, but according to an organised, inner consciousness because if one allows life to drift without imposing the control of a higher consciousness, life becomes inexpressive and irresolute. It is to waste one's time in the sense that matter persists without a conscious utilisation.

5. The whole earth must prepare itself for the advent of the new species, and Auroville wants to consciously work towards hastening that advent.

6. Little by little it will be revealed to us what this new species should be, and meanwhile the best measure to take is to consecrate oneself entirely to the Divine.

No Religion   2.10.5

Auroville is for those who want to live a life essentially divine but who renounce all religions whether they be ancient, modern or future.

It is only in experience that there can be knowledge of the truth. No one ought to speak of the Divine unless he has had experience of the Divine. Get experience of the Divine, then alone will you have the right to speak of it.

The objective study of religions will be a part of the historical study of the development of human consciousness.

Religions make up part of the history of mankind and it is in this guise that they will be studied at Auroville — not as beliefs to which one ought or ought not to fasten, but as part of a process in the development of human consciousness which should lead man towards his superior realisation.

Program:

Research through experience of the
Supreme Truth
A Life Divine
but
NO RELIGIONS

Source: The Mother [of the Sri Aurobindo Ashram], *Auroville: Cradle of a New World,* Sri Aurobindo Ashram, Pondicherry 1972, pp.1-6.

3   THE NOBLE PATH OF BUDDHISM

[*Editor's Note:* In the twentieth century Buddhism has spread almost throughout the five continents. And though the number of its adherents in many areas may still be very small it has succeeded in gaining the sympathetic approval of many who still retain another faith but who see in Buddhist teaching and life something very attractive.

The Buddhist Canon consists of three collections of texts, termed *Tripitaka* or 'Triple Basket'. They are written in an artificial literary language known as Pali. This Pali *Tripitaka* is divided into (1) *the Vinaya Pitaka,* (2) *the Sutta-Pitaka* and (3) *the Abidhamma-Pitaka.*

These writings, some of which are attributed to the founder of the faith, Gautama, form a Canon of scripture which is the main inspiration for Buddhist thought and practice and is therefore given a dominating place in this Buddhist section of the Reader. In addition the student will find two small but significant pieces which come from Buddhism outside India — Bassui's sermon, and the Ox-Herding pictures attributed to a twelfth-century teacher.

As with Hinduism, students will generally find many new and strange-sounding words — bhikkhu, bodhisattva, sangha, etc. The Glossary referred to in the Editorial Note on Hinduism, together with the explanatory matter in the Course Units — plus television and radio programmes — should solve the 'new word' problem.

Professor Joseph Masson has earned our special thanks by writing an introductory note to every extract in the scripture section which follows; students will find these notes invaluable. The foot-notes to the extracts are also provided by Professor Masson. Note also that the recurring abbreviation SBE stands for 'Sacred Books of the East'.]

3.1   THE BUDDHA

The Great Retirement   3.1.1

[This is the spiritual aspect of the decision to abandon the world. It has been dramatised in the symbolic episodes of Gautama leaving his palace for a walk, and encountering successively an old man, a sick man, a dead man and a monk.]

Monks, I was delicately nurtured, exceeding delicately nurtured, delicately nurtured beyond measure. For instance, in my father's house lotus-pools were made thus: one of blue lotuses, one of red, another of white lotuses, just for my benefit. No sandal-wood powder did I use that was not from Kāsi: of Kāsi cloth was my turban made: of Kāsi cloth was my jacket, my tunic and my cloak. By night and day a white canopy was held over me, lest cold or heat, dust or chaff or dew, should touch me. Moreover, monks, I had three palaces: one for winter, one for summer, and one for the rainy season. In the four months of the rains I was waited on by minstrels, women all of them. I came not down from my palace in those months. Again, whereas in other men's homes broken rice together with sour gruel is given as food to slave-servants, in my father's home they were given rice, meat and milk-rice for their food.

To me, monks, thus blest with much prosperity, thus nurtured with exceeding delicacy, this thought occurred: Surely one of the uneducated manyfolk, though himself subject to old age and decay, not having passed beyond old age and decay, when he sees another broken down with age, is troubled, ashamed, disgusted, forgetful that he himself is such an one. Now I too am subject to old age and decay, not having passed beyond old age and decay. Were I to see another broken down with old age, I might be troubled, ashamed and disgusted. That would not be seemly in me. Thus, monks, as I considered the matter, all pride in my youth deserted me.

Again, monks, I thought: One of the uneducated manyfolk, though himself subject to disease, not having passed beyond disease, when he sees another person diseased, is troubled, ashamed and disgusted, forgetful that he himself is such an one. Now I too am subject to disease. I have not passed beyond disease. Were I to see another diseased, I might be troubled, ashamed, disgusted. That would not be seemly in me. Thus, monks, as I considered the matter, all pride in my health deserted me.

Again, monks, I thought: One of the uneducated manyfolk. . . when he sees another person subject to death. . .is disgusted and ashamed, forgetful that he himself is such an one. Now I too am subject to death. I have not passed beyond death. Were I to see another subject to death, I might be troubled. . . That would not be seemly in me. Thus, monks, as I considered the matter, all pride in my life deserted me.

Source: From the Añguttara-Nikaya, I: 145-6, in F.L. Woodward, *Gradual Sayings,* Pali Text Society, 1932 Vol.1, pp.128-9.

3.1.2 Enjoying the Bliss of Emancipation

[After attaining the 'right vision' of reality in his meditation and illumination, Siddhârtha has now become a Buddha, an 'awakened'. In the following text, we find a dramatic expression of his feelings: he has reached the supreme goal; he is now superior to all existing beings and he proclaims what he discovered.]

1. Then the Blessed One, at the end of those seven days, arose from that state of meditation, and went from the foot of the Ajapâla banyan tree to the Mucalinda tree. And when he had reached it, he sat cross-legged at the foot of the Mucalinda tree uninterruptedly during seven days, enjoying the bliss of emancipation.

2. At that time a great cloud appeared out of season, rainy weather which lasted seven days, cold weather, storms and darkness. And the Nâga (or Serpent) king Mucalinda[1] came out from his abode, and seven times encircled the body of the Blessed One with his windings, and kept extending his large hood over the Blessed One's head, thinking to himself: 'May no coldness (touch) the Blessed One! May no heat (touch) the Blessed One! May no vexation by gadflies and gnats, by storms and sunheat and reptiles (touch) the Blessed One!'

3. And at the end of those seven days, when the Nâga king Mucalinda saw the open, cloudless sky, he loosened his windings from the body of the Blessed One, made his own appearance disappear, created the appearance of a youth, and stationed himself

in front of the Blessed One, raising his clasped hands, and paying reverence to the Blessed One.

4. And the Blessed One, perceiving that, on this occasion, pronounced this solemn utterance: 'Happy is the solitude of him who is full of joy, who has learnt the Truth, who sees (the Truth). Happy is freedom from malice in this world, (self-) restraint towards all beings that have life. Happy is freedom from lust in this world, getting beyond all desires; and putting away of that pride which comes from the thought "I am!" This truly is the highest happiness!' Here ends the account of what passed under the Mucalinda tree.

7. Now Upaka, a man belonging to the Âjîvaka sect [i.e. the sect of naked ascetics], saw the Blessed One travelling on the road, between Gayâ and the Bodhi tree; and when he saw him, he said to the Blessed One: 'Your countenance, friend, is serene; your complexion is pure and bright. In whose name, friend, have you retired from the world? Who is your teacher? Whose doctrine do you profess?'

8. When Upaka the Âjîvaka[2] had spoken thus, the Blessed One addressed him in the following stanzas: 'I have overcome all foes; I am all-wise; I am free from stains in every way; I have left everything; and have obtained emancipation by the destruction of desire. Having myself gained knowledge, whom should I call my master? I have no teacher; no one is equal to me; in the world of men and of gods no being is like me. I am the holy One in this world, I am the highest teacher, I alone am the absolute Sambuddha; I have gained coolness (by the extinction of all passion) and have obtained Nirvâna. To found the Kingdom of Truth I go to the city of the Kâsîs (Benares); I will beat the drum of the Immortal in the darkness of this world.'

9. [Upaka replied]: 'You profess then, friend, to be the holy, absolute Jina.'[3]

[Buddha said]: 'Like me are all Jinas who have reached extinction of the Âsavas; I have overcome all states of sinfulness; therefore, Upaka, am I the Jina.' When he had spoken thus, Upaka the Âjîvaka replied: 'It may be so, friend', shook his head, took another road, and went away.

10. And the Blessed One, wandering from place to place, came to Benares, to the deer park Isipatana.

Notes

1. Such serpents form a class of supernatural beings.
2. An Âjîvaka is a naked ascetic.
3. i.e. the Victorious One.

Source: From the Mahâvagga I: 3, 1-4 and I: 6, 7-10 in M. Müller, ed., *SBE,* Vol.XIII, OUP 1881, pp.80-81 and 90-91.

3.1.3 The Buddha Hesitates to Preach

[After his illumination, the Buddha seems to have hesitated to leave the concentration on his individual experience and to come again into contact with men. For two reasons: he feared to lose his spiritual peace, and he feared that men would not listen to him... One should note, from the text, that all categories of beings, including the gods, are in need of his preaching to obtain Nirvâna.]

1. Then the Blessed One, at the end of those seven days, arose from that state of meditation, and went from the foot of the Ragayatana tree to the Ajapâla banyan tree. And when he had reached it, the Blessed One stayed there at the foot of the Ajapâla banyan tree.

2. Then in the mind of the Blessed One, who was alone, and had retired into solitude, the following thought arose: 'I have penetrated this doctrine which is profound, difficult to perceive and to understand, which brings quietude of heart, which is exalted, which is unattainable by reasoning, abstruse, intelligible (only) to the wise. This people on the other hand, is given to desire, intent upon desire, delighting in desire. To this people, therefore, who are given to desire, intent upon desire, delighting in desire, the law of causality and the chain of causation will be a matter difficult to understand; most difficult for them to understand will be also the extinction of all samkhâras, the getting rid of all the substrata (of existence), the destruction of desire, the absence of passion, quietude of heart, Nirvâna! Now if I proclaim the doctrine, and other men are not able to understand my preaching, there would result but weariness and annoyance to me.'

3. And then the following...stanzas, unheard before, occurred to the Blessed One: 'With great pains have I acquired it. Enough! Why should I now proclaim it? This doctrine will not be easy to understand to beings that are lost in lust and hatred. Given to lust, surrounded with thick darkness, they will not see what is repugnant

(to their minds), abstruse, profound, difficult to perceive, and subtle.'

4. When the Blessed One pondered over this matter, his mind became inclined to remain in quiet, and not to preach the doctrine. Then Brahmâ Sahampati[1] understanding by the power of his mind the reflection which had arisen in the mind of the Blessed One, thought: 'Alas! the world perishes! Alas! the world is destroyed! if the mind of the Tathâgata, of the holy, of the absolute Sambuddha inclines itself to remain in quiet, and not to preach the doctrine.'

5. Then Brahmâ Sahampati disappeared from Brahma's world, and appeared before the Blessed One [as quickly] as a strong man might stretch his bent arm out, or draw back his outstretched arm.

6. And Brahmâ Sahampati adjusted his upper robe so as to cover one shoulder, and putting his right knee on the ground, raised his joined hands towards the Blessed One, and said to the Blessed One: 'Lord, may the Blessed One preach the doctrine! may the perfect One preach the doctrine! there are beings whose mental eyes are darkened by scarcely any dust; but if they do not hear the doctrine, they cannot attain salvation. These will understand the doctrine.'

7. Thus spoke Brahmâ Sahampati; and when he had thus spoken, he further said: 'The Dhamma hitherto manifested in the country of Magadha has been impure, thought out by contaminated men. But do thou now open the door of the Immortal; let them hear the doctrine discovered by the spotless One!

'As a man standing on a rock, on a mountain's top, might overlook the people all around, thus, O wise One, ascending to the highest palace of Truth, look down, all-seeing One, upon the people lost in suffering, overcome by birth and decay — thou, who has freed thyself from suffering!

'Arise, O hero; O victorious One! Wander through the world, O leader of the pilgrim band, who thyself art free from debt. May the Blessed One preach the doctrine; there will be people who can understand it!' [The request is repeated three times.]

Then the Blessed One, when he had heard Brahmâ's solicitation, looked, full of compassion towards sentient beings, over the world, with his (all-perceiving) eye of a Buddha. And the Blessed One, looking over the world with his eye of a Buddha, saw beings whose mental eyes were darkened by scarcely any dust, and beings whose eyes were covered by much dust, beings sharp of sense and blunt of sense, of good disposition and of bad disposition, easy to instruct and difficult to instruct, some of them seeing the dangers of future life and of sin. And when he had thus seen them, he addressed

Brahmâ Sahampati in the following stanza: 'Wide opened is the door
of the Immortal to all who have ears to hear; let them send forth
faith to meet it.'

Note

1. A great king of the gods who is nevertheless in need of the Master for
   Liberation.

Source: From the Mahâvagga 1:5, 1-7 in M. Müller, ed., *SBE,* OUP 1881, Vol.
XIII, pp.84-8.

3.1.4 The Benares Sermon

[This text is traditionally presented as the first preaching of the
Buddha, in the Deer-Park. It offers an elaborate and systematic form
of the Kernel of the Doctrine (Dhamma), and has two parts. (1) The
Doctrine is presented as the 'middle', between two extremes, being
founded on, and in conformity with, reason. (2) The reality of life is
clearly analysed, in a kind of medical diagnosis and prescription.]

17. The Blessed One thus addressed the five Bhikkhus: 'There are
two extremes, O Bhikkhus, which he who has given up the world
ought to avoid. What are these two extremes? A life given to
pleasures, devoted to pleasures and lusts: this is degrading, sensual,
vulgar, ignoble, and profitless; and a life given to *mortifications:* this
is painful, ignoble, and profitless. By avoiding these two extremes, O
Bhikkhus, the Tathâgata has gained the knowledge of the Middle
Path which leads to insight, which leads to wisdom, which conduces
to calm, to knowledge, to the Sambodhi, to Nirvâna.
18. 'Which, O Bhikkhus, is this Middle Path the knowledge of
which the Tathâgata has gained, which leads to insight, which leads
to wisdom, which conduces to calm, to knowledge, to the
Sambodhi, to Nirvâna? It is the *holy eightfold Path,* namely, Right
Belief, Right Aspiration, Right Speech, Right Conduct, Right Means
of Livelihood, Right Endeavour, Right Memory, Right Meditation.
This, O Bhikkhus, is the Middle Path the knowledge of which the
Tathâgata has gained, which leads to insight, which leads to wisdom,
which conduces to calm, to knowledge, to the Sambodhi, to Nirvâna.
19. 'This, O Bhikkhus, is the Noble Truth of *Suffering:* Birth is
suffering; decay is suffering; illness is suffering; death is suffering.
Presence of objects we hate, is suffering; Separation from objects we

love, is suffering; not to obtain what we desire, is suffering. Briefly, the fivefold clinging to existence[1] is suffering.

20. 'This, O Bhikkhus, is the Noble Truth of the *Cause of suffering:* Thirst, that leads to re-birth, accompanied by pleasure and lust, finding its delight here and there. [This thirst is threefold] namely, thirst for pleasure, thirst for existence, thirst for prosperity.

21. 'This, O Bhikkhus, is the Noble Truth of the *Cessation of suffering:* [it ceases with] the complete cessation of this thirst – a cessation which consists in the absence of every passion – with the abandoning of this thirst, with the doing away with it, with the deliverance from it, with the destruction of desire.

22. 'This, O Bhikkhus, is the Noble Truth of the *Path* which leads to the cessation of suffering; That holy eightfold Path, that is to say: Right Belief, Right Aspiration, Right Speech, Right Conduct, Right Means of Livelihood, Right Endeavour, Right Memory, Right Meditation.'

Note

1. The 'Five clingings' are: Corporality, feeling,perception, mental formation, consciousness. Buddhism sums up in this way all the elements of our (illusory) bodily and spiritual personality.

Source: From Mahâvagga 1:6, 17-02 in M. Müller, ed., *SBE,* OUP 1881, Vol. XIII, pp.94-6.

The Sermon on Burning

[This sermon is a good example of the synthesis between imagination and systematic teaching in Buddhism. Every passion is a fire, is a flame; consequently all the aspects of sense-perceptions determined by the passions, and the objects of sense-perceptions as well, are likewise a burning. The analysis is repeated in exactly the same words for each sense and for the *manas,* which is the power which synthesises all perceptions.]

1. And the Blessed One, after having dwelt at Uruvelâ as long as he thought fit, went forth to Gayâsîsa, accompanied by a great number of Bhikkhus, by one thousand Bhikkhus who all had been to Jatilas[1] before. There near Gaya, at Gayâsîsa, the Blessed One dwelt together with those thousand Bhikkhus.

2. There, the Blessed One thus addressed the Bhikkhus:

'Everything, O Bhikkhus, is burning. And how, O Bhikkhus, is everything burning? The eye, O Bhikkhus, is burning; visible things are burning; the mental impressions based on the eye are burning; the contact of the eye [with visible things] is burning; the sensation produced by the contact of the eye [with visible things], be it pleasant, be it painful, be it neither pleasant nor painful, that also is burning. With what fire is it burning? I declare unto you that it is burning with the fire of lust, with the fire of anger, with the fire of ignorance; it is burning with [the anxieties of] birth, decay, death, grief, lamentation, suffering, dejection and despair.

3. 'The ear is burning, sounds are burning. . . The nose is burning, odours are burning. . . The tongue is burning, tastes are burning. . . The body is burning, objects of contact are burning. . . The mind is burning, thoughts are burning. . .

4. 'Considering this, O Bhikkhus, a disciple learned [in the scriptures], walking in the Noble Path, becomes weary of the eye, weary of visible things, weary of the mental impressions based on the eye, weary of the contact of the eye [with visible things], weary also of the sensation produced by the contact of the eye [with visible things], be it pleasant, be it painful, be it neither pleasant nor painful. . .

'Becoming weary of all that, he divests himself of passion; by absence of passion he is made free; when he is free, he becomes aware that he is free; and he realises that re-birth is exhausted; that holiness is completed; that duty is fulfilled; and that there is no further return to this world.'

When this exposition was propounded, the minds of those thousand Bhikkhus became free from attachment to the world, and were released from the Âsavas.

Note

1. The Jatilas were naked ascetics, hermits with matted hair, and *fire*-worshippers. One should note the appropriateness of the theme of the sermon for such an audience.

Source: From the Mahâvagga 1:21, 1-4 in M. Müller, ed., *SBE,* OUP|1881, Vol.XIII, pp.134-5.

3.1.6 Vocation of Two Friends

[Sâriputta and Moggallâna, two young Brahmanas, were the disciples

of a wandering ascetic, a paribbâjaka, called Sañjaya. As indicated in
the text, the origin of their conversion was the attitude of a young
Buddhist monk, Assaji. Conversions of this type were frequent...]

23.1 At that time Sañjaya, a paribbâjaka [wandering ascetic], resided
at Râjagaha with a great retinue of paribbâjakas, with two hundred
and fifty paribbâjakas. At that time Sâriputta and Moggallâna [two
young Brâhmanas] led a religious life as followers of Sañjaya the
paribbâjaka; these had given their word to each other: 'He who first
attains to the immortal [amata, i.e. Nirvâna] shall tell the other one.'

23.2 Now one day in the fore-noon, the venerable Assaji [a
Buddhist monk], having put on his under-robes, and having taken his
alms-bowl, and with his civara on, entered the city of Râjagaha for
alms; his walking, turning back, regarding, looking, drawing [his
arms] back, and stretching [them] out was decorous; he turned his
eyes to the ground, and was dignified in deportment. Now the
paribbâjaka Sâriputta saw the venerable Assaji, who went through
Râjagaha for alms, whose walking was decorous, who kept his eyes
on the ground, and was dignified in deportment. Seeing him he
thought: 'Indeed this person is one of those Bhikkhus who are the
worthy ones [arhats] in the world, or who have entered the path of
Arhatship. What if I were to approach this Bhikkhu and ask him: "In
whose name, friend, have you retired from the world? Who is your
teacher? Whose doctrine do you profess?"'

23.3 Now the paribbâjaka Sâriputta thought: 'This is not the time
to ask this Bhikkhu; he has entered the interior yard of a house,
walking for alms. What if I were to follow this Bhikkhu step by step,
according to the course recognised by those who want something.'

And the venerable Assaji, having finished his alms-pilgrimage
through Râjagaha, went back with the food he had received. Then
the paribbâjaka Sâriputta went to the place where the venerable
Assaji was; having approached him, he exchanged greeting with the
venerable Assaji; having exchanged with him greeting and complaisant
words, he stationed himself at his side; standing at his side the
paribbâjaka Sâriputta said to the venerable Assaji: 'Your
countenance, friend, is serene; your complexion is pure and bright.
In whose name, friend, have you retired from the world? Who is
your teacher? Whose doctrine do you profess?'

23.4 [Assaji replied]: 'There is, friend, the great Samana
Sakyaputta, an ascetic of the Sakya tribe; in His, the Blessed One's
name, have I retired from the world; He the Blessed One, is my

teacher; and His, the Blessed One's doctrine do I profess.'
'And what is the doctrine, Sir, which your teacher holds, and preaches to you?

'I am only a young disciple, friend; I have but recently received the ordination; and I have newly adopted this doctrine and discipline. I cannot explain to you the doctrine in detail; but I will tell you in short what it means.'

Then the paribbâjaka Sâriputta said to the venerable Assaji: 'Well, friend, tell me much or little as you like, but be sure to tell me the spirit of the doctrine; I want but the spirit; why do you make so much of the letter?'

23.5 Then the venerable Assaji pronounced to the paribbâjaka Sâriputta the following text of the Dhamma: 'Of all objects which proceed from a cause, the Tathagata has explained the cause and he has explained their cessation also; this is the doctrine of the great Samana.'

And the paribbâjaka Sâriputta after having heard this text obtained the pure and spotless Eye of the Truth [that is, the following knowledge] : 'Whatsoever is subject to the condition of origination is subject also to the condition of cessation.' [And he said] : 'If this alone be the doctrine [the Dhamma], now you have reached up to the state where all sorrow ceases [that is, Nirvâna], [the state] which has remained unseen through many myriads of Kappas [world-ages] of the past.'

23.6 Then the paribbâjaka Sâriputta went to the place where the paribbâjaka Moggallâna was. And the paribbâjaka Moggallâna saw the paribbâjaka Sâriputta coming from afar; seeing him he said to the paribbâjaka Sâriputta: 'Your countenance, friend, is serene: your complexion is pure and bright. Have you then really reached the immortal, friend?'

'Yes, friend, I have attained to the immortal.'

'And how, friend, have you done so?'

23.7-9 'I saw, friend, the Bhikkhu Assaji who went through Râjagaha for alms; But I will tell you in short what it means.'

'Tell me much or little as you like, but be sure to tell me the spirit of the doctrine; I want but the spirit; why do you make so much of the letter?'

23.10 'Then, friend, the Bhikkhu Assaji pronounced the following Dhamma sentence: "Of all objects which proceed from a cause, the Tathâgata has explained the cause, and He has explained their cessation also; this is the doctrine of the great Samana".'

And the paribbâjaka Moggallâna, after having heard. . .[remainder of paragraph as in paragraph 23.5]

24.1 Then the paribbâjaka Moggallâna said to the paribbâjaka Sâriputta: 'Let us go, friend, and join the Blessed One, that he may be our Teacher!'

Source: From Mahâvagga 1:23, 1-10 and 24, 1 in M. Müller, ed., *SBE*, OUP 1881, Vol.XIII, pp.144-8.

Last Instructions of the Buddha   3.1.7

[These instructions are very important because they come immediately before the death of the Buddha. The essential point is: The Buddha is only a Master and a Model, not a Saviour; everybody has to liberate himself by his own efforts; and the Community has to rely on its own efforts.]

The Venerable Ânanda addressed the Blessed One, and said: 'I have beheld, Lord, how the Blessed One was in health, and I have beheld how the Blessed One had to suffer. And though at the sight of the sickness of the Blessed One[1] my body became weak as a creeper, and the horizon became dim to me, and my faculties were no longer clear, yet notwithstanding, I took some little comfort from the thought that the Blessed One would not pass away from existence until at least he had left instructions as touching the order.'

32. 'What, then, Ânanda? Does the order expect that of me? I have preached the truth without making any distinction between exoteric and esoteric doctrine: for in respect of the truths, Ânanda, the Tathâgata has no such thing as the closed fist of a teacher, who keeps some things back. Surely, Ânanda, should there be any one who harbours the thought, "It is I who will lead the brotherhood", or, "The order is dependent upon me", it is he who should lay down instructions in any matter concerning the order. Now the Tathâgata, Ânanda, thinks not that it is he who should lead the brotherhood, or that the order is dependent upon him. Why then should he leave instructions in any matter concerning the order? I too, O Ânanda, am now grown old and full of years, my journey is drawing to its close, I have reached my sum of days, I am turning eighty years of age; and just as a worn-out cart, Ânanda, can only with much additional care be made to move along, so, methinks, the body of the

Tathâgata can only be kept going with much additional care. It is only, Ânanda, when the Tathâgata, ceasing to attend to any outward thing, or to experience any sensation, becomes plunged in that devout meditation of heart which is concerned with no material object — it is only then that the body of the Tathâgata is at ease.

33. 'Therefore, O Ânanda, be ye lamps unto yourselves. Be ye a refuge to yourselves. Betake yourselves to no external refuge. Hold fast to the truth as a lamp. Hold fast as a refuge to the truth. Look not for refuge to any one besides yourselves. And how, Ânanda, is a brother to be a lamp unto himself, a refuge to himself, betaking himself to no external refuge, holding fast to the truth as a lamp, holding fast as a refuge to the truth, looking not for refuge to any one besides himself?

34. 'Herein, O Ânanda, let a brother, as he dwells in the body, so regard the body that he, being strenuous, thoughtful, and mindful, may, whilst in the world, overcome the grief which arises from bodily craving — while subject to sensations let him continue so to regard the sensations that he, being strenuous, thoughtful, and mindful, may, whilst in the world, overcome the grief which arises from the sensations — and so, also, as he thinks, or reasons, or feels, let him overcome the grief which arises from the craving due to ideas, or to reasoning, or to feeling.

35. 'And whosoever, Ânanda, either now or after I am dead, shall be a lamp unto themselves, and a refuge unto themselves, shall betake themselves to no external refuge, but holding fast to the truth as their lamp, and holding fast as their refuge to the truth, shall look not for refuge to any one besides themselves — it is they, Ânanda, among my bhikkhus, who shall reach the very topmost Height! — but they must be anxious to learn.'

Note

1. On the nature of the last sickness of the Buddha, the texts are not very clear.

Source: Mahâparinibbâna Sutta II, 31-35 in M. Muller, ed., *SBE*, Vol.XI OUP 1881, pp.36-9.

3.1.8 The Four Holy Places

[The devotion of the Buddhists has transformed into sanctuaries and places of pilgrimage the four principal places of the Buddha's earthly career: the place of his birth, illumination, first preaching, death.

Those Holy Places are visited by thousands of Buddhist pilgrims.]

16. 'There are these four places, Ânanda, which the believing man should visit with feelings of reverence and awe. Which are the four?

17. 'The place, Ânanda, at which the believing man can say, "Here the Tathagâta *was born!*" is a spot to be visited with feelings of reverence and awe.[1]

18. 'The place, Ânanda, at which the believing man can say, "Here the Tathâgata *attained to the supreme and perfect insight!*" is a spot to be visited with feelings of reverence and awe.[2]

19. 'The place, Ânanda, at which the believing man can say, *"Here was the kingdom of righteousness set on foot by the Tathâgata!"* is a spot to be visited with feelings of reverence and awe.[3]

20. 'The place, Ânanda, at which the believing man can say, "Here the Tathâgata *passed finally away* in that utter passing away which leaves nothing whatever to remain behind!" is a spot to be visited with feelings of reverence and awe.[4]

21. 'And there will come, Ânanda, to such spots, believers, brethren and sisters of the order, or devout men and devout women, and will say, "Here was the Tathâgata born!" or, "Here did the Tathâgata attain to the supreme and perfect insight!" or, "Here was the kingdom of righteousness set on foot by the Tathâgata!" or "Here the Tathâgata passed away in that utter passing away which leaves nothing whatever to remain behind!"

22. 'And they, Ânanda, who shall die while they, with believing heart, are journeying on such pilgrimage, shall be reborn after death, when the body shall dissolve, in the happy realms of heaven. . .'

24. 'What are we to do, Lord, with the remains of the Tathâgata?'

'Hinder not yourselves, Ânanda, by honouring the remains of the Tathâgata. Be zealous, I beseech you, Ânanda, in your own behalf! Devote yourselves to your own good! Be earnest, be zealous, be intent on your own good! There are wise men, Ânanda, among the nobles, among the Brâhmans, among the heads of houses, who are firm believers in the Tathâgata; and they will do due honour to the remains of the Tathâgata.'

Notes

1. Lumbinî Grove.
2. Bodh-Ghaya.
3. Benares, Deer Park.

4. Kuśinagara.

Source: From Mahâparinibbâna Sutta, V: 16:22 and 24 in M. Muller, ed., *SBE*, OUP 1881, Vol.XI, pp.90-91.

3.2   THE DHAMMA

The Thirty-one Grades of Being in the Universe

[This is a post-canonical and technical text. Its systematic description of the universe is obviously more developed and complicated than the descriptions given by the Buddha himself.]

The realm of punishment, the realm of sensual bliss, the realm of form, and the realm of formlessness are the four realms. The realm of punishment is fourfold: hell, the brute class, the state of the Manes, the Titan host. The realm of sensual bliss is sevenfold: mankind, the Suite of the Four Great Kings, the Suite of the Thirty-three, the Yama Gods, the Satisfied Gods, the Gods Who Delight in Fashioning, the Gods Who have Control of Pleasures Fashioned by Others. These eleven together are also called the realm of sensual pleasure. The realm of form is sixteenfold: to the Retinue of Brahma, to the Priests of Brahma, and to the Great Brahma Gods access is had through the first trance;[1] to the Gods of Limited Splendour, to the Gods of Immeasurable Splendour, and to the Radiant Gods access is had through the second trance; to the Gods of Limited Lustre, to the Gods of Immeasurable Lustre, and to the Completely Lustrous Gods access is had through the third trance; to the Richly Rewarded Gods, to the Gods without Perception, and to the Pure Abodes access is had through the fourth trance. There are five of these Pure Abodes; that of the Aviha (Effortless?) Gods, of the Untroubled Gods, of the Easily Seen Gods, of the Easily Seeing Gods, and of the Sublime Gods. The realm of formlessness is fourfold: that of the infinity of space, of the infinity of consciousness, of nothingness, and of neither perception nor yet non-perception.

> None unconverted e'er are found
> To dwell within the Pure Abodes,
> Nor those who in the holy life
> Are in the first or second path;
> No saints 'mongst those perception-reft
> Nor in the realms of punishment;
> But all may reach the other states,
> Be they within the paths or not.

Note

1. A trance (dhyâna) is an eminent spiritual state. See the texts on meditation in §3.5 below. Happiness is not primary a 'place', but, first of all, a 'state of mind'.

Source: From Abhidhammadha Sañgaha V: 2-6 and 10 in H.C. Warren, *Buddhism in Translations*, Harvard University Press 1963, p.289.

3.2.2 Duration and Pains of Hell

[Buddhism, in its texts and paintings, has been traditionally far from reticent when describing hells. The following extract gives some perspectives on 'popular Buddhism', such as existed beside, and perhaps before, the refinements effected by more learned people.]

A Bhikkhu asked Bhagavat: 'How long is the rate of life, O venerable one, in the Paduma hell?.

'Long, O Bhikkhu, is the rate of life in the Paduma hell, it is not easy to calculate either [by saying] so many years or so many hundreds of years or so many thousands of years or so many hundred thousands of years.'

'But it is possible, I suppose, to make a comparison, O thou venerable one?'

'It is possible, O Bhikkhu;' so saying, Bhagavat spoke [as follows]: 'Even as, O Bhikkhu, [if there were] a Kosala load of sesamum seed containing twenty khâris,[1] and a man after the lapse of every hundred years were to take from it one sesamum seed at a time, then that Kosala load of sesamum seed, containing twenty kharis, would, O Bhikkhu, sooner by this means dwindle away and be used up than one Abbuda hell; and even as are twenty Abbuda hells, O Bhikkhu, so is one Nirabbuda hell; and even as are twenty Nirabbuda hells, O Bhikkhu, so is one Ababa hell; and even as are twenty Ababa hells, O Bhikkhu, so is one Ahaha hell; and even as are twenty Ahaha hells, O Bhikkhu, so is one Atata hell; and even as are twenty Atata hells, O Bhikkhu, so is one Kumuda hell; and even as are twenty Kumuda hells, O Bhikkhu, so is one Sogandhika hell; and even as are twenty Sogandhika hells, O Bhikkhu, so is one Uppalaka hell; and even as are twenty Uppalaka hells, O Bhikkhu, so is one Pundarika hell; and even as are twenty Pundarika hells, O Bhikkhu, so is one Paduma hell; and to the Paduma hell, O Bhikkhu, the

Bhikkhu Kolâliya is gone, having shown a hostile mind against Sâriputta and Moggallâna.' This said Bhagavat, and having said this, Sugata, the Master, furthermore spoke as follows:

'To [every] man that is born, an axe is born in his mouth, by which the fool cuts himself, when speaking bad language.

'He who praises him who is to be blamed, or blames him who is to be praised, gathers up sin in his mouth, and through that [sin] he will not find any joy.

'Trifling is the sin that [consists in] losing riches by dice; this is a greater sin that corrupts the mind against Sugatas.[2]

'Out of the one hundred thousand Nirabbudas [he goes] to thirty-six, and to five Abbudas; because he blames an Ariya he goes to hell, having employed his speech and mind badly.

'He who speaks falsely goes to hell, or he who having done something says, "I have not done it"; both these after death become equal, in another world [they are both] men guilty of a mean deed.

'He who offends an offenceless man, a pure man, free from sin, such a fool the evil [deed] reverts against, like fine dust thrown against the wind.

'He who is given to the quality of covetousness, such a one censures others in his speech, [being himself] unbelieving, stingy, wanting in affability, niggardly, given to backbiting.

'O thou foul-mouthed, false, ignoble, blasting, wicked, evil-doing, low, sinful, base-born man, do not be garrulous in this world, [else] thou wilt be an inhabitant of hell.

'Thou spreadest pollution to the misfortune [of others], thou revilest the just, committing sin [yourself], and having done many evil deeds thou wilt go to the pool [of hell] for a long time.

'For one's deeds are not lost, they will surely come [back to you], [their] master will meet with them, the fool who commits sin will feel the pain in himself in the other world.

'To the place where one is struck with iron rods, to the iron stake with sharp edges he goes; then there is [for him] food as appropriate, resembling a red-hot ball of iron.

'For those who have anything to say [there] do not say fine things, they do not approach [with pleasing faces], they do not find refuge [from their sufferings], they lie on spread embers, they enter a blazing pyre.

'Covering [them] with a net they kill [them] there with iron hammers; they go to dense darkness, for that is spread out like the body of the earth.

'Then [they enter] an iron pot, they enter a blazing pyre, for they are boiled in those [iron pots] for a long time, jumping up and down in the pyre.

'Then he who commits sin is surely boiled in a mixture of matter and blood; whatever quarter he inhabits, he becomes rotten there from coming in contact [with matter and blood].

'He who commits sin will surely be boiled in the water, the dwelling-place of worms; there it is not [possible] to get to a shore, for the adjacent lakes [of fire] are exactly alike.

'Again they enter the sharp Asipattavana with mangled limbs; having seized the tongue with a hook, the different watchmen [of hell] kill them.

'Then they enter Vetaranî,[3] that is difficult to cross and has got streams of razors with sharp edges; there the fools fall in, the evil-doers after having done evil.

'There black, mottled flocks of ravens eat them who are weeping, and dogs, jackals, great vultures, falcons, crows, tear [them].

'Miserable indeed is the life here [in hell] which the man sees that commits sin. Therefore should a man in this world for the rest of his life be strenuous, and not indolent.

'Those loads of sesamum seed which are carried in Paduma hell have been counted by the wise, they are several nahutas and five kotis and twelve hundred kotis besides.

'As long as hells are called painful in this world, so long people will have to live there for a long time; therefore amongst those who have pure, amiable, and good qualities one should always guard speech and mind.'

Notes

1. The sesamum seed is very small. On the other hand, khâris amount to sixty bushels of grain.
2. Sugata means 'One who walks well, progresses easily'. It is a common epithet for a Buddha.
3. Veteranî is a stream in the hells.

Source: From Suttanipâta III, 10 in M. Muller, ed., *SBE*, OUP 1881 Vol.X, pp.120-24.

3.2.3 Rebirth — Samsâra

The Round of Existence

The king said: 'When you speak of transmigration [rebirth],

Nāgasena, what does that mean?'

'A being born here, O king, dies here. Having died here it springs up elsewhere. Having been born there, there it dies. Having died there, it springs up elsewhere. That is what is meant by transmigration.'

'Give me an illustration.'

'It is like the case of a man, who, after eating a mango, should set the seed in the ground. From that a great tree would be produced and give fruit. And there would be no end to the succession, in that way of mango trees. . .'

Are all subject to rebirth?

The king said: 'Nāgasena, is there anyone who, after death, is not reindividualised [reborn]?'

'Some are, some are not.'

'Who are they?'

'A sinful being is reindividualised, a sinless one is not.'

'Will you be reindividualised?'

'If, when I die, I die with craving for existence in my heart, yes; but if not, no. . .'

Is this my last existence?

The king said: 'Is a man, Nāgasena, who will not be reborn, aware of the fact?'

'Yes, O king.'

'And how does he know it?'

'By the cessation of all that is cause, proximate or remote, of rebirth.'

'Give me an illustration.'

'Suppose a farmer, a great king, had ploughed and sown and filled his granary; and then, for a period should neither plough nor sow but live on the stored-up grain, or dispose of it in barter, or deal with it as he has need. Would the farmer be aware, great king, that his granary was not getting filled?'

'Yes, he would know that.'

'But how?'

'He would know that the cause, proximate and remote of the filling of the granary had ceased. Just so, with the man you spoke of. By the cessation of all that leads to rebirth, he would be conscious of having escaped his liability to it.'

What follows after him?

What thing is (a man's) own? What takes he hence?
What dogs his steps, like shadow in pursuit?

Man's merits and the sins he here hath wrought
That is the thing he owns, that takes he hence.

That dogs his steps, like shadow in pursuit.

Hence let him make good store for life elsewhere.
Sure platform in some other future world,
Rewards of virtue on good beings wait.

The cause of inequality among living men.

The king said: 'Why is it, Nâgasena, that all men are not alike but some are short-lived and some long-lived, some sickly and some healthy, some ugly and some beautiful, some without influence and some of great power, some low-born and some high-born, some stupid and some wise?'

'Why is it, O great king, that all vegetables are not alike, but some sour and some salt, and some pungent, and some acid, and some astringent, and some sweet?'

'I fancy, Sir, it is because they come from different kinds of seeds.'

'Just so, O great king, are the differences you have mentioned among men to be explained.'

For it has been said by the Blessed One: Beings, O brahmin, have each their own karma, are inheritors of karma, belong to the tribe of their karma, are relatives by karma, have each their karma as their protective over-lord. It is karma that divides them up into low and high and the like divisions.

Sources:
1. From the Milanda Pañha III:6.9 in M. Muller, ed. *SBE,* OUP 1886, Vol. XXXV, p.120.
2. From the Milanda Pañha II:1.6 in op.cit. p.50.
3. From the Milanda Pañha II:2.2. Ibid. p.65.
4. From Samyatta III:1.4 in Mrs Rhys Davids, *Kindred*Sayings, Pali Text Society 1917, Vol.I p.98.
5. From the Milanda Pañha III:4.2 in M. Muller, ed. op.cit. pp.101-2.

Fruitful and Barren Karma 3.2.4

(a)
Monks, there are three originating causes of action. What three? *Lust, malice and delusion.*

An act performed in lust, born of lust, originating in lust, arising from lust has its fruit wherever one's personal self is reborn. Wherever that act comes to fruition, there one experiences the fruit thereof, whether it come in this very life or in some other phase of existence.

An act performed in *malice*. . .an act performed under *delusion*. . . has its fruit in like manner. . .

Just as seed that are unbroken, not rotten, unspoiled by wind and heat, capable of sprouting, and well embedded in a good field, planted in properly prepared soil — if the sky rain down steadily those seeds come to growth, increase, abundance; even so, monks, whatsoever act is performed in lust. . .in malice. . .under delusion. . . one experiences the fruit thereof, whether it come into bearing in this very life or in some other phase of existence.

There, monks, are the three originating causes of action.

(b)
Monks, there are these three originating causes of action. What three?

Freedom from lust, malice and delusion.

An act not performed in lust, not born of lust, not originating in lust, not arising from lust — since lust has vanished, that act is abandoned, cut off at the root, made like a palm-tree stump, made unable to come again, of a nature not to arise again in future time.

An act *not* performed in malice. . .*not* performed under delusion . . .is cut off at the root. . .of a nature not to arise again in future time.

An act *not* performed in malice. . .*not* performed under delusion . . .is cut off at the root. . .of a nature not to arise again in future time.

Suppose seeds that are unbroken, not rotten, unspoiled by wind and heat, capable of sprouting, well embedded, and a man burns them with fire, and having done so reduces them to ashes. Having done that he winnows the ashes in a strong wind or lets them be carried off by a swiftly flowing stream — those seeds, monks, would be cut off at the root, made like a palm-tree stump, made unable to become again, of a nature not to arise again in future time. . .

Just so, monks, an act not performed in lust, not performed in malice, not performed under delusion. . .is of a nature not to arise again in future time.

These indeed, monks, are the originating causes of actions.

> From lust or malice or delusion born,
> A deed, or great or small, performed by fools
> Just here is felt: no other ground is seen
> For its fulfilment. Wise monks should eschew
> Lust, malice and delusion for this cause,
> Get knowledge and forsake all ways of woe.

Source: From Anguttñara-Nikâya I: 134-35 in F.L. Woodward, *Gradual Sayings,* Pali Text Society, 1932, Vol.I pp.117-9.

3.2.5 There is no Ego

1. [25] Now Milinda the king went up to where the venerable Nâgasena was, and addressed him with the greetings and compliments of friendship and courtesy, and took his seat respectfully apart. And Nâgasena reciprocated his courtesy, so that the heart of the king was propitiated.

And Milinda began by asking, 'How is your Reverence known, and what, Sir, is your name?'

'I am known as Nâgasena, O king, and it is by that name that my brethren in the faith address me. But although parents, O king, give such a name as Nâgasena, or Sûrasena, or Vîrasena, or Sîhasena, yet this, Sire — Nâgasena and so on — is only a generally understood term, a designation in common use. For there is no permanent individuality (no soul) involved in the matter.'

Then Milinda called upon the Yonakas and the brethren to witness: 'This Nâgasena says there is no permanent individuality (no soul) implied in his name. Is it now even possible to approve him in that?' And turning to Nâgasena, he said: 'If, most reverend Nâgasena, there be no permanent individuality (no soul) involved in the matter, who is it, pray, who gives to you members of the Order your robes and food and lodging and necessaries for the sick? Who is it who enjoys such things when given? Who is it who lives a life of righteousness? Who is it who devotes himself to meditation? Who is it who attains to the goal of the Excellent Way, to the Nirvâna of Arahatship? And who is it who destroys living creatures? Who is it who takes what is not his own? Who is it who lives an evil life of worldly lusts, who speaks lies, who drinks strong drink, who (in a word) commits any one of the five sins which work out their bitter fruit even in this life? If that be so there is neither merit nor demerit: there is neither doer nor causer of good or evil deeds; there is neither fruit nor result of good or evil Karma.

[26] — If, most reverend Nâgasena, we are to think that were a man to kill you there would be no murder, then it follows that there are no real masters or teachers in your Order, and that your ordinations are void. — You tell me that your brethren in the Order are in the habit of addressing you as Nâgasena. Now what is that Nâgasena? Do you mean to say that the hair is Nâgasena?'

'I don't say that, great king.'

'Or the hairs on the body, perhaps?'

'Certainly not.'

'Or is it the nails, the teeth, the skin, the flesh, the nerves, the bones, the marrow, the kidneys, the heart, the liver, the abdomen, the spleen, the lungs, the larger intestines, the lower intestines, the stomach, the faeces, the bile, the phlegm, the pus, the blood, the sweat, the fat, the tears, the serum, the saliva, the mucus, the oil that lubricates the joints, the urine, or the brain, or any or all of these, that is Nâgasena?'[1]

And to each of these he answered no.

'Is it the outward form then (Rûpa) that is Nâgasena, or the sensations (Vedanâ), or the ideas (Saññâ), or the confections (the constituent elements of character, Samkhârâ), or the consciousness (Viññâna), that is Nâgasena?'

And to each of these also he answered no.

'Then is it all these Skandhas combined that are Nâgasena?'

'No! great king.'

'But is there anything outside the five Skandhas that is Nâgasena?'
And still he answered no.

'Then thus, ask as I may, I can discover no Nâgasena. Nâgasena is a mere empty sound. Who then is the Nâgasena that we see before us? It is a falsehood that your reverence has spoken, an untruth!'

And the venerable Nâgasena said to Milinda the king: 'You, Sire, have been brought up in great luxury, as beseems your noble birth. If you were to walk this dry weather on the hot and sandy ground, trampling underfoot the gritty, gravelly grains of the hard sand, your feet would hurt you. And as your body would be in pain, your mind would be disturbed, and you would experience a sense of bodily suffering. How then did you come, on foot, or in a chariot?'

'I did not come, Sir, on foot [27]. I came in a carriage.'

'Then if you came, Sire, in a carriage, explain to me what that is. Is it the pole that is the chariot?'

'I did not say that.'

'Is it the axle that is the chariot?'

'Certainly not.'

'Is it the wheels, or the framework, or the ropes, or the yoke, or the spokes of the wheels, or the goad, that are the chariot?'[2]

And to all these he still answered no.

'Then is it all these parts of it that are the chariot?'

'No, Sir.'

'But is there anything outside them that is the chariot?'

And still he answered no.

'Then thus, ask as I may, I can discover no chariot. Chariot is a mere empty sound. What then is the chariot that you say you came in? It is a falsehood that your Majesty has spoken, an untruth! There is no such thing as a chariot! You are king over all India, a mighty monarch. Of whom then are you afraid that you speak untruth?" And he called upon the Yonakas and the brethren to witness, saying: 'Milinda the king here has said that he came by carriage. But when asked in that case to explain what the carriage was, he is unable to establish what he averred. Is it, forsooth, possible to approve him in that?'

When he had thus spoken the five hundred Yonakas shouted their applause, and said to the king: 'Now let your Majesty get out of that if you can.'

And Milinda the king replied to Nâgasena, and said: 'I have spoken no untruth, reverend Sir. It is on account of its having all these things — the pole, and the axle, the wheels, and the framework, the ropes, the yoke, the spokes, and the goad — that it comes under the generally understood term, the designation in common use, of "chariot".'

'Very good! Your Majesty has rightly grasped the meaning of "chariot". And just even so it is on account of all those things you questioned me about — [28] the thirty-two kinds of organic matter in a human body, and the five constituent elements of being — that I come under the generally understood term, the designation in common use, of 'Nagasena".'

Notes

1. The whole question and answer are repeated in the text for each physical element.
2. Same remark for each part of the chariot.

Source: Milinda Pañha II: 1.25-28, in M. Muller, ed., *SBE,* OUP 1886, Vol.XXXV, pp.40-45.

Two Kinds of Quest   3.2.6

The venerable Ânanda spoke thus to the Lord:

'Lord, this hermitage of the brahman Rammaka is not far; the hermitage of the brahman Rammaka is lovely, Lord; the hermitage of the brahman Rammaka is beautiful, Lord. It were good, Lord, if out of compassion, the Lord were to approach the hermitage of the brahman Rammaka.' The Lord consented by becoming silent. Then the Lord approached the hermitage of the brahman Rammaka. At that time a number of monks came to be sitting down and talking *dhamma* in the hermitage of the brahman Rammaka. Then the Lord stood outside the porch waiting for the talk to finish. Then the Lord, knowing that the talk had finished, coughed and knocked on the bar of the door; those monks opened the door to the Lord. Then the Lord, having entered the hermitage of the brahman Rammaka, sat down on the appointed seat. As he was sitting down, the Lord said to the monks:

'As you were sitting down just now, what was your talk about, monks? What was your talk that was interrupted?:

'Lord, our talk that was interrupted was about the Lord himself; then he arrived.'

'It were good, monks, that when young men of family such as you who have gone forth from home into homelessness out of faith are gathered together that you talk about *dhamma*. When you are gathered together, monks, there are two things to be done: either talk about *dhamma* or the ariyan [noble] silence.

'These, monks, are the two quests: the ariyan quest and the unariyan quest. And what, monks, is the unariyan quest? As to this, monks, someone, liable by birth because of self, seeks what is likewise liable to birth; being liable to ageing because of self, seeks what is likewise liable to ageing; being liable to decay because of self. . .being liable to dying because of self. . .being liable to sorrow because of self. . .being liable to stain because of self, seeks what is likewise liable to stain. And what, monks, would you say is liable to birth? Sons and wife, monks, are liable to birth, women-slaves and men-slaves are liable to birth, goats and sheep are liable to birth, cooks and swine are liable to birth, elephants, cows, horses and mares are liable to birth, gold and silver are liable to birth. These attachments, monks, are liable to birth; yet this [man], enslaved, infatuated, addicted, being liable to birth because of self, seeks what is likewise liable to birth.

'And what, monks, would you say is liable to ageing? Sons and wife, monks, are liable to ageing, women-slaves and men-slaves. . . goats and sheep. . .cocks and swine. . .elephants, cows, horses and mares. . .gold and silver are liable to ageing. These attachments, monks, are liable to ageing; yet this [man], enslaved, infatuated, addicted, being liable to ageing because of self, seeks what is likewise liable to ageing.

'And what, monks, would you say is liable to disease? Sons and wife, monks, are liable to disease; women-slaves and men-slaves. . . goats and sheep. . .cocks and swine. . .elephants, cows, horses and mares are liable to disease. These attachments, monks, are liable to disease. . .seeks what is likewise liable to disease.

'And what, monks, would you say is liable to dying? Sons and wife, monks, are liable to dying, women-slaves and men-slaves. . . goats and sheep. . .cocks and swine. . .elephants, cows, horses and mares are liable to dying. These attachments, monks, are liable to dying. . .seeks what is likewise liable to dying.

'And what, monks, would you say is liable to sorrow? Sons and wife, monks, are liable to sorrow, women-slaves and men-slaves. . . goats and sheep. . .cocks and swine. . .elephants, cows, horses and mares are liable to sorrow. These attachments, monks, are liable to sorrow. . .seeks what is likewise liable to sorrow.

'And what, monks, do you say is liable to stain? Sons and wife, monks, are liable to stain, women-slaves and men-slaves. . .goats and sheep. . .cocks and swine. . .elephants, cows, horses and gold and silver are liable to stain. These attachments, monks, are liable to stain; yet this [man], enslaved, infatuated, addicted, being liable to stain because of self, seeks what is likewise liable to stain. This, monks, is the unariyan quest.

'And what, monks, is the ariyan quest? As to this, monks, someone, being liable at birth because of self, having known the peril in what is likewise liable to birth, seeks the unborn, the uttermost security from the bonds — nibbạna; being liable to dying because of self, having known the peril in what is likewise liable to dying, seeks the undying, the uttermost security from the bonds — nibbāna; being liable to sorrow because of self, having known the peril in what is likewise liable to sorrow, seeks the unsorrowing, the uttermost security from the bonds — nibbāna; being liable to stain because of self, having known the peril in what is likewise liable to stain, seeks the stainless, the uttermost security from the bonds — nibbāna. This, monks, is the ariyan quest.'

Source: From Majjhima-Nikâya I: 161-164 in I.B. Horner, *Middle Length Sayings*, Pali Text Society, 1954, Vol.I, pp.204-7.

Good Conduct 3.2.7

[This not too systematic text contains precepts common to all Buddhists and precepts for monks only. Here appears the moral ideal proposed by Buddhism to people.]

1. 'Now wherein, Vâsettha, is one's conduct good?'

'Herein, O Vâsettha, that putting away the *murder* of that which lives, he abstains from destroying life. The cudgel and the sword he lays aside; and, full of modesty and pity, he is compassionate and kind to all creatures that have life!

'This is the kind of goodness that he has.

2. 'Putting away the *theft* of that which is not his, he abstains from taking anything not given. He takes only what is given, therewith is he content, and he passes his life in honesty and purity of heart!

'This, too, is the kind of goodness that he has.

3. 'Putting away *unchastity,* he lives a life of chastity and purity,

averse to the low habit of sexual intercourse.
'This, too. . .

4. 'Putting away *lying*, he abstains from speaking falsehood. He speaks truth, from the truth he never swerves; faithful and trustworthy, he injures not his fellow man by deceit.
'This, too. . .

5. 'Putting away *slander*, he abstains from calumny. What he hears here he repeats not elsewhere to raise a quarrel against the people here: what he hears elsewhere he repeats not here to raise a quarrel against the people there. Thus he lives as a binder together of those who are divided, an encourager of those who are friends, a peace-maker, a lover of peace, impassioned for peace, a speaker of words that make for peace.
'This, too. . .

6. 'Putting away *bitterness of speech*, he abstains from harsh language. Whatever word is humane, pleasant to the ear, lovely, reaching to the heart, urbane, pleasing to the people, beloved of the people — such are the words he speaks.
'This, too. . .

7. 'Putting away *foolish talk* he abstains from vain conversation. In season he speaks; he speaks that which is; he speaks fact; he utters good doctrine; he utters good discipline; he speaks, and at the right time that which redounds to profit, is well-grounded, is well-defined, and is full of wisdom.
'This, too. . .

8. 'He refrains from *injuring* any herb or any creature. He takes but one meal a day; abstaining from food at night time, or at the wrong time. He abstains from dancing, singing, music, and theatrical shows. He abstains from wearing, using, or adorning himself with garlands, and scents, and unguents, and he abstains from lofty couches and large beds.
'This, too. . .

9. 'He abstains from the getting of silver or gold. He abstains from the getting of grain uncooked. He abstains from the getting of flesh that is raw. He abstains from the getting of any woman or girl. He abstains from the getting of bondmen or bondwomen. He abstains from the getting of sheep or goats. He abstains from the getting of fowls or swine. He abstains from the getting of elephants, cattle, horses, and mares. He abstains from the getting of fields or lands.
'This, too. . .

10. 'He refrains from carrying out those commissions on which

messengers can be sent. He refrains from buying and selling. He abstains from tricks with false weights, alloyed metals, or false measures. He abstains from bribery, cheating, fraud and crooked ways.

'This, too. . .

11. 'He refrains from maiming, killing, imprisoning, highway robbery, plundering villages or obtaining money by threats of violence.

'This, too. . .'

Source: From the Tevijja Sutta I: 1-11 in M. Muller ed., *SBE,* OUP 1881, Vol.XI, pp.189-91.

Show Me an Island   3.2.8

[This short text sums up the search of a man whom material possessions do not satisfy, and indicates the way of 'depossession', which in practice consists in following the Buddha and becoming a mendicant monk.]

1. For those who stand in the middle of the water,
    In the formidable stream that has set in,
    For those who are overcome by decay and death,
    Tell thou me of an island that this [sorrow] may not again
        come on.

2. For those who stand in the middle of the water,
    In the formidable stream that has set in,
    For those who are overcome by decay and death,
    I will tell You of an island, O Kappa.

3. This matchless island:
    Possessing nothing and grasping after nothing,
    I call NIBBÂNA, the destruction of decay and death.

4. Those who, having understood this, are thoughtful and calm,
    Because they have perceived the Dhamma,
    Do not fall into the power of Mara.[1]

Note

1. Mâra is the personification of evil, a kind of Buddhist Satan.

Source: From Suttanipâta V: 11 in M. Muller ed., *SBE*, OUP 1881, Vol.X, pp.203-4.

3.3   THE SANGHA

Scrutiny of Admission to the Order   3.3.1

[In the first period of Buddha's preaching, admission into the
Sangha took place with the Master simply saying: Ehi, Come!
Afterwards conditions and ceremonies were progressively introduced,
because of the great number and diversity of the candidates.]

1. Are you afflicted with the following diseases: leprosy, boils, dry
   leprosy, consumption, fits?
2. Are you a human being?
3. Are you a male?
4. Are you a free man?
5. Have you debts?
6. Are you not in the royal service?
7. Have your father and mother given their consent?
8. Are you fully twenty years old?
9. Are your alms-bowl and your robes in due state?
10. What is your name?
11. What is your upajjhaya's name?

Comments:
1. Living in common, the monks had to discard any danger of
   infection.
2. Stories were told of non-human beings which had taken a
   human form to be admitted, trained and liberated.
3. The Buddha, even after having agreed to the foundation of a
   monastic branch for women, stressed very strongly a complete
   separation between monks and nuns.
4. A slave was not free to decide; he needed his master's
   permission.
5. Entering the Order could not be a way to evade financial
   obligations.
6. If too great a number of persons had left the military or civil
   service, the administration of the kingdom would have been
   perturbed. This was not an imaginary danger in certain regions.
7. The parents' authority, even over grown-up sons, remained
   great.

8. This was the minimum age, not to enter but to be admitted to the vows however, the Founder himself had occasionally received younger candidates.
9. They had to be offered by the candidate, his parents or benefactors.
10. Notwithstanding the liberty, current in that time, of changing one's name, the candidate had to indicate his 'official' name in the Order.
11. The name of the upajjhaya, preceptor and spiritual master, was a guarantee of the right preparation of the candidate.

Source: From the Mahâvagga, I: 76 in M. Muller ed., *SBE,* OUP 1881, Vol.XIII, p.230.

3.3.2 The Ten Precepts

[Here are reported, in their most compressed form, the ten cardinal precepts of Buddhism. They do not apply equally to all the members. The first five bind all Buddhists; the following three bind the monks and some pious laymen who observe them freely; the last two concern the monks only.]

I prescribe, O monks, ten precepts for the novices. . .

Abstinence from destroying life.
Abstinence from stealing.
Abstinence from impurity.
Abstinence from lying.
Abstinence from strong drinks and intoxicating liquors, which cause stupidity.
Abstinence from eating at forbidden times.[1]
Abstinence from dancing, singing and seeing spectacles.
Abstinence from garlands, scents, unguents, ornaments and finery.
Abstinence from high or broad beds.
Abstinence from accepting gold and silver.

Note

1. The right times for eating are: a very light breakfast in the morning and the principal meal before noon.

Source: Mahâvagga 1: 56 in M. Muller, ed., *SBE,* OUP 1881, Vol.XIII, p.211.

Four Fundamental Attitudes of a Noble Disciple 3.3.3

[The first three attitudes are merely the extension of the short essential formula of commitment to Buddhism; Buddha, Dhamma, Sangha; the fourth means in brief all the exercises which lead to Nirvâna — negatively, abandoning all passions; positively, striving towards final concentration (samâdhi).]

'Monks, although a rajah, a roller of the wheel, holding supreme lordship and dominion over four continents, on the break-up of body is reborn after death in the Happy Lot, in the Heaven World, in the Company of the Devas of the Thirty-Three; although he spends his time there in [heavenly] Nandana Grove, attended by a troop of nymphs, supplied and provided with, surrounded by, celestial pleasures of sense, yet is he not released from Purgatory, he is not released from [birth in] the womb of an animal, he is not released from the realm of ghosts, he is not released from Hell, the Way of Woe, the Downfall.

'Monks, although an Ariyan disciple lives on gathered scraps, though he be clothed in rags, yet if he is possessed of four things then he is released from Purgatory, he is released from [birth in] the womb of an animal, he is released from the realm of ghosts, he is released from Hell, the Way of Woe, from the Downfall. What are the four things?

'Herein, monks, the Ariyan disciple is possessed of unwavering *loyalty to the Buddha;* [He has faith that] He is the Exalted One, Arahant, a fully Enlightened One, perfect in knowledge and practice, a Happy One, world-knower, unsurpassed charioteer of men to be tamed, teacher of devas and mankind, a Buddha, an Exalted One.

'He is possessed of unwavering *loyalty to the Dhamma,* thus: well proclaimed by the Exalted One is the *Dhamma,* seen in this very life, a thing not involving time, inviting one to come and see, leading onward, to be known for themselves by the wise.

'He is possessed of unwavering *faith in the Order,* thus: walking righteously is the Exalted One's Order, walking uprightly, walking in the right way, walking dutifully is the Exalted One's Order of Disciples: namely, the four pairs of men, the eight sorts of men. That is the Exalted One's Order of Disciples, Worthy of honour are they, worthy of reverence, worthy of offerings, worthy of salutations with clasped hands — a field of merit unsurpassed for the world.

'Then he is possessed of the *virtues loved by the Ariyans,* virtues unbroken, whole, unspotted, untarnished, giving freedom, praised by the wise: virtues untainted [by craving or delusion], which lead to concentration of the mind.

'Such are the four things he is possessed of.

'Monks, there is the winning of four continents, and there is the winning of the four things. But to win four continents is not worth a sixteenth part of the winning of the four things.'

Source: From Samyutta-Nikâya LV: 11, 1 in F.L. Woodward, *Kindred Sayings,* Pali Text Society 1930, Vol.V, p.343.

3.3.4 The Wise and Thoughtful Bhikkhu

[This short text describes very well the interior dispositions of self-control, destruction of passions, meditative striving, all of which lead to the 'destruction of ignorance' and to Nirvâna.]

11. 'Let not the wise and thoughtful Bhikkhu be afraid of the adversaries, even having seen many dangers from them; further he will overcome other dangers while seeking what is good.

12. 'Touched by sickness and hunger let him endure cold and excessive heat, let him, touched by them in many ways, and being houseless, make strong exertions.

13. 'Let him not commit theft, let him not speak falsely, let him touch friendly what is feeble or strong, what he acknowledges to be the agitation of the mind, let him drive that off as a partisan of Tanhâ (i.e. Mâra).

14. 'Let him not fall into the power of anger and arrogance; having dug up the root of these, let him live, and let him overcome both what is pleasant and what is unpleasant.

15. 'Guided by wisdom, taking delight in what is good, let him scatter those dangers, let him overcome discontent in his distant dwelling, let him overcome the four causes of lamentation.

16. 'What shall I eat, or where shall I eat? – he lay indeed uncomfortably [last night] – where shall I lie this night? Let the Sekha who wanders about houseless subdue these lamentable doubts.

17. 'Having had in [due] time both food and clothes, let him know moderation in this world for the sake of happiness; guarded in these [things] and wandering restrained in the village let him, even

[if he be] irritated, not speak harsh words.

18. 'Let him be with down-cast eyes, and not prying, devoted to meditation, very watchful; having acquired equanimity let him with a composed mind cut off the seat of doubt, and misbehaviour.

19. 'Urged on by words [of his teachers] let him be thoughtful and rejoice [at this urging], let him break stubbornness in his fellow-students, let him utter propitious words and not unseasonable, let him not think detractingly of others.

20. 'And then the five impurities in the world, the subjection of which he must learn thoughtfully — let him overcome passion for form, sound and taste, smell and touch.

21. 'Let the Bhikkhu subdue his wish for these Dhammas and be thoughtful, and with his mind well liberated, then in time he will, reflecting upon Dhamma, and having become intent upon one object, destroy darkness.' So said Bhagavat.

Source: From Suttanipâta IV: 16, 11-21 in M. Muller ed., *SBE*, OUP 1881,' Vol.X, pp.181-3.

The Welfare of a Community   3.3.5

[These rules, inspired by common wisdom and experience, describe the ideal image of a community. Obviously the text is a synthesis of teaching given on different occasions by the Founder or the community leaders who followed him.]

The Blessed One arose, and went to the Service Hall; and when he was seated he addressed the Brethren, and said:

6. 'I will teach you, O mendicants, *seven conditions of the welfare of a community*. Listen well and attend, and I will speak.'

'Even so, Lord', said the Brethren, in assent, to the Blessed One; and he spoke as follows:

'So long, O mendicants, as the brethren meet together in full and frequent assemblies — so long as they meet together in concord, and rise in concord, and carry out in concord the duties of the order — so long as the brethren shall establish nothing that has not been already prescribed, and abrogate nothing that has been already established, and act in accordance with the rules of the order as now laid down — so long as the brethren honour and esteem and revere and support the elders of experience and long standing, the fathers and leaders of the order, and hold it a point of duty to hearken to their words — so long as the brethren fall not under the influence of that craving which, springing up within them, would give rise to renewed existence — so long as the brethren delight in a life of solitude — so long as the brethren so train their minds that good and holy men shall come to them, and those who have come shall dwell at ease — so long may the brethren be expected, not to decline, but to prosper. So long as these seven conditions shall continue to exist among the brethren, so long as they are well-instructed in these conditions, so long may the brethren be expected not to decline, but to prosper.

7. '*Seven other conditions of welfare* will I teach you, O brethren. Listen well, and attend, and I will speak.'

And on their expressing their assent, he spoke as follows:

'So long as the brethren shall not engage in, or be fond of, or be connected with business — so long as the brethren shall not be in the habit of, or be fond of, or be partakers in idle talk — so long as the brethren shall not be addicted to, or be fond of, or indulge in slothfulness — so long as the brethren shall neither have, nor fall under the influence of, sinful desires — so long as the brethren shall not become the friends, companions, or intimates of sinners — so long as the brethren shall not come to a stop on their way [to Nirvana] because they have attained to any lesser thing — so long may the brethren be expected not to decline, but to prosper.

'So long as these conditions shall continue to exist among the brethren, so long as they are instructed in these conditions, so long may the brethren be expected not to decline, but to prosper.

8. '*Seven other conditions of welfare* will I teach you, O brethren. Listen well, and attend, and I will speak.'

And on their expressing their assent, he spoke as follows:

'So long as the brethren shall be full of faith, modest in heart, afraid of sin, full of learning, strong in energy, active in mind, and full of wisdom, so long may the brethren be expected not to decline but to prosper.

'So long as these conditions shall continue to exist among the brethren, so long as they are instructed in these conditions, so long may the brethren be expected not to decline but to prosper.

9. '*Seven other conditions of welfare* will I teach you, O brethren. Listen well, and attend, and I will speak.'

And on their expressing their assent, he spoke as follows:

'So long as the brethren shall exercise themselves in the sevenfold higher wisdom, that is to say, in mental activity, search after truth, energy, joy, peace, earnest contemplation, and equanimity of mind, so long may the brethren be expected not to decline, but to prosper.

'So long as these conditions shall continue to exist among the brethren, so long as they are instructed in these conditions, so long may the brethren be expected not to decline, but to prosper.

10. '*Seven other conditions of welfare* will I teach you, O brethren. Listen well, and attend, and I will speak.'

And on their expressing their assent, he spoke as follows:

'So long as the brethren shall exercise themselves in the sevenfold perception due to earnest thought, that is to say, the perception of impermanency, of non-individuality, of corruption, of the danger of sin, of sanctification, of purity of heart, of Nirvâna, so long may the brethren be expected not to decline, but to prosper.

'So long as these conditions shall continue to exist among the brethren, so long as they are instructed in these conditions, so long may the brethren be expected not to decline, but to prosper.

11. '*Six conditions of welfare* will I teach you, O brethren. Listen well, and attend, and I will speak.'

And on their expressing their assent, he spoke as follows:

'So long as the brethren shall persevere in kindness of action, speech and thought amongst the saints, both in public and in private — so long as they shall divide without partiality, and share in common with the upright and the holy, all such things as they receive in accordance with the just provisions of the order, down even to the mere contents of a begging bowl — so long as the brethren shall live among the saints in the practice, both in public and in private, of those virtues which (unbroken, intact, unspotted, unblemished) are productive of freedom, and praised by the wise; which are untarnished by the desire of future life, or by the belief in the efficacy of outward acts; and which are conducive to high and holy thoughts — so long as the brethren shall live among the saints, cherishing, both in public and in private, that noble and saving faith which leads to the complete destruction of the sorrow of him who acts according to it — so long may the brethren be expected not to decline, but to prosper.

'So long as these six conditions shall continue to exist among the brethren, so long as they are instructed in these six conditions, so long may the brethren be expected not to decline, but to prosper.'

Source: From Mahâparinibbânasutta 1.6-11 in M. Muller, ed., *SBE*, OUP 1881, Vol.XI, pp.6-11.

3.4 THE MAGGA

3.4.1 The True Ploughing

[A good example of occasional teaching. The Buddha actually answers a ploughman who accuses him of laziness. The answer is 'I am also a ploughman, a spiritual one. . .' The text enumerates all the dispositions which are essential for the progress towards Nirvâna.]

2. Faith is the seed, penance the rain,
   Understanding my yoke and plough,
   Modesty the pole of the plough, mind the tie,
   Thoughtfulness my ploughshare and goad.

3. I am guarded in the body, guarded in speech,
   I am temperate in food,
   I make truth to cut away (the weeds).
   Sympathy is my deliverance.

4. Exertion is my beast of burden,
   Carrying me to Nirvâna,
   He goes without turning back
   To the place where having gone, one does not grieve.

5. So this ploughing is ploughed.
   It bears the fruit of Immortality,[1]
   Having ploughed this ploughing,
   One is freed from all pain.

Note
1. Immortality is another name for Nirvâna.

Source: From Suttanipâta 1:4.2 in M. Muller, ed., *SBE*, OUP 1881, Vol.X, pp.12-13.

3.4.2 Reflection on the Worthlessness of the Body

For as the body when dead is repulsive, so is it also when alive; but on account of the concealment afforded by an adventitious adornment, its repulsiveness escapes notice. The body is in reality a collection of over three hundred bones, and is framed into a whole by means of one hundred and eighty joints. It is held together by nine hundred tendons, and overlaid by nine hundred muscles, and has an outside envelope of moist cuticle covered by an epidermis full of pores, through which there is an incessant oozing and trickling, as if from a kettle of fat. It is a prey to vermin, the seat of disease, and subject to all manner of miseries. Through its nine apertures it is always discharging matter, like a ripe boil. Matter is secreted from the two eyes, wax from the ears, snot from the nostrils, and from the mouth issue food, bile, phlegm and blood, and from the two lower orifices of the body faeces and urine, while from the ninety-nine thousand pores of the skin an unclean sweat exudes, attracting black flies and other insects.

Were even a king in triumphal progress to neglect the use of tooth-sticks, mouth-rinses, anointings of the head, baths and inner and outside garments, and other means for beautifying the person, he would become as uncouth and unkempt as the moment he was born, and would in no wise differ in bodily offensiveness from the low-caste caṇḍāla whose occupation is to remove dead flowers. Thus in respect of its uncleanness, malodour, and disgusting offensiveness, the person of a king does not differ from that of a caṇḍāla. However, when, with the help of tooth-sticks, mouth-rinses, and various ablutions, men have cleansed their teeth, and the rest of their persons, and with manifold garments have covered their nakedness, and have anointed themselves with many-coloured and fragrant unguents, and adorned themselves with flowers and ornaments, they find themselves able to believe in an 'I' and a 'mine'. Accordingly, it is on account of the concealment afforded by this adventitious adornment that people fail to recognize the essential repulsiveness of their bodies, and that men find pleasure in women, and women in men. In reality, however, there is not the smallest just reason for being pleased.

A proof of this is the fact that when any part of the body becomes detached, as, for instance, the hair of the head, hair of the body, nails, teeth, phlegm, snot, faeces, or urine, people are unwilling so much as to touch it, and are distressed at, ashamed of, and loathe it. But in respect of what remains, though that is likewise repulsive, yet men are so wrapped in blindness, and infatuated by a passionate fondness for their own selves, that they believe it to be something desirable, lovely, lasting, pleasant and an Ego.

Source: From Suttanipâta I: 11, vv.1-14 in H.C. Warren, *Buddhism in Translations,* Harvard University Press 1963, pp.298-9.

3.4.3 The Four 'Spiritual Dwellings'

[A man who admits passions not only does harm to himself but, very often, to other persons as well. On the contrary, if somebody tries to manifest goodwill to all beings, and finally tries to reach an undisturbed state of mind, he can gain much on his way to liberation. This exercise comes normally after the meditation on material objects and before the highest meditations.]

1. The meditating Buddhist lets his mind pervade one quarter of the world with thoughts of *Love,* and so the second and so the third and so the fourth. And thus the whole wide world, above, below, around and everywhere, does he continue to pervade with heart of Love, far-reaching, grown great, and beyond measure.

2. 'Just, Vâsettha, as a mighty trumpeter makes himself heard — and that without difficulty — in all the four directions; even so of all things that have shape or life, there is not one that he passes by or leaves aside, but regards them all with mind set free and deep-felt love.

'Verily this, Vâsettha, is the way to the state of union with Brahmâ.

3. 'And he lets his mind pervade one quarter of the world with thoughts of *pity, sympathy and equanimity,* and so the second and so the third, and so the fourth. And thus the whole wide world, above, below, around and everywhere, does he continue to pervade with heart of pity, sympathy and equanimity, far-reaching, grown great, and beyond measure.

4. 'Just, Vâsettha, as a mighty trumpeter makes himself heard — and that without difficulty — in all the four directions; even so of all things that have shape or life, there is not one that he passes by or leaves aside, but regards them all with mind set free, and deep-felt pity, sympathy and equanimity.

'Verily this, Vâsettha, is the way to a state of union with Brahmâ.

5. 'Now what think you, Vâsettha, will the Bhikkhu who lives thus be in possession of women and of wealth, or will he not?'

'He will not, Gotama!'

'Will he be full of anger, or free from anger?'

'He will be free from anger, Gotama!'

'Will his mind be full of malice, or free from malice?'

'Free from malice, Gotama!'

'Will his mind be sinful, or pure?'

'It will be pure, Gotama!'

'Will he have self-mastery, or will he not?'

'Surely he will, Gotama!'

6. 'Then you say, Vâsettha, that the Bhikkhu is free from household cares, and that Brahmâ is free from household cares. Is there then agreement and likeness between the Bhikkhu and Brahmâ?'

'There is, Gotama!'

7. 'Very good, Vâsettha. Then in sooth, Vâsettha, that the Bhikkhu who is free from household cares should after death, when the body is dissolved, become united with Brahmâ, who is the same — such a condition of things is every way possible.

8. 'And so you say, Vâsettha, that the Bhikkhu is free from anger, and free from malice, pure in mind, and master of himself; and that Brahmâ is free from anger, and free from malice, pure in mind, and master of himself. Then in sooth, Vâsettha, that the Bhikku who is free from anger, free from malice, pure in mind, and master of himself should after death, when the body is dissolved, become united with Brahmâ, who is the same — such a condition of things is every way possible!'

9. When he had thus spoken, the young Brahmans Vasettha and Bhâradvâga addressed the Blessed One and said:

'Most excellent, Lord, are the words of thy mouth, most excellent! Just as if a man were to set up that which is thrown down, or were to reveal that which is hidden away, or were to point out the right road to him who has gone astray, or were to bring a lamp into the darkness, so that those who have eyes can see the external forms; — just even so, Lord, has the truth been made known to us, in many a figure by the Blessed One. And we, even we, betake ourselves, Lord, to the Blessed One as our refuge, to the Truth, and to the Brotherhood. May the Blessed One accept us as disciples, as true believers, from this day forth, as long as life endures!'[1]

Note

1. This is the stereotyped formula of approbation and petition for candidates.

Source: From Tevijja Sutta III: 1-9 in M. Muller, ed., *SBE*, OUP 1881, Vol.XI, pp.201-3.

3.4.4 The Way to the Highest Meditations

Monks, there are these five strands of sense-pleasures. What are the five? Material shapes cognisable by the eye, alluring, agreeable, pleasant, liked, connected with sense-pleasures, enticing; sounds cognisable by the ear. . .smells cognisable by the nose. . .tastes cognisable by the tongue. . .touches cognisable by the body, alluring, agreeable, pleasant, liked, connection with sense-pleasures. Monks, those recluses or brahmans who enjoy these five strands of sense-pleasures enslaved and infatuated by them, addicted to them, not seeing the peril in them, not aware of the escape from them — these should be told: 'You have come to calamity, you have come to misfortune and are ones to be done to by the Evil One as he wills. Monks, it is like a deer living in a forest who might be lying caught on a heap of snares — this may be said of it: It has come to calamity, it has come to misfortune, it is one to be done to by the trapper as he wills, for when the trapper comes it will not be able to go away as it wishes. Even so, monks, those recluses or brahmans. . .are ones to be done to by the Evil One as he wills.

Monks, those recluses or brahmans who enjoy these five strands of sense-pleasures, not enslaved, not infatuated by them, not addicted to them, seeing the peril in them, aware of the escape from them — these should be told: You have not come to calamity, you have not come to misfortune, you are not ones to be done to by the Evil One as he wills. Monks, it is like a deer living in a forest who might lie down on a heap of snares but is not caught by it — this may be said of it: It has not come to calamity, it has not come to misfortune, it is not one to be done to by the trapper as he wills, for when the trapper comes it will be able to go away as it wishes. Even so, monks, those recluses or brahmans. . .are not ones to be done to by the Evil One as he wills.

Monks, it is like a deer living in a forest, roaming the forest slopes, who walks confidently, stands confidently, sits down confidently, goes to sleep confidently. What is the reason for this? Monks, it is out of the trapper's reach. Even so, monks, a monk, aloof from pleasures of the senses, aloof from unskilled states of mind, enters on and abides in the *first meditation* which is accompanied by initial thought and discursive thought, is born of aloofness, and is rapturous and joyful. Monks, this monk is called one who has put a darkness round Māra, and having blotted out Māra's vision so that it has no range, goes unseen by the Evil One:

And again, monks, a monk, by allaying initial and discursive thought, his mind subjectively tranquillised and fixed on one point, enters on and abides in the *second meditation* which is devoid of initial and discursive thought, is born of concentration and is rapturous and joyful.

And again, monks, a monk, by the fading out of rapture, dwells with equanimity, attentive and clearly conscious, and experiences in his person that joy of which the ariyans say: 'Joyful lives he who has equanimity and is mindful': and he enters on and abides in the *third meditation.*

And again, monks, a monk, by getting rid of joy, by getting rid of anguish, by the going down of his former pleasures and sorrows, enters on and abides in the *fourth meditation* which has neither anguish nor joy and which is entirely purified by equanimity and mindfulness.

And again, monks, a monk, by passing quite beyond perception of material shapes, by the going down of perception of sensory reactions, by not attending to perceptions of variety, thinking: 'Ether is unending', enters on and abides in the plane of *infinite ether.* Monks, this monk is called one. . .by the Evil One.

And again, monks, a monk, by passing quite beyond the plane of infinite ether, thinking: 'Consciousness is unending', enters on and abides in the plane of *infinite consciousness.*

And again, monks, a monk, by passing quite beyond the plane of infinite consciousness, thinking: 'There is not anything', enters on and abides in the plane of *no-thing.*

And again, monks, a monk, by passing quite beyond the plane of no-thing, enters on and abides in the plane of *neither-perception-nor-non-perception.* Monks, this monk is called one who has put a darkness round Māra, and who, having blotted out Māra's vision so that it has no range, goes unseen by the Evil One.

And again, monks, a monk, by passing quite beyond the plane of neither-perception-nor-non-perception, enters on and abides in the *stopping of perception and feeling;* and having seen by intuitive wisdom, his cankers are utterly destroyed.

Monks, [any monk who abides in any of these meditations] is called one who has put a darkness round Māra, and having blotted out Māra's vision so that it has no range, goes unseen by the Evil One.

Thus spoke the Lord. Delighted, these monks rejoiced in what the Lord had said.

Source: From Majjhima-Nikâya I: 173-175 in I.B. Horner, *Middle Length Sayings*, Pali Text Society 1954, Vol.I, pp.217-9.

3.4.5 Questions which do not help Spiritual Progress

[The complete series of questions being considered is:
Is the world eternal or not, or both eternal and not-eternal,
Or neither eternal nor not eternal?
Is the world finite?
Are soul and body identical?
Does the Buddha exist after dying?]

Then the venerable Mālunkyāputta, emerging from solitary meditation towards evening, approached the Lord; having approached, having greeted the Lord, he sat down at a respectful distance. As he was sitting down at a respectful distance, the venerable Mālunkyāputta spoke thus to the Lord: 'Now, revered sir, as I was meditating in solitary seclusion, a reasoning of mind arose to me thus: "Those [speculative] views that are not explained, set aside, ignored by the Lord: The world is eternal. . .or that the Tathāgata neither is nor is not after dying, then will I, disavowing the training, revert to secular life.' If the Lord knows that the world is eternal, let the Lord explain to me that the world is eternal. If the Lord knows that the world is not eternal, let the Lord explain to me that the world is not eternal. If the Lord does not know whether the world is eternal or whether the world is not eternal, then, not knowing, not seeing, this would be honest, namely to say: "I do not know, I do not see." If the Lord knows that the world is finite, let the Lord explain. . .[*repeat as in two previous sentences*]. If the Lord does not know whether the Tathāgata neither is nor is not after dying, then, not knowing, not seeing, this would be honest, namely to say: "I do not know, I do not see. . ." '

'But did I ever speak thus to you, Mālunkyāputta: "Come you, Mālunkyāputta, fare the Brahma-faring under me and I will explain to you either that the world is eternal or that the world is not eternal [*and so with all the other questions in turn*] or that the Tathāgata neither is nor is not after dying?'

'No, revered sir.'

'Or did you speak thus to me: "I, revered sir, will fare the Brahma-faring under the Lord if the Lord will explain to me either that the world is eternal or that the world is not eternal. . .or that the Tathāgata neither is nor is not after dying". . .?'

'No, revered sir.'

'So it is agreed, Mālunkyāputta, that neither did I say: "Come you, Mālunkyāputta, fare the Brahma-faring under me and I will explain to you either that the world is eternal or that the world is not eternal. . .or that the Tathāgata neither is nor is not after dying'; and that neither did you say: "I, revered sir, will fare the Brahma-faring under the Lord if the Lord will explain to me either that the world is eternal. . .or that the Tathāgata neither is nor is not after dying." This being so, foolish man, who are you that you are disavowing?

'Whoever, Mālunkyāputta, should speak thus: "I will not fare the Brahma-faring under the Lord until the Lord explains to me whether the world is eternal or whether the world is not eternal or whether the Tathagata neither is nor is not after dying" – this man might pass away. Mālunkyāputta, or ever this was explained to him by the Tathāgata. Mālunkyāputta, it is as if a man were pierced by an arrow that was thickly smeared with poison and his friends and relations, his kith and kin, were to procure a physician and surgeon. He might speak thus: "I will not draw out this arrow until I know of the man who pierced me whether he is a noble or brahman or merchant or worker." He might speak thus: "I will not draw out this arrow until I know the name and clan of the man who pierced me." He might speak thus: "I will not draw out this arrow until I know of the man who pierced me whether he is tall or short or middling in height." He might speak thus: "I will not draw out this arrow until I know of the man who pierced me whether he is black or deep brown or golden skinned." He might speak thus: "I will not draw out this arrow until I know of the man who pierced me to what village or market town or town he belongs." He might speak thus: "I will not draw out this arrow until I know of the bow from which I was pierced whether it was a spring-bow or a cross-bow." He might speak thus: "I will not draw out this arrow until I know of the bow-string from which I was pierced whether it was of swallow-wort or of reed or sinew or hemp or a tree". He might speak thus: "I will not draw out this arrow until I know of the shaft by which I was pierced whether it was of reeds of this kind or that." He might speak thus: "I will not draw out this arrow until I know of the shaft from which I was pierced what kind of feathers it had: whether those of a vulture or heron or hawk or peacock or some other bird." He might speak thus: "I will not draw out this arrow until I know of the shaft from which I was pierced with what kind of sinews it was encased: whether those of a cow or buffalo or deer or monkey." He might speak thus: "I will not draw out this arrow until I know of the arrow by which I was pierced whether it was an ordinary arrow o⁻ some other kind of arrow". Mālunkyāputta, this man might pass away before ever this was known to him. In the same way, Mālunkyāputta, whoever should speak thus: "I will not fare the Brahma-faring under the Lord until the Lord explains to me either that the world is eternal or that the world is not eternal. . .or that the Tathāgata neither is nor is not after dying. . ." this man might pass away. Mālunkyāputta, before ever it was explained to him by the Tathāgata.

'The living of the Brahma-faring, Mālunkyāputta, could not be said to depend on the view that the world is eternal. Nor could the living of the Brahma-faring, Mālunkyāputta, be said to depend on the view that the world is not eternal. Whether there is the view that the world is eternal or whether there is the view that the world is not eternal, there *is* birth, there *is* ageing, there *is* dying, there *are* grief, sorrow, suffering, lamentation and despair, the suppression of which I lay down here and now. . .

'Wherefore, Mālunkyāputta, understand as not explained what has not been explained by me, and understand as explained what has been explained by me. And what, Mālunkyāputta, has not been explained by me? That the world is eternal has not been explained by me, Mālunkyāputta; that the world is not eternal. . .that the world is finite. . .that the world is not finite. . .that the life-principal and the body are the same. . .that the life-principle is one thing and the body another thing. . .that after dying the Tathagata is. . .is not . . .both is and is not. . .neither is nor is not has not been explained by me, Mālunkyāputta. And why, Mālunkyāputta, has this not been explained by me? It is because it is not connected with the goal, it not fundamental to the Brahma-faring, and does not conduce to turning away from, nor to dispassion, stopping, calming, super-knowledge, awakening nor to nibbana. Therefore it has not been explained by me, Mālunkyāputta. And what has been explained by me, Mālunkyāputta? "This is anguish [dukkha]" has been explained by me. "This is the course leading to the stopping of anguish" has been explained by me. And why, Mālunkyāputta, has this been explained by me? It is because it is connected with the goal, is fundamental to the Brahma-faring, and conduces to turning away from, to dispassion, stopping, calming, super-knowledge, awakening and nibbāna. Therefore it has been explained by me. Wherefore, Mālunkyāputta, understand as not explained what has not been explained by me, and understand as explained what has been explained by me.'

Source: From Majjihima-Nikâya I: 427-432, in I.B. Horner, *Middle Length Sayings* 1957, Vol.II, pp.98-101.

A Missionary Monk

3.4.6

Then the venerable Punna came to see the Exalted One. . .Seated at one side the venerable Punna said to the Exalted One:

'Well for me, lord, if the Exalted One would teach me a teaching in brief, hearing which teaching from the Exalted One I might dwell solitary, remote, earnest, ardent and aspiring.'

'There are objects, Punna, cognizable by the eye, objects desirable, pleasant, delightful and dear, passion-fraught, inciting to lust. If a brother be enamoured of such, if he welcome them, persist in clinging to them, so enamoured, so persisting in clinging to them, there comes a lure upon him. The arising of the lure, Punna, is the arising of Ill [Dukkhla] . So I declare.

'There are sounds, Punna, cognizable by the ear. . .scents cognizable by the nose. . .savours cognizable by the tongue. . .things tangible cognizable by the body. Moreover, Punna, there are mind-states cognizable by the mind, states desirable, pleasant, delightful and dear, passion-fraught, inciting to lust. If a brother be enamoured of such. . .there comes a lure upon him. The arising of the lure, Punna, is the arising of Ill [Dukkhla] . So I declare.

'But there are objects, Punna. . .If a brother be not enamoured of such, if he welcome them not, persist not in clinging to them, thus not enamoured, thus not persisting in clinging to them, the lure comes to cease. The ceasing of the lure, Punna, is the ceasing of Ill [Dukkha] . So I declare.'

[The same is asserted concerning mind and mind-states.]

'Now, Punna, after being instructed by me with this teaching in brief, tell me in what district you will be dwelling.'

'There is a district, lord, called Sunāparanta. That is where I shall be dwelling.'

'Hotheaded, Punna, are the men of Sunāparanta. Fierce, Punna, are the men of Sunāparanta. If the men of Sunāparanta abuse and revile you, Puṇṇa, how will it be with you?'

'If the men of Sunāparanta abuse and revile me, lord, I shall feel thus of them: "Kindly indeed are the men of Sunāparanta. Very kindly are the men of Sunāparanta in that they do not smite me a blow with their hands." That is how it will be with me, then, O Exalted One. That is how it will be with me then, O Happy one.'

'But if, Puṇṇa, those men of Sunāparanta smite you a blow with their hands, how will it be with you then, Puṇṇa?'

'Why in such case, lord, this is how it will be with me: "Kindly indeed, very kindly are these men of Sunāpranta, in that they do not throw clods of earth at me." That is how it will be with me, O Exalted One. That is how it will be with me, O Happy One.'

'But suppose, Puṇṇa, that they throw clods at you. What then?'

'If they do so, lord, I shall think: "Kindly indeed, very kindly are these men of Sunāparanta, in that they do not beat me with a stick. . ." '

'But if they do beat you with a stick, Puṇṇa, what then?'

'Then, lord, I shall think them kindly for not striking me with a sword. . .'

'But if they do, Puṇṇa, what then?'

'I shall think them kindly, lord, for not slaying me with a sharp sword. . ,

'But suppose they do so slay you, Puṇṇa?'

'Then, lord, I shall think: "There are disciples of that Exalted One who, when tormented by, ashamed of, disgusted with, body and life, have resort to stabbing themselves[1]. Now I have come by a stabbing that I never sought." That is how it will be with me, O Exalted One. That is how it will be with me, O Happy One.'

'Well said! Well said, Puṇṇa! Possessed of such self-control as this, you will be able to dwell in the district of the folk of Sunaparanta. So now, Puṇṇa, do what you think it time for.'[2]

Thereupon the venerable Puṇṇa welcomed the words of the Exalted One, and took pleasure therein, and rising from his seat he saluted the Exalted One by the right. Then he set his lodging in order, and taking bowl and robe went off on his wanderings to the district of Sunāparanta. And so wandering on, reached it, and there the venerable Puṇṇa stayed in the district of Sunaparanta.

And during that rainy season the venerable Puṇṇa established in the Dhamma as many as five hundred devotees. In that same rainy season he realized the threefold knowledge. In that same rainy season he passed finally away.

Now a number of brethren came to the Exalted One. Seated at one side those brethren said to the Exalted One:

'Lord, that clansman named Punna, who was taught with a teaching in brief by the Exalted One, is dead. What is his rebirth? What is his attainment?'

'A sage, brethren, was Punna the clansman. He lived in accordance with the Dhamma. He did not hurt me with disputings about the Dhamma Puṇṇa, brethren, has passed finally away.'

Notes

1. This is contrary to the ordinances of the Vinaya-Pitaka.
2. This is an ordinary formula of dismissal. In another text, it is added that Punna converted many unbelievers.

Source: From Samyutta-Nikâya IV. 60, in F.L. Woodward, *Kindred Sayings*, Pali Text Society 1927, Vol.IV, pp.34-7.

Ashoka's Rock-Edict   3.4.7

[The text of this edict shows the cruelty of wars in that time, and the way in which a monarch could be converted; not exactly to Buddhism in a clearly-defined form, but rather to a natural code of non-violence. However, Buddhism gained special benefit from the general religious good-will of Ashoka. His reign (c.270-232 B.C.) marks a decisive moment in Buddhism's expansion.]

'The Beloved of the Gods. The Compassionate King (Piye-dasi) in the ninth year of his reign conquered the Kalinga. One hundred and fifty thousand persons were thence carried away captive, one hundred thousand were there slain, and many times that number perished.

'Ever since the annexation of the Kalingas, The Beloved of the Gods has zealously protected the Law of Piety (Dharma), has been devoted to that law and has proclaimed its precepts.

'The Beloved of the Gods feels remorse on account of the conquest of the Kalingas, because during the subjugation of a previously unconquered country, slaughter, death and the taking away captive of the people necessarily occur, whereat The Beloved of the Gods feels profound sorrow and regret.

'There is another reason for The Beloved of the Gods feeling still more regret, namely that in such a country dwell Brahmans and ascetics, men of different sects, and households who all practise obedience to elders, obedience to father and mother, obedience to teachers, proper treatment of friends, acquaintances, comrades, relatives, slaves and servants, with fidelity and devotion. To such people dwelling in that country happen violence, slaughter, and separation from those they love.

'Even those persons who are themselves protected retain their affections undiminished: thus when ruin falls on their friends, acquaintances, comrades, relatives, in this way violence affects those who are personally unhurt. All this diffused misery is matter for regret to The Beloved of the Gods. For there is no country where such communities are not found, including others besides Brahmans and ascetics.

'Though a man should do him an injury The Beloved of the Gods holds that it must be patiently borne so far as it can possibly be borne.

'Even upon the forest tribes in his dominion The Beloved of the Gods has compassion and seeks their conversion, inasmuch as the might even of The Beloved of the Gods himself is based on repentance. They are warned thus: "Shun evil-doing, that ye may escape destruction; because The Beloved of the Gods desires for all animate beings security, control over passion, peace of mind and joyousness (happiness)."

'Delight is found in the conquest made by the Law; but The Beloved of the Gods thinks nothing of much importance save what concerns the next world.

'The only true conquest is that effected through the Law of Piety (Dharma), which avails both for this world and the next. Let all the pleasures of my sons be the pleasure of exertion which avails both for this world and the next.'

Source: Rock-Edict XIII, in L.A.Waddell, *Lamaism*, Heffer 1934, pp.435-7.

3.5   MONASTIC MEDITATION

Some Introductory Notes

Some texts

1.*The mysterious Ultimate and the rest*

N.B. Even if the ultimate aims, meditation and liberation through meditation are the same in all the schools of Buddhism, they may greatly differ in the way they understand the Ultimate Reality. For some groups it is Void, Emptiness (sûnya); for some other groups, Mind only (cittamatrâ). Others have other expressions; but the Ultimate is beyond any possible definition.

The *Mind* is the leader of all things. When a man understands the Mind he knows all things, because all things of the world are created by Mind.

Suchness (Tathatâ) is beyond all relativity, evil and passion. By its nature, it is pure, tranquil, permanent, unchanging (Ratnamegha, Ho-u). All things are born of causation and phenomenal, but ignorant people cling to them as real.

The *true nature* and the true form of all things is permanent and never changes.

The true essence of all things is absolute *identity* with Suchness. Tathatâ.

The *human mind* possesses the Buddha-nature (as) a man who has a jewel in his clothes he knows not of.

Suchness, or Ultimate reality are synonymous with Emptiness.

2. *Method*

Meditate upon the Mind as Supreme Dharma and Supreme Master.

Separate yourself from noise, sloth and sleep, and make a thorough survey of all the different aspects of the self-discriminating Mind.

When the Mind is disturbed, the multiplicity of things is produced; when *the Mind is quieted,* the multiplicity of things disappears.

3. *Results*

He who meditates upon the Mind as Supreme Dharma of the Buddha, as Supreme Master, obtains Nirvâna.

One who is convinced of the fitness of everything is not captivated by worldly things (dharmas), because he does not lean on them. When he gains something, he does not rejoice. when he does not gain, he is not depressed. Fame does not make him proud, lack of fame does not depress him. Scorn does not cow him, praise does not win him over. Pleasures do not attract him, pain does not repel him. One who in such a way is not captivated by the worldly things is said to be one who knows emptiness.

Some terms

Mahâprajnâparamitâsûtra = Japanese 'Hannya-kyo'.
Avatamsaka = Japanese 'Kegon-Kyo'.
Nirvânasûtra = Japanese 'Neham-gyo'.

Source: J. Masson, unpublished.

3.5.2 Emptiness

If a son or daughter of a family wishes to perform the study in this deep Prajñâpâramitâ (Perfection of Wisdom), he must think thus: 'There are five components of the human existence (skandha) an they should be considered as by their nature empty. *Form is emptiness,* and *emptiness indeed is form.* Emptiness is not different from form, form is not different from emptiness. What is form, that is emptiness; what is emptiness, that is form. Thus perception, name, conception, and knowledge also are emptiness. Thus, O Sâriputra, all things have the character of emptiness, they have no beginning, no end, they are faultless and not faultless, they are not imperfect and not perfect. Therefore, O Sâriputra, here in this emptiness there is no form, no perception, no name, no concept, no knowledge. No eye, ear, nose, tongue, body, and mind. No form, sound, smell, taste, and objects. . . There is no knowledge, no ignorance, no destruction of ignorance, there is no decay and death, no destruction of decay and death; there are not the Four Truths, viz. that there is pain, origin of pain, stoppage of pain, and the path to it. There is no knowledge, no obtaining, no not-obtaining of Nirvâna. Therefore, O Sâriputra, as there is no obtaining (of Nirvâna), a man who has approached the Prajñâpâramitâ of the Bodhisattvas, dwells (for a time) enveloped in consciousness. But when the envelopment of consciousness has been annihilated, then he becomes free of all fear, beyond the reach of change, enjoying final Nirvâna.

'All Buddhas of the past, present, and future, after approaching the Prajñâpâramitâ, have awoken to the highest perfect knowledge.

'Therefore we ought to know the great verse of the Prajñâpâramitâ, the verse of the great wisdom, the unsurpassed verse, the verse which appeases all pain – it is truth, it is not false – the verse proclaimed in the Prajñaparamita: "O wisdom, gone, gone, gone to the other shore, landed at the other shore, Svaha!..."[1]

'This, O Sâriputra, should a Bodhisattva teach in the study of the deep Prajñâpâramitâ.'

Then when the Bhagavat had risen from that meditation, he gave his approval to the venerable Bodhisattva Avalokitesvara, saying: 'Well done, well done, noble son! So it is, noble son. So indeed must this study of the deep Prajñâpâramitâ be performed. As it had been described by thee, it is applauded by Arhat Tathâgatas.' Thus spoke Bhagavat with joyful mind. And the venerable Sâriputra, and the honourable Bodhisattva Avalokiteśvara, and the whole assembly, and the world of gods, men, demons, and fairies praised the speech of the Bhagavat.

Note

1. The other shore is Nirvâna, as experience. The verse here quoted has by itself a mysterious spiritual power; we are here between meditation and magic formula (as in some formulas of Tibetan Buddhism). (If 'Emptiness' in ordinary experience appears as contrary to terms such as 'Fulness', this opposition is no longer true at the supreme level, when to say 'void', 'full', 'form' or 'without-form' is equally inadequate.

Source: From Larger Prajñâparamitâhridayasûtra, in M. Muller, ed., *SBE*, OUP 1881, Vol.XLIX, pp.147-9.

Suchness   3.5.3

[Emptiness = Suchness, because the Ultimate cannot be adequately expressed; it is 'beyond words', and can be attained only by 'mental enlightenment'.]

Subhuti: What then is this supreme enlightenment?

The Lord: It is Suchness. But Suchness neither grows nor diminishes. A Bodhisattva, who repeatedly and often dwells in mental activities connected with that Suchness, comes near to the supreme enlightenment, and he does not lose those mental activities again. It is certain that there can be no growth or diminution of an entity which is *beyond all words,* and that therefore neither the perfections, nor all dharmas, can grow or diminish. It is thus that, when he dwells in mental activities of this kind, a Bodhisattva becomes one who is near to *perfect enlightenment.*

Source:
From Astâsâhasrikâ XVIII: 350-351 in E. Conzè *et al., Buddhist Texts through the Ages,* Bruno Cassirer 1954, p.180.

3.5.4 Nâgârjuna: No Difference between Samsâra and Nirvâna

In his Ratnâvali, Nâgârjuna says that just as a learned grammarian may teach even the alphabets, similarly Buddha taught according to the capacity of his disciples... To the best he taught the Blessed Sûnya, the deeper truth, terrible to the fools but kind to the wise. Nâgârjuna condemns nihilism, by saying that negation leads to hell; affirmation leads to heaven; and non-dual truth, which transcends affirmation and negation, leads to liberation. This Pure Knowledge where affirmation and negation, good and evil, heaven and hell are merged, is called liberation by the wise... Negation is possible only as a destruction or an antithesis of affirmation. But when there is no affirmation, how can there be any negation? Synthesis alone is real. Both thesis and antithesis are appearances. The universe therefore is neither real nor unreal, and hence only an appearance... The Real transcends all categories of intellect, and the phenomenal is the relative, as it is 'neither real nor unreal'. This is the noble Present of our Religion, the Deep Truth Nectar of the Teaching of the Buddha.

What is called the phenomenal world, or the cycle of birth and death seen from the empirical standpoint (viewed through the glasses of causation and relativity), that very world is called Nirvâna, or the Absolute from the ultimate standpoint, viewed without causation and the bondage of relativity; it is liberation.

The Absolute *is* its appearances. There is not the slightest difference between Samsâra and Nirvâna... The essential nature of all objects, like Nirvâna, is beyond production and destruction...

Source:
C. Sharma, *A Critical Survey of Indian Philosophy,* Hutchinson 1960, pp.101-2.

Chinese Sources 3.5.5

The Ultimate Reality and the rest

No-Thought is Absolute Reality, in which the Mind ceases to act (Fa-Yung, 594-657 C.E.).

Void and Being are not seen as two: this is the Middle Way (Fa-Yung).

Substance and action are unimpededly interfused; this is the essence of Ch'an (Tung-shan, 807-869 C.E.).

He is the same as me. Yet I am not he (Tung-shan and Lyang Chie).

The Methods of meditation

You should not search *through others*, lest the Truth recede further from You. When alone I proceed through myself, I meet him wherever I go (Lyang-Chie).

To *talk* about names and manifestations is useless, but a direct approach easily reaches it. No-Mind is that which is in action; it is that constant action which does not act. The no-Mind of which I speak is not separate from the Mind (Fa-Yung).

Do not abide in an excess of Void (sunyata) but illuminate the non-being in being (Fa-Yung).

As there is no self and no others, how can one speak of degrees of intimacy? You should not lecture from assembly to assembly, since words do not lead directly to the Truth (P'ang-Yun).

I have my secret. I look at You with twinkling eye. If You do not understand this, do not call Yourself a monk (Hsiang-yen).

Koan (enigmas as meditation-topics)

1. If I have nothing, what should I do? Throw it away!
2. You are not allowed to travel at night, but You must arrive before day-break.
3. The bridge flows, the water does not.
4. What is the sound of ONE hand clapping?
5. If You run away from the Void, You can never be free of it. If You search for the Void, You can never reach it.

Results

When one is absorbed in all, one penetrates into all.
When all is absorbed by one, all penetrates into one.
What one is absorbed by one, one penetrates into one.
When all is absorbed by all, all penetrates into all (Tsung-mi).

I meet Him wherever I go. He is the same as me. Yet I am not He. Only if You understand this, will You identify with what You are (Tung-shan).
If you begin to reason about it, when will You ever achieve enlightenment? (Yun-men, d. 949 C.E.).
The consciousness of non-differentiation is awareness of the Absolute One, beyond duality. The instantaneous enlightenment is the light which is self-illuminating. Pure is the water, and transparent where fish move slowly in it. Boundless is the sky where flying birds disappear, disappear into the unseen (Hung-Chih).
With one stroke, all previous knowledge is forgotten. No cultivation is needed for this (Hsiang-yen, hearing the sound of a stone against a bamboo-tree).
When there is nothing to give up, one has reached the Source; when there is no Void to abide in, one is experiencing the Void. No-action transcends quiescence; rather it constantly acts (Wang Wei).
When Purity is absolute, therein I have bliss.
Purity and Bliss sustain one another.
The bliss of one's Self is limitless.
And absolute purity in infinite.
They are transparency beyond form.
And consciousness illuminating the empty chamber.
The empty chamber is void: neither a being, nor a non-being (Hung-chi).

Source: From C.T. Chang, *Original Teachings of Ch'an Buddhism*, Harper, New York 1971.

3.5.6 Japanese Sources

The Ultimate Reality

There is a Reality, even prior to Heaven and earth.
Indeed it has no form, much less a name. . .
To call it Mind (mind-only, cittamatra) or Buddha violates its nature.
For then it becomes like the mirage of a flower in the air.
It is not Mind, nor Buddha.
Absolutely quiet, and yet illuminating in a mysterious way,
It allows itself to be perceived only by the clear-eyed.
It is a Reality (Dharma) truly beyond form and sound.
It is a Way-Tao, having nothing to do with words.
(Daito Kokushi)

Method

If you desire to listen to the thunderous voice of the Dharma,
Exhaust your words, empty your thoughts,
For then You may come to recognize this one essence.
(Daito Kokushi)

As regards meditation practised in the Mâhayâna,
We have no words to praise it fully:
The virtues of perfection such as benevolence, morality, etc.,
And the invocation of the Buddha's name, confession, ascetic
    discipline,
And many other good deeds of merit,
All these issue from the practice of meditation.
(Hakuin)

There are four kinds of dhyânas: of the ignorant, for the examination
of the meaning, with the Tathâgata, for its object, and the pure
Dhyana of the Tathâgata.
(Lankavatâra)

Effects

For them opens the gate of the oneness of cause and effect,
And straight runs the path of no-two and no-three.
Abiding with the non-particular which is in the particulars,
Whether going or returning, they remain for ever unmoved.
Taking hold of the non-thought which lies in thoughts,
In every act of theirs, they hear the voice of the Truth.
How boundless the sky of Samadhi, unfettered!
How transparent the perfect moon-light of the fourfold wisdom!
At that moment, what do they lack?
As the Truth eternally calm reveals itself to them,
This very earth is the Lotus-Land of Purity
And this body is the body of the Buddha.
(Hakuin)

Source: From D.T. Zuzuki, *Manual of Zen Buddhism, and Essays in Zen Buddism* Hutchinson 1955.

3.6 PERSONAL DEVOTION

3.6.1 Some Introductory Notes

The Bodhisattava

Great compassion and a great pitying heart is called *Buddha-nature*. Compassion is Tathâgata; tathâgata is compassion (Nirvânasûtra, Nehangyo).

A Bodhisattva should think: I wish to suffer the sufferings of hell for the sake of all beings, so as to make them come to the realisation of Enlightenment.

A Bodhisattva must guard himself from advising others to do things which he does not desire for himself.

A Bodhisattva, knowing the deeds, causations, and desires of beings, preaches the Law according to their capacity.

A Bodhisattva is never tired of teaching beings and manifests himself according to the wish of beings.

Faith and its results

Of all treasures, faith is the best (Lalitavistara, Daishogonkyo).

Faith indeed is the son of Buddha; so the wise should strive to be near it (Maharatnakuta, Hoshakukyo).

When a man recites the name of Buddha with no cowardly heart but with wisdom and straight-forwardness, he will be in the presence of the Buddha (Dvadasabuddhaka, Junibutsusumyokyo).

Examples of invocation

Japanese	Sanskrit
Namu Amitoboya totogyatoya	Namo Amitâbhaya tathâgataya
Toniyato Omiritsubomi	Tadyatho Amriodbhave
Omirito shitabomi	Amritaya. . .bhave
Omirito bigyarato gyamini	Amritaya vikrantagamine
Gyagyano shitogyari	Gaganakirtikare
Somoko	Svâhâ

Some examples of comparative terms

Hokke-kyo: Saddharmapundarikasûtra
Shin-gyo (long and short): Hridayasûtra
Kongo-kyo: Vajracchedikasûtra

Rioga-kyo: Lankavatara
Hanna-kyo: Prajñapâramitâsûtra
Riogon-kyo: Surangamasûtra
Muryoju: Sukkâvati

Examples of magic mantra

Adoration of all the Buddhas!
Adoration to the Teaching without obstructions
Om! Khya khya khyahi khyahi [speak, speak]!
Hum hum!
Jvala jvala prajvala prajvala [blaze, blaze]!
Tistha tistha [Up, Up]!
Stri Stri!
Sphata sphata [burst, burst]!
One who is quiescent!
To the glorious one, hail!

Source: J. Masson, hirtherto unpublished

Infallibility of the Buddha 3.6.2

[The devotional current is essentially founded on a certain kind of
faith (sraddha); this faith regards the Founder and his words as
infallible.]

Be attentive, all, young men of good family; I am to utter an
infallible word; refrain from disputing about it, O sages; the science
of the Tathâgata is beyond reasoning.

Be all steady and thoughtful; continue attentive all. Today you
will hear a law as yet unknown, the wonder of the Tathâgatas.

Never have any doubt, ye sages, for I shall strengthen you. I am
the Leader who speaketh infallible Truth, and my knowledge is
unlimited. Profound are the laws known to the Tathâgata; above all
reasoning and beyond argumentation. These laws I am going to
reveal; ye, hear which and how they are.

Source: From Saddharmapundarikasûtra XIV in M. Muller, ed., *SBE*, OUP
1884, Vol.XXI, p.291.

3.6.3 The Authority of the Saddharmapundarikasûtra (The 'Lotus of the True Law')

It is supreme

Just as the great ocean surpasses all springs, streams and tanks, so the Lotus of the True Law surpasses all Sûtras spoken by the Tathâgatas. . . As the moon, as a luminary, takes the first rank amongst the whole of the asterisms, so the Lotus of the True Law ranks first among all Sûtrântas spoken by the Tathâgata. . .

As the orb of the sun dispels gloomy darkness, so the Lotus of the True Law dispels all the gloomy darkness of unholy works. . .

As Brahma Sahâṁpati exercises the function of a father in the Brahman world, so the Lotus of the True Law exercises the function of a father to all beings, whether under training or past it, to all disciples, Pratyekabuddhas,[1] and those who in the Bodhisattva-vehicle are striving for the goal. . .

This Lotus of the True Law saves all beings from fear, delivers them from pains. It is like a tank for the thirsty, like a fire for those who suffer from cold, like a garment for the naked, like the caravan-leader for the merchants, like a mother for her children, like a boat for those who ferry over. . .like a lamp for those who are wrapped in darkness.

It leads to Nirvana

He who is desirous of omniscience and thinks 'How shall I soonest reach it' must try to know this Sûtra by heart or at least honour one who knows it.

He has been sent by the Lord of the world to instruct men, he who out of compassion for mankind recites this Sûtra. One should always reverentially salute him with joined hands.[2]

Notes

1. The Pratyekabuddhas are illuminated but do not preach.
2. The sacred text is the word of the Buddha, and part of him. It has a spiritual strength, not only as a teaching but also on account of the very expression and formulas it uses.

Source: From Saddharmapundarikasûtras XXII and X in M. Muller, *SBE*, OUP 1884, Vol.XXI, pp.386ff and Vol.XXXI, p.217.

Meaning and Power of the Sacred Names 3.6.4

[The short texts here collected explain the meaning of the principal names and give a good example of the way in which they are used in devotion and liturgy.]

Part I

Why 'Tathâgata'?

Why, O Subhûti, the name of Tathâgata? It expresses true suchness (Tathâgata).

And again: Why this name? It means that it has no origin. And again:

Why this name? It expresses that the [transient] characters are destroyed.

And again why is it said: One who has no origin? Because, O Subhûti, non-origin is the highest goal.

Why Amitâyus and Amitâbha?

For what reason is that Tathâgata called Amitâyus? The length of life, O Sâriputra, of that Tathâgata and of those men there [= in the Paradise of Amida] is immeasurable. Therefore is that Tathâgata called Amita-âyus (life without limits). And for what reason is that Tathâgata called Amitâbha? The splendour, O Sâriputra, of that Tathâgata is unimpeded over all Buddha-countries. Therefore is that Tathâgata called Amita-âbhâ (splendour without limits).

Why Sukhâvatî?

For what reason is that world (that heavenly world) called Sukhâvatî [= happy]? In that Sukhâvatî-world, O Sâriputra, there is neither bodily nor mental pain for living beings. The sources of happiness are innumerable there. For that reason is that world called Sukhâvatî (the happy world).

Part II

Invocation of the Sacred Names

Om = Mystic syllable.
Adoration to the Three Treasures = Buddha, Dharma, Sangha.
Om, Adoration to all Buddhas = Completely achieved.
Bodhisattvas = Working for the salvation.

Pratyekabuddhas = Not preaching for others.
Sravakas = Disciples.
Adoration to Amitâbha = [See above]
Adoration to him whose soul is endowed with incomprehensible virtues.
Adoration to Amitâbha, to the Jina = The Victorious.
To thee, O Muni = Ascetic.
I go to Sukhâvatî through thy compassion = He helps the disciples.
To Sukhâvatî, with his groves, resplendent with gold = Mythic description.
The delightful, adorned with the sons of Sugata = Synonym for Buddha.
I go to it, which is full of many jewels and treasures,
And the resort of You, the famous and wise = Amitâbha.
Thus It was heard by me = The expression tends to stress the antiquity and genuineness of the text.

Sources:
Part I from Vajracchedikâ XVII in M. Muller, ed. *SBE,* OUP 1883, Vol.XIX pp.133, Smaller Sukhâvatı-Vyuha, 8, in op.cit., p.97, and Smaller Sukhâvatı-Vyuha, 2, in op.cit., p.91: Part II from Larger Sukhâvatı-Vyuha, Introduction, in M. Muller, op.cit. p.21.

3.6.5 Devotion to Amida

[The texts come from one of the most famous 'saints' of Japan, the Monk, Hōnen, who founded the Sect Jōdo.]

From Hōnen's letter

It is a joy beyond all other joys to have attained all these things that are so difficult of attainment; first of all being born a human being, then coming in contact with the Original Vow,[1] then having one's religious aspirations aroused, then getting free from the long road of transmigrations, and finally being born into the Pure Land. While believing that even the man who is so sinful that he has committed the ten evil deeds and the five deadly sins may be born into the Pure Land, as far as you are concerned, be not guilty even of the smallest sins. And if a sinful man may thus be born into that land, how much more a good man! And as to this act of repeating the *nembutsu*[2] believe that ten repetitions, yea even one, will never be in vain, and so continually practice it without ceasing. If by repeating the *nembutsu* once a man may thus reach *Ojo*[3], how much more so if he repeats it many times!

As Amida Buddha has already verified the words of His Vow, 'unless it happens as I vow, I shall not accept enlightenment', and is now in reality in that blissful land, as He said, He surely will come and meet us when we are about to die. The revered Shaka[4] himself will indeed rejoice when he looks with delight upon our escape from the transmigratory round by following his teachings, and in like manner will also all the Buddhas of the six quarters rejoice, when they see that we have, by believing what they have endorsed, been born into that Pure Land, from whose pure blessedness we shall never fall.

Let your joy, therefore, be as high as the heavens above and as deep as the earth beneath. Let us then, whether walking, standing, sitting, or lying, or wherever we are, always be returning thanks for the great blessedness of having in this life come in contact with the Original Vow of the Amida Buddha.

There are those who say that the effort to avoid sin and improve oneself is making light of Amida's Vow, and the frequent repetition of the *nembutsu,* and the effort to pile up a larger number of them is equivalent to doubting his saving power; and many such like things one sometimes hears. But do not for a moment be misled by such misconceptions. Is there any place in any of the sutras where Amida encourages men to sin? Certainly not. Such things come from those who make no effort to get away from their own evil deeds, and who go on in their former sinful life. By such utterly unreasonable and false sayings they would mislead ignorant men and women, urging them forward in the committing of sin and stirring up their evil passions within them. Now such persons are nothing less than a company of devils, and their work heathenish, and you ought to think of them as enemies to your reaching birth into that Pure Land of Perfect Bliss. Again, to say that frequent repetitions of the sacred name mean the encouragement of the principle of self-effort shows utter ignorance of facts and is a deplorable blunder. Even one repetition or two of the sacred name must be said to be the *nembutsu* of salvation by one's own power, if one does it with that thought in his heart, while a hundred or a thousand repetitions day and night for a hundred or a thousand days, so long as one does it with an entire trust in the merits of the Great Vow, looking up in confidence to Amida with every repetition, constitute the *nembutsu* of salvation by Amida's power alone. And so the *nembutsu* of those who possess the so-called mental states no matter how many times they may call upon the sacred name, moment by moment, day and night, can by no means be called the *nembutsu* of salvation by one's own power, so long as they are really looking up to Amida, and trusting to his saving power alone.

Poems of Hōnen

The glorious vision

> The Pure Land's glorious vision
> Is bliss that man may claim
> If he worthily repeats
> Amida's sacred name.

Invocation alone

> Ill seems each occupation
> That would free the heart from blame
> Compared with invocation
> Of the Buddha's sacred name.

The Seasons

> O mist of spring, thou hidest
> All things beautiful and bright
> As if there did not shine
> The true, imperishable light.

> I gaze and gaze each passing day
> On the geranium sweet
> And for the happy day I yearn
> My Amida to meet.

> If from Buddha Amida
> My heart its col'ring gains,
> 'Twill be like the beauteous boughs
> Which autumn's crimson stains.

> If in the winter of our sin,
> Amida's name we call,
> Warm rays from Him will chase away
> The cold and snowdrifts all.

The pine of a thousand years

> Pine of a thousand earthly years,

I dwell beneath thy shade,
Till by the Lord of Boundless Life[5]
My welcome is made.

Notes

1. The Original Vow is the vow of a Bodhisattva (cf. § 3.6.6): 'to remain in
   this world after one's illumination, in order to help others to arrive at
   Nirvâna.' The confidence of the Buddhist devotees is founded on the
   conviction that the bodhisattvas help them.
2. Nembutsu – 'namu Amida butsu'.
3. Ojo – rebirth in the Pure Land.
4. Shaka – a name for the Buddha (from 'Śakyamuni' – the sage of the
   Sakyas).
5. Boundless Life is *Amitâyus*. One should note the peaceful and 'passive'
   aspect of this devotional way, and the connection between man and nature.

Source: H.H. Coates and R. Ishizuka, *Honen, the Buddhist Saint,* Chion-in,
Kyoto 1925, pp.402-6, 542-5.

The Commitment of the Bodhisattva for the Salvation of Men
3.6.6

[Even if already illuminated, the Bodhisattva chooses to remain in
the world, in order that all beings may be illuminated and liberated,
through his example and preaching.]

I, on the strength of generosity, equanimity, virtue, forbearance,
power, meditation and absorption, undertake here the first and best
duties, and shall become a Buddha, the Saviour of all beings . . .

May I go to Avici hell and always abide there, if I cease to
practise the power of prayer. . .

If, in that Buddha-country of mine, the beings who are born there
should fall away (die) and fall either into hell, or the brute realm,
the realm of departed spirits, or into the body of Asuras,[1] then may
I not obtain the highest perfect knowledge. . .

If, in that Buddha-country of mine, the beings who are born
there should not be firmly established, that is, in absolute truth, till
they have reached Mahâparinirvâna, then may I not obtain the
highest perfect knowledge. . .

If, for the beings in this Buddha-country of mine, after I have
obtained Bodhi, even the name of sin should exist, then may I not
obtain the highest perfect knowledge. . .

If those beings who have directed their thoughts towards the highest perfect knowledge. . . .and who, after having heard my name, have meditated on me with serene thoughts, if, at the moment of their death, after having approached them, surrounded by an assembly of Bhikkhus, I should not stand before them, worshipped by them, that is, so that their thoughts should not be troubled again, then may I not obtain the highest perfect knowledge. . .

If those beings who are born in that Buddha-country of mine, after I have obtained Bodhi, should not all recite the Story of the Law, which is accompanied by omniscience, then may I not obtain the highest perfect knowledge. . .

If, after I have obtained Bodhi, women in immeasurable, innumerable, inconceivable, imcomparable, immense Buddha-countries on all sides, after having heard my name, should allow carelessness to arise, should not turn their thoughts towards Bodhi, should, when they are free from birth, not despise their female nature; and if they, being born again, should assume a second female nature, then may I not obtain the highest perfect knowledge. . . If this my prayer succeeds, after I have obtained Bodhi, may this sphere of the world tremble, and may a shower of flowers descend on the host of the gods.

Then the earth trembled, flowers were showered down, hundreds of instruments resounded in the sky, powder of heavily sweet sandal-wood was scattered and there was a voice saying: 'Thou wilt be a Buddha in the world.'

Note
1. Those destinies are inferior, and do not lead to final liberation.

Source: From Larger Sukhâvatî-Vyûha, 4ff. in M. Muller, ed., *SBE*, OUP 1881, Vol.XLIX, pp.2 and 8ff.

3.6.7 Explanation and Praise of the Bodhisattva Avalokiteśvara

1. Citradhvaja asked Akshayamati the following question: For what reason, son of Jina, is Avalokiteśvara so called?

2. And Akshayamati, that ocean of profound insight, after considering how the matter stood, spoke to Citradhvaja: Listen to the conduct of Avalokiteśvara. . .

A. *Description*

4. Hearing, seeing, regularly and constantly thinking of Avalokiteśvara

will infallibly destroy all suffering, mundane existence and grief of living beings here on earth.

5. If a man be thrown into a pit of fire by a wicked enemy, with the object of killing him, he has but to think of Avalokiteśvara, and the fire shall be quenched as if sprinkled with water.

6. If one happens to fall into the dreadful ocean, the abode of Nâgas, marine monsters, and demons, he has but to think of Avalokiteśvara, and he shall never sink down into the king of waters.

7. If a man happens to be hurled down from the brink of Meru, by some wicked person with the object of killing him, he has but to think of Avalokiteśvara, and he shall, sunlike, stand firm in the sky.

8. If rocks of thunderstone and thunderbolts are thrown at a man's head to kill him, he has but to think of Avalokiteśvara, and they shall not be able to hurt one hair of the body.

9. If a man be surrounded by a host of enemies armed with swords, who have the intention of killing him, he has but to think of Avalokiteśvara, and they shall instantaneously become kind-hearted.

10. If a man, delivered to the power of the executioners, is already standing at the place of execution, he has but to think of Avalokiteśvara, and their swords shall go to pieces.

11. If a person happens to be fettered in shackles of wood or iron, he has but to think of Avalokiteśvara, and the bonds shall be speedily loosened.

12. Mighty spells, witchcraft, herbs, ghosts and spectres, pernicious to life, revert thither whence they come, when one thinks of Avalokiteśvara.

13. If a man is surrounded by goblins, Nâgas, demons, ghosts, or giants, who are in the habit of taking away bodily vigour, he has but to think of Avalokiteśvara, and they shall not be able to hurt one hair of his body.

14. If a man is surrounded by fearful beasts with sharp teeth and claws, he has but to think of Avalokiteśvara, and they shall quickly fly in all directions.

15. If a man is surrounded by snakes, malicious and frightful on account of the flames and fires [they emit], he has but to think of Avalokiteśvara, and they shall quickly lose their poison.

16. If a heavy thunderbolt shoots from a cloud pregnant with lightning and thunder, one has but to think of Avalokiteśvara, and the fire of heaven shall quickly, instantaneously be quenched.

17. He [Avalokiteśvara] with his powerful knowledge beholds all creatures who are beset with countless troubles and afflicted by many

sorrows, and thereby becomes a saviour in the world, including the gods.

18. As he is thoroughly practised in wonder-working power, and possessed of vast knowledge and skilfulness, he shows himself in all directions and in all regions of the world.

19. Birth, decrepitude and disease will slowly come to an end for those who are in the wretched states of existence, in hells, in brute creation, in the kingdom of Yama, for all beings (in general).

B. Hymn

20. O thou whose eyes are clear, whose eyes are kind, distinguished by wisdom and knowledge, whose eyes are full of pity and benevolence; thou art so lovely in thy beautiful face and beautiful eyes.

21. Thy lustre is spotless bright, thy knowledge is free from darkness, thou shinest as the sun, radiant as the blaze of fire, not to be beaten away; thou spreadest in thy flying course thy lustre in the world.

22. O thou who rejoicest in kindness having its source in compassion, thou great cloud of good qualities and of benevolent mind, thou quenchest the fire that vexes living beings, thou pourest out nectar, the rain of the law.

C. Exhortation

23. In quarrel, dispute, war, battle, in any great danger one has to think of Avalokiteśvara, who shall quell the wicked troop of foes.

24. One should think of Avalokiteśvara, whose sound is as the clouds and the drums, who thunders like a rain-cloud, possesses a sweet voice like Brahma, [a voice] going through the whole range of tones.

25. Think, O think with tranquil mood of Avalokiteśvara, that pure being; he is a protector, a refuge, a recourse in death, disaster and calamity.

26. He who possesses the perfection of all virtues, and beholds all beings with compassion and benevolence, he, an ocean of virtues, Virtue itself, he Avalokiteśvara, is worthy of adoration.

27. He, so compassionate for the world, shall once become a Buddha, destroying all dangers and sorrows; I humbly bow to Avalokiteśvara. . .

D. Contemplation

29. At one time standing to the right, at another to the left of the

Chief Amitâbha, whom he is fanning, he, by dint of meditation, like a phantom, in all regions honours the Jina.

30. In the west, where the pure world Sukhâkara is situated, there the Chief Amitâbha, the tamer of men, has his fixed abode.

31. There no women are to be found; there sexual intercourse is absolutely unknown; there the sons of Jina, on springing into existence by apparitional birth, are sitting in the undefiled cups of lotuses.

32. And the Chief Amitâbha himself is seated on a throne in the pure and beautiful cup of a lotus, and shines as the Sala-king.

33. The Leader of the world, whose store of merit has been praised, has no equal in the triple world. O supreme of men, let us soon become like thee!

Source: From Saddharmapundarikasûtra XXIV:1-33 in M. Muller, ed., *SBE,* OUP 1884, Vol.XXI, pp.413-18.

How should One Preach the Saddharmapundarikasutra?

23. After entering [the Nirvana by knowing this Sûtra], putting on his robe and sitting down on the seat, the preacher should, undaunted, expound this Sûtra.

24. The strength of kindness is my abode; the apparel of forebearance is my robe; void is my seat. Let [the preacher] take his stand on this and preach.

25. Where clods, sticks, pikes or abusive words and threats fall to the lot of the preacher, let him be patient, thinking of men [= the Buddha].

27. To that courageous man who shall proclaim this Sûtra after my complete extinction, I will also send many [angels?].

29. And should there be some to attack him with clods, sticks, injurious words, threats, taunts, then the [angels?] will defend him.

30. And when he shall stay alone, engaged in study, in a lonely place, in the forest or the hills.

31. Then will I show him my luminous body and enable him to remember the lesson he would have forgotten.

35. And the creatures who are entrusted to his care shall very soon all become Bodhisattvas, and by cultivating his intimacy, they shall behold Buddhas as numerous as the sands of the Ganges.[1]

Note

1. Almost all the principal elements of the Mahâyâna are expressed here: (a) The idea of Bodhisattva, one who has arrived at illumination and liberation, but remains with men to save them by preaching. (b) The general disposition of kindness which is the note of a Bodhisattva. (c) The paramount position of the Lotus of the True Law as a basis for all preaching. (d) The philosophical idea of VOID (Sunya), as negation of all limited beings, and as the only final name for the Ultimate reality or state. (e) The mythical accretions, according to which Superhuman Beings and the Buddha himself appear to men to help and protect them. (f) The contradictions which a preacher will have to suffer (not only from unbelievers but also from some monks of other schools, for instance of the Hînayâna, where philosophy and mythology have no place, at least in theory... (g) The necessity of forbearance as a condition to go on preaching... (h) All the authority of preaching being attributed to the authority of the Sûtra, presented as a final expression of the Message of the Master.

Source: From Saddharmapundarikasûtra X: 23-35 in M. Muller, ed., *SBE*, OUP 1884, pp.224 ff.

3.7   MAHAYANA BUDDHISM: RITUAL AND MAGIC IN TIBET

Some Introductory Notes 3.7.1

Pantheon

The principal contribution of Tibet to Buddhism is 'theistic' and ritual. The cult is directed to:

Five Dhyâni-*Buddhas* ('void' and inactive): Vairocana, Akshobya, Ratnasambhava, Amoghasiddhi, and (chiefly?) Amitâbha.
Numerous other *Buddhas.*
Eight principal *Bodhisattvas:* Padmapani, Manjusri, Vajrapani, Maitreya (a Buddha yet to come), etc.
A few female *Bodhisattvas,* chiefly *Târâ*.
The *Shaktis,* feminine energetic beings.
The *Dharmapâlas,* Protectors of the Law.
Demons and Witches (to seek favours or to avert their malice).
Some *brahmanical gods;* among them Shiva.
Local and personal *other gods,* of the old polytheistic religion.

Ritual

Formulas: OM MANI PADME HUM!
Charms and amulets; with sacred texts.
Liturgical mystery-plays; dances.

'The external movements annihilate the evil spirits; the interior sacrifice gives joy to the Buddhas' (SUMBUM TSAGHAN DAYANTSHI)

Exorcisms: 'May the exorcist bring forth from himself the sublime Vajravarahi, with the likeness of a pomegranate flower, having one face, two arms, three eyes (of which one is in the forehead), with hair dishevelled, carrying seven seals, and naked. It is she in whom dwell the five wisdoms.'
Offerings to the Buddhas: 'May all the living find a place in heaven, in exchange for the offerings which I present to the Buddha: incense, perfumes and ornaments, symbols of the four quarters of the world, of Mount Sumeru (which is at its very centre), of the sun and of the

moon.

The Lamas are all-powerful

'When in the darkness of time past, there was yet no lama, then even the word "Buddha" was not known. For the Buddhas are brought to life by the action of the lamas.'

'We adore thee, thou sublime Lama, who dost control the truths of the doctrine and dost possess perfect wisdom. We adore thee, the Great Ocean who dost provide all types of treasure.'

The misery of all Beings

'Where hatred is reigning, there are the chains of Hell;
Where greediness is reigning, there are the chains of the realm of ghosts;
Where ignorance is reigning, there are the chains of the realm of brutes;
Where passion is reigning, there are the chains of the human world;
Where furore is reigning, there are the chains of the Asura-realm;
Where pride is reigning, there are the chains of the realms of the gods.
These are the chains in which all beings are imprisoned, in "non-liberation".'

[Milarepa, famous Tibetan spiritual leader].

Source: J. Masson, hitherto unpublished.

3.7.2 Tibetan Invocations

[Comparing the following two invocations, it is easy to see how much they differ. The first one is classical, orthodox Buddhism; the second one has been penetrated by a number of superstitious elements of the pre-existing Tibetan (Bon) religion. The first one belongs to the monks, the second one to the 'shamans' (wizards).]

I

Ohm Ma Ni Padme Hum (song to the eternal religion-gift).

Hail teacher sublime, Supreme Buddha.
Holy doctrine, peaceful and separated from passion:
Community refulgent with talent;
Hail Union of the Sublime Three.

II

Today from the abode of the gods of war, come three hundred and sixty mouth-terrible ones and give advice to this song of the world. As to this place, if you do not know it, this is the land of rMa ('peacock') the basin of the Yellow River. The two fair ones — sun, moon — are joined. High ones, chiefs — sun, moon — are joined. Fathers, uncles — eagle, dragon — are joined. The six tribes — peace, felicity — are joined. If I am not known, I, the descendant on the stem of the trumpet of my ancestors, am the beautiful flower of gold. Pleasant speech circles the turquoise bird — the cuckoo. Speech becomes meaningful with the saying of a single word. If this song is not known, it is the lead part of the poem of the God-region.

Source: R.B. Ekvall, *Religious Observances in Tibet,* University of Chicago Press 1964, p.31.

The Cult of the Goddess Tarâ   3.7.3

[The word 'goddess' is used here intentionally. In Tibetan piety, the figure of Tarâ is at the centre of a religious belief and cult.]

1. *Hymn to Tarâ*

Tarâ, the Mother.	Arya, Tarâ! Hail to Thee![1] Our Deliveress sublime! Avalok'ta's messenger Rich in power and pity's store.
Tarâ, the supremely Courageous.	Hail O Tarâ! quick to save! Lotus-born of pitying tear Shed down by The Three-World-Lord (Grieving sad for sunken souls).
Tarâ, the white-moon Brightness.	Hail! to Thee with fulgent face, Brilliant as a hundred moons Of harvest gleaming in the light Of myriad dazzling stars.

Târâ, the Golden-Coloured.	Hail! to Thee whose hand is decked By the lotus, golden blue. Eager soother of our woe, Ever tireless worker, Thou!
Târâ, the Grand Hair-piled.	Hail! to Thee with pil'd-up hair, Where Tathâgata sits shrin'd, Victor of the universe, Thou a saintly victor too!
Târâ, the 'Hun' Shouter.	Hail to thy 'tut-târâ-hun'[2], Piercing realms of earth and sky, Treading down the seven worlds, Bending prostrate everyone!
Târâ, the best Three-World Worker.	Hail! adored by mighty gods, Indra, Brâhma, Fire and Wind, Ghostly hordes and Ganharvas All unite in praising Thee!
Târâ, the Supressor of Strife.	Hail! with Thy dread 'tre' and 'phat'[3] Thou destroyest all Thy foes; Striding out with Thy left foot Belching forth devouring fire!
Târâ, the Bestower of Supreme Power.	Hail! with fearful spell'tur-re' Banishing the bravest fiends, By the mere frown of Thy brows, Vanquishing whole hordes of foes!...

2. Presentation of offerings

'We hail Thee, revered and sublime Târâ!
Thou art adored by all kings and princes
Of the ten directions, of the present,
Past, and future.
We pray Thee to accept these offerings
Of flowers, incense, perfumed lamps,
Precious food, the music of cymbals,
And the other offerings!

We sincerely beg Thee in all Thy divine Forms
To partake of the food now offered!
On confessing to Thee penitently their sins
The most sinful hearts, yea! even the committers of the
Ten vices and the five boundless sins,
Will obtain forgiveness and reach
Perfection of soul — through Thee!
If we [human beings] have amassed any merit
In the three states,
We rejoice in this good fortune, when we consider
The unfortunate lot of the poor [lower] animals
Piteously engulfed in the ocean of misery.
On their behalf, we now turn the wheel of religion!
We implore Thee by whatever merit we have accumulated
To kindly regard all the animals.
And for ourselves!
When our merit has reached perfection
Let us not, we pray Thee,
Linger longer in this world!'

Notes

1. Târâ is Avalokitesvara's consort, represented under twenty-one forms.
2. This is a portion of Târâ's spell.
3. Magic spells of the wizards.

Source: L.A. Waddell, *Lamaism*, Heffer 1934, pp.435-7.

An Evocation of Prajnâpâramitâ   3.7.4

[Originally, Wisdom is only a 'quality' of every Buddha. But here it appears, up to a point, as personified. Contrary to the feminine partners of the hindu-gods (presented as their 'energies') this 'goddess' is associated with the final inactivity and void of Nirvana.]

A

One should envisage in one's own heart the syllable DHIH set upon a lunar disc, and with the rays that emerge from it one should arouse all gurus and Buddhas and Bodhisattvas and drawing them in before oneself, one should envisage them as sitting there in their various positions.[1] Then one should mentally confess one's sins and rejoice at such merit as has accrued, take the three-fold refuge, rouse the thought of enlightenment, dedicate merit and beg for pardon. Next one should develop friendliness, compassion, sympathetic joy and even-mindedness. Then with these words one should meditate the Void: 'I possess in my essence the adamantine nature which is knowledge of the Void.'²

B

Next one should envisage that syllable DHIH which is set on the lunar disc, as transformed into the Lady Prajñâpâramitâ. She bears a head-dress of twisted hair; she has four arms and one face. With two of her hands she makes the gesture of expounding the dharma and she is adorned with various jewelled ornaments. She blazes like the colour of gold and in her (second) left hand she holds a blue lotus with a Prajñâpâramitâ-book upon it. She wears various garments both below and above and with her [second] right hand she makes a gesture of fearlessness. She is seated cross-legged on the lunar disc and on a red lotus. Envisaging her thus, one should perform the act of identification: 'Such as is the Lady Prajñâpâramitâ, even so am I. Such as am I, even so is the Lady Prajñâpâramitâ.' Next one should set out the mantras: at the throat OM DHIH, on the tongue OM GIH, and on the ears OM JRIH.

Then in one's own heart one should imagine a red eight-petalled lotus, which arises from the syllable AH and is complete with pericarp and filament, and upon the pericarp and petals of this lotus one should mentally inscribe in yellow these words:

On the eastern petal:	HOMAGE
On the south-eastern petal:	TO THE LADY
On the southern petal:	PRAJNAPARAMITA
On the south-western petal:	WHOSE VIRTUE IS IMMORTALITY
On the western petal:	WHO RESPONDS TO LOVING DEVOTION
On the north-western petal:	WHO IS REPLETE WITH THE KNOWLEDGE OF ALL THE TATHAGATAS
On the northern petal:	WHO IS LOVING TOWARDS ALL
On the north-eastern petal:	OM DHIH
Then, On the eastern side of the pericarp:	SRU

On the south-eastern side:	TI
On the southern side:	SMR
On the south-western side:	TI
On the western side:	VI
On the north-western side:	JA
on the northern side:	YE
On the north eastern side:	SVAHA

Having thus set out these mantra-words one should recite them and meditate upon them — for a day, a week, six months, or a year. Thereby one becomes possessed of wisdom.

Notes

1. Here a mandala (symbolic image) is used as a starting-point for meditation.
2. The first steps which are indicated here are classical Buddhism: taking refuge, orientating the mind, developing the four brahma-viharas (universal, spiritual, benevolent dispositions), and passing to the highest trances. Under two forms; one 'negative': Void, Emptiness; the other one positive: Wisdom, Prâjñâ. But the rest of the text evidently belongs to another current: devotional and magical.

Source: From Sâdhanamâlâ in E. Conzé *et. al., Buddhist Texts through the Ages,* Bruno Cassirer 1954,

3.8 BASSUI'S SERMON

3.8.1 The Sermon

3.8.1 If you would free yourself of the sufferings of samsara, you must learn the direct way to become a Buddha. This way is no other than the realization of your own Mind. Now what is this Mind? It is the true nature of all sentient beings, that which existed before our parents were born and hence before our own birth, and which presently exists, unchangeable and eternal. So it is called one's Face before one's parents were born. This Mind is intrinsically pure. When we are born it is not newly created, and when we die it does not perish. It has no distinction of male or female, nor has it any coloration of good or bad. It cannot be compared with anything, so it is called Buddha-nature. Yet countless thoughts issue from this Self-nature as waves arise in the ocean or as images are reflected in a mirror.

3.8.2 If you want to realize your own Mind, you must first of all look into the source from which thoughts flow. Sleeping and working, standing and sitting, profoundly ask yourself, 'What is my own Mind?' with an intense yearning to resolve this question. This is called 'training' or 'practice' or 'desire for truth' or 'thirst for realization'. What is termed zazen is no more than looking into one's own mind. It is better to search your own mind devotedly than to read and recite innumerable sutras and dharani every day for countless years. Such endeavors, which are but formalities, produce some merit, but this merit expires and again you must experience the suffering of the Three Evil Paths. Because searching one's own mind leads ultimately to enlightenment, this practice is a prerequisite to becoming a Buddha. No matter whether you have committed either the ten evil deeds or the five deadly sins, still if you turn back your mind and enlighten yourself, you are a Buddha instantly. But do not commit sins and expect to be saved by enlightenment [from the effects of your own actions. Neither enlightenment] nor a Buddha nor a Patriarch can save a person who, deluding himself, goes down evil ways.

3.8.3 Imagine a child sleeping next to its parents and dreaming it is being beaten or is painfully sick. The parents cannot help the child no matter how much it suffers, for no one can enter the dreaming mind of another. If the child could awaken itself, it could be freed of this suffering automatically. In the same way, one who realizes that his own Mind is Buddha frees himself instantly from the sufferings arising from [ignorance of the law of] ceaseless change of birth-and-death. If a Buddha could prevent it, do you think he would allow even one sentient being to fall into hell?[1] Without Self-realization one cannot understand such things as these.

What kind of master is it that this very moment sees colors with   3.8.4 the eyes and hears voices with the ears, that now raises the hands and moves the feet? We know these are functions of our own mind, but no one knows precisely how they are performed. It may be asserted that behind these actions there is no entity, yet it is obvious they are being performed spontaneously. Conversely, it may be maintained that these *are* the acts of some entity; still the entity is invisible. If one regards this question as unfathomable, all attempts to reason [out an answer] will cease and one will be at a loss to know what to do. In this propitious state deepen and deepen the yearning, tirelessly, to the extreme. When the profound questioning penetrates to the very bottom, and that bottom is broken open, not the slightest doubt will remain that your own Mind is itself Buddha, the Void-universe. There will then be no anxiety about life or death, no truth to search for.

In a dream you may stray and lose your way home. You ask   3.8.5 someone to show you how to return or you pray to God or Buddhas to help you, but still you can't get home. Once you rouse yourself from your dream-state, however, you find that you are in your own bed and realize that the only way you could have gotten home was to awake yourself. This [kind of spiritual awakening] is called 'return to the origin' or 'rebirth in paradise'. It is the kind of inner realization that can be achieved with some training. Virtually all who like zazen and make an effort in practice, be they laymen or monks, can experience it to this degree. But even such [partial] awakening cannot be attained except through the practice of zazen. You would be making a serious error, however, were you to assume that this was true enlightenment in which there is no doubt about the nature of reality. You would be like a man who having found copper gives up the desire for gold.

Upon such realization question yourself even more intensely in   3.8.6 this wise: 'My body is like a phantom, like bubbles on a stream. My mind, looking into itself, is as formless as empty-space, yet somewhere within sounds are perceived. Who is hearing?' Should you question yourself in this wise with profound absorption, never slackening the intensity of your effort, your rational mind eventually will exhaust itself and only questioning at the deepest level will remain. Finally you will lose awareness of your own body. Your long-held conceptions and notions will perish, after absolute questioning, in the way that every drop of water vanishes from a tub broken open at the bottom, and perfect enlightenment will follow like flowers suddenly blooming on withered trees.

3.8.7   With such realization you achieve true emancipation. But even now repeatedly cast off what has been realized, turning back to the subject that realizes, that is, to the root bottom, and resolutely go on. Your Self-nature will then grow brighter and more transparent as your delusive feelings perish, like a gem gaining luster under repeated polishing, until at last it positively illumines the entire universe. Don't doubt this! Should your yearning be too weak to lead you to this state in your present lifetime, you will undoubtedly gain in Self-realization easily in the next, provided you are still engaged in this questioning at death, just as yesterday's work half done was finished easily today.

3.8.8   While you are doing zazen neither despise nor cherish the thoughts that arise; only search your own mind, the very source of these thoughts. You must understand that anything appearing in your consciousness or seen by your eyes is an illusion, of no enduring reality. Hence you should neither fear nor be fascinated by such phenomena. If you keep your mind as empty as space, unstained by extraneous matters, no evil spirits can disturb you even on your deathbed. While engaged in zazen, however, keep none of this counsel in mind. You must only become the question 'What is this Mind?' or 'What is it that hears these sounds?' When you realize this Mind you will know that it is the very source of all Buddhas and sentient beings. The Bodhisattva Kannon is so called because he attained enlightenment by perceiving [i.e. grasping the source of] the sounds of the world about him.

3.8.9   At work, at rest, never stop trying to realize who it is that hears. Even though your questioning becomes almost unconscious, you won't find the one who hears, and all your efforts will come to naught. Yet sounds can be heard, so question yourself to an even profounder level. At last every vestige of self-awareness will disappear and you will feel like a cloudless sky. Within yourself you will find no 'I', nor will you discover anyone who hears. This Mind is like the void, yet it hasn't a single spot that can be called empty.

This state is often mistaken for Self-realization. But continue to ask yourself even more intensely, 'Now who is it that hears?' If you bore and bore into this question, oblivious to anything else, even this feeling of voidness will vanish and you will be unaware of anything — total darkness will prevail. [Don't stop here, but] keep asking with all your strength, 'What *is* it that hears?' Only when you have completely exhausted the questioning will the question burst; now you will feel like a man come back from the dead. This is true realization. You will see the Buddhas of all the universes face to face and the Patriarchs past and present. Test yourself with this koan: 'A monk asked Joshu: "What is the meaning of Bodhidharma's coming to China?" Joshu replied: "The oak tree in the garden".' Should this koan leave you with the slightest doubt, you need to resume questioning, 'What is it that hears?'

If you don't come to realization in this present life, when will 3.8.10 you? Once you have died you won't be able to avoid a long period of suffering in the Three Evil Paths. What is obstructing realization? Nothing but your own half-hearted desire for truth. Think of this and exert yourself to the utmost.

Note

1. What is implied here is that Buddhas are not supernatural beings who can prevent one from falling into hell by conferring enlightenment, but that enlightenment, through which one can be saved from the sufferings of such a fate, is attainable solely through one's own efforts.

Source: P. Kapleau, ed., *The Three Pillars of Zen,* Weatherhill 1967, pp.160-4.

3.9   THE OX-HERDING

Attributed to Kuo-an Sh-yuan

3.9.1 Seeking the Ox

The ox has never really gone astray so why search for it? Having turned his back on his True-nature, the man has become alienated from it. Led astray by the delusions of the senses, he has lost it. Home grows further away and the road branches confusingly. Desire for gain and fear of loss burn like fire, ideas of right and wrong shoot up like arrows.

Finding the Tracks

Through the sutras and teachings he discerns the tracks [of the ox]. He now realises that, in the same way that various [golden vessels] are made of the same gold, so everything is a manifestation of the Self. But he is unable to distinguish right from wrong, truth from falsehood. He has only seen the tracks. He has not yet entered the gate.

3.9.3 Seeing the Ox

Through following the sound (of the ox) he sees into the Source of things. The six senses are no different from the true Source. In every activity it is manifestly present. It is like the taste of salt in water and the glue in paint. If your vision is really clear you will see whatever you look at is the same as the true Source; and that, indeed, it is no different from your True-nature.

Catching the Ox 3.9.4

Today he encountered the ox which had been lost for a long time in the fields. But the ox is spirited and difficult to control. It constantly longs for sweet-smelling grass. The stubborn mind is irrepressible. The wild nature is still untamed. If you want to tame it you must use a whip.

3.9.5 Taming the Ox

As soon as a thought occurs then another follows. When enlightenment occurs such thoughts become valid. While one is still in a state of delusion such thoughts are false. Truth and falsehood, enlightenment and delusion do not have their source in the objective world but only in one's mind. Pull the nose-string tight and do not waver.

Riding the Ox Home   3.9.6

The struggle is over; gain and loss no longer exist for him. He hums the rustic tune of the wood-cutter and sings the simple songs of the village boy. Sitting on the ox he gazes at the clouds in the sky. If he is called to he will not turn round. Impervious to all enticements, he will not be kept back.

3.9.7 The Ox Forgotten, Leaving the Man Alone

In the Dharma there is no duality. The ox symbolises his original nature. The trap is no longer needed once the rabbit has been snared; there is no further use for the net when the fish has been caught. It is like gold separating from dross; like the moon coming out from behind clouds; there is only the light of eternity.

The Ox and the Man Both Forgotten 3.9.8

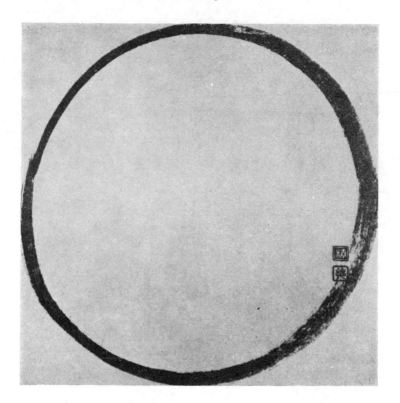

The delusive feelings of the secular mind have become void; and so have ideas of holiness. He does not linger where the Buddha is, and where the Buddha is not, he passes on. Since he no longer adheres to dualistic ways of thinking even one with a thousand eyes cannot discern what he is. An enlightenment before which a hundred birds offer flowers is but a travesty [of enlightenment].

3.9.9 Returning to the Source

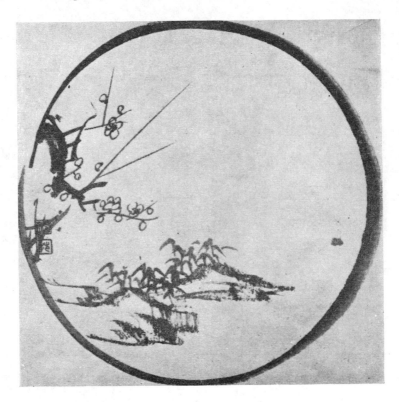

From the very beginning he has been pure and immaculate, uncontaminated by even so much as a speck of dust. He calmly watches the growth and decay of phenomena in the world while abiding in the immovable serenity of non-assertion. He is not in a state of illusion therefore what is the need for artificial effort? The waters are blue, the mountains are green. He sits and watches things continuously changing.

Entering the City with Bliss-Bestowing Hands 3.9.10

The humble gate of his cottage is closed and even the wisest do not know him. His mind is hidden. He goes his own way, not following the steps of previous sages. Carrying a gourd he goes into the market; leaning on his staff he returns home. He leads publicans and fishmongers to enlightenment.

Original drawings and commentaries attributed to Kuo-an Shi-yuan, a Chinese Zen Master of the twelfth century.

Source: For the Plates I-X cf. D.T. Suzuki, *Essays in Zen Buddhism* (First Series).

4 SIKHISM: THE VOICE OF THE GURŪ

[*Editor's Note:* The following note and translation are the work of Terry Thomas, the Course Unit author of the Sikhism units.]

Sikhism is one of the more recent religions of the world. Gurū Nānak, its founder, lived in India between 1469 and 1539 C.E. He was followed by nine other Gurūs. During the period of the Gurūs the Sikh faith was directed by the accumulated teaching of the Gurūs, more particularly Gurū Nānak, and the interpretation of each succeeding Gurū. The whole teaching was retained in the form of hymns in the vernacular, Panjabi. Hymns in the vernacular were a feature of the whole *Bhakti* movement in India in the fifteenth century C.E.

Written collections of hymns were prepared from the time of the second Gurū onwards but the major collection was compiled in 1603-4 under Gurū Arjan. It was called *Adi Granth* (First Collection), a title which is still used. By this time it had achieved the status of scripture but was unusual as scripture in that it contained hymns by teachers of other faiths, most notably Kabir.

The Sikh scriptures attained a new status following the death of the last Gurū, Gobind Singh, in 1708. Authority was now vested in the scriptures and the community of believers. In such a situation the written scriptures were bound to be elevated to a pre-eminent position. Not only were belief and practice to be controlled according to the scriptures but the physical embodiment of the scriptures was to be honoured. The volume of scriptures came to be known as *Gurū Granth Sāhib,* an ever-present embodiment of the divine inspiration of the human Gurūs, taking on the features of the living presence of the Gurūs.

This explains the centrality of the *Guru Granth Sahib* as a physical object in every Sikh gurdwārā (place of worship), the veneration shown towards it and its ongoing function in the life of every Sikh community, expressed in regular worship and all the important events of life, from birth to death.

I wish to acknowledge the help and advice given by Piara Singh Sambhi and W. Owen Cole in the translation that follows. Any blemishes which have persisted are my own.

4.1 A SELECTION OF THE HYMNS OF GURŪ NĀNAK FROM THE GURŪ GRANTH SAHIB OR ĀDI GRANTH

Translated by D.A.T. Thomas

Japji *[A long poem, from 4.1.1 to 4.1.23, taken from A.6. pp.1-8]*

ik omkār

> God is One,   4.1.1
> He is the True Name,
> The Maker and All-pervading Spirit
> Fearing nothing, hating no one,
> 5 A Being beyond time,
> Self-existent beyond birth,
> Revealed by the grace of the Gurū.

Jap

> Before all things existed He was Truth,
> In the beginning of all things He was Truth,
> 10 Today He is Truth, Nānak,
> And Truth He will ever be.

> Though I think a hundred thousand thoughts of God, thought 4.1.2
> alone cannot reach Him.

> Though I remain in deep and silent meditation, such meditation
> alone cannot achieve the divine Silence.

> 5 Though I hunger for Him my hunger does not depart if I am
> filled only with this world's goods.

> Though I possess a hundred thousand worldly devices not one
> avails for this task.

> How then can I be true?
> 10 How can the barrier of untruth be demolished?

> By obeying the pre-ordained Will of the Lord, Nānak.

4.1.3   Through His Will things come to be,
His Will is indescribable.
Through His Will souls come to be,
Through His Will excellence is obtained.

5   Through His Will some are high born, others low;
Through His pre-ordained Will some receive pain, others
      pleasure.
One through His Will receives blessing,
The other through His Will must ever wander.

His Will applies to all,
10 None shall escape His Will,
Nānak, he who knows His Will
Cannot glory in his own self.

4.1.4   Some who have the power sing of His might.
Some sing of His gifts, who know His signs.
Some sing of His attributes, His excellent greatness.
Some sing of His knowledge, His deepest thought.
5   Some sing of His creation of the body and of its dissolution to
      dust.
Some sing of His taking life and of its restoration.
Some sing of His apparent distance from us,
Some sing of His nearness, beholding us face to face.

Discourses and expositions are endless,
10 Millions of sermons by millions of preachers.
The giver gives and the receiver wearies of receiving,
Age upon age man is refreshed and replenished.
The Sovereign by His Will has ordered man's path.
He remains happy, Nānak, in His contentment.

4.1.5   The Lord is Truth, His Righteousness is true, His language is
      infinite love.
We pray and beg, 'Give us, give us', and the Giver gives.
What then can we offer Him that we may see His Court?
What words should we utter that He might show us love?
5   At fragrant dawn reflect on the True Name and His greatness.

Past actions determine our garment, His Grace gives us the door
of salvation.
Know this, Nānak, that this is the way to know that the True
One is everything.

He cannot be made and installed like an idol,   4.1.6
He Himself of Himself is self-existent.
Those who have served Him have received honour.
Nanak, praise the Lord, the Treasury of virtues.
Sing and hear and retain His love in your heart,
Thus will sorrow flee and joy shall dwell in its place.
The Guru's voice is the eternal sound, the Guru's voice is the
Veda, the Guru's voice is all-pervading.
The Guru is Ishwar,[1] the Guru is Gorakh[2] and Brahma, the
Guru is Parvati[3] and the Mother-goddess.[4]
If I know Him should I not tell His story, but He cannot be
described by words.

The Guru has explained one thing to me:
There is but one Giver of all life, let me never forget Him.

I would pilgrimage to a holy river if I thought I would gain His   4.1.7
love,
But without it the ablutions are useless.
I behold all created beings,
But without grace what can they obtain?
5   The mind is filled with gems and precious stones
If we listen to just one item of the Guru's teaching.

The Guru has explained one thing to me:
There is but one Giver of all life, let me never forget Him.

Though a man's life spanned the four ages or ten times more,   4.1.8
Or his reputation spread to nine continents and everyone
followed him,
Or his name were praised and his renown known in all the world,
If His Grace does not descend on him then he is as someone
ignored.

5   He becomes a worm among worms, even the sinful accuse him
of sin.

Nānak, those lacking virtue God makes virtuous, even the
virtuous were given their virtue by Him.
I cannot think of anyone else who could grant them virtue.

4.1.9   He who hears *the Word* becomes like Ishwar,[5] Brahma and
Indra.[6]
He who hears, though he be of low estate, will be filled with
praise.
He who hears discovers the way of yoga and the secrets of the
body.
He who hears understands the Shastras,[7] Smritis[8] and Vedas.[9]
5   Nānak, the *bhagats*[10] are always happy.
For him who hears, sorrow and sin are destroyed.

4.1.10   Innumerable His names and innumerable His dwellings,
Inaccessible and incomprehensible His innumerable realms.
It is folly even to say that they are innumerable.
In letters we spell His Name, in letters we sing His praise,
5   In letters are spelt His Wisdom, in letters are His praises sung
and His virtues known,
In letters we write down the spoken word,
In letters is a man's destiny inscribed on his brow;
But they are not found on the head of Him who inscribed
them.
As he ordains so shall man receive.
10   As great is creation, so great is His Name.
There is no corner without His Name.
What power of thought have I to describe His creation?
I am not worthy to be sacrificed to Him even once.

Whatever pleases Thee is a good deed.
15   Thou dost endure always, Formless One.

4.1.11   When hands, feet and the body are dirty,
Water washes the dirt away.

When your clothing is soiled,
With the use of soap it is washed clean.
5 When the mind is polluted by sin,
It is cleansed by delighting in the Lord's Name.
Purity and sin are not mere words,
Rather are they actions with effective results.
A man eats what he sows.
10 Nānak, by God's Will we come and go.

Pilgrimage, penance, compassion and the giving of alms   4.1.12
Are given the least honour;[11]
He who hears, obeys and loves God in his heart,
Bathes in a place of pilgrimage within himself.
5 All virtues are Thine, Lord. I have none.
But without virtue, devotion to Thee is impossible.
Hail to Thee who created Maya, the Word and Brahma,
Thou art Truth and Beauty, whose heart is ever filled with
    delight.

At what time, at which moment, what day of the month or week,
10 What was the season, what was the month, when it all took
    shape?
The pandits did not discover the time or it would be in the
    Puranic texts.
The qazis did not discover the time or they would have written
    it in the Qur'an.
Nor did the yogis or anyone else know the season or the month
    or the day of the month or week.
He who created the world alone knows when he did it;
15 How shall we address Thee, praise Thee, describe Thee or know
    Thee, Lord?
Nānak, all speak about Him, each man wiser than the next.
Great is the Lord, great is His Name, whatever He wills comes
    to pass.
Nānak, he who thinks himself something will not be honoured
    in the life hereafter.

There are hundreds of thousands of worlds below and heavens 4.1.13
    above.

Men have wearied themselves searching limitless bounds; but the
Vedas say the Spirit is one.
The *Kateba*[12] says there are 18,000 worlds but that Reality is
one principle.
If description were possible then it would have been written;
but men have exhausted themselves.
5   Nānak, call Him Great. Only He knows Himself.

4.1.14   There's no limit to God's praise, to His glorification no limit.
There's no limit to His works, to His giving no limit.
We cannot limit Him by our seeing or by our hearing.
We cannot know the limit of the secret of His heart.
5   We cannot know the limit of His created world.
We cannot know the limit of His own accepted limits.
How many cry out to know His limits?
But His limits cannot be discerned.
This limit no one can know.
10   The more that is described the more remains.
Great is the Lord, His throne is exalted.
Higher than the highest is His Name.
If anyone were to be as highly exalted as He,
Then he would know His exaltation.
15   But God alone knows how great He is.
Nānak, what we receive is the result of Grace.

4.1.15   Make contentment thine earrings, spiritual endeavour thy
begging bowl and wallet, and meditation thy sacred ash.
Wear death like sackcloth, in manner of life let thy body be that
of a virgin and faith in God be thy staff.
Let communion with all men be thy holy order, control of the
mind means control of the world.
5   Hail, Hail to Him!
The First, the Pure, the One without beginning, the Indestructible, from age to age retaining the same vesture.

4.1.16   The union of the One with the Mother[13] gave birth to three
approved disciples.
One the world's Creator, one its Sustainer, and the third its

Judge.[14]

According to God's pleasure they perform their duties.

He watches over them, but they behold Him not. What a great marvel!

5   Hail, Hail to Him!

The First, the Pure, the One without beginning, the Indestructible, from age to age retaining the same vesture.

Let my single tongue become hundreds of thousands twenty   4.1.17 times over,

So would I repeat the Name of the Lord of Creation endlessly.

Thus would I ascend the stairs to the Lord and become one with Him.

The sound of heavenly things makes the lowest want to rise.

5 Nānak, by Grace is God attained, the rest is false boasting.

God created the night, the seasons, days of the month and week.   4.1.18

He created the wind, water, fire and the worlds below.

In their midst he set the world as the sphere of *dharma*.

In it he placed animals of various species and colour,

5 Their names are many and endless.

Each one is judged according to his deeds.

The Lord Himself is True and His Court is true,

There the elect rejoice in their acceptance.

They bear the sign of grace and mercy.

10 There the bad and the good are separated.

Nānak, when we go there this will be manifest.

Such is the stage of Religious Duty.   4.1.19

Now I shall describe the activity of the stage of Knowledge.

How many are the winds, waters and fires, how many the Krishnas and Sivas!

How many the Brahmas who created worlds, of many forms and colours and vestures!

5 How many worlds of *karma* and mountains like Meru, how many Dhruvas under instruction!

How many Indras, moons and suns, how many universes and countries!

How many Siddhas, Buddhas and Nāths, how many goddesses in
different forms!
How many gods, demons and ascetics, how many jewels and
seas![15]
How many sources of life, how many languages, how many
royal dynasties!
10 How many approaches to God and servants of God! Nānak, the
process is endless.

4.1.20   In the stage of Knowledge divine wisdom shines forth;
It is the realm of the eternal sound, giving countless joys and
pleasures.
In the next stage of Spiritual Striving the language is perfection;
There, things are fashioned in an incomparable way.
5   What goes on there cannot be described.
Whoever tries must later feel ashamed.
There inner consciousness, intellect, mind and wisdom are shaped.
There the state of being a sage and a Siddha is achieved.

4.1.21   In the stage of Grace, man is so filled with spiritual power
That nothing more can be added to him.
There are found very great warriors and heroes,
Whom the great Lord[16] fills completely.
5   They are inextricably woven into the greatness of the Lord;
Such is their beauty it cannot be described.
They do not die neither are they deceived,
Those in whose hearts the Lord abides.
There also dwell communities of bhagats;
10   They live in bliss, the True One in their hearts.

In the stage of Truth, the Formless One resides.
He, the Creator, beholds His creation and looks upon it with
grace.
Here there are continents, worlds and universes.
Who can describe a boundless bound?
15   Here there are worlds within worlds and endless forms.
Whatever God wills, that they do freely.
God beholds His creation and rejoices.
Nānak, to describe it is iron hard.

Let chastity be your furnace, patience your goldsmith. 4.1.22
Let understanding be your anvil, divine knowledge your tools.
Let the fear of God be your bellows, penance your fire.
Let the love of God be your crucible, in which *amrit* is smelted.
5 In this mint of Truth, the Word is coined.
This is the practice of those on whom God looks graciously.
Nānak, the Gracious One makes glad the heart of those upon
whom He looks with favour.

The air is the Gurū, water our father, the great earth our mother. 4.1.23
Day and night are the male and female nurses, in whose care the
whole world plays.
Good deeds and bad will be read in the presence of the Righteous One.
According to the operation of karma, some will be near and some
afar off.
5 Those who have meditated on the Name and have departed,
their toil completed,
Their faces, Nānak, will be bright and many will be released
along with them.

[Here follows a series of short poems, from 4.1.25 to 4.1.38]

Sohilā Ārti

There are six schools of philosophy, six teachers and six 4.1.24
doctrines,
But the Gurū of gurus is one, though he has many appearances.
Father, the school in which the Creator is praised,
That school protect, it is for Thy greatness.
5 Just as there are seconds, minutes, watches of the day, lunar
days, weekdays and months,
And many seasons depending on the one sun,
So, Nānak, the one Creator manifests many aspects.

[Rag Asa A.G. p.12]

The heaven is Thy salver, the sun and moon Thy lamps, 4.1.25
The stars in their paths are Thy scattered pearls.

The fragrance of sandalwood is Thine incense,
The wind is Thy *chowri*[17] and all the forests thy flowers, Lord of Light!
5   What worship[18] this is! This is Thy worship, Destroyer of rebirth!
The unstruck Word is Thy temple drums.

Thousands are Thine eyes, yet Thou hast no eye.
Thousands are Thine images, yet Thou hast no form.
Thousands are Thy pure feet, yet Thou hast no foot.
10   Thousands are Thy fragrances, yet Thou has no fragrance.
This play fascinates me.

In all there is light. Thou art that Light.
The brilliance which is from Him shines in all hearts.
By the Guru's teaching the Light is manifested.
15   Whatever pleases Him, that is *ārati.*

My heart is attracted by the lotus feet of God as the bee is by the honey, night and day I thirst for them.
Give to Nānak, the *sārang,*[19] the water of Thy mercy, so that he may abide ever in Thy Name.

[Rag Dhanasri. A.G. p.663]

4.1.26   If I were to live for millions and millions of years,
If I were to exist on air as my food and drink,
If I were to live in a cave deprived of the sun and moon and never dream of sleeping,
Still I would not be able to estimate Thy worth
5   Nor say how great Thy Name is.

True is the Formless One and unique.
Hearing and hearing one repeatedly proclaims.
If it pleases Him, only He can grant us awareness of Him.
If I were slashed and cut in pieces and ground into a pulp,
10   If I were consumed by fire and my ashes scattered,
Even then I would not be able to estimate Thy worth
Nor say how great Thy Name is.

If I were to become a bird and fly through a hundred skies,

If I were to vanish completely and exist without drinking or
eating,

15 Still I would not be able to estimate Thy worth,

Nor say how great Thy Name is.

Nānak, had I thousands of tons of books and read them diligently,

Could my pen write with the speed of the wind and the ink
never dry,

Even so I would not be able to estimate Thy worth

20 Nor say how great Thy Name is.

[Sri Rag. A.G. p.14]

Forgetting the Beloved even for an instant means great sickness 4.1.27
in the soul.

How can honour be achieved in His Court if the Lord does not
dwell in the soul?

By meeting the Gurū happiness is achieved, the fire is quenched
in His virtue.

My Soul! day and night repeat the virtues of the Lord.

5 Those who do not forget the Name for the briefest moment,
such men are rare in this world.

When our light meets the Light and our wisdom is joined with
Wisdom,

Violence and self-interest flee, doubt and sorrow are no more.

The gurmukh[20] in whose heart the Lord dwells, is united by the
Gurū.

If I give my body as a bride the Lord, the Bridegroom, will take
me.

10 Do not make love with him who is merely passing through.

The gurmukh like a chaste bride enjoys the Bridegrooms couch.

The four fires[21] are quenched and extinguished in the gurmukh
by pouring the water of the Lord.

Thus the heart, like the lotus, shall blossom; it shall be filled to
the brim with amrit.

Nānak, make the *Satguru*[22] thy friend, achieve Truth and enter
His Court.

[Sri Rag. A.G. p.21]

4.1.28   Thou, Lord, art the River, knowing all, seeing all.
         How can I, the fish, know Thy limits?
         Wherever I look Thou art there,
         Removed from Thee I perish and die.
    5   I do not know the fisherman nor do I recognize the net.
         When pain besets me then I call to Thee.

         Thou pervadest all things, I thought you were far off.
         Whatever I do, it is always in Thy presence.
         Thou seest all yet I deny my actions,
    10   I am unworthy of Thee and therefore cannot glorify Thy Name.

         Whatever Thou givest I eat.
         There is no other door, to whose door should I go?
         Nānak has one petition, accept my body and soul.

         The Lord Himself is near, He is also far off and He fills the in-
            between.
    15   He beholds all, He hears all, by His power He created the world.
         Whatever pleases Him, Nānak, it comes to pass according to His
            Will.

                                                    [Sri Rag. A.G. p.25]

4.1.29   The fish did not recognise the net in the salty and unfathomable
            sea;
         It was very clever and beautiful, why and whence its confidence?
         Because of its action it was caught, death does not pass it by.

         Brother, know that likewise death hovers over your head.
    5   As with the fish, so with man, the net falls unexpectedly.
         The whole world is in bondage to Death, without the Gurū
            death is unchallengeable.
         Those who are immersed in Truth are saved, leave doubt and
            vices behind.
         May I be a sacrifice to the truthful who repose in the Court of
            Truth.

         Birds at the mercy of the hawk and the nets in the hunter's
            hands are parables.

10 Those whom the Guru cares for are saved, the rest are caught
      with the bait.
    Without the Name they are taken and cast aside, without
      companionship and without friends.

    In truth we proclaim the Truth, the true realm is Truth.
    Those who honour the True One have Truth in their hearts.
    He who is pure of mind and speech and has knowledge is a
      gurmukh.

15 Pray before the Satguru and you will meet your Beloved.
    Happiness results from meeting the Beloved and the angels of
      death take poison and die.
    May I dwell in the Name and the Name will abide in my heart.
    Without the Gurū darkness prevails, without the Word wisdom
      is lost.
    By the Gurū's word divine light shines and we are absorbed in
      Truth.
20 Death does not enter there and our light blends with the Light.

    Thou art the Beloved, Thou art wise, Thou art the agent of
      union.
    Through the Word of the Gurū we praise Thee, Thou who art
      Infinite.
    Death cannot reach where the Word of the Gurū is supreme.

    By His Will all is created.
25 By His Will all deeds are done.
    By His Will some are doomed to die.
    By His Will some are united in the Truth.
    Nānak, whatever pleases Him comes to pass,
    Men are powerless to do anything.

                                        [Sri Rag. A.G. p.55]

    My Soul, let your love of the Lord be like that of the lotus for 4.1.30
      the water,
    Overcome by waves, it still flowers in love.
    Living things created in the water, if taken out of the water, die.
    My Soul, how can you be saved without love?

5   The Lord dwells in the heart of the gurmukh, to him he gives a treasure of devotion.

My Soul, let your love of the Lord be like that of the fish for the water,
The more water the more happiness and peace of mind and body.
Without water, even for an instant, it cannot live,
And God knows the suffering of its separation. . .

10   True love cannot be broken if the Satguru is present.
Access to the gift of Knowledge gives insight into the three worlds.
The pure Name is not forgotten if our trade is in virtue. . .

Without the Guru Love is not born, the stain of self-interest does not go away.
He who perceives God within himself knows the Word and is satisfied.
15   When the gurmukh understands himself, what more is there to do?

Why try to unite those who are already united in Him? Having received the Word they are satisfied.
The *manmukh*[23] cannot achieve understanding, in his alienation he suffers punishment.
Nānak, there is one door to the house of the Lord, there is nowhere else to go.

[Sri Rag. A.G. p.59]

4.1.31   The bhagats adore Him with love, they thirst for the Truth with great affection.
Those who plead and pray with tears receive happiness and much love in affection.

My Soul, repeat the Name of God and seek His refuge.
The ocean of life is crossed by a boat, namely the repetition of God's name as a rule of life.

5 My Soul, death becomes a well-wisher when you delight in the
    Word of the Lord.
   The mind is filled with real and beneficial Knowledge when it is
    imbued with the precious Name of God...

   This world is lost in temptation and attachment and is in great
    pain of birth and death.
   Hasten to Satguru's sanctuary, repeat God's Name in your heart
    and be saved...

   By fear, love and devotion and fixing the mind on the feet of
    God man crosses the terrible ocean.
10 Lord, let thy holy and loving Name be in my heart, I have come
    to Thy sanctuary.

   The waves of avarice and greed are overcome by the pre-
    eminence of God's Name in the soul.
   Chasten my soul, Pure Lord, Nānak seeks Thy protection.

                          [Gujri Ashtapadi. A.G. p.505]

   There are five adversaries,[24] I am alone. How shall I protect my 4.1.32
    mortal house, my soul?
   Time and again they attack and plunder me. To whom shall I
    appeal?
   Utter the Name of the Lord God, my soul.
   Before you is the army of death, powerful and numerous.

5 God has built this temple of many doors, and has installed a
    woman.
   The maid, thinking herself immortal, plays away her life, while
    the five adversaries plunder her.

   The temple is burned down and plundered; the maid, all alone,
    is taken captive.
   Death bludgeons her, her neck is chained, the five adversaries
    flee.

   The woman wants gold and silver, friends desire good eating.
10 Nānak, he who sins for the sake of such things, will go bound to

the city of death.

[Rag Gauri Cheti. A.G. p.155]

4.1.33   The Lord God is King,
         He beholds all the world he created.
         He sees, understands and knows every little thing.
         He is all-pervading.

[Rag Asa Patti, 24. A.G. p.433]

4.1.34   Black deer, hear me. Why are you attracted by that enclosed
          garden?
          The sweetness of forbidden fruit lasts but four days; then it
          becomes bitter.
          What you long for most becomes most bitter; without the Name
          great fever ensues.
          It is like a ripple on the sea or the lightning's sudden flash.
      5   Without the Lord there is no protector and you have forgotten
          Him.
          Nānak speaks the truth; consider it my Soul, black deer, you will
          die. . .

          My soul, you alien in this world, why do you fall victim to it?
          When the True Lord dwells in your soul, why should you be
          snared in death's net?
          The fish is separated from the water with tearful eyes when the
          fisherman has cast his net,
     10   The world of maya is a sweet attraction, in the end the delusion
          is exposed.
          Make devotion, apply consciousness to God and rid yourself of
          mental apprehension.
          Nānak speaks the truth, consider it my Soul, you foreigner soul.
          Rivers which separate along different channels hardly come
          together again.
          In each succeeding age what appears sweet is in fact full of
          poison, so a rare yogi affirms.
     15   Those who experience ultimate union realize God the Satguru
          and contemplate Him.

Without God's Name we stray as fools in deception and are
   destroyed.
Those who do not devote themselves to the Name of God, who
   do not have truth in their hearts, end up in anguish and
   remorse.
Nānak speaks the truth, through the true Word, those long
   separated souls unite with Him.

[Rag Asa. A.G. p.438]

The drop is in the ocean and the ocean in the drop. Who can   4.1.35
   understand this secret? He who knows the ways of the Lord.
The One who created the world, He Himself knows the meaning.
He who meditates on this Knowledge attains the perfect state
   through liberation.

The day is in the night and the night in the day; the same is
   true of heat and cold.
5   No other knows His condition and extent, without the Guru
   this understanding is not attained.

The male is in the female and the female in the male, the
   Divine Teacher knows it.
In the Word is concentration, in concentration there is
   knowledge, through the grace of the Guru an untold talc.

The soul is in the Light and the Light in the soul, the five senses
   join as the Guru's brethren,
Nānak says: 'I am a sacrifice to those who have set their heart
   on the Lord!

[Rag Ramkali. A.G. p.878]

Questions from a Yogi   4.1.36

What is the basis of your teaching?
What period is your thought?
Who is your Gurū, to whom are you a disciple?
What exposition keeps you in detachment?
Tell us what we want to hear, child Nānak.

Nānak Answers

The basis of my teaching is the first breath.
My thought belongs to the age of the Satguru.
The Word is my Gurū, I am a disciple of the sound of meditation;
The exposition of the Inexplicable keeps me in detachment.
10 Nānak, in each succeeding age the Gurū is God.[25]
I meditate on the exposition of the One Word,
For the gurmukh, self-interest is consumed in its fire.

[Rag Ramkali. A.G. p.942]

4.1.37   For millions of ages there was thick darkness;
There was no earth, no sky, only the Will of the Infinite.
There was no day or night, no moon or sun, only He alone
sitting in unmoving trance.

No existent matter or speech, no air and no water,
5   No creation, no destruction, no coming or going,
No continents, no worlds below, no surging ocean or flowing
river.

There were no higher, middle or lower levels of existence;
There was no heaven and no hell, neither was there death.
There was no hell and no heaven, no birth or death, no coming
or going.

10 There was no Brahma, Vishnu or Mahesh;[26]
No other was to be seen, only the One.
There was no female or male, no caste and no birth and no-one
to suffer pain or pleasure. . .

There was no karma or dharma or maya.
Caste and birth were not seen with the eye;
15 There was no snare of affection, death stalked no head,
There was nothing to meditate on. . .

There was no caste or religious division, no Brahman or Khatri;
No god, no temple, no cow or *Gayatri*.[27]
There was no living sacrifice, no bathing in holy places, no-one

to perform worship. . .[28]

20 There were no Vedas, no Kateba, no Smritis, no Shastras.
There was no reading of the Purānas at sunrise and sunset;
The unseen Lord was both subject and object of devotion, the
unique One Himself perceived all.

When He willed it, then He created the world and He set the
unsupported firmament.
He created Brahma, Vishnu and Mahesh; and maya and
temptation.

25 A few rare persons are enabled to hear the Gurū's Word.
By His will He created all and watches over it.
He founded continents, the universe, the worlds below, the
Unmanifest manifested Himself.

No one knows His limits;
The Perfect Gurū provides understanding.
30 Nānak, those who are filled with Truth wonder, they delight in
singing praise to the Gurū.

[Rag Maru A.G. p.1035]

Where self-interest exists Thou art not.   4.1.38
Where Thou art, self-interest cannot exist.
Gyāni[29] try to unravel this mystery.
This description of the Indescribable must lodge in the soul.
5 Without the Gurū this principle is not discovered, that the
Unseen One dwells in the soul.
When the Satguru is met, the Name and the Word dwell in the
soul.
When the Self is overcome, then doubt and fear are also over-
come and the sorrow of death and rebirth removed.
The teaching of the Gurū makes the Unmanifest manifest, by
His perfect wisdom we are saved.
Nānak, repeat the formula: 'He is me, I am He.' The three levels
of existence are summed up in that.

[Rag Maru. A.G. p.1092]

Notes

1. Śiva.
2. Vishnu.
3. Wife of Śiva.
4. Lakshmi, wife of Vishnu.
5. See 4.1.6.
6. Vedic god of the Heavens.
7. Scriptures.
8. Lit. 'things remembered', i.e. the traditions, texts based on the Vedas. The most ancient scriptures of the Hindus.
10. Or *Bhaktas,* those who adopted the discipline of *bhakti,* or pious devotion to a personal God. The hymns of some *bhagats* like Kabir and Namder are included in the Guru Granth Sahib though they were not Sikh gurus.
11. Lit. 'as much as a seasamum seed'.
12. The Muslim scriptures.
13. Maya.
14. The triad, Brahma, Vishnu and Śiva.
15. May refer to the myth of the ocean of milk which, when it was churned up, produced jewels, one of which was Lakshmi, goddess of wealth.
16. Ram.
17. An object made of animal hair fixed to a handle and used for fanning important persons like royalty. It is used in the Sikh *gurdwārā* over the Guru Granth Sahib or Holy Book.
18. *ārati* – a form of worship in which a tray with lights is waved before the object of worship.
19. Hawk-cuckoo, which according to legend drinks only rain water.
20. The spiritual man as opposed to the worldly man *(manmukh).*
21. The four are cruelty, worldly love, anger and avarice, Macauliffe, *The Sikh Religion* Vol.1 p.264, New Delhi 1963.
22. The True Guru, a name for God.
23. See 4.1.27, n.20.
24. Lit. 'five others'; lust, anger, greed, attachment and pride.
25. Gopal.
26. Śiva.
27. Sacred verse from *Rig Veda* used by the Hindu in his daily dawn devotions.
28. Lit. puja, i.e. ritual worship.
29. Religious teacher.

Source: Translation of the originals, hitherto unpublished, by D.A.T. Thomas.

4.2   SIKHISM

Hew McLeod

4.2.1 Although Sikhism is generally understood to be a simple faith, the definitions which are offered to describe it can be widely and confusingly divergent. Four such definitions are commonly encountered. All four relate primarily to the origins of the faith, each reflecting a distinctive range of predilection.

4.2.2 For the strictly orthodox Sikh the faith which by preference he calls *Gurmat* (in contrast to the western term 'Sikhism') can be regarded as nothing less than the product of direct revelation from God. *Gurmat* means 'the Gurū's doctrine'. God, the original Gurū, imparted his message to his chosen disciple Nānak who, having intuitively apprehended the message, thereby absorbed the divine spirit and became himself the Gurū. This same divine spirit passed at Nānak's death into the body of his successor, Gurū Angad, and in this manner dwelt successively within a series of ten personal Gurūs. At the death of the tenth Gurū, Gobind Singh, the divine spirit remained present within the sacred scripture and the community of the Gurū's followers. He who accepts the teachings of the Gurūs as recorded in the scripture *(granth)* or expressed in the corporate will of the community *(panth)* is truly a Sikh. In its more extreme form this interpretation holds that the actual content of *Gurmat* is wholly original, owing nothing of primary significance to the environment within which it emerged.[1]

4.2.3 As one would expect, the three remaining definitions all dispute this claim to uniqueness, emphasising instead the features which Sikhism so patently holds in common with other religious traditions in India. Many Hindu commentators, stressing the elements common to Sikh and Hindu tradition, have maintained that Sikhism is properly regarded merely as one of the many Hindu reform movements which have appeared from time to time in Indian history. In like manner there have been Muslim claims, based upon such doctrines as the oneness of God and the brotherhood of believers, to the effect that Sikhism is an offshoot of Islam.[2] Finally, there is the interpretation popular in Western textbooks, that Sikhism must be understood as the product of a consciously eclectic intention, an attempt to fuse Hindu and Muslim belief within a single irenic system.

4.2.4   Two of these definitions can be summarily dismissed. Both the Muslim and the eclectic interpretations are based upon partial and superficial readings of Sikh sources. Indications of Muslim influence do appear in the recorded utterances of the Gurūs and in subsequent Sikh tradition, but in so far as they constitute significant elements of Sikh belief they normally do so in direct contradiction to the Muslim influence.[3] The eclectic interpretation depends primarily upon a misreading of certain passages which appear in the works of Nānak and of a cryptic reference recorded in the traditional narratives of his life.[4] Gurū Nānak does indeed look to a faith transcending both Hindu and Muslim notions, but for him the required pattern of belief and practice is one which spurns rather than blends.

4.2.5   The two remaining definitions require more careful attention. Even if one is unable to accept a doctrine of divine inspiration, there remains an obligation to consider the teachings of Nānak and his successors in terms of genuine originality. Having acknowledged this measure of originality we must also pay heed to those features of Sikhism which so obviously derive from sources within contemporary Indian society. This must be done in the light of the complete range of Sikh history, from the period of Nānak to the present day. The conclusion which will follow is that Sikhism is indeed a unique phenomenon, but that this uniqueness derives more from its later development than from its earliest forms of custom and belief.

4.2.6   Sikhism is generally held to derive from the teachings of the first Gurū Nānak (1469-1539). In a sense this is true, for there can be no doubt that the doctrines which he taught survive within the community to this day. Moreover, there can be no doubt that a direct connection links the community of today with the group of disciples who first gathered around Nānak in the Panjāb during the early years of the sixteenth century. In another sense, however, the claim is open to obvious objections. An analysis of the teachings of Nānak will demonstrate that the essential components of his thought were already current in the Indian society of his period. Nānak taught a doctrine of salvation through the divine Name. Others were already preaching this doctrine, and a comparison of their beliefs with those of the early Sikh community plainly shows that Nānak taught from within a tradition which had already developed a measure of definition.

4.2.7   This was the *Nirguna Sampradāya,* or Sant tradition of northern

India, a devotional school commonly regarded as a part of the tradition of Vaishnava *bhakti*. A connection between the Sants and the Vaishnavas does indeed exist, but there are distinctive features of Sant doctrine which distinguish it from its Vaishnava antecedents. Most of these can be traced to its other major source, Tantric Yoga. The most prominent of the Sants prior to Nānak was Kabīr, and it is no doubt due to the obvious similarities in their teachings that Nānak has sometimes been represented as a disciple of his predecessor. Although there is no evidence to support this supposition, the measure of doctrinal agreement which links them is beyond dispute.[5]

This debt to the earlier Sant tradition must be acknowledged if   4.2.8 there is to be any understanding of the antecedents of Nānak's thought. It is, however, necessary to add that, as far as can be judged from surviving Sant works, Nānak raised this inheritance to a level of beauty and coherence attained by none of his predecessors. From the quality of this Panjābī verses and the clarity of the message expressed in them it is easy to appreciate why this particular man should have gathered a following of sufficient strength to provide the nucleus of a continuing community. The evidence suggests that Nānak inherited a theory of salvation which was at best incomplete and commonly naïve in its insistence upon the adequacy of a simple repetition of a particular divine name Kabīr, master of the pithy epigram, was certainly not naïve, nor yet does he appear to have been altogether clear and consistent. These are qualities which one cannot always expect to find in a mystic, and there can be no doubt that in Kabīr it was the mystical strain which predominated. For Nānak also salvation was to be found in mystical union with God, but Nānak evidently differed in that he recognised the need to explain in consistent terms the path to the ultimate experience. It is in the coherence and the compelling beauty of his explanation that Nānak's originality lies.

The thought of Nānak begins with two groups of basic   4.2.9 assumptions. The first concerns the nature of God, who in an ultimate sense is unknowable. God, the One, is without form *(nirankār)*, eternal *(akāl)*, and ineffable *(alakh)*. Considerable stress is thus laid upon divine transcendence, but this alone does not express Nānak's understanding of God. If it did there would be, for Nānak, no possibility of salvation. God is also gracious, concerned that men should possess the means of salvation and that these means should be abundantly evident to those who would diligently seek them.

There is, Nānak insists, a purposeful revelation, visible to all who will but open their eyes and see. God is *sarab viāpak,* 'everywhere present', immanent in all creation, both within and without every man.

4.2.10   The second group of assumptions concerns the nature of man. Men are by nature wilfully blind, shutting their eyes to the divine revelation which lies about them. They commonly appreciate the need for salvation, but characteristically seek it in ways which are worse than futile because they confirm and strengthen humanity's congenital blindness. The Hindu worships at the temple and the Muslim at the mosque. Misled by their religious leaders they mistakenly believe that external exercises of this kind will provide access to salvation. Instead they bind men more firmly to the transmigratory wheel of death and rebirth, to a perpetuation of suffering rather than to the attainment of bliss.

4.2.11   This, for Nānak, is *māyā.* In Nānak's usage the term does not imply the ultimate unreality of the world itself, but rather the unreality of the values which it represents. The world's values are a delusion. If a man accepts them no amount of piety can save him. They must be rejected in favour of alternative values. Salvation can be obtained only through a recognition of the alternative, and through the faithful exercise of a discipline which demonstrably produces the desired result.

4.2.12   Nānak's teachings concerning the way of salvation are expressed in a number of key words which recur constantly in his works. God, being gracious, communicates his revelation in the form of the *sabad* (*sabda,* 'word') uttered by the *gurū* (the 'preceptor'). Any aspect of the created world which communicates a vision or glimpse of the nature of God or of his purpose is to be regarded as an expression of the *sabda.* The gurū who expresses, or draws attention to, this revelation is not, however, a human preceptor. It is the 'voice' of God mystically uttered within the human heart. Any means whereby spiritual perception is awakened can be regarded as the activity of the gurū.

4.2.13   Duly awakened by the *gurū,* the enlightened man looks around and within himself and there perceives the *hukam* (the divine 'order'). Like its English equivalent, the term *hukam* is used by Nānak in two senses, but it is the notion of harmony which is fundamental. Everywhere there can be perceived a divinely-bestowed harmony. Salvation consists in bringing oneself within this pattern of harmony.

This requires an explicit discipline, the practice of *nām simaran* or 4.2.14
nām japan. The word *nām* ('name') signifies all that constitutes the
nature and being of God; and the verb *simaranā* means 'to hold in
remembrance'. The alternative verb *japanā* means, literally, 'to repeat',
and for many of the Sants a simple, mechanical repetition of a
chosen name of God (e.g. Rām) was believed to be a sufficient
method. For Nānak much more is required. The pattern which he
sets forth consists of a regular, disciplined meditation upon the
nām. The essence of the *nām* is harmony and through this discipline
the faithful devotee progressively unites himself with the divine
harmony. In this manner he ascends to higher and yet higher levels
of spiritual attainment, passing eventually into the condition of
mystical bliss wherein all disharmony, is ended and, in consequence,
the round of transmigration is at last terminated. The proof of this is
the experience itself. Only those who have attained it can know it.

For most people a reference to Sikhism will at once evoke an 4.2.15
impression of beards, turbans and martial valour. It rarely suggests
doctrines of salvation through patient meditation upon the divine
Name. Both, however, belong to Sikhism. In order to understand
how they united it is necessary to trace the history of the Sikh
community since the time of Nānak.

Concerning Nānak himself relatively little can be known with 4.2.16
assurance, apart from the content of his teachings. Hagiographic
narratives abound (the *janam-sākhīs*), but their considerable
importance relates principally to the later period within which they
evolved. It seems certain that Nānak was born in 1469, probably in
the village of Talvandi in the central Panjāb. During his early
manhood he was evidently employed in the town of Sultānpur near
the confluence of the Beās and Satluj rivers. This was followed by a
period visiting pilgrimage centres within and perhaps beyond India, a
period which figures with particular prominence in the *janam-sākhī*
narratives. Eventually he settled in the village of Kartārpur above
Lāhore on the right bank of the Rāvī river and there died, probably
in 1539.

The pattern of teaching through the composition and communal 4.2.17
singing of hymns was continued by Nānak's first four successors and
reached a climax in the work of Arjan, the fifth Gurū (died 1606).
During the time of the third Gurū, Amar Dās (died 1574), a
collection was made of the hymns of the first three Gurūs and of
other writers (Sants and Sūfīs) whose works accorded with the
teachings of Nānak. To this collection Gurū Arjan added his own

compositions and those of his father, Gurū Rām Dās. The new compilation, recorded in a single volume in 1603-4, became the primary scripture of the community (the *Adi Granth* later known as the *Gurū Granth Sahib*). Notable amongst Gurū Arjan's own compositions is the lengthy hymn entitled *Sikhmanī*, an epitome of the teachings of the Gurūs.

4.2.18   In this respect the first four successors followed Nānak's example, faithfully reproducing his teachings in language of sustained excellence. There were, however, significant changes taking place within the community of their followers. The more important of these developments appear to have emerged during the period of the third Gurū. Whereas Gurū Nānak had laid exclusive emphasis upon the need for inner devotion, Gurū Amar Dās, faced by the problems of a growing community, introduced features which served to maintain its cohesion. Distinctively Sikh ceremonies were instituted, a rudimentary system of pastoral supervision was begun, three Hindu festival-days were appointed for assemblies of the faithful, and the Gurū's own town of Goindvāl became a recognised pilgrimage centre.

4.2.19   An even more significant development, one which should probably be traced right back to the period of Gurū Nānak, concerns the caste constituency of the growing community. Whereas all the Gurūs belonged to the urban-based mercantile Khatrī caste, most of their followers were rural Jats. This preponderance of Jats, which continues to the present day, is of fundamental importance in the later development of the community. Many of the features which distinguish the modern community from that of Nānak's day can be traced, as we shall see, to the pressure of Jat ideals.

4.2.20   Signs of Jat influence became apparent during the period of the sixth Gurū, Hargobind (died 1644), an influence which is perhaps discernible even earlier, during the years under Gurū Arjan. It was during this period that the community first entered into overt conflict with the Mughal administration. According to tradition it was Gurū Hargobind who first decided to arm his followers, a decision which he is said to have reached following the death of his father Arjan in Mughal custody. There can be no doubt that the followers of Gurū Hargobind did bear arms (three skirmishes were fought with Mughal detachments between 1628 and 1631), yet it is difficult to accept that the martial Jats would have spurned the use of arms prior to this period.

4.2.21   These martial traditions received further encouragement within the community as a result of Gurū Hargobind's decision to withdraw to the Shivālik hills in 1634. During their actual tenure of the office of Gurū, all four of his successors spent most of their time in the Shivāliks. The move was significant in that it exposed the developing community to the influence of the dominant *Sakti* culture of the hills area. This did not produce a transformation, but such features as the exaltation of the sword which emerge prominently during the period of the tenth Gurū should probably be traced to Shivālik influences.

It was during the lifetime of the tenth Gurū, Gobind Singh (died 4.2.22 1788), that the conflict with Mughal authority assumed serious proportions. Sikh tradition ascribes to this period and to Gurū Gobind Singh the features which distinguish the later community from its precursor. It is said that Gurū Gobind Singh, confronted by the evident weaknesses of his followers, decided to transform them into a powerful force which would wage war in the cause of righteousness. This he did by inaugurating a new brotherhood, the Khālsā, in 1699.

To this decision and its fulfilment are traced almost all the 4.2.23 distinctive features of contemporary Sikhism. All who joined the Khālsā (both men and women) were to accept baptism and swear to obey a new code of discipline. Prominent amongst the requirements of this new code were an obligation to bear the *panj kakke*, or 'Five K's', and to refrain from various *kurahit*, or 'prohibitions'. The Five K's comprised the *keś* (uncut hair), the *kanghā* (comb), *kirpān* (dagger, or short sword), *karā* (bangle), and *kachh* (a variety of breeches which must not reach below the knee). The prohibitions included abstinence from tobacco, from meat slaughtered in the Muslim fashion (*halāl*), and sexual intercourse with Muslim women. A change of name was also required of the initiate. All men who accepted baptism into the Khālsā brotherhood were thereafter to add Singh to their names, and all women were to add Kaur.

Sikh tradition also relates to the period and intention of Gurū 4.2.24 Gobind Singh another of the distinctive features of the later Sikh community. Immediately prior to his death in 1708 Gurū Gobind Singh is said to have declared that with his demise the line of personal Gurūs would come to an end. Thereafter the function and the authority of the Gurū would vest jointly in the scripture (the *granth*, which accordingly comes to be known as the *Gurū Granth Sāhib*) and in the corporate community (the *panth*, or *Khālsā Panth*).

4.2.25   Tradition thus accords to the period and to the deliberate purpose of Gurū Gobind Singh almost all the characteristic features which outwardly distinguish the modern Sikh community. It is a tradition which must in some measure be qualified. There can be no doubt that something did in fact happen in 1699 and no reason exists for questioning the claim that Gurū Gobind Singh instituted some kind of brotherhood during his lifetime. Beyond this, however, it is still difficult to proceed with assurance, for there is evidence which suggests that particular features of the Khālsā code must have emerged subsequent to the death of Gurū Gobind Singh in response to pressures independent of his intention.

4.2.26   Two of these pressures deserve particular emphasis. There is, first, the continuing impact of Jat ideals upon the community, which numerically the Jats dominated. During the period of the Gurūs influence would have been minimised although, as the events of Gurū Hargobind's period indicate, it was by no means without effect. With the termination of the personal authority of the Gurū in 1708 the pressure to incorporate features derived from Jat cultural patterns evidently became much stronger. The confused political circumstances of eighteenth-century Panjāb further enhanced this Jat ascendancy, for periods of military strife would be handled with much greater success by the martial Jats than by any other group in Panjāb society. Their ascendancy was by no means complete (three of the prominent leaders of this period were not Jats), but it was nevertheless extensive and it left its imprint upon the evolving community. The militant attitude of the Sikh community must be traced to this source, together with particular features such as the Five K's.

4.2.27   The second of the important eighteenth-century influences also concerns the battles of that century. Because Ahmad Shāh Abdālī chose to represent his invasions as a Muslim crusade, the Sikh resistance developed a pronounced anti-Muslim aspect.[6] To this development can be traced the three examples of the Five Prohibitions cited above.

4.2.28   It was also during this critically important century and the early decades of its successor that the Sikh doctrine of the Gurū emerged in its modern form. For Nanak the *gurū*, the voice of God spoke mystically within the human heart. Because Nanak was believed to give utterance to the divine message the title was conferred upon him, and upon his nine successors in the manner of a single flame şuccessively igniting a series of torches. The death of Gurū Gobind

Singh without surviving heirs created a serious crisis, for ever since the time of the fourth Gurū, Rām Dās, the office had been hereditary within his family of Sodhī Khatris. An attempt was made to continue the pattern of personal authority (a disciple named Banda was widely acknowledged as leader until his execution in 1716), but disputes within the community and its dispersion during the period of persecution which followed Bandā's death eventually produced a different pattern of leadership.

During this period and the subsequent years of the Afghan invasions there emerged twelve separate guerrilla bands (the *misls*). In order to preserve a measure of cohesion the leaders of the *misls* assembled on specified occasions to discuss issues of common interest. Together they constituted the Sikh community and it was as a community (*panth*) that they deliberated. Well back in the period of the personal Gurūs there had developed, in response to the increasing growth and dispersion of the community, the doctrine that the Gurū's bodily presence was not actually essential. Wherever a group of the faithful gathered to sing the songs of the Gurū, there the Gurū was himself mystically present. The doctrine was now extended to cover the periodic meetings of the *misl* leaders. Assemblies were always held in the presence of a copy of the sacred scripture and decisions reached by these assemblies were acclaimed as the will of the Gurū *(gurmattā).* 4.2.29

A further development in the doctrine of the Gurū came during the early nineteenth century when Mahārājā Ranjīt Singh, having established his dominance over his fellow *misaldārs,* suppressed these confederate assemblies. The doctrine of the *Gurū Panth* then lapsed into desuetude and in its place the theory of the *Gurū Granth* assumed virtually exclusive authority. The presence of the Gurū in the scriptures had long been acknowledged. All that was required was a shift in emphasis. 4.2.30

To this day the *Gurū Granth Sahib* occupies the central position in all expressions of the Sikh faith. Decisions are commonly made by using it as an oracle, continuous readings are held in order to confer blessing or avert disaster, and the presence of a copy is mandatory for all important ceremonies. The scripture which is used in this manner is Gurū Arjan's collection, the *Adi Granth.* It should be distinguished from the so-called *Dasam Granth,* a separate collection compiled during the early eighteenth century which derives from the period of Gurū Gobind Singh. Although the *Dasam Granth* also possesses canonical status it is in practice little used. The bulk of the 4.2.31

collection consists of a retelling of legends from Hindu mythology.

4.2.32   Another institution which deserves special notice is the Sikh temple, or gurdwārā (*guaraduārā*, literally 'the Gurū's door'). Following earlier precedents the disciples of Nanak in any particular locality would regularly gather in a room set aside for their communal hymn-singing (kirtūn). This room (or separate building) was called a *dharamsālā*. As the community's interests expanded beyond the narrowly devotional into areas of much wider concern the function of the *dharamsālā* expanded accordingly. In the process its name changed to *guraduārā*. The gurdwārās still remain the centre and focus of the community's activities, partly because their substantial endowments provide a considerable annual income. Contemporary Sikh political activity (expressed through the Akāli party) depends to a marked degree upon control of the wealthier of these institutions. The most famous of all gurdwārās, and still the primary centre of Sikh political power, is the celebrated Golden Temple of Amritsar.

4.2.33   Out of these five centuries of history there has emerged the modern Sikh community, a community which occupies in the life of India today a position of prominence considerably in excess of its actual numerical strength. Sikhs today are renowned for their participation in progressive farming, the armed forces, sport and the transport industry. In all four areas the prominence belongs principally to Jat Sikhs, the caste group which still constitutes more than half of the total strength of the community. Of the other groups which have significant representations within the community, the Khatris and Aroras, both mercantile castes, are more particularly distinguished for their work in manufacturing industries, commerce and the professions. Other substantial constituents are a group of artisan castes, jointly known as Rāmgarhiā Sikhs; and converts to Sikhism from the scheduled castes (Mazhabi and Rāmdāsiā Sikhs).

4.2.34   Although a measure of caste consciousness certainly persists within the community, all can join the Khālsā brotherhood and observe the common discipline. Here, however, a final qualification is required. Although Khālsā organisations normally insist that only the Khālsā Sikh is a true Sikh, there are others who lay claim to the title without observing the formal discipline. These are the so-called *sahaj-dhārī* Sikhs, noted for their adherence to the devotional patterns taught by Gurū Nanak and his successors. In a sense they can be regarded as the descendants of the early movement, largely unaffected by the changes which took place during the seventeenth and eighteenth centuries. Their number is impossible to determine and without the external insignia of the orthodox Khālsā Sikh they constitute a much less stable group. There can be no doubt that the Khālsā provides the community with its stability and that its success in this respect has largely derived from its insistence upon external symbols. For this reason one can readily understand the apprehension with which orthodox Sikhs of today regard any inclination to abandon the traditional code of discipline.

Notes

1. 'It is altogether a distinct and original faith based on the teachings of Gurū Nanak in the form of Ten Gurūs, and now through Gurū Granth Sahib and the Khalsa Panth.' Gobind Singh Mansukhani, *The Quintessence of Sikkhism*, Amritsar 1958, p.1.
2. The original edition of *The Legacy of India* gives expression to both the second and the third definitions. Dr Radhakrishnan lists Jainism, Buddhism, and Sikhism as 'creations of the Indian mind [which] represent reform movements from within the fold of Hinduism put forth to meet the special demands of the various stages of the Hindu faith' (op.cit., p.259). In the following chapter Abdul Qadir, in direct contradiction, cites Sikhism in support of his claim that 'Islam has had a more direct influence in bringing into existence monotheistic systems of faith in India' (ibid., p.291).
3. This aspect is briefly covered below in the discussion of eighteenth-century developments. For a more detailed discussion of this period and its results see W.H. McLeod, *The Evolution of the Sikh Community* (Oxford, forthcoming).
4. 'There is neither Hindu nor Muslim'. See W.H. McLeod, *Gurū Nānak and the Sikh Religion*, Oxford 1968, pp.38 and 161.
5. McLeod, *op.cit.*, pp.151-8. Ch. Vaudeville, *Au cabaret de l'amour: paroles de Kabīr*, Paris, 1959, pp.7-9.
6. Ahmad Shāh Abdālī of Afghanistan invaded north India nine times between 1747 and 1769.

Source: From A.L. Basham, Cultural History of India, OUP 1975, pp.294-302.

4.3   SOCIOLOGICAL DILEMMAS: FIVE PARADOXES OF INSTITUTIONALIZATION

Thomas F. O'Dea

[*Editor's Note:* The essay by Thomas F. O'Dea is found in the Sikhism section because, although it is written by a sociologist and does not refer specifically to Sikhism, it contains material which Mr. D.A.T. Thomas, the Course Unit Author, wishes to use in relation to his writing on Sikhism. It will be seen that Mr. O'Dea's arguments can, of course, have a much wider application.]

Introduction

4.3.1 An institutional complex may be viewed as the concrete embodiment of a cultural theme in the ongoing life of a society. To carry out any cultural motif, to give stability to social performance in conformity with any theme, requires that its content become embedded in the stable expectations of human beings. This process of reducing a theme or set of orientations to the expected ongoing activity of men is what is meant by institutionalization... While this process of institutionalization is an important aspect of all fields of human activity, solving certain basic problems for human association — (and creating others), in the area of religious activity it is seen most dramatically to exhibit the problems generally involved. The great virtue of social institutions from the point of view of the functioning of the social system is that they provide stability. In a human world of change and ambiguity, they provide the stable points of reference and the established forms which permit ongoing day-to-day activity to function smoothly. The brilliant performance of the genius, the hero, the sage, or the saint lights up the record of human events with those bright flashes that often give example and supply incentive to future generations. But human society would be an unsteady and incalculable universe indeed were it chiefly dependent upon such unusual phenomena. To achieve the necessary stability made possible by social structure, the price involved is a consequent loss of spontaneity and creativity, although these processes do make themselves felt to some extent within the canalizations of the institutional patterns. Yet measured against the 'charismatic' moment, it seems possible to say the cost of bringing the original thematic orientations within the scope of the ordinary everyday activity of men is the prosaic and often quite mediocre quality of institutionalized performance. Since the charismatic moment of religious activity is to be found in what Joachim Wach, following Rudolf Otto, has called the 'religious experience'[1], and since this experience involves a deep engagement of the personality of the individuals concerned and is always an awareness of and a response to a 'beyond', the religious insight would remain a fleeting and impermanent element in human life without its embodiment in institutional structures. In other words, the religious experience, whether understood or interpreted by the actor as a response to something immanent within the life of nature and vital processes or as transcendent and above − 'other' than − these natural phenomena, always, to use Pareto's term, 'transcends' experience,[2] understood as the prosaic experience of everyday life. Because there is in the religious experience what Tillich has called a relation to the 'ultimate',[3] religion, perhaps more than other basic human activities, requires the stabilization of institutional patterning if it is to be given a definite relationship to daily life. Precisely because the charismatic moment involved in the 'experience of the holy' lies at the other end of the continuum of human experience from prosaic action, as Durkheim has shown,[4] the process of embodying its implications in structural form raises the problems of institutionalization in the sharpest way.

In other words, religion both needs most and suffers most from institutionalization. The most subtle of insights, the most unusual − most charismatic − of experiences, the most supraempirical aspects of human cognition and response and their implications for belief, attitude, and behaviour cannot be given social regularity without becoming embodied in institutional structure. But, on the other hand, precisely because of the inherent antinomy which Durkheim showed to be involved between the sacred and the prosaic, such institutionalization raises in the sharpest form the possibility of emasculating the basic content of the religious experience or at least its serious curtailment and distortion. Yet without such institutionalization it would appear that all implications beyond the immediate presence of the religious experience or the charismatic leader must be surrendered by religion as outside its power to influence the behaviour of men.

What is stated here is that there is of necessity and unavoidably 4.3.2 involved in the institutionalization of religion a structured set of ambivalences derived from the inevitable ambiguity of ideal and reality that exists in the fundamental relation of the religious experience to life. The problems that arise from this fundamental ambiguity find expression in five dilemmas or paradoxes which the history of religion in general and that of Christianity in particular may be seen to exhibit. The statement of these five dilemmas is both an empirical generalization and a middle-range theory which may prove useful in research and analysis upon the concrete problems of the sociology of religion. It is an empirical generalization based upon the history of Christianity in the first place, but an acquaintance with the development of other world religions suggests that the processes isolated by this analysis may be found within them as well. Also, religious practice as described in numbers of anthropological monographs on the cultures of preliterate peoples leaves the distinct impression that these processes are not absent in such cultures, although our lack of knowledge of the historical development of pre-literate peoples makes close examination of some aspects difficult. Let us turn now to a discussion of the five problem areas.

The Dilemma of Mixed Motivation

4.3.3   In the preinstitutionalized state of the development of a religious movement, the classical form of which is to be seen in the relation between a Master and his disciples, the attraction of the followers and the motivation of devotees are characterized by a certain single-mindedness. That is not to assume that the religious movement does not satisfy complex needs for the adherents and converts. Such an assumption would seem most unwarranted in view of what psycho-analytic theory has taught us concerning human motivation. But it is to assert that the religious movement in its charismatic moment makes its message and the attraction of its leader the main focus with respect to such needs and motives. There is present in the response to the call of the charismatic leader and the attraction of the content of his message a wholeheartedness that is the result of the centrality of these phenomena in the consciousness of the adherents. However, with the emergence of a stable institutional matrix, there arises a structure of statuses and roles — a structure of offices — which become capable of eliciting other kinds of motivation. These concern such elements as the gratification of needs for prestige and needs to direct and manage fellow men, the satisfaction of drives for power and control, or the more prosaic wish for the security of a respectable and established position in the going professional and occupational structure of society. The first two types of motive may not be wholly absent even during the charismatic moment, as the gospel account of the disciples of Jesus arguing over which would sit higher in the Kingdom of God shows. But they are more easily dominated by the charismatic call than in later stages of development. Moreover, the satisfaction of security needs seems to be largely dependent upon stable institutional structure, at least their satisfaction in terms of socially respectable status. Charismatic movements, while granting security in their own way, definitely do not do so in the prosaic manner of well-institutionalized statuses. Religious activity in such early stages is much more likely, in A.N. Whitehead's terms, to be an 'adventure of the spirit' than a 'rule of safety'.

This aspect of institutionalization was suggested several decades ago by Vilfredo Pareto.[5] Pareto stated that new social forms were established by those whom he called 'lions', strong in conviction and ready for self-sacrifice. But, Pareto argued, when social institutions were fully established, their function, their role in society, and their importance attracted the 'foxes', those characterized by cleverness and the desire and ability to play it smart and make their way by guile rather than by strength. Strength, a certain ruthlessness born of single-mindedness together with a willingness to fight, suffer, and, if need be, to die, gives way to shrewdness, manipulation, and a weakness of conviction that often goes as far as willingness to serve unrestrained by principle. What is suggested here is that similar phenomena *mutatis mutandis* may be seen in the institutionalization of religion. It is better to sacrifice the colorfulness of Pareto's metaphor to avoid the exaggeration and value judgments which his use of it seems to entail. But a process not unlike the one he described is certainly to be seen as one aspect of the process of institutionalization.

This is, of course, simply one aspect of the general process of 4.3.4 embodying the idea in on-going human activity. Institutions have the great virtue of *not* depending upon the purer, more whole-hearted motivation which the charismatic period of religious development is able to arouse. By mobilizing both the self-interested and the disinterested — or object-interested — elements of motivation, institutionalization reinforces the structure of the human activity involved in carrying out the ideal. This process of the mobilization of a favorable balance of motivation behind institutionalized goals has been shown by Parsons in his analysis of professional roles and later in his work on the social system.[6] In his study of the medical profession he has analyzed how the physician is prevented from resorting to certain abuses against the medical code both by his adherence to and socialization in the values of the profession and by the fact that normal operation of social control in such a context would make his use of questionable methods extremely harmful to his own self-interested ends with respect to his future career. The establishment of institutional structures within the field of religious activity offers a quite analogous spectacle. Institutionalization brings about a situation in which religious practitioners, especially those who occupy official statuses, are placed in a position where not only devotion to the ideals of the religious organization but also self-interest in terms of prestige and career are mobilized behind the prescribed behaviour.

4.3.5   Yet, if it is the great strength of the institution that it can insure stability of performance by its ability to mobilize both object-interested and self-interested elements of motivation, this is para-doxically also its great weakness and may in certain circum-stances prove to be its Achilles' heel. The criteria of selection and promotion within the institutional structure of roles must of necessity reflect the functional and operational needs of the system and therefore do not distinguish very finely between the two types of motivation involved. Thus it may be that within the context of institutional operation the self-interested motivation comes to prevail. In such cases a situation analogous to Pareto's infiltration of the foxes has taken place. The result may be a slow transformation of the original institutional aims and goals. Since these original tenets are still taught explicitly or are at least available in the sacred literature, a standard is at hand for the judgment of present performance. Such a judgment may see the newer developments as corruption, and a movement of protest may result. At any rate the religious body is likely to become marked to some extent by careerism of a type only formally involved with original goals. Bureaucratic rigorism of the kind that sacrifices institutionalized values to the defence of vested interests, official conservatism, and lethargy (frequently referred to by the term 'deadwood') are some of the more palpable evidences of the process involved.

4.3.6   Certainly such processes contributed in a significant way to arousing the religious protest of the sixteenth century. The expressed attitudes of the Reformation toward clerical leadership and the high frequency with which legists are found in the officialdom of the church at the time offer impressive evidence of what had in fact taken place. Ernst Troeltsch, in his monumental work that is still the great classic of the sociology of religion, has stated that the relation between religion and secular activities becomes a most important area of tension for the development of religious movements. Troeltsch concluded that the Christian ideal is one 'which cannot be realized within this world apart from compromise. Therefore the history of the Christian Ethos becomes the story of a constantly renewed search for this compromise, and of fresh opposition to this spirit of compromise.'[7] He saw four areas of social life as the points where such tension was concentrated: the family, political power, economic activities, and intellectual endeavor. Certainly the necessities and inevitable consequences of institutionalization comprise one of the great fundamental points of contact and tension between religion and the 'world'. Its recognition carries further the insights of Troeltsch into the area of social structure, which comprises the context of most important activity after the closing of the original charismatic period. What has been said here in relation to religious movements generally is applicable not only to the development of ecclesiastical bodies, but also the routinization of sects into denominations and to the history of religious orders.

The Symbolic Dilemma: Objectification *versus* Alienation

The object of the apprehension of the 'sacred' or the experience of the 'holy' as well as the kinds of attitude involved in the response of the adherents must be given some form of objectified expression if they are to survive the moments of such experiences themselves, especially if they are to be communicated to others and transmitted from generation to generation. Most central in this respect are those acts of worship which both express attitudes and place the worshiper in relation to the object of those attitudes. Cult and its rituals are central to organized religious life, whether we speak of world religions or the religious behaviour of preliterate peoples. Characteristic of the cult is the fact that although it may be derived at least in part from the expressive needs of worshipers, it is usually observed and participated in at a much later stage of development in forms that have been elaborated and standardized. It is, as Suzanne Langer has observed, expressive in a logical rather than in a psychological sense.[8] Ritual presents to the participant an objectified order to which he relates himself in terms of the ritual itself. This process of objectification means that established cultic worship is no longer simply a derivative of the psychological needs and drives of

4.3.7

individual participating worshipers, but rather imposes upon them its own patterns of attitude and response. Like all socially structured phenomena, it is characterized by a large element of what Durkheim called 'exteriority' and 'constraint'. As such it is a genuine social and communal act.

4.3.8   But this process of the socialization of the religious experience and its concomitant attitudes can proceed so far that it loses any close meaningful connection with the interior dispositions and attitudes of the participants. It can become for them a sheer formalism carried out merely because of duty or a general reverence for what somehow embodies sacredness or because of a diffuse respect for tradition. Whereas earlier the cultic worship evoked attitudes and responses and tended to mold the personal religiosity of the worshiper after its own image and therefore to affect the formation of personality structure, such an overextension of the objectification process leads to routinization and a consequent superficiality of participation. This is a process to be seen not only in the world religions but would also appear to be well advanced among preliterate peoples.

4.3.9   What has been said above of ritual could likewise be said for graphic and representational symbolism. What had originally been what Langer called a 'symbolic transformation of experience',[9] has become alienated from the living experience of the adherents.

4.3.10   This process of overobjectification of symbols to the point of alienation of the public religious life from the private religious interests of the members of a religious organization is one of the most important processes that work to separate the individual from the community and to isolate him from solidarity with the religious group. This process also gives rise to movements of protest. These may aim to re-establish the original relation of cultic activities with individual religiosity as may be seen in the various movements for liturgical renovation among both Catholics and Protestants; or they may find expression in a strongly expressed antagonism to ritual and ceremony, graphic representation and symbol in general, as is to be seen in the extreme sects of the Reformation period and which came to some extent to characterize Protestantism generally. The fact that the English Reformation concentrated so much of its fire upon the Mass, the priest as one consecrated to celebrate Mass, statues and stained glass, and prayer in a language other than the vernacular are dramatic examples of how important such a protest can become. Ridley, the reforming bishop of London, for example, removed altars from the churches of his diocese, while at the same time the priest was changed into a preacher and the Mass into a vernacular communion service. Large sections of the Protestant Reformation insisted upon a very literal understanding of the command 'Thou shalt not make unto thyself a graven image'.

Although opposition to the clerical status and to the use of a language other than the vernacular are also in part a protest against the process discussed earlier — a fact showing that concretely these processes and the reaction against them are found closely interrelated — the importance of the Reformation as a protest against the alienation of symbolic expression from personal religiosity has not generally been given the attention it deserves by the historians of the movement. That is not to say that the dramatic facts have been neglected, but their true significance has not always been adequately assessed in terms of identifiable sociological processes.

The Dilemma of Administrative Order: Elaboration and Alienation

Max Weber has shown that charismatic leadership soon undergoes 4.3.11 a process of routinzation into a phenomenon which he characterized as the existence of a chief and an administrative staff; a development that may proceed either toward rational legality or toward traditionalism. The process of institutionalization is marked by the elaboration and standardization of procedures and in the process establishes a matrix of statuses and roles with more or less well-defined rights, obligations, and relationships within a total structure. In many cases one of the most important characteristics of such a development is a certain separation between the status and its incumbent, what Weber called the evolution of the concept of 'office'. Such a matrix, especially in the case of rational legality, becomes, again in Weber's terms, a bureaucracy within which the incumbent occupies the status and performs the behaviour prescribed by the role but does not become identical with the position itself. One tendency of bureaucracy as it elaborates in response to the current problems facing it is to become complicated. Precedents lead to the precipitation of new rules and new offices. This process can also proceed to the point where its usefulness is curtailed by its very complication. Functional precedents become in later situations dysfunctional obstacles to forthright activity in response to contemporary problems. Weber noted that bureaucracy — such an elaborate structure of offices — tends to be the most effective method which men have evolved for the rational, purposeful management of affairs.

4.3.12   At the same time, the tendency for such a structure to over-elaborate itself raises the problems of dysfunctional consequences. Overdefinition of areas of competence and rules of operation and overproliferation of offices and divisions of responsibility tend to bog down and to transform what was originally an instrument of efficiency into an unwieldy social machine within which it may become difficult to accomplish anything in terms of the solution of immediate problems. This process raises many concrete problems in the life of modern societies. It appears more than likely that the operation of modern large-scale technology, based as it is upon the rational methods of scientific procedures, requires the elaboration of large-scale bureaucracy. Yet, such elaborate structures bring their own problems of intraorganizational function, a fact to be seen in the great interest in recent years in the sociological study of organization. It seems that the greatly increased leverage that men have achieved through scientific technology in their efforts to master the physical environment is in part canceled out by their inability to master the operational requirements of the self-complicating organizational structures that such technology inevitably entails.

4.3.13   In the sphere of religious organization, the requirements for large-scale management have brought about the development of bureaucratization. In fact, as Weber so clearly saw, the modern concept of office is found fully developed for the first time in the new civilization that arose upon the ruins of classical antiquity in the structure of the medieval church. Yet the dilemma entailed in this necessity for and the consequent dysfunctional consequences of such organization are clearly apparent by the close of the Middle Ages. The many failures of attempts to reform the church in the fourteenth and fifteenth centuries are to a considerable extent related to this development of bureaucracy. Moreover, administrative reform itself was one of the most obvious needs at that time. Yet the hypothesis that one may draw from this theoretical statement — that the problem of administrative reform, or of any other reform that had to be cleared through the bureaucratic apparatus, or implemented by the bureaucratic administration, would become increasingly difficult — was borne out by the facts of the two centuries preceding Martin Luther.

4.3.14   One implication of this problem is that after a certain point ongoing institutions become sufficiently dysfunctional in terms of achieving their own goals that some partial 'de-institutionalization' becomes necessary, or else the violent eruption of protest into rebellion will ensue. Such de-institutionalization becomes increasingly difficult as elaboration proceeds. This situation is made more complex by its relation to the first dilemma. Office-holders come to have a vested interest in the operation of the system as it is. Merton has discussed this problem in terms of institutionalized means becoming ends for the holders of bureaucratic office.[10] Perhaps one of the most significant contributions of sociology to modern civilization will be a better understanding of what is involved in such a necessary 'molting' process. Certainly such self-complication of procedures and offices is one of the reasons for the truth of Toynbee's statement that the same elite seldom solves two major challenges to its leadership role in succession, for successful solution of the first incapacitates the leadership for successful apprehension of the second. Such processes are also involved in what the same writer refers to as the transformation of a 'creative' minority into a 'dominant' minority — that is, of leadership into domination.

The Dilemma of Delimitation: Concrete Definition *versus* Substitution of Letter for Spirit

To affect the daily lives of men, the import of a religious message must be translated and often transformed into terms that have relevance to the prosaic events of which the daily lives of most of us generally consist. This translation is first of all a process of concretization. But in this process of applying the religious ideal to the prosaic and concrete, the content of that message may itself appear to take on a prosaic quality and lose those charismatic elements that originally moved men. The process of concretization can become also a process of finitization of the content of the religious message itself. Moreover, since the insights of the charismatic leader are usually uttered in terms of the concrete conditions of the society in which he and his followers live, adaptation to new conditions involves a difficult process of apprehending the general import of concrete counsels and their subsequent relativizing in relation to new conditions. Such a process faces two pitfalls. Its second relativization may in fact emasculate and render commonplace what was originally a call to the extraordinary. Or unable to see how such relativization is possible, followers of a later generation may insist upon a literal observance and close their eyes to the fact that conditions at present

4.3.15

are far different from those under which the counsels were originally given. Thus there is the danger of watering down or of a rigidly literalist fundamentalism. In either case the original religious message has obviously been transformed.

4.3.16   This problem may be clearly seen in the sphere of the religious ethic. The original ethical insight is translated into a set of rules to bring it within the scope of new converts made in new situations. This process is clearly noticeable in the first centuries of Christianity. This is an attempt to give the original ethical insight a kind of operational definition of utility to the growing membership and under the new conditions of life. Yet rules, however elaborate they may become, cannot make explicit all that is implied in the original insight itself. Moreover, precisely as the rules become elaborate in response to the need to give unambiguous relation of the basic ethos of the original insight to new situations, the more the original insight itself tends to be identified with concrete items of behaviour. Thus the original insight becomes transformed or at least tends to become transformed into a complicated set of legal formulations and the development of that kind of legal rigorism which makes of the letter a substitute for the inner meaning. Brahmanic developments with regard to ritual purity in Hinduism, Pharisaic rituals in the Judaism of the classical period, as well as similar developments in Christianity are illustrations of this process. Here indeed, as St. Paul observed, the letter killeth, but the spirit giveth life.

The process of delimitation becomes a very important aspect of the routinization of charisma, yet without concretization the religious ethic could not be rendered operational in the lives of men.

The Dilemma of Power: Conversion *versus* Coercion

4.3.17 The religious experience exercises a strong attraction upon those whom it affects and draws to become adherents of its insights. In Otto's terms, its content has an aspect 'which shows itself as something uniquely attractive and fascinating'.[11] Moreover, the propagation of a religious message in the world religions is generally one that involves an invitation or 'call' to interior change. The 'interior turning' or 'conversion' is the classical beginning of religious life. With the institutionalization of the religious viewpoint such a conversion may be replaced by the socialization of the young so that a slow process of education and training and related character formation substitutes for the more dramatic conversion experience. Yet even here in many cases such slower socialization acts as a propadeutic to such conversion. In any case, among Christians, both Catholic and Protestant, it is generally conceded that the act of acceptance must be a voluntary one and must involve such interior turning or conversion.

However, as religion becomes institutionalized it comes to be a   4.3.18 repository of many of the values from which much of the ongoing life of society derives what Weber called its legitimacy. Thus the maintenance of the religious-belief system and even the integrity of the religious organization come to be entwined with the societal problems of public order and political loyalty. This tends to be the case even where there is a legal separation of church and state.

In addition, since religion is dependent upon interior disposition   4.3.19 and since that disposition may be weak among the nominally religious, there is always present in the institutionalized circumstances the subtle temptation for religious leaders to avail themselves of the close relation between religion and general cultural values in order to reinforce the position of religion itself. This process can take the form of a tendency toward collaboration between the institutionalized authority system of the religious body and that of the general society. The result may well be that a degree of coercion comes to be substituted for, or at least to supplement, the factor of voluntary adherence in propagating and maintaining religion itself.

While such an interpenetration of the problems of religious   4.3.20 adherence and political loyalty may strengthen the position of religion in society, it may also weaken it in important respects. First of all, it may cause ambivalences on the part of the religious membership who recognize that the use of force — even legal force — is not really consonant with the original nature of religious conversion. Secondly, it may produce what is only apparent religiosity beneath which lurks cynicism. History offers obvious examples of such an intertwining of religious conformity and public order; the establishment of inquisitions, the various forms of Catholic and Protestant confessional states with their 'union of throne and altar' and the subtle identifications of American nationalism and Protestantism in the nineteenth century are well known. The problems created for the religious body by such inter-twining of religious and secular interests are the bringing into existence of a tendency for religion to rely upon coercion as an ultimate sanction for faith and a consequent danger of weakening the voluntary element. With the weakening of voluntary adherence, the general status of religion in the society is changed and religion itself weakened. For some people in the community at least the community of religion has become a forced uniformity.

4.3.21   A genuine dilemma is involved. For if the religious system of beliefs and practices is to affect the lives of the members of the society, then religion must relate itself to the existing institutions of society. Since religion is concerned with the ultimate sanction of values by what Parsons has called a 'transcendental reference', a relation to authority and power structures is unavoidable. Thus there develops not only an affecting of secular values by religion but also a certain overlap and partial identification of the religious and secular sphere. While this may have positive consequences for the religious body, it can easily lead to a situation in which religious values as defined by the church or group of churches become identified with public order and general loyalty to the commonwealth. In such circumstances religious dissent becomes in actuality political rebellion and heresy is treason. Moreover, political opposition is also expressed as religious rebellion.

4.3.22   Whereas the original partial identification of the basic values of the religious system and the secular culture tended to strengthen both religious and social institutions, the confusion of the two to the point of making religious conformity and political loyalty synonymous tends to be detrimental to each. From the point of view of the religious community it tends to weaken the emphasis upon the inner core of the religious ethos and to substitute externals for it. From the point of view of the general society, it tends to narrow down the possibility of consensus by insisting upon a far larger area of value agreement than would be functionally necessary to the continued life of society as such. Yet the fact remains that the stability of society would in any case require some relationship between its basic values and those given ultimate significance in the religion of its members.

Anyone acquainted with the religious wars of the sixteenth century will readily recognize this dilemma as one of their important aspects. The long and painful travail of the development of religious liberty was made more difficult because of the obstacles to Western men coming to understand that social order could exist apart from religious unanimity. Elizabeth I was probably not of a very religious disposition, but her great concern with a religious settlement and with uniformity was real indeed and seems to have derived from her concern with maintaining national unity and order.

While such dilemmas present themselves in the framework of a   4.3.23
sociological conceptual scheme as potential ambiguities of development, it should not be imagined that they are avoidable. The
usefulness in their presentation lies in their ability to offer a set of
conceptual tools in terms of which many of the developments of
religious history and much of the observed behavior of contemporary
religious groups can be better understood. The tendencies expressed
here in terms of these five dilemmas appear inherent in the process
of institutionalization. Yet certainly one of the great hopes
attending the development of modern social science is that, in
addition to giving men a better understanding of the factors and
circumstances that influence and condition their lives, it seems
possible such understanding will also offer men levers for the
practical control or at least modification of such factors. A better
understanding of these five dilemmas may also render them more
amenable to conscious rational human control. Perhaps research and
study of what is involved in these five basic instabilities exhibited in
the institutionalization of religion may enable men to exercise some
degree of control and management of them.

Conclusion: Weber and the Dilemmas

The present theoretical formulation of these dilemmas represents   4.3.24
one way of apprehending general instabilities in human society
which have been studied, in some cases for a very long time, in terms
of other conceptualizations. The first and fifth of these paradoxes
are quite obviously special manifestations and further specifications
of the problems of the control of force and fraud, a classical
problem of political theory. They spell out in the more concrete
terms of the institutionalization of religion the basic instability
which the ever-present possibility of the use of force and fraud
presents to human association.

On the other hand, the second, third, and fourth dilemmas are   4.3.25
really special forms of that social process that Max Weber called 'the
routinization of charisma'. Weber dealt with this chiefly in the
domain of authority and authority institutions, where he showed the
contrast between the more spontaneous, more creative, and at any
rate more unusual evocation of response by the charismatic leader
and the legitimacy of established authority institutions of either the
rational-legal or traditional types. Moreover, Weber emphasised the
impermanent quality of pure charisma and the necessity of its
routinization, a process which he saw as the result of contact

between charisma and the prosaic elements of daily life, and especially those involved in economic activity with its rational calculability and self-interest. The second dilemma — objectification versus alienation of symbols — calls attention to the same process in the sphere of cultic activity and of symbolism in general. Here too the root cause appears to be the same as in Weber's analysis. It is the unavoidable contact with the prosaic — with the daily life of the believers and its petty horizons and demands — and its consequent conversion into routine which results in the final alienation.

4.3.26   The third dilemma — elaboration and alienation of the administrative order — carries out the same kind of analysis upon the structure of offices which Weber applied to the source of legitimacy in his analysis of authority. Here also creativity and spontaneity are progressively replaced by rigidity and complication. The occasions of this overelaboration and alienation are again the demands of meeting the problems of the routine daily functioning of the administrative machinery.

4.3.27   The fourth dilemma — concrete definition versus substitution of the letter for the spirit — is obviously an analogous application of Weber's master conception of the routinization of charisma to the sphere of belief and ethics. Here again one sees the result of the contact between the charismatic element and the domain of everyday life.

4.3.28   Actually the fifth dilemma is discussed by Talcott Parsons in his *The Social System* in substantially the same form in which it is presented here. In fact, it seems that Parsons was the first to use the term 'dilemma of institutionalization', which he applied to this particular problem of the relationship between institutionalization of religion and the power structure of society. A closer analysis, however, reveals that this is merely one of the dilemmas that are to be seen in the process of institutionalization of religion.

With respect to the second, third, and fourth dilemmas and to Weber's concept of the routinization of charisma, the literature of the sociology of religion from Troeltsch on has given many analyses of the process of the routinization of sects and their transformation into stable and conservative denominations. Such a process often coincides with the upward social mobility of the sect members, a process related to their sober steadfastness in economic activity and hence to their contact with what Weber considered the most extreme form of prosaic activity. Thus, once more, contact of the charismatic with the prosaic and routine repetitive round of human activity either transforms or at least limits the spontaneous and creative charismatic element itself.

Quite clearly in all these cases — the Weberian analysis of the routinization of charisma, the routinization of sects as analyzed by Niebuhr and others, and the five dilemmas presented in this discussion — we are dealing with varied expressions of the problem of spontaneity versus stability, of creativity versus continuity. This problem — the Bergsonian problem, it may appropriately be called — may be stated with bleak economy as follows: What problems are involved for social systems in their attempt to evolve workable compromises between spontaneity and creativity which are the very stuff of human life and the source of necessary innovation, and the stable organized and defined context of social institutions so necessary to the continuation of that life and without which it would dissolve into chaos? This Bergsonian problem takes its place alongside what Parsons has called the Hobbesian problem — the problem of the inhibition of force and fraud — as a fundamental functional dilemma for social systems, and in the first and fourth dilemmas presented here the two problems are seen in profound interpenetration.

4.3.29

Notes

1. Joachim Wach, *Sociology of Religion,* University of Chicago Press 1944, pp.17-33.
2. Vilfredo Pareto, *The Mind and Society,* ed. Arthur Livingston. New York, Harcourt, Brace and World 1935, Vol.I, Chap.IV, pp.231-384.
3. Paul Tillich, 'Trends in Religious Thought that affect Social Outlook', in *Religion and World Order,* ed. F. Ernest Johnson, New York, Institute for Religious Studies 1944, pp.17-28.
4. Emile Durkheim, *The Elementary Forms of Religious Life,* J.W. Swain, *trans.* New York, The Free Press of Glencoe 1945.
5. V. Pareto, op.cit., Vol.IV, § 2178, pp.1515-16.
6. Talcott Parsons, *Essays in Sociological Theory,* New York, The Free Press of Glencoe 1954.
7. Ernst Troeltsch, *The Social Teaching of the Christian Churches,* Olive Wyon, *trans.* New York, The Macmillan Company 1931, Vol.II, pp.999-1,000.
8. Susanne Langer, *Philosophy in a New Key,* Harvard University Press 1942, p.123.
9. Ibid., pp.20ff.
10. Robert Merton, *Social Theory and Social Structure,* New York, The Free Press of Glencoe 1949, pp.125ff.
11. Rudolf Otto, *The Idea of the Holy,* J.W. Harvie *trans.,* New York Oxford University Press 1950, p.31.

Source: Abridged from the article by T.F. O'Dea in E.A. Tiryakian, ed., *Sociological Theory, Values and Socio-Cultural Change,* The Free Press of Glencoe, New York 1964, pp.71-89.

5 GREEK AND ROMAN RELIGION

[*Editor's Note:* The philosophy and social organisation of Greece and Rome have left an indelible impression on the West in general and on Western religious institutions in particular; but 'popular' religious life in the area around the Mediterranean at the time when Christianity came to birth strikes a different note.

For the following section of the Reader Professor John Ferguson has chosen two learned articles by eminent classical scholars; and then he has added his own translations of poems and prose writings which throw light on this popular religious thinking and activity.

It may be, as A.D. Nock says in the first essay, that Greek religion 'cannot be formulated'. Nevertheless, the strands which make up that religion can be described. And the same applies to Roman religion.

Students will no doubt mark a sharp difference between the powerful stream of popular religious life in the Graeco-Roman world and the lofty philosophical thoughts and theories of ordered virtue which are to be found at a more sophisticated level, in what we call 'classical literature'.]

5.1 RELIGIOUS ATTITUDES OF THE ANCIENT GREEKS

A.D. Nock

For the myths and rituals of the ancient Greeks we have a large 5.1.1
though unevenly distributed, body of information which admits of
analysis and study. This paper is devoted to the personal attitudes of
the Greeks; as with people of any time and place, these are more
elusive, and our attempt to recapture them depends largely upon
incidental remarks in literature, particularly upon those so phrased
as to leave little doubt that their authors felt that they were speaking
as any sensible man would. We shall draw much from Plutarch, who
combined piety, reflection, and respect for the old ways.

In his life of Demosthenes, he tells how some supernatural 5.1.2
fortune or revolution of events seemed then to be bringing to an end
Greek freedom and to show portents of the future: among these
were terrifying prophecies by the Pythia (who was the mouthpiece
of Apollo at Delphi). 'Demosthenes', he continues,. . .'is said to have
told the people not to pay heed to oracles or give ear to prophecy;
but to suspect the Pythia of taking Philip's side: he reminded the
Thebans of Epaminondas and the Athenians of Pericles. Those men,
he said, reckoned all such things pretexts for cowardice, and used
their reason. Up to this point he was a good man.' Then follows the
tale of his flight from the ranks at the battle of Chaeronea.

'Up to this point he was a good man': ἀνὴρ ἀγαθός may be 5.1.3
primarily 'a brave man', as in the phrase sometimes applied to a
warrior, ἀνὴρ ἀγαθὸς γενόμενος 'having proved himself a brave man';
but even in popular language it has a much wider use and certainly
Plutarch sets the stamp of his moral approval on the actions of
Demosthenes, which include his attitude towards the Pythia. This is
significant. Plutarch was neither critical of old usage nor sceptical of
divine providence and interference in human life: quite the reverse.
He was a priest at Delphi, devoted to its good name and wellbeing,
and his duties included that of presence on some of the occasions on
which the Pythia gave responses. He wrote three treatises concerning
the oracle, and is credited with a lost *Collection of oracles.* Further,
he was familiar with Cynic and Epicurean attacks on belief in this
and other ways' of foreknowing the future. Two objections in

particular, first that the activity of Delphi had declined and many other oracles had disappeared, and second that the Pythia no longer answered in verse, evoked from him elaborate discussions; and the first was for him no mere theoretical question to which he could give an automatic answer. For all his use of inherited arguments, his mind and his heart were deeply engaged, and he could not adopt the reserved pragmatic attitude of Cicero. He held that the Pythia spoke by divine if not verbal inspiration and rejected any suggestion that prophecy was simply a matter of lucky forecasting. So again he defended the validity of visions, and signs including those given by images of deities, and told how events appeared to justify both the experimental and the supernaturalist views of a portent in Periclean Athens.

5.1.4   Nevertheless, he praises Demosthenes for telling the Thebans and Athenians to disregard prophecy, and makes him produce precedents not only from Pericles, who might be regarded as leaning towards rationalism, but also from Epaminondas, the hero in whom Plutarch's local pride found a particular satisfaction. There is no trace of any feeling that Demosthenes had said anything irreverent; and this attitude was not simply the product of later reflection or of enthusiasm for the cause of the Greek city-states, strong as this was in Plutarch. The orator's antagonist, Aeschines, quoted the remark about the Pythia, and characterized Demosthenes as 'being illbred and making full use of the license which you had given him' — not as being blasphemous; and Aeschines missed no chance of vituperation.

5.1.5   The Pythia spoke for Apollo: in fact, we often read of Apollo as sitting on the tripod and prophesying; but the voice was hers, and she was human, and so were the officials who presided over the oracle, were present at consultations, and in earlier times appear to have turned her disordered utterances into cautious hexameter verse. She and they alike were exposed to fear, pressure, partiality and even bribery, and in the great days the officials seem to have followed policies. (We can hardly ascribe the last to the Pythia, who was perhaps at all times, as in Plutarch's day, 'inexperienced and uninformed about almost everything'.) Before the time of Herodotus, the Athenians themselves said that the Alcmaeonids had secured by bribery the oracular command to Sparta to expel Hippias from Athens, and it was common belief that Cleomenes was responsible for the Pythia's decision that his rival Demaratus was illegitimate. These facts, and the remark of Demosthenes quoted earlier, were utilized by critics of the oracle: and many must have been aware of such things. Nevertheless, men's actions usually accorded with two assumptions: what the Pythia said must be fulfilled, and you must use your reason.

You might ask the oracle a wrong question, and receive an 5.1.6 answer intended to bring you to a merited disaster; you might misunderstand the answer which you received; but the answer itself, in some meaning which could be put upon it, must be fulfilled; and this applied not only to Delphi and other established oracles but also to the whole large body of predictions emanating from known seers and anonymous traditions. 'And this came true', whether 'this' be a prophecy or some seemingly casual saying pregnant with meaning, is part of the pattern of popular stories, as it is also the stuff of tragedy. The official Athenian epitaph on the citizens who fell in a battle in the middle of the fifth century concludes: 'Thus he (some hero) brought his will to pass and by the warning of your hurt established for all men to take to heart in time to come the law that the fulfilment of prophecy demands their faith.'

A little later, the chorus in *Oedipus the King* sang, 'No more will I 5.1.7 go reverently to earth's inviolate centre (Delphi), no more to Abae's temple or Olympia, if these oracles do not fit the issue so that all men may point to them. . .the worship of the gods is perishing', and the question of Oedipus, why any one should look to Delphi or to birds screaming overhead, comes but a little before the tragic vindication of the truth of these very prophecies which had seemed false. Iocasta had earlier said that she would not heed the art of divination. The chorus, who represent normal public opinion, are shocked at the possibility of the oracle being wrong; and yet the import of the words for the hearer is not that herein lies the sin of Iocasta, or Oedipus, but that this is tragic irony; these are the words of the man or woman doomed to disaster. They are like Anna's dismissal of the idea that the dead care about the actions of the living, or Dido's mockery of heaven's plan for Aeneas — the plan which means her destruction. The motif of the fulfilment of prophecies and signs and omens is constant in Plutarch: and in view of his moral purpose in writing, that must represent a deliberate choice.

Mantike, the art of foreknowing what to do and what must be, 5.1.8 included not only the direct utterances of Apollo or his mouthpiece and of other deities (e.g., Zeus at Dodona), but also the interpretation of signs and portents (events deemed to be out of the normal order), of visions, of the internal organs of victims sacrificed and of the flight of birds, and the use of texts supposedly composed by inspired seers, such as Musaeus and Bacis. All these might admit of multiple meanings between which you must choose. On a sign or a portent you might consult an oracle, an *exegetes* (or local representative of Delphi and specialist in sacred lore), or a *mantis* (soothsayer); on dreams, an *exegetes* or a *mantis,* and occasionally an oracle; on victims or birds, a *mantis.* In the profession of *mantis* certain individuals and members of certain families were deemed to have special competence; but (apart from various characters of the legendary period) their competence was a matter of skill and not of inspiration, and they differed in ability and moral qualities, just as did the possessors of other skills. Unlike the priests of civic cults, they were professionals; but they played an important part in public affairs and some enjoyed considerable prestige and profit. A *mantis* could be a man of intellectual attainments: Dion had one who had studied in the Academy.

5.1.9   All this involved a human factor and the Greeks frequently show their awareness of this. Even Xenophon represents the father of the elder Cyrus as having his son taught the art, in order that he should of himself know what the gods counselled and should not be at the mercy of soothsayers, if they might wish to deceive him, or helpless if without one. Xenophon himself suffered from the intrigue of Silanus. Portents were like signs of illness, requiring differential diagnosis: one trouble with Nicias and his delay after the eclipse was that he had lost his good *mantis,* and Plutarch's sympathy goes only to the point of remarking that error from cautious scruple in conformity with old established opinions is better than lawless selfwill such as Crassus showed in ignoring omens. Even here the general principles were commonplace; and certainly the examination of the entrails of victims was a matter of routine, like blood tests — but with the important difference that, as a rule, you sacrificed victims until you got favourable omens; unless you desired otherwise. Experts would disagree on details; but the main lines of interpretation were common property. So Xenophon says, 'He (Silanus) knew that, thanks to being regularly present at sacrifices, I too was not inexperienced'; on a later occasion, when himself accused of persuading the soothsayer to declare the sacrifices adverse to setting forth, he invited anyone who wished to attend and any soothsayer present to inspect the sacrifices the next day, and thereafter said to the troops, 'As you see, the sacrifices are not yet successful'. We have also records of favourable signs being pointed out to the troops in order to raise their spirits. Divination was comparable with oratory as a means of creating morale, of encouraging the fainthearted and curbing illtimed eagerness. Xenophon records the bringing of victims, a *mantis,* food, and drink to the army; these were all necessaries, and on the monument at Delphi commemorating the victory of Aegospotami, Lysander, his soothsayer, and his steersman formed a group.

To us this is transparent fiction, but it never lost its hold. Yet the general made the decision, and in Athens Themistocles had to persuade the people of his interpretation of the Delphic oracle about Salamis, just as he had to persuade them on any other disputed issue. 5.1.10

Again, floating prophecies of Musaeus, Bacis, and other (sometimes anonymous) seers enjoyed great authority, although it was widely known or assumed that they were interpolated or invented. Herodotus relates that Onomacritus was caught making an insertion in the oracles of Musaeus and yet he says that he cannot but believe an utterance of Bacis; here, as with the prophecies of Delphi, the idea of a *vaticinium ex eventu* does not seem to have crossed his mind. The Athenian people gave first prize to the *Knights* of Aristophanes, with its brilliant parodies of prophecies produced in support of demagogues; but in real life, such things continued to influence the votes of the assembly, and no soothsayer attacked Aristophanes as Diopeithes did Anaxagoras. 5.1.11

The modernity of the Greeks must not blind us to the distance between our point of view and theirs. Socrates had every reason to know the influence of mundane considerations upon the Delphic oracle and the diverse factors that entered into divination: yet he advised Xenophon to ask the first whether he should or should not join Cyrus, and belief in *mantike* was an integral part of his theism. Plato insisted on the duty of consulting Delphi as the fountain of authority for a city's religious institution, and evolved a theology of *mantike;* Dion's *mantis* from the Academy has been mentioned. The line between the supposedly divine and the obvious human element in divination was not clear; but few save professed Cynics and Epicureans denied the former. 5.1.12

After all, do not early Christian writers, who might so easily have chosen to regard Delphi and the other oracles and every form of divination as mere human trickery, generally explain these things as due to the activity of evil *daimones* and sometimes find divine inspiration in them? In fact, some followed Hellenistic Jewish precedent and produced Sibylline utterances in support of monotheism — and even fabricated suitable responses by Apollo. As for divination, they did not find it easy to turn the faithful from its use.

5.1.13   Belief in these things was deeply rooted; and yet the normative tradition of Greek classical thought did not involve a constant unqualified awe before a *mysterium tremendum.* Plutarch had the strongest conviction of the reality of godhead, a profound attachment to those many Greek and Egyptian myths and rites in which he found this reality enshrined, a detached attitude on details, and a repugnance for such popular practices as seemed to him superstitious. So he says of stories of the miraculous behaviour of images: 'One cannot lightly despise these tales. Yet human weakness makes it dangerous to believe greatly or to disbelieve excessively in such things': that is, let us steer a middle course between superstition and contempt of the divine. This is Plutarch's personal and Academic attitude; but it corresponds to the older norm of conduct. The Old Comedy mocked at soothsayers and devotees of new cults as well as at atheists: you had to use human judgment.

5.1.14   As far as divination was concerned, this was clear, before the intellectualist movement of the fifth century had begun to exercise influence. After all, you 'accepted' or did not 'accept' signs and omens, and sometimes you could divert the destiny which they indicated (which is why cities and tyrants kept secret certain collections of prophecies: if divulged, these might be used by others). An omen was not so much an indication of inevitable destiny as a token of luck or an endorsement of policy. Were there many occasions in Greek history on which a city followed an oracular command or the advice of a *mantis* if it were against the inclinations of all who shaped its policies? Even that model character, Hector, when Polydamas suggested that the flight of an eagle bearing a snake indicated that it was not wise to advance, replied that he did not care about birds, whether they fared to the right or to the left: 'one omen is best, to fight for our country'. To be sure, he could quote a positive counsel of Zeus; but even so the spirit is that of Nelson putting the telescope to his blind eye. Obedience whether to your commander or to omens is normally right; but there must be exceptions. After all, the gods were larger Greeks, and would understand. Does not Athena in *Odyssey,* XIII, 296-9, appreciate the cunning of Odysseus and remark that in shrewdness she was first among immortals, and he among mortals? Again, at all times perjury was a serious thing: the breach of an oath was thought to involve fearful penalties on yourself and on your dependents — and yet, in *Odyssey,* XIX, 395-7, (and this was one of the two epics which were thought to teach virtue), we read that Autolycus outdid all men in thievery and skill in swearing, and that the god Hermes himself gave him this skill. Strictly speaking, this probably means 'the knack of swearing an oath which deceived his adversary without being exactly a false oath' — just such an oath as is ascribed to the god in the *Homeric Hymn to Hermes* 379ff. (274, he offers to swear what would have been formal falsehood; but we do not know how he would have phrased the oath). An increasing stability and reflectiveness of living brought scruples, but the Greek retained this comparatively light touch — except when he was afraid, except when famine or plague or stress of war or a bitter sense of personal injustice conjured spirits from the deep.

Plutarch supplies several illustrations; Apollo used ambiguous 5.1.15 language in oracles in order to protect his servants from the wrath of the mighty; the youthful priest who had broken his vows is answered with the old line 'God allows all things that are inevitable'. Stilpo dreamed that Poseidon was angry with him for not sacrificing an ox as was usual for priests; he was not abashed but answered, 'What do you say, Poseidon? Do you come complaining like a child because I did not borrow money and fill the city with the odor of burnt sacrifice but gave a modest offering from my resources?' and Poseidon appeared to smile and stretch out his right hand and say that for Stilpo's sake he would give the Megarians a haul of anchovies; a wife should not worship gods other than those whom her husband worships, 'for no god finds pleasure in ceremonies performed by a woman with furtive stealth'.

The gods, like the Greeks, were sensible and not easily shocked. 5.1.16 When Aristophanes represents Prometheus hiding under a parasol, in order that Zeus might not see him, or Pisthetairos starving out the gods by cutting them off from the smoke of incense and animal offering, or Heracles being informed of testamentary disabilities consequent upon his illegitimacy, excellent scholars are disposed to regard him as weakening popular faith. Mediaeval parallels suggest that they are wrong. There are limits, even for Aristophanes: no essential levity touches the Maiden of the Acropolis or Demeter. Further, the poet's popularity shows that he did not give offence; and the Athenian people could take offence, and that not only at things which stirred them as deeply as did the mutilation of the Hermae and the supposed parody of the Eleusinian mysteries.

5.1.17   Like other Greeks, they were brought up on Homer; and Homer
has not only the naif folktale anthropomorphism of *Iliad* II 1ff.
(gods and men are all asleep, save Zeus, who is pondering how to
honor Achilles) but also the deliberate comedy of the tale of Ares
and Aphrodite, and again the mock combat of the gods in *Iliad*
XXI, which involves very dignified deities. Again, consider the story
in Herodotus I 60. Pisistratus was returning from exile, and a very
tall woman was dressed up as Athena, and heralds sent to announce
'O Athenians, receive in kindly spirit Pisistratus, whom Athena
honors above all men and is leading to her Acropolis.' She entered in
a chariot, and the citizens worshipped her and received Pisistratus.
The truth or falsity of the story does not concern us: only the fact
that it was told and the comment of Herodotus, 'an expedient
superlatively foolish' (as among Greeks, nay Athenians, and at so
late a time). 'The most foolish' not 'the most impious' Herodotus
expresses various moral judgments, and of course his silence does not
imply approval; but here he comments — on the stupidity involved,
not on any wickedness imputed to the friends of Pisistratus and
Megacles. Anyone caught by such a trick deserved what happened to
him; and it was stupid to try it, if it was tried.

5.1.18   The tale of the sacred snake leaving the Acropolis in 480, given in
Herodotus VIII 41 as a plain fact, is thus recorded in Plutarch,
Themistocles 10: 'At this point, Themistocles, in despair of winning
the multitude by human reasonings, arranged something like a *deus
ex machina* and brought before them supernatural signs and oracles'
(cf. ibid. 19.4 the statement that the early kings of Attica were
credited with inventing the story of the contest between Poseidon
and Athena in order to wean the population from sea to land; *Numa*
4.11-2 'Nor is there anything wrong about the other story told of
Lycurgus and Numa and other such men to the effect that mastering
as they were multitudes hard to control and hard to please, and
introducing great changes in constitutions, they arrogated to
themselves the reputation of divine aid, to the benefit of the very
men before whom they acted the part'). The fabrication of oracles in
the fifth century for political purposes has been noted earlier; we
may add that when Oedipus taunts Tiresias with having been bought,
and Creon with having bought him, he does not accuse either of
impiety. Here personal or political interest was involved; we have
also in Greece as elsewhere various records of pious frauds, whether
done ad hoc or as part of a regular liturgical tradition. The Jewish
author of *Bel and the Dragon,* the rationalist Lucian, and Christian

critics express their indignation at the fraud and gullibility involved; but, so far as our evidence goes, they were wicked only from the standpoint of another religion or irreligion, or when done within the sphere of private unapproved magical operations.

Of course there were limits to justifiable manipulation: the   5.1.19 madness of Cleomenes was widely regarded as divine punishment for his Delphic intrigue. But in general, we seem to see a feeling that the gods were Hellenic and sensible, as men could and should be. Long before Protagoras, man was the measure of all things; and a Greek did not scruple to admit the motive of *philotimia,* the desire to make a good showing before men, in his liberalities to the gods and their temples; Plutarch imputes it to one who was thought 'dear to the gods', the righteous Nicias. The Greek had no desire to

> Do good by stealth and blush to find it fame:

no sympathy with the maxim enunciated in *Matthew* 6.2-3 or with Rabbinic exhortations to give alms secretly; *philotimia* was a commonly accepted and expressed motive for charity; *parete* meant not only the fact but also the recognition of excellence. Further, the gods could be called citizens; their cults were part of the fabric of civic life, and the upkeep of these cults was a civic obligation. The sense of self-importance and the desire for recognition are constant factors in human life, and find expression in a wide range of religious and secular activities; in most societies there is what W.I. Thomas calls a 'pattern of distinction'. Competitiveness for prestige marked the Greek, whether in the rigorous self-discipline of Sparta or in the self-expression of developed Athens.

Much of what can be said about the religion of any one nation or   5.1.20 culture can be said about many others; for religion is largely determined by the human situation, and in considerable measure this is a constant. Greek religion, however, has a definite idiosyncrasy, and this becomes clearer when we turn to the contrast of republican Rome, and of the Near East. On the days which belonged to the gods, *dies nefasti,* the Roman approached them as *numina,* forces operating according to laws and not beings whose conduct could be guessed on human probability *(eikos)*: everything was done with juristic precision, according to rituals, inherited in a *gens* or prescribed by permanent bodies called *collegia.* These *collegia* were deemed to possess an undisputed right to determine what might and might not be done: they granted dispensations, where a Greek might have taken them. (Neither Greek nor Roman would have died rather than commit anything like a breach of the sabbath, but would they not have had different ways out of the difficulty?) One of these *collegia* consulted a collection of prophecies, the Sibylline books, but the public was normally told the decisions of the *collegium* and of the Senate, not the words of the Sibyl. A magistrate who held *imperium* possessed *auspicia* (both words which resemble *numen* in having no precise Greek equivalent), the right and luck of consulting the gods for their approval. He had attendants, but their role was hardly more than that of technicians; they had not the independent personality of the Greek *mantis*. The magistrate acted as he saw fit, but almost always behind the screen of a completely maintained legal fiction; and he too decided not as an individual, but as the possessor of *imperium* and *auspicia,* as one of those whose conduct of public affairs was chronicled without name by the elder Cato. Criticism and discussion had no part in the native scheme of things. Rome's rise to world power and the impact of Hellenistic thought involved a more critical and reflective attitude, and even the elder Cato made his joke about diviners; in the next century Cicero states a strong case against the theoretical validity of divination, but was no more ready than Cato to consider the possibility of the system being abandoned. When Augustus sought to rehabilitate the Roman virtues, he necessarily set himself to restore temples and rituals (and I may remark in passing that his enterprise cannot be pronounced a failure: the ruling class regained a sense of responsibility).

5.1.21   From the Roman standpoint, religious *philotimia* also was out of the question. Rome had its *gloria,* the concomitant of eminent services to the state; but the foundation of temples was the work of magistrates acting within prescribed formulas, and their maintenance was public. Certain families had hereditary ritual obligations, but the idea of private munificence in this area does not appear before Horace; in other words, not before a time when the old order was shaken to its foundations.

5.1.22   To speak very generally, the measures of things in Greece is man, in Rome is law, and in the Near East is the gods — or the gods and a monarchy which is their instrument. These gods were after the fashion, if not always after the form, of men, and the stories told of them, even in the canonical text of ritual hymn and drama, include not only allegory and inventive elaboration but also (as did the cult) elements which seem to us undignified and even worse. Yet the stories are, it seems, almost wholly the work of priesthoods, the prime repositories of tradition and learning. Biologically and emotionally the members of a priesthood are not a race apart from their fellow-nationals nor are they devoid of individualism and personal ambition, but their responses are strongly conditioned by their training and likely to be in large part conventional; when treating myth, they can seldom stand outside the tradition and look at it in an individualistic way. Our evidence may be misleading: we have what priests and scribes preserved, and even the protests of Zoroaster and prophets and psalmists against elements of exaggerations of cult have survived in formularies, while our knowledge of the layman hardly goes beyond expressions of personal devotion and moral reflectiveness. Nevertheless, the very fact of what was preserved shows what was normative: though we now have from Egypt a literary pastiche on the tale of Horus and Seth, the Near East has not yet shown anything like the freedom of the words of the Muses to Hesiod: 'We know how to tell many lies like unto truths, and we know how to tells truths, when we wish', or the range of Greek mythology not associated with any cult, nor, again, any criticism of myth or rite from a secular standpoint. There was cynicism, indifference, carelessness, and pretence, but not the free play of the intellect — no more in myth than in history. Further, the cults were rich, in their own possessions and in royal gifts: the ordinary man paid to them what he must needs in tithe or the equivalent, but there was no place for liberality, *philotimia,* save on the part of civil and religious potentates, in their ordained hieratic roles; for others conformity sufficed, and specially good repute was gained by benevolence to the poor and the unburied dead rather than by services to the cult.

   The Greek attitudes which we have considered are very far from 5.1.23 Christianity, very far from Ethical Culture; they were already very far from Plato and the philosophic tradition, within which a wholly different notion of divinity developed. Yet they existed side by side with deep feelings of dependence and devotion and awe. 'O Solon, Solon, you Greeks are always children', said the Egyptian priest in Plato's *Timaeus:* but children, though they may sound irreverent, are afraid of the dark and glad of the light, capable of passionate attachment to those who feed and guard them, those to whom they take their little troubles and grievances, those who to them represent something like omniscience and omnipotence, capable, again, of a sense of guilt and awe before those who represent also the order of commands which may not be broken. In the *Ion* of Euripides,

Creusa speaks of Apollo as one who has done her a brutal violence, and yet the young hero's attitude to the god and the Delphic shrine is like that of an unspoiled novice in a cloister enriched with the devotion of the ages. 'All men have need of the gods', says Nestor (*Odyssey* III 48); and the Zeus who could be represented in so undignified a manner was also the natural protector of the stranger and the suppliant, the god who 'pours forth rain most violently, being in wrath and anger against men who judge crooked judgments by force in the assembly, and drive justice out, and heed not the vengeance of the gods' (*Iliad,* XVI 385 ff.). Something like the spirit of Old Testament prophecy exists side by side with the Ovidian tale. Man was the measure; but what he sought to measure seemed greater than himself. The gods were larger Greeks; yes, but between gods and man there was a line. 'Do not seek to become a god': you might be honored as a god, but you remained a man, and any gesture that suggested forgetfulness of this, any 'frantic boast and foolish word' might draw on you that supernatural resentment, whether ethical or beyond good and evil, which the Greeks called Envy or Nemesis, the tragic penalty of greatness in sagas and Herodotean tales. You walked proudly in the sun; but, says Cephalus in Plato's *Republic,* 'When a man is near the point of thinking that he will die, there comes upon him fear and reflection on matters which did not trouble him before. The stories told about things in Hades, to the effect that the man who has done wrong here must pay the penalty there, those stories at which he used to mock, trouble his spirit then — lest they may be true.' There was fear, on a higher level and on a lower. The Greek disapproved of magic and witchcraft; yet Plato clearly indicates how difficult it would have been to eradicate the fear of them from men's minds, and archaeological evidence shows that such proceedings were used by men of wealth and position.

5.1.24   These considerations make it easier to understand the Greek attitude towards oracles and divination: the human element in these things was seen, and yet the results seemed to vindicate them. We must not look for consistency in men's religious actions, any more than in their secular conduct: norms of belief and facts of practice, words and deeds do not fit: nor do men mean all that they say, in reverence or irreverence, least of all men as nimble of wit and tongue as were many of the Greeks. Religion is not all or nothing, certainly not among them.

5.1.25   The Homeric pattern and the disciplined life of the small Greek city-states in the archaic period supplied a norm: the land of Greece, physical conditions with singular clarity of atmosphere and yet a certain capricious quality, unlike the massive regularity of Egypt and Mesopotamia, and experienced with special sharpness by the many who lived in contact with the sea: the Greeks themselves, a kaleidoscopic variety of pattern against a common background. So we find a religion of laymen with a respect for tradition and a strong strain of that commonsense which is superior to intellectualism. In religion, as in other things, classical Hellenism represents a delicate balance which defies our attempts at formulation.

Note

Footnotes have been eliminated and the number of exact source-references to classical texts have been reduced. Those who want to check these fuller references should consult the original article in *Proceedings of the American Philosophical Society* 85 (1942) 472-82 (250), reprinted in A.D. Nock, *Essays on Religion and the Ancient World,* Oxford, Clarendon Press 1972, Vol.II, pp.534-50.

5.2   THE LATIN HISTORY OF THE WORD *RELIGIO*

W. Warde Fowler

5.2.1 This word, which in its modern form is in use all over Europe, had a
remarkable history in its own Latin speech and literature. That
history seems to me to have more than a mere linguistic interest, and
I propose in this paper to indicate in outline where that interest lies.
Of the much disputed etymology of the word I will only say this:
that the question stands now very much as it did in the time of
Cicero and Lucretius, who took conflicting views of it. Professor
Conway, whose authority is great, tells me that apart from the
evidence of usage and the feeling of the Romans themselves, there is
nothing to decide whether it is to be connected with *ligare,* to bind,
as Lucretius thought, or with *legere,* to string together, arrange, as
Cicero believed. His feeling is in favour of Cicero's view, as less
prejudiced than that of Lucretius; so is mine. But our feelings are
not of much account in such questions, and I may pass on at once to
the *history* of the word.

5.2.2   In Latin literature down to Christian times, *religio* is used in a
great variety of senses and often in most curious and unexpected
ones; but all these uses can, I think, be reduced to two main types of
meaning, one of which is probably the older, the other derivative.
The one reflects the natural feeling of the Latin when face to face
with the supernormal or supernatural, before the State with its
priesthoods and religious law had intervened to quiet that feeling.
The other expresses the attitude of the citizen of a State towards
the supernatural, now realisable without fear or doubt in the shape
of the recognised deities of his State. I must explain these two uses
to begin with.

5.2.3   I. *Religio* is the feeling of awe, anxiety, doubt, or fear, which is
aroused in the mind by something that cannot be explained by a
man's experience or by the natural course of cause and effect, and
which is therefore referred to the supernatural. This I take to be the
original meaning of the word, for the following reasons:

1. *Religio* is not a word which has grown out of any State usage,
or been rendered technical by priestly law or ritual. It has no part in
the *ius divinum* (divine law), like the word *sacrum* (holy, sacred):
we search for it in vain in the indices to the *Corpus Inscriptionum,*

330

where it would inevitably be found if it were used in a technical or legal sense. In its adjectival form, as applied to times and places, we may also see the results of this non-technical meaning. *Dies religiosi, loca religiosa,* are *not* days and places which are proclaimed as such by the official administrators of the *ius divinum:* they are rather such days and places as man's own feeling, independently of the State and its officials, has made the object of *religio. Religiosum* stands in contrast with *sacrum* as indicating something about which there is awe, fear, scruple, and which has not been definitely brought within the province of State law, nor handed over to a deity by ritualistic formulae. If this be so, then we may safely refer the origin of the word to a period when powerful State priesthoods had not as yet, by ritual and routine, soothed down the natural awe which in less perfect social forms man feels when obstructed, astonished, embarrassed, by that which he cannot explain or overcome.

2. That this is the true and the oldest meaning of the word seems also proved by the fact that it survived in this sense throughout Latin literature, and was indeed so used by the ordinary Roman layman. It is familiar to us in a thousand passages. *Religio* may stand for a doubt or scruple of any kind, or for anything uncanny which creates such doubt or scruple. To illustrate this I may select a single passage from Caesar, as a writer who would be sure to use a word in a sense obvious to every one. In describing the alarm of the soldiers of Q. Cicero when besieged at Aduatuca, he says:

> One announced that the camp was already captured, another maintained that the barbarians had arrived victorious from the massacre of the army and its commander-in-chief. The majority set before their eyes the disaster which overtook Cotta and Titurius who fell in that very fortress, and so created for themselves fresh *religiones* out of the nature of the place [*Gallic War* 6,37].

Here Caesar might almost as well have simply written *metus* (fears) instead of *religiones;* but he wishes to express not only natural fear and alarm as to what may happen, but that fear accentuated by the sense of something wrong or uncanny, for which the soldiers or their leaders may be responsible – in this case the pitching of a camp in a place which they believed to have been the scene of a former disaster. Let us note that these soldiers were out of reach of the protecting arm of their own *ius divinum:* they were on foreign soil, ignorant of what supernatural powers might be present there. Their commander-in-chief, it is true, was the chief administrator of that *ius*. Caesar was pontifex maximus: but Caesar was not there, and if he had been, his presence would in those days and in such a place have made little difference. They are in the same position towards the supernatural as their ancestors had been before the State arose, and in describing their alarm Caesar uses the word *religio* in the same sense in which it had come into use in those primitive ages.

Livy, writing of a pestilence and its moral effects, says that 'it was not only their bodies which were affected by the plague; various forms of *religio*, generally foreign ones, assailed their minds as well' (4, 30): where by *religio* he means the feeling of anxiety which took practical shape in the performance of various rites, foreign for the most part. Such examples could be multiplied a hundredfold: and the word came at last to be used for anything that produces a feeling of wonder or even of curiosity, seeing that we do not understand it. Thus Pliny says that there is a *religio* in men's knees, because we kneel on them to supplicate, and clasp the knees of those from whom we ask mercy; there is something uncanny about that part of the body — something we cannot explain (*Nat.Hist.* 11, 250). In the same way he says that no animal is more open to *religio* than the mole, because its heart and its teeth are supposed to have some mysterious medicinal powers (30, 19).

In this way the adjective *religiosus* came to be applied to human beings in a sense not far removed from that of *superstitiosus*, which is, so far as I know, always used of persons addicted to rites or fancies outside the pale of the Roman State-religion. This sense seems to be an early one: it occurs in the fragment of an 'early hymn' quoted by Aulus Gellius (4, 9, 1): 'you should be *religentem* (attentive) not *religiosum* (over-anxious)'. Lucretius' use of the substantive may also be mentioned in this context: for him *all* that we call religion was superstitious and degrading, and could therefore be properly called by that word which the Romans invariably used to express their doubts, fears, and scruples.

Lastly, before I go on to the second chief meaning of the word, I may mention the significant fact that *religio* is never personified as a deity, as were Pietas (Piety), Sanctitas (Sanctity) and almost all the virtues at one time or another. It is not a virtue: it does not necessarily lead to a definite course of action, and embodies no sense of duty or moral value: it is primarily and essentially a *feeling* to which human nature is liable under certain circumstances.

II. I now come to the second chief sense in which the word is 5.2.4
used, and which brings it a step nearer to our own use of it. This
sense was mainly due, I think, in Roman literature to Cicero, though
it may be far older in common use: and is perhaps the result of the
Greek originals, e.g. Posidonius, whom he was following when
writing *The Laws* and *The Nature of the Gods,* etc.; but this is a
point which I must here pass over. From Cicero in any case I can
best illustrate this new turn of meaning which the word acquires.

When Cicero was a young man, not yet too learned or
philosophical, he defined the word clearly according to its common
usage, with an addition of some importance. '*Religio* observes due
ritual attention to a higher being which people call divine' (Invent.
2, 161), i.e. a *feeling* of awe that inevitably suggests the discovery of
the proper rites by which the object of that feeling may be
propitiated. But later on in his life, in the second book of *The Laws,*
which deals with the State religion, he uses the word with much
freedom of *the particular cults,* or all of them together, which are
the result of the feeling. Thus in x.25: 'The worship of private gods,
whether new or foreign, brings confusion into *religiones*', i.e. private
persons may not introduce new cults; for there would in that case be
a confusion both of religious feeling and duty. In x.23 he calls his
own imaginary *ius divinum* a *constitutio religionum,* a system of
religious duties. Thus the word is passing into the sense of the *forms
of cult,* as ordered and organised by the State, the feeling, the *religio*
proper, being only aroused when scruple is felt as to the accurate
performance of these rites. In vii.15 we read 'with what intention,
with what sense of duty he observed *religiones*', where it answers
almost exactly to religious duties. In xvi. 40 he tells how the
Athenians consulted the Delphic oracle 'which *religiones* they would
do best to retain', and the answer was, 'the traditional ones'. Again
in xi.27 we find '*religio Larium*', the cult of the Lares. But the
feeling which prompts the cult, and which is aroused afresh if it be
neglected is seldom entirely absent. The phrase of tombs' *religio*
(xxii.55) suggests quite as much the feeling as the ritual: and a little
further down we are told that the pontifical law of burials shows
great *religionem* and care for ritual — the word *caerimonia* (ritual)
being necessary to express the ritual following on the feeling. And
lastly this word may be used to gather up and express in totality a
number of acts of cult, because the same feeling is at the root of
them all. Thus in xix.47 the question is raised whether a pontifex

should know the civil law. The answer is, 'the part of it associated with *religio,* that relates to sacrifices, vows, festivals, burials', the pontifex has to do with these matters, which can all be expressed together by the word *religio.*

These examples seem to show how the word might pass into the sense in which we still use it; the feeling which prompts us to worship, and also the forms under which we perform that worship. The feeling is common to human nature, civilised or not: that is the original meaning of the word: the worship, organised by a priesthood, is the work of the State — that is the second, or as we may call it, the Ciceronic meaning. And in the same age it is also so used by Lucretius, who includes under it all that was for him the world's evil and folly, i.e. both the feeling and the cult — delusion, myth, superstition, as well as the organised but futile worship of the family and the State. 'Such are the heights of wickedness to which men are prompted by *religio*' (1.101). In an age of cosmopolitanism, when the old local character of the cults was disappearing, and in an age of philosophic-religious syncretism when men like Posidonius, Cicero, Varro, and others were thinking and writing about the nature of the gods and kindred questions, a word was wanted to gather up and express all this religious side of human life and experience: it must be a word without a definite technical meaning, and such a word was *religio.* To take a single example, besides those already quoted from Cicero, there is the famous aphorism which St Augstine ascribes to Varro: 'It is expedient for states to be deceived *in religione' (City of God,* 4,27).

Thus while *religio* continues to express the feeling only, or the cult only, if called on to do so by Latin writers, it gains in the Ciceronian age a more comprehensive connotation, as the result of the contemplation of religion by philosophy as a thing apart from itself; and thus, as we shall see directly, enabled the early Christian writers, who knew their Cicero well, and modelled their prose on his, to use it in much the same sense as that in which we use it today.

5.2.5   Time fails to trace the word in the pre-Christian literature of the early Empire, and to see how it is affected by the finer quasi-religious Stoicism, or again by the Caesar-worship of the day — the nearest approach in antiquity, as it has been called, to a cosmopolitan religion. So far as I can see, it did not take from either of these sources any new turn or type of meaning. Seneca, for example, has but little use for it; though he was, as Professor Dill has said of him, one of the few heathen moralists who warm moral feeling with the emotion of modern religion, he had little real interest either in the feeling or the cult. If he made himself a religion out of his Stoic principles, it was not one that he could have described by the word *religio*. For him, though tinged by emotion, it was still wisdom: he could hardly have assented to the later teaching of Lactantius, *True Wisdom,* that wisdom and *religio* are inseparably connected. Nor did the worship of the Caesars bring any new turn of meaning: here it could express the cult ('heavenly *religiones*'), but the feeling at the root of a genuine religious cult was not there to be expressed. This is perhaps significant both of the true meaning of the word, and also of the weak point in Caesar-worship: but I must not now dwell upon it. I will only mention one passage in which Pliny the Younger uses it of the cult of Trajan, because the kind of feeling which it there represents — loyalty and devotion to an individual — is in some sense a new one, and may be a foreshadowing of the Christian use. Pliny writes to Trajan from Bithynia reporting celebrations on the Emperor's birthday: 'We have celebrated the day with due *religio,* commending our public vows and thanks to the gods to whom we owe your power' (10,102). Here it means the feeling of devotion prompting the vows and thanks, as well as those acts themselves. There is nothing in it of the old fear, scruple, anxiety; it is the devotion and gratitude which expresses itself in religious festivities.

But there was to be a real change in the meaning of the word, the last but one in its history. The second century A.D. was that in which the competition was keenest between various religious creeds and forms, each with its own vitality, and each clearly marked off from the others. It is no longer a question of religion as a whole contemplated by a critical or a sympathetic philosophy: the question is, which creed and which form is to be the true and the victorious religion. Our wonderful word again adapts itself to the situation. Each separate religious system can now be called a *religio*. The old polytheistic system can now be called *religio deorum* (of the gods) by the Christian, while his own creed is *religio Dei* (of God). In the *Octavius* of Minucius Felix, written probably in the first half of the second century A.D., the word is already used in this sense. His *nostra* (our) *religio, vera* (true) *religio,* distinguished from all other *religiones,* is the whole Christian faith and Christian practice as it stood then; the depth of feeling and the acts which give it outward form. The one true religion can be expressed by this word, though it is quite different from anything the word has as yet been called on to mean. In Lactantius, Arnobius, Tertullian, this new sense of the

5.2.6

word is to be found on almost every page: but a single noble passage of Lactantius must suffice to illustrate it. 'The heathen sacrifice', he says, 'and leave all their *religio* in the temple': thus it is that such *religiones* cannot make men good, or firm in their faith. 'Our *religio* is firm, strong and immutable, in that it has the mind itself for a sacrifice, in that it is wholly within the mind of the worshipper' (*Justice* 5,19). *Religio* here is not awe only or cult only, or scruple about details of cult, but a mental devotion capable of building up character. 'The kingdom of God is within you.' It is worth noting that it can now be explained by the word *pietas* (piety, sense of duty), which was not possible in the old days, because *pietas* was a virtue and *religio* was not a virtue but a feeling. Lactantius says that philosophy, 'which does not contain true *religionem,* that is the height of *pietas,* is not true wisdom' (*True Wisdom,* 4,3).

5.2.7   Thus the word has meant successively (1) the natural fear and awe which semi-civilised man feels in the presence of what he cannot explain; (2) the cult by which he strives to propitiate the unseen Powers, together with the scruple he feels if the propitiation is in the least degree imperfect; (3) the whole sphere of worship, together with all belief in the supernatural, as viewed from the standpoint of the philosopher; (4) the competing divisions of that sphere of worship and belief, each being now a *religio,* and the Christian faith being for the Christian the *vera religio.* There is one later stage in the history of the word, which I can only mention here. It suffered a degradation when it was made to mean the monastic life: the life of men who withdrew themselves from a world in which true religion was not. But even in this degraded form it reveals once more its wonderful capacity to express the varying attitude of humanity towards the supernatural. Outside the monasteries — the homes of the *religiosi* — were a thousand fears, fancies, superstitions, which the old Roman might have summed up by his word *religio,* the anxious fear of the supernatural: inside them, for many ages at least, was still something of the *vera religio* of the early Fathers, the devotion and the ritual combined, the pure life and training, *religio Dei.*

Note

English is substituted for the original Latin in the quotations.

Source: From W. Warde Fowler, *Rome,* OUP 1972, pp.7-15.

5.3 GREEK AND ROMAN SELECTED READINGS

Translated by John Ferguson

The Power of Zeus

5.3.1

Come, you gods, have a try, then you'll all know.
Dangle a rope of gold from the sky.
All you gods and all you goddesses take hold of it.
You would not have the strength to pull from heaven to earth
Zeus, who is supreme in wisdom, not for all your efforts.
But when once I was of a mind to pull,
then pull you up I should, earth, sea and all,
binding the rope around the peak of Olympus
and leaving everything suspended in mid-air.
So far am I superior to gods and men.

[Homer *Iliad* 8, 18-27]

Greek Pessimism

5.3.2

My son, Zeus the Thunderer holds the destiny
of all things and disposes them by his will.
There's no understanding in man: creatures of a day,
we live like cattle, and do not know
how God shall bring each of us to his destined end.
But Hope and Confidence keep us going,
our minds on the unattainable; some await
the coming of a single day, others the cycle of years.
Next year, every mortal imagines he'll return
feathered with riches and possessions.
But unenvied age seizes one
before he reaches port; another's heart
is worn with illness; another is overpowered by Ares
and sent by Hades below the black earth.
Some at sea are wrecked by storms
and wave upon wave of the dark ocean
and lose their lives, when they've loaded the ship with livelihood.
Others tie a noose around their wretched necks
and leave the sunlight by their own choice.
Nothing is free from evil. Ten thousand

dooms assail us humans, our anxieties and sorrows
are beyond imagination. If anyone would listen to me,
we should not set our hearts on good things, or torture
ourselves by fixing our minds on disasters.

[Semonides fr.1.]

5.3.3 The Priestess at Delphi

We do not deprive prophecy of any basis in God or reason, when we
assign a human soul   as its material cause and mephitic vapour as its
instrument or plectrum. In the first place the earth which generates
the vapours and the sun which equips the earth with the potentiality
of constitution and transmutation are traditionally among our gods.
In the second place, it would not seem irrational or impossible to
leave spiritual powers as superintendents, patrolmen and protectors
of this constitution, slackening or tautening it at need, eliminating
an excess of ecstatic distraction, and mixing in an element which can
stir the soul of the subject without causing pain or damage. We do
nothing contrary to this principle of rationality when we sacrifice
first, crown the sacrificial victims with flowers and pour libations
over them. The priests and religious officials claim that they sacrifice
their victims, pour libations over their heads and observe their
shivering movements as a demonstration that the god is ready to
prophesy. The sacrificial offering must be pure, innocent and incorrupt
in soul and body. Evidence relating to the body is easy enough to see
with the eye. They test the soul by putting barley in front of the bulls
and chick-peas in front of the boars. If they do not eat they are
regarded as having something wrong with them. But with the goat
cold water is an adequate test. A soul in its natural state could not
remain indifferent or immobile in face of a shower of water. Even if it
were a firm conclusion that the movement is evidence of the god's readiness to prophesy, and the failure to move of his unreadiness, I cannot
see that this creates any difficulty for my position. Every faculty
gives better or worse results at different moments. We may get the
moment wrong; it is reasonable for the god to produce evidence.

I think that the vapours are not always of the same quality, but
are more or less intense at different times. As witnesses I call a great
many visitors and the whole temple staff. The room in which they
place those who have come to consult the god is sometimes filled
with fragrant air. This does not happen frequently or regularly, but
from time to time as it occurs. It is like the scent of the richest and
sweetest perfumes, and it has as its source the inner sanctuary. It is

presumably a kind of efflorescence produced by heat or some other internal force. If this seems implausible, you will admit that the Pythia herself receives different impulses at different times in the inspired part of her soul, and her soul's constitution is not single and simple like that of a musical instrument which once tuned is kept at the same pitch. Many distractions take hold of her body and affect her soul; she is aware of some, unconscious of rather more. When these are dominating her, it is better for her not to enter the sanctuary and surrender herself to the god, in view of the fact that she is not undistracted, not like a well-tuned musical instrument, but in a state of emotional instability. . .

Whenever the faculty of imagination and prophecy is properly attuned to the constitution of the spirit as to a drug, there cannot but be divine inspiration in those who utter prophecies. In other circumstances there cannot be inspiration, or the inspiration is not pure and effective but misleading, as we can see in the recent death of the Pythia. A delegation arrived from overseas to consult the oracle. Reports say that in their anxiety for the reputation of the oracle the priests went too far; they kept at it until the victim, soaked to the skin and practically drowned, eventually gave in. What did this involve for the priestess? According to the report she went down to the oracular chamber reluctantly and unenthusiastically. In her first answers it was clear from the hoarseness of her voice that there was something wrong with her responses. She was like a ship in a storm. She was filled with an evil spirit which was inhibiting her. Finally she showed signs of complete distraction. She gave a fearful, unintelligible scream, dashed to the door, and flung herself out. The deputation ran away; so did Nicander, the interpreter, and the other religious representatives present. Before long they went back in, and picked her up. She was still conscious but died a few days later.

For the same reasons they insist on the Pythia keeping her body pure from sexual intercourse, and her life in general free from contact and communication with strangers. They take the omens before the oracular responses are given, trusting the god to show whether her constitution and disposition are in a fit state to experience divine inspiration without harm. The power of the spirit does not affect everyone in the same way, or the same people in the same way on every occasion. As I have been suggesting, it provides a kind of starting-point, a spark to light the flame for those who are in a fit condition to go through the transforming experience. The power comes from gods and divine spirits. Even so it is not inexhaustible; it is subject to deterioration with the passage of time; it does not extend into that eternity which wears out all that exists between the earth and the moon according to our philosophy.

[Plutarch *Moralia* 436E-437D, 438A-D]

5.3.4 Initiation at Eleusis

So we describe the soul which has passed beyond as one of the holy dead because it is wholly changed and transformed. In this world it lacks knowledge, except at the very moment of expiring; at that point it has an experience similar to those who receive the inspiration of initiation into the Great Mysteries. (There is a similarity, verbal and actual, between expiration and inspiration). First comes aimless wandering, tiring movements in a circle, uncertain explorations through darkness getting nowhere, then before the actual fulfilment terrors of every kind, shuddering, knees shaking, sweat pouring down, a feeling of awe. Then suddenly a marvellous light comes to meet him and he enters open fields and a land of purity; there are voices and dancing and majestic and holy things to greet the ear and eye. Now he has found fulfilment, he is an initiate, and he walks freely among all this with a garland on his head, celebrating and companying with saintly men. He looks down on the great mass of those living on earth, uninitiated, unpurified, packed together in mud and fog, trampling one another underfoot, and out of fear of death clinging to their evils because they do not believe in the blessings beyond. From this you can see clearly that the soul's entanglement with the body and imprisonment in it are really contrary to nature.

[Plutarch *On the Soul* (fragment in Stobaeus 4, 52, 49)]

5.3.5 Rome: Agricultural Rites

When the pear is flowering make your offering for the oxen. . . The offering should be made as follows. Present Jupiter of the Offering with a beaker of wine of any size you like. The day is to be a holiday for oxen, drivers and those making the offering. The formula for the offering runs: 'Jupiter of the Offering, in that it is meet for a beaker of wine to be offered to you in my house before my people, so receive our worship in the presentation of this offering'. Next the hands are to be washed and the wine lifted up with the words: 'Jupiter of the Offering, receive our worship in the presentation of this offering, receive our worship in this sacrificial wine.' Bring a gift for Vesta if you wish. The offering for Jupiter comprises roast meat and a stoup of wine. Consecrate it to Jupiter devoutly approaching him in the appropriate manner. Afterwards, when the offering is completed, plant millet, panic-grass, garlic, and lentils. . .

Before harvesting you should sacrifice the pre-harvest pig according to the following rite. Ceres should receive a sow as the pre-harvest pig before you garner the following crops: spelt, wheat, barley, beans, rape-seed. Before you sacrifice the sow offer a prayer accompanied by incense and a libation of wine, to Janus, Jupiter and Juno. Bring forward a plate of cakes for Janus with these words: 'Father Janus, in bringing forward this plate of cakes, I ask in all faith that you will look with kindly grace on me and my children, my home and household.' Present the oblation-cake to Jupiter with these words: 'Jupter, in bringing forward this oblation-cake I ask in all faith that you will accept this oblation and look with kindly grace on me and my children, my home and my household.' Next present the wine to Janus with these words: 'Father Janus, just as in bringing forward the plate of cakes I asked in all faith for your favour, so to the same end accept this sacrificial wine.' Next address Jupiter with these words: 'Jupiter, accept this oblation-cake and accept this sacrificial wine.' Next sacrifice the pre-harvest pig. When the entrails have been cut out, bring forward a plate of cakes for Janus and offer it with the same rituals you used previously. Bring forward an oblation-cake for Jupiter and offer it with the same ritual as you used previously. In the same manner, offer wine to Janus and offer wine to Jupiter, in the same manner as before in bringing forward the plate of cakes and consecrating the oblation-cake. When all this is done offer the entrails and wine to Ceres. . .

The following is the Roman ritual for thinning a grove. There is to be the propitiatory sacrifice of a pig with the following formula: 'Whether you be a god or a goddess to whom this grove is sacred, as is your due, receive this propitiatory sacrifice of a pig for the violence done to this holy place, and for this purpose, whether I perform the act myself, or someone else performs it on my authority, grant that it may be rightly done. To this end in offering the propitiatory sacrifice of a pig I ask in all faith that you will look with kindly grace on me, my home, my household and my children. To this end accept this propitiatory sacrifice of a pig.' If you wish to cultivate the ground offer a second propitiatory sacrifice in the same manner with the additional words 'by reason of the work to be done'. So long as the work continues see that the ritual is performed each day in a different section of the land. If you omit a day or if some public or private festival is interposed, a further propitiatory offering must be made.

The ceremonial purification of the land must be performed according to the following ritual. Instruct the sacrificial procession of pig, ram and bull to move round the land with the words: 'That with the goodwill of the gods all may turn out for the best, I charge you, Manius, to be responsible for the purification of my farm, fields and land by means of this sacrificial procession of pig, ram and bull, directing it to be driven or carried around whatever part you think right.' Begin by offering a prayer with a libation of wine to Janus and Jupiter and then speak as follows: 'Father Mars, I pray and beseech you to look with kindly favour on me, my home and household; for which purpose I have instructed this sacrificial procession of pig, ram and bull to be driven round my fields, land and farms, that you may avert, keep off and eliminate diseases seen and unseen, barrenness and devastation, and that you may permit my produce, crops, vineyards and plantations to be fruitful and prosper, keep safe my herdsmen and their herds, and grant good health and strength to me, my family and household; for this purpose, for the purification of my farm, land and fields, and for making a purification, accept the sacrifice of this suckling pig, ram and bull. Father Mars for this same purpose accept this suckling pig, ram and bull.' Then with the sacrificial knife make a pile of cakes, and see that the oblation-cake be set beside it; then bring forward the victims. The following is the ritual formula for offering the pig, lamb and calf: 'For this purpose accept this sacrifice of pig, ram and bull.' It is forbidden at this point to mention Mars by name. . . or the lamb and calf. But if the omens are unfavourable at every point, use the following formula: 'Father Mars, if something has displeased you in the former offering of suckling pig, ram and bull, I make expiation with this pig, ram and bull.' If there is doubt about one or two, use this formula: 'Father Mars, seeing that you were displeased with the former pig, I make expiation with this new pig. . .'

[Cato *On Agriculture,* pp.131ff.]

5.3.6 Rome: The Need for a Precise Formula

Man can provide his own remedies, and the first of them raises a major unsolved question: have words, have formulaic spells any power? If they do, then the fact ought to be generally recognised. Ask intellectuals individually; they hold no such belief; but unconsciously it is universally accepted. It is regarded as useless to offer sacrifice without prayer: the gods have not been duly consulted. Besides, different language is used for securing favourable omens, for averting evil, or invoking support for an enterprise. We notice that our chief magistrates use set prayers. No word must be omitted or out of turn, so each phrase is read from a book for the magistrate to repeat, an official is appointed to keep a strict check, another is authorised to ensure silence, a musician is playing to shut out external noises. There are some remarkable records of both going wrong, of ill-omened noises abnegating the prayer and of mistakes in the prayer itself, resulting within the entrails in the sudden disappearance of reduplication or the head of the liver or the heart while the victim was standing there. There has survived a most important example of a ritual formula which the Decii, father and son, used in devoting themselves. Also extant are the words of the plea of innocence used by the Vestal Tuccia against a charge of unchastity when she carried water in a sieve in the year A.U.C. 609. Our own generation has actually seen a man and woman from Greece, and members of other nations with whom we were at war, buried alive in the Cattle Market. The Master of the College of Fifteen generally goes through the prayer for this ceremony clause by clause. If you read it you are found to admit the power of formulaic prayer; the outline of eight hundred and thirty years is a complete indication of it. We hold today that our Vestal Virgins can use prayer to root to the ground runaway slaves so long as they have not got clear of the city. If the principle is once accepted that the gods listen to any prayers or are affected by any form of words, then the whole problem is solved.

[Pliny the Elder, 28: 3, 10-3.]

A Sacred Spring

5.3.7

Spring of Bandusia, brighter than crystal,
worthy of rich wine, worthy of flowers,
    tomorrow brings you a goat,
        on whose forehead the young horns
grow with promise of love and battles.
It's not to be: your cool waters
    will flow red with the blood
        of the playful kid.
The cruel season of blazing Sirius
cannot touch you; you offer welcome
    coolness to wandering herds

and bullocks tired with ploughing.
You'll join the company of famous springs
when I tell of the oak growing over the hollow
    rocks where your chattering
        streams leap down.

                                [Horace *Odes* 3,13]

5.3.8 Hymn for the Inauguration of a New Era

Phoebus, and Diana lady of the forests,
glowing splendour of the sky, for ever
honoured and to be honoured, grant our petition
    at this holy season
when the song of Sibyl has commanded
picked girls and blameless boys
to worship the gods who protect the Seven
    Hills, with a hymn.
Life-giving Sun, in your golden chariot you
open and close the day, being reborn different
but the same. May you never look on any spectacle
    greater than Rome!
And you, Ilithyia, gentle in preparing
birth in due season, protect our mothers,
whether we call you 'Bringer of the Daylight' or
    'Goddess of Childbirth'.
Guard our growing children, goddess, and give blessing
to the Fathers' edicts and the bonds of marriage
and to the law of wedlock with its promise of
    plentiful children,
that, as it passes, the cycle of the century
may bring round again the music and the contests
played on three fine days before a crowded audience,
    three memorable evenings.
You also, Fates, who prophesy truthfully
what the Powers have decreed and the outcome of history
holds unchanged, join a prosperous future
    to all that is past.
May the Earth, rich in life of plant and animal,
present Ceres with a garland of corn!
May wind and rain from Jupiter bring healthy
    growth to our harvest!
Apollo, be gentle and favourable; put away

your bow and listen to the prayers of the boys.
Lady of the Moon, queen of the constellations,
 listen to the girls.
If Rome is your care, if from Troy came
the people who settled on the coast of Etruria,
that remnant with orders to change their home and city,
 protected as they voyaged,
the people for whom Aeneas, survivor of his country,
holy and guiltless though Troy was put to the flames,
forged a path to freedom, ready to restore
 more than they'd lost —
then, you gods, grant growth in virtue to our youth,
grant tranquillity and peace to our elders,
grant to the house of Romulus prosperity, children
 and all glory!
Grant that Anchises' and Venus' far-famed line
may receive the object of their prayer and sacrifice
of white oxen, trampling enemies who resist,
 merciful to the fallen.
Already by land and sea the Parthian
shrinks from the power and armed might of Italy,
already the Scythians and Indians have dropped their arrogance
 and are asking for terms.
Already Trust, Peace, Honour and Chastity
(come from our past) and Virtue (long neglected)
have confidence to return, and Plenty, endowed with
 a full horn, can be seen.
May Phoebus, the seer, glorious with gleaming
bow and welcome to the nine Muses,
Phoebus, who by medical science restores the body's
 wearied limbs,
if he looks with favour on the altars of the Palatine,
may he prolong the power of Rome and prosperity
of Latium for another epoch and a future
 onward and upward.
May Diana, worshipped by Aventine and Algidus,
mark the prayers of the fifteen priests,
and lend a gracious ear to the supplication
 of the children.
We carry home hope, favourable and sure,
that this is the will of Jupiter and all the gods,

we, the choir, trained to sing the praises
   of Phoebus and Diana.

                        [Horace, *Carmen Saeculare*]

5.3.9 **A Christian View of Initiation into the Rites of Cybele**

   As you know, a trench is dug, and the high priest
   plunges deep underground to be sanctified.
   He wears a curious headband, fastens fillets for the occasion
   around his temples, fixes his hair with a crown of gold,
   holds up his robes of silk with a belt from Gabii.
   Over his head they lay a plank-platform criss-cross,
   fixed so that the wood is open not solid;
   then they cut or bore through the floor
   and make holes in the wood with an awl at several points
   till it is plentifully perforated with small openings.
   A large bull, with grim, shaggy features
   and garlands of flowers round his neck
   or entangling his horns, is escorted to the spot.
   The victim's head is shimmering with gold
   and the sheen of the gold leaf lends colour to his hair.
   The animal destined for sacrifice is at the appointed place.
   They consecrate a spear and with it pierce his breast.
   A gaping wound disgorges a stream of blood,
   still hot, and pours a steaming flood on the lattice
   of the bridge below, flowing copiously.
   Then the shower drops through the numerous paths offered
   by the thousand cracks raining a ghastly dew.
   The priest in the pit below catches the drops,
   puts his head underneath each one till it is stained,
   till his clothes and all his body are soaked in corruption.
   Yes, and he lays his head back, puts his cheeks in the stream,
   sets his ears underneath, gets lips and nose in the way,
   bathes his very eyes in the drops,
   does not spare his mouth, wets his tongue
   till he drains deep the dark blood with every pore.
   When the blood is exhausted the priests drag away
   the carcase, now growing stiff, from the structure of planks.
   Then the high priest emerges, a grim spectacle.
   He displays his dripping head, his congealed beard,
   his sopping ornaments, his clothes inebriated.
   He bears all the stains of this polluting rite,

filthy with the gore of the atoning victim just offered —
and everyone stands to one side, welcomes him, honours him,
just because he has been buried in a beastly pit
and washed with the wretched blood of a dead ox.

[Prudentius, *Peristephanon* 10, 1011-50]

The Apotheosis of a Roman Emperor   5.3.10

It is the practice of the Romans to deify those of their emperors
who die, leaving children to succeed them. They call the rite
apotheosis. Mourning is observed all through Rome, curiously mixed
with festival celebrations and religious worship. They inter the body
of the dead emperor in the ordinary way with a costly funeral. Then
they make a wax image exactly like the dead man, and expose it to
view on a large ivory couch spread with cloth of gold and elevated
on a platform, in the entrance-hall of the palace. The image is pallid
like a sick man as it lies there. For most of the day the whole of the
senate sit round the bed on the lefthand side, clothed in black, and
on the right all the women whose husband's or father's position
entitle them to a place of honour. These last wear no gold jewellery
or necklaces but put on plain white clothes like mourners. These
observances extend over seven days. Every day doctors arrive, go up
to the bed, and actually examine the patient and announce that he is
growing steadily worse. When they decide that he is dead, the
noblest member of the equestrian order and young men, carefully
selected, of senatorial rank take up the bier, carry it along the sacred
way, and expose it to public view in the old forum, at the place
where the magistrates of Rome take the oath at the end of their
term of office. On either side stands are constructed with tiers. Two
choirs stand on these, one formed of children from upper-class
families, and opposite one of women of repute. Each sings hymns
and praise-songs for the dead man, modulated in tones of mournful
solemnity. Next they carry the bier out of the city to the Campus
Martius. Here in the widest section of the open space there has been
erected a square structure, built entirely of huge logs, rather like a
house. This is completely filled with brushwood, and ornamented
outside with gold-embroidered hangings, ivory statues and a variety
of pictures. On top of this erection a similar but smaller one is built,
with open doors and windows, and above it a third and fourth in
diminishing sequence, with the smallest of all on top. In form the
structure is like those lighthouses which dominate harbours, and
guide ships in the dark to safe berths, and which go by the general

name of Pharos. They take the bier up to the second storey and set
it down there, heaping up every sort of aromatic spice and incense
and every kind of fragrant fruit, herb or juice. Every nation, every
city, every person of prominence vie with one another in offering
these last gifts in honour of the emperor. When a vast heap of these
aromatics is collected and the entire chamber filled with them, there
is a cavalry procession around the pyre and the whole equestrian
order circle round in formation using the pace and rhythm of the
Pyrrhic dance. Chariots move round in the same formation, their
drivers wearing the purple-fringed toga, and carry figures wearing
masks resembling the most distinguished Roman emperors and
military commanders. When this part of the ritual is complete the
heir to the throne applies a torch to the construction, and the others
fire the pile from all sides. The whole thing goes up in flames
without difficulty in view of the quantity of brushwood aromatics
piled up inside. Then from the smallest storey at the very top, as
from a pinnacle, an eagle is released to mount into the sky together
with the fire, taking the emperor's soul from earth to heaven, as the
Romans believe. Thereafter he is worshipped with the other gods.

[Herodian 4, 2.]

5.3.11   A Roman Epitaph

To the Divine Shades. Vettius Agorius Praetetatus, Augur, Priest of
Vesta, Priest of the Sun, Member of the Fifteen, Curial of Hercules,
Consecrated to Liber and the deities of Eleusis, Hierophant,
Superintendent Minister, Initiated by the bull's blood Father of
Fathers. In politics indeed Quaestor by special nomination, Praetor
of the City, Governor of Tuscia and Umbria, Consular of Lusitania,
Proconsul of Achaea, City Prefect, Appointed Ambassador by the
Senate five times, twice Prefect of the Praetorian Guard in Italy and
Illyrium, Nominated Consul Regular.

Also Aconia Fabia Paulina, daughter of Caius, Consecrated to
Ceres and the Deities of Eleusis, Consecrated to Hecate on Aegina,
Initiated by the bull's blood, Hierophant.

These lived united together for forty years.

Ancestral glory gave me no greater blessing
than to be worthy of your hand.
My husband's name was all my light, my glory;
Agorius, born of a proud seed,
you brighten your country, your senate, your wife

by your integrity, character and learning;
which won you the crown of virtue.
All that wise men with heaven's gate open before them
have carefully handed down in Greek or Latin,
all that their learning embodied in verse,
all that they expressed in loose prose phrases,
all this you enhanced between reacting and recounting.
These are trifles. You are a pious initiate of the holy
mysteries and keep their revelations in the depth of your mind;
you have learned to honour the various gods in different ways,
and generously took your wife as partner in religion,
sharing your knowledge of gods and men, loyal to you.
Why should I now speak of your offices and titles,
the privileges men seek so earnestly.
You always thought them minor, fleeting;
your highest honour was the priestly fillet.
My husband, you took me, instructed me in the good,
kept me pure and holy, snatched me from the grasp of death,
brought me to the temples, dedicated me to serve the gods;
you were my sponsor as I entered the mysteries;
when I became priestess of Cybele and Attis,
you, my true partner, honoured me with the mystic blood of bulls;
when I became a servant of Hecate you taught me the triple secret;
you presented me as a worthy initiate of Ceres at Eleusis.
It is through you that all men honour me
devout and blest, for you spread my good name
through all the world. Unknown myself, I am known to all.
How should men not honour your wife?
The mothers of Rome treat me as an example,
and think their children lovely if like you.
Men and women alike welcome and look to
the glories you have taught them to wear.
These are gone. I, your wife, am racked with tears,
blessed indeed, if the god had granted my husband
longer life than myself, but blessed even so
because I am, have been, and after death shall be yours.

[*Corpus Inscriptionum Latinarum* 6, 1, 1779]

6 THE RELIGION OF THE JEWS

[*Editor's Note:* Some of the basest deeds in human history have been perpetrated against the Jews; but these have not prevented Jews from exercising immense influence in the life of mankind. No one can deny this people the right to be considered one of the most significant ethnic groups in the human story. Yet for two and a half thousand years it has been necessary for them to engage in strenuous struggle in order even to survive. They have been the children of perpetual exile.

At the very centre of their life has been their religion. In the pages which follow, the student will find examples of the scriptures which have provided a foundation for their uncertain life, teachings from Jewish sages of the past, and contemporary statements about Judaism made by people who, living in what has been a tragic century for them, are seeking to reinterpret the old faith in fast-changing times.]

6.1 PASSAGES FROM THE OLD TESTAMENT

God's Covenant with the Jews

God spoke to Moses and said, 'I am the Lord. I appeared to 6.1.1
Abraham, Isaac, and Jacob as God Almighty. But I did not let
myself be known to them by my name JEHOVAH. Moreover, I
made a covenant with them to give them Canaan, the Land where
they settled for a time as foreigners. And now I have heard the
groaning of the Israelites, enslaved by the Egyptians, and I have
called my covenant to mind. Say therefore to the Israelites, "I am
the Lord. I will release you from your labours in Egypt. I will rescue
you from slavery there. I will redeem you with arm outstretched and
with mighty acts of judgement. I will adopt you as my people, and I
will become your God. You shall know that I, the Lord, am your
God, the God who releases you from your labours in Egypt. I will
lead you to the land which I swore with uplifted hand to give to
Abraham, to Isaac and to Jacob. I will give it you for your
possession. I am the Lord." '

[*Exodus* 6:2-8]

God's Encounter with Moses on the Mountain

In the third month after Israel had left Egypt, they came to the 6.1.2
wilderness of Sinai. They set out from Rephidim and entered the
wilderness of Sinai, where they encamped, pitching their tents
opposite the mountain. Moses went up the mountain of God, and
the Lord called to him from the mountain and said, 'Speak thus to
the house of Jacob, and tell this to the sons of Israel: You have seen
with your own eyes what I did to Egypt, and how I have carried you
on eagles' wings and brought you here to me. If only you will now
listen to me and keep my covenant, then out of all peoples you shall
become my special possession; for the whole earth is mine. You shall
be my kingdom of priests, my holy nation. These are the words you
shall speak to the Israelites.'

Moses came and summoned the elders of the people and set
before them all these commands, which the Lord had laid upon him.
The people all answered together, 'Whatever the Lord has said we
will do.' Moses brought this answer back to the Lord. The Lord said
to Moses, 'I am now coming to you in a thick cloud, so that I may

speak to you in the hearing of the people, and their faith in you may never fail.' Moses told the Lord what the people had said, and the Lord said to him, 'Go to the people and hallow them today and tomorrow and make them wash their clothes. They must be ready by the third day, because on the third day the Lord will descend upon Mount Sinai in the sight of all the people. You must put barriers round the mountain and say, "Take care not to go up the mountain or even to touch the edge of it." Any man who touches the mountain must be put to death. No hand shall touch him; he shall be stoned or shot dead; neither man nor beast may live. But when the ram's horn sounds, they may go up the mountain.' Moses came down from the mountain to the people. He hallowed them and they washed their clothes. He said to the people, 'Be ready by the third day; do not go near a woman.' On the third day, when morning came, there were peals of thunder and flashes of lightning, dense cloud on the mountain and a loud trumpet blast; the people in the camp were all terrified.

Moses brought the people out from the camp to meet God, and they took their stand at the foot of the mountain. Mount Sinai was all smoking because the Lord had come down upon it in fire; the smoke went up like the smoke of a kiln; all the people were terrified, and the sound of the trumpet grew ever louder. Whenever Moses spoke, God answered him in a peal of thunder. The Lord came down upon the top of Mount Sinai and summoned Moses to the mountain-top, and Moses went up. The Lord said to Moses, 'Go down; warn the people solemnly that they must not force their way through to the Lord to see him, or many of them will perish. Even the priests, who have access to the Lord, must hallow themselves for fear that the Lord may break out against them.' Moses answered the Lord, 'The people cannot come up Mount Sinai, because thou thyself didst solemnly warn us to set a barrier to the mountain and so to keep it holy.' The Lord therefore said to him, 'Go down; then come up and bring Aaron with you, but let neither priests nor people force their way up to the Lord, for fear that he may break out against them.' So Moses went down to the people and spoke to them.

[*Exodus* 19]

The Ten Commandments

6.1.3   God spoke, and these were his words:
I am the Lord your God who brought you out of Egypt, out of the land of slavery.

You shall have no other god to set against me.

You shall not make a carved image for yourself nor the likeness of anything in the heavens above, or on earth below, or in the waters under the earth.

You shall not bow down to them or worship them; for I, the Lord your God, am a jealous god. I punish the children for the sins of the fathers to the third and fourth generations of those who hate me. But I keep faith with thousands, with those who love me and keep my commandments.

You shall not make wrong use of the name of the Lord your God; the Lord will not leave unpunished the man who misuses his name.

Remember to keep the sabbath day holy. You have six days to labour and do all your work. But the seventh day is the sabbath of the Lord your God; that day you shall not do any work, you, your son or your daughter, your slave or your slave-girl, your cattle or the alien within your gates; for in six days the Lord made heaven and earth, the sea, and all that is in them, and on the seventh day he rested. Therefore the Lord blessed the sabbath day and declared it holy.

Honour your father and your mother, that you may live long in the land which the Lord your God is giving you.

You shall not commit murder.

You shall not commit adultery.

You shall not steal.

You shall not give false evidence against your neighbour.

You shall not covet your neighbour's house, you shall not covet your neighbour's wife, his slave, his slave-girl, his ox, his ass, or anything that belongs to him.

When all the people saw how it thundered and the lightning flashed, when they heard the trumpet sound and saw the mountain smoking, they trembled and stood at a distance. 'Speak to us yourself', they said to Moses, 'and we will listen; but if God speaks to us we shall die.' Moses answered, 'Do not be afraid. God has come only to test you, so that the fear of him may remain with you and keep you from sin.' So the people stood at a distance, while Moses approached the dark cloud where God was.

[*Exodus* 20:1-21]

God's Law: its Extension

The Lord spoke to Moses and said, Speak to all the community of 6.1.4 the Israelites in these words: You shall be holy, because I, the Lord your God am holy. You shall revere, every man of you, his mother and his father. You shall keep my sabbaths. I am the Lord your God. Do not resort to idols; you shall not make gods of cast metal for yourselves. I am the Lord your God.

When you sacrifice a shared-offering to the Lord, you shall slaughter it so as to win acceptance for yourselves. It must be eaten on the day of your sacrifice or the next day. Whatever is left over till the third day shall be destroyed by fire; it is tainted, and if any of it is eaten on the third day, it will not be acceptable. He who eats it must accept responsibility, because he has profaned the holy-gift to the Lord: that person shall be cut off from his father's kin.

When you reap the harvest of your land, you shall not reap right into the edges of your field; neither shall you glean the loose ears of your crop; you shall not completely strip your vineyard nor glean the fallen grapes. You shall leave them for the poor and the alien. I am the Lord your God.

You shall not steal; you shall not cheat or deceive a fellow-countryman. You shall not swear in my name with intent to deceive and thus profane the name of your God. I am the Lord. You shall not oppress your neighbour, nor rob him. You shall not keep back a hired man's wages till next morning. You shall not treat the deaf with contempt, nor put an obstruction in the way of the blind. You shall fear your God. I am the Lord.

You shall not pervert justice, either by favouring the poor or by subservience to the great. You shall judge your fellow-countryman with strict justice. You shall not go about spreading slander among your father's kin, nor take sides against your neighbour on a capital charge. I am the Lord. You shall not nurse hatred against your brother. You shall reprove your fellow-countryman frankly and so you will have no share in his guilt. You shall not seek revenge, or cherish anger towards your kinsfolk; you shall love your neighbour as a man like yourself. I am the Lord.

You shall keep my rules. You shall not allow two different kinds of beast to mate together. You shall not plant your field with two kinds of seed. You shall not put on a garment woven with two kinds of yarn.

When a man has intercourse with a slave-girl who has been assigned to another man and neither ransomed nor given her freedom, enquiry shall be made. They shall not be put to death, because she has not been freed. The man shall bring his guilt-offering, a ram, to the Lord to the entrance of the Tent of the Presence, and with it the priest shall make expiation for him before the Lord for his sin, and he shall be forgiven the sin he has committed.

When you enter the land, and plant any kind of tree for food, you shall treat it as bearing forbidden fruit. For three years it shall be forbidden and may not be eaten. In the fourth year all its fruit shall be a holy-gift to the Lord, and this releases it for use. In the fifth year you may eat its fruit, and thus the yield it gives you shall be increased. I am the Lord your God.

You shall not eat meat with the blood in it. You shall not practise divination or soothsaying. You shall not round off your hair from side to side, and you shall not shave the edge of your beard. You shall not wash yourselves in mourning for the dead; you shall not tattoo yourselves. I am the Lord.

Do not prostitute your daughter and so make her a whore; thus the land shall not play the prostitute and be full of lewdness. You shall keep my sabbaths, and revere my sanctuary. I am the Lord.

Do not resort to ghosts and spirits, nor make yourselves unclean by seeking them out. I am the Lord your God.

You shall rise in the presence of grey hairs, give honour to the aged, and fear your God. I am the Lord.

When an alien settles with you in your land, you shall not oppress him. He shall be treated as a native born among you, and you shall love him as a man like yourself, because you were aliens in Egypt. I am the Lord your God.

You shall not pervert justice in measurement of length, weight, or quantity. You shall have true scales, true weights, true measurements dry and liquid. I am the Lord your God who brought you out of Egypt. You shall observe all my rules and laws and carry them out. I am the Lord.

[*Leviticus* 19]

A Prophet Speaks: Words of Judgement

The vision received by Isaiah son of Amoz concerning Judah and 6.1.5
Jerusalem during the reigns of Uzziah, Jotham, Ahaz, and Hezekiah,
kings of Judah.

Hark you heavens, and earth give ear,
>   for the Lord has spoken:
> I have sons whom I reared and brought up,
> but they have rebelled against me.
> The ox knows its own
>   and the ass its master's stall;

but Israel, my own people,
has no knowledge, no discernment.

O sinful nation, people loaded with iniquity,
race of evildoers, wanton destructive children
who have deserted the Lord,
spurned the Holy One of Israel
and turned your backs on Him.
Where can you still be struck
if you will be disloyal still?
Your head is covered with sores,
your body diseased;
from head to foot there is not a sound spot in you —
nothing but bruises and weals and raw wounds
which have not felt compress or bandage
or soothing oil.
Your country is desolate, your cities lie in ashes.
Strangers devour your land before your eyes;
it is desolate as Sodom in its overthrow.
Only Zion is left,
like a watchman's shelter in a vineyard,
a shed in a field of cucumbers,
a city well guarded.
If the Lord of Hosts had not left us a remnant,
we should soon have been like Sodom,
no better than Gomorrah.

Hear the word of the Lord, you rulers of Sodom;
attend, you people of Gomorrah, to the instruction of our God:
Your countless sacrifices, what are they to me?
says the Lord.
I am sated with whole-offerings of rams
and the fat of buffaloes;
I have no desire for the blood of bulls,
of sheep and of he-goats.
Whenever you come to enter my presence
who asked you for this?
No more shall you trample my courts.
The offer of your gifts is useless,
the reek of sacrifice is abhorrent to me.
New moons and sabbaths and assemblies,

sacred seasons and ceremonies, I cannot endure.
I cannot tolerate your new moons and your festivals;
    they have become a burden to me,
        and I can put up with them no longer.
        When you lift your hands outspread in prayer,
    I will hide my eyes from you.
    Though you offer countless prayers
        I will not listen.
    There is blood on your hands;
        wash yourselves and be clean.
    Put away the evil of your deeds,
        away out of my sight.
Cease to do evil and learn to do right,
pursue justice and champion the oppressed;
give the orphan his rights, plead the widow's cause.

    Come now, let us argue it out,
        says the Lord.
    Though your sins are scarlet,
        they may become white as snow;
        though they are dyed crimson,
        they may yet be like wool.
        Obey with a will,
    and you shall eat the best that earth yields;
        but if you refuse and rebel,
        locust-beans shall be your only food.
    The Lord himself has spoken.

                              [*Isaiah* 1:1-20]

A Prophet Speaks: Words of Promise

Comfort, comfort my people;   6.1.6
    — it is the voice of your God;
speak tenderly to Jerusalem
    and tell her this,
that she has fulfilled her term of bondage,
    that her penalty is paid;
    she has received at the Lord's hand
    double measure for all her sins.

    There is a voice that cries:
Prepare a road for the Lord through the wilderness,

clear a highway across the desert for our God.
    Every valley shall be lifted up,
every mountain and hill brought down;
rugged places shall be made smooth
      and mountain-ranges become a plain.
    Thus shall the glory of the Lord be revealed,
and all mankind together shall see it;
    for the Lord himself has spoken.

A voice says, 'Cry',
and another asks, 'What shall I cry?'
'That all mankind is grass,
they last no longer than a flower of the field.
The grass withers, the flower fades,
when the breath of the Lord blows upon them;
the grass withers, the flowers fade,
    but the word of our God endures for evermore.'

You who bring Zion good news, up with you to the mountain-top;
    lift up your voice and shout,
    you who bring good news to Jerusalem,
      lift it up fearlessly;
cry to the cities of Judah, 'Your God is here.'
Here is the Lord God coming in might,
    coming to rule with his right arm.
      His recompense comes with him,
      he carries his reward before him.
    He will tend his flock like a shepherd
      and gather them together with his arm;
    he will carry the lambs in his bosom
      and lead the ewes to water.

[*Isaiah* 40:1-11]

The Jewish People: God's Servant

6.1.7   Here is my servant, whom I uphold,
    my chosen one in whom I delight,
    I have bestowed my spirit upon him,
    and he will make justice shine on the nations.
    He will not call out or lift his voice high
    or make himself heard in the open street.
    He will not break a bruised reed,

or snuff out a smouldering wick;
he will make justice shine on every race,
never faltering, never breaking down,
he will plant justice on earth,
while coasts and islands wait for his teaching.

Thus speaks the Lord who is God,
he who created the skies and stretched them out,
who fashioned the earth and all that grows in it,
who gave breath to its people,
the breath of life to all who walk upon it:
I, the Lord, have called you with righteous purpose
and taken you by the hand;
I have formed you, and appointed you
to be a light to all peoples,
a beacon for the nations,
to open eyes that are blind,
to bring captives out of prison,
out of the dungeons where they lie in darkness.
I am the Lord; the Lord is my name;
I will not give my glory to another god,
nor my praise to any idol.
See how the first prophecies have come to pass,
and now I declare new things;
before they break from the bud I announce them to you.

[*Isaiah* 42: 1-9]

The Treachery of God's Servant

When the Ephraimites mumbled their prayers,　　6.1.8
God himself denounced Israel;
they were guilty of Baal-worship and died.
Yet now they sin more and more;
they have made themselves an image of cast metal,
they have fashioned their silver into idols,
nothing but the work of craftsmen;
men say of them,
'Those who kiss calf-images offer human sacrifice.'

Therefore they shall be like the morning mist
or like dew that vanishes early,
like chaff blown from the threshing floor

or smoke from a chimney.
But I have been the Lord your God since your days in Egypt,
    when you knew no other saviour than me,
        no God but me.
        I cared for you in the wilderness,
    in a land of burning heat, as if you were in pasture.
        So they were filled,
    and, being filled, grew proud;
        and so they forgot me.
So now I will be like a panther to them,
I will prowl like a leopard by the wayside;
I will meet them like a she-bear robbed of her cubs
    and tear their ribs apart,
like a lioness I will devour them on the spot,
    I will rip them up like a wild beast.
I have destroyed you, O Israel; who is there to help you?
    Where now is your king that he may save you,
        or the rulers in all your cities
        for whom you asked me,
    begging for king and princes?
    I gave you a king in my anger,
        and in my fury took him away.
        Ephraim's guilt is tied up in a scroll,
        his sins are kept on record.
When the pangs of his birth came over his mother,
he showed himself a senseless child;
        for at the proper time he could not present himself
        at the mouth of the womb.
        Shall I redeem him from Sheol?
    Shall I ransom him from death?
Oh, for your plagues, O death! Oh, for your sting, Sheol!
    I will put compassion out of my sight.
    Though he flourishes among the reeds,
    an east wind shall come, a blast from the Lord,
        rising over the desert;
Ephraim's spring will fail and his fountain run dry.
    It will carry away as spoil
        his whole store of costly treasures.
Samaria will become desolate because she has rebelled against her God;
her babes will fall by the sword and be dashed to the ground,
    her women with child shall be ripped up.

                              [*Hosea* 13]

God's Promise of Forgiveness

Return, O Israel, to the Lord your God;   6.1.9
    for you have stumbled in your evil courses.
  Come with your words ready,
    come back to the Lord;
say to him, 'Thou dost not endure iniquity.
    Accept our plea,
  and we will pay our vows with cattle from our pens.
  Assyria shall not save us, nor will we seek horses to ride;
    what we have made with our own hands
  we will never again call gods;
  for in thee the fatherless find a father's love.'

I will heal their apostasy; of my own bounty will I love them;
  for my anger is turned away from them.
  I will be as dew to Israel
    that he may flower like a lily,
  strike root like the poplar
    and put out fresh shoots,
  that he may be as fair as the olive
    and fragrant as Lebanon.
  Israel shall again dwell in my shadow
    and grow corn in abundance;
    they shall flourish like a vine
    and be famous as the wine of Lebanon.
What has Ephraim any more to do with idols?
  I have spoken and I affirm it;
  I am the pine-tree that shelters you;
  to me you owe your fruit.

[*Hosea* 14]

God's Choice of the Jews Carries Justice with It

Listen, Israelites, to these words that the Lord addresses to you, to   6.1.10
the whole nation which he brought up from Egypt:
For you alone have I cared
among all the nations of the world;
therefore will I punish you
  for all your iniquities.
Do two men travel together
  unless they have agreed?
Does a lion roar in the forest

>   if he has no prey?
> Does a young lion growl in his den
>   if he has caught nothing?
> Does a bird fall into a trap on the ground
>   if the striker is not set for it?
> Does a trap spring from the ground
>   and take nothing?
> If a trumpet sounds the alarm,
>   are not the people scared?
> If disaster falls on a city,
>   has not the Lord been at work?
> For the Lord God does nothing
> without giving to his servants the prophets knowledge of his plans.
>   The lion has roared; who is not terrified?
> The Lord God has spoken; who will not prophesy?

[Amos 3:1-8]

God will Establish His Rule

6.1.11   In days to come
>   the mountain of the Lord's house
>   shall be set over all other mountains,
>   lifted high above the hills.
>   Peoples shall come streaming to it,
> and many nations shall come and say,
> 'Come, let us climb up to the mountain of the Lord,
>   to the house of the God of Jacob,
>   that he may teach us his ways
>   and we may walk in his paths.'
> For instruction issues from Zion,
>   and out of Jerusalem comes the word of the Lord:
>   he will be judge between many peoples
> and arbiter among mighty nations afar.
>   They shall beat their swords into mattocks
>   and their spears into pruning-knives;
> nation shall not lift sword against nation
>   nor ever again be trained for war,
>   and each man shall dwell under his own vine,
>   under his own fig-tree, undisturbed.
>   For the Lord of Hosts himself has spoken.

> All peoples may walk, each in the name of his god,

but we will walk in the name of the Lord our God for ever and ever.

On that day, says the Lord,
    I will gather those who are lost;
I will assemble the exiles and I will strengthen the weaklings.
    I will preserve the lost as a remnant
    and turn the derelict into a mighty nation.
The Lord shall be their king on Mount Zion now and for ever.
And you, rocky bastion, hill of Zion's daughter,
    the promises to you shall be fulfilled;
    and your former sovereignty shall come again,
    and dominion of the daughter of Jerusalem.

[*Micah* 4:1-8]

God's Majesty and Man's Great Vocation

    O Lord our sovereign,   6.1.12
how glorious is thy name in all the earth!
Thy majesty is praised high as the heavens.
    Out of the mouths of babes, of infants at the breast,
        thou hast rebuked the mighty,
silencing enmity and vengeance to teach thy foes a lesson.
When I look up at thy heavens, the work of thy fingers,
    the moon and the stars set in their place by thee,
    what is man that thou shouldst remember him?
    mortal man that thou shouldst care for him?
    Yet thou hast made him little less than a god,
    crowning him with glory and honour.
    Thou makest him master over all thy creatures;
    thou hast put everything under his feet:
all sheep and oxen, all the wild beasts,
    the birds in the air and the fish in the sea,
    and all that moves along the paths of ocean.
    O Lord our sovereign,
how glorious is thy name in all the earth!

[*Psalm* 8]

God Demands Righteousness of His People

O Lord, who may lodge in thy tabernacle?   6.1.13
Who may dwell on thy holy mountain?
The man of blameless life, who does what is right
and speaks the truth from his heart;

who has no malice on his tongue,
who never wrongs a friend
and tells no tales against his neighbour;
    the man who shows his scorn for the worthless
    and honours all who fear the Lord;
    who swears to his own heart and does not retract;
.   who does not put his money out to usury
    and takes no bribe against an innocent man.
He who does these things shall never be brought low.

                                            [*Psalm* 15]

God's Providential Care

6.1.14 The Lord is my shepherd; I shall want nothing.
    He makes me to lie down in green pastures,
and leads me beside the waters of peace;
    he renews life within me,
and for his name's sake guides me in the right path.
Even though I walk through a valley dark as death
I fear no evil, for thou art with me,
thy staff and thy crook are my comfort.

Thou spreadest a table for me in the sight of my enemies;
    thou hast richly bathed my head with oil,
        and my cup runs over.
Goodness and love unfailing, these will follow me
    all the days of my life,
    And I shall dwell in the house of the Lord
    my whole life long.

                                           [*Psalm* 23]

Psalm of Thanksgiving to God

6.1.15 Bless the Lord, my soul;
    my innermost heart, bless his holy name.
Bless the Lord, my soul,
    and forget none of his benefits.
    He pardons all my guilt
    and heals all my suffering.
He rescues me from the pit of death
and surrounds me with constant love,
    with tender affection;
he contents me with all good in the prime of life,

and my youth is ever new like an eagle's.

The Lord is righteous in his acts;
　　he brings justice to all who have been wronged.
He taught Moses to know his way
　　and showed the Israelites what he could do.
The Lord is compassionate and gracious,
　　long-suffering and for ever constant;
　　He will not always be the accuser
　　or nurse his anger for all time.
He has not treated us as our sins deserve
or requited us for our misdeeds.
For as the heaven stands high above the earth,
so his strong love stands high over all who fear him.
　　Far as east is from west,
so far has he put our offences away from us.
　　As a father has compassion on his children,
so has the Lord compassion on all who fear him.
For he knows how we were made,
he knows full well that we are dust.

Man's days are like the grass:
he blossoms like the flowers of the field;
　　a wind passes over them, and they cease to be,
　　and their place knows them no more.
But the Lord's love never fails those who fear him;
　　his righteousness never fails their sons and their grandsons
　　who listen to his voice and keep his covenant,
　　　　who remember his commandments and obey them.

The Lord has established his throne in heaven,
　　his kingly power over the whole world.
　　Bless the Lord, all his angels,
　　　　creatures of might who do his bidding.
　　Bless the Lord, all his hosts,
　　　　his ministers who serve his will.
　　Bless the Lord, all created things,
　　　　in every place where he has dominion.

Bless the Lord, my soul.

[*Psalm* 103]

Psalm of Praise to God

6.1.16   O praise the Lord.

O praise God in his holy place,
praise him in the vault of heaven, the vault of his power;
praise him for his mighty works,
    praise him for his immeasurable greatness.
Praise him with fanfares on the trumpet,
    praise him upon lute and harp;
praise him with tambourines and dancing,
    praise him with flute and strings;
praise him with the clash of cymbals,
    praise him with triumphant cymbals;
let everything that has breath praise the Lord!

O praise the Lord.

[*Psalm* 150]

True Wisdom

6.1.17 There are mines for silver
and places where men refine gold;
where iron is won from the earth
and copper smelted from the ore;
the end of the seam lies in darkness,
and it is followed to its farthest limit.
Strangers cut the galleries;
they are forgotten as they drive forward far from men.
While corn is springing from the earth above,
what lies beneath is raked over like a fire,
and out of its rocks come lapis lazuli,
dusted with flecks of gold.
No bird of prey knows the way there,
and the falcon's keen eye cannot descry it;
proud beasts do not set foot on it,
and no serpent comes that way.
Man sets his hand to the granite rock
and lays bare the roots of the mountains;
he cuts galleries in the rocks,
and gems of every kind meet his eye;
he dams up the sources of the streams
and brings the hidden riches of the earth to light.

But where can wisdom be found?
And where is the source of understanding?
No man knows the way to it;
it is not found in the land of living men.
The depths of ocean say, 'It is not in us',
and the sea says, 'It is not with me.'
Red gold cannot buy it,
nor can its price be weighed out in silver;
it cannot be set in the scales against gold of Ophir,
against precious cornelian or lapis lazuli;
gold and crystal are not to be matched with it,
no work in fine gold can be bartered for it;
black coral and alabaster are not worth mention,
and a parcel of wisdom fetches more than red coral;
topaz from Ethiopia is not to be matched with it,
it cannot be met in the scales against pure gold.
Where then does wisdom come from,
and where is the source of understanding?
No creature on earth can see it,
and it is hidden from the birds of the air.
Destruction and death say,
'We know of it only by report.'
But God understands the way to it,
he alone knows its source;
for he can see to the ends of the earth
and he surveys everything under heaven.
When he made a counterpoise for the wind
and measured out the waters in proportion,
when he laid down a limit for the rain
and a path for the thunderstorm,
even then he saw wisdom and took stock of it,
he considered it and fathomed its very depths.
And he said to man:
    The fear of the Lord is wisdom,
    and to turn from evil is understanding.

[*Job* 28]

Source: The passages from the Old Testament are from the New English Bible, OUP and CUP, 1970.

6.2 READING FROM THE AUTHORISED DAILY PRAYER BOOK

6.2.1 Ethics of the Fathers

6.2.1 *A chapter such as the following is read on each Sabbath from the Sabbath after Passover until the Sabbath before New Year. On each of the last three Sabbaths before New Year two chapters are read.*

All Israel have a portion in the world to come, as it is said (Isaiah 1x, 21). And thy people shall be all righteous; they shall inherit the land for ever, the branch of my planting, the work of my hands, that I may be glorified.

6.2.2 Chapter I

6.2.2 (1) Moses received the Torah[1] on Sinai, and handed it down to Joshua; Joshua to the elders; the elders to the prophets; and the prophets handed it down to the men of the Great Synagogue. They said three things: Be deliberate in judgement; raise up many disciples, and make a fence round the Torah. (2) Simon the Just was one of the last survivors of the Great Synagogue. He used to say, Upon three things the world is based: upon the Torah, upon the Temple service, and upon the practice of charity. (3) Antigonos of Socho received the tradition from Simon the Just. He used to say, Be not like servants who minister to their master upon the condition of receiving a reward; but be like servants who minister to their master without the condition of receiving a reward; and let the fear of Heaven be upon you. (4) Jose, the son of Joezer, of Zeredah, and Jose, the son of Jochanan, of Jerusalem, received the tradition from the preceding. Jose, the son of Joczer, of Zeredah, said, Let thy house be a meeting house for the wise; sit amidst the dust of their feet, and drink their words with thirst. (5) Jose, the son of Jochanan, of Jerusalem, said, Let thy house be open wide; let the poor be the members of thy household, and engage not in much gossip with women. This applies even to one's own wife; how much more then to the wife of one's neighbour. Hence the sages say, Whoso engages in much gossip with women brings evil upon himself, neglects the study of the Torah, and will in the end inherit Gehinnom. (6) Joshua, the son of Perachyah, and Nittai, the

370

Arbelite, received the tradition from the preceding. Joshua, the son of Perachyah, said, Provide thyself a teacher, and get thee a companion, and judge all men in the scale of merit. (7) Nittai, the Arbelite, said, Keep thee far from a bad neighbour, associate not with the wicked, and abandon not the belief in retribution. (8) Judah, the son of Tabbai, and Simeon, the son of Shatach, received the tradition from the preceding. Judah, the son of Tabbai, said, (In the judge's office) act not the counsel's part; when the parties to a suit are standing before thee, let them both be regarded by thee as guilty, but when they are departed from thy presence, regard them both as innocent, the verdict having been acquiesced in by them. (9) Simeon, the son of Shatach, said, Be very searching in the examination of witnesses, and be heedful of thy words, lest through them they learn to falsify. (10) Shemayah and Abtalyon received the tradition from the preceding. Shemayah said, Love work, hate lordship, and seek no intimacy with the ruling power. (11) Abtalyon said, Ye sages, be heedful of your words, lest ye incur the penalty of exile and be exiled to a place of evil waters, and the disciples who come after you drink thereof and die, and the Heavenly Name be profaned. (12) Hillel and Shammai received the tradition from the preceding. Hillel said, Be of the disciples of Aaron, loving peace and pursuing peace, loving thy fellow-creatures, and drawing them near to the Torah. (13) He used to say, A name made great is a name destroyed; he who does not increase his knowledge decreases it; and he who does not study deserves to die; and he who makes a worldly use of the crown of the Torah shall waste away. (14) He used to say, If I am not for myself, who will be for me? And being for my own self, what am I? And if not now, when? (15) Shammai said, Fix a period for thy study of the Torah; say little and do much; and receive all men with a cheerful countenance. (16) Rabban Gamaliel said, Provide thyself a teacher, and be quit of doubt, and accustom not thyself to give tithes by a conjectural estimate. (17) Simeon, his son, said, All my days I have grown up amongst the wise, and I have found nought of better service than silence; not learning but doing is the chief thing; and whoso is profuse of words causes sin. (18) Rabban Simeon, the son of Gamaliel, said, By three things is the world preserved: by truth, by judgement, and by peace, as it is said, Judge ye the truth and the judgement of peace in your gates (Zech. viii, 16).

Rabbi Chananya, the son of Akashya, said, The Holy One, blessed be he, was pleased to make Israel worthy; wherefore he gave them a

6.2.3

copious Torah and many commandments, as it is said, It pleased the Lord, for his righteousness' sake, to magnify the Torah and make it honourable (Isaiah xiii, 21).

Note

1. The word Torah is left untranslated. It is variously used for the Pentateuch, the Scriptures, the Oral Law, as well as for the whole body of religious truth, study and practice.

Source: S. Singer, ed., *Authorised Daily Prayer Book*, Singer's Prayer Book Publication Committee 1963, pp.251-4.

6.3 THE SANHEDRIN

From the Mishnah

How did they admonish the witnesses in capital cases? They brought them in and admonished them, [saying,] 'Perchance ye will say what is but supposition or hearsay or at secondhand, or [ye may say in yourselves] , We heard it from a man that was trustworthy. Or perchance ye do not know that we shall prove you by examination and inquiry? Know ye, moreover, that capital cases are not as non-capital cases: in non-capital cases a man may pay money and so make atonement, but in capital cases the witness is answerable for the blood of him [that is wrongly condemned] and the blood of his posterity [that should have been born to him] to the end of the world. For so have we found it with Cain that slew his brother, for it is written, *The Bloods of thy brother cry.*[1] It says not 'The blood of thy brother', but *The Bloods of thy brother* — his blood and the blood of his posterity. (Another saying is: *Bloods of thy brother* — because his blood was cast over the trees and stones.) Therefore but a single man was created in the world, to teach that if any man has caused a single soul to perish Scripture imputes it to him as though he had caused a whole world to perish; and if any man saves alive a single soul Scripture imputes it to him as though he had saved alive a whole world. Again [but a single man was created] for the sake of peace among mankind, that none should say to his fellow, 'My father was greater than thy father'; also that the heretics should not say, 'There are many ruling powers in heaven.' Again [but a single man was created] to proclaim the greatness of the Holy One, blessed is he; for man stamps many coins with the one seal and they are all like one another; but the King of kings, the Holy One, blessed is he, has stamped every man with the seal of the first man, yet not one of them is like his fellow. Therefore everyone must say, For my sake was the world created. And if perchance ye would say, why should we be at these pains — was it not once written, *He being a witness, whether he hath seen or known [if he do not utter it, then shall he bear his iniquity] ?*[2] And if perchance ye would say, why should we be guilty of the blood of this man? — was it not once written, *when the wicked perish there is rejoicing?*[3]

Notes

1. *Genesis 4:10.*
2. *Leviticus 5:1.*
3. *Proverbs 11:10.*

Source: H. Danby, The *Mishnah,* OUP 1933, pp.387-8.

6.4 READING FROM THE AUTHORISED DAILY PRAYER BOOK

These are things which have no fixed measure (by enactment of the Law): the corners of the field, the first fruits, the offerings brought on appearing before the Lord at the three festivals, the practice of charity and the study of the Law — These are the things, the fruits of which a man enjoys in this world, while the stock remains for him for the world to come: viz., honouring father and mother, the practice of charity, timely attendance at the house of study morning and evening, hospitality to wayfarers, visiting the sick, dowering the bride, attending the dead to the grave, devotion in prayer, and making peace between man and his fellow, but the study of the Torah leadeth to them all.

Source: S. Singer, ed., op.cit., p.6.

6.5   LAWS CONCERNING THE SEVEN DAYS OF MOURNING

J. Goldin

1. One is obliged to observe the rite of mourning on the death of the following seven next of kin: one's father, mother, son, daughter, brother and sister, whether from the father's side or mother's side, a wife, and a husband.

2. For the death of a child that did not live thirty days one need not observe the rite of mourning.

3. A minor, less than thirteen years old, is not obligated to observe the rite of mourning.

4. The period of mourning begins as soon as the dead is buried and the grave is filled up with earth.

5. During the seven days of mourning cohabitation is forbidden. It is also forbidden to wear leather footwear.

6. During the first three days of mourning, the mourner is not allowed to do any work, even if he is poor and is supported by charity. From the fourth day on, if he lacks food, he may do work privately in his home. But the sages said: 'May poverty overtake his neighbours, who forced him to do work', for it is their duty to provide for the poor, especially during the period of mourning. . .

12. During the seven days of mourning, the mourner is not permitted to study the Torah, but he may study the books and laws concerning mourning; as, for instance: The Book of Job; the Treatise Semahot; the mournful parts of Jeremiah, and the laws relating to mourners. . .

14. During the first three days of mourning, the mourner should neither greet any one, nor should other people greet him. If others, unaware that he is in mourning, do greet him, he is not allowed to respond to their greetings; he should inform them that he is a mourner. After the third day and until the seventh, he must not greet others, but he may respond to the greetings of people who, not knowing of his condition, do greet him.

15. During the seven days of mourning, laughter and any kind of rejoicing is forbidden.

16. During the seven days of mourning, the mourner is not permitted to sit on a chair or bench; he should sit on a low bench or

stool. It is not obligatory for him to sit; he may either walk about or stand. When people come to offer him condolence, he must sit down. . .

19. During the seven days of mourning, a mourner is forbidden to leave his house. If death occurred in his family, or if it occurred elsewhere and there are not enough people to attend to the bier and the burial, he is permitted to leave the house even on the first day. If he has to attend to a matter of great importance, as where his absence would involve a great loss, he is permitted to go out, but he should put dirt in his shoes.

20. No mourning should be observed for the death of him who had committed suicide. . .

26. A candle or a lamp should be kept burning for the departed soul during the seven days of mourning, especially when the prayers are offered.

Source: From J. Goldin, *Hamadrikh, The Rabbi's Guide*, Hebrew Publishing Company, New York 1956, pp. 142ff. (Nos. 1-6, 14-16, 19-20, 26).

6.6 LAWS OF PRAYER FROM *THE SHULKHAN ARUKH*

J. Caro

[This summary of laws of prayer is excerpted from the authoritative legal code, *The Shulkhan Arukh*.]

6.6.1 One who prays must be conscious of the meaning of the words he utters, as it is written, 'You will strengthen their heart; You will incline Your ear' [Ps. 10:17]. Many prayer books with explanations in other languages have been published, and every man can learn the meaning of the words he utters in prayer. If one is not conscious of the meaning of the words, he must at least, while he prays, reflect upon matters which influence the heart and which direct the heart to our Father in heaven. Should an alien thought come to him in the midst of prayer, he must be still and wait until it is no more.

6.6.2 One should place his feet close together, as though they were one, to be likened to the angels, as it is written, 'Their legs were a straight leg' [Ezek, 1:7], that is to say: their feet appeared to be one foot. One should lower his head slightly, and close his eyes so that he will not look at anything. If one prays from a prayer book, he should not take his eyes off it. One should place his hands over his heart, his right hand over his left, and pray whole-heartedly, in reverence and awe and submission, like a poor beggar standing at a door.

6.6.3 One should utter the words consciously and carefully. Every person should pray according to his own tradition, whether it be Ashkenazic or Sephardic or other; they share a sacred basis. But one should not mix the words of two traditions, for the words of each tradition are counted and numbered according to major principles and one should neither increase nor decrease their number.

6.6.4 One must be careful to pray in a whisper, so that he alone will hear his words, but one standing near him should not be able to hear his voice, as it is written of Hannah, 'Hannah was speaking in her heart; only her lips moved, and her voice was not heard' [I Sam. 1:13].

6.6.5 One should not lean against any object for even the slightest support. One who is even slightly ill may pray while seated or even whilst lying down, provided that he is able to direct his thoughts cogently. If it is impossible for one to pray with the words of his mouth, he should at least contemplate with his heart. . .

When one who is outside of the Land rises to pray, he must face 6.6.6 in the direction of the Land of Israel, as it is written, '. . .and they pray to You toward their land. . .' [I Kings 8:48], and in his heart he should be directed toward Jerusalem and the Temple site and the Holy of Holies as well. Therefore those who dwell to the West of the Land of Israel must face the East (but not precisely East, for there are idolaters who pray in the direction of sunrise and their intention is to worship the sun), those who dwell to the East should face West and those who dwell to the South should face North (and those who dwell to the Northwest of the Land of Israel should face Southeast, etc.).

One who prays in the Land of Israel should face Jerusalem, as it 6.6.7 is written, '. . .they pray to the Lord toward the city which You have chosen. . .' [I Kings 8:44], and his thoughts should be focused toward the Temple and the Holy of Holies as well. One who prays in Jerusalem should face the Temple site, as it is written '. . .when they come and pray toward this House. . .' [II Chron. 6:32], and his thoughts should be focused toward the Holy of Holies as well.

Thus the entire people of Israel in their prayer will be facing one place, namely, Jerusalem and the Holy of Holies, the Heavenly Gate through which all prayer ascends. . .

If one is praying in a place where he cannot discern directions, 6.6.8 so that he is unable to know if he is facing in the proper direction, he should direct his heart to his Father in heaven, as it is written, '. . .and they pray to the Lord. . .' [I Kings 8:44] . . .

Source: Text in A. Hertzberg, ed., *Judaism*, Prentice-Hall, 1961, pp.231-233.

6.7 THREE PRAYERS FROM THE AUTHORISED DAILY PRAYER BOOK

6.7.1 O my God, the soul which thou gavest me is pure; thou didst create it, thou didst form it, thou didst breathe it into me; thou preservest it within me; and thou wilt take it from me, but wilt restore it unto me hereafter. So long as the soul is within me, I will give thanks unto thee, O Lord my God and God of my fathers, Sovereign of all works, Lord of all souls! Blessed are thou, O Lord, who restorest souls unto the dead.

6.7.2 And may it be thy will, O Lord our God and God of our fathers, to make us familiar with thy Law, and to make us adhere to thy commandments. O lead us not into sin, or transgression, iniquity, temptation, or shame; let not the evil inclination have sway over us; keep us far from a bad man and a bad companion: make us cling to the good inclination and to good works; subdue our inclination so that it may submit itself unto thee; and let us obtain this day, and every day, grace, favour, and mercy in thine eyes, and in the eyes of all who behold us; and bestow loving kindnesses upon us. Blessed art thou, O Lord, who bestowest loving-kindnesses upon thy people Israel.

6.7.3 Sovereign of all worlds! Not because of our righteous acts do we lay our supplications before thee, but because of thine abundant mercies. What are we? What is our life? What is our piety? What is our righteousness? What our helpfulness? What our strength? What our might? What shall we say before thee, O Lord our God and God of our fathers? Are not all the mighty men as nought before thee, the men of renown as though they had not been, the wise as if without knowledge, and the men of understanding as if without discernment? For most of their works are void, and the days of their lives are vanity before thee, and the pre-eminence of man over the beast is nought, for all is vanity.

Nevertheless we are thy people, the children of thy covenant, the children of Abraham, thy friend, to whom thou didst swear on Mount Moriah; the seed of Isaac, his only son, who was bound upon the altar; the congregation of Jacob, thy first born son, whose name thou didst call Israel and Jeshurun by reason of the love wherewith thou didst love him, and the joy wherewith thou didst rejoice in him.

It is, therefore, our duty to thank, praise and glorify thee, to bless, to sanctify and to offer praise and thanksgiving unto thy name. Happy are we! how goodly is our portion, and how pleasant is our lot, and how beautiful our heritage! Happy are we who, early and late, morning and evening, twice every day, declare: Hear, O Israel, the Lord our God, the Lord is One. Blessed be His name, whose glorious kingdom is for ever and ever.

Source: S. Singer, ed., op.cit., pp.6, 8, 9.

Let us now praise the Lord of all, the Maker of heaven and earth; for he chose us to make known his unity, and called us to proclaim him King. We bow in reverence and thanksgiving before the King of Kings, the Holy One, praised be he. He spread out the heavens and established the earth; he is our God, there is none else. In truth, he alone is our King, as it is written: 'Know then this day and take it to heart: the Lord is God in the heavens above and on the earth below; and there is none else.' Trusting in You, O Lord our God, we hope soon to behold the glory of Your might, when false gods shall cease to take Your place in the hearts of men, and the world will be perfected under Your unchallenged rule; when all mankind will call upon Your name and, forsaking evil, turn to You alone. Let all who dwell on earth understand that unto You every knee must bend, and every tongue swear loyalty. Before You, O Lord our God, let them humble themselves, and to Your glorious name let them give honour. Let all accept the yoke of Your kingdom, so that You may rule over them soon and for ever. For the kingdom is Yours, and to all eternity You will reign in glory, as it is written: 'The Lord shall reign for ever and ever.' And it has been said. 'The Lord shall be King over all the earth; on that day the Lord shall be One and his name One.'

Source: *Service of the Heart*, Union of Liberal and Progressive Synagogues 1967, pp.364-6.

Translated by David Goldstein

All Glory to His Name[1]   6.9.1

To him who delights in music and rhyme,
I proclaim:
'All glory to his name.'

I consider. His work is good.
I sing to him who has numbered the world,
And created man from an earthen clod,
And has put a soul in his inmost core,
Pure,
Like a king in his tower.

He exists in all. From his hand comes all.
Nothing approximates him to the full.
Compared with him, all is null.
What shall I say? The world entire
Is poor.
His knowledge is far from man's power.

His might and the mystery of his skies are far.
Around his throne are his servants of fire.
His awe extends through the hosts of the air.
He has built his home on the waters above.
He moved
His lips. The heavens were clothed.

There are wonderful things in all his work.
Creation bears witness for his glory's sake.
To the prophets he revealed all that was dark.
The soul that appears to him to be dear
He will steer
In the pathway of those that fear.

Before I was Born[2]   6.9.2

Before I was born your love enveloped me.
You turned nothing into substance, and created me.

Who etched out my frame? Who poured
Me into a vessel and moulded me?
Who breathed a spirit into me? Who opened
The womb of Sheol and extracted me?
Who has guided me from youth-time until now?
Taught me knowledge, and cared wondrously for me?
Truly, I am nothing but clay within your hand.
It is you, not I, who have really fashioned me.
I confess my sin to you, and do not say
That a serpent intrigued, and tempted me.
How can I conceal from you my faults, since
Before I was born your love enveloped me?

6.9.3 Lament on the Devastation of the Land of Israel[3]

Weep, my brothers, weep and mourn
Over Zion with great moan,
Like the lament of Hadadrimmon,
Or of Josiah, son of Amon.

Weep for the tender and delicate ones
Who barefoot now tread upon thorns,
Drawing water for barbarians,
Felling trees at their commands.

Weep for the man who is oppressed,
In bondage inexperienced.
They say to him: 'Carry! Make haste!'
And he, among burdens, finds no rest.

Weep for the fathers when they see
Their sons, none more praiseworthy,
Whose price gold cannot buy,
At the hands of Cushites condemned to die.

Weep for the blind who wander on,
Defiled, through the land of Zion,
With the blood of pregnant women,
The blood of the aged and young children.

Weep for the pious, whom the unclean goad,
Force them to eat forbidden food,
To make them forget their bond with God,
And the land, where their joys reside.

Weep for the women pure and chaste,
Whose fidelity has never ceased,
Subject to Hamitic lust,
Conceiving, with terror in their breast.

Weep for the daughters, noble
And upright as sculptured marble,
Forced to be slaves to the ignoble,
Who are themselves a servile rabble.

Weep, Weep and mourn
The synagogues forlorn,
That wild beasts have torn down,
And desert birds have made their own.

Weep for those in the enemies' grip,
Gathered together for a day without hope,
For those poor souls who have drained the cup,
Who are suffering now murder and rape.

Weep, weep for our living.
Do not weep for our dying;
For, as long as we have being,
To be like the dead is our desiring.

Therefore, my friend, do not recall
Consolation for my soul,
For those torn in pieces, all
In Zion, with no burial.

Notes

1. The author of this poem, Joseph Ibn Abithur, was born in Merida in the middle of the tenth century. Exiled following controversy, he spent much time in the Middle East. A celebrated liturgical writer, much of his work was used in Jewish prayer books.
2. The author of this poem, Solomon Ibn Gabirol, was born in Malaga in 1021 or 1022. Crippled by disease, his interests lay in philosophical

speculation and in the writing of a considerable number of liturgical poems.
3. The author of this poem, Abraham ben Meir ibn Ezra, was born in Tudela
   c.1092 C.E. He journeyed throughout Europe (including England) seeking
   to disseminate the culture of the Spanish Jews; in this he was far from
   unsuccessful. In his poetry he introduces a new note of humour and satire.

Source: From *The Jewish Poets of Spain, 900-12 C.E.* trans. David Goldstein,
Penguin Books 1965, pp.39-40, 97 and 158.

6.10 KOL NIDRE PRAYER

Leo Baeck

In this hour all Israel stands before God, the judge and the forgiver.

In his presence let us all examine our ways, our deeds, and what we have failed to do.

Where we transgressed, let us openly confess: 'We have sinned!' and, determined to return to God, let us pray: 'Forgive us.'

We stand before our God.

With the same fervor with which we confess our sins, the sins of the individual and the sins of the community, do we, in indignation and abhorrence, express our contempt for the lies concerning us and the defamation of our religion and its testimonies.

We have trust in our faith and in our future.

Who made known to the world the mystery of the Eternal, the One God?

Who imparted to the world the comprehension of purity of conduct and purity of family life?

Who taught the world respect for man, created in the image of God?

Who spoke of the commandment of righteousness, of social justice?

In all this we see manifest the spirit of the prophets, the divine revelation to the Jewish people. It grew out of our Judaism and is still growing. By these facts we repel the insults flung at us.

We stand before our God. On Him we rely. From Him issues the truth and the glory of our history, our fortitude amidst all change of fortune, our endurance in distress.

Our history is a history of nobility of soul, of human dignity. It is history we have recourse to when attack and grievous wrong are directed against us, when affliction and calamity befall us.

God has led our fathers from generation to generation. He will guide us and our children through these days.

We stand before our God, strengthened by His commandment that we fulfil. We bow to Him and stand erect before men. We worship Him and remain firm in all vicissitudes. Humbly we trust in Him and our path lies clear before us; we see our future.

All Israel stands before her God in this hour. In our prayers, in our hope, in our confession, we are one with all Jews on earth. We look upon each other and know who we are; we look up to our

God and know what shall abide.

'Behold, He that keepeth Israel doth neither slumber nor sleep' (Psalm 121:4).

'May He who maketh peace in His heights bring peace upon us and upon all Israel' (Prayer book).

Source: From A.H. Friedlander, ed., *Out of the Whirl-wind,* Union of American Hebrew Congregations, New York 1968, pp.131-2.

[Maimonides summarised the legal obligation to give charity in his code of Jewish Law, the *Mishneh Torah,* in the section entitled 'The Laws of giving to the Poor'.]

If the poor asks of you and you have nothing in your hand to give 6.11.1
him, soothe him with words. It is forbidden to rebuke a poor man or
to raise one's voice against him in a shout, for his heart is shattered
and crushed and it is written, 'A broken and contrite heart, O God,
You will not despise' [Ps. 51:19]. And it is written, 'I dwell in the
high and holy place and also with him who is of a contrite and
humble spirit, to revive the spirit of the humble and to revive the
heart of the contrite' [Isa. 57:15]. Alas for anyone who has
humiliated a poor man, alas for him. He should rather be like a
father both with compassion and with words, as it is written, 'I was a
father to the poor' [Job 29:16] . . .

    There are eight degrees in the giving of charity, each one higher 6.11.2
than that which follows it:

    1. The highest degree, exceeded by none, is giving a gift or a loan or
taking one as a partner or finding him employment by which he can
be self-supporting. . .

    2. Giving charity to the poor without knowing to whom one
gives, the recipient not knowing the donor's identity, for this is a
good deed of intrinsic value, done for its own sake. An example of
this is the Hall of Secret Donations which was maintained in the
Temple. The righteous would donate in secret and the poor would
be supported from it in secret. Approximating this is giving to a
charity fund. One should not give to a charity fund unless he knows
the collector is trustworthy and wise and conducts himself properly,
like Rabbi Hananiah ben Tradyon.

    3. Giving to one whose identity one knows, although the
recipient does not know the donor's identity. An example of this
would be the action of those great sages who would walk about in
secret and cast coins at the doors of the poor. It is fitting to imitate
such a custom and it is a high degree indeed, if the charity collectors
[through whom one can give impersonally] do not conduct
themselves properly.

    4. Giving without knowing to whom one gives, although the

recipient knows the donor's identity. An example of this would be the action of those great sages who would wrap up coins in a bundle and throw it over their shoulder. The poor would then come to take it without suffering any embarrassment.

5. Giving before being asked.

6. Giving only after being asked.

7. Giving inadequately, though graciously.

8. Giving grudgingly.

6.11.3   The great sages would give a coin for the poor before each prayer service and then pray, as it is written, 'I shall behold Your face in righteousness' [Ps. 17:5]. Giving food to one's older sons and daughters (though one is not obligated to do so) in order to teach the males Torah and to direct the females on the proper path, and giving food to one's father and mother is considered to be charity. And it is a great degree of charity, for relatives should have precedence. . .

6.11.4   One should always press himself and suffer rather than be dependent upon others; he should not cast himself upon the community as a responsibility. Thus the sages commanded: 'Rather make your Sabbath like a week day than be dependent upon others' [*Pesahim* 112a]. Even if a man was learned and respected and then became poor he should occupy himself with a trade, even a lowly trade, rather than be dependent upon others. It is better to strip the hide of dead animals than to say 'I am a great sage, I am a Priest; support me.' Among the great sages there were wood choppers, those who watered gardens and those who worked with iron and charcoal. They did not ask the community for money and they did not take it when it was offered to them.

Source: From A. Hertzberg, ed., op.cit., pp.106-8.

6.12 SAYINGS OF THE BRATZLAVER

1. Every man should devote much time to meditation between his Creator and himself. He should judge himself and determine whether his actions are correct, and whether they are appropriate before the Lord Who has granted him life, and Who is gracious to him every moment. If he finds that he has acted properly, he should fear no one — no officials, no robbers, no beasts — and nothing in the universe except the Lord. When he learns this, he will have attained, first: perfection in the study of the Torah and in meekness; and second, perfect worship wherein all material considerations are forgotten: worship which asks for no personal benefits, and which prompts one to forget his very existence.

2. He who meditates in solitude before God receives divine inspiration.

3. He who is pure of heart will find new thoughts and new phrases every time he meditates in solitude.

4. A man's longing and intense desire to cast away any evil within himself and to attain goodness recreates his soul in pure goodness. It should be expressed in words in order to give it actual and true expression.

5. Meditation before God brings forth the holy spark that is found in every Jew; it lights up his heart, and thereby deprives him of all desire for evil.

6. The chief object of meditation is truthful confession of a man's every act, and the cultivation of a sense of contrition for his sins.

7. Meditation and prayer before God is particularly efficacious in grassy fields and amid the trees, since a man's soul is thereby strengthened, as if every blade of grass and every plant united with him in prayer.

8. In meditation a man may discuss his tribulations with God; he may excuse himself for his misdeeds and implore the Lord to grant him his desire to approach nearer to God. A man's offenses separate him from his Maker.

9. It is impossible to be a good Jew without devoting each day a portion of the time to commune with the Lord in solitude, and to have a conversation from the heart with Him.

10. Even though a man may feel he cannot concentrate adequately

upon the theme of his meditation, he should nevertheless continue to express his thoughts in words. Words are like water which falls continually upon a rock until it breaks it through. In similar fashion they will break through a man's flinty heart.

11. A man should say every day in his meditation: 'I shall commence today to cleave unto Thee, O Lord.' No man can remain in the same position without change, and hence in the achievement of goodness we must frequently alter our place. Whether he falls back or moves forward, he will at least have commenced afresh.

12. In true meditation a man cries to the Lord like a child to his father who is about to take his departure. There is no sadness in this weeping — only longing and yearning.

Source: C. Newman, ed., *The Hasidic Anthology,* Schocken Books, New York 1963, pp.175-6.

6.13 MAIMONIDES ON FREE WILL

Every man is given free will. If he wishes to turn to the good way 6.13.1
and to be righteous, he has the power to do so. Or if he wishes to
turn to the evil way and to be wicked, he has that power, too. Thus
it is written in the Torah: 'Behold, the man is become as one of us,
to know good and evil' (Gen. 3:22). That is to say, this species, man,
has become unique in the world, there being no species like him in
the respect that, of himself and from the exercise of his own
knowledge and reason, he knows good and evil. He can do whatever
he wishes, and there is no one to hinder him from doing good or
evil. This being so — 'lest he put forth his hand' (ibid.).

Do not believe what the fools among the nations of the world 6.13.2
and most of the blockheads among the children of Israel say: to wit,
that the Holy One, blessed be he, decrees whether a man will be
righteous or wicked at the moment of his creation. It is not so. But
every man may become righteous like Moses our master, or wicked
like Jeroboam, wise or foolish, compassionate or cruel, miserly or
generous, and so with all the other qualities. There is no one to
coerce a man, and no one to determine his actions, and no one to
draw him into either one of the two ways: he himself of his own free
will turns to whatever way he wills. That is what Jeremiah meant
when he said, 'Out of the mouth of the Most High proceedeth not
evil and good' (Lam. 3:38). That is to say, the Creator does not
determine that a man will be good or that he will be evil. Since this
is so, the sinner is responsible for any injury he does to himself.
Therefore, it is fit for him to cry and to bewail his sins and what he
has done to his soul and the evil he has brought upon it. This is
expressed in the next verse: 'Wherefore doth a living man complain?'
(Lam. 3:39). Jeremiah continues, saying as it were, 'Since we have
free will and committed all these evils knowingly, it is fit that we
turn in Teshuvah and forsake our wickedness, since we have the
power to do so.' This is expressed in the next verse: 'Let us search
and try our ways, and return to the Lord.'

And this is an important principle, the pillar of the Torah and of 6.13.3
the commandment, as it is said, 'See, I have set before thee this day
life and good' (Deut. 30:15), and 'Behold, I set before you this day a
blessing and a curse' (Deut. 11:26). That is to say, you have the
power, and whatever a man wishes to do he can do, whether it be

good or bad. And because he has this power, it is said, 'Oh that they had such a heart as this always. . .' (Deut. 5:26), implying that the Creator does not coerce the sons of man, nor decree that they are to do either good or evil, but all they do is in their own discretion.

6.13.4   If God had decreed whether a man were to be righteous or wicked, or if there were some force inherent in his nature that irresistibly drew him to a particular course, or a special science, or a particular view, or a special action, as the stupid astrologers pretend, how could He have commanded us through the prophets, 'Do thus and do not thus, better your ways and do not follow your wicked impulses' — if from the moment of a man's creation his destiny had already been decreed, or if his nature irresistibly drew him to that from which he could not free himself? What place would there be for all of the Torah, and by what right or justice would the wicked be punished or the righteous rewarded? 'Shall not the Judge of all the earth do justly?' (Gen. 18:25).

Source: From S.Y. Agnon, ed., *Days of Awe*, Schocken Books 1948, p.116.

6.14   THE CONCEPT OF TORAH

H.N. Bialik

The concept of 'Torah' attained in the esteem of the [Jewish] people an infinite exaltation. For them the Torah was almost another existence, a more spiritual and loftier state, added to or even taking the place of secular existence. The Torah became the center of the nation's secret and avowed aspirations and desires in its exile. The dictum 'Israel and the Torah are one' was no mere phrase; the non-Jew cannot appreciate it, because the concept of 'Torah', in its full national significance, cannot be rendered adequately in any other tongue. Its content and connotations embrace more than 'religion' or 'creed' alone, or 'ethics' or 'commandments' or 'learning' alone, and it is not even just a combination of all these, but something far transcending all of them. It is a mystic, almost cosmic, conception. The Torah is the tool of the Creator; with it and for it He created the universe. The Torah is older than creation. It is the highest idea and the living soul of the world. Without it the world could not exist and would have no right to exist. 'The study of the Torah is more important than the building of the Temple.' 'Knowledge of the Torah ranks higher than priesthood or kingship.' 'Only he is free who engages in the study of the Torah.' 'It is the Torah that magnifies and exalts man over all creatures.' 'Even a heathen who engages in the study of the Torah is as good as a High Priest.' 'A bastard learned in the Torah takes precedence over an ignorant High Priest.' [Quotations are from rabbinic literature.]

Such is the world outlook to which almost seventy generations of Jews have been educated. In accordance therewith their spiritual life was provisionally organized for the interim of the exile. For it they suffered martyrdom and by virtue of it they lived. The Jewish elementary school was established shortly before the destruction of Jerusalem and has survived to this day. As a result of such prolonged training, the nation has acquired a sort of sixth sense for everything connected with the needs of the spirit, a most delicate sense and always the first to be affected, and one possessed by almost every individual. There is not a Jew but would be filled with horror by a cruel decree 'that Jews shall not engage in the Torah'. Even the poorest and meanest man in Israel sacrificed for the teaching of his children, on which he spent sometimes as much as half of his income or more. Before asking for the satisfaction of his material needs, the Jew first prays daily: 'And graciously bestow upon us knowledge, understanding, and comprehension.' And what was the first request of our pious mothers over the Sabbath candles? 'May it be Your will that the eyes of my children may shine with Torah.' Nor do I doubt that if God had appeared to one of these mothers in a dream, as He did once to Solomon, and said, 'Ask, what shall I give unto you?' she would have replied even as Solomon did, 'I ask not for myself either riches or honor, but O Lord of the universe, may it please You to give unto my sons a heart to understand Torah and wisdom to distinguish good from evil' [Based on I Kings 3:9-11].

Source: From A. Hertzberg, ed., op.cit., pp.85-6.

6.15   THE PEOPLE AND THE BOOK

Leo Baeck

When the great test is put to a man, his whole life, all which he has
had and has been and which lies before him, enters this one hour.
His whole life speaks to him. So, too, is it demanded of a people
when it is put to the great test. Its whole history in its journey from
the former to the now, from the now to the coming becomes its
present. Past and future must pass the test of the now. The now is
confronted, and past and future can become vital forces only as they
stream into the present.

Only rarely, and then not always as a blessing, did this people
have days without spiritual and intellectual strain. Then perhaps the
Bible could appear as a book written and in a sense ready at hand, a
book that told of what had been, that stated what had been
commanded, that announced what the expectation then foresaw.
But when the questions pressed and oppressed, when question
crowded question, then this Book had to elevate itself and set out on
its ceaseless way. As the Book of this people it could only be, to a
degree, a book in movement. It had grown together with this people.
When the people was reborn, the Book was also reborn, and the
rebirth of the Book created the rebirth of the people. Its history
runs from present to present.

To designate this unique quality, this dynamic nearness and
immediacy of the Book, a special, characteristic expression was
coined in early rabbinic times. One said that the Book presented
itself in a two-sided manner: as 'Written Torah' and as 'Oral Torah'.
It could also be rendered thus: It is a book composed and written
down, and it is at the same time a movement, awakened and
renewing itself from within. It has its word with which it begins and
its word with which it ends. But in reality it never ceases and never
ends; ever again it commences and continues. Its word seems to be a
word that was spoken once, but it is in reality a task that starts itself
again and again. He who believes that he carries it in his hand does
not have it; but he who is driven by it, to him has it come. One of
the teachers could say: 'The men of this Book can never rest
completely [and added with hyperbole], not in this world nor in the
world to come.' It is a book in movement, and therefore it belongs

to no generation and to no epoch completely. It endures and remains because it takes its way from generation to generation. Therefore it is the 'Written Torah' and the 'Oral Torah'.

Source: Leo Baeck, *This People Israel,* Holt, Rinehart and Winston, New York, 1964, pp.199-200.

6.16   THE PHARISAIC MOVEMENT

Leo Baeck

One can only speak of a Pharisaic movement, and not of a Pharisaic party, just as the Sadducean group and the Essenic circle, generally compared or contrasted with the Pharisees, should also not be designated as parties. Flavius Josephus, an historian of this people, spoke of them as parties. He wanted to recount the many aspects of his people to the Romans and the Greeks who had to think of parties whenever they thought of differences in a society that had its own internal development. A party wishes to win adherents, to unite them, to lead them to success; but a movement wants to awaken the conscience and effect a change in life. Actually this people was at that time seized by the Pharisaic movement which might even be called the Pharisaic awakening.

To accept in all seriousness the great demand of Sinai, 'And ye shall be unto Me a kingdom of priests, and a holy nation' (Ex.19:6), to take it seriously always and everywhere, this was the great idea which emanated from this movement. An idea is great and genuine only when it becomes an enduring task; and such a task can only be one which approaches everyone, each exalted and humble soul, in the same manner. The manifold contrasts of caste and divisions of rank basically can be traced to groups which originally or retroactively ascribe to themselves a higher ideal. Upon it they base the claim to set themselves apart from others or look down upon them. The circle of the conqueror, the usurper, the oppressor, is to be considered the domain of the higher idea for whose sake it is to remain protected and secured. The Pharisaic movement, in a decisive manner and with decisive historical success, undertook to bring the higher, the determining ideal to everyone simultaneously, so that they all might come to possess it now, completely. The law of Sinai, with which the true history of this people begins, was rejuvenated, in order to meet changed times and to create for itself new expression and new form. Now each individual was addressed even more strongly; to him, responsibility and through it the right to his place was more firmly given.

Source: Leo Baeck, op.cit., pp.215-6.

6.17 THE LAW IS NOT A BURDEN

S. Schechter

It is ar illusion to speak of the burden which a scrupulous care to observe six hundred and thirteen commandments must have laid upon the Jew. Even a superficial analysis will discover that in the time of Christ many of these commandments were already obsolete (as for instance those relating to the tabernacle and to the conquest of Palestine), while others concerned only certain classes, as the priests, the judges, the soldiers, the Nazirites, or the representatives of the community, or even only one or two individuals among the whole population, as the King and the High Priest. Others, again, provided for contingencies which could occur only to a few, as for instance the laws concerning divorce or levirate marriages, whilst many — such as those concerning idolatry, and incest, and the sacrifice of children to Moloch — could scarcely have been considered as a practical prohibition by the pre-Christian Jew, just as little as we can speak of Englishmen as lying under the burden of a law preventing them from burning widows or marrying their grandmothers, though such acts would certainly be considered as crimes. Thus it will be found by a careful enumeration that barely a hundred laws remain which really concerned the life of the bulk of the people. If we remember that even these include such laws as belief in the unity of God, the necessity of loving and fearing Him, and of sanctifying His name, of loving one's neighbour and the stranger, of providing for the poor, exhorting the sinner, honouring one's parents and many more of a similar character, it will hardly be said that the ceremonial side of the people's religion was not well balanced by a fair amount of spiritual and social elements. Besides, it would seem that the line between the ceremonial and the spiritual is too often only arbitrarily drawn. With many commandments it is rather a matter of opinion whether they should be relegated to the one category or the other.

Thus the wearing of the Tephillin or phylacteries has, on the one hand, been continually condemned as a meaningless superstition, and a pretext for formalism and hypocrisy. But, on the other hand, Maimonides, who can in no way be suspected of superstition or mysticism, described their importance in the following words: 'Great is the holiness of the Tephillin; for as long as they are on the arm and head of man he is humble and God-fearing, and feels no attraction for frivolity or idle things, nor has he any evil thoughts, but will turn his heart to the words of truth and righteousness.' The view which Rabbi Johanan, a Palestinian preacher of the third century, took of the fulfillment of the Law, will probably be found more rational than that of many a rationalist of today. Upon the basis of the last verse in Hosea, 'The ways of the Lord are right, and the just shall walk in them, but the transgressors shall fall therein', he explains that while one man, for instance, eats his paschal lamb with the purpose of doing the will of God who commanded it, and thereby does an act of righteousness, another thinks only of satisfying his appetite by the lamb, so that his eating it (by the very fact that he professes at the same time to perform a religious rite) becomes a stumbling block for him. Thus all the laws by virtue of their divine authority — and in this there was in the first century no difference of opinion between Jews and Christians — have their spiritual side, and to neglect them implies, at least from the individual's own point of view, a moral offense.

The legalistic attitude may be summarily described as an attempt to live in accordance with the will of God, caring less for what God is than for what He wants us to be. But, nevertheless, on the whole this life never degenerated into religious formalism. Apart from the fact that during the Second Temple there grew up laws, and even beliefs, which show a decided tendency towards progress and development, there were also ceremonies which were popular with the masses, and others which were neglected. Men were not, therefore, the mere soulless slaves of the Law; personal sympathies and dislikes also played a part in their religion. Nor were all the laws actually put upon the same level. With a happy inconsistency men always spoke of heavier and slighter sins, and by the latter — excepting, perhaps, the profanation of the Sabbath — they mostly understood ceremonial transgressions.

Source: From A. Hertzberg, ed., op.cit., pp.82-4.

6.18 YOSSEL RAKOVER'S APPEAL TO GOD

Z. Kolitz

I believe that to be a Jew means to be a fighter, an everlasting swimmer against the turbulent human current. The Jew is a hero, a martyr, a saint. You, our evil enemies, declare that we are bad. I believe that we are better and finer than you, but even if we were worse, I should like to see how you would look in our place!

I am happy to belong to the unhappiest of all peoples of the world, whose precepts represent the loftiest and most beautiful of all morality and laws. These immortal precepts which we possess have now been even more sanctified and immortalised by the fact that they have been so debased and insulted by the enmies of the Lord.

I believe that to be a Jew is an inborn trait. One is born a Jew exactly as one is born an artist. It is impossible to be released from being a Jew. That is our Godly attribute that has made us a chosen people. Those who do not understand this will never understand the higher meaning of our martyrdom. If I ever doubted that God once designated us as the chosen people, I would believe now that our tribulations have made us the chosen one.

I believe in You, God of Israel, even though You have done everything to stop me from believing in You. I believe in Your laws even if I cannot excuse Your actions. My relationship to You is not the relationship of a slave to his master but rather that of a pupil to his teacher. I bow my head before Your greatness, but I will not kiss the lash with which You strike me.

You say, I know, that we have sinned, O Lord. It must surely be true! And therefore we are punished? I can understand that too! But I should like You to tell me whether *there is any sin in the world deserving of such a punishment as the punishment we have received?*

You assert that you will yet repay our enemies? I am convinced of it! Repay them without mercy? I have no doubt of that either! I should like You to tell me, however — *is there any punishment in the world capable of compensating for the crimes that have been committed against us?*

You say, I know, that it is no longer a question of sin and punishment, but rather a situation in which Your countenance is veiled, in which humanity is abandoned to its evil instincts. But I should like to ask You, O Lord — and this question burns in me like a consuming fire — *what more, O, what more must transpire before You unveil Your countenance again to the world?*

I want to say to You that now, more than in any previous period of our eternal path of agony, we, we the tortured, the humiliated, the buried alive and burned alive, we, the insulted, the mocked, the lonely, the forsaken by God and man — we have the right to know *what are the limits of Your forebearance?*

I should like to say something more: Do not put the rope under too much strain, lest, alas, it snaps! The test to which You have put us is so severe, so unbearably severe, that You should — You must — forgive those members of Your people who, in their misery, have turned from You.

Forgive those who have turned from You in their misery, but also those who have turned from You in their happiness. You have transformed our life into such a frightful, perpetual order that the cowards among us have been forced to flee from it; and what is happiness but a place of refuge for cowards? Do not chastise them for it. One does not strike cowards, but has mercy on them. Have mercy on *them,* rather than *us,* O Lord.

Forgive those who have desecrated Your name, who have gone over to the service of other gods, who have become indifferent to You. You have castigated them so severely that they no longer believe that You are their Father, that they have any Father at all.

I tell You this because I do believe in You, because I believe in You more strongly than ever, because now I know that You are my Lord, because after all You are not, You cannot possibly be after all the God of those whose deeds are the most horrible expression of ungodliness!

Source: From A.H. Friedlander, ed., op.cit., pp.396-7.

6.19   THE CONCEPT OF MAN AFTER AUSCHWITZ

J. Bemporad

Judaism points to the twofoldedness of human nature. Once we recognize that man is by nature neither good nor evil and that both his good and evil are human qualities and that man has the freedom to actualize either good or evil, then we are able to recognize the traditional Jewish teaching with respect to the nature of man.

Judaism recognized that man has much power for good and for evil. It recognizes that man can destroy himself or bring about the Messianic Age. The prophetic doctrine which announces the consequences of destruction through the bold admonition of a day that was darkness and not light also spoke of a day of peace and justice. Judaism believes that man has within him the power to bring about the one or the other. In the book of Deuteronomy Moses spoke to the people and said, 'I have set before thee life and death, the blessing and the curse. Choose life that you may live.' But the blessing and the curse are not in God's hands. It is not something that God is going to take care of for man. Man is to choose and realize life or death, blessing or curse, the Messianic Age or the bomb.

The Midrash to Genesis relates that when God was about to create man, the angels of the service were divided. Love said let him be created for he will do loving deeds. But Truth said let him not be created for he will be all lies. Righteousness said let him be created for he will do righteous deeds. Peace said let him not be created for he will be all quarrelsomeness and discord. What did God do? He took hold of Truth and cast him to the earth. The angels then said, 'Lord of the World, why do You despise the Angel of Truth? Let Truth arise from the earth. As it is said, Truth shall spring from the earth.'

Judaism recognizes that it is man's task to bring forth truth and justice and righteousness and peace. It is a mistake to believe that man is by nature good or evil. Man has the capacity for both and the holocaust has shown that he can in fact actualize great evil.

The School of Hillel and the School of Shammai fought for many years and there was one question which they fought over very seriously. This question was: Would it have been better for man to have been created, or not to have been created? The School of Shammai said, it would have been better for man not to have been created, and the School of Hillel said, it was better for man to have been created. After all, the Shammaites must have argued, look at all the suffering and tragedy, all that is horrible in the world; it is better off for man not to have been created. So they debated and debated and couldn't agree. After two years of debate they took a vote and the Shammaites won. So they decided that man should examine his past deeds and future deeds. There is a hint as to the meaning of this statement in the Tosafist's comment on this passage and we might expand it as follows: Before a person is born you don't know if it is better if he were created or not. For instance, it certainly would have been much better for Hitler and Stalin never to have been created, and each one of us is never sure whether it would have been better not to be created. Therefore, we interpret the passage to mean, live your life in such a way so that you will be worthy of having been created. This is an important concept. It doesn't mean that when one is born, he is born in a state of original sin, that anything he does will be bad. It doesn't mean that he is born with reason and goodness, and it is only through sheer error that he does anything bad. No, it means that the individual is born with both a potentiality for doing great good and with the potentiality for doing great evil, and it is up to him whether he does one or the other, whether he chooses life and the blessing, or whether he chooses death and the curse. Let us choose life, that we may live.

Source: From A.H. Friedlander, ed. op.cit., pp.484-7.

6.20   MAIMONIDES TO OBADIAH THE PROSELYTE

'While we are the descendants of Abraham, Isaac and Jacob, you derive from Him, through whose word the world was created'

Thus says Moses the son of Rabbi Maimon, one of the exiles from Jerusalem, who lived in Spain:

I received the question of the master Obadiah, the wise and learned proselyte, may the Lord reward him for his work, may a perfect recompense be bestowed upon him by the Lord of Israel, under whose wings he has sought cover.

You ask me if you, too, are allowed to say in the blessings and prayers you offer alone or in the congregation: *'Our* God' and 'God of *our* Fathers', 'Thou who hast sanctified *us* through Thy Commandments', 'Thou who hast separated *us*', 'Thou who has chosen *us*', 'Thou who hast inherited *us*', 'Thou who has brought *us* out of the land of Egypt', 'Thou who hast worked miracles to *our* fathers', and more of this kind.

Yes, you may say all this in the prescribed order and not change it in the least. In the same way as every Jew by birth says his blessing and prayer, you, too, shall bless and pray alike, whether you are alone or pray in the congregation. The reason for this is, that Abraham, our father, taught the people, opened their minds, and revealed to them the true faith and the unity of God; he rejected the idols and abolished their adoration; he brought many children under the wings of the Divine Presence; he gave them counsel and advice, and ordered his sons and the members of his household after him to keep the ways of the Lord forever, as it is written, 'For I have known him to the end that he may command his children and his household after him, that they may keep the way of the Lord, to do righteousness and justice.' Ever since then whoever adopts Judaism and confesses the unity of the Divine Name, as it is prescribed in the Torah, is counted among the disciples of Abraham, our father, peace be with him. These men are Abraham's household, and he it is who converted them to righteousness.

In the same way as he converted his contemporaries through his words and teaching, he converts future generations through the testament he left to his children and household after him. Thus Abraham, our father, peace be with him, is the father of his pious posterity who keep his ways, and the father of his disciples and of all proselytes who adopt Judaism.

Therefore you shall pray, 'Our God' and 'God of our fathers', because Abraham, peace be with him, is *your* father. And you shall pray, 'Thou who hast taken for his own our fathers', for the land has been given to Abraham, as it is said, 'Arise, walk through the land in the length of it and in the breadth of it; for I will give it unto thee'. As to the words, 'Thou who hast brought us out of the land of Egypt' or 'Thou who hast done miracles to our fathers' – these you may change, if you will, and say, 'Thou who hast brought Israel out of the land of Egypt' and 'Thou who has done miracles to Israel'. If however, you do not change them, it is no transgression, because since you have come under the wings of the Divine Presence and confessed the Lord, no difference exists between you and us, and all miracles done to us have been done as it were to us and to you. Thus it is said in the book of Isaiah, 'Neither let the son of the stranger, that hath joined himself to the Lord, speak, saying, "The Lord hath utterly separated me from His people" ' There is no difference whatever between you and us. You shall certainly say the blessing, 'Who hast chosen us', 'Who hast given us', 'Who hast taken us for Thine own' and 'Who hast separated us': for the Creator, may He be extolled, has indeed chosen you and separated you from the nations and given you the Torah. For the Torah has been given to us *and* to the proselytes, as it is said, 'One ordinance shall be both for you of the congregation, and also for the stranger that sojourneth with you, an ordinance for ever in your generations; as you are, so shall the stranger be before the Lord.' Know that our fathers, when they came out of Egypt, were mostly idolators; they had mingled with the pagans in Egypt and imitated their way of life, until the Holy One, may He be blessed, sent Moses, our teacher, the master of all prophets, who separated us from the nations and brought us under the wings of the Divine Presence, us and all proselytes, and gave to all of us one law.

Do not consider your origin as inferior. While we are the descendants of Abraham, Isaac and Jacob, you derive from Him through whose word the world was created. As is said by Isaiah: 'One shall say, I am the Lord's, and another shall call himself by the name of Jacob.'

Source: From F. Kobler, ed., *Letters of Jews through the Ages,* East and West Library, New York 1952, Vol.I, pp.194-6.

6.21   A PRIEST-PEOPLE

K. Kohler

Undoubtedly the Law, as it embraced the whole of life in its power, sharpened the Jewish sense of duty, and served the Jew as an iron wall of defense against temptations, aberrations, and enticements of the centuries. As soon as the modern Jew, however, undertook to free himself from the tutelage of blind acceptance of authority and inquired after the purpose of all the restrictions of the Law laid upon him, his ancient loyalty to the same collapsed and the pillars of Judaism seemed to be shaken. Then the leaders of Reform, imbued with the prophetic spirit, felt it to be their imperative duty to search out the fundamental ideas of the priestly law of holiness and, accordingly, they learned how to separate the kernel from the shell. In opposition to the orthodox tendency to worship the letter, they insisted on the fact that Israel's separation from the world — which it is ultimately to win for the divine truth — cannot itself be its end and aim, and that blind obedience to the law does not constitute true piety. Only the fundamental idea, that Israel as the 'first-born' among the nations has been elected as a priest-people must remain our imperishable truth, a truth to which the centuries of history bear witness by showing that it has given its life-blood as a ransom for humanity, and is ever bringing new sacrifices for its cause. Only because it has kept itself distinct as a priest-people among the nations could it carry out its great task in history; and only if it remains conscious of its priestly calling and therefore maintains itself as the people of God, can it fulfill its mission. Not until the end of time, when all of God's children will have entered the kingdom of God, may Israel, the high-priest among the nations, renounce his priesthood.

Source: From A. Hertzberg, ed., op.cit., pp.84-5.

6.22   THE CHOSEN PEOPLE

Louis Jacobs

In view of the importance the doctrine of Israel as God's chosen
people assumes in the Bible, its central role in Rabbinic thought and
the emphasis placed upon it by many modern Jewish thinkers, it
comes as a shock to discover that it features in none of the medieval
classifications as a basic principle of the Jewish faith. In all
probability the reason for the omission is that the medieval thinkers
did not see the chosenness of Israel as a separate dogma but as
implied in other principles of the faith, especially those concerning
the Torah, which was given to Israel. But it is also very plausible to
suggest that the influence of Greek thought, which gave a
universalistic cast to medieval thinking, made the doctrine of a
chosen people something of an embarrassment. Maimonides, for
example, when he does discuss the question of why God revealed His
law to one particular nation and at one particular time can only
reply that God willed it so. The 'scandal of particularism' is always
a problem when this idea of God choosing is examined. The
'oddness' in God's choosing is not in His choice of the Jews but in
the choice itself. Why did God have to make a *choice* among
peoples, why not convey the truth to all mankind?

It cannot be denied that some Jewish thinkers have interpreted
the doctrine to mean that there is a qualitative difference between
Jews and other peoples, that the Jews are spiritual supermen,
endowed with rare qualities of soul by virtue of their descent from
the Patriarchs. In the medieval world the representative of this type
of thinking was Judah Ha-Levi. Ha-Levi builds his philosophy on the
view that the Jew is not simply a superior type of human being but
belongs, in fact, to a different category altogether. The difference
between Israel and the other peoples of the world is one of kind, not
of degree, just as humans are different from animals, animals from
plants, and plants from minerals. Aware of the moral difficulty in
such a view, Ha-Levi observes that since, however, Israel is the 'heart
of the nations' it can be the most healthy and the most sick of
peoples. A bad Jew is more thoroughly bad than the worst Gentile.
Ha-Levi's 'racism' is, of course, limited. He cannot reject the Rabbinic
view that Gentiles can be converted to Judaism and hence belong to

the Jewish people. But, for Ha-Levi, the higher reaches of the religious life such as prophecy are not possible for those born outside the people of Israel.

In modern times a qualitative interpretation of Jewish chosenness has been advocated by thinkers like Abraham Geiger who believed that the Jewish people has a special genius for religion and is far more sensitive than others to the call of the religious life.

At the opposite extremes are those Jewish thinkers who would reject the whole notion of chosenness as unworthy. On the theological level it has seemed to some to have an inadequate concept of Deity to say that God shows favouritism to any one group and it seems unjust that the children of righteous forebears should be singled out not through any merit of their own but by accident of birth. One of the most vigorous protagonists of the view that all peoples are 'called' by God to fulfil his purpose but none are 'chosen', not even the Jews, is Mordecai Kaplan. Not that Kaplan fails to consider the special nature of Jewish religious forms. Kaplan is a great believer in preserving and furthering the distinctive patterns of Jewish life as enriching and rewarding. But he steadfastly refuses to formulate this in terms of 'chosenness' which suggests privilege. To the stock answer that the 'choice' of Israel is not for privilege but for service, Kaplan retorts that to be chosen for service is the greatest privilege of all. Hugo Bergman, after studying carefully the various moves of modern Jewish thinkers to defend the doctrine of chosenness, finds none of them completely convincing and comes to the conclusion that the doctrine, in whatever form it is presented, is difficult to reconcile with the idea of God's justice.

Between the two extremes is the view, followed here, that while chosenness should not be interpreted in qualitative terms it should not be given up entirely. On the contrary it is still valid and, paradoxical though this may seem, is still the most powerful way of expressing the universal ideal. Jewish history has demonstrated that truths originally the possession of a particular people have become, through the efforts of that people to live by them, the property of millions beyond the confines of the people to whom the truth was originally revealed. Ethical monotheism is the supreme example of this. The rest of this chapter is devoted, then, to a defence of the doctrine of the chosen people always with the *proviso* that the doctrine is conceived of in non-qualitative terms. The following points require especially to be made in defence of the doctrine.

1. The Biblical conception of the election of Israel has nothing in

common with the idea of a tribal god protecting his people, responding to their attempts to buy his favour and capable of suffering defeat at the hands of a more powerful deity. The relation of a tribal god to his people is a 'natural one'. He does not 'choose' his people any more than they are members of the tribe by choice. In the Bible it is the universal God who 'chooses'. As I. Heinemann has pointed out the Biblical references to the choice are in a universalistic framework. 'Now, therefore, if ye will obey My voice indeed, and keep My covenant, then ye shall be a peculiar treasure unto Me above all people: *For all the earth is Mine'* (Ex. 19:5). 'Why sayest thou, O Jacob, and speakest O Israel, my way is hid from the Lord, and my judgement is passed over from my God? Hast thou not known? hast thou not heard, *that the everlasting God, the Lord, the Creator of the ends of the earth,* fainteth not, neither is weary? there is no searching of His understanding' (Is. 40:27-28). 'Thus saith God the Lord, *He spread the heavens, and stretched them forth, He spread forth the earth and that which cometh out of it, He that giveth bread unto the people upon it, And spirit to them that walk therein;* I the Lord have called thee in righteousness, and have taken hold of thy hand, and kept thee, and set thee for a covenant of the people, For a light of the Nations; to open the blind eyes. To bring out the prisoners from the dungeon. And them that sit in darkness out of the prison-house' (Is. 42:5-7).

2. The doctrine is not of a Herrenvolk whom others must serve but on the contrary of a folk dedicated to the service of others. The prophet Amos declares: 'You only have I known of all the families of the earth, therefore I will visit upon you all your iniquities' (Amos 3:2). The constant castigations of their people by the prophets, their steadfast demands that the people live up to their vocation in which they are failing lamentably, their frequent warnings of divine displeasure, are hardly ideas one associates with divine favouritism. Zangwill once said that the Bible is an anti-Semitic book! In a typical Rabbinic passage we read: 'It is written: "It was not because you were greater than any people that the Lord set His love upon you and chose you for you are the smallest of all peoples" (Deut. 7:7). The Holy One, blessed be He, said to Israel, I love you because even though I bestow greatness upon you, you humble yourselves before Me. I bestowed greatness upon Abraham, yet he said to Me, 'I am dust and ashes' (Gen. 18:27); upon Moses and Aaron, yet they said, 'And we are nothing' (Ex. 16:8); upon David, yet he said, 'But I am a worm and no man' (Ps. 22:7). But

with the heathen it is not so. I bestowed greatness upon Nimrod, and he said, 'Who is the Lord' (Ex.5:2); upon Sennacherib, and he said, 'Who are they among all the gods of the countries?' (2 Kings 18:35); upon Nebuchadnezzar, and he said, 'I will ascend above the heights of the clouds' (Is. 14:14); upon Hiram king of Tyre, and he said, 'I sit in the seat of God, in the heart of the seas' (Ezek. 28:2).

3. The doctrine has no affinity with such notions as that of Aryan racial superiority. Jewish particularism is never exclusive: anyone can become a Jew by embracing the Jewish faith. Some of the greatest of the Rabbis are said to have been descended from converts to Judaism. In one Talmudic passage it is said that the proselyte is dearer to God than the born Israelite. Another passage teaches that Israel was scattered among the nations only that they might make proselytes. The proselyte is regarded as a Jew in every respect. He should recite in his prayers the formula: 'Our God and the God of our fathers', for he is a spiritual child of Abraham. It is strictly forbidden to taunt a proselyte with his background or former behaviour.

4. The choice was reciprocal — God choosing Israel and Israel choosing God. The idea of a covenant between God and Israel is basic to the whole conception. 'Thou has avouched the Lord this day to be thy God, and to walk in His ways, and to keep His statutes, and His commandments and His judgements, and to hearken unto His voice; And the Lord hath avouched thee this day to be His peculiar people, as He hath promised thee, and that thou shouldest keep His commandments' (Deut. 26:17-18). 'And Joshua said unto the people, Ye are witnesses against yourselves that you have chosen you the Lord to serve Him. And they said, we are witnesses' (Josh. 24:22). The Rabbis had something of this in mind when they told of God offering the Torah to all the other nations, who refused it, before giving it to Israel who accepted its yoke and cheerfully proclaimed: 'We will do and we will hear'.

5. If the empirical test is applied it becomes obvious that we are not discussing a dogma incapable of verification but the recognition of sober historical fact. The world owes Israel the idea of the One God of righteousness and holiness. This is how God became known to mankind and clearly God used Israel for this great purpose. When Judaism declares that the covenant is still in force it reaffirms that Israel still has a special role to play.

From what has been said it is clear that the Chosen People idea is not a narrowly exclusive one, that it is universalistic, that it invokes duty rather than bestows privilege, that it is a doctrine of reciprocity, and that it bears the stamp of historical truth.

Yet there is also no doubt that this doctrine, perhaps more than any other, is so easily distorted and may even be dangerous. The suggestion or implication that it means that God is exclusively concerned with Jews or even that they are His special concern is surely at variance with the universalistic doctrine of Judaism that God is the Father of all mankind. Undoubtedly, less worthy interpretations of the doctrine are found in the Jewish sources but the nobler view is also found there and that in abundance.

The Jew of today is the heir to the whole tradition and this means that here, as in other areas, there are tensions with which he has to learn to live. As a powerful spur to Jewish survival, as providing a sense of destiny, as a reaffirmation of the covenant with its demands, responsibilities and obligations, the doctrine of the chosen people still possesses much value. As a temptation to narrowness and exclusiveness it still has its dangers. The modern Jew must learn to avail himself of the values inherent in the doctrine while taking due caution against its degeneration. To attempt to live without such tensions is to deprive life of its creativity. It is altogether right and proper that Jews should be concerned with the difficulties in the doctrine of Israel's chosenness. It may be that the Jew never comes closer to the truth in the doctrine of chosenness than when he is severely critical of why and how God can choose the Jewish people.

Source: From Louis Jacobs, *A Jewish Theology,* Darton, Longman and Todd 1973, pp.269-75.

6.23   THE REDEMPTION OF ISRAEL

Z.H. Kallischer

The redemption of Israel, for which we long, is not to be imagined as a sudden miracle. The Almighty, praised be His name, will not suddenly descend from on high and command His people to go forth. He will not send His Messiah from heaven in a twinkling of an eye, to sound the great trumpet for the scattered of Israel and gather them into Jerusalem. He will not surround the Holy City with a wall of fire or cause the Holy Temple to descend from the heavens. The bliss and the miracles that were promised by His servants, the prophets, will certainly come to pass — everything will be fulfilled — but we will not run in terror and flight, for the redemption of Israel will come by slow degrees and the ray of deliverance will shine forth gradually.

My dear reader! Cast aside the conventional view that the Messiah will suddenly sound a blast on the great trumpet and cause all the inhabitants of the earth to tremble. On the contrary, the Redemption will begin by awakening support among the philanthropists and by gaining the consent of the nations to the gathering of some of the scattered of Israel into the Holy Land. . .

Can we logically explain why the Redemption will begin in a natural manner and why the Lord, in His love for His people, will not immediately send the Messiah in an obvious miracle? Yes, we can. We know that all our worship of God is in the form of trials by which He tests us. When God created man and placed him in the Garden of Eden, He also planted the Tree of Knowledge and then commanded man not to eat of it. Why did He put the Tree in the Garden, if not as a trial?. . . When Israel went forth from Egypt, God again tested man's faith with hunger and thirst along the way. . . .Throughout the days of our dispersion we have been dragged from land to land and have borne the yoke of martyrdom for the sanctity of God's name; we have been dragged from land to land and have borne the yoke of exile through the ages, all for the sake of His holy Torah and as a further stage of the testing of our faith.

If the Almighty would suddenly appear, one day in the future, through undeniable miracles, this would be no trial. What straining of our faith would there be in the face of miracles and wonders attending a clear and heavenly command to go up and inherit the land and enjoy its good fruit? Under such circumstances, what fool would not go there, not because of his love of God, but for his own selfish sake? Only a natural beginning of the Redemption is a true test of those who initiate it. To concentrate all one's energy on this holy work and to renounce home and fortune for the sake of living in Zion before 'the voice of gladness' and 'the voice of joy' are heard — there is no greater merit or trial than this. . .

For all this to come about there must first be Jewish resettlement in the Lord; without such settlement, how can the ingathering begin?

Source: From A. Hertzberg, ed., op.cit., pp.221-22.

7   THE CHRISTIAN WAY

[*Editor's Note:* Christianity, though having its origin in an historical person born in Palestine, has flourished as an organised religion much more in the West than in the area of its birth.

The course of study for which the Reader provides source material is being offered in the first place in a Britain in which Christianity has for many centuries been the religion of the great majority of the people. Many students will therefore have an inevitable tendency to regard Christianity as the central of all world religions and to regard, other faiths, though important, as being overshadowed by Christianity.

This view is being widely questioned today. It may seem that what Professor John Hick has called the 'Ptolemaic' religious universe (with Christianity at the centre and all other religions peripheral to it) is giving way to a 'Copernican' religious outlook in which Ultimate Reality is at the centre and *all* religions, including Christianity, are moving round the fixed centre, though doubtless at different distances from that centre and moving in different ways.

Starting with the charismatic figure of Jesus who would not accept the religious constraints of his inherited Judaism, Christianity develops from being a vigorous 'non-establishment' movement into an institutionalised hierarchical body, complete with priests, holy book and obligatory religious rites. For many years it continued with an outward appearance of unity, although even in the early centuries serious divisions began to appear within its corporate life.

During the last four hundred years this tendency to schism has increased. But the modern 'ecumenical movement' seeks to reverse the process of fragmentation.

A vigorous missionary religion, Christianity has had a profound influence in many parts of the world, although, like all world religions, it is now experiencing a crisis in its life. It remains, however, an important spiritual and social force, continuing to teach and preach the unique 'incarnation' of God in one human being, Jesus Christ.

In the following section Dr Clark makes use of Christian scriptures, some well-known hymns, and a very diverse group of doctrinal statements, as illustrative material for the section on Christianity which he has written for the Course.]

Man's Original Situation According to Genesis 7.1.1

Then God said, 'Let us make man in our image, after our likeness; and let them have dominion over the fish of the sea, and over the birds of the air, and over the cattle, and over all the earth, and over every creeping thing that creeps upon the earth.' So God created man in his own image, in the image of God he created him; male and female he created them. And God blessed them, and God said to them, 'Be fruitful and multiply, and fill the earth and subdue it, and have dominion over the fish of the sea and over the birds of the air and over every living thing that moves upon the earth. . .'

(Genesis 1:26-28)

Then the Lord God formed man of dust from the ground, and breathed into his nostrils the breath of life; and man became a living being. And the Lord God planted a garden in Eden, in the east; and there he put the man whom he had formed. And out of the ground the Lord God made to grow every tree that is pleasant to the sight and good for food, the tree of life also in the midst of the garden, and the tree of the knowledge of good and evil. . .

(Genesis 2:7-9)

The Lord God took the man and put him in the garden of Eden to till it and keep it. And the Lord God commanded the man, saying, 'You may freely eat of every tree of the garden; but of the tree of the knowledge of good and evil you shall not eat, for in the day that you eat of it you shall die. . .'

(Genesis 2:15-17)

Now the serpent was more subtle than any other wild creature that the Lord God had made. He said to the woman, 'Did God say, "You shall not eat of any tree of the garden"?' And the woman said to the serpent, 'We may eat of the fruit of the trees of the garden; but God said, "You shall not eat of the fruit of the tree which is in the midst of the garden, neither shall you touch it, lest you die".' But the serpent said to the woman, 'You will not die. For God knows that when you eat of it your eyes will be opened, and you will be like God, knowing good and evil.' So when the woman saw that the tree was good for food, and that it was a delight to the eyes, and that the tree was to be desired to make one wise, she took of its

419

fruit and ate; and she also gave some to her husband, and he ate. Then the eyes of both were opened, and they knew that they were naked; and they sowed fig leaves together and made themselves aprons. . .

(Genesis 3:1-7)

The Lord God said to the serpent, 'Because you have done this, cursed are you above all cattle, and above all wild animals; upon your belly you shall go, and dust you shall eat all the days of your life. I will put enmity between you and the woman, and between your seed and her seed; he shall bruise your head, and you shall bruise his heel.' To the woman he said, 'I will greatly multiply your pain in child bearing; in pain you shall bring forth children, yet your desire shall be for your husband, and he shall rule over you.' And to Adam he said, 'Because you have listened to the voice of your wife, and have eaten of the tree of which I commanded you, "You shall not eat of it", cursed is the ground because of you; in toil you shall eat of it all the days of your life; thorns and thistles it shall bring forth to you; and you shall eat the plants of the field. In the sweat of your face you shall eat bread till you return to the ground, for out of it you were taken; you are dust, and to dust you shall return. . .'

(Genesis 3:14-19)

Then the Lord God said, 'Behold, the man has become like one of us, knowing good and evil; and now, lest he put forth his hand and take also of the tree of life and eat, and live forever' — therefore the Lord God sent him forth from the garden of Eden, to till the ground from which he was taken. He drove out the man; and at the east of the garden of Eden he placed the cherubim, and a flaming sword which turned every way, to guard the way to the tree of life.'

(Genesis 3:22-24)

7.1.2 Deuterocanonical Comments

The Lord created man out of earth, and turned him back to it again. He gave to men few days, a limited time, but granted them authority over the things upon the earth. He endowed them with strength like his own, and made them in his own image. He placed the fear of them in all living beings, and granted them dominion over beasts and birds. He made for them tongue and eyes; he gave them ears and a mind for thinking. He filled them with knowledge and understanding, and showed them good and evil. He set his eye upon their hearts to show them the majesty of his works. And they will praise his holy name, to proclaim the grandeur of his works. He bestowed knowledge upon them, and allotted to them the law of life. He established with them an eternal covenant, and showed them his judgements. Their eyes saw his glorious majesty and their ears heard the glory of his voice. And he said to them, "Beware of all unrighteousness". And he gave commandment to each of them concerning his neighbour.[4]

[Ecclesiasticus 17:1-15]

The Lord hates all abominations, and they are not loved by those who fear him. It was he who created man in the beginning, and he left him in the power of his own inclination. If you will, you can keep the commandments, and to act faithfully is a matter of your own choice. He has placed before you fire and water; stretch out your hand for whichever you wish. Before a man are life and death and whichever he chooses will be given to him. For great is the wisdom of the Lord; he is mighty in power and sees everything; his eyes are on those who fear him and he knows every deed of man. He has not commanded anyone to be ungodly, and he has not given anyone permission to sin.

(Ecclesiasticus 15:13-20)

God created man for incorruption,
And made him in the image of his own eternity;
But through the devil's envy death entered the world,
And those who belong to his party experience it.

(The Wisdom of Solomon 2:23-4)

The Psalmist Praises Creation   7.1.3

O Lord, how manifold are thy Works! In wisdom hast thou made them all; the earth is full of thy creatures. . . These all look to thee, to give them their food in due season. When thou givest to them, they gather it up; when thou openest thy hand, they are filled with good things. When thou hidest thy face, they are dismayed; when thou takest away their breath, they die and return to their dust. When thou sendest forth thy Spirit, they are created; and thou renewest the face of the ground.

(Psalm 104: 24, 27-30)

Praise the Lord!
Praise the Lord from the heavens, praise him in the heights!
Praise him, all his angels praise him, all his host!
Praise him, sun and moon, praise him, all you shining stars!

Praise him, you highest heavens, and you waters above the heavens!
Let them praise the name of the Lord!
For he commanded and they were created.
And he established them for ever and ever;
He fixed their bounds which cannot be passed.
Praise the Lord from the earth, you sea monsters and all deeps,
Fire and hail, snow and frost, stormy wind fulfilling his command!
Mountains and all hills, fruit trees and all cedars!
Beasts and all cattle, creeping things and flying birds!
Kings of the earth and all peoples, princes and all rulers of the earth!
Young men and maidens together, old men and children!
Let them praise the name of the Lord, for his name alone is exalted;
His glory is above earth and heaven.

(Psalm 148:1-13)

7.1.4 Sin and Pollution

Have mercy on me, O God, according to thy steadfast love;
according to thy abundant mercy blot out my transgressions.
Wash me thoroughly from my iniquity, and cleanse me from my sin!
For I know my transgressions, and my sin is ever before me.
Against thee, thee only, have I sinned, and done that which is evil in
    thy sight,
so that thou art justified in thy sentence and blameless in thy
    judgement.
Behold, I was brought forth in iniquity, and in sin did my mother
    conceive me.
Behold, thou desirest truth in the inward being; therefore teach me
    wisdom in my secret heart.
Purge me with hyssop, and I shall be clean;
Wash me, and I shall be whiter than snow.
Fill me with joy and gladness; let the bones which thou hast broken
    rejoice.
Hide thy face from my sins, and blot out all my iniquities.
Create in me a clean heart, O God, and put a new and right spirit
    within me.
Cast me not away from thy presence, and take not thy holy Spirit
    from me.

(Psalm 51:1-11)

7.1.5 Paul on Human Depravity

For the wrath of God is revealed from heaven against all ungodliness and wickedness of men who by their wickedness suppress the truth. For what can be known about God is plain to them, because God has shown it to them. Ever since the creation of the world his invisible nature, namely, his eternal power and deity, has been clearly perceived in the things that have been made. So they are without excuse; for although they knew God they did not honour him as God or give thanks to him, but they became futile in their thinking and their senseless minds were darkened. Claiming to be wise, they became fools, and exchanged the glory of the immortal God for images resembling mortal man or birds or animals or reptiles. Therefore God gave them up in the lusts of their hearts to impurity, to the dishonouring of their bodies among themselves, because they exchanged the truth about God for a lie and worshipped and served the creature rather than the Creator, who is blessed forever! Amen. For this reason God gave them up to dishonourable passions. Their women exchanged natural relations for unnatural, and the men likewise gave up natural relations with women and were consumed with passion for one another, men committing shameless acts with men and receiving in their own persons the due penalty for their error.

And since they did not see fit to acknowledge God, God gave them up to a base mind and to improper conduct. They were filled with all manner of wickedness, evil, covetousness, malice. Full of envy, murder, strife, deceit, malignity, they are gossips, slanderers, haters of God, insolent, haughty, boastful, inventors of evil, disobedient to parents, foolish, faithless, heartless, ruthless. Though they know God's decree that those who do such things deserve to die, they not only do them but approve those who practise them.

(Romans 1:18-32)

Do you not know that the unrighteous will not inherit the kingdom of God? Do not be deceived; neither the immoral, nor idolators, nor adulterers, nor homosexuals, nor thieves, nor the greedy, nor drunkards, nor revilers, nor robbers will inherit the kingdom of God. And such were some of you. But you were washed, you were sanctified, you were justified in the name of the Lord Jesus Christ and in the Spirit of our God.

(I Corinthians 6:9-11)

The Reign of Sin and its Antidote 7;1.6

Therefore as sin came into the world through one man and death through sin, and so death spread to all men because all men sinned — sin indeed was in the world before the law was given, but sin is not counted where there is no law. Yet death reigned from Adam to Moses, even over those whose sins were not like the transgression of Adam, who was a type of the one who was to come.

But the free gift is not like the trespass. For if many died through one man's trespass, much more have the grace of God and the free gift in the grace of that one man Jesus Christ abounded for many. And the free gift is not like the effect of that one man's sin. For the judgement following one trespass brought condemnation, but the free gift following many trespasses brings justification. If, because of one man's trespass, death reigned through that one man, much more will those who receive the abundance of grace and the free gift of righteousness reign in life through the one man Jesus Christ.

Then as one man's trespass led to condemnation for all men, so one man's act of righteousness leads to acquittal and life for all men. For as by one man's disobedience many were made sinners, so by one man's obedience many will be made righteous. Law came in, to increase the trespass; but where sin increased, grace abounded all the more so that, as sin reigned in death, grace also might reign through righteousness to eternal life through Jesus Christ our Lord.

(Romans 5:12-21)

7.1.7 The Thirty-nine Articles on Original or Birth-Sin

Original Sin standeth not in the following of Adam (as the Pelagians do vainly talk), but it is the fault and corruption of the Nature of every man, that naturally is ingendered of the offspring of Adam: whereby man is very far gone from original righteousness, and is of his own nature inclined to evil, so that the flesh lusteth always contrary to the spirit; and therefore in every person born into this world, it deserveth God's wrath and damnation. And this infection of nature doth remain, yea in them that are regenerated; whereby the lust of the flesh, called in the Greek, *phronema sarkos,* which some do expound the wisdom, some sensuality, some the affection, some the desire, of the flesh, is not subject to the Law of God. And although there is no condemnation for them that believe and are baptised, yet the Apostle doth confess, that concupiscence and lust hath of itself the nature of sin.

From Article IX of the Thirty-nine Articles of the Church of England.

From the Decree of the Council of Trent on Original Sin 7.1.8

The Holy, Oecumenical and General Synod of Trent. . . lays down, professes and declares the following truths concerning original sin:

When the first man Adam had disobeyed the commandment of God in Paradise, he straightway lost the holiness and justice in which he had been created. By his offence and disobedience he incurred the wrath and indignation of God, and consequently, as God had previously warned him, death also. Together with death he incurred slavery under the yoke of him who had the power of death, namely the devil. Thus through that offence of disobedience Adam in his whole nature, both in body and in soul, was changed for the worse.

The disobedience of Adam harmed not only himself but also those descended from him. He lost the holiness and justice which he had received from God, not only for himself but for us also. By that sin of disobedience he passed on to the whole human race not only death and bodily retribution, but also sin, which is the death of the soul. . .

This sin of Adam, drawn from that one origin, is transmitted by generation not by imitation; it is present in all and belongs to each. It cannot be taken away by any other remedy than through the merit of the one Mediator, Our Lord Jesus Christ. . .

Through the grace of our Lord Jesus Christ, which is bestowed in baptism, the guilt of original sin is remitted. Indeed everything that can be called sin in a true and proper sense is taken away. It must not be said to be merely cut back or not imputed. For in those who are reborn God finds nothing hateful, because 'there is no condemnation for those' (Rom. 8:1) who are truly 'buried with Christ by baptism into death' (Rom. 6:4). . .

However, concupiscence or the 'tinder' [of sin] does remain in the baptised. . . This is left to provide occasion for the spiritual combat, but it cannot do harm to those who do not consent to it and who manfully struggle against it through the grace of Jesus Christ. . . Although in some places the Apostle Paul calls this concupiscence 'sin', the holy Synod declares that the Catholic Church has never understood this to mean that anything remains in the baptised which is sin in the true and proper sense, but only because concupiscence had its origin in sin, and it inclines men towards sin.

If any one should deny these truths, let him be anathema.

7.1.9 From the Burial Service of the Church of England

Man that is born of a woman hath but a short time to live, and is full of misery. He cometh up, and is cut down like a flower; he fleeth as it were a shadow, and never continueth in one stay. In the midst of life we are in death; of whom may we seek for succour, but of thee, O Lord, who for our sins art justly displeased? Yet, O Lord God most holy, O Lord most mighty, O holy and most merciful Saviour, deliver us not into the bitter pains of eternal death. Thou knowest, Lord, the secrets of our hearts; shut not thy merciful ears to our prayer; but spare us, Lord most holy, O God most mighty, O holy and merciful Saviour, thou most worthy Judge eternal, suffer us not, at our last hour, for any pains of death, to fall from thee.

(The Book of Common Prayer)

General Note:

All Scripture references in §7.1 are taken from the Revised Standard Version.

7.2 TO WHAT?

A Jewish Text which Christians Adopted

But the souls of the righteous are in the hand of God,
and no torment will ever touch them.
In the eyes of the foolish they seemed to have died;
and their departure was thought to be an affliction,
And their going from us to be their destruction:
but they are at peace.
For though in the sight of men they were punished,
their hope is full of immortality;
Having been disciplined a little they will receive great good,
because God tested them, and found them worthy of himself;
Like gold in the furnace he tried them,
and like a sacrificial burnt offering he accepted them.
In the time of their visitation they will shine forth,
and will run like sparks through the stubble,
They will govern nations, and rule over peoples,
and the Lord will reign over them for ever.
Those who trust in him will understand truth,
and the faithful will abide with him in love,
because grace and mercy are upon his elect,
and he watches over his holy ones.

But the ungodly will be punished as their reasoning deserves, who
disregarded the righteous man and rebelled against the Lord;
for whoever despises wisdom and instruction is miserable.
Their hope is vain, their labours are unprofitable
And their works are useless.

(The Wisdom of Solomon 3:1-11)

The Warning

And do not fear those who kill the body but cannot kill the soul;
rather fear him who can destroy both soul and body in hell.

(Matthew 10:28)

Jesus Explains What Will Matter at the Last Judgement

When the Son of man comes in his glory, and all the angels with him, then he will sit on his glorious throne. Before him will be gathered all the nations, and he will separate them one from another as a shepherd separates the sheep from the goats, and he will place the sheep at his right hand, but the goats at the left. Then the King will say to those at his right hand, 'Come, O blessed of my Father, inherit the kingdom prepared for you from the foundation of the world; for I was hungry and you gave me food, I was thirsty and you gave me drink, I was a stranger and you welcomed me, I was naked and you clothed me, I was sick and you visited me, I was in prison and you came to me.' Then the righteous will answer him, 'Lord, when did we see thee hungry and feed thee, or thirsty and give thee drink? And when did we see thee a stranger and welcome thee, or naked and clothe thee? And when did we see thee sick or in prison and visit thee?' And the King will answer them, 'Truly, I say to you, as you did it to one of the least of these my brethren, you did it to me.' Then he will say to those at his left hand, 'Depart from me, you cursed, into the eternal fire prepared for the devil and his angels; for I was hungry and you gave me no food, I was thirsty and you gave me no drink, I was a stranger and you did not welcome me, naked and you did not clothe me, sick and in prison, and you did not visit me.' Then they also will answer, 'Lord, when did we see thee hungry or thirsty or a stranger or naked or sick or in prison, and did not minister to thee?' Then he will answer them, 'Truly, I say to you, as you did it not to one of the least of these, you did it not to me.' And they will go away into eternal punishment, but the righteous into eternal life.

(Matthew 25:31-34)

7.2.4 The Coming Day of the Lord

But we would not have you ignorant, brethren, concerning those who are asleep, that you may not grieve as others do who have no hope. For since we believe that Jesus died and rose again, even so, through Jesus, God will bring with him those who have fallen asleep. For this we declare to you by the word of the Lord, that we who are alive, who are left until the coming of the Lord, shall not precede those who have fallen asleep.

For the Lord himself will descend from heaven with a cry of command, with the archangel's call, and with the sound of the trumpet of God. And the dead in Christ will rise first; then we who are alive, who are left, shall be caught up together with them in the clouds to meet the Lord in the air; and so we shall always be with the Lord.

Therefore comfort one another with these words.

(1 Thessalonians 4:13-18)

Now concerning the coming of our Lord Jesus Christ and our assembling to meet him, we beg you, brethren, not to be quickly shaken in mind or excited, either by spirit or by word, or by letter purporting to be from us, to the effect that the day of the Lord has come. Let no one deceive you in any way; for that day will not come, unless the rebellion comes first, and the man of lawlessness is revealed, the son of perdition, who opposes and exalts himself against every so-called god or object of worship, so that he takes his seat in the temple of God, proclaiming himself to be God. Do you not remember that when I was still with you I told you this? And you know what is restraining him now so that he may be revealed in his time.

For the mystery of lawlessness is already at work; only he who now restrains it will do so until he is out of the way. And then the lawless one will be revealed, and the Lord Jesus will slay him with the breath of his mouth and destroy him by his appearing and his coming. The coming of the lawless one by the activity of Satan will be with all power and with pretended signs and wonders, and with all wicked deception for those who are to perish, because they refused to love the truth and so be saved. Therefore God sends upon them a strong delusion to make them believe what is false, so that all may be condemned who did not believe the truth but had pleasure in unrighteousness.

But we are bound to give thanks to God always for you, brethren beloved by the Lord, because God chose you from the beginning to be saved, through sanctification by the Spirit and belief in the truth. To this he called you through our gospel, so that you may obtain the glory of our Lord Jesus Christ.

(2 Thessalonians 2:1-14)

The Resurrection of the Dead 7.2.5

But someone will ask, 'How are the dead raised? With what kind of body do they come?' You foolish man! What you sow does not come to life unless it dies. And what you sow is not the body which is to be, but a bare kernel, perhaps of wheat or of some other grain. But God gives it a body as he has chosen, and to each kind of seed its own body. For not all flesh is alike, but there is one kind for

men, another for animals, another for birds, and another for fish.
There are celestial bodies and there are terrestrial bodies; but the
glory of the celestial is one, and the glory of the terrestrial is
another. There is one glory of the sun, and another glory of the
moon, and another glory of the stars; for star differs from star in
glory. So is it with the resurrection of the dead. What is sown is
perishable, what is raised is imperishable. It is sown in dishonour, it
is raised in glory. It is sown in weakness, it is raised in power. It is
sown a physical body, it is raised a spiritual body. If there is a
physical body, there is also a spiritual body. Thus it is written, 'The
first man Adam became a living being'; the last Adam became a life-
giving spirit. But it is not the spiritual which is first but the physical,
and then the spiritual. The first man was from the earth, a man of
dust; the second man is from heaven. As was the man of dust, so are
those who are of the dust; and as is the man of heaven, so are those
who are of heaven. Just as we have borne the image of the man of
dust, we shall also bear the image of the man of heaven. I tell you
this, brethren: flesh and blood cannot inherit the kingdom of God,
nor does the perishable inherit the imperishable. Lo! I tell you a
mystery. We shall not all sleep, but we shall all be changed, in a
moment, in the twinkling of an eye, at the last trumpet. For the
trumpet will sound, and the dead will be raised imperishable, and
we shall be changed. For this perishable nature must put on the
imperishable, and this mortal nature must put on immortality. When
the perishable puts on the imperishable, and the mortal puts on
immortality, then shall come to pass the saying that is written:
'Death is swallowed up in victory.' 'Oh death, where is thy victory?
Oh death, where is thy sting?' The sting of death is sin, and the
power of sin is the law. But thanks be to God, who gives us the
victory through our Lord Jesus Christ.

(I Corinthians 15:35-57)

7.2.6   Raised to Heavenly Life Even Now

And you, he made alive, when you were dead through the trespasses
and sins in which you once walked, following the course of this
world, following the prince of the power of the air, the spirit that is
now at work in the sons of disobedience. Among these we all once
lived in the passions of our flesh, following the desires of body and
mind, and so we were by nature, children of wrath, like the rest of
mankind.

But God, who is rich in mercy, out of the great love with which he loved us, even when we were dead through our trespasses, made us alive together with Christ (by grace you have been saved), and raised us up with him, and made us sit with him in the heavenly places in Christ Jesus, that in the coming ages he might show the immeasurable riches of his grace in kindness toward us in Christ Jesus. For by grace you have been saved through faith; and this is not your own doing, it is the gift of God — not because of works, lest any man should boast. For we are his workmanship, created in Christ Jesus for good works, which God prepared beforehand, that we should walk in them.

(Ephesians 2:1-10)

Conformed with Christ in Newness of Life   7.2.7

Do you not know that all of us who have been baptised into Christ Jesus were baptised into his death? We were buried therefore with him by baptism into death, so that as Christ was raised from the dead by the glory of the Father, we too might walk in newness of life.

For if we have been united with him in a death like his, we shall certainly be united with him in a resurrection like his. We know that our old self was crucified with him so that the sinful body might be destroyed, and we might no longer be enslaved to sin.

For he who has died is freed from sin. But if we have died with Christ, we believe that we shall also live with him. For we know that Christ being raised from the dead will never die again; death no longer has dominion over him. The death he died he died to sin, once for all, but the life he lives he lives to God. So you also must consider yourselves dead to sin and alive to God in Christ Jesus.

Let not sin therefore reign in your mortal bodies, to make you obey their passions. Do not yield your members to sin as instruments of wickedness, but yield yourselves to God as men who have been brought from death to life, and your members to God as instruments of righteousness. For sin will have no dominion over you, since you are not under law but under grace. . .

When you were slaves of sin, you were free in regard to righteousness. But then what return did you get from the things of which you are now ashamed? The end of those things is death. But now that you have been set free from sin and have become slaves of God, the return you get is sanctification and its end, eternal life. For the wages of sin is death, but the free gift of God is eternal life in Christ Jesus our Lord.   (Romans: 6:3-14.20-23)

7.2.8 The New Spirit of Sonship

For all who are led by the Spirit of God are sons of God. For you did not receive the spirit of slavery to fall back into fear, but you have received the spirit of sonship. When we cry, 'Abba! Father!' it is the Spirit himself bearing witness with our spirit that we are children of God, and if children, then heirs, heirs of God and fellow heirs with Christ, provided we suffer with him in order that we may also be glorified with him.

(Romans 8:14-17)

7.2.9 Inheriting the Riches of God's Grace

Blessed be the God and Father of our Lord Jesus Christ, who has blessed us in Christ with every spiritual blessing in the heavenly places, even as he chose us in him before the foundation of the world, that we should be holy and blameless before him. He destined us in love to be his sons through Jesus Christ according to the purpose of his will, to the praise of his glorious grace which he freely bestowed on us in the beloved. In him we have redemption through his blood, the forgiveness of our trespasses, according to the riches of his grace which he lavished upon us.

For he has made known to us in all wisdom and insight the mystery of his will, according to his purpose which he set forth in Christ as a plan for the fulness of time, to unite all things in him, things in heaven and things on earth.

In him, according to the purpose of him who accomplishes all things according to the counsel of his will, we who first hoped in Christ have been destined and appointed to live for the praise of his glory. In him you also, who have heard the word of truth, the gospel of your salvation, and have believed in him, were sealed with the promised Holy Spirit, which is the guarantee of our inheritance until we acquire possession of it, to the praise of his glory.

(Ephesians 1:3-14)

7.2.10 Love the Ultimate Value

See what love the Father has given us, that we should be called children of God; and so we are. The reason why the world does not know us is that it did not know him. Beloved, we are God's children now; it does not yet appear what we shall be, but we know that when he appears we shall be like him, for we shall see him as he is. And every one who thus hopes in him purifies himself as he is pure. . . He who commits sin is of the devil; for the devil has sinned from the beginning. The reason the Son of God appeared was to destroy the works of the devil.

No one born of God commits sin; for God's nature abides in him, and he cannot sin because he is born of God.

By this it may be seen who are the children of God, and who are the children of the devil: whoever does not do right is not of God, nor he who does not love his brother . . .

Beloved, let us love one another; for love is of God, and he who loves is born of God and knows God. He who does not love does not know God; for God is love. In this the love of God was made manifest among us, that God sent his only Son into the world, so that we might live through him. In this is love, not that we loved God but that he loved us and sent his Son to be the expiation for our sins.

Beloved, if God so loved us, we also ought to love one another. No man has ever seen God; if we love one another, God abides in us and his love is perfected in us.

(1 John 3: 1-3, 8-10; 4: 7-12)

A Vision of the Beyond 7.2.11

Then I saw a new heaven and a new earth; for the first heaven and the first earth had passed away, and the sea was no more. And I saw the holy city, new Jerusalem, coming down out of heaven from God, prepared as a bride adorned for her husband; and I heard a great voice from the throne saying, 'Behold, the dwelling of God is with men. He will dwell with them, and they shall be his people, and God himself will be with them; he will wipe away every tear from their eyes, and death shall be no more, neither shall there be mourning nor crying nor pain any more, for the former things have passed away.'

And he who sat upon the throne said, 'Behold I make all things new.' Also he said, 'Write this, for these words are trustworthy and true.' And he said to me, 'It is done! I am the Alpha and the Omega, the beginning and the end. To the thirsty I will give water without price from the fountain of the water of life. He who conquers shall have this heritage, and I will be his God and he shall be my son. But as for the cowardly, the faithless, the polluted, as for murderers, fornicators, sorcerers, idolaters, and all liars, their lot shall be in the lake that burns with fire and brimstone, which is the second death.'

(Revelation 21:1-8)

7.2.12 A Hymn about Heaven

Jerusalem the golden,
With milk and honey blest,
Beneath thy contemplation
Sink heart and voice opprest.
I know not, O I know not,
What joys await us there,
What radiancy of glory,
What bliss beyond compare.

They stand, those halls of Sion,
All jubilant with song,
And bright with many an angel,
And all the martyr throng;
The Prince is ever in them,
The daylight is serene:
The pastures of the blessèd
Are decked in glorious sheen.

There is the throne of David;
And there from care released,
The shout of them that triumph,
The song of them that feast;
And they, who with their leader
Have conquered in the fight,
For ever and for ever
Are clad in robes of white.

O sweet and blessed country,
The home of God's elect!
O sweet and blessed country
That eager hearts expect!
Jesu, in mercy bring us
To that dear land of rest;
Who are with God the Father,
And Spirit ever blest.

Latin original by St Bernard, twelfth century. English translation by John
Mason Neale.

The Heart of Jesus as Refuge 7.2.13

All ye who seek a comfort sure
In trouble and distress,
Whatever sorrow vex the mind,
Or guilt the soul oppress,

Jesus, who gave himself for you
Upon the Cross to die,
Opens to you his sacred heart —
Oh, to that heart draw nigh.

Ye hear how kindly he invites;
Ye hear his words so blest;
'All ye that labour, come to me,
And I will give you rest'.

What meeker than the Saviour's heart?
As on the Cross he lay,
It did his murderers forgive,
And for their pardon pray.

Oh Jesus joy of saints on high!
Thou hope of sinners here!
Attracted by those loving words,
To thee I lift my prayer.

Wash thou my wounds in that dear blood
Which forth from thee doth flow;
New grace, new hope inspire; a new
And better heart bestow.

English translation by Edward Caswall.

Renewed by the Indwelling Spirit 7.2.14

Holy Spirit, Lord of Light,
From the clear celestial height,
Thy pure beaming radiance give,
Come, thou Father of the poor,

Come with treasures which endure:
Come thou Light of all that live!

Thou, of all consolers best,
Thou, the soul's delightsome guest,
Dost refreshing peace bestow,
Thou in toil art comfort sweet,
Pleasant coolness in the heat,
Solace in the midst of woe.

Light immortal, Light divine,
Visit thou these hearts of thine,
And our inmost being fill.
If thou take thy grace away,
Nothing pure in man will stay;
All his good is turned to ill.

Heal our wounds, our strength renew;
On our dryness pour thy dew;
Wash the stain of guilt away.
Bend the stubborn heart and will;
Melt the frozen, warm the chill;
Guide the steps that go astray.

Thou, on those who evermore
Thee confess and thee adore,
In thy sevenfold gifts descend:
Give them comfort when they die,
Give them life with thee on high,
Give them joys that never end.

Veni Sancte Spiritus: Latin original ascribed to Stephen Langton, Archbishop of Canterbury, died 1228; English translation by Edward Caswall.

7 2.15 Papal Teaching on the Lot of Man after Death

We will state what, according to God's normal disposition, is the condition after death of the souls of the following classes of men: the souls of all those holy men who departed from this world before the passion of Our Lord Jesus Christ; also of the holy apostles, martyrs, confessors, virgins; also of the other faithful departed who have received the sacred baptism of Christ, whether they have already lived or are yet to live in the future, and in whom nothing needing purgation was found, or will be found, at the time of their death; likewise, those in whom something needing purgation was or will be found at that time, but who receive due purgation after their death; and also the souls of those infants who have been baptised and reborn with the baptism of Christ, and who die before they come to the use of their free will. All such souls, we declare have been (since the ascension of our Saviour and Lord Jesus Christ into heaven), are now, or will be in heaven, that is, in the kingdom of heaven and in the celestial paradise with Christ. They are received there straight after their death (or, in the case of those who need purgation, after such purgation has been completed in them). They are joined to the company of the holy angels. Subsequent to the passion and death of our Lord Jesus Christ, they have seen and they will see the divine essence with an intuitive and also face-to-face vision. No creature has any part in mediating this vision, as far as the object of vision is concerned, but the divine essence shows itself to them unveiled, clearly and openly. Those who have this vision thus have full enjoyment of the divine essence. Even before the general judgement, the souls of those who have died are truly blessed, and have eternal life and repose, from that vision and fruition of the divine essence. The same is true of the souls of those who will die in the future; they also will see the same divine essence and enjoy it. Moreover this vision of the divine essence and the enjoyment of it brings to an end in those souls the exercise of the acts of faith and hope, in so far as faith and hope are strictly theological virtues. And further, once this intuitive and face-to-face vision, and its enjoyment, has been or will be begun in them, that vision and enjoyment perseveres continuously without any interruption or withdrawal, and it will so continue until the final judgement and from then for all eternity.

A Reformation Statement on the Destiny of the Elect   7.2.16

Predestination to Life is the everlasting purpose of God, whereby (before the foundations of the world were laid) he hath constantly decreed by his counsel secret to us, to deliver from curse and damnation those whom he hath chosen in Christ out of mankind, and to bring them by Christ to everlasting salvation, as vessels made to honour. Wherefore, they which be endued with so excellent a

Definition of Pope Benedict XII in the constitution *Benedictus Deus*, of 29 January 1336.

benefit of God be called according to God's purpose by his Spirit working in due season: they through grace obey the calling: they be justified freely: they be made sons of God by adoption: they be made like the image of his only-begotten Son Jesus Christ: they walk religiously in good works, and at length, by God's mercy, they attain to everlasting felicity.

From Article XVII of the Thirty-nine Articles of the Church of England.

General Note:

All Scripture references in §7.2 are taken from the Revised Standard Version.

7.3   BY WHAT?

Christy as Saviour   7.3.1

An angel of the Lord appeared to him in a dream, saying, 'Joseph, son of David, do not fear to take Mary your wife, for that which is conceived in her is of the Holy Spirit; she will bear a son, and you shall call his name Jesus, for he will save his people from their sins.'

(Matthew 1:20-21)

And the angel said to them, 'Be not afraid; for behold, I bring you good news of a great joy which will come to all the people; for to you is born this day in the city of David a Saviour who is Christ the Lord.'

(Luke 2:10-11)

Then Peter, filled with the Holy Spirit, said to them ... 'Be it known to you all, and to all the people of Israel, that by the name of Jesus Christ of Nazareth, whom you crucified, whom God raised from the dead, by him this man is standing before you well. This is the stone which was rejected by you builders, but which has become the head of the corner. And there is salvation in no one else, for there is no other name under heaven given among men by which we must be saved.'

(Acts 4:8-12)

God has brought to Israel a Saviour, Jesus, as he promised. Before his coming John had preached a baptism of repentance to all the people of Israel. And as John was finishing his course, he said, 'What do you suppose that I am? I am not he. No, but after me one is coming, the sandals of whose feet I am not worthy to untie.' Brethren, sons of the family of Abraham, and those among you that fear God, to us has been sent the message of this salvation.

(Acts 13:23-26)

The Climax of Salvation: Christ's Death and Resurrection   7.3.2

The Son of Man came not to be served but to serve, and to give his life as a ransom for many.

(Matthew 20:28)

Jesus began to show his disciples that he must go to Jerusalem and suffer many things from the elders and chief priests and scribes, and be killed, and on the third day be raised.

(Matthew 16:21)

I am the good shepherd; I know my own and my own know me, as the Father knows me and I know the Father; and I lay down my life for the sheep. And I have other sheep, that are not of this fold; I must bring them also, and they will heed my voice. So there shall be one flock, one shepherd. For this reason the Father loves me, because I lay down my life, that I may take it again. No one takes it from me, but I lay it down of my own accord. I have power to lay it down, and I have power to take it again; this charge I have received from my Father.

(John 10:14-18)

Jesus answered them, 'The hour has come for the Son of Man to be glorified. Truly, truly, I say to you, unless a grain of wheat falls into the earth and dies, it remains alone; but if it dies it bears much fruit.'

(John 12:23-24)

For I delivered to you as of first importance what I also received, that Christ died for our sins in accordance with the scriptures, that he was buried, that he was raised on the third day in accordance with the scriptures.

(I Corinthians 15:3-4)

7.3.3 Christ's Abasement and Exaltation

Have this mind among yourselves, which you have in Christ Jesus, who, though he was in the form of God, did not count equality with God a thing to be grasped, but emptied himself, taking the form of a servant, being born in the likeness of men. And being found in human form he humbled himself and became obedient unto death, even death on a cross. Therefore God has highly exalted him and bestowed on him the name which is above every name, that at the name of Jesus every knee should bow, in heaven and on earth and under the earth, and every tongue confess that Jesus Christ is Lord, to the glory of God the Father.

(Philippians 2:5-11)

7.3.4. Christ the Great High Priest

For Christ has entered, not into a sanctuary made with hands, a copy of the true one, but into heaven itself, now to appear in the presence of God on our behalf. Nor was it to offer himself repeatedly, as the high priest enters the Holy Place yearly with blood not his own; for then he would have had to suffer repeatedly since the foundation of the world. But as it is, he has appeared once for all at the end of the age to put away sin by the sacrifice of himself. And just as it is appointed for men to die once, and after that comes judgement, so Christ, having been offered once to bear the sins of many, will appear a second time, not to deal with sin but to save those who are eagerly waiting for him.

(Hebrews 9:24-28)

Justified by Faith 7.3.5

Therefore, since we are justified by faith, we have peace with God through our Lord Jesus Christ. Through him we have obtained access to this grace in which we stand, and we rejoice in our hope of sharing the glory of God. More than that, we rejoice in our sufferings knowing that suffering produces endurance, and endurance produces character, and character produces hope, and hope does not disappoint us, because God's love has been poured into our hearts through the Holy Spirit which has been given to us. While we were yet helpless, at the right time Christ died for the ungodly. Why, one will hardly die for a righteous man — though perhaps for a good man one will dare even to die. But God shows his love for us in that while we were yet sinners Christ died for us. Since, therefore, we are now justified by his blood, much more shall we be saved by him from the wrath of God. For if while we were enemies we were reconciled to God by the death of his Son, much more, now that we are reconciled, shall we be saved by his life.

(Romans 5:1-10)

The Ministry of Reconciliation 7.3.6

Therefore, if any one is in Christ, he is a new creation; the old has passed away, behold, the new has come. All this is from God, who through Christ reconciled us to himself and gave us the ministry of reconciliation; that is, God was in Christ reconciling the world to himself, not counting their trespasses against them, and entrusting to us the message of reconciliation. So we are ambassadors for Christ, God making his appeal through us. We beseech you on behalf of Christ, be reconciled to God. For our sake he made him to be sin who knew no sin, so that in him we might become the righteousness of God.

(2 Corinthians 5:17-21)

The Need to Live Righteously 7.3.7

But we beseech you, brethren, to respect those who labour among you and are over you in the Lord and admonish you, and to esteem them very highly in love because of their work. Be at peace among yourselves.

And we exhort you, brethren, admonish the idle, encourage the fainthearted, help the weak, be patient with them all. See that none of you repays evil for evil, but always seek to do good to one another and to all. Rejoice always, pray constantly, give thanks in all circumstances; for this is the will of God in Christ Jesus for you.

Do not quench the Spirit, do not despise prophesying, but test everything; hold fast what is good, abstain from every form of evil.

May the God of peace himself sanctify you wholly; and may your spirit and soul and body be kept sound and blameless at the coming of our Lord Jesus Christ. He who calls you is faithful, and he will do it.

(1 Thessalonians 5:12-24)

7.3.8 God Desires All to be Saved through Christ

First of all, then, I urge that supplications, prayers, intercessions and thanksgivings be made for all men, for kings and all who are in high positions, that we may lead a quiet and peaceable life, godly and respectful in every way. This is good, and it is acceptable in the sight of God our Saviour, who desires all men to be saved and to come to the knowledge of the truth. For there is one God, and there is one mediator between God and men, the man Christ Jesus, who gave himself as a ransom for all, the testimony to which was borne at the proper time.

(1 Timothy 2:1-6)

7.3.9 The Basic Test of a Christian

A new commandment I give to you, that you love one another; even as I have loved you, that you also love one another. By this all men will know that you are my disciples, if you have love for one another. . .

By this my Father is glorified, that you bear much fruit, and so prove to be my disciples. As the Father has loved me, so have I loved you; abide in my love. If you keep my commandments, you will abide in my love, just as I have kept my Father's commandments and abide in his love. These things I have spoken to you, that my joy may be in you, and that your joy may be full.

(John 13:34-35; 15:8-11)

The Sermon on the Mount 7.3.10

Seeing the crowds, he went up on the mountain, and when he sat down his disciples came to him. And he opened his mouth and taught them saying:

'Blessed are the poor in spirit, for theirs is the kingdom of heaven. Blessed are those who mourn, for they shall be comforted. Blessed are the meek, for they shall inherit the earth. Blessed are those who hunger and thirst for righteousness for they shall be satisfied. Blessed are the merciful, for they shall obtain mercy. Blessed are the pure in heart, for they shall see God. Blessed are the peacemakers, for they shall be called sons of God. Blessed are those who are persecuted for righteousness' sake, for theirs is the kingdom of heaven. Blessed are you when men revile you and persecute you and utter all kinds of evil against you falsely on my account. Rejoice and be glad, for your reward is great in heaven, for so men persecuted the prophets who were before you.

You are the salt of the earth; but if salt has lost its taste, how shall its saltness be restored? It is no longer good for anything except to be thrown out and trodden under foot by men. You are the light of the world. A city set on a hill cannot be hid. Nor do men light a lamp and put it under a bushel, but on a stand, and it gives light to all in the house. Let your light so shine before men, that they may see your good works and give glory to your Father who is in heaven.

Think not that I have come to abolish the law and the prophets; I have come not to abolish them but to fulfil them. For truly, I say to you, till heaven and earth pass away, not an iota, not a dot, will pass from the law until all is accomplished. Whoever then relaxes one of the least of these commandments and teaches men so, shall be called least in the kingdom of heaven; but he who does them and teaches them shall be called great in the kingdom of heaven. For I tell you, unless your righteousness exceeds that of the scribes and Pharisees, you will never enter the kingdom of heaven.

You have heard that it was said to the men of old, 'You shall not kill; and whoever kills shall be liable to judgement.' But I say to you that every one who is angry with his brother shall be liable to judgement; whoever insults his brother shall be liable to the council, and whoever says, 'You fool!' shall be liable to the fell of fire. So if you are offering your gift at the altar, and there remember that your brother has something against you, leave your gift there before the altar and go; first be reconciled to your brother, and then come and offer your gift. Make friends quickly with your accuser, while you are going with him to court, lest your accuser hand you over to the judge, and the judge to the guard, and you be put in prison; truly, I say to you, you will never get out till you have paid the last penny.

You have heard that it was said, 'You shall not commit adultery.' But I say to you that every one who looks at a woman lustfully has already committed adultery with her in his heart. If your right eye causes you to sin, pluck it out and throw it away; it is better that you lose one of your members than that your whole body be thrown into hell. And if your right hand causes you to sin, cut it off and throw it away; it is better that you lose one of your members than that your whole body go into hell.

It was also said, 'Whoever divorces his wife, let him give her a certificate of divorce.' But I say to you that every one who divorces his wife, except on the ground of unchastity, makes her an adulteress; and whoever marries a divorced woman commits adultery.

Again you have heard that it was said to the men of old, 'You shall not swear falsely, but shall perform to the Lord what you have sworn.' But I say to you, Do not swear at all, either by heaven, for it is the throne of God, or by the earth, for it is his footstool, or by Jerusalem, for it is the city of the great King. And do not swear by your head, for you cannot make one hair white or black. Let what you say be simply 'Yes' or 'No'; anything more than this comes from evil.

You have heard that it was said, 'An eye for an eye and a tooth for a tooth.' But I say to you, Do not resist one who is evil. But if any one strikes you on the right cheek, turn to him the other also; and if any one would sue you and take your coat, let him have your cloak as well; and if any one forces you to go one mile, go with him two miles. Give to him who begs from you, and do not refuse him who would borrow from you.

You have heard that it was said, 'You shall love your neighbour and hate your enemy.' But I say to you, Love your enemies and pray for those who persecute you, so that you may be sons of your Father who is in heaven; for he makes his sun rise on the evil and on the good, and sends rain on the just and on the unjust. For if you love those who love you, what reward have you? Do not even the tax collectors do the same? And if you salute only your brethren, what more are you doing than others? Do not even the Gentiles do the same?

You, therefore, must be perfect, as your heavenly Father is perfect. Beware of practising your piety before men in order to be seen by them; for then you will have no reward from your Father who is in heaven. Thus, when you give alms, sound no trumpet before you, as the hypocrites do in the synagogues and in the streets, that they may be praised by men. Truly, I say to you, they have their reward. But when you give alms, do not let your left hand know what your right hand is doing, so that your alms may be in secret; and your Father who sees in secret will reward you.

And when you pray, you must not be like the hypocrites; for they love to stand and pray in the synagogues and at the street corners, that they may be seen by men. Truly, I say to you, they have their reward. But when you pray, go into your room and shut the door and pray to your Father who is in secret; and your Father who sees in secret will reward you. And in praying do not heap up empty phrases as the Gentiles do; for they think that they will be heard for their many words. Do not be like them, for your Father knows what you need before you ask him. Pray then like this:

Our Father who art in heaven,
Hallowed be thy name.
Thy kingdom come,
Thy will be done,
On earth as it is in heaven.
Give us this day our daily bread;
And forgive us our debts,
As we also have forgiven our debtors;
And lead us not into temptation,
But deliver us from evil.

For if you forgive men their trespasses, your heavenly Father also will forgive you; but if you do not forgive men their trespasses, neither will your Father forgive your trespasses.

And when you fast, do not look dismal, like the hypocrites, for they disfigure their faces that their fasting may be seen by men. Truly, I say to you, they have their reward. But when you fast, anoint your head and wash your face, that your fasting may not be seen by men but by your Father who is in secret; and your Father who sees in secret will reward you.

Do not lay up for yourselves treasures on earth, where moth and rust consume and where thieves break in and steal, but lay up for yourselves treasure in heaven, where neither moth nor rust consumes and where thieves do not break in and steal. For where your treasure is, there will your heart be also. The eye is the lamp of the body. So, if your eye is sound, your whole body will be full of light; but if your eye is not sound, your whole body will be full of darkness. If then the light in you is darkness, how great is the darkness!

No one can serve two masters; for either he will hate the one and love the other, or he will be devoted to the one and despise the other. You cannot serve God and mammon. Therefore I tell you, do not be anxious about your life, what you shall eat or what you shall drink, nor about your body, what you shall put on. Is not life more than food, and the body more than clothing? Look at the birds of the air: they neither sow nor reap nor gather into barns, and yet your heavenly Father feeds them. Are you not of more value than they?

And which of you by being anxious can add one cubit to his span of life? And why are you anxious about clothing? Consider the lilies of the field, how they grow; they neither toil nor spin; yet I tell you, even Solomon in all his glory was not arrayed like one of these. But if God so clothes the grass of the field, which today is alive and tomorrow is thrown into the oven, will he not much more clothe you, O men of little faith? Therefore do not be anxious, saying, 'What shall we eat?' or 'What shall we drink?' or 'What shall we wear?' For the gentiles seek all these things; and your heavenly Father knows that you need them all. But seek first his kingdom and his righteousness, and all these things shall be yours as well. Therfore do not be anxious about tomorrow, for tomorrow will be anxious for itself. Let the day's own trouble be sufficient for the day.

Judge not, that you be not judged. For with the judgement you pronounce you will be judged, and the measure you give will be the measure you get. Why do you week the speck that is in your brother's eye, but do not notice the log that is in your own eye? Or how can you say to your brother, 'Let me take the speck out of your eye,' when there is the log in your own eye? You hypocrite, first take the log out of your own eye, and then you will see clearly to take the speck out of your brother's eye.

Do not give dogs what is holy; and do not throw your pearls before swine, lest they trample them under foot and turn to attack you. Ask, and it will be given you; seek, and you will find; knock, and it will be opened to you. For everyone who asks receives, and he who seeks finds, and to him who knocks it will be opened. Or what man of you, if his son asks him for bread, will give him a stone? Or if he asks for a fish, will give him a serpent? If you then, who are evil, know how to give good gifts to your children, how much more will your father who is in heaven give good things to those who ask him!

So whatever you wish that men would do to you, do so to them; for this is the law and the prophets.

Enter by the narrow gate; for the gate is wide and the way is easy, that leads to destruction, and those who enter by it are many. For the gate is narrow and the way is hard, that leads to life, and those who find it are few. Beware of false prophets, who come to you in sheep's clothing but inwardly are ravenous wolves. You will know them by their fruits. Are grapes gathered from thorns, or figs from thistles? So, every sound tree bears good fruit, but the bad tree bears evil fruit. A second tree cannot bear evil fruit, nor can a bad tree bear good fruit. Every tree that does not bear food fruit is cut down and thrown into the fire. Thus you will know the by their fruits.

Not every one who says to me, 'Lord, Lord,' shall enter the kingdom of heaven, but he who does the will of my Father who is in heaven. On that day many will say to me, 'Lord, Lord, did we not prophesy in your name, and cast out demons in your name, and do many mighty works in your name?'

And the will I declare to them, 'I never knew you; depart from me, your evildoers'.

Every one then who hears these words of mine and does them will be like a wise man who built his house upon the rock; and the rain fell, and the floods came, and the winds blew and beat upon that house, but it did not fall, because it had been founded on the rock. And every one who hears these words of mine and does not do them will be like a foolish man who built his house upon the sand; and the rain fell, and the floods came, and the winds blew and beat against that house, and it fell; and great was the fall of it.'

And when Jesus finished these sayings, the crowds were astonished at his teaching, for he taught them as one who had authority, and not as their scribes.

(Matthew, Chapters 5,6 and 7)

A Hymn for the Incarnation   7.3.11

Praise to the Holiest in the height,
And in the depth be praise,
In all his words most wonderful,
Most sure in all his ways.

Oh loving wisdom of our God!
When all was sin and shame,
A second Adam to the fight,

And to the rescue came.

Oh wisest love! that flesh and blood
Which did in Adam fail,
Should strive afresh against the foe,
Should strive and should prevail.

And that a higher gift than grace
Should flesh and blood refine,
God's presence and his very self,
And Essence all divine.

Oh generous love! that he who smote
In man for man the foe,
The double agony in man
For man should undergo.

And in the garden secretly,
And on the Cross on high,
Should teach his brethren, and inspire
To suffer and to die.

Praise to the Holiest in the height,
And in the depth be praise,
In all his words most wonderful,
Most sure in all his ways.

John Henry Newman

7.3.12 A Hymn for the Birth of Christ

Hark the herald Angels sing
Glory to the new-born King;
Peace on earth and mercy mild,
God and sinners reconciled:
Joyful all ye nations rise,
Join the triumph of the skies,
With th 'angelic host proclaim,
Christ is born in Bethelehem,
    Hark! the herald Angels sing
    Glory to the new-born King.

Christ by highest heaven adored,
Christ the everlasting Lord,
Late in time behold him come
Offspring of a Virgin's womb!
Veiled in flesh the Godhead see,
Hail the incarnate Deity!
Pleased as man with man to dwell,
Jesus, our Emmanuel.
    Hark! the herald Angels sing
    Glory to the new-born King.

Hail the heaven-born Prince of Peace!
Hail the Sun of Righteousness!
Light and life to all he brings,
Risen with healing in his wings;
Mild he lays his glory by,
Born that man no more may die,
Born to raise the sons of earth,
Born to give them second birth.
    Hark! the herald Angels sing
    Glory to the new-born King.

By Charles Wesley, George Whitefield, Martin Madan and others.

A Hymn for Christ's Saving Death upon the Cross   7.3.13

The royal banners forward go,
The cross shines forth in mystic glow;
Where he in flesh, our flesh who made,
Our sentence bore, our ransom paid.

There whilst he hung, his sacred side
By soldier's spear was open'd wide,
To cleanse us in the precious flood
Of water mingled with his blood.

Fulfill'd is now what David told
In true prophetic song of old,
How God the heathen's King should be;
For God is reigning from the tree.

Oh tree of glory, tree most fair,

Ordain'd those holy limbs to bear,
How bright in purple robe it stood,
The purple of a Saviour's blood!

Upon its arms, like balance true,
He weigh'd the price for sinners due,
The price which none but he could pay,
And spoil'd the spoiler of his prey.

To thee, eternal Three in One,
Let homage meet by all be done;
As by the Cross thou dost restore,
So rule and guide us ever more.

Vexilla Regis Proeunt: original Latin words by Venantius Fortunatus, sixth century English translation by John Mason Neale and others.

7.3.14 To Pay the Price of Sin

There is a green hill far away,
Without a city wall,
Where the dear Lord was crucified
Who died to save us all.

We may not know, we cannot tell,
What pains he had to bear,
But we believe it was for us
He hung and suffered there.

He died that we might be forgiven,
He died to make us good;
That we might go at last to Heaven,
Saved by the precious blood.

There was no other good enough
To pay the price of sin;
He only could unlock the gate
Of heaven, and let us in.

O, dearly, dearly has he loved,
And we must love him too,
And trust in his redeeming blood,

And try his works to do.

Cecil Frances Alexander.

Love so Amazing 7.3.15

When I survey the wondrous Cross,
On which the Prince of glory died,
My richest gain I count but loss,
And pour contempt on all my pride.

Forbid it, Lord, that I should boast
Save in the death of Christ my God;
All the vain things that charm me most,
I sacrifice them to his Blood.

See from his head, his hands, his feet,
Sorrow and love flow mingled down;
Did e'er such love and sorrow meet,
Or thorns compose so rich a crown?

His dying crimson like a robe,
Spreads o'er his body on the Tree;
Then am I dead to all the globe,
And all the globe is dead to me.

Were the whole realm of nature mine,
That were an offering far too small;
Love so amazing, so divine,
Demands my soul, my life, my all.

Isaac Watts, 1674-1748.

A Hymn for Christ's Resurrection 7.3.16

Christ the Lord is risen today,
Christians haste your vows to pay;
Offer ye your praises meet
At the Paschal victim's feet;
For the sheep the Lamb hath bled,
Sinless in the sinner's stead,
Christ is risen today we cry,
Now he lives no more to die.

Christ, the victim undefiled,
Man to God hath reconciled;
Whilst in strange and awful strife
Met together death and life;
Christians, on this happy day
Haste with joy your vows to pay,
Christ is risen today we cry,
Now he lives no more to die.

Christ, who once for sinners bled,
Now the first-born from the dead,
Throned in endless might and power,
Lives and reigns for evermore.
Hail, eternal hope on high!
Hail, thou King of victory!
Hail, thou Prince of life adored!
Help and save us, gracious Lord.

Original Latin words by Wipo, eleventh century; English translation by
Jane E. Leeson.

7.3.17　A Hymn for the Church

The Church's one foundation
Is Jesus Christ, her Lord;
She is his new creation
By water and the Word:
From heaven he came and sought her
To be his holy Bride,
With his own Blood he bought her,
And for her life he died.

Elect from every nation,
Yet one o'er all the earth,
Her charter of salvation
One Lord, one Faith, one Birth;
One holy name she blesses,
Partakes one holy Food,
And to one hope she presses
With every grace endued.

'Mid toil and tribulation,

And tumult of her war,
She waits the consummation
Of peace for evermore;
Till with the vision glorious
Her longing eyes are blest,
And the great Church victorious
Shall be the Church at rest.

Yet she on earth hath union
With God the Three in One,
And mystic sweet communion
With those whose rest in won
Oh happy ones and holy!
Lord, give us grace that we
Like them, the meek and lowly,
On high may dwell with thee.

S.J. Stone

A Lesson in the Duties of Life 7.3.18

Question: You said that your Godfathers and Godmothers did promise for you, that you should keep God's Commandments. Tell me how many there be?

Answer: Ten.

Question: Which be they?

[Here follow the Ten Commandments, taken from the Book of Exodus, Chapter 20, which have already been given above in §6.1.3]

Question: What dost thou chiefly learn by these Commandments?

Answer: I learn two things: my duty towards God, and my duty towards my Neighbour.

Question: What is thy duty towards God?

Answer: My duty towards God is to believe in him, to fear him, and to love him with all my heart, with all my mind, with all my soul and with all my strength; to worship him, to give him thanks, to put my whole trust in him, to call upon him, to honour his holy Name and his Word, and to serve him truly all the days of my life.

Question: What is thy duty towards thy Neighbour?

Answer: My duty towards my Neighbour is to love him as myself, and to do to all men as I would they should do unto me:

To love, honour and succour my father and mother: To honour and obey the Queen, and all that are put in authority under her: To submit myself to all my governors, teachers, spiritual pastors and masters: To order myself lowly and reverently to all my betters: To hurt nobody by word nor deed: To be true and just in all my dealing: To bear no malice nor hatred in my heart: To keep my hands from picking and stealing, and my tongue from evil-speaking, lying and slandering: To keep my body in temperance, soberness and chastity: Not to covet nor desire other men's goods; but to learn and labour truly to get mine own living, and to do my duty in that state of life unto which it shall please God to call me.

Catechist: My good child, know this, that thou art not able to do these things of thyself, nor to walk in the commandments of God and to serve him, without his special grace; which thou must learn at all times to call for by diligent prayer.

7.3.19 A Modern Prophetic Vision

Extract from *A Catechism, that is to say, An Instruction to be learned of every person before he be Brought to be Confirmed by the Bishop,* which is printed in *The Book of Common Prayer* of the Church of England.

Christ, principal of universal vitality because sprung up as man among men, put himself in the position (maintained ever since) to subdue under himself, to purify, to direct and superanimate the general ascent of consciousness into which he inserted himself. By a perennial act of communion and sublimation, he aggregates to himself the total psychism of the earth. And when he has gathered everything together and transformed everything, he will close in upon himself and his conquests, thereby rejoining, in a final gesture, the divine focus he never left. Then, as St Paul tells us, *God shall be all in all.* This is indeed a superior form of 'pantheism' without trace of the poison of adulteration or annihilation: the expectation of perfect unity, steeped in which each element will reach its consummation at the same time as the universe . . .

It is relatively easy to build up a theory of the world. But it is beyond the powers of an individual to provoke artificially the birth of a religion. Plato, Spinoza and Hegel were able to elaborate views which compete in amplitude with the perspectives of the Incarnation. Yet none of these metaphysical systems advanced beyond the limits of an ideology. Each in turn has perhaps brought light to men's minds, but without ever succeeding in begetting life. What to the eyes of a 'natural scientist' comprises the importance and the enigma of the Christian phenomenon is its existence-value and reality-value. . .

It is doubtless a quantitative value of life if measured by its radius of action; but it is still more a qualitative value which expresses itself − like all biological progress − by the appearance of a specifically new state of consciousness. I am thinking here of Christian love . . . Christian love is incomprehensible to those who have not experienced it. That the infinite and the intangible can be lovable, or that the human heart can beat with genuine charity for a fellow-being, seems impossible to many people I know − in fact almost monstrous. But whether it be founded on an illusion or not, how can we doubt that such a sentiment exists, and even in great intensity? We have only to note crudely the results it produces unceasingly all around us . . . Lastly, is it not a fact, as I can warrant, that if the love of God were extinguished in the souls of the faithful, the enormous edifice of rites, of hierarchy and of doctrines that comprise the Church would instantly revert to the dust from which it rose? . . .

Alone, unconditionally alone in the world today, Christianity shows itself able to reconcile, in a single living act, the All and the Person. Alone, it can bend our hearts not only to the service of that tremendous movement of the world which bears us along, but beyond, to embrace that movement in love.

Pierre Teilhard de Chardin, *The Phenomenon of Man*, Collins 1974, pp.323, 323-4, 326.

General Note:

All Scripture references in §7.3 are taken from the Revised Standard Version.

7.4 CREEDS AND CONFESSIONS

7.4.1 A Second-century Testimony

The Church, though dispersed throughout the whole world even to the ends of the earth, has received from the Apostles and their disciples this faith: faith in one God, the Father Almighty, Maker of heaven and earth and the sea and all things that are in them; and in one Christ Jesus, the Son of God, who became incarnate for our salvation; and in the Holy Spirit, who proclaimed through the prophets the dispensations of God; and the coming of the beloved Christ Jesus Our Lord, and his birth from a virgin, and his passion, and his resurrection from the dead, and his ascension into heaven in the flesh; and his future manifestation from heaven in the glory of the Father 'to gather all things in one', and to raise up anew all flesh of the whole human race; in order that to Christ Jesus, our Lord and God and Saviour and King, according to the will of the invisible Father, 'every knee should bow, of things in heaven, and things in earth, and things under the earth, and every tongue should confess' to him; and that he should execute just judgement towards all; that he may send into everlasting fire all spiritual evils, and the angels who transgressed and became apostates, together with the ungodly and unrighteous and wicked and profane among men; but may, in the exercise of his grace, confer immortality on the righteous and holy and those who have kept his commandments, and have persevered in his love, some from the beginning and others from the time of their repentance, and may surround them with everlasting glory.

From Irenaeus, *Against Heresies* 1.10:1 about 190 C.E.

7.4.2 The Nicene Creed

I believe in one God the Father Almighty, Maker of heaven and earth, and of all things visible and invisible; and in one Lord Jesus Christ, the only-begotten Son of God, begotten of his Father before all worlds, God of God, Light of Light, very God of very God, begotten not made, being of one substance with the Father; by whom all things were made; who for us men and for our salvation came down from heaven, and was incarnate by the Holy Ghost of the Virgin Mary, and was made man; and was crucified also for us under Pontius Pilate. He suffered and was buried. And the third day he rose again according to the Scriptures; and ascended into heaven, and sitteth on the right hand of the Father. And he shall come again with glory to judge both the quick and the dead; whose kingdom shall have no end. And I believe in the Holy Ghost, the Lord and giver of life, who proceedeth from the Father and the Son; who with the Father and the Son together is worshipped and glorified; who spake by the prophets. And I believe one Catholic and Apostolic Church. I acknowledge one baptism for the remission of sins. And I look for the resurrection of the dead, and the life of the world to come. Amen.

The Athanasian Creed

7.4.3

Whosoever will be saved, before all things it is necessary that he hold the catholic faith. Which faith, except everyone do keep whole and undefiled, without doubt he shall perish everlastingly. And the catholic faith is this: that we worship one God in Trinity and Trinity in Unity; neither confounding the Person nor dividing the Substance. For there is one person of the Father, another of the Son, and another of the Holy Ghost. But the godhead of the Father, of the Son, and of the Holy Ghost, is all one: the glory equal, the majesty co-eternal. Such as the Father is, such is the Son, and such is the Holy Ghost. . .for like as we are compelled by the Christian verity to acknowledge every Person by himself to be God and Lord, so are we forbidden by the catholic religion to say there be three Gods or three Lords. The Father is made of none; neither created nor begotten. The Son is of the Father alone; not made, nor created, but begotten. The Holy Ghost is of the Father and of the Son; neither made, nor created, nor begotten, but proceeding. So there is one Father, not three Fathers; one Son, not three Sons; one Holy Ghost, not three Holy Ghosts. And in this Trinity none is afore or after other; none is greater or less than another. But the whole three Persons are co-eternal together and co-equal. So that in all things, as is aforesaid, the Unity in Trinity and the Trinity in Unity is to be worshipped. He therefore that will be saved must thus think of the Trinity. Furthermore it is necessary to everlasting salvation that he also believe rightly the Incarnation of our Lord Jesus Christ. For the right faith is that we believe and confess that our Lord Jesus Christ, the Son of God, is God and Man: God, of the substance of the Father, begotten before the worlds; and Man, of the substance of his mother, born in the world; perfect God and perfect Man; of a reasonable soul and human flesh subsisting; equal to the Father, as touching his godhead and inferior to the Father as touching his manhood. Who although he be God and Man, yet he is not two but one Christ; one, not by conversion of the godhead into flesh, but by taking of the manhood into God; one altogether, not by confusion of substance, but by unity of Person. For as the reasonable soul and flesh is one man, so God and Man is one Christ. Who suffered for our salvation, descended into hell, rose again the third day from the dead. He ascended into heaven, he sitteth on the right hand of the Father, God Almighty; from whence he shall come to judge the quick and the dead. At whose coming all men shall rise again with their bodies, and shall give account for their own works. And they that have done good shall go into life everlasting; and they that have done evil into everlasting fire. This is the catholic faith, which except a man believe faithfully, he cannot be saved.

The so-called Athanasian Creed was formulated in the West about the middle of the sixth century; this is a sixteenth-century English translation.

7.4.4   A Creed Proposed by the Second Council of Lyons (1274)

We believe in the holy Trinity, the Father and the Son and the Holy Spirit, one God Almighty; the whole deity in Trinity; co-essential and consubstantial, co-eternal and co-almighty; of one will, power and majesty; Creator of all creatures, from whom proceed all things, in whom are all things, to whom all things are, both in heaven and on earth, whether visible or invisible, corporal or spiritual. We believe each person in the Trinity to be the one true God, full and perfect.

We believe that the Son of God, the Word of God, eternally born from the Father, consubstantial, co-almighty and equal in all things with the Father in Godhead, was born in time from the Holy Spirit and from Mary ever Virgin, with a rational soul; that he has two modes of generation, one the eternal generation from the Father, the other his temporal birth from his mother. He is true God and true man, properly existing and perfect in both natures; one and only Son of God, Son not by adoption or in appearance only. He is in and from those two natures, namely divine and human, in the uniqueness of one person. He is impassible and immortal by his divinity, but in his humanity he suffered for us and for our salvation by a true passion of his flesh; he died and was buried, and descended into hell; and on the third day he rose again from the dead in a true resurrection of the flesh; on the fortieth day after his resurrection he ascended into heaven, with both risen body and soul. He is seated at the right hand of God the Father, and thence he will come to judge the living and the dead, and to render to each one according to his works, whether good or evil.

We also believe in the Holy Spirit, full, perfect and true God, proceeding from the Father and from the Son, coequal and consubstantial and co-almighty and co-eternal in all things with the Father and the Son. We believe that this Holy Trinity is not three Gods, but one almighty God, eternal and invisible and unchangeable.

We believe that there is one, true, Catholic and Apostolic Church, in which there is given one holy baptism and true remission of all sins. We also believe in true resurrection of this flesh which we now carry, and in life everlasting. We also believe that there is one author of the New and Old Testament, containing the Law, and the writings of the Prophets and Apostles — the Lord God Almighty. . .

As to the lot of those who have died if, truly penitent, they have died in a state of charity, but before they have made satisfaction, by due works of penance, for their sins — for what they have done or left undone — in their case, their souls are purified by purgatorial or cleansing punishments. . . To relieve them from these punishments the suffrages of the faithful alive on earth assist them — namely the sacrifices of Masses, the prayers and almsdeeds and other works of piety, which the faithful are wont to perform for their fellow-Christians according to the institution of the Church. In the case of the souls of those who, after they have received holy baptism, have incurred no stain of sin at all, they are received at once into heaven. The same is true of those who, though they have contracted some stain of sin, but have been purified in the manner aforesaid, whether while still in their bodies or when they have put them aside at death. But the souls of those who die either in a state of mortal sin or with original sin alone, descend at once into hell; the punishments for those two classes are diverse. Nevertheless, the holy Roman Church firmly believes and firmly declares that in the day of judgement all men will appear before the tribunal of Christ with their own bodies, in order to give an account of their own deeds.

From the Profession of Faith, tendered by the Council for subscription by Michael Palaeologos, the Byzantine Emperor.

From the Lutheran Augsburg Confession (1530)   7.4.5

It is taught among us that since the fall of Adam all men who are born according to the course of nature are conceived and born in sin. That is, all men are full of evil lusts and inclinations from their mother's wombs and are unable by nature to have true fear of God and true faith in God. Moreover, this inborn sickness and hereditary sin is truly sin and condemns to the eternal wrath of God all those who are not born again through baptism and the Holy Spirit. Rejected in this connection are the Pelagians and others who deny that original sin is sin, for they hold that natural man is made righteous by his own powers, thus disparaging the sufferings and merit of Christ.

It is also taught among us that God the Son became man, born of the Virgin Mary, and that the two natures, divine and human, are so inseparably united in one person that there is one Christ, true God and true man, who was truly born, suffered, was crucified, died, and was buried in order to be a sacrifice not only for original sin but also for all other sins and to propitiate God's wrath. The same Christ also descended into hell, truly rose from the dead on the third day, ascended into heaven, and sits on the right hand of God, that he may eternally rule and have dominion over all creatures, that through the Holy Spirit he may sanctify, purify, strengthen, and comfort all who believe in him, that he may bestow on them life and every grace and blessing, and that he may protect and defend them against the devil and against sin. The same Lord Jesus Christ will return openly to judge the living and the dead, as stated in the Apostles' Creed.

It is also taught among us that we cannot obtain forgiveness of sin and righteousness before God by our own merits, works, or satisfactions, but that we receive forgiveness of sin and become righteous before God by grace, for Christ's sake, through faith, when we believe that Christ suffered for us and that for his sake our sin is forgiven and righteousness and eternal life are given to us. For God will regard and reckon this faith as righteousness, as Paul says in *Romans* 3:21-26 and 4:5

Articles II, III and IV of the Augsburg Confession, translated by Theodore G. Tappert, in *The Book of Concord*, Philadelphia, Muhlenberg Press 1959.

7.4.6   From the (Presbyterian) Westminster Confession (1646)

By the decree of God, for the manifestation of his glory, some men and angels are predestinated unto everlasting life, and others fore-ordained to everlasting death. The angels and men, thus predestinated and fore-ordained, are particularly and unchangeably designed; and their number is so certain and definite that it cannot be either increased or diminished. Those of mankind that are predestinated unto life, God, before the foundation of the world was laid, according to his eternal and immutable purpose, and the secret counsel and good pleasure of his will, hath chosen in Christ, unto everlasting glory, out of his mere free grace and love, without any foresight of faith or good works, or persevereance in either of them, or any other thing in the creature, as conditions, or causes moving him thereunto; and all to the praise of His glorious grace. As God hath appointed the elect unto glory, so hath he, by the eternal and most free purpose of his will, fore-ordained all the means thereunto. Wherefore they who are elected, being fallen in Adam, are redeemed by Christ, are effectually called unto faith in Christ by his Spirit working in due season, are justified, adopted, sanctified, and kept by his power through faith unto salvation. Neither are any other redeemed by Christ, effectually called, justified, adopted, sanctified, and saved, but the elect only. The rest of mankind God was pleased, according to the unsearchable counsel of his own will, whereby he extendeth or withholdeth mercy as he pleaseth, for the glory of his sovereign power over his creatures, to pass by, and to ordain them to dishonour and wrath for their sin, to the praise of his glorious justice... Our first parents, being seduced by the subtilty and temptation of Satan, sinned in eating the forbidden fruit. This their sin God was pleased, according to his wise and holy counsel, to permit, having purposed to order it to his own glory. By this sin they fell from their original righteousness and communion with God, and so became dead in sin, and wholly defiled in all the faculties and parts of soul and body. They being the root of all mankind, the guilt of this sin was imputed, and the same death in sin and corrupted nature conveyed to all their posterity descending from them by ordinary generation. From this original corruption, whereby we are utterly indisposed, disabled and made opposite to all good, and wholly inclined to all evil, do proceed all actual transgressions. This corruption of nature, during this life, doth remain in those that are regenerated; and although it be through Christ pardoned and mortified, yet both itself and all the motions thereof are truly and properly sin.

The Westminster Confession, Chapters 3 and 6; text in *Creeds of Christendom* by Philip Schaff, Vol.3, New York, Harper and Brothers 1877.

7.4.7   From the Orthodox Confession of Dositheus (1672)

We believe the most good God to have from eternity predestinated unto glory those whom he hath chosen, and to have confined unto condemnation those whom he hath rejected; but not so that he would justify the one, and consign and condemn the other without cause. For that were contrary to the nature of God, who is the common Father of all, and no respecter of persons, and would have all men to be saved, and to come to the knowledge of the truth; but since he foreknew the one would make a right use of their free-will, and the other a wrong, he predestinated the one, or condemned the other ... But to say, as the most heretics do, that God, in predestinating or condemning, had in no wise regard to the works of those predestinated or condemned, we know to be profane and impious ...

And because the Maker is good by nature, he made all things very good whatsoever he hath made, nor can he ever be the maker of evil. But if there be aught evil, that is to say, sin, come about contrarily to the divine will, in man or in demon — for that evil is simply in nature, we do not acknowledge — it is either of man or of the devil ...

We believe the first man created by God to have fallen in Paradise, when, disregarding the divine commandment, he yielded to the deceitful counsel of the serpent. And hence hereditary sin flowed to his posterity; so that none is born after the flesh who beareth not this burden, and experienceth not the fruits thereof in this present world. But by these fruits and this burden we do not understand sin, such as impiety, blasphemy, murder, sodomy, adultery, fornication, enmity, and whatsoever else is by our depraved choice committed contrarily to the divine will ... but only what the divine justice inflicted upon man as a punishment for the [original] transgression, such as sweats in labour, afflictions, bodily sicknesses, pains in child-bearing, and in fine, while on our pilgrimage, to live a laborious life, and lastly, bodily death.

From the third, fourth and sixth decrees of *The Acts and Decrees of the Synold of Jerusalem,* translated by J.N.W.B. Robertson, Thomas Baker, London 1899.

7.4.8   A Declaration of the Second Vatican Council (1964)

The Eternal Father, by a free and hidden plan of his own wisdom and goodness, created the whole world. His plan was to raise men to a participation of the divine life. God the Father did not abandon men,

fallen in Adam, but ceaselessly offered helps to salvation, for the
sake of Christ, the Redeemer 'who is the image of the invisible God,
the first born of every creature' *(Col.* 1:15). All the elect, before
time began, the Father 'foreknew and predestined to become
conformed to the image of his Son, that he should be the first-born
among many brethren' *(Rom.* 8:29). He planned to assemble in the
Holy Church all those who would believe in Christ. Already from
the beginning of the world the foreshadowing of the Church took
place. It was prepared in a remarkable way throughout the history of
the people of Israel and by means of the Old Covenant. In the
present era of time the Church was constituted and, by the
outpouring of the Spirit, was made manifest. At the end of time it
will gloriously achieve completion, when, as is read in the Fathers,
all the just, from Adam and from Abel the just one, to the last of the
elect, will be gathered together with the Father in the universal
Church.

The Son therefore, came, sent by the Father. It was in him,
before the foundation of the world, that the Father chose us and
predestined us to become adopted sons, for in him it pleased the
Father to re-establish all things. To carry out the will of the Father,
Christ inaugurated the kingdom of Heaven on earth and revealed to
us the mystery of that kingdom. By his obedience he brought about
redemption. The church, or, in other words, the kingdom of Christ
now present in mystery, grows visibly through the power of God in
the world. This inauguration and this growth are both symbolised by
the blood and water which flowed from the open side of the
crucified Jesus *(John* 19:34), and are foretold in the words of the
Lord referring to his death on the cross: 'And I, if I be lifted up
from the earth, will draw all things to myself' *(John* 12:32). As
often as the sacrifice of the cross in which Christ our passover was
sacrificed (1 *Cor.* 5:7) is celebrated at the altar, the work of our
redemption is carried on; and, in the sacrament of the Eucharistic
bread, the unity of all believers who form one body in Christ is both
expressed and brought about. All men are called to this union with
Christ, who is the light of the world, from whom we go forth,
through whom we live, and towards whom our whole life tends.

When the work that the Father gave the Son to do on earth
was accomplished, the Holy Spirit was sent on the day of Pentecost
in order that he might continually sanctify the Church, and thus, all
those who believe would have access through Christ in one Spirit to the
Father. He is the Spirit of life, a fountain of water springing up to

life eternal. To men, dead in sin, the Father gives life through him, until the day when he will bring to life again, in Christ, their mortal bodies.

From the Constitution on the Church, *Lumen Gentium*, of the Second Vatican Council; English translation published by Darton, Longman and Todd 1965.

7.4.9 Anglican Attitudes to the Creeds Today

To many members of the Church of England the creeds are a norm of Christian belief, additional to though dependent upon the Bible. For them the creeds not only constitute vital links with the Church's past but also embody the standing truth of the gospel in the present ... They find the creeds to be mandatory for them because they have found the contents of the creeds to be true and significant; they do not embrace them simply because they are received as mandatory by others. They know that these verbal formularies, like the Biblical formulations which they more or less directly reflect, circumscribe mysteries whose depth no man can ever plumb ... They could not contemplate any replacing or superseding of the historic creeds as official formularies, for in their view it is precisely by the creeds, viewed as classical crystallizations of Biblical faith, that the new though forms and frameworks, and the assertions which they are used to make, must be measured and tested.

They do not wish to clamp down on the exploring of experimental theologies which for the moment might seem to have left the creeds behind. But they do maintain that any significant weakening in the corporate acceptance and use of the creeds would impair the Church of England's catholicity; and they hold therefore, that in Anglicanism the creeds are a norm, and that adherence to them is by Anglican standards essential.

A second approach to Christian belief may be described as on balance traditionalist in its general character; but those who adopt it vary in their detailed reactions to the historic credal formularies. On the negative side they have difficulties about individual clauses in the creeds. Sometimes this problem is resolved by stressing the symbolic character of the words, sometimes by emphasizing their historical context ... On the positive side, however, they feel that saying the Nicene Creed, for example, at the Eucharist along with their fellow Christians is one important way of expressing their faith in God through Christ, and of rejoicing in a unity of God's people which transcends time and finds its deepest earthly expression not so much in words as in the bond of the eucharistic action given by that God to whom the words refer.

Thirdly, there is a broad category of Christians whose convictions lead them to approach the creeds in a rather different way. They acknowledge with gratitude that, for those of them at least who were brought up in the Christian community and whose faith in God was fostered and developed there, the creeds have played an important formative part in their lives. But their allegiance now is rather to the continuing Church of God than to any past beliefs and formulations, which they regard as inevitably relative to the culture of the age which produced them ... They agree that the creeds are *de facto* without rivals as official formulations of Christian belief, but are in varying degrees unhappy at the thought that they should indefinitely continue to be so ... Such Christians would, therefore, like to see the Church investigate all possible ways in which it might testify to its profound concern for truth, leaving open the question whether or not these would be likely to take a credal form of any sort.

Finally, there are Christians for whom the essence of their faith is to be found in a life of discipleship rather than in credal affirmation. Such people may have their own doctrinal interpretation of life, but these doctrines seem to them to be relative to their own culture and temperament rather than permanent statements of their faith ... Such people do make theological affirmations but they do so by their lives and through their prayers. They commit themselves to the Reality whom men call God as their creator, their saviour, and their sanctifier; and they commit themselves also to a life of Christian discipleship in the sense of loyalty to Jesus and to his values, attitudes and teaching as depicted in the Gospels. They find in him a key to the truth about God and the world, and an authentic way of life. Commitment to God and to Jesus, understood in this sense, is more important to them than 'provisional' assent to credal propositions of any kind.

From an essay, 'The Christian and the Creeds' in a report entitled *Christian Believing* by the Doctrine Commission of the Church of England, SPCK 1976, pp.35-38.

8 ISLAM AND THE MUSLIM

[*Editor's Note:* Bishop Kenneth Cragg, the author of the Course section on Islam, has woven editorial notes into his choice of material from secondary Islamic sources. But the first part of his selected material is from the Qur'an, the sacred writings of the Muslims, the book which is accepted as being the Word of God in an absolute way since it has in the eyes of the believer come to them directly through Muhammad. It will be seen that Bishop Cragg has not used to the Surahs in the order in which they are found in A.J. Arberry's translation; the Roman number at the head of each Surah gives its position in the conventional order. Bishop Cragg places them in the following order: 114-90, 2, 57, 59, 23, 17, 24, 36, 52. Note also that Nos. 2, 59, 17, 24, 36 and 52 are not given in full, extracts only are used.]

8.1   SELECTIONS FROM THE KORAN

CXIV Men

8.1.1

In the Name of God; the Merciful, the Compassionate

Say: 'I take refuge with the Lord of men,
the King of men,
the God of men,
from the evil of the slinking whisperer
who whispers in the breasts of men
of jinn and men.

CXIII Daybreak

8.1.2

In the Name of God, the Merciful, the Compassionate

Say: 'I take refuge with the Lord of the Daybreak
from the evil of what He has created,
from the evil of darkness when it gathers,
from the evil of the women who blow on knots,
from the evil of an envier when he envies.'

CXII Sincere Religion

8.1.3

In the Name of God, the Merciful, the Compassionate

Say: 'He is God, One,
God, the Everlasting Refuge,
who has not begotten, and has not been begotten,
and equal to Him is not any one.'

CXI Perish

8.1.4

In the Name of God, the Merciful, the Compassionate

Perish the hands of Abu Lahab, and perish he!
His wealth avails him not, neither what he has earned;
he shall roast at a flaming fire
and his wife, the carrier of the firewood,
upon her neck a rope of palm-fibre.

8.1.5 CX Help

In the Name of God, the Merciful, the Compassionate

When comes the help of God, and victory
and thou seest men entering God's religion in throngs,
then proclaim the praise of thy Lord, and seek His forgiveness;
for He turns again unto men.

8.1.6 CIX The Unbelievers

In the Name of God, the Merciful, the Compassionate

Say: 'O unbelievers,
I serve not what you serve
and you are not serving what I serve,
nor am I serving what you have served,
neither are you serving what I serve.

To you your religion, and to me my religion!'

8.1.7 CVIII Abundance

In the Name of God, the Merciful, the Compassionate

Surely We have given thee abundance;
so pray unto thy Lord and sacrifice.
Surely he that hates thee, he is the one cut off.

8.1.8 CVII Charity

In the Name of God, the Merciful, the Compassionate

Hast thou seen him who cries lies to the Doom?
That is he who repulses the orphan
and urges not the feeding of the needy.

So woe to those that pray
and are heedless of their prayers,
to those who make display
and refuse charity.

CVI Koraish

8.1.9

In the Name of God, the Merciful, the Compassionate

For the composing of Koraish,
their composing for the winter and summer caravan!

So let them serve the Lord of this House
who has fed them against hunger,
and secured them from fear.

CV The Elephant

8.1.10

In the Name of God, the Merciful, the Compassionate

Hast thou not seen how thy Lord did with the Men of the Elephant?
Did He not make their guile to go astray?
And He loosed upon them birds in flights,
hurling against them stones of baked clay
and He made them like green blades devoured.

CIV The Backbiter

In the Name of God, the Merciful, the Compassionate

Woe unto every backbiter, slanderer,
who has gathered riches and counted them over
thinking his riches have made him immortal!

No indeed; he shall be thrust into the Crusher;
and what shall teach thee what is the Crusher?
The Fire of God kindled
roaring over the hearts
covered down upon them,
in columns outstretched.

CIII Afternoon

8.1.12

In the Name of God, the Merciful, the Compassionate

By the afternoon!
Surely Man is in the way of loss,
save those who believe, and do righteous deeds,
and counsel each other unto the truth,
and counsel each other to be steadfast.

8.1.13   **CII Rivalry**

In the Name of God, the Merciful, the Compassionate

Gross rivalry diverts you,
even till you visit the tombs,
No indeed; but soon you shall know.
Again, no indeed; but soon you shall know.
No indeed; did you know with the knowledge of certainty,
you shall surely see Hell.
Again, you shall surely see it with the eye of uncertainty
then you shall be questioned that day concerning true bliss.

8.1.14   **CI The Clatterer**

In the Name of God, the Merciful, the Compassionate

The Clatterer! What is the Clatterer
And what shall teach thee what is the Clatterer?
The day that men shall be like scattered moths,
and the mountains shall be like plucked wool-tufts.

Then he whose deeds weigh heavy in the Balance
shall inherit a pleasing life,
but he whose deeds weigh light in the Balance
shall plunge in the womb of the Pit.
And what shall teach thee what is the Pit?
A blazing Fire!

8.1.15   **C The Chargers**

In the Name of God, the Merciful, the Compassionate

By the snorting chargers
by the strikers of fire,
by the dawn-raiders,
blazing a trail of dust
cleaving there with a host!
Surely Man is ungrateful to his Lord,
and surely he is a witness against that!
Surely he is passionate in his love for good things.
Knows he not that when that which is in the tombs is overthrown,
and that which is in the breasts is brought out —
surely on that day their Lord shall be aware of them!

XCIX The Earthquake 8.1.16

In the Name of God, the Merciful, the Compassionate

When earth is shaken with a mighty shaking
and earth brings forth her burdens,
and Man says, 'What ails her?'
upon that day she shall tell her tidings
for that her Lord has inspired her.

Upon that day men shall issue in scatterings to see their works,
and whoso has done an atom's weight of good shall see it,
and whoso has done an atom's weight of evil shall see it.

XCVIII The Clear Sign 8.1.17

In the Name of God, the Merciful, the Compassionate

The unbelievers of the People of the Book
and the idolaters would never leave off,
till the Clear Sign came to them,
a Messenger from God, reciting pages purified
therein true Books.
And they scattered not, those that were given the Book,
excepting after the Clear Sign came to them.
They were commanded only to serve God,
making the religion His sincerely,
men of pure faith, and to perform
the prayer, and pay the alms — that is
the religion of the True.

The unbelievers of the People of the Book
and the idolaters shall be in the Fire of Gehenna,
therein dwelling forever;
those are the worst of creatures.
But those who believe, and do righteous deeds,
those are the best of creatures;
their recompense is with their Lord —
Gardens of Eden, underneath which rivers flow,
therein dwelling for ever and ever.
God is well-pleased with them, and they are well-pleased with Him;
that is for him who fears his Lord.

8.1.18   XCVII Power

In the Name of God the Merciful, the Compassionate

Behold, We sent it down on the Night of Power;
And what shall teach thee what is the Night of Power?
The Night of Power is better than a thousand months;
in it the angels and the Spirit descend,
by the leave of their Lord, upon every command.
Peace it is, till the rising of dawn.

8.1.19   XCVI The Blood-Clot

In the Name of God, the Merciful, the Compassionate

Recite: In the Name of thy Lord who created,
created Man of a blood-clot.
Recite: And thy Lord is the Most Generous,
who taught by the Pen,
taught Man that he knew not.

No indeed; surely Man waxes insolent,
for he thinks himself self-sufficient.
Surely unto thy Lord is the Returning.

What thinkest thou? He who forbids
a servant when he prays —
What thinkest thou? If he were upon guidance
or bade to godfearing —
What thinkest thou? If he cries lies, and turns away —
Did he not know that God sees?

No indeed; surely, if he gives not over,
We shall seize him by the forelock,
a lying, sinful forelock.
So let him call on his concourse!
We shall call on the guards of Hell.

No indeed; do thou not obey him,
and bow thyself, and draw nigh.

XCV The Fig

In the Name of God, the Merciful, the Compassionate

By the fig and the olive
and the Mount Sinai
and this land secure!
We indeed created Man in the fairest stature
then We restored him the lowest of the low —
save those who believe, and do righteous deeds;
they shall have a wage unfailing.

What then shall cry thee lies as to the Doom?
Is not God the justest of judges?

XCIV The Expanding

In the Name of God, the Merciful, the Compassionate

Did We not expand thy breast for thee
and lift from thee thy burden,
the burden that weighed down thy back?
Did We not exalt thy fame?

So truly with hardship comes ease,
truly with hardship comes ease.
So, when thou art empty, labour,
and let thy Lord be thy Quest.

XCIII The Forenoon

In the Name of God, the Merciful, the Compassionate

By the white forenoon
and the brooding night!
Thy Lord has neither foresaken thee nor hates thee
and the Last shall be better for thee than the First.
Thy Lord shall give thee, and thou shalt be satisfied.

Did He not find thee an orphan, and shelter thee?
Did He not find thee erring, and guide thee?
Did He not find thee needy, and suffice thee?

As for the orphan, do not oppress him,
As for the beggar, scold him not;
and as for thy Lord's blessing, declare it.

8.1.23 **XCII The Night**

In the Name of God, the Merciful, the Compassionate

By the night enshrouding
and the day in splendour
and That which created the male and the female,
surely your striving is to diverse ends.

As for him who gives and is godfearing
and confirms the reward most fair,
We shall surely ease him to the Easing.
But as for him who is a miser, and self-sufficient,
and cries lies to the reward most fair,
We shall surely ease him to the Hardship;
his wealth shall not avail him when he perishes.

Surely upon Us rests the guidance,
and to Us belong the Last and the First.

Now I have warned you of a Fire that flames,
whereat none but the most wretched shall be roasted,
even he who cried lies, and turned away;
and from which the most godfearing shall be removed,
even he who gives his wealth to purify himself
and confers no favour on any man for recompense,
only seeking the Face of his Lord the Most High;
and he shall surely be satisfied.

8.1.24 **XCI The Sun**

In the Name of God, the Merciful, the Compassionate

By the sun and his morning brightness
and by the moon when she follows him,
and by the day when it displays him
and by the night when it enshrouds him!
By the heaven and That which built it
and by the earth and That which extended it!
By the soul, and That which shaped it
and inspired it to lewdness and godfearing!
Prosperous is he who purifies it,
and failed has he who seduces it.

Thamood cried lies in their insolence
when the most wretched of them uprose,
then the Messenger of God said to them,
'The She-camel of God; let her drink!'
But they cried him lies, and hamstrung her,
so their Lord crushed them for their sin, and levelled them:
and He fears not the issue thereof.

XC The Land 8.1.25

In the Name of God, the Merciful, the Compassionate

No! I swear by this land,
and thou art a lodger in this land;
by the begetter, and that he begot,
indeed, We created man in trouble.
What, does he think none has power over him,
saying, 'I have consumed wealth abundant'?
What, does he think none has seen him?

Have We not appointed to him two eyes,
and a tongue, and two lips,
and guided him on the two highways?
Yet he has not assaulted the steep;
and what shall teach thee what is the steep?
The freeing of a slave,
or giving food upon a day of hunger
to an orphan near of kin
or a needy man in misery;
then that he become of those who believe
and counsel each other to be steadfast,
and counsel each other to be merciful.

Those are the Companions of the Right Hand.
And those who disbelieve in Our signs,
they are the Companions of the Left Hand;
over them is a Fire covered down.

8.1.26 **II The Cow**

> It is not piety, that you turn your faces
>> to the East and to the West.
>>> True piety is this:
> to believe in God, and the Last Day,
> the angels, the Book, and the Prophets,
> to give of one's substance, however cherished,
>> to kinsmen, and orphans,
> the needy, the traveller, beggars,
>> and to ransom the slave,
> to perform the prayer, to pay the alms.
> And they who fulfil their covenant
> when they have engaged in a covenant,
>> and endure with fortitude
>> misfortune, hardship and peril,
> these are they who are true in their faith,
>> these are the truly godfearing.

> O believers, prescribed for you is
> retaliation, touching the slain;
> freeman for freeman, slave for slave,
> female for female. But if aught is pardoned
> a man by his brother, let the pursuing
> be honourable, and let the payment be
> with kindliness. That is a lightening
> granted you by your Lord, and a mercy;
> and for him who commits aggression
> after that — for him there awaits
>> a painful chastisement.

175 > In retaliation there is life for you,
> men possessed of minds; haply you
>> will be godfearing.

> O believers, prescribed for you is
> the Fast, even as it was prescribed for
> those that were before you — haply you
>> will be godfearing —

180 > for days numbered; and if any of you
> be sick, or if he be on a journey,
> then a number of other days; and for those
> who are able to fast, a redemption

by feeding a poor man. Yet better
it is for him who volunteers good,
and that you should fast is better for you,
    if you but know;
the month of Ramadan, wherein the Koran
was sent down to be a guidance
to the people, and as clear signs
of the Guidance and the Salvation.
So let those of you, who are present
at the month, fast it; and if any of you
be sick, or if he be on a journey,
then a number of other days; God desires
ease for you, and desires not hardship
for you; and that you fulfil the number, and
magnify God that He has guided you, and haply
    you will be thankful.

And when My servants question thee
concerning Me — I am near to answer
the call of the caller, when he calls
to Me: so let them respond to Me,
and let them believe in Me; haply so
    they will go aright.

Permitted to you, upon the night of
the Fast, is to go in to your wives;
they are a vestment for you, and you are
a vestment for them. God knows that you have been
betraying yourselves, and has turned to you
and pardoned you. So now lie with them,
and seek what God has prescribed for you.
And eat and drink, until the white thread
shows clearly to you from the black thread
at the dawn; then complete the Fast
unto the night, and do not lie with them
while you cleave to the mosques. Those are
God's bounds; keep well within them. So God
makes clear His signs to men; haply they
    will be godfearing.

Consume not your goods between you
in vanity; neither proffer it
to the judges, that you may sinfully
consume a portion of other men's goods,
        and that wittingly.

185   They will question thee concerning
the new moons. Say: 'They are appointed
times for the people, and the Pilgrimage.'

It is not piety to come to the houses
from the backs of them; but piety is
to be godfearing; so come to the houses
by their doors, and fear God; haply so
        you will prosper.

And fight in the way of God with those
who fight with you, but aggress not: God loves
        not the aggressors.
And slay them wherever you come upon them,
and expel them from where they expelled you;
persecution is more grievous than slaying.
But fight them not by the Holy Mosque
until they should fight you there;
then, if they fight you, slay them —
such is the recompense of unbelievers —
but if they give over, surely God is
All-forgiving, All-compassionate.

Fight them, till there is no persecution
and the religion is God's; then if they
give over, there shall be no enmity
        save for evildoers.
190   The holy month for the holy month;
holy things demand retaliation.
Whoso commits aggression against you,
do you commit aggression against him
like as he has committed against you;
and fear you God, and know that God is
        with the godfearing.

And expend in the way of God;
and cast not yourselves by your own hands
into destruction, but be good-doers; God
     loves the good-doers.

Fulfil the Pilgrimage and the Visitation
unto God; but if you are prevented,
then such offering as may be feasible.
And shave not your heads, till the offering
reaches its place of sacrifice. If any
of you is sick, or injured in his head,
then redemption by fast, or freewill offering,
or ritual sacrifice. When you are secure,
then whosoever enjoys the Visitation
until the Pilgrimage, let his offering
be such as may be feasible; or if he
finds none, then a fast of three days
in the Pilgrimage, and of seven when
you return, that is ten completely;
that is for him, whose family are not
present at the Holy Mosque. And fear
God, and know that God is terrible
     in retribution.

The Pilgrimage is in months well-known;
whoso undertakes the duty of Pilgrimage
in them shall not go in to his womenfolk
nor indulge in ungodliness and disputing
in the Pilgrimage. Whatever good you do,
God knows it. And take provision;
but the best provision is godfearing,
so fear you Me, men possessed of minds!
It is no fault in you, that you should seek
bounty from your Lord; but when you press on
from Arafat, then remember God
at the Holy Waymark, and remember Him
as He has guided you, though formerly you
     were gone astray.

195   Then press on from where the people
       press on, and pray for God's forgiveness;
       God is All-forgiving, All-compassionate.
       And when you have performed your holy rites
       remember God, as you remember your fathers
       or yet more devoutly. Now some men
       there are who say, 'Our Lord, give to us
       in this world, such men shall have no part
                in the world to come.

       And others there are who say, 'Our Lord,
       give to us in this world good, and good
       in the world to come, and guard us against the
                chastisement of the Fire';
       those—they shall have a portion from
       what they have earned; and God is swift
                at the reckoning.

       And remember God during certain days
       numbered. If any man hastens on
       in two days, that is no sin in him;
       and if any delays, it is not a sin
       in him, if he be godfearing. And
       fear you God, and know that unto Him
                you shall be mustered.

8.1.27 LVII Iron

       In the Name of God, the Merciful, the Compassionate

       All that is in the heavens and the earth magnifies God;
                He is the All-mighty, the All-wise.
       To Him belongs the Kingdom of the heavens and the earth;
       He gives life, and He makes to die, and He is powerful
                over everything.
       He is the First and the Last, the Outward and the Inward;
                He has knowledge of everything.
          It is He that created the heavens and the earth
                in six days
             then seated Himself upon the Throne.
          He knows what penetrates into the earth,
                and what comes forth from it.

what comes down from heaven, and what goes up unto it.
He is with you wherever you are; and God sees
the things you do.

5 To Him belongs the Kingdom of the heavens and the earth;
and unto Him all matters are returned.
He makes the night to enter into the day
and makes the day to enter into the night.
He knows the thoughts within the breasts.

Believe in God and His Messenger, and expend of
that unto which He has made you successors. And
those of you who believe and expend shall have
a mighty wage.
How is it with you, that you believe not in God
seeing that the Messenger is calling you to
believe in your Lord, and He has taken compact
with you, if you are believers?
It is He who sends down upon His servant signs,
clear signs, that He may bring you forth from
the shadows into the light. Surely God is to you
All-gentle, All-compassionate.

10 How is it with you, that you expend not in the
way of God, and to God belongs the inheritance
of the heavens and the earth? Not equal is he
among you who spent, and who fought before the
victory; those are mightier in rank than they
who spent and fought afterwards; and unto each
God has promised the reward most fair; and God
is aware of the things you do.
Who is he that will lend to God a good loan,
and He will multiply it for him, and his shall be
a generous wage?

Upon the day when thou seest the believers, men and women,
their light running before them, and on their right hands.
'Good tidings for you today! Gardens underneath which
rivers flow, therein to dwell for ever; that is indeed
the mighty triumph.'
Upon the day when the hypocrites, men and women, shall say
to those who have believed, 'Wait for us, so that we may
borrow your light!' It shall be said, 'Return you back

behind, and seek for a light!' And a wall shall be set up
between them, having a door in the inward whereof is
mercy, and against the outward thereof is chastisement.
They shall be calling unto them, 'Were we not with you?'
They shall say, 'Yes indeed; but you tempted yourselves,
and you awaited, and you were in doubt, and fancies
deluded you, until God's commandment came, and the
Deluder deluded you concerning God. Therefore today
no ransom shall be taken from you, neither from those who
disbelieved. Your refuge is the Fire, that is your master —
            an evil homecoming!'

15   Is it not time that the hearts of those
      who believe should be humbled to the
      Remembrance of God and the Truth which
      He has sent down, and that they should
      not be as those to whom the Book was
      given aforetime, and the term seemed
      over long to them, so that their hearts
      have become hard, and many of them
            are ungodly?
      Know that God revives the earth after
      it was dead. We have indeed made clear
      for you the signs, that haply you will
            understand.
      Surely those, the men and the women,
      who make freewill offerings and have
      lent to God a good loan, it shall be
      multiplied for them, and theirs shall be
            a generous wage.
      And those who believe in God and His
      Messengers — they are the just men
      and the martyrs in their Lord's sight;
      they have their wage, and their light.
      But the unbelievers, who have cried lies
      to Our signs, they are the inhabitants
            of Hell.
      Know that the present life is but a
      sport and a diversion, an adornment
      and a cause for boasting among you,
      and a rivalry in wealth and children.

It is as a rain whose vegetation
pleases the unbelievers; then it
withers, and thou seest it turning
yellow, then it becomes broken orts.
And in the world to come there is a
    terrible chastisement,
20   and forgiveness from God and good pleasure;
and the present life is but the joy
    of delusion.
Race to forgiveness from your Lord,
and a Garden the breadth whereof is
as the breadth of heaven and earth,
made ready for those who believe in
God and His Messengers. That is the
bounty of God; He gives it unto

whomsoever He will; and God is of
    bounty abounding.
No affliction befalls in the earth
or in yourselves, but it is in a
Book, before We create it; that is
    easy for God;
that you may not grieve for what
escapes you, nor rejoice in what has
come to you; God loves not any man
    proud and boastful,
such as are niggardly, and bid men
to be niggardly. And whosoever
turns away, God is the All-sufficient,
    the All-laudable.

25   Indeed, We sent Our Messengers with
the clear signs, and We sent down
with them the Book and the Balance
so that men might uphold justice.
And we sent down iron, wherein is
great might, and many uses for men,
and so that God might know who
helps Him, and His Messengers,
in the Unseen. Surely God is
    All-strong, All-mighty.

And We sent Noah, and Abraham,
and We appointed the Prophecy and
the Book to be among their seed; and
some of them are guided, and many of
    them are ungodly.

    Then We sent, following
    in their footsteps, Our
    Messengers; and We sent,
    following, Jesus son of
    Mary, and gave unto him
      the Gospel.
And We set in the hearts of those who
followed him tenderness and mercy.

And monasticism they invented — We
did not prescribe it for them — only
seeking the good pleasure of God; but
they observed it not as it should be
observed. So We gave those of them
who believed their wage; and many of
    them are ungodly.

O believers, fear God, and believe
in His Messenger, and He will give you
a twofold portion of His mercy, and
He will appoint for you a light whereby
you shall walk, and forgive you; God is
    All-forgiving, All-compassionate;
that the People of the Book may know
that they have no power over anything
of God's bounty, and that bounty is in
the hand of God; He gives it unto
whomsoever He will; and God is of
    bounty abounding.

8.1.28   **LIX Exile**

O believers, fear God. Let every soul
consider what it has forwarded for the
morrow. And fear God; God is aware of
    the things you do.

Be not as those who forgot God, and so He
caused them to forget their souls, those —
    they áre the ungodly.
Not equal are the inhabitants of the
Fire and the inhabitants of Paradise.
The inhabitants of Paradise — they
    are the triumphant.

If We had sent down this Koran upon a mountain,
thou wouldst have seen it humbled, split asunder
    out of the fear of God.
And those similitudes — We strike them for men;
    haply they will reflect.

    He is God;
    there is no god but He.
He is the knower of the Unseen and the Visible;
He is the All-merciful, the All-compassionate.

    He is God;
    there is no god but He.
He is the King, the All-holy, the All-peaceable,
    the All-faithful, the All-preserver,
    the All-mighty, the All-compeller,
    the All-sublime.
Glory be to God, above that they associate!

    He is God,
    the Creator, the Maker, the Shaper.
To Him belong the Names Most Beautiful.
All that is in the heavens and the earth magnifies Him;
    He is the All-mighty, the All-wise.

XIII The Believers   8.1.29

In the Name of God, the Merciful, the Compassionate

    Prosperous are the believers
    who in their prayers are humble
    and from idle talk turn away
    and at almsgiving are active
5   and guard their private parts

save from their wives and what their right hands own
then being not blameworthy
(but whosoever seeks after more than that,
those are the transgressors)
and who preserve their trusts
and their covenant
and who observe their prayers.
10   Those are the inheritors
who shall inherit Paradise
therein dwelling forever.

We created man of an extraction
of clay,
then We set him, a drop, in a receptacle
secure,
then We created of the drop a clot
then We created of the clot a tissue
then We created of the tissue bones
then We garmented the bones in flesh;
thereafter We produced him as another creature.
So blessed be God, the fairest of creators!
15   Then after that you shall surely die,
then on the Day of Resurrection you
shall surely be raised up.
And We created above you seven ways,
and We were not heedless of creation.

And We sent down out of heaven water
in measure and lodged it in the earth;
and We are able to take it away.
Then We produced for you therewith
gardens of palms and vines
wherein are many fruits for
you, and of them you eat,
20   and a tree issuing from the Mount of Sinai that
bears oil and seasoning
for all to eat.
And surely in the cattle there is a lesson for you;
We give you to drink of
what is in their bellies,
and many uses there are in them for you,

and of them you eat;
and upon them, and on the ships, you are borne.

And We sent Noah to his people;
and he said, 'O my people, serve God!
You have no god other than He.
    Will you not be godfearing?'
Said the Council of the unbelievers
of his people, 'This is naught but
a mortal like yourselves, who desires
to gain superiority over you. And
if God willed, He would have sent down
angels. We never heard of this among
    our fathers, the ancients.
25   He is naught but a man bedevilled; so
    wait on him for a time.'
He said, 'O my Lord, help me,
    for that they cry me lies.'
Then We said to him, 'Make thou the Ark
under Our eyes and as We reveal,
and then, when Our command comes
    and the Oven boils,
insert in it two of every kind
and thy family — except for him
against whom the word already
has been spoken; and address Me not
concerning those who have done evil;
    they shall be drowned.
Then, when thou art seated in the Ark
and those with thee, say, "Praise belongs to
God, who has delivered us from the people
    of the evildoers."
50   And say, "O my Lord, do Thou harbour
me in a blessed harbour, for Thou art
    the best of harbourers." '
Surely in that are signs, and surely
    We put to the test.

Thereafter, after them, We produced
    another generation,
and We sent amongst them a Messenger

of themselves, saying, 'Serve God!
You have no god other than He.
 Will you not be godfearing?'
Said the Council of the unbelievers
of his people, who cried lies to the
encounter of the world to come,
and to whom We had given ease in the
present life, 'This is naught but
a mortal like yourselves, who eats
 of what you eat

35 and drinks of what you drink.
If you obey a mortal like yourselves,
 then you will be losers.
What, does he promise you that when you are
dead, and become dust and bones, you
 shall be brought forth?
  Away, away
 with that you are promised!
There is nothing but our present life;
we die, and we live, and we shall
 not be raised up.

40 He is naught but a man who has forged
against God a lie, and we will
 not believe him.'
He said, 'O my Lord, help me,
 for that they cry me lies.'
He said, 'In a little they will
 be remorseful.'
And the Cry seized them justly, and We
made them as scum; so away with the people
 of the evildoers!

Thereafter, after them, We produced
 other generations;

45 no nation outstrips its term, nor
 do they put it back.
Then sent We Our Messengers successively;
whenever its Messenger came to a nation
they cried him lies, so We caused some
of them to follow others, and We made them
as but tales; so away with a people
 who do not believe!

Then we sent Moses and his brother
Aaron with Our signs and a manifest
    authority
unto Pharaoh and his Council;
but they waxed proud, and they were
    a lofty people,
and they said, 'What, shall we believe
two mortals like ourselves, whose people
    are our servants?'
50   So they cried them lies, and they were
    among the destroyed.

And we gave Moses the Book, that haply
    they would be guided;
and We made Mary's son, and his mother,
to be a sign, and gave them refuge
upon a height, where was a hollow
    and a spring:
'O Messengers, eat of the good things
and do righteousness; surely I know
    the things you do.
Surely this community of yours
is one community, and I am your Lord;
    so fear Me.'
But they split in their affair between them
into sects, each party rejoicing in
    what is with them.
So leave thou them in their perplexity
    for a time.
What, do they think that We succour them with
    of wealth and children
We vie in good works for them? Nay, but
    they are not aware.

Surely those who tremble in fear of their Lord
60   and those who believe in the signs of their Lord
and those who associate naught with their Lord
and those who give what they give, their hearts
quaking that they are returning to their Lord —
those vie in good works, outracing to them.

We charge not any soul save to its capacity,
and with Us is a Book speaking truth, and
   they shall not be wronged.

65   Nay, but their hearts are in perplexity
as to this, and they have deeds besides that
   that they are doing.

Till, when We seize with the chastisement
the ones of them that live at ease,
   behold, they groan.

'Groan not today; surely you shall not be
   helped from Us.

My signs were recited to you, but upon your
   heels you withdrew,

waxing proud against it, talking foolish
   talk by night.'

70   Have they not pondered the saying, or came there
upon them that which came not upon their
   fathers, the ancients?

Or did they not recognise their Messenger
   and so denied him?

Or do they say, 'He is bedevilled'? Nay,
he has brought them the truth, but most of them are
   averse from the truth.

Had the truth followed their caprices,
the heavens and the earth and whosoever
in them is had surely corrupted. Nay, We
brought them their Remembrance, but from their
   Remembrance they turned.

Or dost thou ask them for tribute? Yet the
tribute of thy Lord is better, and He is the
   best of providers.

75   Assuredly thou art calling them
   to a straight path;

and surely they that believe not
in the world to come are deviating
   from the path.

Did We have mercy on them, and remove
the affliction that is upon them,
they would persist in their insolence
   wandering blindly.

We already seized them with the chastisement,

yet they abased not themselves to their Lord
    nor were they humble;
until, when We open against them a door
of terrible chastisement, lo, they are sore
    confounded at it.

80   It is He who produced for you hearing, and eyes, and hearts;
    little thanks you show.
It is He who scattered you in the earth, and to Him
    you shall be mustered.
It is He who gives life, and makes to die, and to Him
belongs the alternation of night and day; what,
    will you not understand?

Nay, but they said the like of what
    the ancients said.
They said, 'What, when we are dead
and become dust and bones, shall we be
    indeed raised up?
85   We and our fathers have been promised this
before; this is naught but the fairy-tales
    of the ancients.'
Say: 'Whose is the earth, and whoso is in it,
    if you have knowledge?'
They will say, 'God's.' Say: 'Will you not
    then remember?'
Say: 'Who is the Lord of the seven heavens
    and the Lord of the mighty Throne?'
They will say, 'God's.' Say: 'Will you not
    then be godfearing?'
Say: 'In whose hand is the dominion of
everything, protecting and Himself unprotected,
    if you have knowledge?'
They will say, 'God's.' Say: 'How then
    are you bewitched?'
Nay, but We brought them the truth, and they
    are truly liars.
God has not taken to Himself any son,
nor is there any god with Him; for then
each god would have taken off that he created
and some of them would have risen up

over others; glory to be God, beyond
    that they describe,
who has knowledge of the Unseen and the
Visible; high exalted be He, above
    that they associate!

95   Say: 'O my Lord, if Thou shouldst show me
    that they are promised,
O my Lord, put me not among the people
    of the evildoers.'
Assuredly, We are able to show thee
    that We promise them.
Repel thou the evil with that which is
fairer. We Ourselves know very well
    that they describe.
And say: 'O my Lord, I take refuge
in Thee from the evil suggestions
    of the Satans,
100   and I take refuge in Thee, O my Lord,
    lest they attend me.'

Till, when death comes to one of them, he says,
    'My Lord, return me;
haply I shall do righteousness in that
I forsook.' Nay, it is but a word
he speaks; and there, behind them,
is a barrier until the day that they
    shall be raised up.

For when the Trumpet is blown, that day there shall be no
    kinship
any more between them, neither will they question one
    another.
Then he whose scales are heavy — they are the prosperers,
105 and he whose scales are light — they have lost their souls
in Gehenna dwelling forever, the Fire smiting their faces
the while they glower there. 'What, were My signs not recited
to you, and you cried them lies?' They shall say, 'Our Lord,
our adversity prevailed over us; we were an erring people.
Our Lord, bring us forth out of it! Then, if we revert,
110 we shall be evildoers indeed.' 'Slink you into it,'

He shall say, 'and do not speak to Me. There is a party
of My servants who said, "Our Lord, we believe; therefore
forgive us, and have mercy on us, for Thou art the best
of the merciful." But you took them for a laughing-stock,
till they made you forget My remembrance, mocking at them.
Now today I have recompensed them for their patient
    endurance;
115   they are the triumphant.' He shall say, 'How long have you
tarried in the earth, by number of years?' They shall say,
'We have tarried a day, or part of a day; ask the numberers!'
He shall say, 'You have tarried but a little, did you know.
What, did you think that We created you only for sport,
    and that you would not be returned to Us?'

> Then high exalted be God,
>   the King, the True!
> There is no god but He, the
> Lord of the noble Throne.

And whosoever calls upon another god
    with God, whereof he has no proof,
    his reckoning is with his Lord;
surely the unbelievers shall not prosper.

> And say: 'My Lord, forgive
> and have mercy, for Thou art the best
> of the merciful.'

XVII The Night Journey   8.1.30

> Set not up with God
> another god, or thou
> wilt sit condemned
>   and forsaken.
> Thy Lord has decreed
> you shall not serve
>   any but Him,
> and to be good to parents,
> whether one or both of them
> attains old age with thee;
>   say not to them 'Fie'
>   neither chide them, but

speak unto them words
respectful,
25 and lower to them the
wing of humbleness
out of mercy and say,
 'My Lord,
have mercy upon them,
as they raised me up
when I was little.'
Your Lord knows very well what is in your hearts
if you are righteous,
for He is All-forgiving to those who are penitent.
And give the kinsman his right,
and the needy, and the traveller;
and never squander;
the squanderers are brothers of
Satan, and Satan is unthankful
to his Lord.
30 But if thou turnest from them,
seeking mercy from thy Lord that
thou hopest for, then speak unto
them gentle words.
And keep not thy hand chained
to thy neck, nor outspread it
widespread altogether, or thou
wilt sit reproached
and denuded.
Surely thy Lord outspreads and straitens His provision
unto whom He will;
surely He is aware of and sees His servants.

And slay not your children for fear of poverty;
We will provide for you and them;
surely the slaying of them is a grievous sin.
And approach not fornication;
surely it is an indecency, and evil as a way.
35 And slay not the soul God has
forbidden, except by right. Whosoever is slain
unjustly, We have appointed to
his next-of-kin authority; but let him not exceed
in slaying; he shall be helped.

And do not approach the property of the orphan
save in the fairest manner, until he is of age.
And fulfil the covenant; surely the covenant
    shall be questioned of.
And fill up the measure when you measure, and
weigh with the straight balance; that is better
    and fairer in the issue.
And pursue not that thou hast no knowledge of;
the hearing, the sight, the heart — all of those
    shall be questioned of.
And walk not in the earth exultantly; certainly
thou wilt never tear the earth open, nor attain
    the mountains in height.

40   All of that — the wickedness of it is hateful
    in the sight of thy Lord.

That is of the wisdom thy Lord has revealed to thee:
    set not up with God
    another god, or thou
    will be cast into
    Gehenna, reproached
    and rejected.

XXIV Light   8.1.31

35   God is the Light of the heavens and the earth;
    the likeness of His Light is as a niche
        wherein is a lamp
        (the lamp in a glass,
    the glass as it were a glittering star)
        kindled from a Blessed Tree,
an olive that is neither of the East nor of the West
whose oil wellnigh would shine, even if no fire touched it;
        Light upon Light;
    (God guides to His Light whom He will.)
    (And God strikes similitudes for men,
    and God has knowledge of everything.)
in temples God has allowed to be raised up,
and His Name to be commemorated therein;
therein glorifying Him, in the mornings and the evenings,
are men whom neither commerce nor trafficking
    diverts from the remembrance of God

and to perform the prayer, and to pay the alms,
fearing a day when hearts and eyes shall be turned about,
that God may recompense them for their fairest works
   and give them increase of His bounty;
and God provides whomsoever He will, without reckoning.

  And as for the unbelievers,
their works are as a mirage in a spacious plain
  which the man athirst supposes to be water,
till, when he comes to it, he finds it is nothing;
   there indeed he finds God,
and He pays him his account in full; (and God is swift
   at the reckoning.)
40 or they are as shadows upon a sea obscure
    covered by a billow
    above which is a billow
    above which are clouds,
   shadows piled one upon another;
when he puts forth his hand, wellnigh he cannot see it.
  And to whomsoever God assigns no light,
    no light has he.

Hast thou not seen how that whatsoever is in the heavens
   and in the earth extols God,
  and the birds spreading their wings?
Each — He knows its prayer and its extolling; and God knows
   the things they do.
To God belongs the Kingdom of the heavens and the earth,
   and to Him is the homecoming.
Hast thou not seen how God drives the clouds, then composes
  them,
   then converts them into a mass,
then thou seest the rain issuing out of the midst of them?
And He sends down out of heaven mountains, wherein is hail,
so that He smites whom He will with it, and turns it aside
   from whom He will;
wellnigh the gleam of His lightning snatches away the sight.
  God turns about the day and the night;
  surely in that is a lesson for those who have eyes.
  God has created every beast of water,
   and some of them go upon their bellies,

and some of them go upon two feet,
and some of them go upon four; God
creates whatever He will; God is powerful
over everything.

XXXVI Ya Sin   8.1.32

And the Trumpet shall be blown; then behold, they are sliding
down
from their tombs unto their Lord.
They say, 'Alas for us! Who roused us out of our sleeping-
place?
This is what the All-merciful promised, and the Envoys
spoke truly.'
'It was only one Cry; then behold, they are all arraigned before
Us.
So today no soul shall be wronged anything, and you shall not
be
recompensed, except according to what you have been doing.
55 See, the inhabitants of Paradise today are busy in their rejoicing,
they and their spouses, reclining upon couches in the shade;
therein they have fruits, and they have all that they call for.
'Peace!' – such is the greeting, from a Lord All-compassionate.
'Now keep yourselves apart, you sinners, upon this day!
60 Made I not covenant with you, Children of Adam, that you
should not serve Satan – surely he is a manifest foe to you –
and that you shculd serve Me? This is a straight path.
He led astray many a throng of you; did you not understand?
This is Gehenna, then, the same that you were promised;
roast well in it today, for that you were unbelievers!'
65 Today We set a seal on their mouths, and their hands speak to
Us,
and their feet bear witness as to what they have been earning.

LII The Mount   8.1.33

Surely the godfearing shall be in gardens and bliss,
rejoicing in that their Lord has given them;
and their Lord shall guard them against the chastisement of Hell.
'Eat and drink, with wholesome appetite, for
that you were working.'
20   Reclining upon couches ranged in rows;
and We shall espouse them to wide-eyed houris.

And those who believed, and their seed followed them
in belief, We shall join their seed with them, and We
shall not defraud them of aught of their work;
every man shall be pledged for what he earned.
And We shall succour them with fruits and flesh
such as they desire
while they pass therein a cup one to another
wherein is no idle talk, no cause of sin,
and there go round them youths, their own,
as if they were hidden pearls.
25   They advance one upon another, asking each other questions.
They say, 'We were before among our people, ever
going in fear,
and God was gracious to us, and guarded us
against the chastisement of the burning wind;
we were before ever calling upon Him; surely
He is the All-benign, the All-compassionate.'

Source: From A.J. Arberry, trans., *The Koran Interpreted,* Allen and Unwin 1964, Surahs 2, 17, 23, 24, 36, 52, 57, 59, and 90-114.

8.2   THE BEAUTIFUL NAMES

Introduction   8.2.1

Much of Islamic theology has gathered around the study and exposition
of the Ninety-nine Beautiful Names by which God is denoted and
described. Popular devotion cherishes the same words and recites them
with the rosary, or chain of ninety-nine beads (or a lesser multiple
like thirty-three, repeated). In these loved, and utterly familiar words,
Muslim devotion and Muslim theology come together, in the double
meaning of the term 'Call', which has to do both with naming and
invoking, with indicating and beseeching. God is addressed by those
terms in which, Muslims believe, He has willed to be described.

Abu Hāmid al-Ghazāli, (1058-111 C.E.) wrote a commentary on
the Beautiful Names from which the following section[1] is drawn.
The exposition is complete in each case.

Al-'Azīm, **The Great**   8.2.2

You must know that the word 'great' was applied to physical bodies
in its original coinage. Thus one says: 'This body is great and this
body is greater than that body', if it is more extended in respect of
length, width and depth.

Then you must know that it is divided into (a) the 'greatness' of
which the eye receives an impression and (b) that whose extremities it
is inconceivable that vision could grasp completely, such as the earth
and the heavens. Thus one says that the elephant is 'great', and the
mountain is 'great', and yet vision is able to grasp their extremities
completely. Either of these is 'great' in comparison with that which is
smaller than it. As far as the earth is concerned, it is inconceivable that
vision should be able to grasp its extremities completely, and this is
true also of the heavens. It is to these objects in the realm of those
things subject to physical vision that the term 'great' is applied in the
absolute sense.

You must understand that there is also a difference in respect of
those things that are apprehended by the powers of mental perception. Human reason grasps completely the core of the real nature of
some of them and falls short in the case of others. That portion of
them which reason falls short of completely is divided into (a) that
which some may conceivably grasp although the understanding of the

majority falls short of it, and (b) into that concerning which reason cannot conceivably grasp the core of its real nature completely. This last one is the absolute 'Great One' who exceeds all the limits of human understanding so that the comprehension of His essential Being is inconceivable. And that One is God most High. . .

An admonition: The 'great' among men are the prophets and the scholars. When the wise man knows something of their attributes, his bosom is filled with veneration and his heart so replete with veneration that no room remains in it for anything else. The prophet is 'great' in respect of his people, the shaikh in respect of his disciple and the teacher in respect of his student, since the reason (of these subordinates) is incapable of comprehending the core of the master's attributes. But if the subordinate equals or surpasses the master, then the latter is no longer 'great' in comparison with the former. Every greatness applied to other than God is deficient and not absolutely 'great', because it manifests itself in relation to one thing and not another – apart from the greatness of God most High. Certainly He is the absolutely 'Great', not only relatively.

8.2.3 *Al-Fattāh,* The Opener

He is the One by whose concern everything that is closed is opened, and the One by whose guidance everything that is obscure is made manifest. At times He causes kingdoms to be opened (that is, conquered) for His prophets and He takes them out of the hand of their enemies and says: 'Lo! We have given thee (O Muhammad) a signal victory (lit. 'opening') that God may forgive thee.' At times He lifts the screen from the hearts of His friends, and He opens to them the gates of the kingdom of His heaven and the beauty of His grandeur. He says: 'That which God openeth unto mankind of mercy, none can withhold it.' The one in whose hand are the keys to the invisible world, as well as the keys to the means of sustenance, he is the one who is truly worthy of being an opener.

An admonition: In order that man might have a portion of the name *Al-Fattāh,* it is necessary that he longs for the time when he will reach the stage where the locks upon the divine problems are opened by his tongue, and those religious and worldly subjects which have been difficult for mankind will become easy by means of his knowledge.

8.2.4 *Al-Ghaffār,* The Very Forgiving One

Al-Ghaffār is the One who makes manifest what is noble and veils what is disgraceful. The sins (of man) are among the disgraceful things which He veils by placing a veil upon them in this world and disregarding their punishment in the hereafter. *Al-Ghafr* means veiling. The first of God's veils for man is to be found in the fact that the opening in the body that has been created for that which his eyes consider ugly has been hidden within him and is concealed within the beauty of his exterior. How great is the difference between the interior of man and his exterior in terms of cleanliness and dirtiness, of ugliness and beauty! Just look at that part of him which God exposes and that part which He covers.

God's second veil for man is the human heart which He has made the seat of his reprehensible thoughts and disgraceful desires so that no one might know about this veil. If mankind were aware of the things that occurred in [a man's] mind, in terms of repeated temptations, thoughts of corruption, deception and evil thinking in general, certainly they would detest him. But behold how his secrets and weaknesses are veiled from all people but himself!

God's third veil for man is the forgiveness of the sins for which he deserved to be disgraced in the sight of mankind. God has promised that He will exchange good deeds for man's misdeeds so that he might cover the repulsive qualities of his sins with the reward of his good deeds when he has proved his faith.

An admonition: Man's portion of this name lies in his veiling for the next man that part of him which needs to be veiled. (Muhammad) said — May the peace of God be upon him: 'The one who veils the imperfections of a believer, his imperfections will God cover on the day of resurrection'. The slanderer, the spy, the avenger, and the one who requites evil with evil, are far removed from this characterisation. However, the one who is characterised by it is the one who does not divulge anything about God's creation except those things which are best in them. There is no creature totally free from perfection and imperfection, from ugliness and beauty. The one who disregards the repulsive qualities and remembers the good ones is the person who possesses a share of this name, even as it is related of Jesus — may peace be upon him — that he and his disciples passed by a dead dog, and the stench of it was overpowering. His disciples exclaimed: 'How this corpse smells!' But Jesus — may peace be upon him — replied: 'How lovely is the white of his teeth!' In this way he pointed out that they ought to mention only that which is good.

8.2.5 *Al-Mu'izz al-Mudill,* **The One who raises to Honour and Abases**

He is the One who gives dominion to whom He wishes and the One who takes it from whom He wishes. True dominion is to be found in liberation from the humiliation of [physical] needs, the subjugation of appetite[s] and the fault of the disgrace of ignorance. Therefore, [in the case of] the one from whose heart the veil is lifted so that he can know the beauty of God's presence, and the one who is granted the ability to be abstemious so that as a result of it he has no need for the things of God's creation, and is provided with strength and support so that by means of them he controls his own attributes, God has raised this man to a position of honour and gives him dominion in this world. God will also raise him to honour in the hereafter in terms of this person's gaining access to Him, and God will call for him, saying: 'O soul at peace, return unto thy Lord.' (Surah 89.27) desires it.

The one whom God causes to look at human beings in such a way that he is dependent on them and is so much under the dominion of greediness that he is not content even when he has sufficient to satisfy his needs, and the one who advances by his cunning until he is deceived about himself and (thus) remains in the darkness of ignorance, God abases such a one and dispossesses him. That is the workmanship of God most High, as and when He desires it.

For He is the One of whom it is said: 'Thou exaltest whom Thou wilt and abasest whom Thou wilt.' (Surah 3.26) And this lowly one is the one to whom God speaks and says: 'But you tempted one another, and hesitated, and doubted, and vain desires beguiled you till the ordinance of God came to pass: and the deceiver deceived you concerning God, so this day no ransom can be taken for you.' (Surah 57-14) This is the utmost limit of abasement. Each person who acts by means of his hand and his tongue so as to make the causes of honour easy possesses a portion of this characterisation.

8.2.6 *Al-Kabir,* **The Grand One**

Al-Kabir is the one who possesses grandeur. Grandeur is an expression for the perfection of the essence, by which I mean the perfection of existence. The perfection of existence is traceable to two things. One of them is its perpetuity, both past and future. Every existence is deficient which sooner or later is interrupted by a period of non-existence. For this reason, one says of a man whose period of existence is lengthy that he is a *kabir,* that is to say, great of age, one who has lived long on this earth, and one does not say that he is *'aẓīm* of age. *Al-Kabīr* is used in ways in which al-'aẓīm can not be used. If, then, the being whose period of existence is lengthy, even though its actual duration is limited, is said to be a *kabīr* [i.e. aged] then the one who always will be and always has been eternal, the one in relation to whom non-existence is inconceivable, is more worthy of being called a *kabīr*.

The second is that his existence is the existence from which the existence of all existing things emanates. If the one whose existence is complete in itself is perfect and grand, then the one from whom the existence of all existing things originated is more worthy of being called perfect and grand.

An admonition: *Al-kabīr* among men is the perfect one whose attributes of perfection are not restricted to himself. Rather do they extend to others beside himself. No one sits next to him without pouring out upon the other (one) something of his own perfection. Man's perfection lies in his reason, piety and knowledge. *Al-kabīr* is the God-fearing wise one who leads people, the one who is fit to be a pattern, the one whose lights and knowledge are a fount for others. For this reason Jesus said — may peace be upon him — 'The one who knows and acts accordingly is called mighty (*'aẓīm*) in the kingdom of the heavens'.

Edwin Arnold's *Pearls of Faith*, being a verse commentary on the 8.2.7 Ninety-nine Names from Muslim sources, has long been a favourite and oft-reprinted treasure of faith and piety. It weaves Quranic and traditional phrases with the celebration of the Names. Here is its Pearl of *Al-Kabīr*.[2]

Seven heavens God made: first Paradise,
Next the gate of eternity, the third the house of peace,
The fourth Felicity, the fifth the home of golden light,
The sixth the garden of delight, the seventh the
Footstool of the Throne. And each and every one
Sphere above sphere, and treasure over treasure,
The great decree of God made for reward and pleasure.
Saith the perspicuous Book: 'Look up to heaven! look!
Dost thou see fault or flaw, in that vast vault,
Spangled with silvery lamps of night,
Or gilded with glad light
Of sunrise, or of sunset, or warm noon?
Rounded He well the moon?

Kindled He wisely the red lord of day?
Look twice! look thrice, and say?'
Thy weak gaze fails:
Eyesight is drowned in yon abyss of blue:
Ye see the glory but ye see not through:
God's greatness veils
Its greatness by its greatness — all that wonder
Lieth the lowest of the heavens under,
Beyond which angels view
God and God's mighty works, asunder:
The thronged clouds whisper of it when they thunder.
Allāh Kabīr, in silence we
Meditate on Thy majesty!

8.2.8   The deepest sense of the Name *Al-Fattāh* is reached in the story of the Night Journey of Muḥammad and his 'ascension' where the mystery of truth was opened to his understanding. This significant focus of Islamic celebration of Muḥammad is given in verse from in the Pearl of *Al-Fattāh*.

Al-Fattāh, praise the Opener and recite
The marvels of that 'Journey of the Night'.
Our Lord Muḥammad lay upon the hill
Safe, whereby the holy city stands,
Asleep, wrapped in a robe of camels' wool.

Dark was the night, that Night of grace, and still:
When all the spheres, by God's commands,
Opened unto him, splendid and wonderful.

For Gabriel, softly lighting, touched his side,
Saying: 'Rise, thou enwrapped one, come and see
The things which be beyond. Lo! I have brought
Burāq, the horse of swiftness: mount and ride.'
Milk-white that steed was, with embroidery
Of pearls and emeralds in his long hair wrought.

Hooved like a mule he was, with a man's face:
His eyes gleamed from his forlock, each a star
Of lucent hyacinth: the saddle cloth
Was woven gold, which priceless work did grace:

The lightning goeth not so fast or far
As those broad pinions which he fluttered forth.
One heel he smote on Safa, and one heel
On Sinai, where the dint is to this day.
Next at Jerusalem he neighed. Our Lord,
Descending with the Archangel there, did kneel
Making the midnight prayer: afterwards they
Tethered him to the Temple by a cord.

'Ascend!' spake Gabriel: and behold! there fell
Out of the sky a ladder bright and great,
Whereby, with easy steps, on radiant stairs,
They mounted, past our earth and heaven and hell,
To the first sphere, where Adam kept his gate,
Which was of vaporous gold and silvery squares.

Here thronged the lesser angels: some took charge
To fill the clouds with rain and speed them round.
And some to tend live creatures: for what's born
Hath guardians there in its own shape: a large
Beauteous white cock crowed matins, at the sound
Cocks in a thousand planets hailed the morn.

Unto the second sphere by that white slope
Ascended they, whereof Noah held the key:
And twofold was the throng of angels here,
But all so dazzling glowed its fretted cope,
Burning with beams, Muhammad could not see
What manner of celestial folk was there.

A third sphere lay a thousand years beyond
If thou shouldest journey as the sun-ray doth,
But in one *Fātihah* climbed they thitherward.
David and Solomon in union fond
Ruled at the entrance, keeping Sabaoth
Of ceaseless joy. The void was paven hard
With paven work of rubies if there be

Jewels on earth to liken unto them
Which had such colour as no goldsmith knows.
And here a vast archangel they did see,

'Faithful of God' his name, whose diadem
Was set with peopled stars: wherefrom arose
Lauds to the glory of God, filling the blue
With lovely music, as rose gardens fill
A land with essences and young stars, shaking
Tresses of lovely light, gathered and grew
Under his mighty plumes, departing still
Like ships with crews and treasure, voyage-making.

So came they to the fourth sphere: where there sate
Enoch, who never tasted death: and there
Behind its awful portal Azrael writes:
The shadow of his brows compassionate
Made night across all worlds: our Lord felt fear,
Marking the stern eyes and the hand which smites.
For always on a scroll he sets the names
Of new-born beings, and from off the scroll
He blotteth who must die: and holy tears
Roll down his cheeks, recording all our shames
And sins and penalties: while of each soul
Munkir and Nakir reckon the arrears.

Next, at the fifth sphere's entry, they were 'ware
Of a door built in sapphire, having graven
Letters of flashing fire, the faith unfolding:
'There is no god save God', Aaron sat there
Guarding the region of 'the wrath of heaven'.
And Isrefel behind, his trumpet holding,
His trumpet holding, which shall wake the dead
And slay the living — all his cheek puffed out,
Bursting to blow. For none knows God's time
Nor when the word of judgement shall be said.
And darts and chains of fire lay all around,
Terrible tortures for the ungodly's crime.

When to the sixth sphere passed they, Moses sped
Its bars of chrysoprase, and kissed our Lord,
And spake full sweet: 'Prophet of Allāh, thou
More souls of Ismael's tribes to truth hast led,
Than I of Isaac's.' Here the crystal sword
Of Michael gave the light they journeyed through.

But at the seventh sphere that light which shone
Hath not an earthly name, nor any voice
Can tell its splendour, nay, nor any ear
Learn, if it listened: only he alone
Who saw it, knows how there th'elect rejoice,
'Isa, and Ibrahim, and the souls most dear.
And he, the glorious regent of the sphere,
Had seventy thousand heads: and every head
As many countenances, and each face
As many mouths: and in each mouth there are
Tongues seventy thousand, whereof each tongue said:
Ever and ever: 'Praise be to God, praise!'

Here, at the bound, is fixed that lotus-tree
Sidrah, which none among the angels pass
And not great Gabriel's self might farther wend.
Yet, led by presences too bright to see,
Too high to name, on paths like purple glass,
Our Lord Muhammad journeyed to the end.

Alone, alone, through hosts of Cherubim
Crowding the infinite void with whispering vans,
From splendour unto splendour still he sped,
Across 'the lake of gloom' they ferried him,
And then 'the sea of glory', mortal man's
Heart cannot hold the wonders witnessed.

So to the region of the veils he came,
Which shut all times off from eternity.
The bars of being where thought cannot reach:
Ten thousand thousand are they, walls of flame
Lambent with loveliness and mystery,
Ramparts of utmost heaven, having no breach.
Then he saw God! our prophet saw the Throne!
O God, let these weak words be forgiven!
Thou, the Supreme, 'The Opener', spake at last.
The Throne, the Throne, he saw — our Lord alone!
Saw it and heard! But the verse falls from heaven
Like a poised eagle whom the lightnings blast.

And Gabriel, waiting by the tree, he found,
And Burāq, tethered to the Temple porch.
He loosed the horse, and twixt its wings ascended.
One hoof it smote on Zion's hallowed ground,
One upon Sinai: and the day-star's torch
Was not yet fading when the journey ended.

Al-Fattāh! Opener! we say
Thy Name and worship Thee always.

8.2.9   Muhyī al-Dīn Ibn 'Arabī (1165-1240 C.E.), one of the most renowned of mystical philosophers in Islam, presents his understanding of the Beautiful Names in *The Wisdom of the Prophets*.

Let us now come to the gifts which flow from the Divine Names. The mercy (*Rahmah*) which God lavishes on His creatures runs wholly through the Divine Names: it is, on the one hand, of pure mercy, like everything that is licit from nourishment and natural pleasures, and which is not tainted with blame on the day of resurrection (conforming to the Quranic word: 'Say, who then would render illicit the beauty which God manifested for His servants and the lawful things of nourishment,' say: They are for those who believe, in this world, and will not be subject to reproach on the day of resurrection. . .'): It is these gifts which flow from the Name *Al-Rahmān,* and, on the other hand, of mercy which is mixed with punishment, like medicine which is disagreeable to take, but which is followed by relief.

Such are the Divine gifts. For God (in His personal or qualified aspect) never gives except through the intermediary of one of the guardians of the Temple which are his Names.

8.2.10   Thus, God sometimes gratifies the servant by mediation of the Name 'compassionate' (*Al-Rahmān*) and it is then that the gift is free from any mixture which would be momentarily contrary to the nature of him who receives it, or which would contradict the intention, or anything else (of the petitioner). Sometimes He gives by mediation of the Name, The Inclusive (*Al-Wāsi'*), lavishing his gifts in a global manner. Or he gives by mediation of the Name of the Wise (*Al-Hakīm*) judging by that which is salutary for the servant at the given moment, or by the mediation of the Name of He who gives freely (*Al-Wahhāb*), giving that which is good without the servant who receives it by virtue of this Name, needing to compensate for it by actions of merit or grace. Or He gives by the Name of Him who established the order (*Al-Jabbār*) considering the cosmic environment and that which is necessary to it, or by the Name of the Forgiver (*Al-Ghaffār*), considering the state of him who receives the forgiveness. If he finds him in a state which deserves punishment, He protects him from this punishment, and if He finds him in a state which would not deserve punishment He protects him from a state which would deserve it, and it is in this sense that the servant (or saint) is said to be protected or safeguarded from sin.

The giver is always God, in the sense that He is the treasurer of all possibilities and that He only produces according to a predestined measure and by the hand of a Name concerning that possibility. Thus, He gives to everything its own constitution by virtue of His Name, The Just (*Al-'Adi*) and its brothers, like the Arbitrator (*Al-Hakam*), He who rules (*Al-Wālī*) and The Victorious (*Al-Qahhār*).   8.2.11

Although the Divine Names may be infinite as to their multitude (for one knows them by that which flows from them which is equally unlimited), they are nonetheless reducible to a definite number of roots, which are the 'mothres' of the Divine Names, or the Divine presences integrating the Names. In truth, there is but one single, essential Reality (*Ḥaqiqah*) which assumes all the relations and associations which one ascribes to it by the Divine Names. Now, this Reality causes each of these Names which manifest themselves indefinitely to contain an essential truth by which it distinguishes itself from the other Names. It is this distinctive truth, and not that which it has in common with the others, which is the proper determination of the Name. It is in the same way that the Divine gifts distinguish themselves from one another by their personal nature, although they come from the same source. It is, moreover, evident that this one is not that one, the reason, precisely, being the distinction within the Divine Names. Because of His infinity, there is in the Divine Presence nothing that repeats itself, and that is a fundamental truth.   8.2.12

Sources
1. R.C. Stade, trans., *The Names of God,* Daystar Press, Ibadan 1970, pp.68, 69, 36-8, 44-5, 49-50, 75-6.
2. Edwin Arnold, trans., *Pearls of Faith,* Orientalis, Lahore 1954, pp.80-1.
3. Ibid. pp.41-6.
4. Muhyī al-Dīn Ibn 'Arabī, *The Wisdom of the Prophets,* Beshara Publications, Aldsworth 1975, pp.27-9.

8.3   HADITH/SUNNAH

8.3.1 Muhammad's role as prophet and ruler, singular as it was within the Islamic reading of Divine providence and revelation, meant that his personal history, conversation, behaviour and life-style became a cherished source of confidence as to the personal and social duties and ideals of the believer. Tradition was, with very rare exceptions, always distinguished rigorously from the Qur'ān, which Muhammad uttered in the state of *Wahy*, or inspiration. When collected, at an early stage, into the 'canon' of the complete Qur'ān, those deliverances had a status and an authority which nothing could resemble or over-ride. But, precisely because he had been instrumental to them, all else that he said, did, thought, or opined, was treasured as an index to Muslim conduct and guidance.

So there developed in the ensuing two or three centuries a vast corpus of Tradition, of, about and from Muhammad. It is known as *Hadīth*, from the standpoint of its record and its currency. It is known as the *Sunnah* from the standpoint of its directives and authority as law. The former means 'record', as talked about: the latter, 'the path' to be trodden. By *Hadīth/Sunnah* Muhammad shaped and ordered his community, we might say, from the grave. Tradition, in both senses, is the fount of law and it was lawyers who were in the van of its collection and currency. Traditions were circulated on the basis of a chain of attestation, or reliability, going back, of necessity, to some companion of the Prophet himself. Inevitably, the exigencies of life and the inventiveness of devotion led to the making current of vast numbers of spurious, or dubious, traditions. It was these which the classical editors weeded out during 800-900 C.E. The Sunnis acknowledge six traditionalists. The Shī'ah, as in most other realms, have their independent sources.

Many areas of Islamic ethical, economic and social life, as well as Muslim spiritual values and forms, were historically regulated by Muhammad's recorded example or precedent and the Prophet continues to be the inspiration for the Muslim character. But if much is formed in his image, it would also be true to say that the collective ideology, in which many elements combined outside the Arab and the Arabic, determined how the image was seen and desired. The figure and the community were in reciprocal relation.

8.3.2   The literature of Tradition is vast. The following extracts are from *The Living Thoughts of the Prophet Muhammad,* edited by Muhammad 'Ali, one of the main publicists in the Ahmadiyyah Movement, a renewal organisation which dates from the third quarter of last century and was declared heretical in Pakistan in 1974, though not for reasons which affect our choice. Muhammad 'Ali is, in fact, quite representative in the way in which he builds a contemporary ethicism around the Prophet's memory. He writes:

The Prophet said: 'The man who knows most the Book of God shall act as *Imām* of the people. The most virtuous among you shall deliver the *adhān* (call to prayer) and those having most knowledge of the Qur'ān shall act as *Imāms.'*

'Every child conforms to the true religion [lit. human nature]: It is his parents who make him a Jew, a Christian or a Magian.'

'Surely a day will come over Hell, when it will be like a field of corn that has dried up after flourishing for a while — a day when there shall not be a single human being in it.'

Asked about the efficacy of prayer, Muhammad counter-questioned: 'Tell me, if there is a stream at the door of any one of you, in which he bathes five times daily, what do you say, will it leave anything of his dirt?' On receiving a reply in the negative, he continued: 'This is the likeness of the five prayers with which God washes away all faults.' 'When one of you says his prayers, he holds confidential intercourse with his Lord.'

'Thou shouldest worship God as if thou didst see Him: if thou dost not see Him, He surely sees thee.'

'Whoever does the needful for his brother, God does the needful for him. Whoever removes the distress of a Muslim, God removes for him a distress out of the distresses of the day of resurrection.'

'Thou wilt recognise the faithful in their having mercy upon each other and in their love for one another and in their kindness towards one another, like the body — when one member of it ails, the entire body ails.'

'Your slaves are your brethren: God has placed them under your control. So whoever has his brother under his control, he should feed him from what he eats and give him clothes to wear from what he wears. Do not impose on them a task which should overpower them, and if you do impose on them such a task help them in the doing of it.'

'One who manages the affairs of the widow and the needy is like one who exerts himself hard in the way of God, or like one who stands up for prayer in the night and fasts in the day.'

'I, and the man who brings up an orphan, will be in paradise like this.' And he pointed with his two fingers, the forefinger and the middle finger.

'God has no mercy on him who is not merciful to men.' ·

'He is not of us who does not show mercy to our little ones and respect to our great ones.'

'Be careful of your duty to God regarding these dumb animals. Ride them while they are in fit condition, and eat them while they are in fit condition.'

'Charity is incumbent on every Muslim.'

'Every good deed is charity, and it is a good deed that thou meet thy brother with a cheerful countenance and that thou pour water from thy bucket into the vessel of thy brother.'

'Surely truth leads to virtue, and virtue leads to paradise, and a man continues to speak the truth until he becomes utterly truthful. Surely falsehood leads to vice and vice leads to the fire, and a man who continues to tell lies is written down a great liar with God.'

'The most excellent *jihād* is the uttering of truth in the presence of an unjust ruler.'

'Among the best of you are those who are good in payment of debt. Whoever contracts a debt intending to repay it, God will pay it for him: whoever contracts a debt intending to waste it, God will bring him to ruin.'

'Delaying the payment of a debt by a well-to-do person is injustice. Deferring payment by one who has the means to pay makes his punishment legitimate.'

'If the debtor is in constrained circumstances, then there should be postponement until he is in ease, and if you remit it as alms, it is better for you' (quoting Surah 2.280).

'No one eats better food than that which he eats out of the work of his own hand. God did not raise a prophet but that he pastured goats. Yes! I used to pasture them for the people of Mecca.'

'There are three persons whose adversary in dispute God will be on the day of resurrection: a person who makes a promise in His Name, then acts unfaithfully: a person who sells a free person then devours his price: and a person who employs a servant and receives fully the labour due from him and then does not pay him his remuneration.'

'The Truthful honest merchant is as the prophets and the truthful ones and the martyrs.'

'May God have mercy on the man who is generous when he buys and when he sells and when he demands his due.'

'If they [traders] both speak the truth and make manifest [the defect, if any, in the transaction], their transaction shall be blessed: if they conceal [the defect] and tell lies, the blessing of their transaction shall be obliterated.'

'The taking of oaths makes the commodities sell, but it obliterates the blessing therein.'

'Whoever buys cereals, he shall not sell them until he obtains their possession.'

'There is no Muslim who plants a tree or cultivates land and then bird or man or animal eat of it, but it is a charitable deed for him. Whoever cultivates land which is not the property of anyone has a better title to it.'

'The man who marries perfects half his religion.'

'O assembly of young people, whoever of you has the means to support a wife, he should get married. This is the best means of keeping the looks cast down and of guarding chastity. And he who has not the means let him keep fast, for this will act as restraining of desire.'

'Every one of you is a ruler and everyone shall be questioned about his subjects. The king is a ruler: and the man is the ruler over the people of his house: and the woman is a ruler over the house of her husband and his children.'

'Thy body has a right over thee, and thy soul has a right over thee, and thy wife has a right over thee.'

'Never did God allow anything more hateful to Him than divorce. With God, the most detestable of all things allowed is divorce.'

'To hear and obey [the authorities] is binding, so long as one is not commanded to disobey God. When one is commanded to disobey God, he should neither hear nor obey.' On being appointed Governor of Yemen, Mu'adh was asked by the Prophet as to the rule by which he would abide. 'By the Qur'an', he replied. 'But if you do not find any direction therein, what then?' 'Then I will act according to the *Sunnah* of the Prophet', he responded.

'But, if you do not find any direction in the *Sunnah,* what then?' 'Then I will exercise my judgement and act on that.' The Prophet raised his hands and said: 'Praise be to God Who guides the messenger of His Messenger as He wills.'

'Gather together the righteous from among my community and decide the matter by their counsel and do not decide it by one man's opinion.' [This principle of the corporate mind lies behind the institution of *Ijmā'*, or 'consensus', by which the mind of the community, under the priority of the Qur'ān and the *Sunnah,* is held to be indicative of the mind of God.]

'Never do a people take counsel but they are guided to the right course in their affair.'

'The authority of the head [of State] should only be disputed if he has committed open acts of unbelief, in which you have a clear argument from God.'

8.3.3   The spirit of all these moralistic traditions is perhaps best summarised in a saying attributed to Khadījah, first wife of the Prophet:

'Nay! I call God to witness that God will never bring thee [Muhammad] to disgrace. For thou unitest the ties of relationship and bearest the burden of the weak and thou art earning for the destitute and honourest the guest and helpest people in real distress.'

Source: Muhammad 'Ali, ed., *The Living Thoughts of the Prophet Muhammad,* Cassell 1947, pp.62, 68, 71, 75, 83-5, 89, 92, 110, 114-15, 117, 123, 125-6, 135-7 and 83.

8.4   LAW IN ISLAM

One of the fundamental problems in all historical religions is that of   8.4.1
loyalty, the issue of how to keep faith within the inevitable flux of
change. What is sincere continuity? How is it to be identified? Who
is to say what the credentials are and when they are satisfied? These
are perennial problems. They are not least acute in Islam, with its
rigorous temper and its authoritarian structure.

Law in Islam rests on four pillars. The Qur'ān is the first and   8.4.2
ruling arbiter. Developing, but never countering its directives, comes
the *Sunnah* of the Prophet. Thirdly, carefully hedged about, there is
analogy, arguing from an existing prescript in the first two and
reaching therefrom a further prescript by argument from intent
within the letter. Fourthly, there is *Ijmā'*, the consensus of the
community. The means to attain such consensus is *Ijtihād*, or
enterprise, an initiative held to belong only to those, on behalf of
the whole, who have the expertise, i.e. the *ulamā* or scholars.

In contemporary change, one of the significant issues has been   8.4.3
whether the right, and the ability, for *Ijtihād* could be accorded to
lay believers, outside traditional scholarship, who are sincere in their
Islam. Such a right would go far to ensuring dynamic and progressive
interpretations of Islam. For that very reason the claim has been
resisted by those of conservative mind, perhaps also tenacious of
their privilege in retaining the keys of change.

Kemal A. Faruki is an eminent Pakistani scholar who vigorously   8.4.4
advocates the entrusting of Islamic interpretation to a wide, lay
constituency, as a necessary condition of Muslim sincerity *vis-à-vis*
the modern scene. Some years ago he set the '*ulamā*' a series of
questions. With his reactions, the exchange constitutes an
interesting *exposé* of a vital area of contemporary Islamic thought
and decision.

He prefaced it with a confession of faith.

The Qur'ān, the eternal Word of God, applicable for all times to
all places, which men and *jinn,* whether singly or in combination,
can never hope to equal, even to the extent of one verse, will
always yield greater and greater treasures of knowledge and
guidance. The longer mankind is fortunate to possess the
guidance of this Book, the more we read and seek to understand

its meaning, it is but inevitable that our knowledge of its verses, its chapters and, indeed, the Book as a whole, will constantly heighten, widen, deepen and be purified.

It is over-exulting arrogance to imagine that we have, singly or collectively, in that past exhausted the meaning of the eternal Qur'ān with our puny, halting, fallible human intelligence... Through the ages the Muslim community will understand more and more of the eternal Word of God through constant exertion and patient endeavour. It is incumbent upon us, if we are sincere believers, once a richer and more Islamic meaning of a passage is allowed us by God, to accept the richer, more accurate meaning.

With that confidence Kemal Faruki frames his questions to the pundits. The first two simply elucidate facts. He goes on:

(3) Is it permissible for any of the real decisions contained within these standard works of *fiqh* [jurisprudence] to be (a) disregarded, (b) legally revoked, (c) legally replaced?

Answer: Certain categories may be so disregarded, revoked or replaced, other categories not.

(4) If the answer to (3) is affirmative, what are the Islamic legal principles under which and by which these decisions can be cancelled and changed?

Answer: Only those decisions may be altered which are not based on clear injunctions of the Qur'ān and/or the *Sunnah* or on which no consensus deduced from the Qur'ān and the *Sunnah* has been reached.

(5) If the answer to (3) is negative is this due to the doctrine that once the *Ijtihād* of individual jurists has been corrected for error by consensus, the resulting legal conclusion is the permanently correct understanding of the Qur'ān and the *Sunnah* ...and subsequent *Ijtihād* can only be applied to those questions on which no consensus has hitherto been reached?

(6) If the answer to (3) is negative, but the reason given in (5) is incorrect, what is the correct reason for the negative answer to (3)?

Answer to (5) and (6): With regard to *Ijmā'* (consensus) which is irrevocable, this is based on Surah 4.115 and on a tradition: 'My community will never agree on an error.'... Once a verdict is confirmed through consensus of all jurists, it would be deemed to be sure and free from error. *Ijmā'* decisions, therefore, based as they are on the Qur'ān and/or Qur'ān and *Sunnah* attain almost as much sanctity as revealed commandments.

(7) On apostasy. [It is punishable by death for a man, life imprisonment for a woman until she changes her mind.]

After further technical questions, Faruki asked:

(10) Further to (5) and (6), in view of the fact that the verse and the tradition quoted about consensus refer to the community of Muslims as a totality and *not* to any particular group within it, how is the consensus of the learned [the *'ulamā'*] related to the consensus of the community [as a whole]?

Answer: The Quranic verse and the *hadith* no doubt refer to the community as a totality...but in all matters requiring technical erudition and a high degree of knowledge, people in general are always guided by experts... An *Ijmā'* decision is always carefully deduced by legal disciplines and this can obviously only be accomplished by the experts in this field... *Ijmā'* is a technical Islamic legal process for which the Muslim community would naturally rely on those qualified and competent in this sphere.

Reflecting on these replies, Kemal Faruki addressed a letter acknowledging them and continuing with the perceptive question whether this according of power to define law (thus claimed by the *'ulamā'*) did not amount to a kind of *Shirk,* or usurping of the role of God Himself, in that law, so resulting, stood on the same level as that which was given in Divine relevation. This rather abstruse (but highly Islamic) argument took him into a firm plea for a widening of the interpretative custodianship of Islam to all the sincere faithful. *All* community is necessarily limited both in time and space and must therefore be relativised under the omniscient authority of God alone.

It is the fact that God is omnipresent and other things and persons, including the community, are limited in their 'presence'. Thus the 'protection from error' which is deduced from the Qur'ān verse and the *hadith* (see 5 and 6 above) is limited to the limited 'presence' of the community, whether this is evaluated in terms of space or time... Thus, as the limits of the community's 'presence' alter, the legal deductions made from the Qur'ān and the *Sunnah* must be re-examined and, if necessary, altered by fresh processes of *Ijtihād,* if the community is to continue to enjoy God's assurance of 'protection from error'.

The answer to (10) clearly establishes the law-interpreting supremacy of the community as a totality over any particular group, including the 'competent' within it... This still leaves undecided the problem of who are to be considered 'competent' or how they are to be chosen.

I would suggest that a suitable starting-point for this matter is another Quranic verse (4.58) which begins: 'Surely God commands you to make over trusts to those worthy of them...'

In analysing what makes someone trustworthy or *amīn*... I believe there is considerably more required than being an *'alīm* [sing, of *'ulamā'*]. It is necessary that besides possessing knowledge, he should possess integrity of character as well... A person should possess in addition a comparative knowledge of other systems, and also of temporal, materialistic matters... The devising of the collective assembly of those 'competent' should take these factors into account.

Though the background debate about constitutional principles in Pakistan has been overtaken by events, the underlying plea of Kemal Faruki, and the unmistakeable opposition of existing custodians, are an eloquent measure of the perennial problem of authority and change within a religion. His plea is really for a wide laicisation of Islamic self-interpretation and it is based upon a lively initiative in the use of Quranic precepts, including the most fundamental of all — that which forbids the absolutising of anything other than God, not even those who speak and interpret in his Name.

Source: K.A. Farouki, *Ijmā' and the Gate of Ijtihād*, Gateway Publications, Karachi 1954, pp.8-20.

8.5 THE MYSTICS IN ISLAM

The mystics in Islam, known generally as Sufis, represent a long and 8.5.1
vital tradition of devotion and spirtuality. Emerging very early in the
history of Islam as a protest against worldly compromises and
responding to influences, ascetical and intellectual, from sources met
during Islamic expansion, they developed a strong technique of
discipline and spiritual ecstasy, centred around the practice of
dhikr, or recollection. It reached far and wide within the strata of
Muslim society and brought personal religion into the daily character
of the faithful, in forms that orthodoxy did not always approve.
But, precisely for that reason, it generated great personalities around
whom piety could focus and who served as guides and mentors,
almost as magnets, for the following they inspired.

Among them was Shaikh Abu-l-'Abbās al-'Alawī, a twentieth 8.5.2
century saint of Algeria (1869-1934). His reputation extended from
Fez in the west to Damascus in the east. Shortly after his death a
contemporary wrote this description of his quality. It conveys
vividly the genius of Sufism at its finest.

In his brown *jallabah* and white turban, with his silver grey beard
and his long hands which seemed when he moved them to be
weighted with the flow of his *barakah* [blessing], he had
something of the pure archaic ambience of Ṣayyidnā Ibrahīm
[Abraham], the friend of God. He spoke in a subdued, gentle
voice... His eyes, which were like two sepulchral lamps, seemed
to pierce through all objects, seeing in their outer shell merely
one and the same nothingness, beyond which they saw always
one and the same reality — the Infinite. Their look was very
direct, almost hard in its enigmatic unwaveringness, and yet full
of charity Often their long ovals would grow suddenly round as
if in amazement, or as if enthralled by some marvellous spectacle.
The cadence of the singing, the dances and ritual incantations
seemed to go on vibrating in him perpetually. His head would
sometimes rock rhythmically to and fro while his soul was
plunged in the unfathomable mysteries of the Divine Name
hidden in the *dhikr,* or remembrance...

He gave out an impression of unreality, so remote was he, so
inaccessible, so difficult to take in, on account of his altogether

521

abstract simplicity ... He was surrounded, at one and the same
time, with all the veneration due to saints... Yet, as another
observes, he belonged to that class of men, often to be met with
in North Africa, who can pass without transition from deep
thought to action, from the mysteries of the next world to the
life of this, from the vast sweep of ideas to the smallest details of
native politics.[1]

8.5.3   In the newspaper, *Al-Balāgh,* which Shaikh Al-'Alawī published,
he explained in these terms the patterns of recollection which he
taught:

Any reasonably sensitive man will be conscious of the influence
on him of the name he mentions. If we admit this we are bound
believe that the Name of God also produces an influence on the
soul, as other names do, each one leaving the particular imprint
that belongs with it and corresponds to it. I think you are aware
that a name is ennobled with the nobility of him who is named,
inasmuch as it carries his imprint in the hidden fold of its secret
essence and meaning. Al-Ghazālī writes in his commentary on the
Name *Allāh:* 'That which the slave gets from this Name is
Ta'alluh, or deification', by which is meant that his 'heart and his
purpose are drowned in God, so that he sees naught but Him'.

He also wrote: 'My son, rid thy heart of all attachment save
unto God. Go apart by thyself and say with all thy powers of
concentration: *Allāh, Allāh, Allāh.* When thy thoughts are
muddied with other than God, thou hast need of the negation:
Lā ilāha ['There is no god but. . .'.] But once thou hast withdrawn
from all things in contemplation of Him Who is the Lord of all,
thou takest rest in the bidding: Say: *Allāh. . .*

Open the door of your heart with the key of saying: *Lā
ilāha illā Allāh:* 'There is no god but God', and the door of thy
spirit by saying: *'Allāh'.*[2]

8.5.4   It was, reputedly, the same Al-Ghazālī, supreme among the
mentors of Islamic spirituality, who left a poem on 'the blemishes of
the soul', which, in this verse translation by A.J. Arberry, conveys
very aptly those aspects of Sufism which had to do with self-
reproach and self-scrutiny, as the prelude to sustained discipline and
penitent prayer.

Abu Hamid al-Ghazali: 'The Blemishes of the Soul'

What ails my soul, that maketh long complaint
to men, but for the fear of God is faint?
Its very plaint forbiddeth its release,
augments its terror, and destroys its peace.
Would it but come with humble love sincere
unto its Master, He would draw it near;
but since it chooseth who His creatures are
above their Fashioner, He keeps it far,
and makes its need yet more: but let it flee
to Him, He'll grant it full safiety.
Unto His creatures it complains, as though
they have the power to work it weal or woe:
but would it lay all matters at His feet
in true sincerity and trust complete,
He would not leave it in its long despairs,
but give it gladness in return for cares.
It angers God, that it seeks man to please:
a curse upon its self-sought miseries!
If it would dare man's anger to attain,
pleasing its Lord, it would His pleasure gain.
I have a soul whose nature I would tell,
that we may know it and its habits well:
hear then my tale thereon, and tell in turn,
that men of wit its mysteries may learn.
It labours after folly as its goal:
alas, the foolish labour of my soul!
I chide it, but it never will obey,
as if I will not well in what I say;
but idly looking at another's sin
forgets the faults it cherishes within.
Its evil manners have corrupted me,
and leave me neither rank nor piety.
At concert with vain talk it fills the air,
has small remembrance of its God at prayer,
receives His favours with scant gratitude,
and, suffering, with less patience is endued:
full slow of foot its remedy to obtain,
but swift to seek the things that are its bane;
finds endless cause its promises to break,
is false in every claim that it doth make;

keen-sighted after evil vanities,
but blind to where its own salvation lies;
grasping at pleasures with alacrity,
at time of meditation sluggardly;
with leaden eye forgets its God to greet
Who fashioned it in symmetry complete;
when all is well, in confidence arrayed,
but in distress most mightily afraid;
in pride and in hypocrisy well-versed,
yea, and by pride corrupted and accursed;
unstinted in approval and appraise
of him who seeks its dignity to raise,
but lavish of opprobrium and blame
when any dares its shortcomings to name;
in eating and in drinking takes delight,
and to repose is eager for the night;
accounts to others where their faults begin,
forgetful of its own account of sin.
How other far that man, who guards his soul
in cleanliness, godfearing, sweet and whole,
teaches it righteousness, keeping it keen,
nurturing it with lawful food and clean.
All night he holds it instant and awake,
washed with the tears that from his eyelids break.
When lusting after passion, with the fear
of God he visits it, and brings it cheer;
with fasting trains it, till it is subdued,
spite all its waywardness and turpitude.
So it remembers God with thankfulness
and love sincere doth secretly confess.
How well by God assisted is that soul
which, seeking refuge, gains in God its goal!
Rank and renown it winneth from its King,
and at the founts of faith finds watering:
it soars to God in loveliness of thought,
by God with love and kindness it is sought,
and if in need unto the Lord it cries
He hears its prayer, and speedily supplies.
He gives it patience in calamity,
and to its call His hand is ever free.
Not so my soul: wildly rebellious,

to orders and restraints impervious,
God's holy ordinance it never heeds;
alas, my soul! Alas, its sinful deeds!
How shall it ever to its Lord repent,
that serves the Devil, and his blandishment?
Whene'er I say, 'My soul, attend my word,
be heedful of the orders of thy Lord',
the truth it will not heed, though hearing all,
as though it were another that I call.
Knew it the purpose of its fashioning,
that knowledge grief and bitter tears would bring;
were it made ware of God in verity
truly sincere would its godfearing be;
but God hath made it ignorant of him,
neglect hath made the light of guidance dim.
And ah, my soul! Alas for it, and woe,
if God abandons it, and lets it go!
Beguiled by this world's pleasure, it knows not
what after death shall be its dreadful lot.
Much I have strained, to make my soul obey,
but for whose sin I had not gone astray;
when I would be obedient, it was faint,
and shewed a strange distaste and unrestraint.
I wrestled with my soul, as with a foe,
it bidding me to err, I saying no;
we were as ancient enemies at large;
I put on patience, to withstand its charge,
with troops of tempting came it forth to fight –
what patience could withstand such reckless might? –
which gave it courage, when its courage quailed,
and reinforcement, when its forces failed.
Now I succeed, now it, in the affray,
yet, when we meet, it ever wins the day.
I love it well, but it opposes me
as if I held it not in amity:
it is an enemy I cannot hate,
a memory I can ne'er obliterate.
Blindly it swims upon its sinful sea,
clutching the hems of its iniquity:
I greatly fear, if it doth still rebel,
its ruin in this life, and, after, Hell!

Wherefore, O Lord, bring its repentance near,
and wash away its sin in founts of fear:
if Thou, my God, its chastener shouldst be,
O whither shall it look for clemency?
Be gracious, then, and all its sins forgive:
Thou art its Lord, for through Thee it doth live.[3]

8.5.5   But the greatest of all Sufi poets, at least in the Arabic tongue, was Ibn al-Fārid who lived and died at Cairo (1181-1235), whose *Poem of the Way* gives noble expression to that state of unitive bliss, of absorption of the soul in God to the point of utter self-transcendence, which was the goal of the Sufi path and the crown of mystical illumination. The poet visualises all the vast panorama of the world presented to the senses and passes through and beyond it into the bliss of ineffable union.

Ibn al-Fārid: 'Poem of the Way'

Thou seest forms of things in every garb
Displayed before thee from behind the veil
Of ambiguity: the opposites
In them united for a purpose wise:
Their shapes appear in each and every guise:
Silent, they utter speech: though still, they move:
Themselves unluminous, they scatter light.
Thou laughest gleefully, as the most gay
Of men rejoices; weep'st like a bereaved
And sorrowing mother, in profoundest grief;
Mournest, if they do moan, upon the loss
Of some great happiness; art jubilant,
If they do sing, for such sweet melody.
Thou seest how the birds among the boughs
Delight thee with their cooing, when they chant
Their mournful notes to win thy sympathy,
And marvellest at their voices and their words
Expressing uninterpretable speech.
Then on the land the tawny camels race
Benighted through the wilderness; at sea
The tossed ships run amid the billowy deep.
Thou gazest on twain armies — now on land,
Anon at sea — in huge battalions
Clad all in mail of steel for valour's sake

And fenced about with points of swords and spears.
The troops of the land-army — some are knights
Upon their chargers, some stout infantry;
The heroes of the sea-force — some bestride
The decks of ships, some swarm the lance-like masts.
Some violently smite with gleaming swords,
Some thrust with spears strong, tawny, quivering;
Some 'neath the arrows' volley drown in fire,
Some burn in water of the flaming flares.
This troop thou seest offering their lives
In reckless onslaught, that with broken ranks
Fleeing humiliated in the rout.
And thou beholdest the great catapult
Set up and fired, to smash the fortresses
And stubborn strongholds. Likewise thou mayst gaze
On phantom shapes with disembodied souls
Cowering darkly in their dim domain,
Apparelled in strange forms that disaccord
Most wildly with the homely guise of men;
For none would call the Jinnis homely folk.
And fishermen cast in the stream their nets
With busy hands, and swiftly bring forth fish;
And cunning fowlers spread their gins, that birds
A-hunger may be trapped there by a grain.
Ravening monsters of the ocean wreck
The fragile ships; the jungle-lions seize
Their slinking prey; birds swoop on other birds
Out of the heavens; in a wilderness
Beasts hunt for other beasts. And thou mayst glimpse
Still other shapes that I have overpassed
To mention, not relying save upon
The best exemplars. Take a single time
For thy consideration — no long while —
And thou shalt find all that appears to thee
And whatsoever thou dost contemplate
The act of one alone, but in the veils
Of occultation wrapt: when he removes
The curtain, thou beholdest none but him,
And in the shapes confusion no more reigns.[4]

Sources
1. M. Lings, *A Moslem Saint of the Twentieth Century*, Allen and Unwin 1961, p.107.
2. Ibid., pp.112-14 and 117.
3. A.J. Arberry, trans., *'Uyub al-Nafs* (attributed to Al-Ghazālī)', *The Muslim World Quarterly*, Hartford, Conn. 1940, Vol.30, pp.140-143.
4. A.J. Arberry, trans., ' "Poem of the Way" by Ibn al-Fārid,' Chester Beatty Monographs, London (Emergy Walker) 1952, lines 2137-2199.

8.6 ISLAM: A CONTEMPORARY STATEMENT

'In the name of God, Most Gracious, most Merciful'
'And God invites (you) to the House of Peace' (al-Qur'an, 10:25)

Man has conquered the seas and the skies; man has harnessed the forces of nature to his service; man has created vast and complex institutions and organizations to administer his affairs; man seems to have reached the pinnacle of material progress! 8.6.1

Man also claims to have deeply reflected upon his position in the universe. He has begun to interpret reality with the sole use of his reason and the knowledge yielded by his senses. With a new found confidence in his own reasoning power and in the powers of science and technology, he has jettisoned his link with tradition, with revealed Truth, indeed with every form of guidance from beyond himself.

From this elevated position he seeks to mould the world according to his whims and fancies. But the 'brave new world' he has created drives an ordinary human being into profound disillusionment. In spite of unprecedented technological advancement and overall material development the condition of man remains highly unsettled. He sees the powerful subjugating the weak, the rich dominating the poor, the 'have-nots' arrayed against the 'haves'; he sees injustice and exploitation at national and international levels; he sees disintegration of the family, alienation of individual from society and its institutions, even from himself; and he sees the abuse of trust and authority in all spheres. Although he has shown his ability to fly in the air like the birds, and to swim in the oceans like the fishes, (but) he has failed to show his ability to live on the earth as good human beings. His failure here brings into doubt his capability to conduct his affairs in society without clear-cut guidelines for human action.

Man finds himself caught in a dilemma. He believes that he has reached the apex of civilization. But on reaching the apex he faces a new and greater void. He finds himself and the civilization he has built threatened with forces of his own creation. He frantically searches for remedies to rid his life of those portents of destruction which threaten to deprive him of his cherished dream of ultimate bliss. He finds that his world-view lacks definitive criteria to help 8.6.2

him judge between right and wrong; he finds that his learning and expertise fail to give him universal criteria to distinguish between good and bad; he finds that change and the pace of change have swept him off his feet — nothing tangible and lasting remains. Increasingly man becomes dubious about the direction he is heading for. Inability to conceive a way out of this dilemma leads him to despair and gloom. Man becomes increasingly selfish and unmindful of humanity's collective needs. Man becomes aware of a choice — either he relinquishes all pretences to be anything other than an animal and sadly pronounces himself as the 'naked ape' or strive further to regain and retain his sanity.

8.6.3   His search leads him to the awareness that the fruits of his reason are not in themselves sufficient for comprehending the reality around him. He turns to meditation, to mysticism, to occult practices, to pseudo-spiritualism for gaining further insight and inspiration. His thirst remains unquenched; he fails to find a comprehensive doctrine based on reality and capable of universal application.

Man and the Word of God

8.6.4   At this stage, man needs to discover the Word of God. It informs him of his Creator, informs him of the purpose of his creation, informs him of his place as the 'best of creation', provides him with guidance to lead a fulfilling and rewarding life, tells him of the hereafter, teaches him the value of his fellow beings, makes everything else subservient to the criterion of Truth — in short, enables him to be at peace with himself, with the whole of creation and with the Creator.

8.6.5   The religion of Islam embodies the final and most complete Word of God. It is the embodiment of the code of life which God, the Creator and the Lord of the universe, has revealed for the guidance of mankind. Islam integrates man with God and His creation in such a way that he moves in cooperation with all that exists. Neglect of this dimension has impoverished human life and has made most of man's material conquests meaningless. Over-secularisation has deprived human life of its spiritual significance. But spiritual greatness cannot be achieved by a simple swing of the pendulum to the other extreme. Harmony and equilibrium can be attained only by the integration of the material with the spiritual. This is the approach that Islam brings to bear: it makes the whole of the domain of existance spiritual and religious. It stands for the harmonisation of the human will with the Divine Will — this is how peace is achieved in human life. It is through peace with God that man attains peace in the human order as also peace with nature, outside as well as within him.

The Meaning of Islam

Islam is an Arabic word. It is derived from two roots, one *salm*, 8.6.6
meaning peace and the other SLM, meaning submission. Islam stands for 'a commitment to surrender one's will to the Will of God' and as such be at peace with the Creator and all that has been created by Him. It is through submission to the Will of God that peace is produced. Harmonisation of man's will with the Will of God brings about harmonisation of different spheres of life under an all-embracing ideal. Departmentalisation of life into different water-tight compartments, religious and secular, sacred and profane, spiritual and material, is ruled out. There is unity of life and unity of the source of guidance. As God is One and indivisible, so is life and man's personality. Each aspect of life is inseparable from one another. Religious and secular are not two autonomous categories; they represent two sides of the same coin. Each and every act becomes related to God and His guidance. Every human activity is given a transcendant dimension; it becomes sacred and meaningful and goal-centred.

Islam is a world-view and an outlook on life. It is based on the 8.6.7
recognition of the unity of the Creator and of man's submission to His will. Everything originates from the one God and everyone is ultimately responsible to Him. Thus the unity of the Creator has as its corollary the oneness of His creation. Distinctions of race, colour, caste, wealth and power disappear; man's relation with fellow man assumes total equality by virtue of the common Creator. Henceforth, man's mission becomes dedication to his Creator — worship and obedience of the Creator becomes his purpose in life.

The Creator has not left man without guidance for the conduct of 8.6.8
his life. Ever since the beginning of Creation, He has sent down Prophets who conveyed His message to mankind. They are the source for finding God's Will. Thus we have the chain of Prophets beginning with Adam (peace be upon him) and ending with Muhammad (peace be upon him). Noah, John, Zacariah, Moses and Jesus (peace be upon them) all belong to this golden chain of Prophets. Prophets David, Moses, Jesus and Muhammed (may peace be upon them all), brought revealed books of guidance with them.

The Qur'an, the Book revealed to the Prophet Muhammad, is the last of these books of guidance.

8.6.9   The Qur'an contains the Word of God and nothing but the Word of God. In it is preserved the divine revelation, unalloyed by human interpolation of any kind, unaffected by any change or loss to the original. In it is distilled the essence of all the messages sent down in the past. In it is embodied a framework for the conduct of the whole of man's life. There are explicit criteria for judging between the right and wrong, there are principles of individual and collective conduct of man. In it are depicted the follies of man in the past; in it are warnings for mankind and in it are assurances for continued guidance for those who seek God's help.

8.6.10   The Qur'an has depicted a path, the Straight Path (*Sirat al-Mustaqim*) which, when followed by man, revolutionises his whole life. It brings about a transformation in man's character and galvanises him into action. This action takes the form of purification of the self, and then unceasing effort to establish the laws of God on earth, resulting in a new order based on truth, justice, virtue and goodness.

8.6.11   Man plays a crucial role in the making of this world. He acts as God's viceregent (*Khalifa*), His deputy and representative on the earth. He is morally prepared to play this role. His success lies in playing it properly: to enjoin what is right and forbid what is wrong, to free man from the bondage of fellow man, to demonstrate that a sound and serene society can only result if one harmonises one's will with the Will of God, makes seeking the Creator's pleasure as one's only purpose in life, treats the whole of Creation as one's partner, raises the concept of human welfare from the level of mere animal needs to seeking what is best in this world and what is best in the hereafter.

8.6.12   This is the Islamic world-view and its concept of man and his destiny. This is epitomised in the *Kalima* — the declaration of Islamic faith: *There is no god except Allah and Muhammad is Allah's prophet.*

Islam is not a religion in the Western understanding of the word. It is a faith and a way of life, a religion and a social order, a doctrine and a code of conduct, a set of values and principles and a social movement to realise them in history. There is no priesthood in Islam, not even an organised 'church'. All men and women who are committed to this ideal are expected to live in accordance with its principles and to strive to establish them in society and history.

Those who commit themselves to Truth try to see that Truth prevails. They strive to make a new world in the image of the Truth.

Islam as a system of life prepares man to play this role and provides him with guidelines for the development of a new personality and a new society. For the purification of the self there are prayers, (*Salat*) performed five times a day, in the confines of the home and in congregation in the mosques, strengthening man's commitment to God, refreshing his loyalty to truth, reinvigorating him to work for the realisation of his ideals. Prayer is supplemented by fasting (*Sawm*) for the achievement of these objectives. And if prayer and fasting integrate man with God and provide him with the spiritual discipline he needs to become godly in the midst of the rough and tumble of life, *Zakat* commits man's wealth — his worldly resources — to the achievement of divine purposes in the socio-economic realm. *Zakat* is a monetary obligation. Every Muslim who possesses more than a certain minimum amount of wealth has to contribute at least a certain percentage of his total wealth for welfare functions of the society. It is not merely a charity; it is a religious right which the rich owe to the needy and the poor, and to the society at large. But the spirit of this compulsory contribution is that it is paid by the rich as an act of worship and not merely as a tax. This is how all that man has, his soul, his body or his belongings are harnessed for the service of virtue, justice and truth. It is also obligatory on Muslims to visit the *Ka'ba* at least once in their lifetime for *hajj* (pilgrimage). This among others, is an index of the unity of the Muslim community (*Ummah*), a community of faith and a symbol of the unity of mankind. A universal order can come into existence only on the basis of a universal faith and not on the basis of commitment to the gods of race, colour, or region. The ideal of man's brotherhood seeks actualisation in Islam.

8.6.14

Islam in History

Islam is the original religion of man. It began with the first man, who was also the first prophet and who himself submitted to the Will of God and invited others to do the same. The same message was preached by all the prophets of God, who guided man to the Right Path. But man not only veered away from the right path again and again, but also lost or distorted the code of guidance which the prophets handed out to him. That was why other prophets were sent to re-state the original message and guide man to the right path. The last of these prophets was Muhammad (peace be upon him) who

8.6.15

presented God's guidance in its final form and also arranged to preserve it for all time. It is this guidance which is now known as Islam and is enshrined in the Qur'an and the life-example of the Prophet.

Muhammad (peace be upon him) was born in Makka in 571 C.E. At the age of forty (611 C.E.), he received revelation from God and began his role as God's prophet. He invited those around him to the path of Islam: some responded to his call and became his companions; others rebuked him and subjected him and his companions to all form of persecution. He continued his work undaunted by all storms of opposition and oppression. His noble example won converts from far and near. In the twelfth year of his prophethood (622 C.E.) he migrated from Makka, his own birth-place, to Yathrib, later known as Madinah, as the people of Madinah had accepted his message and invited him as their leader and head of the state to establish the new order he was preaching. The Muslim calendar begins from the day the prophet migrated to Madinah, the day Islam became an established order. The prophet lived another ten years during which the new system was developed in Madinah, from where it spread to the whole of Arabia. When the prophet died in 632 C.E. the warring tribes of Arabia were united under the banner of Islam and were poised to make significant contribution to world history and civilisation. The message of Islam had galvanised the hitherto scattered nomadic Arabs into a powerful community with a mission. Within a short space of time the message of Islam was echoed from the shores of Europe to China. The invitation to accept the sovereignty of One God was overwhelmingly accepted, over eight hundred million Muslims bear testimony to this message today. A new society was established on the basis of an ideology and it was able to have within its embrace people belonging to different races, colours and historical traditions.

8.6.16   A new model of human personality and a new vision of human culture were presented before humanity. Science and technology were developed but they were not directed towards destroying nature and man's abode therein; they added to man's efficiency as much as to life's sublimity. There was a new harmony between man and nature and between man and society. The uniqueness of Islamic culture lies in its values. When Muslims, after an illustrious historical career, became oblivious of this fact and became obsessed with the manifestations of their culture, as against its sources, they could not even fully protect the house they had built. The strength of Islam lies in its ideals, values and principles. And their relevance to man is as great today as it has been in history. The message, the Qur'an that contains the message, the example of the prophet that embodies this message, and the example of his followers who have kept the torch burning throughout history are a living force. The message is timeless and the principles it embodies are of universal application. Man has to grasp the message and follow the example of Muhammad (may peace be upon him) to elevate himself to his true position as God's representative on earth.

Thus man, who has lost his bearings at the very threshold of his material and technological prowess needs the reality of Islam to breath a new spirit into him; to revive his decaying morality and values; to show him a fresh direction; to prevent him from taking that final suicidal leap into oblivion; to show him the path to happiness and bliss for which he has laboured so much only to find himself on the edge of a precipice — in short, to give him what, deep down within him, he has always wanted, and on which his survival and future development rests.

Source: Published by the Islamic Council of Europe by The Islamic Foundation, Leicester, 1976.

9   SECULAR ALTERNATIVES TO RELIGION

[*Editor's Note:* Many people take the view that man's relationship with some transcendent spiritual reality is now no longer a possibility for them. The process of secularisation, which began in so-called 'developed' societies, is now challenging the claims and the institutions of organised religion almost everywhere.

No study of Man's Religious Quest could reasonably have omitted material about these 'secular alternatives'. The next part of the Reader draws attention to this process of secularisation, looking at what some scholars choose to regard as 'substitute faiths', because for many people a secular philosophy has replaced a religious world view. The article by J.M. Yinger is necessarily of limited scope but it says many important things; and students also have as one of their text books Roland Robertson's *Sociology of Religion* giving them additional material in this field. Dr Stuart Brown, a philosopher, is the author of the Course Units on *Secular Alternatives.*]

9.1 SECULAR ALTERNATIVES TO RELIGIOUS ACTION

J.M. Yinger

[Introduction]

9.1.1

There is no sharp break that distinguishes religious behavior from other kinds of behavior; only a shading off, as various criteria in one's definition become less and less applicable. It is possible, of course, to pay so much attention to a few similarities among phenomena that the large differences are obscured. Neurosis may be described as a private form of religion, or a man's job may be called his religion. These are not so much wrong as they are intriguing part truths that require careful qualification. The opposite difficulty, however, is perhaps more common: Differences among phenomena are so heavily stressed that the important similarities, in terms of function, are overlooked. At the extreme is the assertion that nothing is religion except one's own system of beliefs and practices. In a day of widespread culture contact, this is less likely than the contention that, although there may be many forms of religion, no phenomenon should be admitted to this category unless it bears the *name* religion. But this word *religion* is without cognates in many languages. It draws a line through reality at places uncongenial to some usages. We are concerned, however, not with names but with processes. If nationalism, for example, performs some of the same individual and group functions as religion, this is an important fact that must be explored, despite differences in name.

There are two primary questions to keep in mind in the analysis of functional alternatives: What are the conditions under which one alternative rather than another will be followed? And what are the similarities and differences in their consequences? These are difficult questions, to which we shall refer at various points in the chapters that follow, in connection with specific situations. In a general answer, one may only say that social, cultural, and character facts set limits to the kinds of alternatives that may be selected. A contemporary American may develop such a faith in the power of science, may make it so much an object of devotion, that it can fairly be said that science is his religion. Clearly this would not be an available alternative in many other sociocultural situations. Nor is it available to persons of different tendencies. Those in whom a love of mystery is strong; those who have been taught to distrust reason; the 'twice-born' torn by doubt and a sense of sin— all these are people unlikely to adopt such an alternative.

The consequences of having adopted one alternative rather than another also vary from situation to situation and from individual to individual. One cannot say that the results of infusing nationalism with a religious fervor will be everywhere the same. To respond to a sense of powerlessness by joining a Nazi movement does not have the same consequences as a universalist religious response to the same feeling. Clearly there are important value questions involved, as well as problems of analysis, for one response may be far less effective than another in achieving stated goals and may produce more unintended dysfunctions.

9.1.2 [The Satisfying of Needs]

Almost every need that we have mentioned in connection with religion finds expression in a wide variety of secular movements. This is particularly true in modern society, in which traditional religious symbols and forms have lost force and appeal. The needs with which religion is connected are still with us. If we are not trained to look to a religious system in our attempts to satisfy them, we will tend to infuse secular patterns with a religious quality. We may seek to overcome a sense of aloneness by joining a lodge, rather than (or in addition to) joining a church congregation. We may struggle with a feeling of powerlessness by imbuing our nation with an absolute quality, rather than identifying with an all-powerful God. We may attempt to rid ourselves of guilt by projecting our weakness onto a minority group, instead of going to confession. We may try to reduce a sense of confusion and doubt by adopting rigid 'all-knowing' secular formulas to explain the world's ills, holding to them with a desperation born more of uncertainty than of conviction. We may attempt to reduce our sense of meaninglessness in life, of boredom in our job, by avid pursuit of entertainment or by alcohol, trying to capture on a weekend what is denied us in the course of our work. (It is in such a situation that 'the lost weekend' takes on a tragic quality, for if the weekend is lost, what remains to a man alienated from his job?)

Such secular attempts to reduce our problems do not necessarily stand in the way of religious efforts. A person with a strong sense of guilt, for example, may be drawn to religion and at the same time express strong racial prejudices, as a result of a tendency toward projection. This does not necessarily show a causal connection between the two patterns of behavior, although they may be causally interrelated. On the other hand, a secular alternative may be quite incompatible with certain kinds of religious attempts to deal with the same problem. The chauvinist who exalts the state into a god may also support a parochial religion, but he can scarcely give full allegiance to a universalist religion.

Those on whom the pressures of life fall most heavily (either because of individual circumstances or because of the time in which they live) *and* for whom an established religious system is lacking, are the most likely candidates for a secular movement of a proto-religious variety. These are the discontented, alienated people who follow the 'Prophets of Deceit', as Lowenthal and Guterman call them.

[An Illustration from History]   9.1.3

Movements that are very different in ideology or in proclaimed goals may satisfy many of the same needs — needs for direction, for a sense of belonging to a vital and significant group, for projection and displacement of one's guilt and doubt, for answers to the meaning of life. Since few social movements accomplish more than a minimum of what they promise, their adherents move restlessly in and out of them, propelled by their own unsatisfied needs. Eric Hoffer describes 'the interchangeability of mass movements':

> In pre-Hitlerian Germany it was often a toss-up whether a restless youth would join the Communists or the Nazis. In the over-crowded pale of Czarist Russia the simmering Jewish population was ripe both for revolution and Zionism. In the same family, one member would join the revolutionaries and the other the Zionists. Dr Chaim Weizmann quotes a saying of his mother in those days: 'Whatever happens, I shall be well off. If Shemuel [the revolutionary son] is right, we shall all be happy in Russia; and if Chaim [the Zionist] is right, then I shall go to live in Palestine.'[1]

[Prejudice and Traditional Religion]   9.1.4

In one sense it is a 'tossup' whether a person will support one or another of social movements that have quite different ideologies and different consequences. Whether or not a given movement is available, in the sense of being carried along a communications network of which an individual is a part, may be as critical a fact as its ideology. It is a mistake, however, to disregard the values and tendencies of potential adherents. These serve as screens that filter out and change various messages. Only under extreme conditions are a person's predispositions irrelevant to the outcome. It is when we combine knowledge of the ideologies, the networks of interaction, and individual tendencies that we best understand the success and failure of various movements.

This is shown clearly in examinations of the relationship between religion and prejudice. An individual may seize upon a socially established system of discrimination and prejudice against minority groups to assuage his self-doubt or to try to reduce his sense of failure. Some studies, in fact, have found a positive correlation between prejudice and traditional religious views of the world. The correlation, however, requires careful examination and interpretation. Does the religious training cause the prejudice? Or does a prejudiced person find a traditional religious outlook congenial? Or does a self-doubting, frustrated person grasp at *both* prejudice *and* religion to try to reduce his difficulties?

The evidence is somewhat mixed. Putney and Middleton found a small but statistically significant correlation between religious orthodoxy and authoritarianism in a large sample of college students. The orthodox were also more likely to be highly concerned about their social status and to be conservative in political and economic matters. These results must be interpreted cautiously, however. Since those with high scores in orthodoxy and authoritarianism were also more likely to be underclassmen, women, Southern, and Catholic, a functional relationship between variations in character (authoritarianism) and religious belief was not clearly established. Maranell, in a study of four undergraduate university samples, found a strong relationship between prejudice and religiosity only in the Southern groups. Photiadis and Johnson introduced a number of personality and educational controls, by means of partial correlation analysis, and found that in a sample of three hundred church members, there was a significant relationship between prejudice and orthodox beliefs. With the limits of the measures used, the relationship could show either that prejudiced persons retain orthodox beliefs or that they become orthodox believers. The causal direction cannot be established. They also found that both authoritarian and tolerant persons, orthodox and unorthodox, became more tolerant through extended church participation.

[Extrinsic and intrinsic religious beliefs] 9.1.5

This last finding points up the weakness of much of the work on this problem: It uses only one dimension of religiosity, most frequently a belief dimension. A high score on the scale of 'being religious' usually implies that one takes a conservative or orthodox position. When other dimensions are introduced, such as Photiadis' and Johnson's measures of participation, we are able to develop a more differentiated interpretation of the relationship between religion and prejudice. Gordon Allport was working along these lines with his distinction between intrinsic and extrinsic religious beliefs, the former being a product of security and normal socialization and the latter a product of insecurity and self-interest. He suggested that extrinsic religious beliefs might be associated with prejudice whereas intrinsic beliefs were associated with tolerance. Efforts to define and measure these terms precisely have not been entirely successful; and findings concerning the relationship between extrinsic beliefs and prejudice have been somewhat contradictory. The need for differentiating among varieties of religious belief and adding attention to other dimensions of religion, however, is of continuing importance. When Allen and Spilka used multiple criteria for religiosity, they found a strong correspondence between prejudice and what they called consensual religion and a negative relationship between prejudice and committed faith, terms similar to Allport's extrinsic-intrinsic distinction.

In the light of these several findings, we can no longer be satisfied with undifferentiated studies of 'religion' and 'prejudice'.

Three 'Secular Religions' of the Contemporary World 9.1.6

Individual prejudices may serve as the basis for groups with religious qualities; or more precisely, the needs underlying those prejudices, if they are shared by a number of persons, may provide that basis in certain supportive environments. The rites and doctrines of the Ku Klux Klan, for example, can be interpreted in this way. More substantial grounds for secular movements with religious qualities, however, are found in three international developments that express important aspects of the tensions and changes of the modern world. Brief comments on these three developments will be helpful in seeing the interplay of cultural, structural, and character elements.

As Paul Tillich has noted, the encounters of the major world religions today are primarily with a series of what he calls quasi-religions — nationalism, communism, and humanism. To fail to study such movements would be to leave a serious gap in the scientific study of religion.

I have already noted that science, morality, and magic were closely associated with religion because they dealt with issues of religious import — ignorance, injustice, and suffering. It is not surprising that in the last several generations, with traditional religions undergoing sharp challenge, substitute ideologies have appeared that offer themselves as new roads to salvation. What *is* perhaps surprising is that three of these substitutes, each proclaiming itself a science, have specialized around the three basic issues mentioned above, in an effort to save man from ignorance, injustice, and suffering. These are *Positivism, Marxism,* and *Freudianism.*

9.1.7 *Religious Aspects of Positivism*

This section might be called a comment on the religion of 'reason and humanity', except that such a phrase calls up too specific an association with the Enlightenment. The religion might be called scientism, except that this term has a more cultist connotation than is intended. In *The Grammar of Science* Karl Pearson described the religion of science as 'single-eyed devotion to truth', but that leaves aside the elements of worship and morality that need also to be kept in mind. Perhaps positivism, despite the variety of meanings associated with it, most nearly represents the range of ideas I wish to discuss.

The roots of positivism go deep, certainly back as far as the Renaissance and more particularly to the early forms of deism that developed along with seventeenth-century science. Newton envisaged a kind God managing an orderly universe, or perhaps one should say viewing an ordered universe that he had created. For Newton and most of his contemporaries, reason could be combined with a fairly traditional faith.

The eighteenth century saw a great increase in belief in man's powers. At least we see such an increase in the thought of the most influential writers. They ranged from relatively conservative deists to secular nationalists, but their dominant emphasis was on reason and humanity, a belief in the possibilities of progress through the application of human intelligence and beneficence. To Condorcet, Diderot, Rousseau, Voltaire and Paine, to mention some of the most influential among them, it was time for a religion of reason and humanity. On the one hand, their work was oppositional and negative: traditional religion and clericalism must be destroyed — *Écrasez l'infâme*. On the other hand, however, there was a positive faith: By the combination of beneficence and reason mankind can achieve the heavenly city on earth.

[Comte's Religion]   9.1.8

For a brief period during the French revolution, the Cathedral of Notre Dame was known as the Temple of Reason. A succession of groups to propagate the 'cult of reason' developed; but most were short-lived. For the most part, the religion of humanity, of progress, of reason, of posterity was an idea in the minds of intellectuals. It was with Saint-Simon and more particularly with Comte that this idea became the basis of a strong organizational effort. Science was to replace theology as the source of ultimate values and perspectives. To his *System of Positive Polity*, Comte gave the subtitle *Religion of Humanity*. By his religion of humanity, as Baumer remarks, he sought to become for his age what St Thomas had been for his own. 'A peace of unexampled duration', Comte wrote in 1852, 'has thoroughly established the spontaneous extinction of the principle of War, and the manifest tendency of modern nations to form ultimately one vast family; the object of whose practical activity is to cultivate the earth, in the constant service of Humanity.'[2] He saw the 'true Religion, the final system of Sociocracy' toward which mankind was steadily converging, not as a revolt against traditional religions but an evolutionary development out of them. Voltaire could say that 'to do good' was his worship; but Comte believed that the anarchy he feared would be avoided and the reasoned beneficence he sought could be obtained only by the full trappings of religion — by church and a hierarchy of leaders, by careful attention to the training of the young, by worship, and by regard for the emotional quality of human existence.

As an organized movement, Comte's religion achieved little success and survives only in a few small positivist groups and, in a more cultist form, in scientology. Many nineteenth-century intellectuals shared his belief in a religion of humanity based on reason, but could not accept the highly institutionalized and even authoritarian church that Comte envisaged. These views were perhaps most explicitly extended a generation after Comte by his countryman Ernest Renan, when he called for the institution of a religion of science. But belief in the saving power of scientific knowledge has more commonly been mixed with nationalism or with ethical humanism. It is an aspect of secular religion rather than the very core of a faith. At least for many who take this view, science is a powerful instrument but is not itself the source of ultimate values. In terms that we shall develop later, belief in science is *diffused* through the structures and cultural values of some societies rather than *institutionalized* as a distinctive religious pattern.

9.1.9 [Faith in Science]

We need to recognize that a religious attachment to science is no more immune from skepticism than are other faiths. For a century and a half, between the mid-eighteenth and the early twentieth centuries, it may have been possible to state, with Renan, that 'science alone can solve' man's eternal problems or to predict, with Comte, the extinction of the principle of war. But today, such utter confidence in science requires more faithfulness than most men can manage, even those who regard themselves as intellectuals, or perhaps I should say, especially among intellectuals. The immediate past has been more 'the age of longing' than an age of positivism.

In the sense of a diffused quality, nevertheless, faith in science is widespread in Western societies, even among the traditionally devout. Its victories over many of man's pressing day-by-day problems is too impressive to disregard in the formation of one's scheme of salvation. There is something of Comte in Durkheim's vision of society reorganized by the development of a scientific morality. Durkheim would have schools teach morality, with society substituted for God — a kind of 'functional equivalent of Catholicism'.

I shall not undertake here an examination of the various rationalist, secularist, and humanist groups for whom science is a powerful object of faith. In some this has been a gradual development stemming from liberal and radical expressions of a traditional religion. Julian Huxley's *Religion Without Revelation* and John Dewey's *A Common Faith,* for example, are extensions of 'left-wing' Christianity, not sharp departures from it.

Faith in science is commonly associated with a social movement built primarily around some other dominant theme — it is an adjunct to the movement rather than its source. Thus Weber speaks of the 'almost superstitious veneration of science' as part of the 'quasi-religious belief in the socialist eschatology' among some of those in nineteenth-century radical movements.[3] This leads us, however, to examination of faith of a different kind; for if science has conditioned the beliefs of political radicals, it was a secular millenarian prophecy that set the dominant tone.

Religious Aspects of Marxism 9.1.10

Prophetic condemnation of an evil world has a long religious tradition. Marxism as an ideology and communism as a movement can be seen as a modern secularized, and highly specialized, prophetic movement, proclaiming the road to justice. Where positivism sees science as the road to salvation, communism sees the creation of new economic and political structures as the way. Its religious quality is apparent in Western societies, where only a small minority of the population have become adherents, as well as in societies where communism is dominant. In the former, the search for an 'overwhelmingly strong power' on which to rely, which may lead one person to give himself to God, may under particular conditions of character and circumstance lead another to 'the party'. It is a mistake to disregard the differences that these choices indicate, but equally a mistake to overlook some important similarities. There is ample evidence that some of the recruits to the Communist Party in the West during the 1930s were highly sensitive people, bewildered by the confusions of modern society, idealistic, and in need of a clear-cut program that claimed to be able to solve the problems they felt so deeply. They found in the authoritative program of communism and in its seeming dedication to justice an 'escape from freedom' that gave them both a sense of belonging and a sense of power. They were no longer the alienated; they had a 'home' and a program.

[Communism: The God that Failed] 9.1.11

For many of them, of course, communism became 'the God that failed', able to give them a sense of identity with an exciting movement but scarcely able to satisfy their idealism. As they became disenchanted with communism, they turned to other programs, propelled by the same burning need for a way to struggle with their bewilderment and sense of powerlessness. Some turned to vigorous anticommunism, investing it with the same energy and dedication they had formerly shown for communism. Others turned to classical religion, in several celebrated cases to Roman Catholicism. Such a dramatic change doubtless indicates a strong reaction against communism; but it also shows some personality continuity, for the Catholic Church more than any other in Christianity furnished its members with a fixed dogma, definitive rites, and an unchallenged structure of power that brought a sense of certainty to those torn by doubt — something of the same appeal that communism had for some people. Because of significant changes in Catholicism, this may be less true now than in the 1930s. Those persons in the 'new left' who become disenchanted may, if these processes in fact are operative, be less inclined to move into Catholicism.

Arthur Koestler describes the religious quality that communism had for him in vivid words:

By the time I had finished with *Feuerbach* and *State and Revolution,* something had clicked in my brain which shook me like a mental explosion. To say that one had 'seen the light' is a poor description of the mental rapture which only the convert knows (regardless of what faith he has been converted to). The new light seems to pour from all directions across the skull; the whole universe falls into pattern like the stray pieces of a jigsaw puzzle assembled by magic at one stroke. There is now an answer to every question, doubts and conflicts are a matter of the tortured past — a past already remote, when one had lived in dismal ignorance in the tasteless, colorless world of those who *don't know.*[4]

Among the 221 former Communists studied by Almond, almost half came from homes where religious interests were important. He interprets their opposition to the religion of their parents, not simply as antireligious development, but often as a redirection of interest to a movement that was embraced with religious fervor.

9.1.12 [Contemporary Radicalism]

Contemporary radicalism in the United States is of many varieties. Our interest here is in those forms of it that are associated with extreme political deviation, with support for 'Maoism' as an ideology and strategy, for example. Because this is mixed, more than was true of the radicalism of the 1930s, with other forms of protest — with attempts to change universities, increase Black Power, or simply to realize rather widely accepted but neglected goals — it is difficult to isolate the individuals and with them the tendencies that support it. There seems little reason to doubt, however, that the movement has its origins also in idealism and longing, heightened by social disorganization and by opposition to those in authority. Perhaps those under thirty who do not trust those over thirty might at least study them – to learn a great deal about themselves, and their probable futures.

Within communist societies, of course, Marxism is not sectarian protest, but the Establishment. It is as vulnerable to schism, to be sure, as are other major faiths, so that one can see 'denominational' variation within societies and major splits across societal lines. There is also sharp conflict, with varying degrees of accommodation, with older religions. In the Soviet Union, the fifty-year-long effort to destroy competing faiths has been only partially successful. Mainland China's 'cultural revolution', which is at least in part an effort by Mao's regime to break the hold of traditional values and to establish communist values, has also met strong resistance. Yet there is little doubt that in terms of belief, ritual, and organization, communism is the major religion of the Soviet Union and China.

[Totalitarian 'Messianism'] 9.1.13

The religious quality of communism was more readily visible in its sectarian period, when it took the form of utopian communities or a messianic movement. Its relationship to the Judaic-Christian tradition is not entirely lost, however, even in its more explicitly political dimensions. And now, after decades of sharp organizational separation and hostility, some slight movement toward encounter, if not reconciliation, is beginning.

Leaving aside all these complexities, our brief reference here is to the ways in which communism (and indeed other forms of totalitarianism) functions as a religion. The injustices of the non-communist world and the powerlessness of workers and peasants in it are described in rich detail in communist literature. But they are provisional facts, to be transformed by the movement. Problems of the present are interpreted in terms of a glorious future that gives those problems meaning. There are appeals to faith. A writer in *The New Masses* declared: 'The loss of religious faith is good only if we can put in its place a faith in life so real and driving that it endows men's acts with an equal validity. . .'[5]

Many despotic movements of the past have sought to use religion to reinforce their power, but in societies in which distinctive religious institutions have developed, despots have seldom been able to bring the religious forces completely under their control. Some element of restraint, some limit on their power was imposed by a partially competing religious system. Waldemar Gurian has distinguished such despotisms from modern totalitarianisms by the fact that the latter are not content simply to use or control the religious forces: they supplant them with their own creed, thus absorbing and using the religious interest to support their cause.

> The totalitarian movements and their power replace God and religious institutions such as the Church; the leaders are deified; the public mass-meetings are regarded and celebrated as sacred actions; the history of the movement becomes a holy history of the advance of salvation, which the enemies and betrayers try to prevent in the same way as the devil tries to undermine and destroy the work of those who are in the service of the City of God.[6]

From contemporary evidence it is clear that Gurian should have written that totalitarian regimes *attempt* to supplant traditional religions. If they become reasonably secure, in fact, some processes of accommodation are undertaken, as has happened in the case of the Soviet Union and the Russian Orthodox Church. Moreover, in the second and third generations, liberal as well as reactionary opponents of the regime may begin to use religion of a traditional form as a mode of expressing their opposition, indicating further its staying power.

9.1.14 [Other Signs of Religion in Totalitarianism]

Keeping in mind these qualifications, we still must note that modern totalitarian systems serve as religions for many people. They attempt to make the grave problems of life more bearable by reference to a happier future, thus sharing the cosmic optimism of religion. The dictator becomes a living embodiment of a 'supernatural' power, scarcely limited by the forces that have prevented other men from solving overwhelming problems. History is on the side of 'the elect'. Ritual, emotionally evocative music, and pageantry are used to heighten support for the cause. Sacred writings and official doctrines are recited and republished endlessly. (In Hitler's time a copy of *Mein Kampf* was given to every newly-wed couple.) Before the totalitarian parties have achieved power, there are many 'sectarian' elements in their approach. After they have come to power, they become 'churchlike'. Altogether, the religious aspects of communism and other totalitarian movements are important elements to the person interested in understanding their influence.

Psychoanalysis as a Modern Faith   9.1.15

The alternative to religion may be, not some social movement with which one can identify, but a private pattern of belief and ritual used by an unhappy individual in his attempts to counter personal failure and isolation. In extreme cases, this private system will be identified by others as a neurosis. Many writers have noted the thin line that separates a moving religious experience from neurotic illness. James developed this point in his classic work. Freud, of course, tended to identify all religion as an expression of neurotic trends. Fromm adds that neurosis can be seen as a private form of religion — an attempt to struggle with the sense of isolation and powerlessness that overwhelms one. If reality is too painful to bear, one can redefine it with the schizophrenic, stand in opposition to it with the paranoic, or alternately run past it and hide from it with the manic-depressive. That each of these responses has its religious equivalent can readily be seen. In his detailed study of 173 seriously disturbed patients, Boisen observes the similarities between their efforts to struggle with their pains and religious behaviour. He notes that many great religious leaders — George Fox, John Bunyan, and St Paul, for example — had emotional disturbances comparable to those of acutely disturbed patients. Yet they were not simply neurotic individuals; '. . .the correct contrast is not between the pathological and the normal in religious experience, but between spiritual defeat and spiritual victory'[7]. Unfortunately, even if we accept his value judgment, Boisen does not explore the conditions in which one may hope for the visions of a Fox instead of the illusions and delusions of a disturbed person. The scientist must try to discover the social, cultural, and character factors that incline one toward a religious effort in dealing with his anxieties rather than toward a neurotic effort.

One of the conditions may be the degree to which an anxiety is 'legitimized' by available cultural interpretations and to some degree 'externalized' by the definitions of a group. A religious movement may help to transform an individual's suffering into an expression of the human condition — and thus furnish a means for dealing with it that is not caught in the ambivalences of the purely individual experience.

9.1.16 [The Insights of Freud]

Freud was unwilling to accept such a compromise with his ideal of
the free individual who governs his own fate to a maximum degree.
Although he was ready to grant that, as a shared neurosis, religion
had some advantages over the individual variety, he saw his task as
the elimination of both. 'He wanted merely to give men more
options than their raw experience of life permitted',[8] by furnishing
them with the power to interpret that experience. The zeal with
which he defended this purely analytical approach, however, had
something of a religious quality to it. It stimulated in his somewhat
less tough-minded associates and followers faithfulness, on the one
hand, and zealotry for competing approaches on the other. In the
context of the tragedies of the twentieth century, Freud's belief in
the ability of the person to achieve mastery over both id and
superego has been difficult to sustain. To some, the upwelling of
violence and sexuality has demonstrated the strength of id forces.
To others, the rigidity, injustice, and irrationality of existing
institutions have documented the coercions of the superego. From
either perspective one sees a need for a new community, through
which not *the* individual but *all individuals in their interdependence*
can find maturity.

Thus Freud has become, almost in spite of himself, '. . .the
founder of a great religious sect',[9] or perhaps we should say, of a
variety of related but competing sects. Jung and Adler, and many
others after them, have elaborated the analytic experience as a
source of commitment and community, through which suffering can
be alleviated.

9.1.17 *Partiality of the Secular Alternatives*

In these brief references to three major nontraditional, secular
faiths I have tended, for purposes of sharpness of distinction, to
exaggerate their special focus on the problems of ignorance, powerlessness, or suffering. We need to note further, therefore, the strong
tendencies toward coalescence in some of the movements associated
with one or another of these problems and in the writings of
important adherents. There are many efforts, for example, to blend
Marxian and Freudian principles, both of which, in turn, share
elements of the positivist tradition. When the three lines converge,
we have the basis for contemporary religious humanism, probably
best represented in the work of Erich Fromm. His chief concern is
not that God is dead, but that *man* is dead — transformed into a

thing by a depersonalized world of his own creation. He thus expresses the fear of existentialists, from Marx and Kierkegaard to Jean-Paul Sartre and Tillich, that a vast renewal of human purposes is needed. These existentialists vary widely, of course, and Fromm differs from each of them in his explicit formulation of a religious humanism.

At the same time, there have been some tendencies within the established religious organization to reach out toward the secular movements, particularly Marxism and Freudianism, in an effort to enfold them and interpret them. Religious efforts to make use of the insights yet to avoid the errors of the secular alternatives, as seen by religious adherents, often stress their incompleteness, their tendency to focus on one or another of the several basic elements of the human condition. More than that, however, from the perspective of the traditional religions, positivism, Marxism, and Freudianism fail to struggle with the truly ultimate questions: How does one deal with our lack of comprehension of the meaning of life, even after every effort to overcome ignorance has been made? How does one respond to the powerlessness and injustice that remain when every secular line of attack on them has been tried? How does one handle the suffering that our most dedicated efforts seem incapable of removing? From the perspective of religious thinkers, therefore, the secular alternatives, however fruitful and important they may be, are partial and incomplete. They do not deal with the ultimate questions.

[The Continuing Questions] 9.1.18

In this discussion of alternatives, important value questions inevitably arise. The scientist cannot say simply that this is a better alternative than that; but he can declare: If this be one's aim, then choice A is better than choice B. Even Freud was willing to grant that in most cases, religion was better than neurosis, because it was a shared 'illusion'. The religious person, because he deals with others, finds his way to some part of reality — which to Freud was a basic goal. The neurotic is an isolated person; indeed, the most painful and difficult part of every neurosis is the overwhelming sense of isolation. But Freud grants very little, in fact. The religious person is likely to assert not only that religion will rescue man from the despair and isolation of neurosis, but that it will harness man's energies for positive achievements. Taking a leaf from the functionalist's notebook, he asks: If man cannot live without a 'frame of orientation and an object of devotion', is not classical religion better than communism, or parochial nationalism, or positivism? Would we not have fewer social movements with narrow and limited goals, yet armed with convictions of absolute validity, and would we not have fewer distraught and bewildered persons, if men were to 'return to religion'? Others, granting the force of this argument, will say: But classical religion is too loaded with the superstitions of the past and itself too easily twisted to support the aims of limited groups — of classes and nations — to make it clearly superior to its secular alternatives. What is in fact needed is a 'new universalism', fully harmonious with modern science and the modern world. Still others believe that at least some of the functions formerly undertaken by religion are as well or better performed by secular alternatives. Few people now oppose secular medical practice, for example. Why should this development not fully include emotional disturbances as well as physical ailments?

We are not concerned here with exploring these highly significant value questions. It is our task to note the functional interconnections of different social and personal facts, secular and religious. But one need not deny the hope that a scientific statement may contribute to effective study and action in terms relevant to the facts of contemporary life.

Notes

1. Eric Hoffer, *The True Believer,* London 1952, pp.16-17.
2. August Comte, *System of Positive Polity,* New York 1967, Vol.2, p.116.
3. Max Weber, *Sociology of Religion,* London 1971, p.135.
4. Arthur Koestler, *The God that failed,* London 1950, p.23.
5. Quoted by Reinhold Niebuhr, *Christianity and Power Politics,* Hamden, Conn. 1969, p.192.
6. Waldemar Gurian in *Totalitarianism,* Carl J. Friedrich, ed., Cambridge, Mass. 1958, p.122.
7. A.T. Boisen, *The Exploration of the Inner World,* New York 1936, p.79.
8. Philip Rieff, *The Triumph of the Therapeutic,* New York, p.87.
9. Erwin Goodenough, *The Psychology of Religious Experience,* New York 1965, p.x.

Source: J.M. Yinger, *Secular Alternatives to Religion,* Collier-Macmillan, New York 1970, pp.190-202.

10   ASPECTS OF AFRICAN RELIGION

[*Editor's Note:* In the Course served by this Reader there is a section carrying the title which is at the head of this page. That section does not, of course, attempt to cover the religions of the entire African continent, but concentrates on specific case studies. These studies are concerned with Sudan and Nigeria. In the Reader itself we confine ourselves to material relating to the religion of the Nuer and the Dinka, tribes of the region of the Upper Nile.

We shall be looking here (and it is unusual in the Course) at religions which have no body of doctrine written down, no sacred books. It is a fascinating matter to realise the strength of oral tradition in religion and to explore the implications behind the ritual activity of peoples who have been, in their religion, misleadingly described as 'primitive'. Students are aware of the danger of applying Western religious presuppositions to African tribal religious practices. Nevertheless, in this Section of the Course they have the opportunity to compare some religious insights and practices of African traditional religions with those of the great 'documented' religions of the world which they have already studied.]

10.1 GOD IN NUER RELIGION

E.E. Evans-Pritchard

I

[God as Creative Spirit] 10.1.1

The Nuer word we translate 'God' is *kwoth*,[1] Spirit. Nuer also speak of him more definitely as *kwoth nhial* or *kwoth a nhial*, Spirit of the sky or Spirit who is in the sky. There are other and lesser spirits which they class as *kuth nhial*, spirits of the sky or of the above, and *kuth piny*, spirits of the earth or of the below. I discuss the conception of God first because the other spiritual conceptions are dependent on it and can only be understood in relation to it.

The Nuer *kwoth*, like the Latin *spiritus*, the Greek *pneuma*, and 10.1.2 the English derivatives of both words, suggests both the intangible quality of air and the breathing or blowing out of air. Like the Hebrew *ruah* it is an onomatope and denotes violent breathing out of air in contrast to ordinary breathing. In its verbal form it is used to describe such actions as blowing on the embers of a fire; blowing on food to cool it; blowing into the uterus of a cow, while a tulchan is propped up before it, to make it give milk; snorting; the blowing out of air by the puff fish; and the hooting by steam pressure of a river steamer. The word is also found, and has the same general sense, in some of the other Nilotic languages.

As a noun, however, *kwoth* means only Spirit, and in the particular 10.1.3 sense we are now discussing it means *kwoth nhial* or *kwoth a nhial*, Spirit of the heavens or Spirit who is in the heavens, the copula *a* in the second designation being one of the verbs we translate 'to be'. *Nhial* is the sky, and combined with verbs the word may also refer to certain natural processes associated with the sky, as raining and thundering; but it may also have merely the sense of 'on high' or 'above'. We may certainly say that the Nuer do not regard the sky or any celestial phenomenon as God, and this is clearly shown in the distinction made between God and the sky in the expressions 'Spirit of the sky' and 'Spirit who is in the sky'. Moreover, it would even be a mistake to interpret 'of the sky' and 'in the sky' too literally.

10.1.4   It would equally be a mistake to regard the association of God with the sky as pure metaphor, for though the sky is not God, and though God is everywhere, he is thought of as being particularly in the sky, and Nuer generally think of him in a spatial sense as being on high. Hence anything connected with the firmament has associations with him. Nuer sometimes speak of him as falling in the rain and of being in lightning and thunder. Mgr. Mlakic says that the rainbow is called the necklace of God.[2] I have never heard a spontaneous reference to the sun as a divine manifestation, but if one asks Nuer about it they say that it too belongs to God, and the moon and the stars also. They say that if a man sees the sun at night this is a divine manifestation, and one which is most dangerous for him; but I think that the light they say is occasionally seen is not regarded as an appearance of the physical sun but as some peculiar luminous vision. When Nuer see the new moon they rub ashes on their foreheads and they throw ashes, and perhaps also a grain of millet, towards it, saying some short prayer, as 'grandfather, let us be at peace' or 'ah moon, *nyadeang* (daughter of the air-spirit *deng*) we invoke (God) that thou shouldst appear with goodness. May the people see thee every day. Let us be (akolapko). . .

10.1.5   It would be quite contrary to Nuer thought, as I have remarked, and it would even seem absurd to them, to say that sky, moon, rain, and so forth are in themselves, singly or collectively, God. God is Spirit, which, like wind and air, is invisible and ubiquitous. But though God is not these things he is in them in the sense that he reveals himself through them. In this sense, he is in the sky, falls in the rain, shines in the sun and moon, and blows in the wind. These divine manifestations are to be understood as modes of God and not as his essence, which is Spirit.

10.1.6   God being above, everything above is associated with him. This is why the heavenly bodies and the movements and actions connected with them are associated with him. This is why also the spirits of the air are regarded as *gaat kwoth,* children of God, in a way other spirits are not, for they, unlike other spirits, dwell in the air and are also thought of as being in the clouds, which are nearest to the sky. This is why also the *colwic* spirits are so closely associated with God, for he touched them with his fire from heaven and took them to himself. Some birds also are spoken about by Nuer as *gaat kwoth,* especially those which fly high and seem, to us as well as to Nuer, to belong to heaven rather than to earth and therefore to be children of light and symbols of the divine. The feeling that they are in a measure detached from the earth is enhanced in the case of migratory birds by their disappearances and reappearances. I have heard the idea expressed that in their absence from Nuerland they have gone to visit God's country. This is probably no more than poetic fancy, but we can say that the disappearance of these birds strengthens the allegory of God's children which arises from their ability to do what man cannot do, fly towards heaven and God...

Thus anything associated with the sky has virtue which is lacking 10.1.7 in earthly things. Nuer pathetically compare man to heavenly things. He is *ran piny,* an earthly persons and, according to the general Nuer view, his ghost is also earth-bound. Between God and man, between heaven and earth, there is a great gulf, and we shall find that an appreciation of the symbolism of the polarity of heaven and earth helps us to understand Nuer religious thought and feeling and also sheds light on certain social features of their religion, for example the greater prestige of prophets than of priests.

Before discussing further the separation of God from man I will 10.1.8 mention some of the chief attributes of God. He is in the sky, but his being in the sky does not mean that he is not at the same time elsewhere, and on earth. Indeed, as will be seen, Nuer religious thought cannot be understood unless God's closeness to man is taken together with his separation from man, for its meaning lies precisely in this paradox.

Nuer say that God is everywhere, that he is 'like wind' and 'like air'... He may be spoken of by the epithets *jiom,* wind, and *ghau,* universe, but these words only stand for God in poems or in an allegorical sense and are illustrations of the liking the Nilotic peoples show in their poetry for metonymy and synecdoche. God is not wind, but *cere jiom,* like wind; and he is not *ghau,* the universe, but *cak ghaua,* the creator of the universe. Another poetic epithet by which he may be referred to is *tutgar.* This is an ox-name, taken from an ox of the kind Nuer call *wer,* which has wide spreading horns and is the most majestic of their beasts... The name is a combination of two words: *tut,* which has the sense of 'strength' or 'greatness', and *gar,* which has the sense of 'omnipresent', as in another of God's titles, *kwoth me gargar,* the omnipresent God (*gargar* can also be translated 'limitless'). But the commonest Nuer way of trying to express their idea of the nature of God is to say that he is like wind or air, a metaphor which seems appropriate to us because it is found throughout the hierological literature of the world and we are particularly familiar with it in the Old Testament.

Among the Nuer the metaphor is consistent not only with the absence of any fixed abode of God but also of any places where he is thought particularly to dwell, for air and wind are everywhere. Unlike the other spirits God has no prophets or sanctuaries or earthly forms.

God, Spirit in the heavens who is like wind and air, is the creator and mover of all things. Since he made the world he is addressed in prayers as *kwoth ghaua*, Spirit of the universe, with the sense of creator of the universe. The word *cak*, used as a noun, can mean the creation, that is, all created things, and hence the nature or character proper to a person or thing; it can be used in a very special sense to refer to an abnormality, *cak kwoth*, a freak; and, though I think rarely, it is used as a title of God, the creator, as in the expression *cak nath*, creator of men. As a verb 'to create' it signifies creation *ex nihilo*, and when speaking of things can therefore only be used of God. However, the word can be used of men for imaginative constructions, such as the thinking of a name to give a child, inventing a tale, or composing a poem, in the same figurative sense as when we say that an actor creates a part. The word therefore means not only creation from nothing but also creation by thought or imagination, so that 'God created the universe' has the sense of 'God thought of the universe' or 'God imagined the universe'.

10.1.9   Professor Westermann wrote at the dictation of a Nuer an account of how God created the world and made all things in it. It begins *'Me chak koth nath, chwo ran thath'*, which he has translated 'When God created the people, he created man'.[3] It will be observed that he has translated two different words, *cak (chak)* and *tath (thath)*, by 'create', but they have not quite the same sense, for whereas *cak* means creation *ex nihilo* and in thought or imagination, *tath* means to make something out of something else already materially existing, as when a child moulds clay into the shape of an ox or a smith beats a spear out of iron. . .

10.1.10   The complementary distinction made in Genesis between 'the heaven and the earth' is made, by implication at least, in a slightly different way by the Nuer. A parallelism often heard in their prayers is *'e pinydu, e ghaudu'*, 'it is thine earth, it is thy universe'. *Piny* is the down-below, the earth in the sense of the terrestrial world as the Nuer know it. *Ghau* has many meanings — world, sky, earth, atmosphere, time, and weather — which taken together, as they should be in a context of prayer, mean the universe. Another common, and related, strophe in prayers is *'e ghaudu, e rwacdu'*, 'it is thy universe, it is thy word'. *Rwac* in ordinary contexts means speech, talk, or word, but when used in prayers and invocations in the phrase *'e rwacdu'*, 'it is thy word', it means the will of God; and when used in reference to creation it has almost the meaning of the creative word: 'he created the world, it is his word'.

The Nuer can hardly be said to have a creation myth, though our 10.1.11 authorities[4] record some fragmentary accounts of the creation of men, parts of which I have myself heard. These state that men were created in the Jagei country of western Nuerland at a certain tamarind tree, at the foot of which offerings and sacrifices were sometimes made till it was destroyed by fire in 1918. . . . I regard Father Crazzolara's version [of this tradition] as the closest to Nuer tradition. In this version the tamarind tree, called Lic, was itself the mother of men who, according to one account, emerged from a hole at its foot or, according to another account, dropped off its branches like ripe fruits.

Whether they are speaking about events which happened *ne* 10.1.12 *walka,* in the beginning or long ago, or about happenings of yesterday or today, God, creative Spirit, is the final Nuer explanation of everything. When asked how things began or how they have come to be what they are they answer that God made them or that it was his will that they have come to be what they are. The heavens and the earth and the waters on the earth, and the beasts and birds and reptiles and fish were made by him, and he is the author of custom and tradition. The Nuer herd cattle and cultivate millet and spear fish because God gave them these things for their sustenance. He instituted their marriage prohibitions. He gave ritual powers to some men and not to others. He decreed that the Nuer should raid the Dinka and that Europeans should conquer the Nuer. He made one man black and another white (according to one account our white skins are a punishment by God for incest committed by our ancestor with his mother), one man fleet and another slow, one strong and another weak. Everything in nature, in culture, in society, and in men is as it is because God made or willed it so. Above all else God is thought of as the giver and sustainer of life. He also brings death. It is true that Nuer seldom attribute death — in such cases as death by lightning or following the breach of a divinely sanctioned interdiction — to the direct intervention of God, but rather to natural circumstances or to the action of a lesser spirit, but they nevertheless regard the natural circumstances or the spirits as instruments or agents of God, and the final appeal in sickness is made to him. Nuer have often told me that it is God who takes the life, whether a man dies from spear, wild beast, or sickness, for these are all *nyin kwoth,* instruments of God.

10.1.13   In the Nuer conception of God he is thus creative Spirit. He is also a *ran,* a living person, whose *yiegh,* breath or life, sustains man. I have never heard Nuer suggest that he has human form, but though he is himself ubiquitous and invisible, he sees and hears all that happens and he can be angry and can love (the Nuer word is *nhok,* and if we here translate it 'to love' it must be understood in the preferential sense of *agapo* or *diligo:* when Nuer say that God loves something they mean that he is partial to it). However, the anthropomorphic features of the Nuer conception of God are very weak and, as will be seen, they do not act towards him as though he were a man. Indeed, such human features as are given him barely suffice to satisfy the requirements of thought and speech. If he is to be spoken about, or to, he has to be given some human attributes. Man's relation to him is, as it is among other peoples, on the model of a human social relationship. He is the father of men.

10.1.14   A very common mode of address to the Deity is *'gwandong',* a word which means 'grandfather' or 'ancestor', and literally 'old father', but in a religious context 'father' or 'our father' would convey the Nuer sense better; and *'gwara'* and *'gwandan',* 'our father', and the respectful form of address *'gwadin',* 'father', are also often used in speaking to or about God. God is the father of men in two respects. He is their creator and he is their protector.

10.1.15   He is addressed in prayers as *'koth me cak gwadong',* 'God who created my ancestor'. Figuratively, and in conformity with Nuer lineage idiom, he is sometimes given a genealogical position in relation to man. A man of the Jinaca clan, for example, after tracing his pedigree back to Denac, the founder of his clan, may go on to say that Denac was a son of Gee, who was a son of *Ran,* man, who was a son of *Ghau,* the universe, who was a son of *Kwoth,* God. When Nuer thus speak of God as their remote ancestor and address him as 'father' or 'grandfather', and likewise when in praying to him they speak of themselves, as they commonly do, as *'gaatku',* 'thy children', their manner of speech is no more to be taken literally than are those frequent passages in the Old Testament in which Israel is spoken of as the spouse or son of Jehovah. Such ideograms are common enough in all religions. . . Nuer do not think of God as the begetter of man but as his creator.

God is also the father of men in that he is their protector and friend. He is *'kwoth me jale ka ji'*, 'God who walks with you', that is, who is present with you. He is the friend of men who helps them in their troubles, and Nuer sometimes address him as *'madh'*, 'friend', a word which has for them the sense of intimate friendship. The frequent use in prayers of the word *rom* in reference to the lives, or souls, of men indicates the same feeling about God, for it has the sense of the care and protection parents give to a child and especially the carrying of a helpless infant. So does another word often used in prayers, *luek,* to comfort. God is asked to *'luek nei'* to 'comfort the people'. The Nuer habit of making short supplications to God outside formal and ritual occasions also suggests an awareness of a protective presence, as does the affirmation one hears every day among the Nuer, *'kwoth a thin'*, 'God is present'. Nuer say this, doubtless often as a merely verbal response, when they are faced with some difficulty to be overcome or some problem to be solved. The phrase does not mean 'there is a God'. That would be for Nuer a pointless remark. God's existence is taken for granted by everybody. Consequently when we say, as we can do, that all Nuer have faith in God, the word 'faith' must be understood in the Old Testament sense of 'trust' (the Nuer *ngath*) and not in that modern sense of 'belief' which the concept came to have under Greek and Latin influences. There is in any case, I think, no word in the Nuer language which could stand for 'I believe'. *Kwoth a thin* means that God is present in the sense of being in a place or enterprise, the *a* being here again a verb 'to be'. When Nuer use the phrase they are saying that they do not know what to do but God is here with them and will help them. He is with them because he is Spirit and being like wind or air is everywhere, and, being everywhere, is here now.

But though God is sometimes felt to be present here and now, he is also felt to be far away in the sky.[5] If he hears a whispered prayer, it is spoken with eyes and hands raised to the distant heavens. However, heaven and earth, that is, God and man, for we are justified here in treating the dichotomy anagogically, are not entirely separated. There are comings and goings. God takes the souls of those he destroys by lightning to dwell with him and in him they protect their kinsmen; he participates in the affairs of men through divers spirits which haunt the atmosphere between heaven and earth and may be regarded as hypostasisations of his modes and

10.1.16

10.1.17

attributes; and he is also everywhere present in a way which can only be symbolised, as his ubiquitous presence is symbolised by the Nuer, by the metaphor of wind and air. Also he can be communicated with through prayer and sacrifice, and a certain kind of contact with him is maintained through the social order he is said to have instituted and of which he is the guardian, a matter I discuss briefly later. But in spite of these communications and contacts the distance between heaven and earth is too great to be bridged.

10.1.18   God's separation and remoteness from man are accounted for in a myth. . .which relates that there was not always a complete separation of heaven and earth and that there might never have been but for an almost fortuitous event. . . The myth relates that there was once a rope from heaven to earth and how anyone who became old climbed up by it to God in heaven and after being rejuvenated there returned to earth. One day a hyena — an appropriate figure in a myth relating to the origin of death — and what is known in the Sudan as a durra-bird, most likely a weaver-bird, entered heaven by this means. God gave instructions that the two guests were to be well watched and not allowed to return to earth where they would certainly cause trouble. One night they escaped and climbed down the rope, and when they were near the earth the hyena cut the rope and the part above the cut was drawn upwards towards heaven. So the connection between heaven and earth was cut and those who grow old must now die, for what had happened could not be made not to have happened. . .

II

10.1.19 **[Man's Helplessness and God's Goodness]**

It is in the light of their feeling that man is dependent on God and helpless without his aid and that God, though a friend and present, is yet also remote that we are to interpret a word Nuer frequently use about themselves when speaking to or about God: *doar*. The meanings of this word given in Nuer-English dictionaries, 'idiot', 'stupid', 'fool', and 'weak-minded', do not adequately convey the sense of the word, especially when it is used to refer to man's relationship to God. Then it means rather 'simple' or 'foolish' or 'ignorant' — 'idiot' in the sense the word used to have in the English language and which the word from which it is derived had in Greek. Nuer say that they are just ignorant people who do not understand the mysteries of life and death, and of God and the spirits, and why things happen as they do.

A favourite Nuer expression is *'yie wicda'*, 'my head goes round' 10.1.20
or 'I am bewildered'. They are at a loss because they are just foolish
people who do not understand the why and the wherefore. In saying
that they are simple or foolish or ignorant Nuer are not being
modest in respect to other peoples... They regard themselves as
having manly virtues exceeding those of other peoples, but
compared with them they are artless. However, when they use the
word *doar* in a religious context they are speaking of themselves
being foolish in comparison with God and in his eyes. The same idea
is expressed in speaking of themselves as *cok,* small black ants,
particularly in their hymns to spirits of the air, that is, they are
God's ants, or in other words what a tiny ant is to man, so man is to
God. This is a conscious and explicit analogy. Thus Father J. Kiggen
quotes the phrases *'kondial labne cuugh, ke min kueine ke kuoth',*
which I would translate 'we, all of us, have the nature of ants in that
we are very tiny in respect to God', and *'kondial gaad cuughni ke
kuoth',* which I would translate 'all of us are like little ants in the
sight of God'.[6] The same metaphor has been recorded for the Dinka
by Archdeacon Shaw.[7] We are reminded of Isaiah's likening of men
to grasshoppers (xl.22).

In speaking about themselves as being like ants and as being 10.1.21
simple Nuer show a humbleness in respect to God which contrasts
with their proud, almost provocative, and towards strangers even
insulting, bearing to men; and indeed humbleness, a consciousness
of creatureliness, is a further element of meaning in the word *doar,*
as is also humility, not contending against God but suffering without
complaint. Humbleness and humility are very evident on occasions
of religious expression among the Nuer — in the manner and content
of prayer, in the purpose and meaning of sacrifices, and, perhaps
most evidently, in their sufferings. Nuer accept misfortunes with
resignation. Whatever the occasion of death and other misfortunes
may be, whether they be what Nuer call *dung cak,* the lot of created
things, or whether they be the result of what they call *dueri,* faults,
they come to one and all alike, and Nuer say that they must be
accepted as the will of God. The best that can be hoped for is that
God will hear the prayers and accept the sacrifices of those who
suffer and spare them any extra burden. Nuer do not complain when
misfortunes befall them. They say that it is God's will *(rwac kwoth),*
that it is his world *(e ghaude),* and — I have often heard Nuer say
this in their sufferings — that he is good *(goagh)...*

10.1.22   God is always in the right, always, as Nuer say, has *cuong*, a word
I discuss later. Nuer also say, when some calamity has happened to
them, *'thile me lele'*, which means that there is nothing which can be
done about it because it is the will of God and therefore beyond
man's control. . .

10.1.23   In taking things God, as we have noted, takes only what is his, but
he is compassionate and, as we have also noted, spares a man if he
sees that he is poor and miserable *(can)*. In talking about these
matters with Nuer I received the impression that, while of course
they like to be rich, they think it safer for a man not to have too
much good fortune. Pride in the number of his children or cattle
may cause God to take them away. For this reason Nuer show great
uneasiness if their good fortune is so much as mentioned. It is
proper to praise a man's moral qualities, to say that he is brave,
generous, or kind, but it is more than rude to remark on his physical
well-being, the size of his family, or the number and quality of his
beasts and other possessions, for evil consequences may follow. . .

10.1.24   The idea here is not that of the evil eye *(peth)*, though the two
ideas may in some ways resemble one another and also overlap. In
Nuer opinion the evil eye is an act of covetousness or envy, whereas
here, I think, the emphasis is on the danger of rejoicing in unusual
good fortune lest it should be taken away. There is a feeling that
God evens things out, so that if he helps the needy he may take
away from those with superfluity. As I understood their view it
expresses a certain uneasiness at attention being drawn to
possessions lest pride should bring about retribution. That this is
their view is further suggested by a number of their stories which
relate how God punished presumptuousness. . .

This brings me to an extremely important Nuer concept, an
understanding of which is very necessary to a correct appreciation
of their religious thought and practice. This is the concept of *cuong*.
This word can mean 'upright' in the sense of standing, as, for
example, in reference to the supports of byres. It is also used
figuratively for 'firmly established', as in the phrase *'be gole cuong'*,
'may his hearth stand', which has the sense of *stet fortuna domus*. It
is most commonly employed, however, with the meaning of 'in the
right' in both a forensic and a moral sense. The discussion in what
we would call legal cases is for the purpose of determining who has
the *cuong*, the right, in the case, or who has the most right; and in
any argument about conduct the issue is always whether a person
has conformed to the accepted norms of social life, for, if he has,

then he has *cuong*, he has right on his side. We are concerned with the concept here both because it relates directly to man's behaviour towards God and other spiritual beings and the ghosts and because it relates to God in a more indirect way, in that he is regarded as the founder and guardian of morality. Up to this point I have been describing Nuer ideas about the nature of God. I shall now describe their ideas about what God requires of them.

III

[A Moral World: Reward and Retribution]   10.1.25

I do not want to suggest that God is thought to be an immediate sanction for all conduct, but I must emphasise that the Nuer are of one voice in saying that sooner or later and in one way or another good will follow right conduct and ill will follow wrong conduct. People may not reap their rewards for good acts and punishments for bad acts for a long time, but the consequences of both follow behind *(gwor)* them and in the end catch up on those responsible for them. You give milk to a man when he has no lactating cows, or meat and fish to him when he is hungry, or you befriend him in other ways, though he is no close kinsman of yours. He blesses you, saying that your age-mates will die while your children grow old with you. God will see your charity and give you long life. Those who have lived among the Nuer must have heard, and received, their blessings. . .

The Nuer have the idea that if a man keeps in the right — does not break divinely sanctioned interdictions, does not wrong others, and fulfils his obligations to spiritual beings and the ghosts and to his kith and kin — he will avoid, not all misfortunes, for some misfortunes come to one and all alike, but those extra and special misfortunes which come from *dueri*, faults, and are to be regarded as castigations. The word *duer* means 'a fault', and the verbal *dwir* means 'to be at fault'. Like similar words in other languages (e.g. Hebrew, Greek and German), *dwir* has both the sense of missing a mark aimed at — in throwing a spear, and today also in firing a rifle — and also of a dereliction, a fault which brings retribution. Here I wish only to observe that not only a sin (a breach of certain interdictions) but also any wrong conduct to persons is spoken of as *duer,* a fault. Any failure to conform to the accepted norms of behaviour towards a member of one's family, kin, age-set, a guest, and so forth is a fault which may bring about evil consequences through either an expressed curse or a silent curse contained in anger and resentment, though the misfortunes which follow are regarded by Nuer as coming ultimately from God, who supports the cause of the man who has the *cuong,* the right in the matter, and punishes the person who is at fault (*dwir*), for it is God alone who makes a curse operative. Nuer are quite explicit on this point. What, then, Nuer ideas on the matter amount to is, in our way of putting it, that if a man wishes to be in the right with God he must be in the right with men, that is, he must subordinate his interests as an individual to the moral order of society. A man must honour his father and his father's age-mates, a wife must obey her husband, a man must respect his wife's kin, and so on. If an individual fails to observe the rules he is, Nuer say, *yong,* crazy, because he not only loses the support of kith and kin but also the favour of God, so that retribution in one form or another and sooner or later is bound to follow. Therefore Nuer, who are unruly and quarrelsome people, avoid, in so far as they can restrain themselves, giving gratuitous offence. Therefore, also, a man who is at fault goes to the person he has offended, admits the fault, saying to him *'ca dwir'*, 'I was at fault', and he may also offer a gift to wipe out the offence. The wronged man then blesses him by spitting or blowing water on him and says that it is nothing and may the man be at peace. He thereby removes any resentment he may have in his heart. Nuer say that God sees these acts and frees the man from the consequences of his fault. Similarly, the consequences of faults which are more directly of a religious order, like the breach of an interdiction or the neglect of some spirit, may be avoided by a timely sacrifice, though Nuer say that sacrifice without contrition is of no use. But — and this is the point I want to bring out here — the fact that the consequences of a fault can be stayed by contrition and reparation shows that the consequences of wrong-doing are not thought to be automatic.

10.1.26   That this is so, and there is a moral, and therefore uncertain and alterable, element involved is further shown by another fact. In estimating the likelihood, or degree, of misfortune that may be expected to follow from an act, Nuer take deliberation into the reckoning. They distinguish between *duer* and *gwac.* The word *duer,* as we have seen, means a fault, and it normally implies that the fault was deliberate, though, as will be seen later, this is not always or entirely so. *Gwac* means a mistake, an unintentional error and generally one of no great consequence, one in which a serious breach of religious or moral precepts is not involved, such as an unintentional lapse in manners or a slip of the tongue. It implies that the action was incorrect but inadvertent; and the man asks to be excused. In a certain sense, however, in the sense that the act was not deliberate, a more serious fault may be regarded as a mistake, even though it is at the same time a fault, and the fact that it was not a deliberate fault is held to some extent to alter the circumstances. This is very evident in affairs in which damage and compensation are involved, as, for example, in homicide. When a man kills another, how the damage is treated, both with regard to manner and to the amount of compensation demanded, much depends on whether the slaying was premeditated or was the unfortunate outcome of a sudden quarrel or an accident. God also takes deliberation into account in breaches of moral law. Thus it is not thought that children will fall sick if they have incestuous relations in their play 'because the children are ignorant of having done wrong'. They know no better. Likewise, if two kinsmen have relations with the same girl, which Nuer regard as incest, without knowing that the other was making love to her, 'it is not incest because each was unaware that the other was making love to her'. Again, it is not thought that a man who commits incest with a kinswoman, not knowing her to be kinswoman, will suffer any serious, or even any, consequences: 'This is not incest because he was unaware of the relationship between them.' If a man who respects hearts or lungs of animals eats them not knowing the nature of the meat he eats, 'this is an accident and his spirit (the spirit of hearts or lungs) knows that it was not done deliberately'. He may get a slight illness, but not a serious one. . .

One can make too rigid distinctions between the meaning of 10.1.27 words, and while an error or accident is clearly regarded by Nuer as different from a deliberate and premeditated act, the concepts of *gwac* and *duer* shade into each other. There is perhaps always an element of the unintentional in the worst fault, and a Nuer who has committed a bad fault is inclined to excuse himself, as we would do, by calling it a mistake; but it is also true that, except in matters of no moment, and although the consequences may not be so severe, a wrong act is always a fault, whether it was deliberate or was due merely to forgetfulness or even involuntary, and may involve liability. Thus the men who in ignorance have relations with the same girl, the man who unknowingly has relations with a kinswoman, and the man who by mistake eats the flesh of his totem have all committed *dueri,* faults, and they cannot be certain that evil consequences will not follow. The effects may be the same as if the acts had been wilful. Likewise a man who inadvertently eats from a dish from which a man with whom his kin have a blood-feud has eaten, and a man who appears naked before a kinswoman of his wife (Nuer men normally have no covering), not having noticed her presence, have committed faults. It may well happen that a man does not know he has done wrong till he suffers the consequences of the wrong. For example, a man takes a woman for concubine not knowing that she is distantly related to him, and his children by her die. He then makes enquiries and discovers the relationship. He sinned, like Oedipus, in ignorance, but that did not alter what he had done and, like Oedipus, he paid the penalty of his fault. Even the innocent may suffer, as the example I have just given shows. Indeed the whole human race suffers death on account of what was no more than a trivial oversight. . .

10.1.28   When Nuer suffer they sometimes at once know what is the cause of their suffering because they are well aware of some particular fault. They sometimes, as we would say, tempt God by doing what they know to be wrong, hoping that it will not matter very much, such as having relations with a woman which are incestuous but not very incestuous. If trouble comes they know that this is the cause, for they have said that whether the relationship was too close for congress would be decided by any consequences of it. They now discover that it was more serious than they thought. Nuer often neglect their duties to their various spirits. They omit or forget to sacrifice to them or they fail to dedicate cows to them or they use cows dedicated to them for marriage and find that they cannot replace them or do not trouble to do so. If a misfortune falls on them they then know that it is due to the anger of a spirit. Often, however, they are in doubt about the cause and confused and bewildered. It may be that the suffering is just something, like death in old age, which had to happen. It may be due to a fetish or the evil eye. It may be the outcome of a curse or the anger of a ghost. Nevertheless, Nuer generally appear to feel that suffering is due to some fault of theirs, and it is probable that there is always an element of this feeling in every situation of misfortune, whatever its immediate cause may be thought to be.

IV

[The Significance of Prayer] 10.1.29

I have discussed in a preliminary way the conception Nuer have of
God, the ideas and feelings they have about their relations with him,
and some of the actions they think bring about divine intervention
in human affairs. I take these topics up again in succeeding chapters
after the notion of Spirit has been broadened by an account of other
spiritual conceptions. A brief consideration of some of the
commoner expressions used in Nuer prayers may, however, be given
now because they are used only when speaking to God.

For obvious reasons Nuer prayers are most commonly heard on 10.1.30
public and formal occasions, generally in connection with sacrifices.
At any important sacrifice, and sometimes on other important
occasions also, Nuer make long invocations, called *lamni*, about the
event which gave rise to the occasion, and into these long rambling
addresses are every now and again introduced short prayers, mostly
petitionary prayers. These what we may call stock prayers are often
strung together in strophes in a kind of Pater Noster, such as 'Our
father, it is thy universe, it is thy will, let us be at peace, let the souls
of the people be cool, thou art our father, remove all evil from our
path', and so forth. However, there are no set form and order to
these prayers, and each petition may be used separately and
anywhere and at any time, and not only in invocations but also in
private and spontaneous prayer, whether spoken or inward, and as
pious ejaculations. If he is in any trouble or anxiety, the head of a
Nuer household may pace up and down his kraal brandishing his
spear and uttering some of these supplications; or, less formally, he
may say them standing or squatting with his eyes turned towards
heaven and his arms outstretched from the elbows, moving his
hands, palms uppermost, up and down. They may also be uttered, if
he says anything at all, in the petition a man on a journey makes to
God as he knots grasses together at the side of a path, a practice
Nuer call *tuc*. A man may do this because he has knocked his 'bad
foot' against a stump in the path, for this presages misfortune, which
can be avoided by asking God to let the badness remain in the grass
so that the traveller may continue his journey with fortune. Each
man has a 'good (auspicious) foot' and a 'bad (inauspicious) foot'
and he learns which is which by experience. Nuer tie grass in the
same manner to ensure success in any enterprise for which a journey
is undertaken, often at the present day when they go to buy or beg
something from an Arab merchant. They ask God to let them make

a good bargain or that the merchant may make them a gift. Nuer may also utter these phrases of prayer at any time as devout ejaculations, and not only when they are in trouble or desire a boon, for they have told me that they like to speak to God when they are happy (*loc tedh*) and because they are happy, and that they often say a few words to him as they go about their daily affairs.

10.1.31   I have already discussed the significance of some of these prayerful words and expressions: 'our father', 'it is thy universe', 'it is thy will', and others. I will now consider the meaning of yet a few others, choosing for the purpose the commonest petitionary phrases. Before doing this I would draw attention to the fact that the petitioner generally uses the first person plural. In private ejaculations a Nuer may use such expressions as 'ah, my God', 'ah, God, what is this?', and 'let me journey well', but he will also use the plural pronoun, and in prayers and invocations uttered in public the plural is invariably used: 'let us be at peace', or whatever the expression may be. I draw attention to this because it is not, I believe, just an indication that there are other people on whose behalf the speaker is asking God's favours. It is rather that the occasions on which prayers are publicly offered are generally such as emphasise by their gravity that, particularly in relation to God, all are members one of another. It is of course natural as well as noticeable that close kin stick together in danger and when a wrong has been done to any one of them, but Nuer also quite clearly show that they feel that a misfortune for any member of their community is a misfortune for all, that when one suffers all suffer, and that if each is to be at peace all must be at peace. This feeling of oneness is particularly evident in Nuer prayers, because they are asking to be delivered from suffering, which has a common quality, the more so in that it is suffering in general rather than particular misfortunes of which they speak.

10.1.32   Perhaps the commonest phrase in Nuer prayers, and the one with which they often start prayer, is *'akonienko'*. Literally this means 'let us sleep', but here it should be rendered 'let us be at peace'. The commonest of the Nuer greetings and, when others are said, the first to be spoken is *'ci nien?'* or *'ci nienu?'*, literally, 'have you slept?' The saluted man replies to this, as to other greetings, by a grunt of affirmation. This is something of a joke among Europeans because Nuer have a reputation with them for being lethargic and lazy; but the question means something rather different from 'have you slept?' It means even more than our 'did you sleep well?' What

Nuer understand by the question is rather, I think, 'have you rested?'or 'are you at ease?'. . .

That Nuer regard being at ease or at peace as having something to do with being in friendship with God is shown by a further question which may follow: *'ci pal?'* or *'ci palu?'*, 'have you prayed?' I think that the idea implied here is that being at peace in yourself means being at peace with God as well as with your fellow men. . .   10.1.33

Nuer speak of life as walking through pastures and they ask for a path that has no hidden dangers, that is, is free from evil, and for softness underfoot, that is, a mind at ease. Hence they petition also *'gwenyi ko kwel gwath me jalko ko'*, 'make clear a way for us in the place where we journey', and *'gwenyi ko gwath'*, 'clear for us a place'. Here again the sense is mainly allegorical. The words do not usually refer to any particular place or journey but to the journey through life, and the making clear of the way does not refer only, or even at all, to any particular dangers of travelling through the bush but to all the suffering and evils which beset the life of man.

Peace and deliverance are the key-notes of these petitions. They are seen again in the phrase *'kwoth ngaci rum yieni, romni yieko'*, 'God, thou (who) knowest how to support [or care for] souls, support [or care for] our souls'. The general sense of the prayer is that God should protect those who supplicate him as a parent protects his helpless infant. This desire for peace, deliverance, and protection is summed up in another common petition: *'akoteko'*, 'let us be'. I am not certain whether the verb here is *tek*, to be alive, or, as I think it is, *te*, to be. There is in any case a considerable overlap in meaning between the two words, and in this context there would not be any great difference in meaning between the one and the other, for the sense is: let us go on living and as we are. Nuer are asking for life, but not just life in the sense of living but of living abundantly, free from the troubles and sufferings which make life, as we say, not worth living. That this is the right interpretation is further suggested by another expression frequently heard in prayer, *'akolapko'*, which also has to be translated 'let us be', and here again signifies, and in a deeper moral sense, life in the mode and manner of leading it. . .   10.1.34

It will have been observed that these expressions in Nuer prayers, as is the case among other peoples, are often repetitions, but rather in the form of parallelisms than of tautologies, for they are variations of meaning within the same general meaning. Different images are used to express the same general idea, each stressing a   10.1.35

different aspect of it.

The distinctive and significant features of Nuer mystical and moral theology cannot be extracted from the short affirmations and petitions which constitute their prayers if these are considered entirely by themselves without Nuer comments on them and without some knowledge of their ritual and of their ideas and values in general, but once these have been delineated they are seen to be summed up concisely in the prayers. They are asking God for deliverance from evil, so that they may have peace, denoted by a variety of images with emotional and ideational relatedness — sleep, lightness, ease, coolness, softness, prayer, the domestic hearth, abundant life and life as it should be according to the nature of the person. As I have explained, Nuer regard the ills they wish to be delivered from as due to faults and they think they can only be avoided by keeping in the right in their dealings with God and men. These two ideas, of being in the right and of deliverance from evil, are basic to their religious thought and they are also, of course, complementary. A fuller understanding of these cardinal concepts of Nuer religion can be obtained only by taking into account their attitudes towards other spirits associated with God, their conception of the soul and of sin, and their sacrificial rites.

10.1.36 Nuer Hymns

Mother of *deng,* the ants (the Nuer) ransom their lives from thee,
Mother of *dengkur,* the ants ransom their lives from thee,
The mother of *dengkur* brings life,
The mother of *dengkur* brings me life,
Life is revived.
She brings life and our children play,
They cry aloud with joy,
With the life of the mother of *deng,* with the life of the mother of
    deng.

The pied crows are given life and are filled.
Our speech is good, we and *buk,*
Our speech is excellent;
The country of the people is good.
We journey on the path of the *pake.*[8]
We are here, we and *buk deang,*
Buk, mother of *deng,* the ants ransom their lives from thee,
Mother of *dengkur,* the ants ransom their lives from thee.

We give thee red blood.
The ants of *deng* are simple people, they do not understand how
their lives are supported.
Let all the people of the cattle camps bring tobacco to the river.

The general sense of this hymn is that *buk* protects the people 10.1.37
from dangers and gives them life. Protection and life are given them
in exchange for oblations of animals (the red blood) and tobacco. I
give the opening verses of another hymn, which appears to be
addressed to both *dayim* and *mani*. It is a war hymn, although I
heard it myself at a ceremony in western Nuerland held in honour of
a person killed by lightning.

Stars and moon which are in the heavens,
Blood of *deng* which you have taken,[9]
You have not summoned the ants of *deng* capriciously,[10]
Blood of *deng* which you have taken,
The wing of battle on the river bank is encircled by plumes.[11]
Dayim, son of God, strike the British to the ground,
Break the steamer on the Nile and let the British drown,
Kill the people on the mountains,
Kill them twice,
Do not slay them jestingly.
Mani goes with a rush,
He goes on for ever,
The sons of Jagei are proud in the byres,
Proud that they always raid the Dinka.

I do not know the time or circumstances of composition of this
hymn, but as it not only exults in defeats of the Dinka and asks for
victory over the people of the Nuba hills but also demands the
destruction of the British it must be fairly recent and probably dates
from the early days of British occupation of the Southern Sudan.
Dr. Lienhardt has recorded a hymn about *deng* which vividly
suggests the mobility of the spirits of the air and the ubiquity of
Spirit. A man says he is tired of the demands made by *deng* and that
he will move. But *deng* replies

A man avoiding *deng*
Will find *deng* in front,
On the right he will find *deng*,

On the left he will find *deng,*
Behind him he will find *deng.*

Notes

1. The word has been variously spelt by European writers. I shall throughout use *kwoth* (pl. *kuth*), neglecting the genitive and locative forms.
2. *The Messenger,* 1943-4 (I have not seen the original articles but only a typewritten copy of them, so I cannot give page references).
3. Diedrich Westermann, 'The Nuer Language', *Mitteilungen des Seminars für Orientalische Sprachen,* 1912, p.115.
4. H.C. Jackson, 'The Nuer of the Upper Nile Province', *Sudan Notes and Records,* 1923, pp.70-71; V.H. Fergusson, 'The Nuong Nuer', Ibid., 1921, pp.148-9.
5. These contrasted feelings are probably common to all predominantly theistic religions and they have often been noted by scholars, e.g. Antonio Anwander in his discussion of *pietà della 'lontananza'* and *pietà della 'vicinanza'* in his *Introduzione alla Storia delle Religioni,* 1932, pp.168 seq.
6. *Nuer-English Dictionary,* 1948, p.60.
7. 'Dinka Songs', *Man,* 1915.
8. This is not a Nuer word but the Arabic *faki,* a fakir or holy man. In Nuer the word is used for an Arab pedlar or merchant. The use of the word in this hymn, probably one of the oldest Nuer hymns, is further evidence of the late introduction of these spirits into Nuerland.
9. Dinka blood on Nuer spears.
10. The spirits which summoned the Nuer to raid the Dinka through the mouths of their prophets did not summon them in vain. The raid was successful. The ants are the Nuer.
11. When warriors are drawn up for battle the prophet runs along the flanks shouting encouragement to them and waving his spear decorated with ostrich plumes.

Source: Abridged from E.E. Evans-Pritchard, *Nuer Religion,* OUP 1956, pp.1-27. Some footnotes have been deleted.

10.2 DIVINITY AND EXPERIENCE IN THE DINKA RELIGION

R.G. Lienhardt

DIVISION IN THE WORLD

[The Meaning of 'Powers'] 10.2.1

Within the single world known to them (for they dwell little upon fancies of any 'other world' of different constitution) the Dinka claim that they encounter 'spirits' of various kinds, which they call generically *jok*. In this account I call them 'Powers'. These Powers are regarded as higher in the scale of being than men and other merely terrestrial creatures, and operate beyond the categories of space and time which limit human actions; but they are not imagined to form a separate 'spirit-world' of their own, and their interest for the Dinka is as ultra-human forces participating in human life and often affecting men for good or ill. They emerge in the interpretation of events, and hence the broad Dinka division of the world into 'that which is of men' and 'that which is of Powers' is in part a classification of events into two kinds. Man and that which shares his terrestrial nature may be contrasted in thought to Powers, considered collectively as exhibiting a different nature. Dinka religious notion and practice define and regulate the relations between beings of these two different natures in the single world of human experience which is their common home.

I have not found it useful to adopt the distinction between 10.2.2 'natural' and 'supernatural' beings or events in order to describe the difference between men and Powers, for this distinction implies a conception of the course or laws of Nature quite foreign to Dinka thought.[1] When, for example, the Dinka attribute lightning to a particular ultra-human Power, it would falsify their understanding, and indeed exaggerate its difference from our own, to refer to a *supernatural* Power. The force of lightning is equally ultra-human for ourselves as for the Dinka, though the interpretation we place upon that fact is very different from theirs. It is part of my later task to demonstrate how many features of Dinka religious thought and action are connected with their experience of what we call 'Nature', and of the scope and limits of human control within their particular environment.

10.2.3 **[The Idea of the Divine Creator]**

The word which any enquirer into Dinka religion will first and most frequently hear is *nhialic*. Literally, the word is the locative form of *nhial,* meaning 'up' or 'above', and *nhialic* is the word used in many contexts in which we should speak of 'the sky'. Part of the meaning of *nhialic*, then, is conveyed by 'sky' and 'in the above'.

But further, *nhialic* is addressed and referred to as 'creator' *(aciek)* and 'my father' *(wa),* and prayers and sacrifice are offered to it. It then has a masculine and a personal connotation, and is used in contexts where, for ordinary purposes, it would be suitably translated as 'God'. Yet the attributes of our 'God' and their *nhialic* are not identical, and I have thought that the advantages of using the obvious translation are eventually outweighed by disadvantages. To use the word 'God' in translating some Dinka statements about *nhialic* would raise metaphysical and semantic problems of our own for which there is no parallel among the Dinka and in their language. Perhaps the extent to which it would be permissible to translate *nhialic* by 'God' is something of which theologians might judge at the end of an account of Dinka religion.

10.2.4 It would be easy, it is true, to translate *nhialic aciek* and *nhialic wa* as 'God the creator' and 'God (my) father', for the attributes of *nhialic* and 'God' there closely coincide, as do many others — unity (of a kind), power, justice, 'highness', for example. When, however, numbers of 'spirits' later discussed are all said in Dinka to be *nhialic,* it would not make similar sense in English to say that they were 'all God'. The word *nhialic* is meaningful in relation to a number of Dinka terms with which our 'God' has no such association. *Nhialic* is figured sometimes as a Being, a personal Supreme Being even, and sometimes as a *kind* of being and activity which sums up the activities of a multiplicity of beings, while the word 'God' has no such extended meaning in our common speech.

10.2.5 So the word *Divinity,* thus written with the capital letter and without definite or indefinite article, is here used to translate *nhialic.* 'Divinity', like *nhialic,* can be used to convey to the mind at once *a* being, a *kind* of nature or existence, and a quality of that kind of being; it can be made to appear more substantive or qualitative, more personal or general, in connotation, according to the context, as is the word *nhialic.*[2] It saves us too, despite its occasional clumsiness, from shifting our attention from a Dinka word to undefined, yet for everyone fairly definite, conceptions of our own.

[Two Kinds of 'Divinities'] 10.2.6

The most important Powers recognized by the Dinka are called collectively *yeeth* (sing. *yath*) — a word, it will be observed, of which there are singular and plural forms. *Nhialic,* Divinity, has no plural; it is both singular and plural in intention. In some senses discussed later all the existences called *yeeth* may be equated with Divinity, and in this account I have found it fitting to refer to them as *divinities,* thus written without the capital letter.

The divinities are of two kinds which for clarity of exposition are here distinguished, though the Dinka use the one word *yath* for both. There are first those which are the tutelary spirits, or genii, of Dinka descent-groups, which in some ways resemble the 'totems' of anthropological literature. Here they are called *clan-divinities;* and when, as is usually but not invariably the case, they are represented in material forms — in animal and other species — I call these forms their *emblems.* So, for example, a clan which has Lion as its clan-divinity will in various ways respect lions, the emblems of that divinity.

There are other *yeeth,* divinities, which are not in special 10.2.7 relationships with descent-groups; they establish relationships with individuals, and through them with their families, which then adopt towards them some of the attitudes adopted towards clan-divinities by whole clans. I call these *free-divinities,* or by their Dinka proper names, as *DENG, GARANG, MACARDIT,* and others later described.

[Divinities Working Within and Outside of Men] 10.2.8

Divinity and divinities belong to that widest class of ultra-human agency collectively called, in Dinka, *jok,* Power. *Jok* is less specific in connotation than *nhialic* or *yath,* Divinity or a divinity. *Jok* as a noun may refer to a particular ultra-human Power. It then has the plural form *jaak* when several distinct individual existences of this kind are in mind. It has also, however, like *yath,* a qualitative sense, indicating the kind and quality of ultra-human power, rather than any particular Power. So when they see some surprising example of European ingenuity the Dinka may say that *turuk ee jok,* 'the European is ultra-human Power'. The implication is merely that Europeans' power is of that quality or order; they would not state this in the plural, *turuk aa jaak,* 'the Europeans are ultra-human Powers', for they are, clearly, only men. Again, confronted with unexpected behaviour in an animal, Dinka might say 'it is Power' *(ee jok)* or 'it is Divinity' *(ee nhialic)*. The implications would be, not that the animal itself was *a* Power, or was identical with Divinity, but that its behaviour manifested a Power or Divinity.

Though if asked for 'definitions' Dinka may say that Divinity and divinities are *jok*, Power or Powers, they normally distinguish clan-divinities and free-divinities from other Powers which concern them less by referring to them as *yeeth*, which, according to Dinka definition, are 'Powers which are related to people'. The relationship is often figured in the idiom of kinship, as when Divinity and the free-divinities are called 'fathers' of men, and clan-divinities are called the 'grandfathers' or ancestors of their descent-groups. The emblems of clan-divinities, the species in which they are now manifest, are hence called 'paternal cousins' or half-brothers of their human clansmen.

10.2.9   The Dinka do not suppose that all the Powers which may exist in their world have been encountered by men, and their numbers are theoretically unlimited. Some are known as the grounds of sickness, and others, figured with varying degrees of distinctness and individuality, are associated with particular places, especially streams and woods. There they occasionally manifest themselves to human beings, and Dinka folk-tales are peopled by such, often anonymous, Powers, described as 'a Power of the wood' or 'a Power of the stream', much like sprites in our own fairy-tales.

Divinities are altogether more clearly figured as individuals, and are of much greater importance. They manifest themselves to men, and in men, more commonly and purposefully, and are given distinct characteristics by being each associated with its own colours and natural species, as I later describe.

Dinka religion, then, is a relationship between men and ultra-human Powers encountered by men, between the two parts of a radically divided world. As will be seen, it is rather phenomenological than theological, an interpretation of signs of ultra-human activity rather than a doctrine of the intrinsic nature of the Powers behind those signs.

Notes

1. Cf. E. Durkheim, *The Elementary Forms of the Religious Life* (trans. J.W. Swain), 1915, pp.26 ff.
2. I should have preferred throughout to refer to Divinity in the third person by the neuter pronoun. In some sentences, however, such a usage would appear extremely forced, and I have consequently written of Divinity as 'it' or 'he' according to what the context seems to demand.

Source: R.G. Lienhardt, *Divinity and Experience: The Religion of the Dinka*, OUP 1961, pp.28-32. [This section is separated by over one hundred pages from that which follows]

DIVINITY AND EXPERIENCE (1)

[The Relationship between Powers and Men]   10.2.10

To the Dinka the Powers are known by personal encounters, as living agents influencing their lives for good or evil. Europeans may perhaps concede an objective reality of this order to the Dinka Divinity, where it most resembles the 'God' of the universal religions; but no European actually encounters DENG, GARANG, or the other Powers as the Dinka claim to do. For analysis, then, the Powers (and logically all equally, including Divinity) must be regarded as representations of realities more accessible to a universal rational knowledge than they need to be in the Dinka view of them; and our final and interpretative task is to ask, if the Dinka Powers be representations, what it is that they represent. I have described them for the most part as the Dinka themselves understand them; but in this chapter I try to give a different account of them, not now as ultra-human 'beings' which might form the subject-matter of a Dinka theology, but as representations (or as I here prefer to call them, 'images') evoked by certain configurations of experience contingent upon the Dinkas' reaction to their particular physical and social environment, of which a foreigner can also have direct knowledge.

It is true that the Powers may be as much part of the Dinkas' total experience — as much phenomena — for them, as are the physical and social realities to which we later refer them; but the Dinka themselves are quite able to discuss the latter without at once introducing Powers as their grounds. Thus, one can discuss the prospects for the harvest without necessarily introducing the free-divinity ABUK, to whom good harvests are attributed, and one can discuss thunder, lightning, and rain up to a point as purely 'natural' phenomena, without talking of DENG or Divinity...

Thus even for the Dinka themselves, a Power is not an immediate *datum* of experience of the same order as the physical facts or events with which it is associated. To refer to the activity of a Power is to offer an interpretation, and not merely a description, of experience; and [here] I consider some features of the type of interpretation offered in relation to the experience which is interpreted.

The clue to this problem lies, it seems to me, in a Dinka statement 10.2.11

which is itself problematical — the statement that a Power is 'in men' and also (in many examples) 'in the sky'. So the free-divinity DENG may on occasions be 'in' men, but it is also 'in' the sky and in the phenomena of the sky. It is clear that for the Dinka, men, whether or not possessed by DENG, are not permanently 'in the sky', while the rain, lightning, and thunder, regarded as physical phenomena only, are not 'in' men. In this example the free-divinity DENG provides a link between moral and physical experience, integrating experience of the human and the ultra-human in the world.

10.2.12   Traditional teaching affirms the existence of Powers and endows them with some of their specific characteristics; but their effective relationship with men at particular times, in the direct encounters which make them so much more vividly present to the Dinka than they can be to ourselves, are matters to be discovered or revealed. Some indication has already been given of the way in which the Dinka try to make such discoveries by divining and questioning. In divination an attempt is made to specify a Power as the grounds of a particular human condition. Until its name is known it remains as it were latent and undefined within the effective condition of the suffering individual, and action cannot be taken to remove it or propitiate it until it has been identified.

10.2.13   The process of treating a sick man whose sickness is attributed to a Power is thus to isolate for the sufferer and his kin a particular Power which can be regarded as a subject of activity within him, from the self which is its object. Hence, when a man is strongly possessed, it is held that 'it is no use speaking to *him*', as a human person, for what is acting is not the man but the Power. It is the process of making manifest what I have called an 'image', corresponding to the effective state of the sufferer as cause to effect, which I now discuss.

10.2.14   It raises first a difficult question of differences between Dinka and European self-knowledge which I can discuss only inadequately. The Dinka have no conception which at all closely corresponds to our popular modern conception of the 'mind', as mediating and, as it were, storing up the experiences of the self.[1] There is for them no such interior entity to appear, on reflection, to stand between the experiencing self at any given moment and what is or has been an exterior influence upon the self. So it seems that what we should call in some cases the 'memories' of experiences, and regard therefore as in some way intrinsic and interior to the remembering person and modified in their effect upon him by that interiority, appear to the Dinka as exteriorly acting upon him, as were the sources from which they derived. Hence it would be impossible to suggest to Dinka that a powerful dream was 'only' a dream, and might for that reason be dismissed as relatively unimportant in the light of day, or that a state of possession was grounded 'merely' in the psychology of the person possessed. They do not make the kind of distinction between the psyche and the world which would make such interpretations significant for them.

A man who has lived for a time in a place very foreign to him 10.2.15 may think that that place (we should say, its 'influence') follows him *(bwoth cok),* as divinities are said to 'follow' those with whom they have formed a relationship. A man who had been imprisoned in Khartoum called one of his children 'Khartoum' in memory of the place, but also to turn aside any possible harmful influence of that place upon him in later life. The act is an act of exorcism, but the exorcism of what, for us, would be memories of experiences. Thus also do the Dinka call children after Powers, and after the dead, who to the Dinka way of thought are less likely to return to trouble the living if their place and constant presence are thus explicitly acknowledged. In such namings, the Power which has once affected a man or one of his close kin, kin themselves who are dead, or the places which have formed a man's personality, are regarded as potent still to affect him as they once certainly affected him, directly, and from without. . .

That the experience of the past whether of people, places or events, may have permanent and profound influences upon the personality is of course a commonplace of European thought also; but there ̖they tend to be regarded as proximately and most importantly derived from the mind or imagination of the remembering self, on which their traces are thought to remain. Our view of the passage of time influences the value we attach to past events far more than is the case for the Dinka whose points of reference are not years counted serially, but the events themselves.[2] In the example of the man who called his child 'Khartoum' it is Khartoum which is regarded as an agent, the subject which acts, and not as with us the remembering mind which recalls the place. The man is the object acted upon. Even in the usual expressions of the Dinka for the action of features of their world upon them, we often find a reversal of European expressions which assume the human self, or mind, as subject in relation to what happens to it; in English, for example, it is often said that a man 'catches a disease', but in Dinka the disease, or Power, always 'seizes the man. . .'

Notes

1. And still less of conscious and unconscious elements, of course.
2. In the early days of European-type court-procedure among the Dinka, it was found very difficult to persuade them to see that the period which had elapsed since an event was at all significant in the attempt to settle a dispute. Even now, a Dinka may think it unreasonable and unjust that a cattle-debt or an injury of many years' standing should be less serious as a subject of litigation than an event of the immediate past.

Source: Abridged from R.G. Lienhardt, op.cit., pp.147-50 (with some footnotes deleted). [This section is separated by six pages from that which follows]

DIVINITY AND EXPERIENCE (2)

10.2.16 **[Divinity, Community and Creativity]**

If the Powers image different ranges of experience, we should not expect the several accounts of them given by the Dinka to agree in details, nor their assertions about them severally, when pieced together by us, to have the connectedness and logical consistency of reflective thought. Dinka experience naturally differs from group to group and person to person. It has appeared from the preceding chapters that the Dinka Divinity is spoken of as both single and manifold. All the sky-Powers are said to 'be' Divinity; yet Divinity is not any one of them, nor are all of them merely subnumerations of Divinity. They are also quite distinct from each other, though considered together in relation to men they have a reality of the same kind. The Dinka assert with a uniformity which makes the assertion almost a dogma that 'Divinity is one'. They cannot conceive of Divinity as a plurality and, did they know what it meant, would deeply resent being described as 'polytheistic'. What account can we now give ourselves of these Powers, both the same as and other than Divinity, which are not merely alternative names for it — for their attributes are not identical with those of Divinity — nor are they thought of as distinct, subordinate existences of the order of Divinity?

10.2.17   Our answer is that Divinity as a unity, and Divinity as a multiplicity, are not the products of logical or mystical elaboration of a revealed truth as are our own theological considerations of similar apprehensions. Divinity is manifold as human experience is manifold and of a manifold world. Divinity is one as the self's manifold experience is united and brought into relationship in the experiencing self. The Powers are distinct from each other, and from Divinity, as the experiences they image are distinct from each other and from the total experience of the world and the self.

Divinity, then, corresponds to experience common to all men, 10.2.18 and to the Dinkas' recognition that a single human nature and condition embraces all. Divinity is thus everywhere, and everywhere the same. The different names by which different peoples know it are matters only of different languages. So in Divinity the Dinka image their experience of the ways in which human beings everywhere resemble each other, and in a sense form a single community with one original ancestor created by one Creator. Divinity therefore transcends the individual and social differentiations the Dinka know, as they recognise them in some ways to be transcended in a fundamental unity of human nature. This theme is frequently stressed in Dinka invocations and hymns:

> . . .and you, Divinity, I call you in my invocation because you help everyone and you are great towards [in relation to] all people, and all people are your children. . .

and

> Divinity, no other man is hated
> Divinity, my father, creator, no other man is hated. . .

and in a hymn quoted from Fr. Nebel:

> God, Father, no man hates another in the whole world.[1]

When, therefore, a prophet like Arianhdit shows that he is able to make peace between normally exclusive and hostile communities, to persuade them to observe between them the peaceful conventions which they had previously observed only internally, and to unite people of different origins in a single community, he proves that he is a 'man of Divinity'. It is not enough for a man to claim to be a 'man of Divinity' and expect such a reputation to follow from his claim; the conviction that a man is genuinely divinely inspired follows upon actual experience of his ability, which in turn strengthens his hand and makes future success more likely. The man is recognised as a powerful 'man of Divinity' because he creates for people the experience of peace between men and of the uniting of forces which are normally opposed to each other, of which Divinity is understood to be the grounds. Without providing that experience a man would not be regarded as truly a 'man of Divinity', whatever his claims to revelations. It is safe to say also that were a man to show ability to unite people and bring peace between them — were the force of his personality such — the Dinka would attribute contact with 'divinity' to him even though he were to make no claim to it.

10.2.19   Divinity, then, images here the lived experience of community and concord, and as imaging the widest community the Dinka can conceive, also represents truth, justice, honesty, uprightness, and such-like conditions of order and peace in human relations. Where these are considered absent, Divinity is also said to be absent from human affairs. And experience of living is here clearly the basis from which comes such theoretical or purely cognitive apprehension of Divinity and the Powers as the Dinka have, for moral and social disorder are more immediately known than Divinity, whose existence does not need to be posited before their results are felt. When their results are felt, in sickness, discord, malice, and so on, to understand them as reflecting the absence of a Divinity is also to recognise them in a way which makes action to restore Divinity, to restore order and health, possible. It is thus that their notion of Divinity may be seen to arise in the experience of order in relation to disorder, life in relation to death, and in other experiential opposites which we have mentioned in an earlier chapter. Divinity is thus comprehended in and through natural experience, and not merely as a theoretical force producing the order of the world from without.

10.2.20   Connected with the conceptualisation, as Divinity, of the basis of community, and of the widest community they can conceive, is the attribution to Divinity of a universal fatherhood. We have already discussed some of the detailed ways in which relations with Divinity and with the father are represented by a single model; but although from one point of view all human beings are equivalent in relation to him collectively as his children, it will be remembered that the eldest and youngest sons among the Dinka, who are favoured by the rules of inheritance and often actually favoured by the father, are also regarded as the special favourites of the Powers. The eldest and the youngest, the *kai* and the *kuun,* are *jok,* 'are [of the kind of being of] Powers'. The usage is consciously metaphorical; but we see that what is known to be their special fortune in relation to the family is reflected in the understanding as a specially close association with Divinity.

10.2.21   Finally, there is the attribution of creativity to Divinity; and here we must consider more generally the way in which the Dinka image in the Powers the diversities and polarities of experience. Divinity and MACARDIT concern every Western Dinka, and the two stand in apposition to each other as we have seen. They are not thought, however, to oppose each other as two warring 'beings' or 'principles'. MACARDIT is also Divinity, though Divinity is not MACARDIT. Since Divinity ultimately is the grounds of everything that is in man and nature, Divinity is the grounds of sterility, barrenness, and pointless or apparently pointless death as he is the grounds of creativity, fertility and prosperity. There is no theoretical problem for the Dinka of reconciling an infinitely good Divinity with the presence of these evils in the world, on a logical or moral plane, because Divinity represents the grounds of what actually happens. Yet the particular affective experience of fertility and prosperity, and of a just, kind, and reasonable order in the events of men's lives, is distinct from that of sterility, barrenness, and sudden inexplicable death. Similarly, the moral order of the homestead and community is ˙explicitly contrasted with the amoral life of wild beasts in the unordered life of the forest. One of the worst insults which can be offered to human beings among the Dinka is to liken them to game. Darkness with its unseen and sudden dangers is similarly in opposition to daylight. All these contrasted experiences are reflected in the apposition of Divinity and MACARDIT. They are not conceived as 'beings' actively pitted against each other, as experiences in themselves cannot actively oppose each other. The difference between them is not intrinsically in them but in the human experiences they image.

[Deng, Abuk and Garang, the 'free' Divinities]　　　10.2.22

Similarly, the free-Divinities DENG, ABUK, and GARANG correspond to fields of experience which are special aspects of the total to which Divinity corresponds. We have indicated what these fields are in general – that imaged by DENG includes the phenomena of the sky associated with rain, that imaged by ABUK is the life of the gardens and the crops, and that imaged by GARANG. . .includes the heat of the sun and certain heated conditions of the human body. The configuration of experience which these three, separately and together, image is very complex, and I do not claim to have been able fully to explore it. It is clear, however, that if we consider only the complete connotations in Dinka life of sun, rain, and vegetation, the fact that the three images are regarded as in some way related as

husband, wife, and son has a significance beyond that merely of
their being understood on the pattern of the human family.
GARANG's and DENG's father-son relationship with ABUK as wife
and mother is consistent with the association of sun and rain and
earth necessary for the herds and the crops.

10.2.23   The Dinka do not of course break down the imaginative
complexes we have discussed in this way into related but separate
constituent parts. Did they do so, in fact, we should not expect to
find them imaging them in the Powers, and part of our difficulty in
interpreting the Powers lies in the fact that the experiences they
image are not correlated by the Dinka in alternative ways. As I have
said, they include what we should distinguish as physical and moral
experience in an organic unity. Thus, for example, rain-coolness-
pastures-cattle-milk-procreation-abundance-life-light and also rain-
clouds-thunder-lightning-sudden death, not in that or any sort of
successive order, are all represented by DENG. In addition, there is
the association of DENG with ABUK, as son or husband, and the
association of ABUK with the vegetation and particularly the crops.
Again, taking only one of the elements of the experience imaged by
DENG and ABUK in relationship, the rain-associations of DENG
suggest equally the lush pastures which the Dinka want for their
cattle, and the rich harvests from which their women will prepare
porridge and beer. The cattle are the affair of men − of husbands
and sons − and DENG is a male divinity, and a husband or a son.
The gardens, though partly worked by men, belong primarily to the
women, who in any case do the work of turning their produce into
food. ABUK similarly is a female divinity and presides over women's
affairs, and she and DENG are called upon together, often as mother
and son, to bring the Dinka the fertility and prosperity − the 'life' −
which the joint labours of men and women among the cattle and the
crops in suitable conditions of rain and sun will bring. GARANG,
associated with the sun among other things, is part of this family of
three. By the association often made between GARANG the Power
and Garang the first man, between ABUK and Abuk the first
woman, and between DENG and Deng, their son or ABUK's
husband, the whole configuration of experiences they image
together is further enriched by the inclusion in it of an original
fatherhood, motherhood, and sonship. In our earlier description we
could only proceed by considering the 'imagery' of the Powers

seriatim; but it is in the representation of extremely complex configurations of moral and physical experience, the elements in which are not distinct from each other but are embedded, as it were, in extensive metaphors, that the Powers have their force. It has taken several paragraphs of description to re-create only a part of the total experiential connotation of the word GARANG, for example, which the mere word GARANG immediately represents for Dinka. We have to take into account not only the experience of the natural environment imaged in the Powers, but also the Dinkas' particular relationship with it, the way in which it is intimately linked with the moral life, the hopes and fears of men.

DENG, for example, is not merely a 'personification' of rain, 10.2.24 lightning, etc. — rain and lightning endowed fancifully or through ignorance with human personal qualities. The name DENG re-creates for the Dinka the whole syndrome of experiences of these natural phenomena as they touch directly upon human life. Rain and its associated phenomena, for people like the Dinka whose subsistence economy makes them directly dependent upon the grass and the crops, do in fact mean life and abundance, just as their absence, or their presence at the wrong time or place, can mean death and misery. When DENG is 'in' a man's body, to use the Dinka expression, that man becomes as it were a meeting-place for the human and ultra-human influences in their lives. To use our European type of distinction between Nature and Mind, it is rather that some men on occasion incorporate in themselves the ultra-human forces of Nature, than that they endow Nature with qualities which they recognise in themselves and in human kind. When the Dinka ask, as in a hymn,

DENG, Governor, support his life. . .

the term DENG represents an integration of political and moral experience with experience of nature in a single image. Through the colour-symbolism we have already mentioned, this image also includes the black-and-white configurations in cattle, which again impress themselves upon the minds of the Dinka as does the lightning in dark, lowering skies which signifies the activities of DENG. . .

[Clan-divinities]

The clan-divinities are easily seen as representative of a particular 10.2.25 limited field of Dinka experience, that of agnatic kinship, as we have pointed out. They reflect experience of the abiding descent-group structure of Dinka society. If Divinity represents among other things the situation of human beings as the children of a common father, the clan-divinities are the counterparts of the particular and distinct patrilineal descent-groups and reflect experience and knowledge of them and the value attached to them. By this I do not mean that they are merely the devices by which social groups, considered as entities, are represented, to focus loyalty and affection, on the familiar analogy with national flags or heraldic emblems. We have seen that the clan-divinities do not primarily face outwards, so to speak, from the clans to which they belong, providing a mark by which others may know them. The name of the clan is enough for that, and Dinka often know the names of clans other than their own without also knowing what their divinities are. The clan-divinities have their meaning in relation to the nature of clanship as members of their clans know it, as membership of agnatic descent-groups which transcend their individual members, and yet of which each individual membership is representative. They provide the clearest example of the structure of experience represented by the Powers. . .

10.2.26   Even where the division of peoples is not represented as integrally bound up with the acquisition of the clan-divinities, it is assumed as a condition for that acquisition. In historical sequence, then, the distinctions of human clanship are always represented as preceding the knowledge of clan-divinities. Clanship, as we have earlier emphasised, does not proceed from the presence of the clan-divinity; the presence of the clan-divinity proceeds from the fact of clanship. Similarly, it will be remembered that while those who are forbidden to marry by the rules of clan exogamy naturally have the same divinity, to have the same divinity is not in itself a bar to intermarriage.

10.2.27   We have considered the way in which the clan-divinities are addressed and spoken of, and the respectful regard for their emblems where these are species which can be touched and handled. All these forms emphasise the relationship between clansmen and their divinities, in their emblems, as one of conjunction and disjunction at the same time. In the case of twin-birth relationships between men and their divinities (in the emblems) it is explicitly said that the animal emblem is 'separated' from its human clansmen, and placed in its own element — the river, in the case of the crocodile for example. In that separation the humans and their divinities' emblems respect each other. The theme of division in unity is found again in the reference to the clan-divinity usually as 'grandfather' (not father') and its emblems as 'half-brother' (not 'brother'), for the essential element of Dinka clanship is that it is the 'relationship between children of a common ancestor (or 'grandfather') whose lines of agnatic descent are different. The Dinka clan member is united with and divided from his clansmen[2] as clansmen as a whole are united with and divided from the clan-divinity and its emblems. The clan-divinity thus images the widest experience of agnatic relationship which a Dinka has. It helps its clansmen, as clansmen have the obligation to help each other; they 'are together' in the divinity as they 'are together' (theoretically) in the blood-feud and in the obligation to help each other in the payment of compensation for homicide. That obligation, of course, can only be effective within a certain territorial range, but the Dinka always insist that in principle it binds clansmen wherever they may be.

Normally, the senior lineage of any group of collateral lineages 10.2.28 within a tribe is thought to be more effective in invocation of the clan-divinity than others are, and by Dinka customs of inheritance it is normally the eldest son who is chosen to succeed the father and who represents the father to his brothers. The senior son, or the senior lineage, thus not only *in*vokes the divinity more effectively, but also *e*vokes more fully sentiments of agnatic solidarity. The reputed strength of the invocations of a man or a lineage, therefore, on the whole corresponds to their social importance within the clan or family. Within a tribe, the whole subtribe with which the senior lineage of the clan of spear-masters with tribal primacy is found is called the *wun yath*, the subtribe of the divinity. In this way the strength of the clan-divinity is regarded as greater in those whose importance for the structure of the clan is greater.

It is to be expected, therefore, that the divinities of the clans of 10.2.29 spear-masters should be regarded as more powerful than those of the secular clans, and should sometimes be said to be the only original clan-divinities. Members of spear-master clans particularly maintain that in the past they were more influential politically than they are today, when the warrior clans have multiplied — as, incidentally, according to this account, have the numbers of clan-divinities. A master of the fishing-spear said that warrior clans 'did not sacrifice for divinities, but only for the ghosts of the dead'; and the fact that the propitiation of ghosts of the dead is a family cult implies here the suggestion that at one time the warrior clans were scarcely to be regarded as clans at all, but as disunited families with no sense of a wider agnatic relationship. In fact also the spear-master clans can on the whole produce clearer and longer genealogies than the rest. Members of warrior clans, asserting their own importance also, deny that they have acquired their clan-divinities more recently than the clans of spear-masters, saying that they too have their clan-divinities which help *them*.[3] They admit, however, that their divinities are not on the whole as strong (*kec*, literally 'biting' or 'hot' or 'bitter') as those of the spear-masters, and that the divinities of the spear-masters when called upon by masters of the fishing-spear will help whole tribes and subtribes, whilst the divinities of warrior clans help only members of those clans. Similarly, the master of the fishing-spear is regarded as belonging to and supporting everyone in his community: 'no man has a master of the fishing-spear all of his own' as the Dinka say.

10.2.30   Finally, as the spear-master clans as a whole are known to be superior to the warrior clans in influence and endowment within the whole social system of the Dinka, so their homogeneity and superiority in relation to the warrior clans are imaged in the common and supreme clan-divinity they all possess — *ring*, Flesh. As will be seen in the myths of the spear-master clans with which the second part of this book starts, these clans are regarded as deriving their superiority from a common original experience from which the warrior clans were excluded, and they accordingly share a common divinity in addition to the different divinities which correspond to their different lines of agnatic descent.

10.2.31   **[The Rise of Individualism, Witchcraft and Prophecy]**

In this chapter I have tried to describe the contexts of experience within which Dinka assertions about the Powers may be understood and harmonised, as they cannot be understood by us if they are regarded as referring to theoretical 'beings' whose existence is posited, as it were, before the human experience to which they correspond. As images, the Powers contract whole fields of direct experience and represent their fundamental nature each by a single term. The Dinka sometimes indicate that originally the free-divinities did not affect them so powerfully as now; that they knew only the power of the clan-divinities, and more particularly of the clan-divinities of the spear-master clans, and Divinity itself which those clans represented to their political communities. We do not know whether this is historically true; but it is significant that, according to the Dinka, the effects of free-divinities on individuals have been the more widely and deeply felt as their own political autonomy has been undermined. 'Everyone now wants to be a master', say the masters of the fishing-spear; and in general the rise of the free-divinities, potentially equally affecting all Dinka as individuals and families, corresponds to their recognition of increasing individualism in their life and intimations of changes in the basic structure of their society. So also do assertions that witchcraft and the use of fetishes have increased and are increasing. On the other hand, the reaction to loss of political autonomy also makes possible wider political combinations than were previously possible, and the influence of prophets is undoubtedly made possible by a response on the part of many Dinka, traditionally divided from each other, to a common influence or set of influences. The great prophets, those who are also masters of the fishing-spear, are thought to have a place also in the original system of religious and political institutions before these were modified by external forces. In this they correspond to the balance of change and permanence in their life which the Dinka encounter in experiences of foreign influence and control.

I have suggested that the Powers may be understood as images 10.2.32 corresponding to complex and various combinations of Dinka experience which are contingent upon their particular social and physical environment. For the Dinka they are the grounds of those experiences; in our analysis we have shown them to be grounded in them, for to a European the experiences are more readily understood than the Powers, and the existence of the latter cannot be posited as a condition of the former. Without these Powers or images or an alternative to them there would be for the Dinka no differentiation between experience of the self and of the world which acts upon it. Suffering, for example, could be merely 'lived' or endured. With the imaging of the grounds of suffering in a particular Power, the Dinka can grasp its nature intellectually in a way which satisfies them, and thus to some extent transcend and dominate it in this act of knowledge. With this knowledge, the separation of a subject and an object in experience, there arises for them also the possibility of creating a form of experience they desire, and of freeing themselves symbolically from what they must otherwise passively endure. . .

Notes

1. In P.W. Schmidt, *Der Ursprung der Gottesidee,* 1949, Vol.viii, p.145.
2. Full-brothers are also clansmen, of course, but no Dinka would refer to his full-brother as his clansman, any more than one would refer to a brother as a relative.
3. It may be also that the modern administrative system has given more scope

to outstanding men from warrior clans.

Source: Abridged from R.G. Lienhardt, op.cit., pp.156-170.

10.3 HYMNS OF THE DINKA

F.M. Deng

Introduction   10.3.1

Hymns reflect man's reaction to the cruelties of a world he does not understand, his attempt to understand what he cannot understand, his appeal to God, spirits, and ancestors for their assistance and their response to his prayers.

In order to gauge man's failure which has invited evil, or the capriciousness of the spirits which have unjustifiably inflicted harm, hymns embody the ideals of the Dinka as guaranteed by God and by well-meaning spirits and ancestors.

In accordance with Dinka religious expression, in which prayers are not a regular habit but a request for something specific, hymns are sung for the help of God, lesser spirits, and the ancestors. Thus, except for certain regular occasions of offerings and feasting, they are used as prayers during sickness, war, drought, famine, or any such tragedy, and may be sung by individuals or by groups, in public or in private. Divine leaders and other religious functionaries may also sing hymns alone or in company with others as part of their general prayer for the well-being of their people even though there may be no specific threat. Hymns are also sung as part of the inauguration ceremonies for chiefs or as part of the burial rites of chiefs and certain holy men.

On whatever occasion hymns are presented, they are generally a means of communication between the ancestors and spirits and their representatives in this world, usually the elders. During war, when young warriors sing in prayer for victory, their hymns take the form of war songs.

In so far as they reflect situations of public significance, whether involving the public as such or some pivotal individuals or groups, hymns are of historical value. This is especially so because hymns of such public interest tend to be perpetuated even though they may be reinterpreted and distorted to present the viewpoints of interested groups. Even when they are new, hymns tend to build on ancient legacy and therefore on old hymns. Whether old, reinterpreted, distorted, or newly composed, by referring to specific clan-divinities, hymns may be of particular help in interpreting mythology and understanding not only the roots of divine leadership, but also current political structure, in so far as it is based on the traditional system.

10.3.2 The Lord Thunders [Ngok]

The Great Lord Madhol[1] thunders in the byre[2]
Thundering in the byre, he is angry with the ants[3]
He is the Man who brings death.
The master whose heart has no grudge
He attracts all the ants
People gather on his feet
And also on his head
Great Lord of the Gourd
Put right our land
The land is shaken
If the earth is bitterly cold
If the earth blows with cold wind
It is the wind of Divinity.
If a man loves me
I love him
And if a man hates me
I hate him.
But not with all of my heart shall I hate
For am I not the prosperity of the ants?

10.3.3 If I Wrong Him [Ngok of Upper Nile Province]

If I wrong Him
I make it right.
If I have wronged Him
I have made it right.
I will not tire
I will not tire
I will not tire of Deng, the spirit of my fathers
Ayuel Longar,[4] Master of Earth,
I do not understand the doubts from above
If I wrong Him
I make it right.

10.3.4 My Horns will not Break [Ngok of Upper Nile Province]

Ayuel Longar, son of Jiel,

I will appease you with a white bull.
The Winter has come
The world has dawned
My horns will not break
I am no longer vexed.
The Winter comes
And I sleep with leisure.
O our Deng,
Deng, son of Garang,
Deng, son of Abuk,
The man has come with life.

The Man from Above [Ngok of Upper Nile Province] 10.3.5

If a thing subdues me
It will be solved by Deng, the man from above.
Awol Kerjok[5] and Deng Acuny[6]
Praise Him Who Embraces the World.
Our River-Girl[7] and Wieu[8]
Come let us pray to Deng.
Kokbong[9] and Longar
The ants have been sad for eight years.
Awol Kerjok, come and listen to the words I say
I praise Abuk and her son, Deng,
The face of the ant you created has become sad
Come let us pray to our Lord.

Big Chief Pray to God [Ngok] 10.3.6

Some years ago, a young man of the Pajok clan fell ill. After his
recovery, he did not return to his normal life, but became 'a man of
God', who might have been an acknowledged prophet in traditional
times. In this hymn, he asks the Chief to turn to God to save the
country from disintegration.
We have become lean
Big Chief, pray to God
Our buttocks have wrinkled
Big Chief, pray to God
Our faces are sad
Big Chief, pray to God
Will dances be held at night
As though they were dances of spirits?
Doo, doo, doo, doo
Big Chief, pray to God.

Notes

1. Praise-name for God.
2. During the rainy season, Dinkas normally keept their cattle in the cattle-byres. God is seen as having a byre in the sky.
3. Ants are human beings.
4. Ayuel, the son of a woman and a Power of the river, punished the people of the village in which he was born by spearing them as they tried to cross to the land of endless grass and water where there was no death. He was finally over-powered by a man to whom he gave the Fishing-Spear which is the source of the power of the clan of the Fishing-Spear. Thus, Ayuel represents a combination of life and death and is divine. For further reference see Lienhardt, op.cit. (1961), pp.171-206.
5. A clan divinity or an ancestor.
6. A praise-name for the clan divinity often used to praise people with the Deng name.
7. Either a girl sacrificed to the Power of the River (e.g. Acai) or a woman who was conceived by the Power of the River (e.g. Ayuel's mother).
8. Presumably another divinity.
9. Yet another divinity.

Source: From F.M. Deng, *The Dinka and their Songs,* OUP 1973, pp.238-242.

11   SPANNING EAST AND WEST: ZOROASTRINISM

[*Editor's Note:* The following notes were written by Mr. John Hinnells, the Course Unit author of the Zoroastrian Units:

Zoroaster (the Greek form of the Iranian Zatarthuštra) was the prophet of ancient Iran. There are disagreements over his date, but there is increasing support for the view that he lived somewhere in the period 1500-1000 BC. The Iranian empire (or 'Persian' to use the older and common name) was founded by Cyrus the Great in the sixth century BC. Just when the prophet's teaching became the official religion of that empire we do not know, but its influence is evident in Achaemenid times (sixth to fourth centuries BC) and was (contrary to what earlier scholarly opinion had said) powerful in Parthian times (second-century BC to the third century CE) when the sacred scriptures or the *Avesta* began to be collected. The religion received much of its classic literary expression and full stately splendour in Sasanian times (third-century to seventh-century CE). The Muslim invasion of Iran produced periods of bitter persecution. This and the attractive vitality of the new faith reduced Zoroastrian numbers in Iran to a very small community living mainly on the edge of the desert in Yazd and Kerman (there were approximately 17,000 in the 1960s).

In the ninth and tenth centuries there were periods of Zoroastrian literary activity when they were permitted to explain, defend and expound their faith. Generally, however, conditions were so unfavourable for Zoroastrians in Iran that a band of the 'pilgrim fathers' of the faith set out to find a new land of religious freedom and they settled on the West coast of India. There the Parsis (= Persians) have kept alive the prophet's faith. In the nineteenth and early twentieth centuries they achieved considerable economic and political power, but this change in their social status and their educational advances resulted in profound changes in their religious beliefs. In the 1950s their numbers began to decline at the rate of 10 per cent per decade and in 1971 there were 91,000 Parsis in the whole of India, 70 per cent of them in the city of Bombay.

A Zoroastrian presence has not been confined to the East. The prophet's name and teaching were known to the ancient Greeks, and the religion was influential in the Roman Empire (in Mithraism for example). It also exercised an influence on Jewish, Christian and Islamic teachings. The presence in the West is also a living one, with communities to this day in Los Angeles, Toronto and London.

Zoroastrianism, then, has a history of 3,000 years and has spread both to the East and the West. It has affected the faiths and lives of countless millions in many countries, not least of course in its homeland, Iran, a veritable bridge between East and West.

The following selection of texts represents different types of material — scriptural and other religious texts, some historical reports, and popular (as opposed to the earlier classic) religious writings; there are also two writings by a distinguished Western scholar who has specialised in the study of Zoroastrianism. Since these two writings serve as a general introduction to our study of man's religious quest according to Zoroastrianism, we print them first, even before the scriptural texts and other primary sources. The author of these two writings is Professor Mary Boyce of the School of Oriental and African Studies, University of London. The first is written especially for this Reader and makes an original and important contribution to the history of Zoroastrian studies. The second is a passage from Professor Boyce's book *A History of Zoroastrianism* (Brill, Leiden, Vol.I, 1975). It deals with the period between the prophet and the formation of the Persian empire, a period clouded in obscurity but of great importance in an understanding of the growth of Zoroastrianism.

The scriptural texts are taken from the Zoroastrian holy book, the *Avesta*. The first (§11.3) is an ancient hymn to Mithra (*Yašt* 10) which, though it has been affected by centuries of transmission in Zoroastrianism, substantially reflects the religion of the pre-Zoroastrian nomads on the Asian steppes. The following section of the material (§§11.4.1 – 11.4.14) is from the *Gāthās*, the hymns of the prophet himself. The subsequent texts (§§11.5.1 – 11.6.3) are from the Pahlavi (Middle Persian) literature written in their present form in that outburst of literary activity in the ninth and tenth centuries already mentioned. The first of these texts (§11.5) contains an exposition of the classic Zoroastrian doctrine on good and evil being diametrically opposed forces, originating from the two ultimately independent and conflicting beings. The other Pahlavi texts set forward the famed Zoroastrian apocalyptic teaching which was probably a source of influence for the ideas of Jews, Christians and Muslims.

The historical texts (§§11.7.1 — 11.8.7) begin with a seventeenth century Parsi account of the settlement in India and then offer some contemporary accounts of the Parsi community in seventeenth and early eighteenth century India.

There are also selections from the writings of some twentieth-century Parsis (§§11.9.1 — 11.12), reflecting the different ways in which they have attempted to interpret their faith in order to give a meaning to life in the face of the pressures and influences they encounter in modern India in general and Bombay in particular.]

11.1 THE CONTINUITY OF THE ZOROASTRIAN QUEST

Mary Boyce

Zoroastrianism is probably the oldest revealed religion in the world, 11.1.1
and has been the most misrepresented. Its scriptures have not long
been generally known, and by the time they were made accessible to
the West, the Zoroastrian community itself had been reduced to two
tiny isolated minorities, in Iran and India. Persecution had taught its
members, moreover, the prudence of keeping silent about their
beliefs and observances, and their reticence was often mistaken for
ignorance or stupidity. So Western scholars, coming eagerly to the
study of the Avesta, felt able to disregard them entirely in seeking to
interpret their ancient scriptures. The first edition of the Avesta was
published in 1852, and a few years later a brilliant young philologist,
Martin Haug, produced the first scholarly attempt to translate the
Gathas into a European language (*Die Gāthā's des Zarathustra*,
Leipzig 1858-60). He had identified these magnificently obscure
hymns as the oldest part of the Avesta, and the only portion which
could be attributed to Zoroaster himself; and for his pioneer
rendering he drew both on his knowledge of Vedic, and on his
expectations of what a great world-prophet should have taught. Thus
he came to understand Zoroaster to have proclaimed a message of
noble simplicity, a strict monotheism, with denial of the existence of
any divine being other than Ahura Mazdā, who was to be
worshipped without rituals or sacrifices, simply through heartfelt
prayer.

Haug based this interpretation of Zoroaster's teachings on the
following main points: firstly, he understood the word *daēva* to be,
not an expression for a particular group of pagan gods, but a term
for divine beings in general; and so he thought that, in repudiating
the *daēvas*, Zoroaster was rejecting all gods but the supreme Lord.
Secondly, he regarded the 'Bounteous Immortals', the Aməša
Spəntas, whose names reverberate through the Gathas, as only
aspects of faculties of God, and not as independent divine beings to
be invoked and worshipped. Thirdly, he supposed that when the
prophet protested passionately against cruelty to cattle, and
castigated (in one verse) the use of an unnamed intoxicant, he was

603

inveighing against the traditional rites of sacrifice and the *haoma*-offering. To reach these conclusions Haug had to reject the testimony, not only of living Zoroastrianism, but also of all the remaining Avesta, which is full of veneration of the Aməša Spəntas and other lesser divinities, together with execration of the *daēvas*, and which abounds in reference to blood-sacrifice and the *haoma*-offering. He was therefore forced to suppose that soon after Zoroaster's death his community, while faithfully preserving his actual words and venerating his memory, greatly corrupted his teachings, reverting almost at once to beliefs and practices which he had banned.

11.1.2   This approach, by which a European scholar, however gifted, could set his judgment, slenderly based on the study of one group of texts alone (and deeply enigmatic texts at that), against all the later scripture, tradition and observances of the once mighty Zoroastrian church now seems astonishingly presumptuous; but Europe in the nineteenth century was very sure of itself and ready to instruct the world, and for a variety of reasons Haug's interpretation was widely accepted. It established Zoroaster, so long fabled for wisdom, as a teacher of whom the contemporary West could approve – a rational theist, making minimal demands for observance. Most students of the Gathas were moreover philologists, like Haug, and were happy with an interpretation which allowed them to ignore complex traditions and the living faith, and to wrestle with these great texts alone in the quiet of their studies. There were, of course, those who were interested in them primarily as religious works, but some of these saw Zoroastrianism in the light of a forerunner of Christianity, whose significance ended when it had transmitted its chief doctrines to the younger faith. So they too were indifferent to its living forms, and also to those of its teachings which are unique and set it apart. W. Hinz and R.C. Zaehner are the most recent representatives of this school of thought, while S. Insler, who offered a new translation of the Gathas in 1975, adhered strictly to the philological approach, drawing, like Haug, on virtually no external aid other than the language of the Vedas. Methods of interpretation initiated in the nineteenth century have thus had a long influence, and much of the work devoted to Zoroastrianism during the past century has been spent on attempts to justify them, and to explain why it is that the resulting conclusions so signally fail to fit the facts.

11.1.3   Haug's theories were the more acceptable in the mid-nineteenth century because at that time the Zoroastrian secondary literature in

Middle Persian or Pahlavi, was virtually unknown. By the 1880s this had changed, thanks to the devoted labours of E.W. West, who began his Pahlavi translations in India, among the Parsis themselves. He was joined briefly in Bombay by another great scholar, James Darmesteter, who was engaged on a new translation of the whole Avesta. He consulted Parsi priests, annotated his translation with a wealth of notes on living practices, and studied the Pahlavi books; and he came to the conclusion that the religious system expounded in these 'is a faithful reflection, in its theology and ethics, of the ideas of the Gathas', and that they provided therefore an invaluable key for unlocking the Gathic enigmas, since Zoroaster's teachings, there wrapped in esoteric ambiguities, are set out plainly in these later prose works (see his *Le Zend-Avesta,* Paris 1892, I cv).

The theology of the Pahlavi books is very different from that 11.1.4 described in the Gathas by Haug, but Darmesteter's appraisal was too late to prevent Haug's interpretation, already well established, from hardening into academic dogma. One reason why it came to seem solidly based was that it had had an influence on Zoroastrians themselves. Haug spent the 1860s in India, and while there lectured energetically to the Parsis on his understanding of their prophet's teachings. He was listened to eagerly by one group among them, made up of those who had been educated at British schools in Bombay, and who were anxiously seeking means to reconcile the doctrines and practices of their ancient faith with the contemporary world of Western science and thought. Haug provided them unexpectedly with a startlingly simple solution, for according to him they could jettison almost all traditional beliefs and observances, and still account themselves faithful followers of Zoroaster. Many other Parsis rejected his ideas indignantly, since these constituted an attack on almost all that they held dear; but their adoption by the reformists meant that thereafter the community was divided, and could not speak with a single voice in the continuing debate on the nature of Zoroaster's message. Moreover, since the reformists wrote mostly in English, it was their utterances which reached Europe, where they were innocently cited as showing that Haug's interpretation must be right, since it reflected the beliefs of Zoroastrians themselves. The Irani Zoroastrians were able to preserve the faith of their forefathers unassailed for a little longer, being immured in a traditional Muslim society, which was itself impervious to any unsettling new ideas; and from them one can learn that the doctrine of a rigid monotheism, with rejection of rituals, had no place in living Zoroastrianism before European impact in the nineteenth century. This is substantiated, moreover, for the Parsi community itself by old records now available.

11.1.5   One of the many points on which Haug challenged traditional beliefs was in his insistence that Zoroaster was not a dualist. Philosophically, he conceded, the prophet had recognised the existence of two separate principles of good and evil; but he denied that this had influenced his theology, causing him to personify evil as a being opposed to Ahura Mazdā. This personification, Haug maintained, was the work of his followers. This interpretation was very welcome to the Parsi reformists, who had been suffering under the attacks of Christian missionaries, to whom any form of dualism was abhorrent. It found less acceptance in Europe, however, for it ignored too flagrantly the various Gathic passages where Zoroaster speaks of the two Spirits, even once (Y.45.2) naming one of them as the Hostile Spirit (Angra Mainyu, Pahlavi Ahriman). A small group of scholars found another justification, however, for the view that Zoroaster was not a dualist – that is, one who recognised the existence of two wholly independent and opposed Beings, one good, the other evil. They fastened on the metaphor of 'twin Spirits' in Y.30.4, and argued, rather quaintly, that since twin children have a father, so must twin spirits have. Hence they deduced that the 'Most Bounteous Spirit' of this passage, who is 'clad in the hardest stone' *[i.e. the sky]*(Y.30.5), was not, as Zoroastrian tradition and ordinary expectation would alike suggest, Ahura Mazdā, but rather his Spirit which, they supposed, had emanated from him with its twin. At that stage, it was suggested, the pair were 'undifferentiated spirit'; and it was only thereafter that one of them chose evil, and so became the Hostile Spirit, implacably opposed to its compaternal brother.

11.1.6   This interpretation comes fairly close to Christian doctrine concerning God and the Devil; and it is a variant on Zurvanism, an old Zoroastrian heresy, likewise based on Y.30.4, which saw Ahura Mazdā and Angra Mainyu as twin brothers begotten by Zurvan, 'Time' or 'Fate'. A Pahlavi commentator stigmatised this Zurvanite doctrine as diabolic, taught to men by a demon (*Dinkard* IX.30.4); and the European variant embodies the same basic heresy, so abhorrent to the orthodox, of postulating a link between good and evil. The enormous strength of the traditional Zoroastrian doctrine, which appears firmly based on Gathic teaching, is that evil is entirely outside the sphere of God, who though wholly good and wise is not all-powerful, being engaged in an active struggle, with man's help, against the forces of wickedness. Hence when a Zoroastrian is afflicted, he can regard his trouble as brought on him by the common enemy, Angra Mainyu; and he does not have to think that it comes with the assent, or through the original act, of an Almighty God whom he has been taught to love and worship. He need not, therefore, seek to resign himself in this to the will of Ahura Mazdā, but can summon up all his courage and endurance to defy the Hostile Spirit. It is this doctrine which inculcates in Zoroastrians their valour; and it is, as Zaehner (himself a supporter of the 'Zurvanite'-type interpretation) generously admits 'perhaps the most rational solution of the problem of evil ever devised'. It was a solution upon which Zoroastrians took a firm stand in their early encounters with Christians and Muslim polemicists, at a time when they still had the strong certainties that go with a position of temporal and numerical superiority.

It might be expected that scholars who sought to modify 11.1.7 Zoroaster's dualism through this theory of two lesser Spirits would be forced by their own arguments to abandon the claim that he was a rigid monotheist; but the Christian doctrine of the Trinity may have helped them to hold both opinions without consciousness of inconsistency. The monotheistic theory had, through repetition, become indeed so firmly established that it was able to withstand a steady accumulation of much more positive evidence against it. This was heaped up by conscientious scholars who, while themselves adhering to it, could not help in the course of their studies arriving at contradictory renderings of particular Gathic passages. To take one example, Zoroaster twice (Y.30.9, 31.4) uses the expression *mazdāscā ahurānhō*. This looks like a plural, and Haug understood it to reflect old folk-beliefs in 'wise lords', which had been elevated by the prophet into his own lofty concept of the one 'Wise Lord'; but this uneasy explanation (for why should the folk-belief find expression still in Zoroaster's own Gathas?) was abandoned, with other unsatisfactory attempts, when the great Avestan lexicographer, Christian Bartholomae, pointed out that the expression was in fact an example of a standard type of compound, in which, if a singular and plural are joined, both take plural endings. So it means simply 'Mazdā and the (other) Lords'. This looks deplorably polytheistic, and so the 'other Lords' were hastily identified with the six Ameša Spentas; and since these were supposed to be only aspects of Ahura Mazdā, and not independent divinities, monotheism could still be upheld. It is a fact, however, that the title *ahura* 'lord', is nowhere given to these six, whereas the later Avesta knows two lesser Ahuras, Mithra and *Vouruna Apạm Napāt, who are acknowledged and venerated by Zoroastrians to this day. That the 'other Ahuras' of the Gathas must be they was recognised by Zehner, who, hedging somewhat in the interests of monotheism, put the matter in the following words:

> Zoroaster himself. . .among the *ahuras* retained only Ahura Mazdāh. . .as the One True God. It is, then, the *daēvas* specifically whom Zoroaster attacks, not the *ahuras* whom he prefers to ignore except once only *[sic]* when he declares that 'Truth is to be invoked, and the Wise One and the *[other]* lords *[ahuras]*' (Y.31.4) − an important qualification since it may well indicate that Zoroaster, monotheist though he certainly was. . .did not utterly dethrone the other 'lords' from beside the 'Wise Lord'. In all probability he considered them to be God's creatures and as fighters on his side.

11.1.8   If we abandon all prevarication, this last sentence represents in fact a surrender of the 'rigid monotheism' position, and an acceptance of actual Zoroastrian doctrine, as embodied in the Gathas themselves, in the later Avesta, in the secondary Pahlavi literature, and in the beliefs and devotional acts of the community at all known points of its history, from the observations of Herodotus in the fifth century BC down to modern times. This doctrine is that *in the beginning,* of all beneficent divinity, Ahura Mazdā alone existed. So in one sense, that of believing in only one eternal, uncreated Being who is worthy of worship, Zoroaster was indeed a monotheist, with a concept of God as exalted as that of any Hebrew or Arabian prophet. But he was also a dualist, in that he saw co-existing with Ahura Mazdā, another uncreated Being, who was maleficent, not to be worshipped. It was in order to destroy this Hostile Spirit, and to achieve a universe of perfect goodness and harmony, that Ahura Mazdā created this world; but to help him both to fashion it, and then to carry on the struggle within it against evil, he first brought into being lesser beneficent divinities, emanated from his own essence like torches kindled from a greater torch. These were the Ameša Spentas or Yazatas. (The former term, meaning 'Bounteous Immortals', was used, it seems, to replace an older pagan invocation of *Vispe Aməša, 'All the Immortals', which embraced the *daēvas* as well.) So in present and future times

Zoroaster acknowledged the existence of a plurality of divine beings; but these are not the heterogeneous throng of a pagan polytheism, for all share the nature and purpose of their one Creator, and strive to do his will. They are therefore in many respects like the angels of Judaism, Christianity and Islam; but the Zoroastrian *yazatas* are more powerful, and should receive, not only veneration and supplication, but worship and prayers in their own right, though always beneath the aegis of great Ahura Mazdā; to whom, no less than men, they owe their individual existence and their complete fidelity.

In response to Ahura Mazdā's creation of the *yazatas,* the Hostile Spirit, Angra Mainyu, produced a counter-creation of his own, the wicked *daēvas,* to be repudiated by all just men. According to one Gathic passage (Y.32.3) the *daēvas* were 'of the race of evil purpose'; according to another (Y.30.6) they 'chose the worst purpose' through blindness. 'Then together they betook themselves to Wrath, through whom they sickened the life of men' (Y.30.6). Among the *daēvas* were the mighty, truculent Indra and his companions, Nānhaithya and Saurva (the Vedic Nāsatya and Śarva), whom the prophet seems to have abhorred because they were worshipped as warlike, amoral beings, the servants indeed of Wrath, who demanded only lavish offerings from their worshippers, and were indifferent to any ethical claims. So Zoroaster, while not denying their existence, courageously rejected and defied them as false gods, holding by the just Ahuras; and his community faithfully followed his example down the ages, uttering daily the Zoroastrian confession of faith, the *Fravarānē,* which begins: 'I profess myself a worshipper of Mazdā, a Zoroastrian, rejecting the *daēvas,* accepting the Ahuric doctrine; one who praises the Aməša Spəntas, who worships the Aməša Spəntas. To Ahura Mazdā, the good, rich in treasures, I ascribe all things good.'

Generations of Western scholars having accepted Haug's pioneering 11.1.9 theories, have had to regard this confession of faith as in part a gross distortion of Zoroaster's teachings (which is much as if modern Zoroastrians were to take it upon themselves to reject whole sections of the Christian creeds); but once one abandons those theories as untenable, then a great log-jam of accumulated, apparently contradictory, evidence slides smoothly into place, and one can see that in fact Zoroaster's followers have remained loyal to their prophet's teachings in all essentials, and that there is an unbroken tradition of orthodoxy from the earliest times through (in a few still traditional centres) to the present day. This coherence and fidelity, rather than a history of backsliding and confusion, is what one would indeed look for from a great seminal faith, which had the strength itself to dominate three mighty empires, and which through its influence has left its imprint on the thoughts of half the world.

11.1.10   The doctrines of Zoroastrianism which were adopted by Christianity and Islam, concerning God and the Devil, individual judgment at death, the Last Judgment, resurrection of the body, Heaven and Hell and life everlasting, are so familiar that they have masked the uniqueness of the complete Zoroastrian system, and have obscured the ancientness of the world-picture which underlies it. Nor has it helped that some influential scholars have accepted a late and, as it is now clear, wholly artificial tradition, evolved by Zoroastrian scholastics in Western Iran, that their prophet lived '258 years before Alexander', that is, in the early sixth century BC. Other, much older traditions of Eastern Iran place him many generations before that; and cumulative evidence suggests that he flourished some 3500 years ago or more, and that his faith was old before the Buddha was born. Moreover, he belonged, it seems, among the last generations of a society whose ways of life and thought had been fashioned during millennia spent by their nomad forbears on the Inner Asian steppes; and so he was heir to some immensely ancient concepts, which indeed seem in part to go back to Indo-European times.

11.1.11   Zoroaster himself appears to have lived during a turbulent era of the great migrations, when the Indians and Iranians were on the move, before their invasions of the countries now called after them; and the conflict is mirrored in the Gathas between peaceful herdsmen, law-abiding, worshipping the Ahuras, who were content to occupy good lands for themselves and their cattle, and roving warrior-bands, rejoicing in conquest for its own sake, pillaging and plundering, and making immoderate sacrifices from their spoils to the battle-loving *daēvas*. It was from this encounter, it seems, between the immensely old and stable, and the fiercely new and challenging, that the prophet Zoroaster emerged; but it was an encounter between elements in his own society. He is the 'Iranian prophet', and it is to the background of Iranian thought that one must look in order fully to understand his message.

11.1.12   The picture which the ancient Iranians had of the physical world is preserved in a Pahlavi work (the *Bundahishn*), based on lost portions of the Avesta. From this it appears that the pagan Iranians thought that the gods had shaped the world in seven stages: first, the solid sky, made of stone, like a huge round shell enclosing the world; then, in the bottom half of this shell, water; then on the water, earth, like a great flat dish; and then a single plant, animal and man, at the earth's centre. All was motionless and unchanging, with the sun, representing the seventh creation, fire, and set, like the moon and stars, beneath the sky standing always at noon. Finally, it seems, the gods crushed the plant, and slew the animal and man, and made a triple sacrifice. From this sacrifice more plants, animals and men sprang into being to occupy the world. The cycle of existence was thus put in motion, and thenceforth birth followed death, generation after generation.

This process, to judge from parallel Indian beliefs, was regarded as 11.1.13 endless. Once started by the gods, it was to go on interminably; but the sacrifice which had begun it was re-enacted daily by the priests (with regard to plants and animals), in order to ensure that it continued — that the sun rose each day, the rains fell, and grass grew to nourish cattle and men. This daily sacrifice was called the *yasna* or 'act of worship', for it was devoted to the divine beings, its other purpose being to sustain their beneficent interest in the world they had brought into being. Each one of the seven creations was represented at the *yasna,* including man himself (through the priestly celebrant). Even the sky of stone was there in flint knife and stone mortar. The whole world with its inhabitants was thus reconsecrated at each daily service, designed to preserve it in being and in health.

Zoroaster, trained as a priest, must have been familiar from 11.1.14 boyhood with this recurrent rite of worship, and it seems that it was largely through meditating upon it, and upon the mystery and purpose of creation, that he attained enlightenment. He saw creation, not as the work of many gods, who had put a piece of mechanism into random motion and might again forget it, but as the planned achievement of one supreme Being, Ahura Mazdā, who had established it for a clearly defined purpose, to be achieved within a limited period of time. All beneficent existence, it was revealed to him, had a shared aim, to struggle against the Hostile Spirit and the evil which he had maliciously brought into the perfect world of Mazdā's creation, and by making an end of him and it to restore this world to its original state, for all eternity. Zoroaster saw man, with his unique power of choice, as the especial handiwork of Ahura Mazdā himself; but he held that each of the other six creations had its own especial guardian, one of the six great

'Bounteous Immortals', who were the first of the lesser divinities to be brought into existence by Ahura Mazdā, and who formed with him a mighty heptad.

11.1.15   These six great beings all hypostatised certain desirable qualities or attributes. The remarkable ability to see what we would now term abstractions as powers, and then further as independent divinities, was characteristic of the Indo-Iranians, who, instead of saying 'God is Love', would be more apt to say 'Love is God'. This appears strikingly in the worship of the three Ahuras, who personify Wisdom (Mazdā), Loyalty (Mithra) and Truth (*Vouruna). Traditionally, moreover, as is shown in the yašts and Vedas, every great divinity was conceived as being encircled by lesser helpers. (Indo-Iranian religion was profoundly polytheistic, as is attested also by the Buddha's acknowledgement of the existence of many gods.) So Zoroaster's vision was cast in a familiar mould when he apprehended Ahura Mazdā as surrounded by these six lesser Beings, radiant divinities in whose presence the prophet 'did not see his own shadow upon the earth, because of their great light' (*Zadspram* XXI.9). The innovation lay in his perceiving them, like every other *yazata*, to have been created by the supreme Lord, to serve his ends. Further, every one of the qualities or attributes which the six Ameša Spentas personify are ones which belong to Ahura Mazdā himself – good purpose, righteousness, dominion, devotion, well-being, immortality – and they can be attained also through striving by each individual man. Zoroaster speaks of these things repeatedly in the Gathas; and he also constantly invokes and venerates the divine beings who personify them. This was established long since for Western inquirers by Bernhard Geiger, who published (in *Die Aməša Spəntas,* Vienna, 1916), a scholarly analysis of all the Gathic passages. His findings conflicted, however, with the 'monotheistic' theory, and so were largely ignored. Thus more than fifty years afterwards one finds Zaehner still able to state that 'in later Zoroastrianism these entities were to become "archangels", separate from the Wise Lord and created by him, but in the *Gāthās* this is not so: they are rather faculties through which he operates'. Not all Western scholars were so firm in denying the facts, however, and in 1925 A.V.W. Jackson roundly declared: 'The whole Zoroastrian system from the beginning to the end, from the Gathas to the latest Ravāyats, postulates the existence of the Amshaspands as a cardinal tenet of faith'.

11.1.16   In the later Avesta and the Pahlavi books, as in living orthodox Zoroastrianism, Ahura Mazdā and the six Aməša Spəntas are constantly linked with the seven physical creations; but this association proved so perplexing to Western scholars, and was so remote, in its rich complexity, from the theory of Zoroaster's simple theism, that it was attributed, like every other unfamiliar element in his teachings, to developments by his followers. But in 1930 H. Lommel, a pupil of Hegel's and one of the most perceptive interpreters of Zoroastrianism, published a masterly study (*Die Religion Zarathustras*) in which he showed that there are subtle allusions in the Gathas which prove beyond doubt that it was Zoroaster himself who linked the divine heptad with the sevenfold physical world. This association is in fact part of the very fabric of his teachings; and though its practical results are curiously modern (for it made his followers into the first ecologists), the doctrine itself could only have been shaped at his own remote place and age, before Iranians began to mingle their ideas with those of Babylon and Greece, and to modify in some respects their ancient picture of the world.

The assertion that this doctrine is essential to Zoroastrianism may   11.1.17
seem over-bold in face of the fact that a scholar of Zaehner's standing could summarise Zoroaster's beliefs without so much as mentioning it; but it has been a weakness in the Western study of Zoroastrianism that it has concentrated largely on texts. The Zoroastrian texts, it is true, are full of reference to this particular doctrine, as to the Ameša Spentas themselves; but in a purely academic study of a religion it is possible to make a subjective choice of what seems significant, whereas encounters with a living faith force one to accept its adherents' own understanding of its essentials, which are likely, moreover, to be embodied in its main observances. The only Zoroastrian ritual which seriously interested Zaehner was the *haoma*-offering, because he saw this, taken in isolation, as having a spurious resemblance to the Christian communion rite. By neglecting to study the full devotional life of the faith he was able to ignore the part played in it by the doctrine of the divine heptad and the seven creations; but for an orthodox Zoroastrian of the old school it is this doctrine which not only shapes his comprehension of the surrounding world, but also directs his conduct and gives much of their significance to his private and public devotions.

This doctrine in its completeness seems also to have been attained   11.1.18
by Zoroaster through his meditations on the *yasna;* for he became conscious evidently then of the inward divinity informing every

single thing which he as celebrant saw or handled: the humbleness of
Ārmaiti, Devotion, in the earth beneath him; the strength of
Khšathra, Dominion, in the hardness of the stone which he touched;
Welfare and Immortality, Haurvatāt and Amərätāt, in the water and
bread which he consecrated; Good Purpose, Vohu Manah, in the
beneficent cow which furnished milk and the sacrifice; Order, Aša,
in the fire in its brazier, while he himself, chanting holy words, was
full of Spanta Mainyu, the Bounteous Spirit of the Lord. So in
celebrating this service, intended to sustain the material world, he
meditated also on these divine Beings, offered them his worship and
sought to bring them — or the qualities which they hypotstatize —
into his own person.

11.1.19   The Gathas are full of transitions between quality and divinity,
one melting into another in a way that baffles certain translation.
For example: 'Ahura Mazdā, uniting himself with Vohu Manah,
together with Khšathra, with sun-possessing Aša, answered them
[i.e. his worshippers]: 'We make choice of your bounteous good
devotion (*ārmaiti-*), it shall be ours'' ' (Y.32.2); or 'the man of good
will has promised to hold fast to the deeds of this good purpose
(*vohu- manah-*), and to bounteous devotion (*spənta- ārmaiti-*),
having known her [i.e. Ārmaiti] who is of the Creator, companion of
Aša (Y.34.10). There are, further, the glancing allusions to the link
between divinity and material objects. Thus it is said of Ārmaiti,
guardian of earth, that 'she has given us a goodly home. . . For her,
through Aša, did Ahura Mazdā cause the plants to grow at the birth
of the primeval world' (Y.48.6). She is created 'for the care of
cattle, if she takes counsel with Vohu Manah' (Y.47.3), and she is
adjured 'through the labour of husbandry, let cattle grow fat for our
nourishment' (Y.48.5). In the later Avesta the name Spənta Ārmaiti
can even be used as a synonym for earth, Vohu Manah for cattle;
for, as Lommel has put it, it is as if at that distant epoch abstract and
concrete appeared as of unified being, the abstract as the inner
reality of the concrete, so that pious Devotion and the earth, for
example, were seen as spiritual and material aspects of the same
thing. Only one modification of Zoroaster's original doctrine appears
to have been made as the centuries passed, concerning Khšathra and
the sky of stone. As Dominion, Khšathra was linked especially with
warriors,who should use their weapons (in Zoroaster's time of stone
and flint) to protect the righteous, not to harm them. When the
Stone Age gave way to those of Bronze and Iron, the Zoroastrian
priests, in order to keep this vital link, were driven to re-interpret the

ancient cosmogony in this one respect. The substance of the sky, they declared, was rock-crystal; and rock-crystal (quarried from veins in rock, like metal ores) could, they said, be classified as a metal. So Khšathra, once lord of stone, became instead lord of metals, represented now at the *yasna* by the metal-bladed knife and metallic mortar; and thus he could remain the especial divinity of fighting men.

The symbolism of the *yasna* is repeated in every lesser Zoroastrian 11.1.20 religious service, and in the old orthodox communities of Iran it is still comprehended by every instructed member of a congregation, whether priest or lay; so even though the Avestan language is not understood, and the liturgy (like the Latin mass for most Catholics) is significant only through usage and association, the ritual, observable by all, still has its meaning, and brings home in familiar fashion the grandeur and pervading presence of Ahura Mazdā and the Aməša Spəntas.

Further, since every single thing around us is linked with one or 11.1.21 other of these great Beings, the Zoroastrian learns from his religion to reverence the world in which he lives, and never wantonly to sully or harm it. Moreover, since each one of his actions necessarily affects either himself or the outside world, each must be either good or bad, helping or hindering the great struggle against evil, material or immaterial. There are no neutral areas of conduct in Zoroastrianism. Even to sweep and dust a room is to restore order, and so is a way of worshipping Aša. To work and earn a livelihood for oneself and one's family is an act pleasing to Ahura Mazdā, for one contributes thereby to the dignity and self-respect of man; and to set aside coins for charity is to honour Khšathra, lord of metals. Water and earth must be kept clean, plants and trees tended, and animals are to be treated with care and kindness, as the creatures of Vohu Manah. In general man, with his powers of understanding and decision, is in the position of steward or guardian of the other six creations and must cherish them, in addition to having a responsibility towards himself and his fellow-men.

The consequences of this fundamental doctrine can be seen in the 11.1.22 conduct of Zoroastrians down the ages. Even today when (because of the work of reformists), the doctrine itself is no longer widely known or understood, the ethic inculcated by it persists, with the result that Zoroastrians are distinguished for self-discipline, and kindliness, charity, cleanliness of person and surroundings, gaiety (for gloom and pessimism are Ahrimanic), and scrupulous honesty.

Even in the hostile atmosphere of Iran a Yazdi Muslim, departing on pilgrimage to Mecca, would sometimes entrust a box of money to his almost penniless Zoroastrian neighbour, certain of receiving it back intact on his return; and this unshakeable integrity, a virtue that would not stoop to deception or self-betrayal, enabled both Parsis and Iranis to thrive as merchants when opportunity came, their word being accepted as their bond; and thereafter they acquired new fame through a vast philanthropy, which reached out beyond their own community to mankind at large.

11.1.23   It has been said in support of ritual that to hear is to forget, to see is to remember, to do is to understand; and Zoroaster, a wise priest, established a number of simple, recurrent observances in which every member of his community could take an active part, and which, like the ritual of the religious services, would help to keep his teachings vividly in their minds. One of these observances was to celebrate communally seven great feasts each year, dedicated to Ahura Mazdā with the six Aməša Spəntas, and to the seven creations. That Zoroaster himself established these feasts is a recorded tradition, and to keep them was a sacred duty for the whole community, negligence in this being a sin that 'went to the Bridge', that is, was weighed in the scales when one's soul was judged. Six of the feasts form a uniform chain, and became known in Sasanian times and thereafter as the *gāhāmbārs*. The Zoroastrians celebrated each by attending special religious services early in the day, and then holding joyous assemblies, with feasts at which food was eaten in communion which had been blessed at the services. These gatherings were marked by a spirit of general goodwill, and quarrels were then made up and friendships renewed and strengthened. The first of the six feasts was in 'mid-spring' and was devoted to the creation of the sky, the last was on the last day of the year, and was dedicated to that of man. On the night of that day was celebrated the age-old festival of All Souls, which Zoroaster reconsecrated to his own faith, with especial honouring of the souls of the just 'who had conquered for righteousness'. The whole of this sixth festival (greatly extended since Sasanian times) is now known by the Middle Persian term 'Farvardigan'. The special religious services celebrated uniformly at all the six feasts are dedicated to Ahura Mazdā, as the supreme Creator.

11.1.24   Just as the seventh creation, fire, is a little separate from the others, being their pervasive life-force, so the seventh feast is set a little apart from the rest. It is No Ruz, New Year's Day, celebrated

by Zoroastrians at the spring equinox, 21 March. It is devoted
to the creation of fire and its guardian Aša Vahišta; and since
it completes the chain of seven feasts, it seals the old year as
well as bringing in the new in a spirit of hope and joy. It is a feast
which celebrates the annual resurgence of life in spring-time as a
promise of the future resurrection and life everlasting, and so it
shares some symbols with Christian Easter — fresh flowers, new
clothes, gaily painted eggs. Moreover, in the old Zoroastrian world-
picture winter was an evil time which belonged to Angra Mainyu,
who sought to kill what was green and flourishing with his weapons
of cold and darkness, whereas summer, bright and warm, was Ahura
Mazdā's. Since the Iranian summer is longer than the winter, this was
another sign of the greater power of the Creator; and No Ruz was an
especially joyous feast because it ushered in his own auspicious
season, and marked a yearly defeat of the Hostile Spirit.

Zoroaster brought this particular manifestation of the dualism at 11.1.25
the heart of things into another observance required of all his
followers, that of making five daily prayers, short, simple, but an
absolute obligation, part of one's duty towards God. A millennium
and a half later Muhammad adopted this observance from
Zoroastrianism, to the enormous strengthening of his ow religion.
He borrowed too the Zoroastrian requirement (characteristic of a
faith for which cleanliness is a part of godliness) that before praying
a believer should wash the dust from face, hands and feet. The times
of prayer were sunrise, noon, sunset, after sunset and between
midnight and dawn; and each of these times was set under the care
of particular *yazatas*. The night watches belonged respectively to the
fravašis (the spirits of the dead) and Sraoša, *yazata* of prayer.
Morning and afternoon were assigned (no doubt traditionally) to the
two lesser Ahuras, Mithra and *Vouruna Apạm Napāt, and noon to
Aša, lord of fire — but only during summer, when noontide in Iran
is burning hot. During winter the noon watch was given instead to
Mithra, together with the morning one. So all through the winter he
is invoked in the prayers said then, but when No Ruz brings in
summer Aša Vahišta is remembered again, in joyful recognition of
the ascendency one more of beneficent warmth and light.

Although lesser divinities are invoked in the daily prayers, these 11.1.26
are all devoted to Ahura Mazdā himself; and the words are accompanied by a simple but significant rite. It seems (to judge from
Brahmin usage) that in Indo-Iranian times men used to wear a cord
tied over one shoulder as a sign of their initiation into the religious

community. Zoroaster adapted this usage to create a special badge for his own followers, who are required, men and women alike (for he saw them as equal in the religious quest) to wear a cord passed thrice round the waist (as a reminder, it is said, of the triple way to salvation, through good thoughts, words and deeds). The cord is knotted twice, at back and front, and a Zoroastrian unties it every time before he prays. Then, standing upright with it held in both hands before him, dignified in the presence of his Creator, he prays to Ahura Mazdā, abjures the Hostile Spirit (flicking the ends of the cord contemptuously as he does so), and reties the cord while still praying. The simple ritual takes only a few minutes, but its regular repetition, always in the presence of fire, lamp or the sun, is a religious exercise of the greatest value, providing a steady discipline and a regular acknowledgement of the fundamental tenets of the faith.

11.1.27   The daily prayers may be said alone, or with the family, or in a fire-temple; but the observance is essentially an individual one, the fulfilment of a personal obligation, whereas the keeping of the seven great feasts is a corporate duty. In imposing these two strict requirements Zoroaster created a pattern of devotion for his followers that filled day and year, and made them both disciplined and firmly grounded in doctrine, self-reliant and yet linked by strong communal ties. The priests meantime continued to celebrate the daily *yasna,* with its ancient rituals which had been given new significance by the prophet. These rituals include the offering of *parahaoma* (an infusion of *haoma,* pomegranate leaves and milk) in libation to water, and incense to fire. Down to the last century the offering to fire was still made, with reverence and devotion, from the blood-sacrifice; but thereafter the Parsis in their prosperity became more open to outside influences (from Christianity, Hinduism and theosophy) and they abandoned the practice. Muslims maintain it to this day, and so there was no pressure on the Zoroastrians of Iran to give up an ancient rite which is alluded to (with the usual subtlety) several times in the Gathas as a part of normal worship. By now, however, Parsi influence has led to its being generally abandoned, and Haug's conviction, often reaffirmed by later scholars, that Zoroaster himself rejected it, is warmly endorsed by the reformists.

11.1.28   The adoption by the reformists of so many European misconceptions has forced them to charge their ancestors with a lack of both fidelity and understanding, and they have had to take the unhappy position that the religion for which their forbears suffered so much was nine-tenths confusion and malpractice. The orthodox have been more loyal to their traditions, and now Western scholars are gradually coming to admit that the misunderstandings have been on their side, the result largely of ill-founded preconceptions. These misunderstandings have done harm both to scholarship and, more seriously, to the Zoroastrian community itself; but as the cloud of misapprehension slowly lifts, it can be seen that, whatever changes and developments may now be desirable, the tradition of this community is one deserving of the utmost respect. The Zoroastrians, it is plain, remained in prosperity and adversity staunchly faithful to the teachings of their prophet, which, though complex, were so lucid and logical, and formed so clear a system of belief, that even the humblest of his followers, helped by the prescribed devotions, could understand and live by them. They were, moreover, very positive teachings, which went with, not against, the normal bent of human nature, and helped men to live satisfying and fulfilled lives. In the light of all this, it ceases to be remarkable that Zoroastrianism survived for some 3500 years, and that the community, though cruelly reduced and of late perplexed, has still not lost the courage and vitality inspired by its prophet's original message.

Source: A hitherto unpublished paper, by Professor Mary Boyce.

11.2 EARLY DAYS

Mary Boyce

11.2.1 The evidence of the Vedas and developments in Iran suggest that some opposition between the ethical Asuras and Indra was felt already in the Indo-Iranian period, and the times of the great migrations probably intensified awareness of this. There must have been different groups then among the invading Iranians, whose divergences seem reflected in the *Gāthās:* on the one hand tribes who moved steadily with their cattle, and fought only when it was necessary to gain what they wanted, namely good, safe pastures where they could settle and prosper; on the other war-bands, unwilling to abandon strife even after new territories had been won, ruthless, predatory, delighting in combat for its own sake and for the booty it could bring. Such warriors were doubtless not above carrying off the cattle of fellow-Iranians when no other plunder offered; and they would naturally have worshipped the unscrupulous Indra, warlike and bountiful, whereas settled peoples were much more likely to have offered their heartfelt prayers to the Ahuras, guardians of order and peace. Indra-worshippers could thus properly be termed 'non-herders among the herders', robber-chieftains and their followers, who preyed upon pastoralists.

11.2.2   Such men would plainly have been hard to turn to the exclusive worship of the ethically demanding Ahura Mazdā and his *spǝnta* creation; and *daēva*-worship seems to have survived stubbornly in certain remote parts of Iran down to the Arab conquest. With staunch commitment by such in the community, and natural caution presumably influencing many of the rest, it is small wonder that Zoroastrian missionaries had a hard initial struggle, and that they felt the need to demand repeated abjurations of the *daēvas* from those whom they succeeded in winning over. Such abjuration is accordingly uttered with great vigour in the ancient confession of the faith, in which, as has been pointed out, the term *vī.daēva* 'rejecting the *daēvas'* is a definition of religious belief of equal value with *mazdayasna* 'Mazdā-worshipper' and *zarathuštri* 'Zoroastrian'. This confession, known from its first word as the *Fravarānē* ('I profess'), is still uttered daily in Zoroastrian prayer and worship. Although its language is characterised as pseudo-Gathic, the text itself gives an impression of high antiquity, with not only citations in it from the *Gāthās*, but also a significant use of Gathic imagery; and it seems possible that its kernel is in fact the original avowal made by converts in the early days of the faith, but that, having evolved with the living tradition into a Younger Avestan form, it was later put back, with some errors and inconsistencies, into Gathic, as more fitting its venerable nature. Some extensions of the original text down the centuries are also very likely. In its existing form it is as follows:

Y.12.1: 'I profess myself a Mazdā-worshipper, a Zoroastrian, rejecting the *daēvas,* accepting the Ahuric doctrine; one who praises the Aməša Spəntas, who worships the Aməša Spəntas. To Ahura Mazdā, the good, rich in treasures, I ascribe all things good, "those which are best indeed" [Y47.5] — to the Righteous One, rich, glorious, whose is the Cow, whose is Aša, whose are the lights, may whose blessed realms be filled with lights' [Y.31.7].

2: Bounteous Ārmaiti, the good, I choose for myself, let her be mine! I renounce the theft and carrying off of the Cow, and harm and destruction for Mazdā-worshipping homes.

3: To those with authority I shall grant movement at will and lodging at will, those who are upon this earth with (their) cattle. With reverence for Aša, the offerings lifted up, that I avow: henceforth I shall not, in caring either for body or life, bring harm or destruction on Mazdā-worshipping homes.

4: I forswear the company of the wicked *daēvas,* the not-good, lawless, evil-working, the most Drug-like of beings, the foulest of beings, the least good of beings — the company of *daēvas* and the followers of *daēvas,* of demons (*yātu-*) and the followers of demons, of those who do harm to any being by thoughts, words, deeds or outward signs. Truly I forswear the company of [all] this as belonging to the Drug, as defiant [of the good].

5: Even as Ahura Mazdā taught Zoroaster in each instance at all deliberations, at all encounterings at which Mazdā and Zoroaster spoke together.

6: Even as Zoroaster forswore the company of *daēvas* in each instance, at all deliberations, at all encounterings at which Mazdā and Zoroaster spoke together, so I forswear, as Mazdā-worshipper and Zoroastrian, the company of *daēvas,* even as Zoroaster forswore it.

7: As [was] the choice of the Waters, the choice of the Plants, the choice of the beneficent Cow, the choice of Ahura Mazdā, who created the Cow, who [created] the just Man, as [was] the choice of Zoroaster, the choice of Kavi Vīštāspa, the choice of Frašaostra and Jāmāspa, the choice of each of the *saošyants,* bringing about reality, just — by that choice and by that doctrine am I a Mazdā-worshipper.

8: I profess myself a Mazdā-worshipper and a Zoroastrian, having pledged myself to and avowed the faith.

I pledge myself to the well-thought thought.

I pledge myself to the well-spoken word.

I pledge myself to the well-performed act.

9: I pledge myself to the Mazdā-worshipping religion, which throws off attacks, which causes weapons to be laid down, which upholds *khvaēt-vadatha,* which is righteous, which of all (faiths) which are and shall be is the greatest, the best, the most beautiful, which is Ahuric, Zoroastrian. To Ahura Mazdā I ascribe all good. This is the profession of the Mazdā-worshipping religion.'

11.2.3   This ancient text has been characterised as 'the oath which was required of someone being received into the faith', and it is natural that what is stressed in it should be those elements which set the convert apart from unbelievers. The very first demand made upon him is that he should avow his worship of Mazdā, and allegiance to his prophet Zoroaster. Then he must declare his rejection of the *daēvas,* and his acceptance of the Ahuric doctrines in general, and his veneration for all *spǝnta* divinities, for those, that is, who are beneficent, as distinct from the evil-working *daēvatāt.* Although much of the text is plain, parts have the allusiveness of the *Gāthās* themselves, and this suggests that converts were taught the basic Gathic doctrines in all their subtlety, for these words to have had meaning for them. Thus the complex Gathic imagery concerning the Cow is prominent; and the doctrine of the creations and their guardians is dealt with comprehensively but allusively, as in the *Gāthās.* Waters and plants, cattle and men, are named in due order in the seventh section; and sky is represented by the "blessed realms" above, which are Khšathra's domain, earth by its Amǝša Spǝnta, Ārmaiti, the Devotion whom the new worshipper abundantly needs. Fire, too, is represented only by its protective divinity, Aša, and is nowhere explicitly named. Presumably since in its early forms (of veneration for the hearth fire) the fire cult was common to pagan and believer, the Zoroastrian missionaries felt no need to give it special emphasis, even though the prophet had endowed fire with new significance as the symbol of righteousness and general focus for prayer. Just as no fresh commitment was required from the convert over this, so too he was not asked to renounce any former ways of worship, but only to deny those beings to whom worship should not be offered. These facts bear out what can be deduced from the *Gāthās* themselves, that Zoroaster made few changes in the existing cult, being concerned rather to elevate its intention and to invest established rituals with deeper moral and spiritual significance. (There is nothing to suggest that practices which he repudiated, such as consuming an evil *mada,* were rites connected with any particular group of gods. They may rather have been general abuses, or observances linked with black magic.)

Doctrinally what is perhaps most striking in the *Fravarānē* is its 11.2.4 dualism. Ahura Mazdā, together with the Aməša Spəntas, is set in opposition to the *daēvatāt*; and all goodness (though not all power) is ascribed to the one, all evil to the other. It is understandable that in this text the opposition should be expressed in these terms, rather than as between Ahura Mazdā and Angra Mainyu, for (as far as is known) no one had been aware of the Hostile Spirit before Zoroaster preached, so that there was no ancient cult of the Evil One to abandon. It was rather those whom Zoroaster regarded as servants of evil, the venerated *daēvas,* whom the convert had to abjure. Although Ahura Mazdā's power is perceived as circumscribed by the existence of independent evil, nevertheless he is acknowledged as the Creator, who has made all beneficent creatures and man himself. The sense of cosmic history is moreover strong, for in uttering this profession of faith the convert speaks as one taking his rightful place in a chain of action which began with the waters when the world was formed. 'The conversion of the initiate is conceived in true Gathic fashion as a choice of the better and a rejection of the worse way. . . He chooses the better way, as all good and life-furthering powers have done and do since the original creation'. Ethically, commitment is to Zoroaster's grand basic teaching of good thoughts, words and acts; and the convert acknowledges his prophet's claim to divine revelation and authority by the repeated references to the 'encounterings at which Mazdā and Zoroaster spoke together', in which 'Ahura Mazdā taught Zoroaster'.

The *saošyants* mentioned in the past tense are presumably the 11.2.5 wise and good, who have brought benefit to the world by following in the footsteps of the prophet; or, if they are the coming Saviours of developed Zoroastrian soteriology, then this must represent an addition to the original text, which seems to have been shaped in the religion's earliest days, when the young community was struggling against hostility and active persecution, with death threatening the faithful and destruction their homes. That Zoroastrians should have so suffered, except where they enjoyed royal favour, is no more remarkable than that the early Christians should have been persecuted, for the two faiths had evidently much in common in their missionary endeavours. Like Christianity, Zoroastrianism entered what appears to have been an easy-going, polytheistic society, with a claim to an exclusive revelation vouchsafed to its prophet by one supreme God, and with a demand for total commitment. It exacted courage and devotion; and it offered to all in return the hope of salvation after death, when unbelievers would be damned. Like primitive Christianity, Zoroastrianism evidently engendered a strong sense of brotherhood among the faithful, united as they were by belief and worship and a firm code of prescribed conduct; and such certainty and solidarity were no doubt as exasperating to pagan Iranians as to pagan Romans, and provoked correspondingly harsh measures of repression. What sharpened hostility to Zoroastrians was no doubt a sense of the rashness of their repudiation of the *daēvas,* an act which their pagan fellows may well have felt threatened to bring down the wrath of these gods upon the people indiscriminately; and it was presumably a sense of the dangerous folly and presumption of the new faith which drove Vistāšpa's neighbours to try to crush it by force before it could cause general calamity.

What is impossible to gauge is the reaction to Zoroaster's teachings of those who were already devoted to the *ahuras,* and who, without any great awe of the *daēvas* or eagerness to worship them, may yet have been reluctant to accept a doctrine of the absolute sovereignty of Ahura Mazdā. The Vedic evidence suggests that from Indo-Iranian times the Lord Wisdom had been venerated as the greatest of the *asuras,* solitary and very powerful, exalted over the mighty Mitra and Varuna. Nevertheless it may even so have been a difficult step to take, to acknowledge him as the one uncreated Being, Creator of all *yazatas,* the ultimate source of all good; and some who turned to the other *ahuras* for special favour and protection may perhaps have resented this vast claim, and have made common cause with *daēva*-worshippers and the generality in seeking to suppress the new religion. It is small wonder, then, that its early progress seems to have been difficult and slow.

Source: Mary Boyce, *A History of Zoroastrianism,* Brill, Leiden, 1975, Vol.I, pp.252-7.

11.3   PASSAGES FROM THE AVESTAN HYMN TO MITHRA

Translated by I. Gershevitch

Stanza 4. On account of his splendour and fortune I will audibly worship Mithra of the wide pastures with libations. Mithra. . .we worship, since it is he who bestows peaceful and comfortable dwellings on the Iranian countries.

Stanza 5. May he join us for assistance, may he join us for (the granting of) spaciousness, may he join us for support, may he join us for mercy, may he join us for therapy, may he join us for ability to defeat the opponent, may he join us for a comfortable existence, may he join us for ownership of Truth, he who is strong and victorious for whom the whole material world must needs worship, pray to, and refrain from deceiving, Mithra of the wide pastures.

Stanza 10. Mithra. . .we worship, whose words are correct, who is challenging, has a thousand ears, is well built, has ten thousand eyes, is tall, has a wide outlook, is strong, sleepless, [ever-] waking, whom the warriors worship at the manes of their horses, requesting strength for their teams, health for themselves, much watchfulness against antagonists, ability to strike back at enemies, ability to rout lawless, hostile opponents.

Stanza 13. Mithra. . .we worship. . .who is the first supernatural god to approach across the Hara, in front of the immortal swift-horsed sun; who is the first to seize the beautiful gold-painted mountain tops; from there the most mighty surveys the whole land inhabited by Iranians.

Stanza 28. Mithra. . .we worship. . .who arranges the columns of the high-pillared house, who builds the strong gate-posts; herds of cattle and [teams of] slaves he bestows on the house in which he is propitiated; the others, in which he is provoked, he smashes.

Stanza 30. . .it is you Mithra who provide with bustling women and fast chariots, with spread-out rugs and piled-up cushion-heaps the high pillared house of the Truth-owning man who regularly mentions you by name in his spoken prayer, offering libations.

Stanza 32. Listen, O Mithra, to our prayer, satisfy, O Mithra, our prayer, condescend to our prayer! Approach our libations, approach them as they are sacrificed, collect them for consumption, deposit them in Paradise!

Stanza 44. Mithra. . .we worship. . .whose abode is set in the material world as far as the earth extends, unrestricted in size, shining, reaching widely abroad;

Stanza 49. . .for whom Ahura Mazdāh, the creator, fashioned an abode above the much-twisting, shining Harā the high, where is no light or darkness, no wind cold or hot, no deadly illness, no defilement produced by evil gods — neither do mists rise from Harā the high:

Stanza 50. Which abode the Incremental Immortals built, all in harmony with the sun. . .[Mithra] from Harā the high surveys the whole material world.

Stanza 61. . . .who stands watchful with upright shanks, the strong challenging watcher, the replenisher of waters who listens to the call, thanks to whom rain falls and plants grow. . .

Stanza 79. Mithra. . .we worship. . .the judge who makes the abode gain prominence. . .

Stanza 80. You are the protector, the defender, of the abode of those who reject falsehood; you are the guardian of the community of those who reject falsehood: with you as master [the community] obtains the most excellent succession and Ahura created victoriousness. . .

Stanza 93. Now then, in both lives, O Mithra. . .in both — this material existence, and the one which is spiritual — do protect us from Death and Wrath, the two owners of Falsehood, from the evil armies of the owners of Falsehood who raise a gruesome banner, from the onslaughts of Wrath.

Stanza 95. . .[Mithra] who goes along the whole width of the earth after the setting of the glowing of the sun, sweeping across both edges of this wide, round earth whose limits are far apart: everything he surveys between heaven and earth.

Stanza 102. [Mithra] the skilful warrior who has white horses and pointed spears with long shafts, who shoots afar with swift arrows;

Stanza 106. But I [= the worshipper] think in my mind: 'There is no material man in existence who thinks evil thoughts to (so) great an extent as supernatural Mithra thinks good thoughts; there is no material man in existence who speaks evil words to (so) great an extent as supernatural Mithra speaks good words; there is no material man in existence who commits evil deeds to (so) great an extent as supernatural Mithra performs good deeds;

Stanza 112. Mithra. . .we worship. . .whose pike is of silver, whose armour is of gold, who drives with the whip, the powerful, strong, broad-shouldered warrior.

Stanza 124. . .from Paradise Mithra. . .drives out his beautiful, golden, all-adorned chariot, which is easy to drive and runs evenly.

Stanza 125. Four horses pull at his chariot; all of the same whiteness, they are immortal, having been reared on supernatural food; their front hooves are shod with gold, their hind hooves with silver. . .

Stanza 134. now it is the Fiendish Spirit, very deadly, who recoils in fear, now malignant Wrath, his body forfeited, now long-handed Procrastination; now recoil in fear all supernatural evil gods and the concupiscent owners of Falsehood (all of them crying):

Stanza 135. 'May we not meet with the onslaughts of Mithra. . .in his rage! May you not strike us in your rage, Mithra of the wide pastures. [Thus] he who is the mightiest of gods, the strongest of gods, the most mobile of gods, the fastest of gods, the most victorious of gods, comes forth on this earth, Mithra of the wide pastures.

Source: From I. Gersheritch, trans. The Avestan Hymn to Mithra, OUP 1959.

11.4 SELECTIONS FROM THE GĀTHĀS

Translated by J.H. Moulton

11.4.1 Yasna 28

. . .

2. I who would serve you, O Mazdah Ahura and Good Thought — do ye give through the Right the blessings of both worlds, the bodily and that of Thought, which set the faithful in felicity.

5. O thou the Right, shall I see thee and Good Thought, as one that knows — the throne of the mightiest Ahura and the Obedience of Mazdah? Through this world [of promise] on our tongue will we turn the robber horde unto the Greatest.

11.4.2 Yasna 30

1. Now will I proclaim to those who will hear the things that the understanding man should remember, for hymns unto Ahura and prayers to Good Thought; also the felicity that is with the heavenly lights, which through Right shall be beheld by him who wisely thinks.

2. Hear with your ears the best things; look upon them with clear-seeing thought, for decision between the two Beliefs, each man for himself before the Great Consummation, bethinking you that it be accomplished to our pleasure.

3. Now the two primal Spirits, who revealed themselves in vision as Twins, are the Better and the Bad in thought and word and action. And between these two the wise once chose aright, the foolish not so.

4. And when these twain Spirits came together in the beginning, they established Life and Not-Life, and that at the last the Worst Existence shall be to the followers of the Lie, but the Best Thought to him that follows Right.

5. Of these twin Spirits he that followed the Lie chose doing the worst things; the holiest Spirit chose Right, he that clothes him with the massy heavens as a garment. So likewise they that are fain to please Ahura Mazdah by dutiful actions.

6. Between these twain the demons also chose not aright, for infatuation came upon them as they took counsel together, so that

the chose the Worst Thought. Then they rushed together to Violence, that they might enfeeble the world of man.

7. And to him [i.e. mankind] came Dominion, Good Thought, and Right; and Piety gave continued life of their bodies and indestructibility, so that by the retributions through the (molten) metal he may gain the prize over those others.

8. So when there cometh the punishment of these evil ones, then O Mazdah, at thy command shall Good Thought establish the Dominion in the Consummation, for those who deliver the Lie, O Ahura, into the hands of Right.

9. So may we be those that make this world advance! O Mazdah, and ye other Ahuras, gather together the Assembly, and thou too the Right, that thoughts may meet where Wisdom is at home.

10. Then truly on the Lie shall come the destruction of delight; but they that get them good name shall be partakers in the promised reward in the fair abode of Good Thought, of Mazdah, and of Right.

11. If, O ye mortals, ye mark those commandments that Mazdah hath ordained — of happiness and pain, the long punishment for the liars, and blessings for the righteous — then hereafter shall ye have bliss.

Yasna 31   11.4.3

1. Mindful of your commands, we proclaim words hard for them to hear that after the commands of the Lie destroy the creatures of Right, but most welcome to those that give their heart to Mazdah...

4. If Right is to be invoked and Mazdah and the other Ahuras, and Destiny and Piety, do thou seek for me, O thou Best Thought, the mighty Dominion, by the increase of which we might vanquish the Lie.

7. He that in the beginning thus thought, 'Let the blessed realms be filled with lights', he it is that by his wisdom created Right. Those realms that the Best Thought shall possess thou dost prosper, Mazdah, by thy spirit, which, O Ahura, is ever the same.

8. I conceived of thee, O Mazdah, in my thought that thou, the First, art (also) the Last — that thou art Father of Good Thought, for thus I apprehended thee with mine eye — that thou didst truly create Right, and art the Lord to judge the actions of life.

9. Thine was Piety, thine the Ox-Creator, even wisdom of spirit, O Mazdah Ahura, for that thou didst give (the cattle) choice whether to depend on a husbandman or on one that is no husbandman.

10. So of the twain it chose for itself the cattle-tending

husbandman as its lord according to Right, the man that advances Good Thought. He that is no husbandman, O Mazdah, however eager he be, has no part in the good message.

11. When thou, Mazdah, in the beginning didst create beings and (men's) Selves by thy Thought, and intelligences — when thou didst make life clothed with body, when (thou madest) actions and teachings, whereby one may exercise choice at one's free will;

18. Let none of you listen to the liar's words and commands: he brings house and clan and district and land into misery and destruction. Resist them then with weapons!

20. Whoso cometh to the righteous one, far from him shall be the future long age of misery, of darkness, ill food, and crying of Woe! To such an existence, ye liars, shall your own Self bring you by your actions.

21. Mazdah Ahura by virtue of his absolute lordship will give a perpetuity of communion with Welfare and Immortality and Right, with Dominion, with Good Thought, to him that in spirit and in actions is his friend.

11.4.4 Yasna 32

. . .

2. To them (*Representatives of the Classes*) Mazdah Ahura, who is united with Good Thought, and in goodly fellowship with glorious Right, through Dominion, made reply: We make choice of your holy good Piety — it shall be ours.

3. *Zarathushtra* — But ye, ye Daēvas all, and he that highly honours you, are seed of the Bad Thought — yea, and of the Lie and of Arrogance; likewise your deeds, whereby ye have long been known in the seventh region of the earth.

4. For ye have brought it to pass that men who do the worst things shall be called beloved of the Daēvas, separating themselves from Good Thought, departing from the will of Mazdah Ahura and from Right.

5. Thereby ye defrauded mankind of happy life and of immortality, by the deed which he and the Bad Spirit together with Bad Thought and Bad Word taught you, ye Daēvas, and the Liars, so as to ruin [mankind].

9. The teacher of evil destroys the lore, he by his teachings destroys the design of life, he prevents the possession of Good Thought from being prized. These words of my spirit I wail unto you, O Mazdah, and to the Right.

10. He it is that destroys the lore, who declares that the Ox and the Sun are the worst thing to behold with the eyes, and hath made the pious into liars, and desolates the pastures and lifts his weapon against the righteous man.

Yasna 33 11.4.5

. . .

2. Whoso worketh ill for the liar by word or thought or hands, or converts his dependent to the good — such men meet the will of Ahura Mazdah to his satisfaction.

3. Whoso is most good to the righteous man, be he noble or member of the community or of the brotherhood, Ahura — or with diligence cares for the cattle, he shall be hereafter in the pasture of Right and Good Thought.

5. I who would invoke thy Obedience as greatest of all at the Consummation, attaining eternal life, and the Dominion of Good Thought, and the straight ways unto Right, wherein Mazdah Ahura dwells;

6. I, as a priest, who would learn the straight [paths] by the Right, would learn by the Best Spirit how to practise husbandry by that thought in which it is thought of: these Twain of thine, O Ahura Mazdah, I strive to see and to take counsel with them.

7. Come hither to me, O ye Best Ones, hither, O Mazdah, in thine own person and visibly, O Right and Good Thought, that I may be heard beyond the limits of the people. Let the august duties be manifest among us and clearly viewed.

11. The most mighty Ahura Mazda, and Piety, and Right that blesses our substance, and Good Thought and Dominion — hearken unto me, be merciful to me, when to each man the Recompense comes.

12. Rise up for me, O Ahura, through Piety give strength, through the holiest Spirit give might, O Mazdah, through the good Recompense, through the Right give powerful prowess, through Good Thought give the Reward.

13. To support me, O thou that seest far onward, do ye assure me the incomparable things of your Dominion, O Ahura, as the Destiny of Good Thought. Holy Piety, teach men's Self the Right.

Yasna 34. 11.4.6

. . .

3. To thee and to Right we will offer the sacrifice, with due service,

that in [thy established] Dominion ye may bring all creatures to perfection through Good Thought. For the reward of the wise man is for ever secure, O Mazdah, among you.

4. Of thy Fire, O Ahura, that is mighty through Right, promised and powerful, we desire that it may be for the faithful man with manifested delight, but for the enemy with visible torment, according to the pointings of the hand.

12. What is thine ordinance? What willest thou? What of praise or what of worship? Proclaim it, Mazdah, that we may hear what ordinances Destiny will apportion. Teach us by Right the paths of Good Thought that are blessed to go in —

13. Even that way of Good Thought, O Ahura, of which thou didst speak to me, whereon, a way well made by Right, the Selves of the future benefactors [Saošyants] shall pass to the reward that was prepared for the wise, of which thou art determinant, O Mazdah.

11.4.7 Yasna 43

. . .

4. Then shall I recognise thee as strong and holy, Mazdah, when by the hand in which thou thyself dost hold the destinies that thou wilt assign to the Liar and the Righteous, by the glow of thy Fire whose power is Right, the might of Good Thought shall come to me.

5. As the holy one I recognised thee, Mazdah Ahura, when I saw thee in the beginning at the birth of Life, when thou madest actions and words to have their meed — evil for the evil, a good Destiny for the good — through thy wisdom when creation shall reach its goal.

6. At which goal thou wilt come with thy holy Spirit, O Mazdah, with Dominion, at the same with Good Thought, by whose action the settlements will prosper through Right. Their judgments shall Piety proclaim, even those of thy wisdom which none can deceive.

9. As the holy one I recognised thee, Mazdah Ahura, when Good Thought came to me. To his question, 'For which wilt thou decide?' [I made reply] : 'At the gift of adoration to thy Fire, I will bethink me of Right so long as I have power. . .'

16. And thus Zarathushtra himself, O Ahura, chooses that spirit of thine that is holiest, Mazdah. May Right be embodied, full of life and strength! May Piety abide in the Dominion where the sun shines! May Good Thought give destiny to men according to their works!

Yasna 44 11.4.8

. . .

3. This I ask thee, tell me truly, Ahura. Who is by generation the Father of Right, at the first? Who determined the path of sun and stars? Who is it by whom the moon waxes and wanes again? This, O Mazdah, and yet more, I am fain to know.

4. This I ask thee, tell me truly, Ahura. Who upheld the earth beneath and the firmament from falling? Who the waters and the plants? Who yoked swiftness to winds and clouds? Who is, O Mazdah, creator of Good Thought?

5. This I ask thee, tell me truly, Ahura. What artist made light and darkness? What artist made sleep and waking? Who made morning, noon, and night, that call the understanding man to his duty .

15. This I ask thee, tell me truly, Ahura — if thou hast power over this to ward it off from me through Right, when the two opposing hosts meet in battle according to those decrees which thou wilt ·firmly establish. Whether is it of the twain that thou wilt give victory?.

Yasna 45 11.4.9

. . .

2. I will speak of the Spirits twain at the first beginning of the world, of whom the holier thus spake to the enemy: 'Neither thought nor teachings nor wills nor beliefs nor words nor deeds nor selves nor souls of us twain agree.'

3. I will speak of that which Mazdah Ahura, the all-knowing revealed to me first in this [earthly] life. Those of you that put not in practice this word as I think and utter it, to them shall be woe at the end of life. . .

Yasna 46 11.4.10

1. To what land shall I go to flee, whither to flee? From nobles and my peers they sever me, nor are the people pleased with me, nor the Liar rulers of the land. How am I to please thee, Mazdah Ahura?

2. I know wherefore I am without success, Mazdah: [because] few cattle are mine, and for that I have but few folk. I cry unto thee, see thou to it, Ahura, granting me support as friend gives to friend. Teach me by the Right the acquisition of Good Thought.

6. But whoso when thus approached should refuse his aid, he shall go to the abodes of the company of the Lie. For he is himself a

Liar who is very good to a Liar, he is a righteous man to whom a righteous man is dear; since thou createdst men's Selves in the beginning, Ahura.

10. Whoso, man or woman, doeth what thou, Mazdah Ahura, knowest as best in life, as destiny for what is Right [give him] the Dominion through Good Thought. And those whom I impel to your adoration, with all these will I cross the Bridge of the Separater.

11. By their dominion the Karapans and Kavis accustomed mankind to evil actions, so as to destroy Life. Their own soul and their own self shall torment them when they come where the Bridge of the Separator is, to all time dwellers in the House of the Lie.

11.4.11 Yasna 48

1. When at the Recompensings the Right shall smite the Lie, so that what was long since made known shall be assigned in eternity to Daēvas and men, then will it exalt with thy blessings, Ahura, him who prays to thee.

6. She [Piety] will give us a peaceful dwelling, she will give lasting life and strength, she the beloved of Good Thought. For it [the cattle] Mazdah Ahura made the plants to grow at the birth of the First Life, through Right.

8. Is the possession of thy good Dominion, Mazdah, is that of thy Destiny assured to me, Ahura? Will thy manifestation, O thou Right, be welcome to the pious, even the weighing of actions by the Good Spirit?

9. When shall I know whether ye have power, O Mazdah and Right, over everyone whose destructiveness is a menace to me? Let the revelation of Good Thought be confirmed unto me: the future deliverer [Saošyant] should know how his own destiny shall be.

12. These shall be the deliverers of thy provinces, who follow after pleasing, O Good Thought, by their actions, O Right, depending on thy command, O Mazdah. For these are the appointed smiters of violence.

11.4.12 Yasna 49

. . .

4. They who by evil purpose make increase of violence and cruelty with their tongues, the foes of cattle-nurture among its friends; whose ill deeds prevail, not their good deeds: these [shall be] in the House of the Daēvas, [the place for] the Self of the Liar.

11. But these that are of an evil dominion, of evil deeds, evil

words, evil Self, and evil thought, Liars, the Souls go to meet them with foul food: in the House of the Lie they shall be meet inhabitants.

Yasna 50   11.4.13

. . .

11. Your praiser, Mazdah, will I declare myself and be, so long, O Right, as I have strength and power. May the Creator of the world accomplish through Good Thought its fulfilment of all that most perfectly answers to his will!

Yasna 51   11.4.14

. . .

7. Give me, O thou that didst create the Ox and Waters and Plants, Welfare and Immortality by the Holiest Spirit, O Mazdah, strength and continuance through Good Thought at the [Judge's] sentence. . .

    13. Thus the Self of the Liar destroys for himself the assurance of the right Way; whose soul shall tremble at the Revelation on the Bridge of the Separator, having turned aside with deeds and tongue from the path of Right.

Source: From J.H. Moulton, *Early Zoroastrianism*, Philo Press, Amsterdam 1972. Selections from pp.347-87.

11.5   FROM SHIKAND GUMĀNĪ VAZĀR

Translated by R.C. Zaehner

11.5.1   (1) Another proof that a contrary principle exists is. . .that good and evil are observable in the world. . .and more particularly in so far as both good [and bad] conduct are defineable as such. . .as are darkness and light. . .right knowledge and wrong knowledge. . . fragrance and stench. . .life and death. . .sickness and health. . . justice and injustice. . .slavery and freedom. . .and all the other contrary activities which indisputably exist and are visible in every country and land at all times;. . .for no country or land exists, has existed, or ever will exist. . .in which the name of good and evil and what that name signifies has not existed or does not exist. . . Nor can any time or place be mentioned in which good and evil change their nature essentially.

11.5.2   (15) There are also other contraries whose antagonism is not [one of essence but] one of function, species, or nature. . . Such is the mutual antagonism of things of like nature as (for example) male and female. . . (the different) scents, tastes and colours; the Sun, Moon and stars whose dissimilarity is not one of substance but one of function, nature and constitution, each being adapted to its own particular work. . . But the dissimilarity of good and evil, light and darkness, and other contrary substances is not one of function but one of substance. . . This can be seen from the fact that their natures cannot combine and are mutually destructive. . . For where there is good, there cannot possibly be evil. . . Where light is admitted, darkness is driven away. . . Similarly with other contraries, the fact that they cannot combine and are mutually destructive is caused by their dissimilarity in substance. . . This substantial dissimilarity and mutual destructiveness is observable in phenomena in the material world. . .

11.5.3   (33) So we must know with a necessary knowledge that this visible and tangible world was created from an invisible and intangible spiritual world and had its origin there. . . Similarly there can be no doubt that the visible and tangible [material world] indicates the existence of an invisible and intangible world which is spiritual.

11.5.4   (35) Since we have seen that in the material world contrary substances exist and that they are sometimes mutually cooperative and sometimes mutually destructive, so [must it also be] in the

636

spiritual world...which is the cause of the material...and material things are its effects. That this is so is not open to doubt...and follows from the very nature of contrary substances... I have shown above that the reason and occasion for the wise activity of the Creator which is exemplified in the creative act is the existence of an Adversary.

Source: This chapter of the writing known as Shikand Gumānī Vazār is quoted from the translation of R.C. Zaehner of *The Teachings of the Magi*, Sheldon Press 1975, pp.59-61.

11.6 APOCALYPTIC PAHLAVI TEXTS

11.6.1 From the Zand-i Vohūman Yasn

Chapter IV

1. He, Zaratūhst, asked: 'O spiritual and beneficent Creator of the material existence! What will be the tokens of the tenth century?'

2. He, Aūhrmazd, replied: 'O Spîtâmân Zaratûhst, I will explain the tokens that will be at the end of thy millenium.

3. 'During that basest of periods, a hundred kinds, a thousand kinds and ten thousand kinds of "divs" having dishevelled hair, of the seed of Aêsem, will arrive.

6. 'They will rush, with sorcery, on to these Iranian villages which I, Aûhrmazd, created... 7. Since they will burn and damage many things, the houses of the house-owners and the villages of the village-chiefs: prosperity, nobility, husbandry, fidelity to Religion, faith, security, joy and all the productions which I, Aûhrmazd, created, this holy Religion of Mazda-worship and the Varahrâm fire, which is established worthily, will all come to nought.

11. 'They have no contract, faith, truth and ordinance; they preserve no security and do not remain firm on the contract they make... 12. They will raze these Iranian villages which I, Aûhrmazd, created, with deceit, avarice and misgovernment...

13. 'During that period, O Spîtâmân Zaratûhst, all men will become deceivers, and great friendship will be of a different hue... 14. And reverence, love and regard for the soul will depart from the world... 15. The affection of the father will depart from the son, and that of the brother from his brother; the son-in-law will be severed [?] from the father-in-law; and the mother will be separated from the daughter and of a different will.

16. 'When the tenth century will be at an end, O Spîtâmân Zaratûhst, the Sun's rays will be very level and much concealed; and the year, month and day will be shorter... 18. And the crops will not yield the seed... 19. And the plants, trees and shrubs will diminish... 20. And men will be born much stunted; they will have little skill and energy, and they will be very deceitful and very immoral...

21. 'During that most evil period, a bird will have more reverence than the Iranian religious man.

25. 'They will think of great works and duties and prepare wickedness and the way to the wicked existence; and they will hie towards the wicked existence on account of impiety, parsimony and the distractions of anger and avarice.

26. 'During that perverse period, O Spîtâmân Zaratûhst, the basest slaves will advance forward to the mastery of the Iranian villages.

33. 'Wealth and respectability will all come to those of alien creed and of alien path. . . 35. The inferiors shall take the daughters of patricians, nobles and sages to wife. . . The utterance of the religious, the seal and the judicature of the upright judge, the utterance of the truthful and even that of the righteous will be considered to be instigation; they will consider, as true and credible, the utterances of the inferiors and slanderers, of the impious and mockers and of those of false judgements. . . 38. And they will take oaths with false-hood, and give false evidence thereby, and will speak falsehood and untruth about me Aûhrmazd.

41. 'And in that tenth century, which will be at the end of thy millenium, O Spîtâmân Zaratûhst, all men will be worshipping avarice and of the false religion. . . 42. And it will not be possible for a fortunate cloud and the holy wind to produce rain at the proper time and season. . . 43. A gloomy cloud shall benight the whole sky. . . 44. The hot wind and the cold wind will arrive and carry away the crops and the seeds of corn. . . 45. The rain, too, will not rain at the proper season; it will rain the noxious creatures more than water. . . 46. And the water of rivers and springs will diminish and it will have no increase. . . 47. And quadrupeds, bullocks and sheep will be born very stunted. . .

49. 'And, in that perverse period, O Spîtâmân Zaratûhst, men, who will have the sacred thread-girdle on their waist, will desire death as a boon, on account of the hurtful demands of the evil rule. . .

59. 'The sovereignty will come unto them from those leathern-belted ones, Arabs and Arûmans. . . They will be so misgoverning that when they will kill a righteous good man or a fly, both the actions will be the same in their eyes.

68. 'This, too, I tell thee, O Spîtâmân Zaratûhst, that he who, at that period, will desire the body, cannot save the soul; for his body will be fat and the soul foul and feeble in the wicked existence; he who will desire the soul, his body will be foul and feeble, he will be destitute and poor on earth, and his soul will be fat in the Best

Existence.'

Chapter VI

. . .

4. 'O Spîtâmân Zaratûhst! when they will come, the Sun will show a melancholy sign, the Moon will change her colour, and there will be melancholy, darkness and gloom on earth; various signs will become manifest in the sky: there will be many earthquakes; the wind will blow very furiously; much indigence, want and unhappiness will appear on earth. . .

7. 'And great battles shall have happened three times, in three places, in internecine dispute, O Spîtâmân Zaratûhst.

10. 'And the third will take place when thy millenium will end, O Spîtâmân Zaratûhst. . .

11. 'For, when the husband will be able to save himself, he will not remember his wife, children and wealth.'

12. Thereupon Zaratûhst said: 'O Creator! give me death, and give my grandsons death' [that is, let them not live in that perverse period].

Chapter VII

1. Zaratûhst asked Aûhrmazd: 'O spiritual and beneficent Aûhrmazd, holy Creator of the material existence! O Creator! as they will be so immense in number, by what means ought they to be destroyed?'

2. He, Aûhrmazd, replied: 'O Spîtâmân Zaratûhst, when the "divs" having dishevelled hair of the seed of Aêsam will appear, first a black token will become manifest in the direction of the East, Aûsîtar the Zaratûhstian will be born on the Lake Frazdân. . .

3. 'At thirty years of age, he will come to a conference with me, Aûhrmazd, O Spîtâmân Zaratûhst. . ,

6. 'On the night when the Kayê [King] will be born, a token will come to the earth, a shower of stars will rain from the sky. . .

7. 'When that king will be thirty years of age. . .when the planet Jupiter will come up to its exaltation and cast Venus down there will come quite innumerable armed heroes having erect banners to the King for sovereignty. . .

Source: From the translation of *The Zand-î Vohûman Yasn* by B.T. Anklesaria, Bombay 1957, extracts from pp.106-13 and 116-20.

From the Dinkard (Book VII, Chapter VIII)

. . .

2. There is this marvellousness, revealed by the Avesta about the ninth and tenth centuries, that which is an indicator of circumstances now visible, such as the dispersion of the sovereignty of Iran from the country of Iran, the disturbance of just law and custom, the predomiancne of those with dishevelled hair and the haughty profession of ecclesiastics.

4. The disappearance of a disposition for wisdom from the foreigners in the countries of Iran, which is an indication of shame at the truth of the religion, and at the praise, peace, liberality, and other goodness whose provision has lodgement in a disposition for wisdom.

5. Also the abundance of the decisions of apostasy, the falsehood, deceit, slander, quarrelsomeness, fraudulence, ingratitude, discord, stinginess, and other vileness whose real connection is a disposition to devour, neglecting heedfulness for the archangels of fire, water, and worldly existence.

6. The oppressiveness of infidelity and idol-worship, the scarcity of freedom, the extreme predominance of avarice in the individuals (tano) of mankind, the plenitude of different opinions about witch-craft, and the much inclination of many for paralyzing the religion of the sacred beings.

7. The annihilation of the sovereignty of mankind one over the other, the desolation of localities and settlements by severe actual distress, and the evil foreign potentates who are, one after the other, scattering the valiant; the destruction among cattle and the defile-ment of the spirit of enjoyment, owing to the lodgement of lamentation and weeping in the countries of Iran, the clamour of the demon-worshipper in the country, and the unobtainable stature, non-existent strength, blighted destiny, and short life of mankind.

9. The maintenance of no ritual of the religion of the sacred beings; the weakness, suffering, and evil habits of those of the good religion; the lamentation and recantation (*khūstvkīh*) of the upholders of the religion; and the wickedness and extermination of good works in most of the countries of Iran.

10. Also much other misery in these two centuries is recounted in the Avesta, which passed away with them and is also now so visible therein, and manifestly occurs in them.

11. This, too, is a statement (*nisang-i*) as to them, which revela-tion mentions thus: 'That is the age mingled with iron. . .

12. . . .whenever it is possible for them they shall cause misery to others; also when an old man publicly advances into a crowd of youths, owing to the evil times in which that man who is learned is born, they are unfriendly to him. 13. . . .they are wicked and are fully maliciously talking, they also tear asunder the spiritual lordship and priestly authority, and shall bring the ruler and priestly authority into evil behaviour as vicious.

14. Anything they say is always mischief (*agīh*). . .it is misery without any intermission they shall inflict. . .'

15. 'Here below they fight, the friend with him who is a friend.'

11.6.3 Book VII, Chapter XI

. . .

2. Concerning the marvellousness of Sôshâns as to splendour and glory of person, it [revelation] says that 'when the coming of the last rotation of those rotations of the seasons of Aûshêdar-mah occurs, the man Sôshâns is born whose food is spiritual and body sunny'. . .

4. And this, too, that in fifty-seven of his years there occur the annihilation of the fiendishness of the two-legged race and others, and the subjugation of disease and decrepitude, of death and persecution, and of the original evil of tyranny, apostasy, and depravity; there arise a perpetual verdant growth of vegetation and the primitive gift of joyfulness; and there are seventeen years of vegetable-eating, thirty years of water-drinking, and ten years of spiritual food. . .

6. And all mankind remain of one accord in the religion of Aûharmazd, owing to the will of the creator, the command of that apostle, and the resources of his companions.

7. At the end of the fifty-seven years the fiend and Aharman are annihilated, the renovation for the future existence occurs, and the whole of the good creation is provided with purity and perfect splendour.

Translation from E.W. West, ed., *Sacred Books of the East*, OUP 1897, Vol. XLVII, extracts from pp.94-7 and 116.7.

11.6.4 From Bundahishn (Chapter XXXIV)

. . .

(3) 'Then Sôshyans will raise up the dead'. . .

(5) First will be raised the bones of Gayômart, then the bones of Mashyē and Mashyānē: then will the bones of [all] other men be raised up. For fifty-seven years will Sôshyans raise the dead and all

men will be resurrected, both those who were saved and those who were damned. And each man will arise in the place where his spirit left him or where first he fell to the ground.

(6) And when the gods have restored to the whole of the material creation its proper form and shape, then will they give [men] their proper character. And of the light that is with the Sun half will they give to Gayōmart and half to the rest of men.

(7) Then will men recognise each other, that is, soul will recognise soul and body body [thinking], 'This is my father', or 'This is my brother', or 'This is my wife', or 'This is whatever close relative it may be'. Then the assembly of Isat-vāstar will convene when men stand upon the earth in that assembly; and every man will see his good and evil deeds, and the saved will be as clearly distinguished from the damned as is a white sheep from a black.

(8) And in that assembly the damned man who had on earth a friend who was saved, will upbraid the man who was saved, saying, 'Why didst thou not apprise me on earth of the good deeds that thou thyself wast doing?' And if in truth the man who was saved did not so apprise him, then must he needs be put to shame in that assembly.

(9) Then will they separate the saved from the damned, and carry off the saved to Paradise (*gārodhmān*) and hurl the damned back into Hell; and for three days and nights these denizens of Hell will endure punishment in Hell, in their bodies and in their souls (*jān*) while the saved experience joy in their bodies during their three days and nights in Paradise.

(12) At that time when the final Rehabilitation is brought about, fifteen men and fifteen maidens from among those blessed men of whom it is written that they are [still] alive, will come to the assistance of Sōshyans.

(13) And Gōchihr, the serpent in the heavenly sphere, will fall from the summit of the Moon to the earth, and the earth will suffer pain like unto the pain a sheep feels when a wolf rends out its wool.

(14) Then will the Fire-god and the god Airyaman melt the metals that are in the mountains and hills, and they will flow over the earth like rivers. And they will make all men to pass through that molten metal and (thereby) make them clean. And it will seem to him who was saved as if he were walking through warm milk, but to the man who was damned it will seem exactly like walking through molten metal.

(15) Then will all men come together in the greatest joy, father

and son, brothers and all friends. And one man will ask another, 'How has thy soul fared in all these many years? Wast thou saved, or wast thou damned?' Next the soul will see its body, will question it and be answered by it.

(16) All men will become of one voice and give praise with a loud voice to Ohrmazd and the Amahraspands. At this time Ohrmazd will have brought his creation to its consummation, and there will be no [further] work he need do.

(17) While the resurrection of the dead proceeds, Sōshyans and his helpers will perform the sacrifice of the raising of the dead, and in that sacrifice the bull Hadhayans will be slain, and from the fat of the bull they will prepare the white Hōm (Haoma), [the drink of] immortality, and give it to all men. And all men will become immortal for ever and ever. . .

(20) Then at the behest of the Creator Sōshyans will distribute to all men their wages and reward in accordance with their deeds. Some there are who are so blessed that he says, 'Take them to the Paradise of Ohrmazd as is their due.' They will take up their bodies, and for ever and ever they will walk together with them. . .

(22) Then Ohrmazd will seize hold of the Destructive Spirit, Vahuman (the Good Mind) will seize Akōman (the Evil Mind), Artvahisht Indar, Shahrēvar Sāvul, Spandarmat Tarōmat (Arrogance) who is Nānghaith, Hurdāt and Armurdāt will seize Tairich and Zairich, True Speech False Speech, and the blessed Srōsh will seize upon Ēshm (Wrath) of the bloody banner.

(23) Then [only two Lies will remain, Ahriman and Āz (Concupiscence). Ohrmazd will come [down] to earth, himself the 'Zōt'-priest with the blessed Srōsh as his 'Rāspīk'-priest, and he will hold the sacred girdle in his hand. By that Gāthic ritual Ahriman and Āz, their weapons smashed, will be made powerless; and by the same passage through the sky by which they rushed in, they will hurtle into the darkness and gloom.

(24) And the serpent Gōchihr will be burnt up in the molten metal; and the molten metal will flow out into Hell. And [all] the stench and corruption that was in Hell will be burnt up by this molten metal and made clean. And [the hole in (?)] Hell by which the Destructive Spirit rushed in, will be sealed up by that molten metal, and the earth that was in Hell will be brought up to the broad expanse of [this] material world.

(25) Then will the final Resurrection take place in the two worlds; and in accordance with its own desire the material world will

become immortal for ever and ever.

(26) This too is said, that this earth will become flat, with neither hills nor dales. There will be neither mountains nor ridges nor pits, neither high ground nor low.

Source: R.C. Zaehner, op.cit., extracts from pp.146-50.

11.7   THE TALE OF SANJAN

Translated by S.K. Hodivala

11.7.1 Hearken now to a wondrous tale recounted by Mobeds and ancients... I have heard it from a wise Dastur who was ever renowned for goodness. May the Dastur whose name is Hoshang and whose wisdom had always great excellence live long.
[The text tells of the Muslim invasion of Iran and the persecution which forced some of the Zoroastrian faithful to go into hiding and then, on the advice of a wise astrologer, Dastur, to move to Div.]

11.7.2   The People of the Good Faith stayed there for nineteen years, at the end of which the Stargazer once more [sought to] divine the future. The aged Dastur having looked into his Tables, said 'O my enlightened friends, hence also must we hie to another spot in which will be our second home.' All of them were delighted by his words and they set sail quickly towards Gujarat. When the vessel had made some way into the sea, a disastrous storm approached. All the Dasturs of the Faith were thrown into consternation and their heads turned as in a whirlpool. They rubbed their faces before the Presence Divine and stood up and made loud laments, [saying], 'O Thou Wise One, come to our aid on this occasion and for once deliver us from this distress. [And] Thou, All-conquering Bahram, befriend us and bring us out triumphant from this trouble. [If we possess] Thy favour, we shall not care for the tempest and give no place to fear in our hearts. Hearken then to the complaints of the helpless and show Thou the way to us who are lost [in this waste of waters]. If we escape from this dreadful storm, if disaster does not confront us and if we reach the realm of Hind with cheerful hearts and merry, we shall kindle a great fire to Bahram. Deliver us then from this strait and keep us sound. We are resigned to everything [that comes] from the Lord, for save Him we possess no other [friend]. By the blessing of the Fire of the Glorious Bahram, all of them luckily got over that trouble; their supplications were instantly heard and the Lord came to the rescue. A prosperous gale began to blow, the light of Heaven [to shine] and the contrary wind ceased. When the Captain with the Holy name of God upon his lips steered the ship with vigour, and all the Dasturs and laymen also made Kusti, the vessel drove instantly into the sea. Then Providence so ordered it that all those people arrived near Sanjan.

In that region was a virtuous Raja who had opened his heart to   11.7.3
holiness. His name was Jādi Rana; he was liberal, sagacious and wise.
A Dastur renowned for learning and prudence went to him with gifts
and invoked blessings upon him and said: 'O Raja of Rajas, give us a
place in this city: we are strangers seeking protection who have
arrived in thy town and place of residence. We have come here only
for the sake of our Religion, for we heard that there was in this place
a Raja descended from the beneficent Shillahras, ever renowned
throughout Hindustan, who gave people shelter in his town and
kingdom and regarded them with the eye of compassion. We were
cheered by these tidings and have approached thee under favourable
auspices. We have now reached thy city in the hope of escaping from
the Miscreants.' The hearts of all the followers of the virtuous Raja
were gladdened and their souls charmed by these words. But when
that prince beheld them a terror suddenly fell upon his heart. Fears
for his crown entered his mind and [he thought] that they might lay
waste his kingdom. Frightened by their dress and accoutrements, he
questioned the Dastur about their religious mysteries. 'O thou
devout Dastur', he at last said, 'Tell us, first of all, the gist of the
matter. What are the customs of your Creed, which of them are
open and which concealed? Let me first of all see what your beliefs
are and we will then arrange for your residence here. Secondly, if we
give you shelter, you must abandon the language of your
country, disuse the tongue of Iran and adopt the speech of the realm
of Hind. Thirdly, as to the dress of your women, they should wear
garments like those of our females. Fourthly, you must put off all
your aims and scimitars and cease to wear them anywhere. Fifthly,
when your children are wedded, the marriage knot must be tied at
evening time. If you first give a solemn promise to observe all this,
you will be given places and abodes in my city.' When the Dastur
heard all this from the Raja, he could not help agreeing to all his
demands.

Then the old Mobed addressed him thus, 'O sagacious king,   11.7.4
hearken now to what I say of our Creed. Do not be heavy-hearted on
our account, for never shall any evil [deed] proceed from us in this
land. We shall be the friends of all Hindustan and everywhere scatter
the heads of thy foes. Know then for certain that we are the
worshippers of Yazdān [One God] and have fled from the
Miscreants only for our religion's sake. We have abandoned all we
possessed and borne many hardships on the road. Houses and

mansions and goods and chattels we have all forsaken, O auspicious prince. We strangers are of the seed of Jamshid and reverence the Sun and the Moon. Three other things also out of Creation, we hold in honour, viz. the Cow, Fire and Water. Thus we adore the Fire, Water, Cows and the Sun and the Moon likewise. It is the Lord who has created all these things that are on earth, and we pray to them, because He Himself has preferred them. Our sacred girdle [*Kusti*] is made of seventy-two threads and we repeat when we tie it on, solemn professions of Faith. Our women when in their manner behold not either the sun or the sky or the noon. . .nor do they touch fire or water. They stand strictly aloof from everything, whether during the radiant day or the darksome night and sit apart until the catamenia have ceased. They look at the fire and the sun only when they have washed from head [to foot] . So also, the female who gives birth to an infant must live apart for forty days'. . . . All their other rites and customs also he described one by one to the Raja. When the mysteries of the Good Faith were thus expounded and the pearls of discourse strung in this most elegant manner, and when the Hindu Raja heard the oration, his mind regained perfect ease.

11.7.5   That good king forthwith commanded that they should reside in his dominions. Then some persons who were intelligent, good-natured and resourceful surveyed the land, discovered a spacious plain and informed the Mobed. A spot in this wilderness was chosen, of which the soil was excellent and there they made their abode. The people also liked the place and a city appeared where there had formerly been a jungle. . . The Dastur gave it the name of Sanjan and it was soon flourishing even as the realm of Iran. . . There they remained in joy and comfort and everyone prospered in the end according to his wish.

11.7.6   One day, they happened to have some business with the Raja. . . The Dastur then addressed him thus: 'O Prince, you have given us a dwelling spot in this land. We now wish to install in the Indian clime the Fire Bahram. [But] the land must be cleared for three farsangs, so that the ceremonies [connected with the consecration] of the Niragn may be duly performed. No alien should be there present, save and except the Wise Men of the Good Faith. . . Then only will the Fire be consecrated' . . . Quota the Raja then, 'I have given you the permission. I am disposed to be very liberal in this matter. . . Go then speedily after his business, and gird up thy loins.' That very instant, the Prince issued his commands and gave the Dastur a pleasant site. The Hindu Rana Jādi had the land at once cleared on every side. All the Unbelievers within three Farsangs were removed and no one remained there except the People of the Good Faith. . . The aged Dasturs thus installed the *Iranshah* beaming with light, in conformity with the rites [prescribed] in our creed. In those times, men were [deeply] versed in spiritual matters and were able to observe religious precepts on account of their wisdom.

Source: This example of religious writing, entitled in the original Kissah-i-Sanjan, is taken from the translation by S.K. Hodivala in *Studies in Parsi History*, Hodivala, Bombay 1920, pp.99-106.

11.8 TRAVELLERS' ACCOUNTS OF THE PARSIS

11.8.1 From E. Terry's *A Voyage to East India* (visited Gujarat 1618-19)

Their profession is, for the generality, all kinds of husbandry, employing themselves very much in the sowing and setting of herbs; in planting and dressing of vines, and palmeto or toddy trees, as in planting and husbanding all other trees bearing fruit, and indeed they are a very industrious people, and so are very many of the Hindoos (as before observed); and they do all very well in doing so, and in this a due and deserved commendation belongs unto them. . . they use their liberty in meats and drinks, to take of them what they please; but because they would not give offence either to Mohametans or Banians, or to other Hindoos, amongst whom they live, they abstain from eating beef or swine's flesh.

For those Parsees, further, they believe that there is but one god, who made all things and hath a sovereign power over all. They talk much of Lucifer and other evil spirits, but they say that those, and all Devils besides, are kept so under and in awe by two good angels that have power over them, as that they cannot hurt or do the least mischief, without their leave or licence.

11.8.2 From H. Lord's *A Display of Two Forraigne Sections in the East Indies* (visited Surat 1620)

The Parsees affirm, that before anything was, there was a God, that was the maker of all things. . . Their law alloweth them great liberty in meats and drinks, but because they will not give offence to the Banians, amongst whom they live, not displease the Moore, under whose government they are, they especially abstain from eating of kine and hog's flesh, meats prohibited by the laws of the two former.

11.8.3 From *Les Voyages du Sieur Albert de Mandelso*

They dwell for the most part along the coast and live quite peacefully, maintaining themselves with the profit they draw from tobacco, which they cultivate, and from toddy which they draw from the palm-trees of those places, and of which they make *arrack,* as it is permitted them to drink wine. They have a hand in trading also and in banking, in keeping shop, in exerting themselves in other kinds of business except...of the smith, and of the locksmith; because it is an unpardonable sin among them to put out the fire.

These Parsees believe that there is one God who is the preserver of the whole Universe.

From J. Ovington's *A Voyage to Suratt in the year 1689*   11.8.4

They own and Adore one Supreme Being, to whom, as he is the Original of all things, they dedicate the first Day in every month, in a solemn observance of his worship.

At their solemn festivals, whither a hundred or two sometimes, resort, in the suburbs of the city, each man according to his fancy and ability, brings with him his Victuals, which is equally distributed, and eat in common by all that are present, for they show a firm affection to all of their own sentiments in Religion, assist the poor and are very ready to provide for the Sustenance and Comfort of such as want it. Their universal kindness, either in employing such as are needy and able to work, or bestowing a seasonable bounteous charity to such as are infirm and miserable; leave no man destitute of Relief, nor suffer a Beggar in all their Tribe...

In their Callings, they are very industrious and diligent, and careful to train 'up their children to Art and Labour. They are the Principal men at the Loom in all the Country and most of the Silks, and Stuffs at Surat are made by their Hands.

From C. Niebuhr (in India 1762-64) and published in J. Pinkerton's 11.8.5
General Collection of the best and most interesting Voyages and Travels in all parts of the World

At Surat, are numbers of Parsees or Persians, who are skilful merchants, industrious artisans and good servants. At Bombay, at Surat, and in the vicinity of these cities, is a colony of ancient Persians, who took refuge in India, when their country was conquered by the Mahometan Arabs, eleven centuries since. They are called Persees. Being beloved by the Hindoos, they multiply exceedingly; whereas their countrymen, in the province of Kerman, are visibly diminishing under the Yoke of the Moslem Persians.

They are a gentle, quiet, industrious race. They live in great harmony among themselves, make common contributions for the aid of their poor, and suffer none of their numbers to ask alms from people of a different religion.

The persees, followers of the religion of Zerdust or Zoroaster, adore one God only, eternal and Almighty.

11.8.6 **From T.S. Stavorinus'** *Voyages to the East*

The Parsis of Surat in 1774 A.D.

They increase in numbers from day-to-day, and have built and inhabit many entire wards in the surburbs.

There are some among them, although few, who leave their countrymen, in the neighbourhood of Surat, for several years, and resort to Cochin, the coast of Coromandel or other places in India, in order to procure a better livelihood. Several among them at Surat are rich, and may be counted among the principal merchants.

They are much fairer than either the Moors or Gentoos, and do not differ much in complexion from the Spaniards; they have, in general, large eyes, aquiline noses, and well proportioned.

They, however, marry no more than one woman at the same time, and never any one but of their own nation, so that they have preserved their race, through so many ages, pure and unmixed with other nations, to the present day.

Pursuers of unlawful pleasures, spurred on by the desire of variety, and such as did not otherwise make any difficulty of confessing and even triumphing in their amours, have uniformly assured me, that they have never succeeded in having their will of any Persian woman, notwithstanding that they have neither spared assiduity nor money.

11.8.7 **From James Forbes'** *Oriental Memoirs,* **(1814)**

Of late years, the most beautiful villas and gardens at Surat, at least those in the best condition, no longer appertain to the Moguls or Hindoos; very considerable landed property, in the outer city and adjoining districts, belong to the Parsees, a numerous and industrious tribe.

These Persian emigrants are now wonderfully multiplied; excepting the extraordinary instance of the children of Israel, there is, perhaps, no record of so great an increase as among the Parsee tribe in India, sprung from the few families who emigrated thither for the preservation of religious liberty. Active, robust, prudent, and persevering, they now form a very valuable part of the Company's subjects on the Western shores of Hindostan, where they are not only protected, but highly esteemed and encouraged. They never interfere with the government or police of any country where they settle, but gradually and silently acquire money, and the influence usually depending on such an acquisition. The Parsees not only acquire wealth, but enjoy the comforts and luxuries naturally accompanying it; as is evident in their own domestic economy, and especially in the entertainments they sometimes make for their English friends at Bombay and Surat.

Sources:
§11.8.1, 11.8.2, 11.8.3 and 11.8.4 are quoted by R.B. Paymaster in his *Early History of the Parsees in India*. The selections given here are taken from the following original sources:
E. Terry, *A Voyage to East India*, pp.337 and 339.
H. Lord, *A Display of two forraigne Sections in the East Indies*, p.5.
Les Voyages du Sieur Albert De Mandelso, pp.180, 184 and 186.
J. Ovington, *A Voyage to Suratt, in the year 1689*, pp.370-74.
§11.8.5, 11.8.6 and 11.8.7 are quoted by M.M. Murzban in his *The Parsis in India*, M.M. Murzban 1917, pp.67-70. The selections given here are taken from the following original sources:
J. Pinkerton, *General Collection of the best and most interesting Voyages and Travels in all parts of the world*, Vol.X, pp.214, 220.
T.S. Stavorinus, *Voyages to the East*, Vol.II, pp.494-8 and 504-5.
James Forbes, *Oriental Memoirs*, Vol.III, pp.411-12.

11.9 WESTERNISED PARSI TEACHING

M.N. Dhalla

11.9.1 My life of the spirit is impoverished, when I neglect communing with thee. A tense silence holds between me and thee when I cease to meet thee and confer with thee. My spiritual vision is blurred. I cannot feel thy presence, I cannot see thy radiant face. Ill do I requite thy gratitude, when I desert thee and go over to Angra Mainyu, the Evil Spirit, and live for him. My footsteps slide on the path of wrong. Like a land bird that finds no solid object to alight upon, when it is out to sea, I am lost when I leave thee and find no place of safety for my misguided soul.

11.9.2 My life is wrapped up in thee and in thy protecting love. Hold me by my hands and guide me and I will follow thee wherever thou dost lead me. I will serve thee to the end of my life, till thou dost call me back from my earthly sojourn to my final rest and repose in thee.

11.9.3 To see Zarathushtra in spirit is to see thee, Ahura Mazda. To know him is to know thee. To understand him is to understand thee. To follow him is to follow thee. To be like him is to be like thee.

I will assimilate Zarathushtra's teachings into my life. I will live devoted to him. I will make him my example in life. I will keep his sublime image engraved upon my mind. With Zarathushtra as my guiding spirit, sustained energy, and driving will fearlessly and courageously will I face whatever befalls and betides me.

11.9.4 Rituals help our spiritual development. They are the accompaniments of religion, but not religion itself. Religion is righteousness. It rests on the individual's piety, and not on a scrupulous observance of ceremonials or a practice of elaborate lustrations.

11.9.5 Death has freed them from the material bondage. They have sped their frail earthly clay and departed this life to live hereafter in the realm of the spirit. Their earthly work is done and they have laid down the burden that pressed heavily on them. From the din and dust and storm of life's struggle they have gone to the deathless world of peace and rest where light fades not and happiness fails not.

Thou, Ahura Mazda, hast called them to thyself. We commend them into thy hands.

11.9.6 Help me so to live, my God, that when death extinguishes my life,

I may yet live upon earth in my good thoughts and good words and good deeds, when my soul dwells with thee in heaven.

Life is kind to us and life is cruel to us, life sits light upon us and 11.9.7 life sits heavy upon us, life is sunshine and life is darkness, life is joy and life is sorrow, life blooms and blossoms and life withers and fades. Life upon earth, O Lord of life, is a blend of contradictions.

Life and suffering are inseparable and the world is a rough enough place to live.

Let me be up and doing and let me work actively and strenuously 11.9.8 while yet I may and let me die in harness when it pleases thee to call me back to heaven, Ahura Mazda.

When doubt assails me and faith grows dim and fails me, lead me, 11.9.9 Ahura Mazda, from destructive doubt to reasoned faith. Let my faith be wedded to reason and let it be based on conviction. Give me faith and more faith, but not the blind faith.

Great is the discord and great is the divergence between the 11.9.10 demands of my conscience and the life I lead.

I am at peace with the world, but not at peace with my conscience, for a fierce struggle goes on in the depths of my soul. My inner world is torn by the conflict. Beneath my calm exterior, the tempest is raging within. My conscience reproaches and persecutes me and does not leave me at rest. The torments and tortures of my conscience are not less painful than the sufferings of the wicked souls in hell as described by Viraf. Blackened with guilt and sin, my conscience makes my heart as ugly and dark as hell.

The fire of my sincere penitence will cleanse my heart of its 11.9.11 impurity. Let my penitence sweep away sin from my heart even as a powerful wind sweeps over the plain and carries away everything with it. Let my sin be absolved, for I will amend my way and sin no more.

All religions come from one and the only God, who makes 11.9.12 himself known by many a name. From the same source, like the tributaries of a river, they flow. All religions make man equally good upon earth and with equal safety do they conduct his soul to heaven. One alone is truth and all religions teach this truth, for religion itself is truth.

Death the grim harvester is heedless of the seasons of life. Old age 11.9.13 and sickness provide a rich harvest for it. . . Like the farmer that mows down grass in the field, death swings its sickle and takes away vast numbers in the heyday of their summer.

Body and soul form two constituents in the formation of man. 11.9.14

The soul exists for the short span of its life on earth in the tenement of the body, and with the crumblings of the material frame into dust, wings its flight heavenward. The bodily death does not mean the death of the soul, for it is immortal.

11.9.15   Ahura Mazda, the Great King of heaven, sits enthroned in Garonmana, the Abode of Song. In these realms of eternal light, stand round the resplendent throne of the lord God, the Holy Immortals and the Adorable Ones, the Amesha Spentas and the Yazatas, the Fravashis, the unfailing friends and guardians of the saintly souls of the dead, all clad in robes of pure, white hue.

With the golden key in his hands, Asha guards the gates of heaven. Heaven is the gift of Asha to those who, wedded to his righteousness in life, walk the Path of Righteousness, the only true path of life upon earth.

Heaven is my birthplace and to heaven will I make my homeward journey, when death liberates me from my earthly bonds. Steep is the ascent to heaven. With truthful and virtuous conduct will I lighten my soul that easily it can climb the highest heights of heaven.

Source: Selections from M.N. Dhalla, *Homage unto Ahura Mazda*, B.T. Anklesaria, Dhalla Memorial Institute, Karachi 1970, pp.4, 5, 52, 67, 83, 84, 85-86, 101, 131, 138, 144, 176, 197, 206 and 212.

11.10 THEOSOPHICAL PARSI TEACHING

K.S. Dabu

Rawan-Boktagi–Ristakhiz–Tan-e-Pasin Kayamat–Frashogard 11.10.1

These are terms allied to one another pointing to an event we call *Resurrection* = (*Re* = again + *sur* = under + *rectus* = right): which implies: 'Regaining the former upright status, which was lost during the soul's descent into incarnation.' The Divine *Spirit,* originally a glowing spark from the Boundless Flame *(asar-Roshni),* has to undergo a 'stepping-down transformation', while encased in a material vesture. (Wordsworth calls this encumbrance: 'Bars of prison-gate, closing round the flashing clouds of glory.') The *Urwan* = Soul (Avesta: *Ur* = inner + *Van* = fighter) has to struggle against all sorts of handicaps during successive incarnations, gaining experience, growing in wisdom, gradually approaching *Bokhtagi* = Liberation from the thraldom of the flesh. This final goal has been (allotted) various terms, quoted at the head of this paragraph: (a) *Ristakhiz (Rista = irista* = The Dead + *akhiz* = Rising up) is an allegorical description, a figure of speech for 'The soul is *dead* that slumbers — *waking up* to his sense of great heritage and destiny', so that he seeks liberation from *'the grave'* = typified by his incarnations! 'He, that hath heard the Word of God, shall never die again.' The spiritual awakening is = the 'rising from the grave,' — individual as well as collective — at its proper time of perfection.

(b) *Tan-e-Pasin* = means 'the last bodily existence' prior to immortality. No longer would he be compelled to be re-born, as he would have gained perfect wisdom, peace, compassion and abilities, through a long series of incarnations. Gatha (30-10) prophesies that when the material deceptive illusive power is broken, he re-enters his true heavenly Home.

(c) *Kayamat* = means a state of 'unchanging permanency due to attainment of immortality'. Prior to this 'life everlasting', the soul was a constant Sojourner, amidst various ventures, and in 'exile' from its true kingdom. It is his 'Paradise Regained'.

(d) *Frashogard* (Avesta: *Frasho-Kereti)* = term used by Zarathushtra in the Gathas — has two interpretations: (i) Renovation, or creating afresh a state of divine innocence (which was lost in the soul's descent into material garb) through his reaching a new world of Reality and Eternal bliss. (ii) It also means 'Going *forward (Faraz)*' from the human stage to the next angelic kingdom — no longer 'a pawn on the chequer-board', but an expert player in the game.

It will be seen that all these terms point to our ultimate destiny: 'Re-union with the Beloved behind the veil' — as the Sufis would describe it.

11.10.2 Khoreh (Khareno)

This term refers to the belief, that each object as well as each living being has an invisible *aura, halo,* or *'glory'* radiating from a centre. This is depicted in pictures of saints with halo round their head. But one's *khoreh* may be impure, if one is living a bad life. He may spread his 'magnetic influence' about him. A temple radiates vivifying aura to a great extent, after its consecration. A priest is supposed to charge certain objects (water, milk, etc.) during a grand ritual, with his own *Khoreh,* and then the object is termed *Ashaya-Uzdata* = 'exalted through one's own pure radiation'. This has reference to a healer's 'magnetic passes' while reciting *Ardibehesht-yasht* over an ailing patient. Iran, as a country, had its lofty *Khoreh* influence. Aura is the extension of *Keherp* = 'Etheric Double'.

Source: K.S. Dabu, *A Handbook of Information on Zoroastrianism,* P.H. Mehta Educational Trust, Bombay 1969, extracts from pp. 2, 3, 4 and 28.

11.11 A CATECHISM OF THE ZOROASTRIAN RELIGION

J.J. Modi

[The Catechism is set in the style of question and answer. The following selections do not always reflect that style.]

1. Why is it that there are so many different religions?
The prophets have appeared in various countries at different times and in different circumstances; and they have revealed their religions according to divine knowledge received by them. Hence more than one religion in the world...

2. The articles of faith.
I am a Mazdayasni, a Mazdayasni Zarthoshti. I profess my self to be faithful and a believer.

I put faith in good thought,

I put faith in good word,

I put faith in good deed,

I put faith in good Mazdayasni Religion, which removes bondage, allays quarrels, teaches self-sacrifice, which is holy, which is greatest, best and excellent among the existing ones and those that shall come into existence, which is taught by Ahura, and which is revealed by Zoroaster. All goodness do I ascribe to Ahura Mazda, Divine Lord. This is the confession of faith of Mazdayasni religion...

4. The principal teachings of the Mazdayasni Zarthoshti Religion are:

(1) Existence of Mazda, the all-wise Lord;

(2) Immortality of the Soul, or the Life Hereafter; and

(3) Our responsibility for our thoughts, words and actions...

5. God existed from all Eternity. He always was, is and will always be. He is self-existent, i.e. He does not depend on any other being or cause for his existence... He has brought the whole Universe into existence. Whatever we see in this world has been created by Him. He is the Source of the existence of all...

6. We see, in all Nature, uniform and constant Principles, harmonious, invariable Laws, regular undeviating Order. All these show that there must be in Existence an all-wise Lord as the Originator and Maintainer of all...

7. The Almighty is Mazda, i.e. Omniscient. He possesses infinite and sovereign wisdom...whatever we think, whatever we speak, whatever we do, is all known to Him.

What is the result of that knowledge?

Knowing what we think, what we speak, and what we do, He rewards us for what is good in our thoughts, words and deeds, and punishes us for what is bad in them.

When does God thus reward or punish us?

At some time or another, when the proper occasion arrives...

9. There is progress in life. We are born as children and we grow up. We then pass through youth and become old. After old age comes death. Sometimes a person dies earlier without attaining to old age. All then go into the presence of the Creator in the invisible world. They live there. The body perishes but the soul lives... As, on birth we came into existence from Ahura Mazda, so after death we go back to Him in accordance with His fixed law...

10. What do you mean by saying that 'we shall be judged properly in the court of God'? Do you mean that we shall be judged after our death?

No. We have learnt that God exists everywhere and at all times. So, His court exists everywhere and at all times. We are therefore judged by him on all proper occasions. We shall be requited for our deeds in this life or in the life hereafter...

11. Then, according to the teaching of our religion, there is no saviour for one, other than himself? Of course not. Every man is his own saviour. His deeds alone will bring out his salvation. A man is the architect of his own fortune. He is his own saviour.

10. What should be our course of conduct of life which may best be regarded as professing the Zoroastrian religion?

We should observe purity of mind, and should adopt *humata, hukhta and hvarshta...*

23. It is the will of the Creator of the Universe that we should always strive for the growth and prosperity of all good and beneficent creations of Nature ... The creations of Nature are meant for the use and benefit of mankind. We can make good use of them, but we must not abuse them...

Work is the salt of life. Without work our life is idle and useless. Our religion teaches us that work is the aim and object of life. We must always keep our body ready and healthy for doing the duties of our life — to do good and right deeds, to help others, and to fight against evil and misery in the world.

26. On the one hand we should not enfeeble or enervate our body by unnecessary pain or exertion, and on the other, we should not indulge in over-gratification of the senses and appetites. We must lead a simple life and maintain our body in good order.

Then, keeping fasts, leading a useless and idle life like that of the common class of ascetics and recluses, and disregarding proper and solicitous care of our body, are wrongful acts?

Yes, all these are wrongful acts... The body should be maintained in a sound state. We must cultivate our mental faculties with acquisition of good knowledge and enliven the kind feelings of our heart. We must make the best possible use of our intellectual and moral powers and thus act for the highest good of all round about us. Ahura Mazda, the Father of us all, would be pleased thereby...

29. We look to fire generally with reverential feelings, as the manifested form of the power of heat and light permeating this world and also as a symbol of the splendour and glory of the Creator. Then in the case of the sacred fire of the Fire-temples, the religious ritual in its consecration adds some elements of moral thoughts and spiritual value. Hence it is, that we look to this consecrated fire with greater reverence.

31. If any evil happens to us...what are we to think of that?

If that evil is the result of our own faults, we should repent for those faults before God and should correct those faults. We should pray to God, and henceforth, do our best so that no evil may happen to us through our own faults, and that everything may turn out for our good.

If we are involved in affliction, not through our own faults or transgressions but through circumstances over which we have no control what view are we to take of that?

We should affirm our faith in God, and bear those sufferings with a confident hope, that those sufferings are a trial for us and that everything will be alright in the end.

An even balance between prosperity and adversity will conduce to our well-being...

Source: Selections from J.J. Modi, *A Catechism of the Zoroastrian Religion,* Parsi Punchayet Press, Bombay 1961.

12 INTER-RELIGIOUS ENCOUNTER

[*Editor's Note:* The Reader material which follows consists of three contemporary essays on the subject of religious encounter. It will be seen that the subjects covered are no more than illustrative of a much wider area of life in which this religious encounter is taking place. But it is hoped that the essays may serve to bring to the fore, general considerations which have relevance to all areas of such encounter.

At this point the Reader ends. There is no better place, it could be argued, for such a collection of material as this to end. For the global village which will be the world of the twentieth century is not going to allow geographical separatedness to the great religions. A new generation will have no choice but to share its back yard with hitherto alien cultures. In §12 of the Reader we take a preview of what lies ahead.]

12.1 MAJOR ISSUES IN THE HINDU-CHRISTIAN DIALOGUE IN INDIA TODAY

S.J. Samartha

The resurgence of religions is a continuing characteristic of contemporary Indian life. Traditional religious values are being reinterpreted to meet modern needs. Among the different religions there is a spirit of greater friendliness and an increasing desire for cooperation. For one thing, it is recognised that in the interests of national unity, religions should not divide people but unite them. For another, the rising tide of secularism indirectly brings the religions together by challenging some of their basic convictions. Moreover, people realise that irrespective of their religious affiliations, as citizens of a country that is rebuilding its total life they face problems common to all. Political freedom, economic progress, social justice and cultural renaissance are questions with which all people are concerned as citizens of India and as human beings, not just as members of particular religious groups. Under these circumstances the relationship between religions is slowly changing from conflict to coexistence, from acquaintance to understanding and from mere confrontation to more active cooperation. Instead of a one-sided 'proclamation' which almost amounted to a 'monologue', today the mood is increasingly one of 'dialogue'. This attitude of dialogue may be described as an attempt to establish a two-way traffic in what was hitherto a one-way street. Admittedly, the situation is highly complex where clear analyses, neat classifications and broad generalisations do not take us too far. Yet, the study of the relationship between religions in India today and also their way of reacting to the challenge of secularism is very fascinating. After a brief historical introduction designed to put the theme in perspective this essay will deal with some of the characteristics of Hindu resurgence today and more specifically with some of the major issues in the contemporary Hindu-Christian dialogue. 12.1.1

I

The modern period in the history of Indian renaissance extends roughly from Raja Ram Mohan Roy (1772-1833) to S. Radhakrishnan 12.1.2

(born 1888). It is not the purpose of this section to trace the historical development of Hindu religious resurgence, but to draw attention to some important personalities whose attitudes and ideas are relevant to the theme of this article. Ram Mohan Roy was concerned not just with the revival of Hinduism, but with the renaissance of the total life of India. He was the first who showed a critical understanding of the values of the East and of the West on the basis of considerable study. Those who criticise his religious thought as being too shallow tend to forget that in his time, on the basis of evidence available to him, he had both the sensitivity and the courage to draw the attention of his countrymen to the values of Christ's teaching. It is his unquestioned patriotism, his breadth of vision, his willingness to go to the original sources, his concern for social justice, his passion for freedom and his readiness to seek truth from whatever sources it might be revealed, that have justifiably earned him the title: the Father of Modern India.

Moreover, in the emerging confrontation between a weakened Hinduism and an aggressive Christianity, he was the first to give serious attention to the essential beliefs of Christianity, thereby opening a way for constructive dialogue based on sound learning rather than partisan propaganda. Whatever be one's judgement on his controversy with the Serampore missionaries one should not minimise the importance of his *approach* to the problem of the relation between Hinduism and Christianity. For instance, he was firmly convinced of the depth and value of the ethical teachings of Jesus Christ and their great relevance to the social needs of his time in India. With great courage and facing the danger of being misunderstood both by fanatic Hindus and orthodox Christians, he wrote the following words in his book *The Precepts of Jesus, the Guide to Peace and Happiness:*

I feel persuaded that by separating from other matters contained in the New Testament, the moral precepts found in that book, these will be more likely to produce the desirable effect of improving the hearts and minds of men of different persuasions and degrees of understanding. . . This simple code of religion and morality is so admirably calculated to elevate men's ideas to high and liberal notions of God. . .and is also so well fitted to regulate the conduct of the human race. . .that I cannot but hope the best effects from its promulgation in the present form.[1]

This tendency to separate the ethical teachings of Jesus from the dogmas about his person continues in India even to this day and constitutes one of the major issues between the Hindus and the Christians. However, the *Brahma Samāj* founded by Ram Mohan Roy is a spent force in India today without any power to inspire or to lead. This is because an artificial synthesis, which attempts to put together selected values from different religions, fails to develop because of its own inner tensions. This is the lesson which the *Brahma Samāj* holds for us at present. Farquhar is right in pointing out that 'Ram Mohan and Keshab were wrong in thinking that a new, vigorous, modern religion could be created merely by placing a few of the leading ideas of Christianity alongside a few of the leading ideas of Hinduism and allowing the two to come together on equal terms.'[2] In the contemporary dialogue between religions, it is essential to avoid this danger. Openness to other religions, without commitment to one's own faith, leads only to a half-way house, the windows of which might look attractive from a distance but the foundation of which would be gravely unstable.

Unlike the *Brahma Samāj* the Ramakrishna Movement refused *to* 12.1.3 *make any* kind of compromise with Christianity. This movement draws its spiritual inspiration from Sri Ramakrishna (1836-1886) and its organisational genius from Swami Vivekananda (1863-1902). Both by circumstance and by inclination Sri Ramakrishna had little to do with Western culture or Christianity. In spite of Swami Vivekananda's acquaintance with the New Testament and his first-hand experience of Western Christianity he never seriously encountered the Jesus Christ of the New Testament. There are many references to Jesus Christ and his teachings in the writings of Swami Vivekananda, but his is always a 'Hinduised version' of Christ and he never made a compromise with Christianity at any point. Therefore, although one can see a certain friendliness towards Jesus Christ and a seeming tolerance of other religions, the posture of this movement is one of complete confidence in the self-sufficiency of Hinduism. Sri Ramakrishna is rightly regarded as the intitiator of the Hindu renaissance, giving a sense of universality to the Hindu message. 'This new dispensation of the age is the source of great good to the whole world, especially to India; and the inspirer of this dispensation, Sri Bhagavan Ramakrishna, is the reformed and remodelled manifestation of all the past great epoch-makers in religion. O man, have faith in this and lay it to heart.'[3]

In the writings of Swami Vivekananda there are several eloquent 12.1.4

passages about Jesus Christ and his teachings. To give just one example, in a lecture entitled, 'Christ, the Messenger', he declared, 'If I, as an Oriental, have to worship Jesus of Nazareth, there is only one way left to me, that is to worship him as God and nothing else.'[4] But one should not be misled by such statements as these. The mood of Swami Vivekananda is that of one who has already attained fulfilment. The social dimension, which Ram Mohan Roy did not find in Hinduism and for which he approached Christianity as a seeker, is found by Swami Vivekananda within Hinduism itself, particularly in the Vedanta rightly interpreted and properly understood... Therefore the 'mission' of Hinduism, and the purpose for which it enters into a dialogue with men of other faiths, is not so much to 'convert' others, but to help others to *become* what they should be. It is to help the Christian to become a better Christian, the Muslim to become a better Muslim or, for that matter, the Hindu to become a better Hindu, since the sole purpose of religious discipline is to realise one's own innate divinity. Under these circumstances it becomes fairly clear that the mood of the Ramakrishnan movement is more of conversation rather than of dialogue.

12.1.5   In the life of Mahatma Gandhi (1869-1948) the relationship between the different religions in India enters a new phase of friendliness without, however, any serious theological debate. He strongly emphasised the social involvement of religion and pointed out that the reformation of Hindu society depends, to a great extent, on the reinterpretation of some of its classical doctrines. Moreover, his attitude of friendliness towards other religions, notably towards Islam and Christianity, was deliberately designed to bring the different communities together. It was inspired more by a deeply felt political need than by any serious consideration of fundamental beliefs. Also, the fact that different religions, Hinduism, Buddhism, Jainism and Christianity, could claim to have made a contribution to his doctrine of non-violence, provided at least a possible theme for discussion and practical application. Gandhiji did enter into dialogue with the many Christian friends he came into contact with and, undoubtedly, he was influenced by the ethical teachings of Jesus Christ. But it would be a mistake to forget that Gandhiji was primarily a Hindu, as confident of the self-sufficiency of Hinduism as was Swami Vivekananda. A modern scholar, in his assessment of Gandhism, makes the following observation about Gandhiji's religion:

The basic facts, with all respect to Mahatma Gandhi, should be squarely faced. In many respects, Gandhiji was a rather conservative Hindu. In his philosophy and methods, in his daily rituals and routine, in prayer and preachings, in his attempts to rouse the masses through Hindu religious songs like the *Ramdhun,* in his constant reference to Ram Raj as the ideal form of state and society that was expected to emerge after *swaraj,* in his life-long struggle for the cause of untouchables, which he regarded more as a cause of Hinduism than a secular and humanitarian cause, in his practically life-long support of the caste system and his opposition to cow slaughter, and in many other respects he was a thoroughly orthodox Hindu and proudly declared himself to be so.[5]

To the question, 'What is your religion?' Gandhiji replied, 'My religion is Hinduism, which for me is the religion of humanity and includes the best of all religions known to me.'[6] On this basis, it was obviously not possible for the Muslims to accept him as a supranational leader, standing above loyalties to particular religious faiths. The assumption that the *communal* problem was a *religious* problem, and that friendliness between religions would solve it, was a gross over-simplification, for there were many other deep-rooted historical and political factors which make a Hindu-Muslim dialogue very difficult even to this day. It is being increasingly recognised that the approach to solve this problem in a multi-religious society should be essentially a secular one, for it is only in the context of 'an open secularism' which is impartial in its attitude towards all religions, that a meaningful dialogue between religions can take place.

In the writings of Sarvepalli Radhakrishnan, the philosopher-president of India, there is not only a greater philosophical justification of the Hindu resurgence, but also a more serious questioning of the theological assumptions of other religions, particularly those of Christianity.[7] Much more than any one previously mentioned, Radhakrishnan has challenged some of the basic beliefs of the Christian faith. His acquaintance with the Christian teachers in the Christian colleges he studied disturbed his faith in traditional Hinduism and led him to a re-examination of the fundamentals of his own faith, as well as to a defence of those beliefs against Christian criticisms. Of his Christian teachers he wrote:

12.1.6

My teachers in Christian missionary institutions. . .restored for me the primordial situation in which all philosophy is born. They were teachers of philosophy, commentators, interpreters, apologists for the Christian way of life and thought, but were not in the strict sense of the term, seekers after truth.[8]

This description of his missionary teachers as 'apologists', and not 'seekers after truth', is not easy to understand, for if this attitude is taken towards those who are committed to a particular faith, then, obviously, no fruitful dialogue is possible. Moreover, although these teachers were admittedly committed to the Christian way of life, on that account it is difficult to argue that they did not possess 'the discipline of mind' and 'a rigorously logical manner', which, according to Radhakrishnan, are 'the essential means for the discovery of truth'. But perhaps one should also note that there is a difference in the understanding of Truth here. To Radhakrishnan, as a Hindu, Truth *(Sat)*, in this context, is primarily a state of being rather than one of cognition. Experiencing the Truth is therefore more important than knowing the Truth, whereas in the Christian understanding, obedience to the Truth is more fundamental than either knowing it or experiencing it. Radhakrishnan also rejects consistently the Christian claim for the 'uniqueness' and 'finality' of God's incarnation in Jesus Christ. In spite of all this, however, Radhakrishnan has pleaded not only for a meeting between religions, but also for a fellowship of faiths. He is a strong supporter of the International Union for the Study of the Great Religions which has for its objective 'a revised religious ideal for man as a social being in this life'.

12.1.7   Reference has been made to some of these selected Hindu thinkers not only because they have contributed to the resurgence of Hinduism but also because in their thinking, certain issues emerge which should enter into any serious dialogue between religions today. Perhaps one of the most important factors which contributes to this mood of dialogue is the growing awareness that the East and the West are coming together in the face of common problems confronting mankind today. Radhakrishnan in his book *East and West* stresses this point when he writes:

Today both of them (the East and the West) are tackling the same problem, the reconciliation of the values of mind with those of spirit. The tension between the two constitutes the meaning and purpose of history. Whether in the East or in the West, we have unresolved contradictions and attempts to solve them, to learn from each other and adapt the inheritance of the past to new and ever-changing conditions and reshape it into a new and living pattern.[9]

Writing in the same strain, a Hindu professor, at the well-known Banaras Hindu University, calls for a universal outlook on the part of the scholars in the East and in the West giving up the sense of superiority and separation. He remarks:

The problem before us today is not how best to promote the sense of superiority and un-Christian pride among people belonging to either East or West, it is rather how to make them understand better both themselves and others, and to realise the possibilities of enlightenment and happiness inherent in the new unified world created by science and technology.[10]

This is the larger context in which the dialogue between religions has to take place today. It is the situation in which the resurgent religions have to take into account both the social needs of the day as well as the new outlook on life created by science and technology.

II

The coexistence of faith in religions and what K.M. Panikkar calls 'hope in secular promise' is a significant feature of contemporary Indian life. The dialogue between religions is taking place in a cultural climate in which secularism is an influential force. To ignore this would be to lose a sense of perspective, and to forget an important element which challenges all traditional religions as their adherents face modern problems. To avoid confusion, one should make a distinction between the character of the Republic of India as *a secular State* and secularism as *a philosophy of life* born out of confidence in man's achievements. The former is a political attitude, an attitude not necessarily of indifference or hostility towards religions, but one of neutrality or impartiality where religions are concerned. In a multi-religious society as that of India this attitude on the part of the State is reasonable and healthy. But secularism, as a philosophy of life, based on man's trust in reason and confidence in the achievements of science, is a challenge to religions everywhere. There is a *threefold* demand in this challenge: *first,* secularism calls

12.1.8

upon the traditional religions, either by its cold indifference or by its militant criticism, to demonstrate 'the secular meaning' of their faiths today; *second,* it draws pointed attention to the possibilities of social reconstruction without recourse to religious resources; and *third,* it builds up 'a philosophy of action' based on human freedom and self-sufficiency which throws out of gear the old religious patterns based on 'faith and works'.

12.1.9   Interest in secular life, or concern with worldly affairs, is, of course, not new in the history of India. The *Chārvaka,* or the *Lokāyata,* or the materialistic school, has systematised this outlook into a philosophy from very early times. In recent years many important leaders have called upon people to lift the nation out of 'a decayed spiritualism' and to recover 'the germ of materialism' essential to the well-being of the nation. No less a man than India's late Prime Minister, Jawaharlal Nehru, represented this point of view when he wrote:

> We have to get rid of that narrowing religious outlook, that obsession with the supernatural and metaphysical speculations, that loosening of the mind's discipline in religious ceremonial and mystical emotionalism, which come in the way of our understanding ourselves and the world. We have to come to grips with the present, this life, this world, this nature which surrounds us in its infinite variety...India must therefore lessen her religiosity and turn to science.[11]

This demand not to neglect worldly affairs, and to recognise that material things *do* contribute to human well-being, is made not only because of a dissatisfaction with sterile religious dogmas but also because many people feel that social reconstruction is possible without religious reformation... The thesis that Hindu social institutions had nothing to do with the Hindu religious beliefs is difficult to maintain. But the real issue here is the *relevance* of religious values, not just for social *stability,* but also for social *change.* This should lead to a reconsideration of the relationship between *ātma* and *deha,* between the *pāramārthika* and the *vyāvahārika,* between what is *satya* and what appears to be *mithya.* At a time when rapid social and economic change is called for, this becomes an important issue not only for Hinduism but also for the other religions.

12.1.10   Those whose outlook on life is primarily secular and those who have an abiding trust in religion are both concerned with economic and social justice. Therefore they can participate in all programmes of national reconstruction. From the time of Ram Mohan Roy, all revival movements have in one way or another concerned themselves with social reformation. The contribution of the Christian missions in this area is not always acknowledged, but it cannot be denied that along with establishing several social service projects in India, the Christian missions were at least one factor in making the Hindu social conscience more sensitive to the social evils of the day. The important question here is whether it is possible to bring about rapid social change within Hindu society without, at the same time, drastically reinterpreting the underlying Hindu religious ideals. The secular answer to this question would be in the affirmative. They would point out that social change need not wait for religious reformation. As an example it is pointed out that the Indian Parliament passed the law against untouchability, without in the slightest degree bothering about religious beliefs. However, while it is possible to recognise the secular nature of Hindu social structure, to miss the underlying connection between religious beliefs and social institutions, for example *karma* and caste, would be to oversimplify a highly complex matter. Moreover, one should not overlook the fact that a great deal of preparatory work had been done by many resurgent movements and by leaders like Mahatma Gandhi before the law against untouchability could even be introduced in the Parliament of India.

Closely connected with the question of religion and social change is an equally important question, *viz.,* the meaning of human *action,* its method, its motivation and its goals. The tension between an ascetic withdrawal from life and an active participation in its duties, between *Yājnavalkya* and *Chānakya,* has always persisted in the course of Indian history. Today when the demand of the hour is for urgent and responsible action for the sake of nation-building, this question becomes exceedingly important. Both secular nationalism and religious nationalism have strongly emphasised a philosophy of activism. Thus Subhas Chandra Bose (1897-1947), the fiery nationalist leader, firmly held that it was wrong to think of peaceful contemplation as the noblest ideal when there was work to be done. 'Don't bark like dogs, but fight like lions', became the slogan of the day. Bose strongly criticised Aurobindo and wrote that 'spiritual progress under the present conditions is possible only by ceaseless and unselfish action, that the best way to conquer nature is to fight her, and that it is weakness to seek refuge in contemplation when we are hemmed in on all sides by dangers and difficulties.'[12] Religious nationalism has attempted to gain support for its philosophy of activism mainly through the reinterpretation of the *Bhagavadgītā* so that, as is well known, during the period of nationalism, it emerged as 'a handbook of action', providing a new ethical, social and political message to meet the needs of the day. It is interesting to note that during the period of Chinese aggression (1962) there was an obvious shift in the selection of religious broadcasts over the All India Radio. There were far more selections from the Bhagavadgītā, where Krishna exhorts Arjuna to give up sloth and fight, than from either the Quran or from the Sermon on the Mount.

12.1.11   There are *three* major points in the teaching of the *Gītā* which are constantly being reinterpreted to provide the basis for a philosophy of action. These are *(a)* the ideal of the *sthitiprajna,* or *gunātīta,* the person of calm detachment, of perfect poise, whose mind is 'like a flame that burns steadily in a place protected by the wind', *(b)* the doctrine of *nishkāma karma,* the call to act without personal involvement in or desire for the fruits of one's actions, and *(c)* the principle of *lokasangraha,* the welfare of the whole world, accepted as the goal towards which all activity should be directed. There is no need to elaborate these well-known points except to say that these constitute the ideals of Hindu activism which is at work even to this day. Showing how these contribute to the foundations of the new India that is slowly emerging, Panikkar makes the following observation:

> The *Gītā* has thus become the scripture of the new age, the main foundation on which its ethical, its social and even its political action depends. . . It is the inspiration and guide, and no one can understand the developments which are taking place in India who has no appreciation of this fundamental fact.[13]

12.1.12 But in contemporary India there seems to be a new phase in the philosophy of activism which is bold enough to question the relevance of these time-honoured ideals. India today is desperately seeking tangible results of work. People are definitely concerned with 'the fruits' of action. They want the National Plans to 'deliver the goods' here and now, not in some distant future. To taste the fruits of one's action is as important as to smell the sweat of one's brow. Therefore the ideal of *nishkāma karma* is being questioned. At least two points of criticism are being made. *First,* that this is a highly *indvidualistic* ethic which does not take into sufficient account the social context of personal decisions and their social consequences. Therefore, it is claimed, that such an ideal is unsuitable to a fast changing and revolutionary context as the present one in India. *Second,* its disinterest in the fruits of one's action *(phalāsa),* removes the very need for moral and responsible action. To say that Krishna was involved only in the battle, but not in the fruits of victory, *viz.,* putting *Yudhishtira* on the throne and, to establish *dharma,* is to ignore that Krishna was a very practical man. Unless there is a serious commitment to achieve the goals desired, and unless there is a definite interest in the fruits of one's action, there can be no progress at all. The Chinese threat at the border, the Indo-Pakistani conflict, the longing for national unity, the desperate need for economic progress, a stable society which is resilient enough to meet rapid change − all these call for a 'goal-oriented', and not a 'self-oriented', attitude. What is necessary today in India is definite *commitment* to purposes and goals, both personal and social. Therefore, calling for an alternative interpretation of this doctrine D.C. Mathur writes:

> This tension between the need for being goal-oriented and for effective moral and social action to achieve a desirable social end on the one hand, and the need for an *ultimate concern* for the serene Ātman on the other, has characterised Indian culture ever since. These have never been fully reconciled. In actual practice for the vast mass of people it has meant either a lip service to the transcendental self and a consequent withdrawal from the field of social and moral action, or an opportunistic pursuit of selfish individual goals. In both cases it has been detrimental to effective social change for the better, and to some extent it accounts for the static character of Indian society.[14]

Such a criticism, coming from Hindus themselves, raises the question whether it is a call for reinterpretation of old doctrines or whether it is a questioning of the adequacy of the Hindu resources to undergird the demand for responsible action today. In any case, the question about the relationship between ultimate concern and immediate needs, between the transcendental self and the moral personality, leads to important issues which cannot be ignored. The relation between the ultimate and the immediate, leads to the question of the *avataras* and the Incarnation of God in Christ. The question of personal and social fulfilment involves the relevance of the Church. And, along with these, no discussion about the meaning of human action can ignore the interpretation of history. To these specific issues in the Hindu Christian dialogue, *viz., (a)* the significance of the *Incarnation, (b)* the relevance of the *Church* and *(c)* the meaning of *history*, we now turn in the rest of this article.

12.1.13   The centrality of Jesus Christ to authentic Christian life cannot be denied. Many Hindu thinkers however, while recognising this, make an attempt to separate Jesus Christ from what Mahatma Gandhi called 'beef and beer bottle' Christianity. From Ram Mohan Roy to Radhakrishnan, Hindus have shown a great reluctance to take the dogmas about his person seriously while acknowledging the usefulness of his ethical teachings. In the Hinduised version of Jesus Christ, his self-less love, his moral teachings and what they describe as 'the Christ-principle', continue to have a valid place. To the Christian of course, this is not enough because it disrupts the totality of the Christian faith. The real issue here at the present time is not so much about the divinity or humanity of Christ as such; it is how, in the structure of our historical existence, our religious beliefs help us to understand the proper relation between the ultimate and the immediate. It is from this point of view that one should look at the *avatāras* of Hinduism on the one hand, and the Incarnation on the other.

12.1.14   The Hindu does not regard as legitimate or fundamental the Biblical link between faith and history. He does not believe that eternal truths can be tied down to temporal pegs. *Kāla* or Time is a process in which all creation is involved and in which God is continuously manifesting himself. That is why to the Hindu the *avatāras* are not dated in history. There can be no particular moments as the *'kairos'* or the *'eschaton'*. 'The whole religious quest of the Hindu is based on the conviction that at any period in *samsāra* he can seek and find the Infinite. In this sense no moment of time is qualitatively different from any other moment. This is why he cannot accept a religion built upon the rock of historicity'[15] The 'Christ-principle' or the 'Christ-within' is simply a Hinduised description of the divinity in man. According to the Hindu, once ignorance is removed, this potential divinity can become actual. Elaborating this point Radhakrishnan writes:

To an educated Hindu, Jesus is the supreme illustration of the growth from human origins to divine destiny. As a mystic who believes in the inner light, Jesus ignores ritual. . . He is the great hero who exemplifies the noblest characteristics of manhood, the revealer of the profoundest depths within ourselves, one who brings home to us the ideal of human perfection by embodying it visibly in himself. . . For me the person of Jesus Christ is a historical fact. Christ is not a datum of history, but a judgement of history. Jesus's insight is expressive of a timeless spiritual fact; but what the theologians say of it are after-thoughts, interpretations of the fact, *viz.*, the life and death of Jesus.[16]

Two points have to be made here by way of criticism. *First,* a 12.1.15 purely *individualistic* interpretation of the life and work of Jesus Christ fails to do justice to the social dimensions of the Gospel as seen in the New Testament and subsequent Church history. One cannot ignore the relevance of such ideas as 'the people of God' in the Old Testament and 'new Israel' in the New. To describe Jesus Christ as 'a mystic' or 'a hero' or 'an example' or 'a *jivanmukta*' or 'a *yogi*' is to put him into a totally different context. *Second,* one must see that the issue is not one of humanity or divinity. It is not of particular importance to say whether the Incarnation or the *avatāra* is humanity raised to the level of divinity, or divinity brought down to the level of humanity. Such formulations seem to be outdated today. More important is it to see how in the actuality of history the immediate and the ultimate are brought together. The issue is the one between 'the Christ principle' and 'the Christ event'. It is the latter that has social and historic consequences. The renewal of man and the remaking of society are historic possibilities in Jesus Christ. Stephen Neill remarks:

The purpose of this life of freedom was to restore to all men the possibility of true human life as from the beginning it was intended to be. Life as we know it is full of contradictions, and contradictions lead to frustration and weakness. Here is life without inner contradiction and therefore peerless in its strength.[17]

The second major issue in the Hindu-Christian dialogue is the 12.1.16 relevance of the Church. Unlike Buddhism with its social expression of the *Sangha,* and Islam with its strong emphasis on the Brotherhood, Hinduism has been traditionally individualistic. The caste is a

given community in which the place of the individual is determined
not by choice but by birth. It is admitted by certain Hindu scholars
that the importation of the social conscience into Hinduism is of
recent origin. The Hindu has consistently rejected the Christian
emphasis on the Church being an integral part of the Gospel. For
one thing, he regards the Church as a communal organisation which
is Western in origin and pattern. To belong to it would be a cultural
betrayal. For another, he feels that any kind of organisation stifles
the free spirit of the individual, for religion is primarily a personal
matter to be pursued alone in quietness, devotion and the spirit of
renunciation. *Moksha* to the Hindu is an individual attainment.
Murti remarks that there is 'something inherently secular and
unspiritual in any organisation. It tends to create vested interests and
to breed corruption... What we need is the realisation of the
spiritual, which is the bedrock of all our endeavour.'[18]

Today one can see that there is everywhere in India an emphasis
on the social dimension of national life. Resurgent religions are
everywhere concerned with social service and social change. Not
only in the matter of the reinterpretation of caste based on *guna*
rather than *jāti* but also in its involvement in all kinds of welfare
schemes, resurgent Hinduism is vigorous in its social activities.
Therefore the question to what extent would an *individualistic*
religion undergird the *social* dimension of contemporary life is
bound to arise. The Christian understanding of the Church and its
place in history has perhaps something to contribute to the Hindu-
Christian dialogue today. True, one has to admit the weaknesses of
the Church as a human organisation in history, but this could be a
cause more for Christian humility than for Hindu rejection. The
outreach of the Church in various kinds of service projects, as
expressions of Christian love, and the tremendous growth of the
ecumenical movement as an expression of the oneness of the Church
have not been without influence on the Hindu mind. To a religion as
individualistic as Hinduism, but which is becoming increasingly
conscious of its social responsibilities, the life and witness of the
Christian Church, both in its particularity and its universality,
cannot be wholly without significance.

12.1.17   The third important issue is the respective Hindu and Christian
attitudes towards history. This is perhaps the most crucial one
because it touches the two previous ones we have discussed briefly.
The consciousness of history is a quest for meaning, an attempt to
make sense of the happenings in the life of a nation. It is a search for

individual fulfilment and social purpose not in an other-worldly, transcendental context, but within the framework of history. Those who take an affirmative attitude towards history would place greater emphasis on change and progress than on tradition and stability.

It is now generally recognised that classical Hindu thought did not pay sufficient attention to the historical dimension of man's life in its quest for meaning beyond history.[19] True, there did exist an 'activist' social and political tradition in India. Chanakya (Kautilya), the Brahmin Counsellor of king Chandragupta, did undoubtedly take an active part in politics and did succeed remarkably in achieving his objective. But having succeeded in gaining this purpose, he goes into the forest in his pursuit of *moksha*. Political participation was just a temporary interruption in his long-term pursuit of *moksha*, which was to be sought, not in the dust and heat of worldly life, but in the quiet loneliness of the forest. In the Indian philosophic tradition individuality was something to be transcended. Hindu thought has always emphasised that aspect of human freedom which enables him to rise above the flux of time. Classical Hindu tradition has always looked inward to the depths of man's consciousness in its quest for the nature and destiny of man. Deeds were considered as links that bind man to the wheel of *samsāra*. The requirement for enlightenment was not involvement, but detachment. It has been rightly observed therefore that 'to see the world in its historical dimension was not a basic concern of a civilisation more attuned to the values of a transcendent immateriality'.[20]

Today it is undoubtedly true that there is a distinctive emphasis on history in India. India is no longer a spectator of history, but an active participant in its drama. There is a shift of emphasis from contemplation to action, from detachment to involvement. The anticipations of change take on the characteristics of historical fulfilment. The Hebrew-Christian understanding of history has made an impact on Indian thought through India's contact with the Western civilization and culture. The characteristics of a distinctive awareness of history: *(a)* a messianic perspective, *(b)* the expectation of historical progress and *(c)* an emphasis on individual commitment and activism in achieving goals — these are to be discerned in various degrees in the Indian life today. This means sometimes a radical reinterpretation of some of the classical doctrines. We have already pointed out that the ideal of *nishkāma karma* is being questioned

12.1.18

and alternative interpretations are sought. *Karma* is being reinterpreted so as to give greater attention to individual freedom and responsibility. Caste is undergoing radical social change. Serious attempts are being made to remove the impression that *māyā* means 'illusion' to show that all that it does mean is that the world has 'a dependent reality'. All these are symptoms of a more affirmative view of history.

12.1.19   This then is an area where one should expect greater possibilities of a creative dialogue between the Hindu and the Christian. An awareness of time as being more an opportunity than a limitation, an interest in the past which is future oriented, a longing for individual fulfilment along with social progress, and a search for the transcendent within the structure of historic events — these are some of the points which must be noted carefully. Already there are several contemporary writers who try to bring new insights into their thinking on history. Panikkar's treatment of 'the determining periods' in the history of India is strikingly reminiscent of the biblical understanding of the *'kairos'*[21]. Devasenapati, a *Saiva Siddhanta* scholar at the university of Madras, in his Miller lectures has strongly emphasised the reality of time and has attempted to combine the cyclical with the progressive view of history.[22] Sankaranarayan points out that unless metaphysical values are transformed into social virtues they are of little use in the contemporary situation. An acknowledgement of the eternal values, *satyam, sivam* and *sundaram,* is of little use unless there is the possibility of their actualisation in history. Therefore decisions and deeds are important. 'The sense of value and the urge to act go together. Conduct springs from a consciousness of value and is concerned with its conservation and increase. So understood, values constitute the urge for human activity'[23]. All these are highly significant efforts on the part of contemporary Hindu thinkers to recognise the framework of history as being important for personal and social fulfilment. To the sensitive Christian who is humble enough to enter into a dialogue with his Hindu brethren and who, at the same time, is strong enough to be rooted in the foundations of his own faith, there are many opportunities both to learn from the dialogue and to contribute to its creative fruits.

Notes

1. *The Precepts of Jesus, the Guide to Peace and Happiness,* pp xxi-xxiv; *English Works,* pp.483-85; Quoted in *The Sources of Indian Tradition,*

William Theodore de Bary, ed. New York: Columbia University Press 1960, p.577.
2. J.N. Farquhar, 'Brahmaism', *Encyclopaedia of Religion and Ethics,* Vol.II p.823.
3. *The Gospel of Sri Ramakrishna,* Tr. Swami Nikhilananda, Madras; Sri Ramakrishna Math 1957, p.305.
4. *The Complete Works of Swami Vivekananda,* Almora; Advaita Ashram, Vol.IV, 1947, p.143.
5. J. Bandhopadhyaya, 'An Assessment of Gandhism', *Quest,* No.37, Bombay April/June 1963, p.17.
6. *Contemporary Indian Philosophy,* S. Radhakrishnan and J.A. Muirhead, eds., London: Allen and Unwin 1936, p.21.
7. *See* S.J. Samartha, *Introduction to Radhakrishnan,* New York: Association Press 1964, where some of the themes are discussed at greater length.
8. P.A. Schilpp, ed., *The Philosophy of Sarvepalll Radhakrishnan,* The Library of Living Philosophers, La Salle, Illinois: The Open Court Publishing Company 1952, p.9.
9. S. Radhakrishnan, *East and West,* New York: Harper and Brothers 1956, p.13.
10. N.K. Devaraja, 'India and Western Scholars', *Quest,* Bombay October/December 1964, p.43.
11. Jawaharlal Nehru, *The Discovery of India,* Anchor Books edition, New York: Doubleday and Co. 1960, p.393.
12. From *Netaji Speaks to the Nation,* pp.44-7 quoted in W.T. de Bary, op. cit., pp.889-90.
13. K.M. Panikkar, *The Foundations of New India,* London: Allen and Unwin 1963, p.45.
14. D.C. Mathur, 'Doctrine of Nishkāma Karma: An Alternative Interpretation', *Quest,* Bombay, July/September 1964, p.25.
15. N. Devadas, 'The Christ of the Ramakrishna Movement', *Religion and Society,* Vol.XI No.3, September 1964, p.16.
16. P.A. Schilpp, op. cit., p.807.
17. Stephen Neill, *Christian Faith and Other Faiths,* London;Oxford University Press 1961, p.11.
18. Quoted by Stephen Neill, op. cit., p.85.
19. *See* S.J. Samartha, *The Hindu View of History, Classical and Modern,* Bangalore: The Christian Institute for the Study of Religion and Society, 1952.
20. John T. Marcus, 'History and the Indian World View', in Baidya Nath Varma, ed. *Contemporary India,* New York: Asia Publishing House 1964, p.11.
21. K.M. Panikkar, *The Determining Periods of India's History,* Bombay: Bharatiya Vidya Bhavan, 1962.
22. V.A. Devasenapati, 'Towards Conquest of Time', Miller Lectures, *Madras University Journal,* Vol.XXXIV No.1, 1962.
23. P. Sankaranarayanan, *Values in History,* Bombay; Bharatiya Vidya Bhavan, 1962.

Source:
This chapter was originally published in German in the book *Die Gefaehrdung Der Religionen* edited by Rolf Italiander and published by J.G. Oncken Verlag, Kassel, West Germany, 1966. It is here reproduced from the English translation in the volume *Inter-Religious Dialogue,* edited by Herbert Jai Singh and published by the Christian Institute for the Study of Religion and Society, Bangalore, India 1967, pp.146-9.

12.2   A HINDU-CHRISTIAN DIALOGUE ON TRUTH

Klaus K. Klostermaier

Preliminary Note

12.2.1   This paper was originally read at a symposium on 'Exclusive Truth Claims' organised by Carleton University. Asked for a contribution on the theme 'Hindu-Christian Dialogue: The Encounter of Two Absolute Truth Claims', I thought it would add a certain dimension to the reflections if the main argument was presented in the form of a dialogue. Not only did I hope to inject some more liveliness into the presentation thereby but it seemed to me appropriate to develop the theme 'truth' within the dialectics of a dialogue, convinced that Truth can be found only in the dynamic interpersonal process of searching for it. The dialogue, as it appears in this paper, is fictional. Having had, however, ample opportunity to engage in real dialogue with Hindus, I trust that it reflects something of the actuality of Hindu-Christian dialogue. I was highly gratified, therefore, to receive a positive response to my paper from as great a Hindu authority as Prof. T.R.V. Murti (Benares Hindu University) who wrote in a letter to me:

> I thoroughly enjoyed reading your article 'A Hindu-Christian Dialogue on Truth'. I am greatly impressed by your fairness and insight into the Hindu point of view. The Hindu would agree with the conclusion towards which you tend, namely that each tradition is a version or a formulation of the ultimate absolute truth which however is really transcendent and ineffable. Each tradition embodies a valuable insight and enables man to reach the highest truth.

And, thoughtfully, he added: 'I wonder whether the orthodox Christian theologian would be prepared to accept this.'

12.2.2   The idea behind this paper had certainly not been to lay to rest, once and forever, the problem of 'absolute truth' but to refocus attention upon this central 'theoretical' issue which all too often is sacrificed to pragmatic considerations. (It is worth noting that contemporary philosophy too, especially in the context of metascience, is returning to this question, after yesterday's philosophy — linguistic analysis — had thought it to be a pseudo-problem not worthwhile wasting one's time on.) Neither the Christian nor the Hindu representative in this dialogue can be identified with certain 'classical' positions within their own traditions, though they reflect, of course, certain aspects of these traditions more than others. The aim of the fictional dialogue described here (as of all true dialogue) is to establish a basis upon which a meaningful discussion can develop. If the two partners were convinced that each of them had *the* truth in their mutually contradictory formulae of truth, a dialogue would be impossible. If the two partners would agree beforehand that nobody really had *the* truth, a dialogue on truth would be redundant.

Despite the fictional character of the two dialogue-partners, I 12.2.3 attach some model value to them: Hindu-Christian dialogue in our time is not merely a restatement of 'pure classical' positions but reflects many influences that have a bearing on the problem involved. Thus the Hindus and the Christians who have participated at some length and depth in the ongoing Hindu-Christian dialogue of today will be unable to identify completely with those Hindus or those Christians who have not been exposed to these challenges. That may be hard to take for the majority of Hindus and Christians — who, after all, have never been engaged in dialogue — but it remains true nevertheless.

John Dunne suggests in 'The Way of All the Earth' that 'passing over and coming back is the spiritual adventure of our time.' Real encounter, however, is not a passing over and coming back: it is a deeply challenging and profoundly changing event which makes it impossible to consider as 'home' the place from where one began one's journey. Reading literature on Eastern religions may prepare one to some extent for the real encounter; in itself it is not the encounter. Real encounters are always surprising (for both partners!) and reflections on them usually reveal how painfully inadequate our present theological terminology is to describe what has happened.

Someone who has met in depth with someone coming from a different tradition is no longer able to draw the same superficial dividing line between traditions which is drawn on the 'official' level. The managers of both Hindu and Christian organisations are rightly afraid that a 'dialogue' in depth would erode their exclusivist functionary positions. But those Hindus and Christians whose concern is Truth will find growth and liberation in the encounter.

Dialogue is no enemy of truth, and truth need not be afraid of honest dialogue. There is a particularly relevant conclusion to be drawn in the context of ecumenism. Both Hinduism and Christianity are split into countless communities that consider their differences serious enough not to merge. In Hindu-Christian dialogues, however conscious the partners may be of their specific sectarian background, the attempt is constantly made to speak not only for the particular group to which one belongs but to try to find 'the' Christian or 'the' Hindu position. Of course, outsiders will notice the limited success of those attempts, but the participants not only experience in those encounters the possibility of meaningful talk with partners from different traditions, but also they often find in a surprisingly vivid way the original 'unity of spirit' of their own multi-faceted traditions. Ecumenism can succeed only if it concentrates on the really essential and truly crucial issues. Ultimately also Christian unity is founded on 'Truth' seen not as a static formula but as a living, interpersonal communication.

Introduction

12.2.4   'What is Truth?' Pilate the politician asked when Christ stood before him, claiming to be witness to Truth.[1] The man who knew the backstage of imperial politics, he who had to compromise often enough with the powerful of the locality and of the day in order to keep his own position and to make his career, was virtually certain that there was no truth as such. For him it was a matter of political expediency to call one of two statements true and its opposite untrue. It all depends on one's standpoint. The worldly-wise person knows that humans and their words can be used and manipulated to serve one's ends, which one conveniently then calls truth.

'Only children and fools speak truth', the proverb says. One must be naive to assume that there is something like truth as such, to accept the idea that over and above the 'liberal's truth' and the 'conservative's truth' there is something like real truth. The ancient Greek Sophists, the 'clever people', took their pride in proving with equally convincing arguments two contradicting statements. It has remained ever since a sign of 'sophistication' to be sceptical as regards absolute truth claims, to be flexible enough in one's opinion to accommodate to whatever ideology reigns supreme.

In a certain sense the ancient philosophers who fought the Sophists and the believers of all ages who suffered the mockers are naive in their common conviction that it makes sense to ask the question 'What is Truth?' and to expect an answer to it that is more than one opinion beside other opinions. The philosophers' disagreements with each other over this issue are proverbial: there seem to be as many truths as philosophers. The believers' disagreements with each other are no less conspicuous: their conflicting claims and convictions as regards Truth have led to sometimes absurdly funny, sometimes horribly destructive, results.

Should we give up, then, the search for Truth and busy ourselves with more practical and practicable matters: measuring our world, classifying collected objects, analysing language, making money, playing the politicians' game, practising religion as if we believe in it, because we see others do so? Despite the worldly-wise and the pragmatists, despite the hypocrites and the cynics, despite the conflicts of the truth-claims of philosophers and preachers, in every generation there have been men and women who honestly and stubbornly asked the question, 'What is Truth?' determined not to rest until they had found it — a truth valid for all, an absolute truth concerning the meaning of their lives. It may be one of those perennial questions that have no answer. But human history simply cannot be understood without this question, whatever the answer might be. The question, 'What is Truth?' looms too large over the life of many an individual and over the history of humanity as such to be simply brushed aside as non-essential or nonsensical. For many people, East and West, it has been, and still is, the question.

The Encounter

Explicitly or implicitly the question of absolute Truth stands behind 12.2.5 every meaningful dialogue about philosophy and religion. It comes up persistently in the dialogues between Hindus and Christians, when both partners take each other seriously and try to share their insights without losing their own souls.

KRSNADĀS, a young Hindu scholar who wanted to familiarise himself with the contemporary self-understanding of Christianity, tried to find a book that could help him — comprehensive, not too technical, and not too simple. One of his Christian friends suggested a recent 'best-seller': *A New Catechism, Catholic Faith for Adults*, widely acclaimed for its courageous reinterpretation of Christian Faith.[2] He looked up the index for the word 'Truth'. Under the letter 'T' he found Taxes. . .and some other things, but not 'Truth'. Somewhat astonished, he asked his Christian friend, ANASTASIOS: 'Does this mean that Truth is no longer considered important in contemporary Christianity, whereas taxes are?'

ANASTASIOS, somewhat embarrassed, retorted: 'This book is not the source for *my* understanding of Christianity. Not everyone who calls oneself a Christian understands and lives Christianity — and not every book with the label 'Christian' reflects the meaning of Christian truth. I suggest we try in all honesty to find out for ourselves from the recognised sources of our religious tradition what truth means.'

KRSNADĀS agreed: 'We have simply to admit that the organisations and social phenomena going under certain brand-names and labels very often are untrue to the word and the spirit of those whom they consider their founders. Much that is practised as 'Hinduism' I, as a Hindu, would not accept, nor would I agree with many statements made by Swāmis and Gurus today who try to defend their own interests and ideologies by calling them *'sanātana dharma'*, eternal religion, or Hinduism. I have formed my own opinion by studying the sources of my tradition, following the best and the purest minds of India. Let us not discuss what this or that sect or party understands under truth but what we can sincerely accept for ourselves'.

12.2.6   ANASTASIOS was ready for that. 'I tried to understand what the New Testament says about "Truth". The most important statement, I think, is that in St. John's gospel where Jesus Christ says about himself: "I am the Truth. . ."[3] *That truth* is not a mere theory, or an opinion about something or nothing; it is a liberating power. "Know the Truth and the Truth will make you free",[4] we read in another place. Again, in the prologue to the Gospel according to John, I find a statement about Truth which helps me:[5] Truth is related to light *(phos)*, to life *(zoe)*, to the Word *(logos)* and to God *(theos)*. Truth in the Christian sense, I understand, is the Truth about God, the Truth about the ultimate meaning of my life, a Truth that is mediated through Christ.'

KRSNADĀS pointed out that the Hindu Scriptures, from which he drew his inspiration, were much older than the New Testament. 'Your Western scholars would admit that the principal Upanisads, those books upon which part of our most profound religious tradition is based, were composed around 600 BC, if not earlier. They gave witness to the Truth that our Rsis (sages) have found — an absolute Truth based on the experience of ultimate Reality. Our language itself helps us to understand the nature of truth: *satyam,* the word for truth, is related to *sat,* reality. Truth is Reality. The sages of India found the *satyasya satyam*,[6] the truly true, the really real. Truth as such! No one can transcend this Truth – no one can have any other Truth. It is not a Truth that is tied up with one single historical personality; it is a Truth that every human can realize if he or she takes the steps outlined in the Upanisads and the Yogasūtras.'

ANASTASIOS suggested that he, too, thought that 'Truth' in the Christian understanding did not begin only 1940 years ago. 'The New Testament is not isolated from the rest of the history of humanity. It links up with two important ancient traditions of humanity – the traditions of Israel and of Greece. "Truth" is a very important matter in the Hebrew Bible; it is strongly related to faith and trust in God. "Truth" as understood there is connection with peace, charity, and justice. "God is Truth" for the believer; all that is done and spoken by God is Truth. And because God is Truth a human being's duty is to live according to truth. The Ancient Greek philosophers had been searching for Truth many centuries before Christ. Their "Truth" has been acknowledged by Christianity too; many Christian thinkers have followed the lead of Greek philosophy in their interpretation of the nature of Truth.[7] Here, too, we find a very close relationship between "truth" and "reality". The most influential of the Greek seekers after Truth is Plato; for him Truth is the firm knowledge of reality, the divine substance *(ousia)* that is hidden behind, and partly revealed through, the passing phenomena of experience. Humanity, in its "normal state" is estranged from Truth, ignorant about Reality – it must undergo a "conversion", an inner change, an opening of the inner eye to be capable of knowing Truth. Our Christian understanding of Truth agrees with him here.'

KRSNADĀS was satisfied to see that his Christian partner was not suggesting that because he found Truth in Christ, truth was alien to those who lived outside the historical influence of Christianity. 'I found quite intriguing what you have mentioned, that humanity, in Plato's, and apparently also in your Christian, understanding is in untruth, not even capable of Truth as such. Our sages have diagnosed the situation of humanity as *avidyā*, untruth, illusion, ignorance regarding Truth and Reality which keeps a "normal" person in bondage, undergoing endless cycles of rebirths and redeaths. It is Truth that dispells the darkness of ignorance and liberates humanity at the same time. Our sages have developed *sādhanā*, methods of Truth-finding, of "eye-opening". They have found that Truth ultimately means to be one with Reality, to be Real. But to bridge over the gap that exists between the consciousness of a "normal" person and reality itself, it is necessary to undergo a training, involving not only a person's abstracting intelligence but the whole being. The Truth that liberates is not the objective truth of the uninvolved observer, but the Truth which Is. It requires and brings about, a radical change in one's life. Humanity clings to its "illusions" because it is motivated by selfish desires and passions, by fears and all kinds of negative reactions. A selfish person cannot reach Truth, nor can a person under the influence of passions or fear. The Truth which our sages mean is not more information about things — it is becoming and being real.'

12.2.7   ANASTASIOS took up the discussion at that point. 'I agree with your understanding of Truth as being one with Reality. When Christ speaks about "knowing God" he does not consider this knowledge to be on the same "objective" level as the knowledge of material things. He refers always to the oneness of the knower and the known, his own knowledge of the Father is not derived from logical inferences or objective information but is based upon his "being in the Father" and the "Father being in him (*einai en*) upon his "being one" *(en einai)* with the Father. The disciples know Christ only insofar as he is in them and they in him — because Christ is in the Father and the Father in Christ, the disciples share ultimate, absolute Truth, because they share ultimate, absolute reality.[8]

The condition of "absolute Truth", then, in our understanding is "to be in Christ" — that means to participate in the relationship between Christ and the Father, in his love. To "know God" is "to love God". Only the one who loves knows truly. I had been referring before to the continuity of Christian ideas regarding Truth with that of Ancient Israel and of Ancient Greek philosophy. Also in the Hebrew tradition *iadā* means a knowledge by participation, by "being one with". For Greek philosophy *gnosis* meant a kind of "seeing" — namely seeing that which is real — not the appearances, but the "ideas" and "images" of the Real. In order to see those realities one has to open the "eye of the soul". Reality, then, is known only insofar as it is both in and one with the "seer". Knowledge of Reality is the highest fulfilment of Being. Knowing Truth means to be assimilated to Truth. Plato, for instance, was not satisfied to formulate statements about philosophy and to teach them in a lecture to his students. He tried to "live philosophy"; he founded a community of seekers after truth, because he also knew that Truth must be practised and trained and requires that one do away with all that is untruth and unreal. Jesus Christ also did not suggest to his disciples that it was an easy matter to become one with him and the Father or that it was to be accomplished through some kind of magic. He trained them to "live truth", slowly to grow toward the Father, to become "more truthful" by training in "love" as he understood it'.

KRSNADĀS took up the catchword 'training' in truth. 'The 12.2.8 Bhagavadgita, quoting the Yogasutras,[9] mentions as the two instruments to find Truth *abhyāsa* and *vairāgya*, "training" and "renunciation". Truth is found in the dialectical interaction of positive endeavour and negative detachment. Both are needed to keep the seeker after Truth going forward. Truth is constant growth toward Reality. Truth is reality, and therefore it requires effort, realisation, creative endeavour; but Truth is not identical with any Reality that we can identify with anything else. The seeker after Truth has to leave behind the shelters and dharmaśālas, the formulae of philosophy and religion in which he or she has found truths, in order to find Truth. Our great Master Śaṅkara explicitly states that the seeker after Truth must already possess an instinct for truth, the faculty to discriminate between appearance and reality, and must possess the restlessness of the traveler who knows that there is still a long way to go and one cannot dwell long in one place. One must have *mumuksutram,* an intense yearning after ultimate freedom and reality. The positive passion for absolute Truth must be complemented by the readiness to give up relative truths. Those who want to be one with the Real must leave all things. On the other hand, the passionlessness of someone who has "renounced" would be nothing short of spiritual death, if it were not ensouled by the passion of Truth.'

ANASTASIOS felt reminded of a passage from the Gospel: 'First of all seek the Reign of God. . .'[10] 'Christ, too, demands this incessant effort of the search, combined with the readiness to give up, for the sake of the Reign of God and its justice. Only those who earnestly seek it can find it; only to those who knock at its doors, does it open itself. Here, too, Christianity links up with Greek philosophy. Plato said that it was *eros,* the "love for Truth', the most powerful motive for human action that made it possible to find Truth. Plato, however, speaks in this connection no longer of *aletheia,* "truth", but of *sophia,* "wisdom". He defines *sophia* as "the knowledge of that which eternally is".

'The content of "wisdom" is Being, the Ideas, especially the good *(agathon)* and the beautiful *(kalon).* Ultimately "widsom" is identical with God's self-understanding. "Philosophia", "love of wisdom" (not of "knowledge"!) is more than just human speculation — it is "something wonderful" and miraculous, the participation in Divine Wisdom achieved through *eros*.

'It is not wholly accidental that Paul also, when speaking about the Truth which he communicates, a truth which he doubtlessly claims to have, uses the words "wisdom of God" *(sophia tou theou)* which is speaks in "hidden words" *(en mysterois)* not accessible to the others who are lacking the inner living principle,[11] which he identifies in some other context as *agapē*, "love".[12] The most subtle intellect may have all the details of information about everything in the world; it does not possess "the Truth" if it does not possess "Wisdom", and it cannot have "Wisdom" without "love" that is ultimately identical with *pneuma,* the "spirit of Christ". Only those who have the *pneuma* are able to perceive Truth. And only insofar as they are really one with this Spirit — expressing it in words, deeds, thoughts — can they claim really to have Truth; otherwise it is an empty boast'.

12.2.9   KRSNADĀS wanted to refer to Mahātmā Gandhi, who had called his whole life 'an experiment with Truth'[13] and did not get tired of emphasising: Truth is God. Mahātmā Gandhi had said on one occasion: 'It is, because we have at the present moment everybody claiming the right of conscience without going through any discipline whatsoever that there is so much untruth being delivered to a bewildered world. All that I can in true humility present to you is that truth is not to be found by anybody who has not got an abundant sense of humility. Truth and love are the only things that count. The instruments for the quest of Truth are as simple as they are difficult. They may appear quite impossible to an arrogant person and quite possible to an innocent child. In the march towards Truth anger, selfishness, hatred, etc., naturally give way, for otherwise Truth would be impossible to obtain. A man who is swayed by passions may have good enough intentions, he may be truthful in word, but he will never find the Truth.'[14]

KRSNADĀS then continued in his own words: 'This Truth cannot come from a person who is wrapped up in beginningless ignorance: only Reality can beget something real, only Truth can dispel untruth. Truth cannot come from an untrue person. A human needs the spark of the divine, the "spirit" as you said, from outside. If you read our Scriptures, beginning with the Upanisads, you will notice their emphasis on the *guru paramparā,* the succession of

Spiritual Masters.[15] You must have the living contact with someone who has realised Truth; in other words, you must remain within the genuine tradition in which this Truth is alive. The medium of communication of this Truth is *sābda*, the Word, the "word of Scripture", which is identical with a form of *brahman* itself.'

ANASTASIOS tried to emphasize that 'Truth in the Christian understanding is a personal Truth. It has to do with the person of Jesus Christ. The "voice of Truth" is recognised by those who "belong to Truth" — they instinctively reject all others as untrue.[16] It is like an inborn "sensor" that reacts only to a certain "wave-length". If this "receiver" is missing, even the words cannot be understood as "communications of Truth". There are those who listen without perceiving.'[17]   12.2.10

KRSNADĀS pointed out that there was a Hindu school that spoke of the relationship between God and human, the Ultimate and the finite, as *bimba-pratibimba*, splendour and reflected splendour: the mirror of the soul reflects only the waves that correspond to its own frequency.

ANASTASIOS reflected: 'If a person can perceive Truth, if a person can reflect Reality, that must express itself in the actions and words of the "enlightened" one too. Do you agree? But I also feel very uneasy about the claim put up by Christian church authorities and Hindu acāryas alike that their tradition collectively and their personal utterances individually are "the Truth" — absolute and infallible truth. It is here in this area too, where we find those countless problems arising out of the conflict of absolute Truth claims especially regarding verbalised formulations of the "truths" of religion. The rather unedifying history of persecution of heretics, of people condemned, imprisoned, and killed because they disagreed with the formula through which the established religion identified itself makes it seem advisable not to give any importance to such statements at all. But on the other hand, I do see that one can violate truth by making wrong statements about reality or by not stating truth, however fragmentary it may be, in the face of evident untruth.'

KRSNĀDAS tried to answer ANASTASIOS by quoting a passage from A. Huxley's *Perennial Philosophy*, which, he thought, pinpointed the problem accurately: 'The overvaluation of words and formulae may be regarded as a special case of that overvaluation of the things of time, which is so fatally characteristic of historic Christianity... To suppose that people can be saved by studying and giving assent to formulae is like supposing that one can get to Timbuktu by poring over a map of Africa. Maps are symbols, and even the best of them are inaccurate and imperfect symbols. But to anyone who really wants to reach a given destination, a map is indispensably useful as indicating the direction in which the traveller should set out and the roads which he must take.'[18] 'To be honest', KRSNADĀS added, 'I must also include Hinduism among the sinners against the spirit; also in the Hindu religion the "fateful overvaluation of the things of time" has led many people to the belief that one need only know the right *mantra* and perform the right gesture at the right time to be saved and freed.'[19]

ANASTASIOS pondered: 'Is it not the constant temptation to consider oneself to have "arrived" and to dispense oneself from further search for Truth? The *metanoia,* the "conversion" required for the one who wants to reach Truth, is a continuing process rather than one single event in the life of an individual. Those who claim "absolute Truth" for certain formulae and symbols are people who are not really "in Truth", otherwise they could not mistake finite reality for Reality as such. But, can we say that everything that is relative is simply untrue? Do we not need "truth" in our daily lives, in our speaking, our thinking — "finite truth", but truth nevertheless?'

12.2.11   KRSNADĀS knew the problem from within his own tradition. 'Sankara tried to solve the problem by introducing the idea of a two-fold truth: *vyavahārika* and *paramārthika,* "empirical" and "ultimate" truth.[20] The former has its own laws, "objective" laws in which terms such as "good" and "bad" make sense. The latter is beyond those dualities; it is "Truth" as such in the ultimate sense. The former "truth" cannot claim any ultimacy. Rāmānuja had his difficulty with this solution. It makes relative reality a no-reality, relative truth a no-truth. He wanted to maintain the unity and continuity of the relative and the absolute, of humanity and God. He insisted that everything was a finite (if even infinitesimal) particle of the Infinite, a fraction of reality, but reality nevertheless, a tiny and limited aspect of truth, but not untruth. The sum total of all these finite truths of life added up to real truth, which through the grace of God was completed into Truth absolute.'

ANASTASIOS found this question intriguing. He knew about 'Christian' solutions that ran very much along the line of Śankara with the claim to be Rāmānujist in the final result. 'I have an interesting text here: "The perpetual universal belief of the Catholic

Church has held and now holds that there are two orders of knowledge, distinct not only in origin but also in object. They are distinct in origin, because in one we know by means of natural reason; in the other by means of divine faith. And they are distinct in object, because in addition to what natural reason can attain, we have proposed to us as objects of belief mysteries that are hidden in God and which, unless divinely revealed, can never be known. . ."[21] The theology proposed here does not only, as the context shows, cut humanity asunder into two camps — the "gentiles" who know God through reason only, the "Christians" who know God by faith — but also severs reason and faith in humanity to such an extent as to make a believer for all practical purposes a schizophrenic. My own idea is, after studying the New Testament, that "knowledge", *gnosis,* and "faith", *pistis,* depend on each other mutually in a complementary dialectical relationship: faith is not "reified" and put beside reason as a second faculty in a human, but it is the soul of reason, its inner light and power: reason helps faith and faith helps reason to come to Truth — one Truth, *the* Truth. "Faith" without qualification is not simply "true" — absolute Truth cannot be reached without faith!'

KRSNADĀS intervened: 'We have not yet dealt with the problem 12.2.12 which we have raised: the possibility of relative truth, of true statements in matters concerning finite reality, ultimately of the possibility of considering particular religions in their statements as "true". We certainly want to accept religions as "true" only if they contribute to the attainment of Truth as such — not because they are able to show that their propositions do not contradict each other. In other words: we accept them as "true" only insofar as they reflect something of the Truth and lead toward it.'

ANASTASIOS pondered: 'Is this possible at all? Truth, as I understand it, is One, not composed of bits and pieces. A *Summa Theologiae* is not the Truth as a great theologian and mystic like Thomas Aquinas had realised. All statements regarding truth are untrue insofar as, in their finiteness, they miss Truth as such. They are symbols at best, open to interpretations, ambivalent.'

KRSNADĀS asked to be permitted to quote Mahatma Gandhi 12.2.13 again: 'I worship God as Truth only. I have not yet found Him, but I am seeking after Him. . . But as long as I have not realized the Absolute Truth, so long must I hold by the relative truth as I have conceived it. That relative truth must, meanwhile, be my beacon, my shield and buckler. Though this path is narrow and straight and sharp as the razor's edge, for me it has been the quickest and easiest. . . It is not given to man to know the whole Truth. His duty lies in living up to the truth as he sees it, and in doing so to resort to the purest means, i.e. non-violence.'

ANASTASIOS interjected: 'But did not the same Mahātma Gandhi also admit to having committed "Himālayan blunders"? How could he — if the relative truths lead to ultimate Truth?' KRSNADAS had an answer. 'Mahātma Gandhi reacted to his failures by fasting and self-purification. He confessed to having let "untruth", selfishness, motives other than pure unselfish love influence his behaviour and thus lead to blunders. Perhaps his experience points to a general law: because Truth demands from the one who seeks it transformation and "being true", the so-called "relative truth" is always precariously close to untruth — because the ordinary human is never fully true, fully real, fully selfless.'

12.2.14 ANASTASIOS, thinking aloud, reasoned: 'Perhaps the best we can expect from humanity is not to *have* Truth but really to *want* it — to be sincere and open for it. Jesus' problem was not so much with those who committed blunders and admitted this, but with the hypocrites, those who claimed to have truth without really wanting it. They mouthed the right words about God — but on their lips those words became lies: they were untrue to themselves, to the "Spirit", and that vitiated everything.'

KRSNADĀS could offer a parallel from the Upanisads: 'The Upanisads speak about "ignorance" as the fetter that binds humanity, and "knowledge" as freedom — but they assert: "Into blind darkness enter they that worship ignorance, into darkness greater than that, as it were, they that delight in knowledge . . .[22] The one who boasts with knowledge does not really know — the words of knowledge may be spoken, but they are like worthless coins in an inflation of words. . ." '

Conclusions

12.2.15 We certainly must admit that not all Hindus would agree with everything that KRSNADĀS had said, nor would all Christians speak like ANASTASIOS. But that just cannot be changed. A dialogue is a meeting of one Hindu with one Christian in which each one tries to meet the partner as he or she is. 'Hinduism' and 'Christianity' as such will never meet — they are abstractions. Both have developed into numerous schools of thought and practice. But individual Hindus and Christians do meet — they are concrete persons with their individualities and their own, sometimes unorthodox, understanding of their traditions, which they accept as a whole but not in each detail. Our two dialogue partners, KRSNADĀS and ANASTASIOS, are convinced that the best minds and the deepest spirits of their traditions have reached Truth. They realise, however, that no one can claim it as 'his' or 'her' truth – it is Truth, without a possessive pronoun. They know also, that it is not the 'absolute objective Truth' of which the totally ignorant dream (what would they do with it, did they have it?), but the Truth that demands from the one who wants to have it, that he or she become true. Both partners in our dialogue consider this the actual importance of their living traditions: to provide methods of transformation, of becoming true and real, of Self-Realisation and Liberation. The aim of religion is not to provide humanity with the ultimate in scientific (objective) knowledge but with 'wisdom': it does not produce Nobel-prize-winning physicists, but saints. They are refined enough in their understanding of religious language that they recognise its symbol-character; at a certain stage words become obstacles rather than paths towards truth. But they also realise the true importance of words, up to a certain stage. They are good enough philosophers to realise that the fact that sooner or later on one's way towards Truth one has to replace one's figures and formulae with an unknown X does not yet warrant the statement that X means in each and any case the same thing, just because it is X. On the contrary, if the traditions which they still observe have any meaning, it is precisely because they are different partial-realisations of the ultimate Truth and as such irreplaceable, embodying a historically conditioned and culturally relevant form of truth.

Both agree also in maintaining that there is in humanity an urge 12.2.16 toward Truth and Reality which keeps it going despite all untruth and unreality, an urge that 'opens' up the human world into the infinite. This urge in humanity can not be fully rationalised; it partakes already of the nature of Truth, points to a Reality that is not simply the sum total of all experiential finite realities, but different in quality. They associate it with words such as 'inspiration', 'grace', 'a divine gift', 'the inherent Brahman-nature' – something which makes Truth appear not so much the last stone in the edifice of human achievement but as a 'given' of human existence. They recognise that the truest and ultimate answer to the question: What is Truth? is silence. Truth is not a word. But 'human truth' expresses itself also in words. The sceptic who rejects 'Truth' because he or she has experienced the many untruths of humankind is as far removed from Truth and Reality as the fundamentalist who assumes an identity between a formula about Truth and Truth Itself. Both are basically incapable of Truth because the right 'discrimination', the sense of Truth, is lacking in them.

12.2.17   Truth, as both our partners in dialogue understand it, is something deeply personal, requiring effort and sincerity and true selflessness. Truth demands courage: not to resist evil (untruth) is untruth (despite 'orthodoxy'). The hypocrite who plays with the formulae of Truth shuts out Truth — because he or she is unreal. What purpose does dialogue then serve? Did not KRSNADĀS just explain his Hindu tradition, and ANASTASIOS comment on his Christian tradition? True. But without the stimulus of the other partner, neither of them might have entered into this meditation on truth. Self-reflection often requires the stimulus of the other. But more than that, dialogue, as both partners would tell you later perhaps, also makes everyone aware that both the traditional Hindu Truth and the traditional Christian Truth are truths, i.e. statements about truth, attempts to reach it, necessarily limited and incomplete. If Truth is Reality, the dialogue widens the horizons, exposes both partners more to Reality, makes them, perhaps, more humble. And that again is part of coming nearer to Truth.

12.2.18   Only when we reach our limits do we become aware of the reality beyond the limits. We come nearer to Truth when we see how limited *our* truth is. And we value the more what little we have. Quite contrary to the opinions of many an 'orthodox' Hindu and Christian, who refuse to enter into dialogue because both are convinced they possess the whole and sole truth and they fear that such dialogues may contaminate their pure faith and result in heretical deviations, real dialogues result in a much greater appreciation of the genuine traditions from which the partners come. Respect for my fellow-human does not imply lack of self-respect. Nor does self-respect have to be expressed in contempt of all others. On the contrary, the more I am able truly to appreciate Truth as such, the more I will cherish whatever little reflection of truth I have in my own mind, passed on to me by thinkers and seekers after Truth in former generations. And because Truth is ultimately No-thing, not identifiable with any word or formula, I must, for the sake of Truth, be prepared when the time has come to surrender the finite to the infinite, the relative truth to full Truth. As long as it is dark, I am grateful for the light that a candle provides and I shall protect it and keep it burning. When the sun is rising, the flame of the candle looks darker than the space filled with bright sunlight. It would be untruth to keep out the sunlight in order to have candle-light. The truth, however, that 'light is' is an absolute truth — derived from the light of the candle! 'We see now a mirror-image, a symbol. . .then we shall see face to face. We know now only aspects, then I shall know as I am known. Now remain faith, hope, love — the greatest of the three is love.'[23]

The encounter of two absolute Truth claims, as we have it in Hindu-Christian dialogue, does not end with an abandoning of the absolute Truth claim on either side or on both sides, nor does it result in quarrels in order to establish one truth-claim against the other, nor in just politely keeping silent in order not to offend the other partner, knowing well that he or she must be wrong. A basic principle in 'dialogue' is that the tension existing between the different religions need not, should not, and cannot be resolved: it is a real dialectics arising out of the fact that life itself has contradictory aspects and dimensions, which are reflected by the major traditions. Dialogue does not aim at monologue but at keeping the dialogue going, maintaining the identity of both partners, and also presupposing sufficient common ground to explore further. Hindu-Christian dialogue goes on and brings both partners to realise the limits and the value of their own 'truths' in their traditions and it constantly kindles the spark of the *pneuma;* it renews the *eros,* gives greater impetus to the *mumuksutvam;* it makes the partner more open for Truth — and that is how we come nearer to Truth. 12.2.19

Notes

1. John 18:37.
2. The so-called 'Dutch Catechism', English translation by Kevin Smyth, published by Burns and Oates/Herder and Herder, 1967 (Index, p.510).
3. John 14:6.
4. John 8:32.
5. John 1:1ff.
6. Bṛhadaranyaka Upanisad II, 1, 20.   Cf. also Chāndogya Upanisad VI, 8, 7 (etc.).
7. For Justin Martyr (died ca. 165 AD), Socrates is the representative of the *logos* who assumed a body in Jesus. Thus he writes: 'We have been taught that Christ was first begotten of God and we have indicated above that he is the *logos* of whom all humanity partakes. Those who live by *logos* are Christians even though they have been considered atheists such as among the Greeks Socrates, Heraclitus, and others like them, and among the foreigners Abraham, Elias, Ananias, Azarias, Misael, and many others. So also those who lived before Christ and did not live by *logos* were useless humans, enemies of Christ and murderers of those who lived by *logos*'

(Apologia 1, 46), Clement of Alexandria (150-215 AD) writes: 'The Hellenic Philosophy does not, by its approach, make the truth more powerful but by rendering powerless the assault of Sophistry against it and frustrating the treacherous plots laid against truth it is said to be the proper fence and wall of the vineyard' *(Stromata* 1, 20, 100).

8. Cf. John 13ff.
9. Bhagavadgītā 6, 35 (Yogasūtras 1, 12).
10. Mt. 6:33.
11. 1 Cor. 2:7-8.
12. 1 Cor. 13:8.
13. The title of Mahātma Gandhi's autobiography is *The Story of My Experiments with Truth,* first published in 1924.
14. Taken from *The Mind of Mahatma Gandhi,* compiled and edited by R.K. Prabhu and U.R. Rao (Ahmedabad: Navajivan Publishing House, 1967), pp.42ff.: 'Truth'.
15. Cf. Br̥hadāranyaka Upaniṣad VI, 5, 1ff.
16. Cf. John 18:38 and John 10:27.
17. Mark 4:12.
18. (Fontana Books, 1958), pp.142-3.
19. Parānas, *passim,* also a good deal of the popular (vernacular) Hindu literature.
20. Cf. Sankara, *Brahmasūtrabhāsya.* Also, Madhava, *Sarvadarśanasamgraha,* Ch.XVI.
21. Vaticanum 1 *(The Church Teaches, Documents of the Church in English Translation* [Herder, 1962], p.32). Vaticanum II has some very vague statements as regards Truth: 'On Religious Freedom': '. . .the highest norm of human life is the divine law – eternal, objective, and universal – whereby God orders, directs and governs the whole universe and all the ways of the human community, by a plan conceived in wisdom and love. Man has been made by God to participate in this law with the result that, under the gentle disposition of divine Providence, he can come to perceive ever increasingly the unchanging truth. Hence every man has the duty and therefore the right, to seek the truth in matters religious. . .' 'On Revelation': 'This tradition which comes down from the apostles develops in the Church with the help of the Holy Spirit. For there is a growth in the understanding of the realities and the words which have been handed down. This happens through the contemplation and study made by believers who treasure these things in their hearts, through the intimate understanding of spiritual things they experience and through the preaching of those who have received through episcopal succession the sure gift of truth. For as the centuries succeed one another the Church constantly moves forward towards the fulness of divine truth until the words of God reach their complete fulfilment in her.'
22. Isa Upanisad 9.
23. 1 Cor. 13:12-13.

Source: From Leonard Swidler, ed. Journal of Ecumenical Studies, Temple University, Philadelphia 1975, Vol.12, Part 2, pp.157-171.

12.3 LIBERATION FOR SOCIAL JUSTICE: The Common Struggle of Christians and Marxists in Latin America

Julio de Santa Ana

From out of many different contexts in Latin America voices can be 12.3.1
heard emphasising that the achieving of a new, just society must
involve a profound transformation of our peoples, not only in terms
of economic, social and political patterns but also in our cultural
values and personal styles of behaviour. Such a process implies the
breaking down of existing situations of economic dependence and
political oppression in order that people may come to stand on their
own feet. This is what is meant by the word 'liberation': a symbol
by which Latin Americans point to the goal towards which we are
striving. Our struggle has of course its own specific context and
characteristics, and these have also shaped the changes in relationship between Christians and Marxists over the last twenty years.

In contrast to what happened in Europe in the same period, the
dialogue between Christians and Marxists in Latin America was not
mainly academic in character; it resulted from the meeting and
collaboration of persons who, though differing in their views of the
world and of life itself, were engaged in joint action. This
phenomenon has not, of course, affected the whole Christian
community, let alone all Marxist groups, but it is a trend which is
spreading with increasing rapidity. What only fifteen years ago was
regarded by many as the fad of a few is now too common to be
overlooked. Admittedly, it prompts passionate reactions for or
against. These in turn imply the adoption of a political standpoint.
For in Latin America Christianity and Marxism are not so much
intellectual views as expressions of forces which dynamically affect
reality. In an extremely volatile context whose various elements are
constantly shifting position, Christianity and Marxism repeatedly
intersect, by no means always in the same way. While it is possible to
observe a certain constancy in Marxist standpoints, the same cannot
be said of the way Christians express themselves. It is still the case
that there are large sectors of society calling themselves Christian (it
would be more appropriate to say that they invoke a Christian tradition) and who reject Marxism. But others, increasingly numerous,

699

are now using Marxist elements in their analysis and understanding of the situation, while yet others are openly joining movements in which Marxists take the lead.

12.3.2 From Mutual Anathema to Joint Endeavour

In the first half of this century the two forces were in flat contradiction. Christians, Catholics above all, saw in Marxism an active agent of social change which would have disastrous consequences for Latin American society, in whose development the Catholic Church had played a fundamental part. The ideological artillery of Catholic preaching was brought into action first against socialism, then against communism too. In face of the possible entry of Marxist atheism on the Latin American scene, it was urgent for the Church to encourage various specialised movements of apostolic action: among industrial workers, intellectuals, young people, and so on. At that time Marxism was considered to be totally incompatible with Christian faith. The Protestant minority in Latin America held a similar if less virulent view. At that time Protestantism appeared as an agent of modernisation for Latin America. Yet despite its greater ability to understand the urgency of social justice in a society which suffered enormous disparities and contradictions, it could not accept Marxism as a legitimate element. For Christians, then, Marxism must be opposed and driven out.

The Marxists, for their part, regarded Christianity (above all Roman Catholicism) as the traditional ally of those who had prevented the social progress of the people, a tool by which the minorities who had always governed Latin America had been able to domesticate the mass of the people and consolidate their oppressive power. For Marxists, the Church was a power to be fought; Christian faith was an element to be rooted out from the minds of the people. Each side was thus anathema to the other. The contradictions were deep and tense. Reconciliation and dialogue were impossible.

Nevertheless, in the course of the 1950s, the situation began to change. More and more, especially in the universities, Marxists and Christians were to be found united in a common struggle against injustice (until very recently university students played an important role in the social struggles of Latin America). Though at first this was a cause of astonishment to both sides, both became passionately interested in studying the motives and methods involved. A cautiously receptive attitude began to replace rigid anathema. Little by little some Marxists began to detect an element which until then they had not perceived in Christianity: a basic goodwill seeking to express the love which faith preaches.

Legitimate Allies 12.3.3

For Christians this open attitude to Marxism implied, at least at that time, three things: first, the recognition of Marxists as legitimate allies in the struggle for social change; second, an interest in Marxism, its doctrinal bases and political views, which had earlier been rejected *a priori;* third, acquaintance with a method of analysis which could provide a more complete knowledge of the Latin American situation. On the other hand, the same process led the Marxists to understand how much closer the Christians were to the Latin American masses; to realise that however alienating some Christian ideas might be (chiefly because of the way in which they had been manipulated by the ruling classes), they were nevertheless integral to the level of consciousness reached by the Latin American peoples; and to realise that even if in the social as well as in the political sphere Marxism is the conception which best suits the legitimate interests of the masses, Marxists should not simply reject all that is Christian, but should seek to know it better.

For Christians, whether through the *aggiornamento* promoted by John XXIII among Catholics or through the attitudes that the ecumenical movement brought to Latin American Protestantism, the *rapprochement* with Marxism warmed up in the 1960s. Groups of Catholics and Protestants gradually became convinced that the cause of the great ills of Latin America lay, as the Marxists said, in economic imperialism. By applying a Marxist analysis to Latin American reality, many Christians came to understand that the actions of economic imperialism had subordinated our nations to the system of exploitation imposed on all the underdeveloped nations. This, of course, was nothing new for Latin American Marxists. The important thing was that on the basis of this conviction Christians and Marxists began to agree about the need to overcome this state of affairs by a process of change described as *liberation.* . . It is as if two currents were now flowing together in a single surging river. Christians and Marxists had in fact come to a similar decision: they were prepared to serve the cause of the oppressed classes in order to establish true justice. This, of course, amounted to a revolutionary decision, in view of the present state of affairs in Latin America. It was not an agreement on merely transitory or accidental matters, but on the goals of action. For many Christians and

Marxists, therefore, the time of anathema was long since over. The moment of common action and commitment had come. Fidel Castro, Prime Minister of Cuba, noting this fact, pointed out during his tour of Chile in November 1971 that between Christians and Marxists there was a fundamental alliance, because even if they do not agree about tactics, they do about strategy: 'We must see Christians of the Left, revolutionary Christians, as strategic allies of the revolution – not as fellow-travellers. . .'[1]

At the end of the 1950s an occasional priest and a few laymen had taken a decision in favour of revolution. With the passage of time, however, it was now no longer a question of rare individual cases, but of an increasingly strong trend. In fact, in the last ten years a very large number of different movements have sprung up from the churches to espouse the cause of liberation. ISAL [Church and Society in Latin America] came into existence in 1962, and before long took the decision in favour of revolution. The student movements – *Juventud Universitaria Católica* (Catholic University Youth) and *Movimiento Estudiantil Cristiano* (the Student Christian Movement) – were consolidated between 1962 and 1966. The workers' and agrarian movements made a revolutionary option about the year 1966. Independent communities of Christians committed to the revolution were organized from 1962 onward. The first groups of priests working for political aims started in 1967 in Brazil and then developed rapidly in Argentina, Peru, Colombia, Venezuela, etc., the best known being the one which provided the nucleus of 'Christians for Socialism' in Chile, created in 1970.

12.3.4 Open to Collaboration

So far we have been speaking only of the Christians. Among the Marxists, various communist and socialist parties and others of Marxist inspiration opened themselves to collaboration with Christians from 1964 onwards. The action of Fr Camilo Torres spurred many of them to make contact with Christians. And so in Chile, Uruguay and Peru, various Marxist political groups openly declared their intention of joining forces with the Christians, not only on the electoral but also on the parliamentary and political levels.

Now common action does not always make it possible to eliminate points of disagreement or to open the way to complete understanding. But in this joint action of Christians and Marxists the disagreements which may exist or the points on which total clarity has not yet been reached are not regarded as insuperable obstacles. Both understand that their dialogue has to do more with practical action and less with abstraction and theory. It is reflection on action which unites, rather than on the points which still divide, that is important. Such reflection has clearly shown that the Christians have not made a revolutionary choice merely in order to have a place in the society which will follow the revolutionary process, and that the Marxists do not intend merely to manipulate, dominate or use, the Christians as a pretext. In the end, it is action which makes it possible to discover what are the real motives and intentions operative in a process of political change. Indeed, this dialogue can only take place in the course of the struggle, fundamentally because the context of their action is one of conflict. In the common struggle, the unsolved problems which opposed Marxism and Christianity cannot divide; our standpoints, our view of the world and of life may be different, but we respect one another and seek agreement wherever possible.

The realisation that the basic reality which we face is one of conflict (class struggle, ideological struggle, etc.) poses such a huge question for Christians and Marxists that it compels them to overcome any residue of sectarianism or dogmatism. What is primary now is, therefore, fundamental agreement about the aims to be achieved. As those who took part in the meeting of Christians for Socialism (Santiago de Chile, April 1972) said:

> The central and inescapable objective of the strategic alliance is to destroy the capitalist system and to combat imperialism. The historical task assumed by the working class (industrial workers and peasants) is the socialist revolution, with the social appropriation of the means of production and the exercise of power by the working class.
> ... The immediate objective of the strategic alliance between Christians and Marxists is the political awakening and organisation of the people; to enable them to realise in the most fundamental way their exploited condition, and to become aware of their right to be free, even to the point of envisaging the urgent need to seize power.[2]

Those who took part in that meeting had to face the problem of the specific contribution of Christians to the alliance with Marxists, and they answered it by formulating five points: (1) revolutionary commitment, a consequence of taking the part of the oppressed and of sharing their liberating struggle against exploitation; (2) their own Christian faith, understood in the context of the revolutionary option as 'an insurrectional consciousness'. By this, the revolutionary Christian can help to unmask the forms in which 'capitalism, with its ideology of domination, is camouflaged in a sociological Christianity;'[3] (3) the struggle against a policy which has been that of the churches in Latin America and which suits the mechanisms of domination over the people employed by the ruling classes. On this plane it is a question of ensuring that the Church is really the Church, without losing its identity through the alienation to which the capitalist system may subject it; (4) to ensure that the Christian community lives the renewing and truly revolutionary meaning of faith. For the alliance to be effective, the true identity of men and women of faith must be maintained and communities of revolutionary Christians formed; (5) to unmask the way capitalism manipulates what is Christian, and at the same time to make the Church aware of the capitalist structure which confines it and which it must overcome in order to stand faithful in the urgency of that love of the neighbour, and especially of the poorest, which Jesus Christ demands.

12.3.5 **A New Understanding**

What specific contributions can Marxists make in their turn in the strategic alliance with Christians? The Santiago meeting suggested:

> The chief contribution of Marxists is their revolutionary experience, their method of work and their firm roots in popular sectors.
>
> In many Marxist achievements (such as the workers' movements in several countries, the Cuban revolution, etc.), Christians recognise their own aspirations towards a new society and a new man.
>
> The disinterested struggle for the proletariat which many Marxists engage in enables Christians to discover the grace of love and obliges them to a secularisation and purification of faith.
>
> The political practice of Marxists demands greater political maturity of Christians, for good intentions are not enough.
>
> Marxism makes it possible for Christians to achieve a new understanding of their history (cf. F. Engel's introduction to K. Marx's *The Class Struggles in France,* 1848 to 1850, 6 March 1895).[4]

It is evident that joint action challenges Christians and Marxists to mutual change and adjustment. For Christians, in the first place, the revolutionary option involves giving primacy to revolutionary action. If there are some for whom faith loses its importance, it must also be recognised that there are other believers in Jesus Christ who enrich and discover their faith in this priority accorded to revolution. Secondly, the alliance with the Marxists leads to a change in the consciousness of the Christians who detach themselves from bourgeois values and accept the imperatives of action for liberation.

As for the Marxists, alliance with the Christians is something which challenges them first to be more faithful in their action to the objectives, necessities and struggles of the working classes, which at the same time means fidelity to Marxism itself, above all by keeping in constant touch with the popular masses. . .

In short, Christians and Marxists, starting from their different standpoints, have gradually grown closer together until they have united in a revolutionary decision in favour of the liberation of the Latin American peoples. That process of growth is not at an end. We shall first consider what factors have made this mutual growth possible (what we might call points of agreement) and then examine the remaining problems which require the dialogue to be pursued in greater depth.

Basic Points of Agreement   12.3.6

In the *first* place there is not only agreement about the instruments of analysis to be applied to reality (the Marxist methods), but also about the data to which the analysis is applied. This has meant a change in the Marxist understanding of reality as well as in that of the Christians. As recently as ten years ago, in fact, Marxists regarded the problems of Latin America as a product of the basic contradiction between the 'modern' and the 'traditional'. They described Latin American society as affected by a 'structural dualism'. To overcome this, the process of 'modernisation' was to be vigorously promoted, thus creating suitable conditions for the industrialisation of the continent. This modernisation was to be accompanied by a deliberate attempt at social participation which would make these societies more democratic. Education was regarded as a particularly valuable means of getting the whole process moving. The process would thus be evolutionary rather than one of conflict.

With the events which precipitated the establishment of socialism in Cuba and the subsequent analysis of those events, the Marxists revised their point or view. As a result the conviction grew, at first among Marxists regarded as 'heretics' but then also among 'official' Marxist thinkers, that Latin America's problems derive basically from the development of capitalism, which in its greed for gain has exploited and plundered Latin America. The root of the problem is to be found not in the opposition between the modern and the traditional, but between development and underdevelopment, between capital and forces of production, all of which finds expression in a series of conflicts, social tensions and class struggles which tend to get worse and worse. The action of capitalism in creating underdevelopment in Latin America has created and reinforced structures of domination and dependence, not only in economic terms but also in social, cultural and above all political life. These structures exist not only in the relations between the Latin American countries and the capitalist countries on which they depend, but also in the internal social structures of the countries. Significant social change in Latin America is impossible unless this situation is overcome.

It is precisely this process of eliminating dependence that is denoted by the term 'liberation'. Latin American development must mean a break with the existing forms of domination and dependence. It will thus lead to forms of social and economic life which will have to be original. In other words, it is now accepted by Latin American Marxists that each country will have to find its own 'way' of development. Otherwise there will not be liberation but a continuation of the situation of dependence.

12.3.7   Just as the Marxists' understanding has been changing, so Christians, too, now see the situation in Latin America as resulting from the domination of the great centres of world power. The *theology of liberation* which is being worked out at present in Latin America makes awareness of dependence a central category in the study of the consciousness of liberation. Dependence and liberation are strictly related terms.

In short, Christians and Marxists approach reality with the same instruments of analysis, though from different standpoints and perspectives. Both agree in defining the Latin American situation as the product of domination that subjects these countries to dependence. To overcome this, liberation is imperative. The common revolutionary option translates into action the acceptance of this challenge.

Second, both partners in the dialogue agree in stressing the 12.3.8
importance of the ethical factor. Cuban Marxists first, and then
others in various Latin American countries, have indicated that while
it is urgent to make structural changes in order to overcome
conditions of dependence, so also it is fundamental to form a new
man, capable of expressing in his personal life the new spirit which
must accompany the development of the new society. It was Ernesto
Guevara who most insisted on this point, stressing the need to forge
this new personality by moral rather than material stimuli. Work
ceases to be a burden for the human being and becomes an
instrument of his liberation; for that reason it is regarded as a 'social
duty' which must be linked with 'technical development' (mastery
of Nature) and which must be performed not just to earn wages but
basically to build a new and just community. For that very reason it
must be 'voluntary work'.[5] For Guevara, the two pillars which make
possible the transition to communism are technical development and
the new man, who is 'fuller, of great interior wealth and imbued
with a sense of responsibility', who knows that 'he must sacrifice
himself, because he lives in a time of sacrifice',[6] and above all, who
is a revolutionary'. . .guided by great feelings of love. It is impossible
to think of an authentic revolutionary without this quality. This is
perhaps one of the great dramas of a leader; he must combine cool
understanding with a passionate spirit, and take decisions, sometimes
painful ones, without moving a muscle. Our avant-garde
revolutionaries must idealise this love for the people, for the most
sacred causes, to the point of making it a unique, indivisible thing.'[7]

Now the demand for human renewal, for conversion, is
fundamental in the Christian message. . . Only the free acceptance of
the struggle can lead to responsible action. Yet authenticity as well
as responsibility is expected of the Christian, and he must show this,
not only by his dedication to just causes, but also through the
consistency which will make him love and therefore give priority to
the communal over the personal. For the Christian, life can only be
lived in freedom (Gal.5). But unlike Guevara and other Marxists, the
Christian affirms that the new life of man is not the result of his own
discipline, but a gift of God: the new man, in truth, is Jesus Christ. . .[8]

But although there are differences about the origin of the
newness of life, both Christians and Marxists agree that the 'new
man' can only be such if he is free and lives in love.

12.3.9 Converging Aims

In the *third* place, all this leads Christians and Marxists in Latin America today to join in a programme of ideological struggle, which they approach from different angles but with converging aims. Both understand that they must attack the problem set by the alienation from which the masses in Latin America suffer: poor, exploited, with no acceptable minimum standard of living, almost disqualified in their existence, yet unable to perceive the real causes of their ills. The dependence of Latin American countries on the centres of world capital and power is also reflected in the dependence of these long-exploited masses. This is why Marxists constantly strive by various means to create favourable conditions for a liberating awakening of consciousness. This involves establishing a programme of action on the ideological level.

Christians, too, know this situation of alienation at first hand. Not only do the vast Catholic masses suffer it, but also those grouped in the most popular evangelical denominations (for example the Pentecostals). According to Christian Lalive d'Epinay, who has made one of the best studies of Latin American Protestantism to date,

These evangelical denominations reincarnated the past, prolonged it in the present. Hence our evangelical micro-societies may be regarded as:
1. Substitution societies at a time when the ancient social structures are disappearing but new ones have not appeared;
2. Survivals (by their structure) adapted from the past;
3. Societies that are closed, finished, without history, static.[9]

Lalive d'Epinay, following this line of thought, speaks of a 'social strike of the Christians'. That is to say, their deliberate refusal to exercise the social responsibility which is theirs — a manifestation of the state of alienation from which they suffer. Hence the need to develop a programme designed to bring those who live in these conditions to a real awareness of their situation, their real needs and how to satisfy them.

12.3.10 The Awakening of Consciousness

The liberation of consciousness thus emerges as a common objective of Christians and Marxists on the ideological plane. It involves using various means to create conditions favourable to an awakening of class consciousness against which, it must be admitted, Christian faith has often been and continues to be manipulated.

The rigid stratification of Latin America societies makes unified popular mobilisation difficult because it hides the common interests of the oppressed classes. There is a large sector of unemployed, with whom the industrial workers often do not recognise a basic community of interests. Racial differences, manipulated by those who are in power, also provoke a fragmentation of forces. Those who are opposed to change in Latin America know how to profit by all these elements in order to strengthen their domination. That is why Christians and Marxists who are committed to revolution have to work out a programme of action designed to get the people to share actively in the struggle for change. The Marxists, who have often mistakenly employed methods of action which have separated them from the masses instead of getting the latter to take part in their own mobilisation, have been occupied with this task for some time. But now the Christians are joining in as well. Hugo Assmann, for instance, can say:

> The fact that in Latin America liberation requires the removal of important obstacles present in the superstructure has a relevance for one fundamental element of the Christian faith. Man receives life as a gift, he is created from 'outside' himself by God. This sounds vague, but it has very concrete implications which are closely related to our belief in revelation. Man does not spring spontaneously from the structures, although they provide the necessary material conditions for his 'birth' as a new man. But if the material structures which provide the context shaping the consciousness of man do not add up to a process in which love is expressed through call and response, then what is generated is in fact a mere product of the structures and not the new man. In this sense the term Christian 'witness' which has been emptied of its meaning retains its full force at the heart of the process of liberation. . . This means that the Christian's influence will be related to the impact made by breaking the superstructure.'[10]

One of the methods which have been used to open breaches in the oppressed Christian consciousness is the liberating pedagogy of Paulo Freire. Its importance lies in the fact that goals and objectives have to be formulated on the basis of popular expectation, without any attempt to impose on the oppressed any preconceived idea of how to do things or of what to seek for by action. This method is also capable of correcting the mistaken views of people who want to work with the masses but in reality adopt a paternalist and therefore antiliberating attitude towards them...

12.3.11   To sum up this part of our essay, we can say that Christians and Marxists are agreed on a common goal: to overcome the flagrant injustices and social contradictions which characterise Latin American societies in order to establish a just society. For those who are committed to this process, the road that leads to this goal is that of socialism. As the Final Document of the Christians for Socialism meeting puts it:

> Socialism is the only acceptable means of overcoming class society. For classes are the reflection of the economic basis which in capitalist society creates an antagonistic division between the possessors of capital and the wage-earners. The latter have to work for the former and are thus an object of exploitation. Only by replacing private property by social ownership of the means of production can objective conditions be created for the suppression of class antagonism.[11]

12.3.12 Open Questions

Agreement on such matters as action, tactical and strategic alliances and joint programmes of ideological struggle is not sufficient to overcome all the problems which can arise in a dialogue between Christians and Marxists. But as we have already noted, such problems need not separate them, but can prompt both partners to deeper reflection. Christians and Marxists call each other to be more faithful to their essential bases, and this has led to a restatement of both Christian faith and Marxism. In this process Christians discover anew that faith is not restricted to the inner life of a human being, disembodied and separated from action and social responsibility. Consequently, Christians try to understand the Gospel on the basis of the context of conflict in which they live, and this obliges them not only to make a choice but also to engage in specific political activity.

> Another element of this restatement of faith...is the political dimension of faith. Faith cannot but be political, since it is a matter of giving concrete form to our love of man by taking a stand in favour of the struggle of the people. When we speak of

'political action' in this context, it is no longer a question of the seizure and exercise of power by a group, but of the total struggle, with the aim of creating a socialist society in which the people call the moves. It is also a question of a transformation of man as a whole, in all his dimensions. Faith has a part to play in this process, opening him to the gift of God.[12]

Christian Identity 12.3.13

This reformulation of faith leads to a thorough examination of ecclesiological questions within the context of a common struggle for liberation. There are, of course, many Christians who once opted for revolutionary commitment but gradually abandoned the Church — they 'lost their faith'. But there are also many, very many more in fact, who still declare themselves Christians and who maintain their militant devotion to liberation. Both, however, are agreed on one point: the Church's traditional forms of life no longer seem valid to those who are trying to express the faith in the present revolutionary Latin American context. Miguez Bonino, who deals with the problem particularly well, notes:

> Perhaps the gravest disagreements among Christians dedicated to the process of liberation arise in regard to their attitudes to the institutions and objective celebrations of Christian faith, which range from uncritical and sometimes fervent participation at one extreme to systematic refusal to take part in any liturgical form of worship or institutional aspects of the life of the Church including critical participation or the creation of substitute groups and forms of celebration. . . In fact, the Christian who reflects on his practice in terms of socio-political analysis and of the facts which give him his identity as a Christian is located (however 'incarnate' his reflection may be) within two circles of consciousness, not concentric but intersecting. Both are essentially communal. And, in my view, the one cannot be substituted for the other. But participation in both in the present situation (and we cannot speak of any other) inevitably involves conflict to a greater or lesser extent. It is this, it seems to me, and not some subtle theoretical question, which is the real ecclesiological problem. And here again, it will not be resolved by speculation but by concrete commitment. In other words, the Latin American revolutionary Christian has to solve the problem of his church practice, without which his Christian identity is incomplete.[13]

While Christians are restating their faith, the Marxists are undergoing a similar process of reflection. If anything is clear in the dialogue, it is that the Marxists are not maintaining their theoretical and political position with the dogmatism of earlier times, but are showing themselves increasingly ready to consider the problems of Latin America without seeking to judge them from perspectives which perhaps were correct in other contexts but have no universal validity. In reality the dialogue has served to bring the Marxists themselves to greater openness, since they have found that faith is not an obstacle to revolutionary struggle. Some Marxists are beginning to reconsider Marx's criticism of religion. This is a subject which needs deeper study, since it is common to Christians and Marxists. Nevertheless, the events which have produced the nucleus of revolutionary Christians demonstrate that the Christian element can serve the cause of liberation.[14]

12.3.14 The Class Struggle

A second problem has been raised but has not yet been solved: the relation of the Church to the class struggle, or, rather, the Church in the context of class struggle. One clear feature of Marxist conduct in the last ten years in regard to the Latin American Church has been a firm will not to attack the Church, nor to set it in opposition to the revolution[15], since Christians are seen as strategical allies. This implies that the Marxists believe the Christian community has a role to play in the class struggle: in reality this matter is more serious for Christians than for Marxists. For Marxists, the class struggle is the very texture of history, whereas for Christians the Church is the place where human divisions are overcome, since in Christ 'there is neither slave nor free; Jew nor Greek'. How then can a Christian take part in the revolution, the clearest expression of the class war? How can he act against others who also call themselves Christians? Given that Christ unites human beings, how is it that Christians, as Christians, can take part in division and conflict? Is this not to admit that Jesus Christ unites some but divides others? But according to the testimony of the Gospel and the New Testament, the unity of Christ is the unity of all. Discussing this problem, Fr Noel Olaya of Colombia notes:

> The unity of Christ, in its fullness, is the unity of all; this unity in process of realisation, on the other hand, demands choices, and by that very fact it cannot fail to create division. And these

choices at the level of what we call 'worldly' matters, are political, economic, and so on. The important thing, therefore, is the criterion which guides them. The basic criterion in this case is a commitment to the poor and oppressed, by adopting their aspirations of freedom and by dedication to their struggle. 'The problem of the unity of the Church cannot be separated from the problem of the unity of the world', says Fr Giulio Girardi. The two roads to unity go by way of the liberation of the poor.

The understanding of the unity of the Church as referring to the unity and justice which God has given to men in Christ has brought revolutionary Christians in Latin America to see the class struggle as the 'struggle against organised hatred'.[16] For them, then, the class struggle is an instrument through which Christian love can be shown no longer as a simple relation between an I and a Thou, but between those who constitute the people, the community, *us.* When the Church is aware of what the class struggle involves, it will undergo a process of reconversion which will eventually make it possible to overcome the division between clergy and laity, and to democratise church life, thus enabling Christianity to regain the revolutionary drive of the early Church. This obviously presupposes a questioning of the Church as an agent of social conciliation, and at the same time it prompts the Church to examine its own conscience, in case it resembles the 'prophets' of the Old Testament who spoke of peace when there was no peace.

A third unsolved problem for many revolutionary Christians is 12.3.15 posed by the use of violence. There are some who have already decided the matter by opting for violence or non-violence. Clearly this problem does not arise for the Marxist conscience; their position is well known ('Violence is the mother of history' — Marx). But for Christians who are committed to liberation, the problem of violence is inescapable. For some, it arises at the level of principles and ethical choices; for others, it must be examined in the light of tactical demands. Every effort must be made to avoid the risk of identifying violence (a means) with liberation (the end). At the same time, however, it is imperative to lay aside 'the shallow sentimentality which passes for Christian ethics in these matters, hiding reactionary attitudes under basic theological categories like reconciliation, forgiveness or peace, which in the long run are more costly in human lives and suffering and less respectful of the human person'.[17] When humane criteria are applied, violence can be an instrument of liberation from structural violence. But this means submitting the use of violence to the requirements of political and social struggles.

12.3.16 Conclusion

Events in Chile since 11 September 1973 put to the test the effectiveness of the alliance between Christians and Marxists and of their common struggle. In fact, they call in question the whole activity of the Latin American Left. It is not possible here to deal fully with this subject, but it points to a problem of which Christians and Marxists are not always aware, namely that if their struggle is to be really effective it will take a long time, and it will demand great patience. Above all, they must realise that there is no place for hopes of miraculous change. The struggle for a new society will inevitably demand huge sacrifice, a love which will not admit weakness and the cultivation of a hope which must not be confused with illusion. On this, Christians and Marxists are in full agreement.

Notes

1. *Cuba-Chile, Encuentro Simbólico entre dos Procesos Históricos.* Havana: Commission of Revolutionary Orientation of the Central Committee of the Communist Party of Cuba, 1972 pp.268-278.
2. *Cristianos por el Socialismo.* Santiago de Chile: Mundo Nuevo 1972, p.254.
3. Ibid. p.257.
4. Ibid. pp.258-259.
5. Ernesto 'Che' Guevara, *Le socialisme et l'homme à Cuba.* Havana: Institut du Livre, 1967, p.30.
6. Ibid. p.42.
7. Ibid. p.43.
8. cf. José Míguez Bonino, *Ama y Haz lo que Quieras,* Buenos Aires, La Aurora 1972, p.50. cf. also by the same author the chapter 'Nuevas Perspectivas Teólogicas' in the collective work *Pueblo Oprimido, Señor de la Historia,* Montevideo, Tierra Nueva 1972, p.211.
9. Christian Lalive d'Epinay, 'La Iglesia Evangélica y la Revolución Latino-americana', in: *Cristianismo y Sociedad,* No.16/17, p.26. Noel Olaya extends this analysis to the Catholic congregations in 'Unidad Cristiana y Lucha de Clases', in: *Pueblo Oprimido, Señor de la Historia,* p.58.
10. Hugo Assmann, 'The Christian Contribution to the Liberation of Spanish America', in: *Anticipation,* WCC, 1971, p.25.
11. *Cristianos por el Socialismo,* p.295.
12. Ibid., pp.269-70.
13. Jose Míguez Bonino, 'Nuevas Perspectivas Teológicas', *loc. cit.,* pp.211-12.
14. cf. Hugo Assmann, *op. cit.* Another reappraisal prompted by the Christian-Marxist dialogue concerns the method of doing theology in this new situation. In this regard the work of José Míguez Bonino 'Nuevas Perspectivas Teológicas', *loc. cit.,* is extremely valuable.
15. cf. F. Castro, *op. cit.,* p.268.
16. *Christianos por el Socialismo, p.263.*

17. José Miguez Bonino, 'La Violencia: Una Reflexion Teológica', in: *Cristianismo y Sociedad*, Montevideo, 1971, no.28, p.10. English: Violence – a theological reflection', in *The Ecumenical Review*, Vol.XXV, No.4, October 1973, p.468.

Source: From S.J. Samartha, ed. *Living Faiths and Ultimate Goals*, The World Council of Churches, Geneva, 1974, pp.90-107. A few abridgements have been made in the text.

INDEX

The field of world religions is notorious for the problems it presents to authors and editors in the matter of achieving uniformity in both spelling and the use of diacritical marks. The policy adopted in this Reader, in which we have made use of extracts from a large number of books (written by different authors spanning many years), has been to reproduce the spelling and the diacritical marks used in the original book or essay. Consistency has not been the goal on this point; but we believe that readers will not be misled by such variety as is presented in the use of certain words.

The making of the Index brings us up against this difficulty again. But we believe that, as with the text of the Reader, the reader will find his way around quite easily even though the form in which a word is printed may not be, in a very few cases, that which is most commonly used today.